Afoot & Afield

Tahoe-Reno

01 Spectacular Outings in the Lake Tahoe Region

SECOND EDITION

Mike White

WILDERNESS PRESS ... *on the trail since 1967*

TO MY TWO SONS, DAVID AND STEPHEN.

Afoot & Afield Tahoe–Reno: 201 Spectacular Outings in the Lake Tahoe Region

2nd edition, 1st printing

Copyright © 2016 by Mike White

Cover and interior photos by Mike White
Maps: Mike White / Bart Wright (Lohnes + Wright)
Cover design: Scott McGrew
Original text design: Andreas Schueller; adapted by Annie Long
Editor: Holly Cross
Proofreader: Lisa Bailey
Indexer: Rich Carlson

ISBN 978-0-89997-791-1; eISBN 978-0-89997-792-8

Manufactured in the United States of America

Published by: **🌲 WILDERNESS PRESS**
        An imprint of Keen Communications, LLC
        2204 First Avenue South, Suite 102
        Birmingham, AL 35233
        800-443-7227; fax 205-326-1012
        info@wildernesspress.com
        wildernesspress.com

Visit our website for a complete listing of our books and for ordering information.

Distributed by Publishers Group West

Cover photos, clockwise from top: Tahoe Rim Trail near South Camp Peak; waterfall on the Mt. Rose Trail; autumn in Thomas Creek Canyon

SAFETY NOTICE: Although Wilderness Press and the author have made every attempt to ensure that the information in this book is accurate at press time, they are not responsible for any loss, damage, injury, or inconvenience that may occur to anyone while using this book. You are responsible for your own safety and health while in the wilderness. The fact that a trail is described in this book does not mean that it will be safe for you. Be aware that trail conditions can change from day to day. Always check local conditions and know your own limitations.

Contents

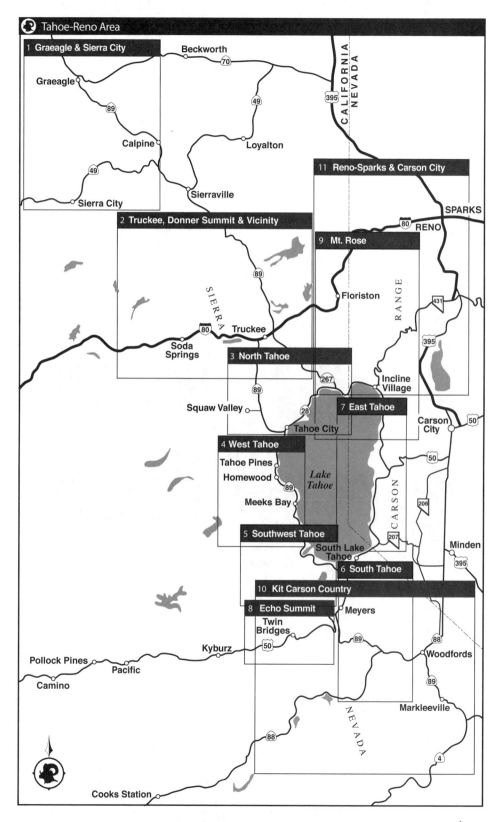

Tahoe-Reno Area

1 Graeagle & Sierra City
2 Truckee, Donner Summit & Vicinity
3 North Tahoe
4 West Tahoe
5 Southwest Tahoe
6 South Tahoe
7 East Tahoe
8 Echo Summit
9 Mt. Rose
10 Kit Carson Country
11 Reno-Sparks & Carson City

Acknowledgments

As with all my writing projects, the most important thank-you goes to my wife, Robin, for her tireless support and encouragement. I greatly appreciated the company of fellow hikers on the trail, including Jan Baguley, Keith Catlin, Bruce Farrenkopf, Dal and Candy Hunter, Diane McCormack, and Andy Montessoro. Thank you to all the folks at Wilderness Press who form my scribblings into a real book.

Mike White
Reno, Nevada
July 2015

Mt. Rose as seen from the summit of Slide Mountain (Trip153)

Preface

Much has happened in the Tahoe–Reno area since the first edition of this guide was published in 2006. The Great Recession certainly halted the out-of-control building boom that previously plagued the Truckee Meadows. Fortunately, unlike the construction industry, trails seemed to fare well during the economic downturn, as several new paths were added to the system. Mostly due to the tireless efforts of volunteers coordinated by nonprofit groups working in conjunction with governmental agencies, such as the Tahoe Rim Trail Association, Truckee Donner Land Trust, and Carson Valley Trails Association, the number of trips described in this guide has increased from 175 in the first edition to 201 in the second. Residents and visitors alike should be grateful for such a turn of events, as many areas of the country are losing, not gaining, recreational trails.

For the first edition of *Afoot & Afield Tahoe–Reno,* I was able to hike every mile of trail that appeared in the guide over the course of three seasons. This time around, with fieldwork limited to one season, hiking every previously described trail along with all of the new trails was simply not possible. However, every effort was made to verify the condition of those trips I was unable to re-hike. Anyone who finds inconsistencies in the descriptions is encouraged to contact Wilderness Press, and updates will be arranged whenever possible.

I feel extremely fortunate to have walked all the trails and viewed the sights contained in the northern Sierra and western valleys of the Great Basin covered in this book. My hope for this guide into the extraordinary terrain of the Tahoe–Reno area is to leave you similarly blessed.

Introducing the Tahoe–Reno Area

Welcome to Tahoe–Reno! Away from the glitz and glamour of the casino districts, this area is a recreational bonanza for a vast array of outdoor enthusiasts, whether they prefer land or water sports. Recently dubbed "America's Adventure Place," Tahoe–Reno offers a wide range of outdoor activities, from world-class skiing in the winter to a host of summer opportunities. Favorable weather and stunning scenery combine to create a remarkable paradise for both locals and visitors seeking to enjoy their favorite open-air pursuit. With a range of terrain that varies from the high desert surrounding Reno to the forests of the Tahoe Basin, there are a vast number of trails from which to choose: lakeside strolls, mountain ascents, forested journeys, or just a place to walk the dog.

To acquaint yourself with the area, consider the following fun facts:

- Tahoe–Reno attracts more than 10 million visitors annually.
- Prior to the Great Recession, Nevada was the fastest-growing state in the Union, with Washoe County reaching a 12% growth rate.
- Twelve miles wide, 22 miles long, and with a 72-mile shoreline, Lake Tahoe is the largest subalpine lake in North America, with a surface elevation of 6,223 feet above sea level.
- With a maximum depth of 1,645 feet, Tahoe is the tenth deepest lake in the world, and the second deepest in the United States, after Crater Lake in Oregon (1,958 feet).
- Lake Tahoe holds 39 trillion gallons of water, which would cover the entire state of California to a depth of more than 14 inches. The daily evaporation rate of the lake is 335 million gallons.
- Known for the clarity of its waters, Lake Tahoe is 99.9% pure.
- Sixty-three streams flow into Tahoe, but only the Truckee River flows out of the lake, taking a 116-mile journey and passing through Reno–Sparks before emptying into Pyramid Lake.

Climate

Combining both high desert and mountain zones, the climate of Tahoe–Reno offers generally pleasant weather conditions during the usual hiking season. Sunny skies and warm daytime temperatures are the norm, although nighttime temperatures can be quite cool. Summer highs in the 90s are common in the Reno area, while thermometers around Lake Tahoe register more moderate temperatures. What little rain that falls in the summer comes from infrequent thunderstorms.

Geology

Geologists speculate that the landform that would ultimately become the Tahoe–Reno area we know today was once beneath a shallow ancient sea in the supercontinent of *Pangaea*. The North American continental plate eventually broke away from Pangaea and headed west, colliding into the Pacific Ocean plate, which was drifting east. Extreme pressure and heat were created as the North American plate rose above the Pacific plate, producing molten rock that slowly solidified beneath the sedimentary surface into granitic rocks that were later exposed through faulting, or fractures in the earth's crust.

Faulting allowed blocks of land to rise and fall, pushing the primarily plutonic rocks of the Sierra Nevada up from the ancient seabed. Eventually two principal faults evolved in the Tahoe area, which produced uplifts that became the main Sierra crest to the west and the Carson Range to the east. In between, the down-thrown fault block formed the deep V-shaped valley of the Tahoe Basin. To the east, similar faulting created a parade of basins and ranges across what is now referred to as the Great Basin.

A lake began to form at the lowest, southern end of the Tahoe Basin, fed by precipitation and creeks draining the surrounding mountains. The level of the lake rose steadily until an outlet for the river draining the lake was reached to the north, near the current town of Truckee. Later, a significant lava flow from Mt. Pluto, site of the Northstar California resort, dammed the outlet and caused the lake to rise again. Eventually the river was able to cut a new outlet through the volcanic rock near the present-day location of Tahoe City. The highest level of Lake Tahoe has been estimated to be about 600 to 800 feet above the current elevation. Additional volcanic activity occurred at both the south end of the basin, around Carson Pass, and the north end of the basin, near Donner Pass.

Although a regional ice sheet was absent, in theory the last Ice Age put the finishing touches on the Tahoe Basin. Separate rivers of ice followed some of the existing V-shaped stream channels, carving them into classic U-shaped canyons. Glacial action scoured several of the canyons on the west side of the basin, revealing the classic granite bedrock associated with the Sierra Nevada today. In the process, some of the area's most picturesque lakes were formed,

including Donner, Cascade, Fallen Leaf, and Echo Lakes, as well as scenic Emerald Bay on Tahoe's southwest shore.

With dramatically less precipitation in the rain shadow of the Sierra crest, glaciers were mostly absent from the Carson Range to the east. Consequently, without the glacial scouring of the west side of the Tahoe Basin, the topography of the Carson Range is composed primarily of granitic and volcanic soils rather than the classic Sierra granite bedrock. While the west side of the Tahoe Basin is sprinkled with an abundance of tarns, lakes, and ponds, the east side is nearly devoid of such features. Additional glacial activity influenced the area when ice dams formed across the Truckee River canyon and broke several times, producing floods that further shaped the canyon, depositing debris downstream as far away as present-day Reno.

Plants

Since the area has such a wide range in elevation (from 4,400 feet in the Truckee Meadows to 10,881 feet atop Freel Peak) and a wide range in annual precipitation (7.5 inches in Reno to nearly 60 inches at Soda Springs), hikers can expect to encounter a similarly wide range of flora. The gamut of flora ranges between the drought-tolerant vegetation of the high desert and the alpine foliage carpeting the highest peaks. The Lake Tahoe Basin is characterized by coniferous forests, almost all of which are second growth, while the ubiquitous sagebrush is commonly associated with the valleys of western Nevada. Generally, the flora of Tahoe–Reno can be classified into the following plant communities, roughly proceeding from east to west.

SAGEBRUSH SCRUB ZONE

No plant is more representative of the Great Basin than the big sagebrush (*Artemisia tridentata*), with the plant's yellow blossoms honored as Nevada's state flower. The plant's pungent aroma following a summer thunderstorm is perhaps the fragrance most associated with the West. At first glance, sagebrush appears to cover everything in sight on the valley floors and surrounding foothills. However, before the area was settled and cattle and sheep grazing were introduced, the vegetation was three-quarters native bunch grass. After the livestock consumed the grass, the unappetizing sagebrush was allowed to fill in the vacant spots where the grass once flourished. Nowadays, the much smaller percentage of grass in the Sagebrush Zone is primarily nonnative species, such as cheatgrass and downy brome, introduced by the westward expansion. The other trademark shrub most associated with the West, the tumbleweed, is also a nonnative plant, having been introduced from the steppes of Russia.

A wide variety of drought-tolerant shrubs may accompany the sagebrush within this zone, commonly including rabbitbrush, blackbrush, ephedra, bitterbrush, spiny hopsage, cotton thorn, desert peach, and snowberry. Wildflower displays vary considerably from year to year, corresponding to the amounts and timing of precipitation. Common wildflowers in this zone include evening primrose, prickly poppy, blazing star, desert paintbrush, mule ears, scarlet gilia, and sulphur buckwheat. Sagebrush oftentimes extends into the pinyon-juniper zone and, under the right conditions, extends even into higher elevations, including the alpine zone.

PINYON-JUNIPER ZONE

Above the sagebrush zone, the pinyon-juniper zone harbors extensive woodlands of the singleleaf pinyon pine (*Pinus monophylla*) and lesser amounts of the Sierra juniper (*Juniperus occidentalis var. australis*) in the Carson Range and Utah juniper (*Juniperus osteosperma*) in the Virginia and Pine Nut ranges. Beginning around 5,000 feet, this zone extends to 8,000 feet and occasionally beyond, thriving in locations along the Sierra foothills that receive more than 12 inches of annual precipitation.

Within the Great Basin, the woodlands of the pinyon-juniper zone form the largest forested zone, exceeding all other forested areas combined. Rarely achieving a height taller than 30 feet, these two species display rounded, spreading crowns—squat forms not generally associated with the perfect shape of a Christmas tree. Pure stands of pinyon pines are common in the higher elevations. Curl-leaf mountain mahogany, which is drought tolerant, is often found intermixed in this zone, usually on rocky, arid slopes and ridges.

Some common shrubs found in this zone include big sagebrush, serviceberry, bitterbrush, snakeweed, snowberry, elderberry, rabbitbrush, and wild rose. Wildflowers are more common here than in the sagebrush scrub zone, and common species include several varieties of penstemon.

Sierra juniper

MONTANE ZONE

The montane zone is found from lake level to about 8,000 feet, being the largest zone in the Lake Tahoe Basin and containing the widest variety of plant types. The montane zone can be grouped into five distinctly different divisions.

Jeffrey pine forest occupies dry slopes that span elevations from approximately 6,000 to 8,000 feet. Open Jeffrey pine forests represent the most common type of coniferous forest on the eastern slope of the Carson Range, intermixing with white fir. In the lower realms of the Tahoe Basin, the Jeffrey pine forest is mixed with sugar pine, ponderosa pine, white fir, and incense cedar. Those conifers are replaced by western white pine, ponderosa pine, and red fir toward the upper limits. On southern exposures, light stands of Jeffrey pine forest often intermix with Sierra juniper or with open areas of montane chaparral.

Montane chaparral is a drought-tolerant community that spans elevations across the spectrum of the montane zone and into the subalpine zone, typically occupying dry slopes with a southern exposure. This community incorporates several common shrubs, including huckleberry oak, tobacco brush, rabbitbrush, manzanita, chinquapin, and sagebrush. Along the eastern fringe of the Carson Range, mountain mahogany and juniper trees may dot the slopes of the montane chaparral community.

White fir forest is named for the dominant member of a mixed forest, which also includes incense cedar, sugar pine, Jeffrey pine, and ponderosa pine, as well as red fir at the upper limits. In the Tahoe Sierra, to elevations around 7,000 feet, white firs prefer a moist habitat, forming either dense stands with little ground cover, or more open stands that allow deciduous trees and shrubs to thrive, including quaking aspen, willow, maple, currant, gooseberry, thimbleberry, and honeysuckle.

Red fir forest extends above the white fir forest to about 8,500 feet. Unlike the white fir, red fir is often found in exclusive stands, usually on cool northern or eastern exposures. The red fir forest is generally dense, allowing very little ground cover, which when present is composed primarily of shade-loving flowers and plants.

Montane meadow is a community that occurs in areas of sufficient groundwater. Similar in some respects to the montane chaparral community, montane meadows span the realm of the upper montane zone into the subalpine zone. The wetter environment allows grasses, rushes, and sedges to thrive, along with several species of moisture-loving wildflowers.

SUBALPINE ZONE

Above the montane zone, the subalpine zone begins around 8,000 feet and continues upward toward timberline, which, depending on a number of variables, starts anywhere from 9,000 to 10,000 feet in the Tahoe Sierra. With characteristically poor soils and a harsh climate, where snow covers the ground for up to nine months of the year, the prolific forests below give way to isolated stands of conifers and the open terrain of meadows and talus slides. Red firs, lodgepole pines, and junipers may extend into this zone in some areas, with lodgepole pines often rimming the shoreline of subalpine lakes. Despite the sporadic appearance of these trees from the lower realm, the two conifer species most closely associated with the subalpine zone are mountain hemlock and whitebark pine. Nearing timberline, dwarfed and wind-battered whitebark pines become the only conifer able to survive the conditions associated with such a harsh environment. Shrubs and plants in this zone also take on a diminished stature, hugging the ground to eke out an existence. Common plants include heathers and laurels. Where seeps and rivulets provide moist soils, a short-lived but stunning display of colorful wildflowers delights passersby. Small patches of soil in rock outcroppings may provide an equally delightful display of plants and flowers.

ALPINE ZONE

Above timberline at the extreme upper elevations of the Tahoe Sierra is the alpine zone. Although there is some debate among botanists as to whether or not the Tahoe area truly has a well-defined alpine zone, only the backcountry traveler who reaches the summit of some of the basin's highest peaks will be able to observe the habitat in question. The vegetation within this zone appears to be a combination of tundra species from the north and desert species from the east. Whatever their origin, these plants are generally compact, low-growing perennials that grow rapidly and flower briefly, with most of their growth occurring below ground. Low-growing shrubs, such as low sagebrush and short-stemmed stenotus, share the extreme conditions and poor soils of the alpine region with an assortment of wildflowers. The uppermost slopes of Mt. Rose and Freel Peak provide some of the best opportunities in the Tahoe Sierra for hikers to experience the flora of the alpine zone.

RIPARIAN ZONES

The last of the classifications within the Tahoe–Reno area is the riparian zone. The vegetation in the zones lining watercourses is generally quite luxuriant, even within the parched sagebrush scrub and pinyon-juniper zones. With the additional moisture provided from perennial streams, lush foliage along the banks includes deciduous trees and shrubs such as aspen, cottonwood, willow, alder, creek dogwood, and mountain ash. Smaller plants and colorful wildflowers are also common in creekside environments.

Animals

Along with a wide variety of plants, the Tahoe–Reno area is home to a varied community of fauna. Alert eyes may be able to spot several different species of animals while traveling the trails.

MAMMALS

The largest mammal in the region is the omnivorous black bear, which may range in color from black to cinnamon. Some members of the black bear population, particularly near developed communities on the west shore of Lake Tahoe, have become quite pesky in seeking food from garbage cans, dumpsters, and campgrounds. However, the vast majority of bears you might see in the backcountry remain timid and wary of human encounters. Although bears here are not nearly as much of a potential nuisance as the more infamous bears in Yosemite, hikers and backpackers should obey the following guidelines:

- Don't leave your pack unattended on the trail.
- At camp, empty your pack and open all flaps and pockets.
- Keep all food, trash, or scented items in a bear-proof canister or safely hung from a tree.
- Pack out all trash.
- Don't allow bears to approach your food—make noise, wave your arms, throw rocks. Be bold, but keep a safe distance and use good judgment.
- If a bear gets your food, you are responsible for cleaning up the mess.
- Never attempt to retrieve food from a bear.
- Never approach a bear, especially a cub.
- Report any incidents to the appropriate authority.

More likely to be seen along the trail than a bear is the mule deer, so named for its floppy ears. Mule deer prefer varied terrain with an ample food supply, which consists mainly of leaves from trees and shrubs, along with grasses, sedges, and other herbs. Watch for deer around dusk in grassy meadows, or during the day in open forest where browse is plentiful. Deer herds in the area are migratory, retreating in winter either west to the California foothills or east to the western valleys of Nevada. Since extinction of the grizzly bear and wolf from the Sierra, the mule deer's only remaining predator, other than humans, is the mountain lion.

Although present in the region, mountain lions, also known as cougars, are rarely seen by humans. I have yet to see a single mountain lion in the wild during many years of hiking and backpacking in the West. Ranging in length from 6.5 to 8 feet and weighing as much as 200 pounds, mountain lions tend to be primarily nocturnal, patrolling a vast range. Although mule deer are their principal food source, mountain lions will stalk smaller mammals as well. At an average weight of 20 pounds, the bobcat is the mountain lion's smaller cousin. Also nocturnal and equally reclusive in nature, bobcats prefer a diet of rodents. You're much more likely to hear their blood-curdling scream during the night than to see bobcats in the wild.

The highly adaptable coyote is often seen loping across clearings and through the woodlands of Tahoe–Reno. From backcountry campsites, backpackers frequently hear the coyote's nighttime chorus of howls and yelps. Although a quite common animal to residents of the West, many people fail to realize that coyotes are omnivores, preferring a diet of small rodents but also dining on berries and plants when such prey is unavailable.

Other common, medium-sized mammals of Tahoe–Reno include beavers, muskrats, martens, marmots, raccoons, porcupines, red fox, weasels, and badgers. Hikers frequently see Douglas squirrels, California ground squirrels, golden-mantled ground squirrels, western gray squirrels, western flying squirrels, and chipmunks. Cottontails and jackrabbits are commonly seen scampering through areas of sagebrush scrub. Smaller rodents include pikas, voles, shrews, mice, moles, and pocket gophers.

At dusk, backpackers camped around the shore of one of the area's backcountry lakes are almost guaranteed a visit from a handful of bats searching the skies for the evening's first course of insects. Midsummer visitors will be comforted to know that large helpings of mosquitoes are on the bats' menu.

BIRDS

Located on the Pacific Flyway, the skies above Tahoe–Reno are home to hundreds of bird species. While hiking around marshlands, rivers, and creeks, or the shores of Lake Tahoe, keep your eyes peeled for waterfowl such as wood ducks, mergansers, mallards, great blue herons, and Canada geese.

Although not particularly common, bald eagles and ospreys are seen from time to time in the Tahoe–Reno skies. Red-tailed hawks are more frequently seen patrolling the skies, particularly around ranchland in the valleys of western Nevada. Great horned owls are primarily nocturnal but may be seen napping on a tree limb during the day.

A walk along a mountain trail without seeing either a Clark's nutcracker, mountain chickadee, or Steller's jay is hard to imagine. Numerous songbirds fly around the Tahoe Basin, but a fine treat would be the sighting of a mountain bluebird flitting about a subalpine meadow or perched on the branch of a young lodgepole pine near the edge.

Viewing deck on the Lake of the Sky Trail

REPTILES AND AMPHIBIANS

Amphibians and reptiles are common residents of the area. The most frequently seen species include Pacific tree frog, western fence lizard, and the common garter snake.

Although possible, encountering a rattlesnake on the trails of Tahoe–Reno is unlikely. Most rattlesnakes will sense the vibration created by your boots on the trail and move away before you arrive. Occasionally, hikers can surprise a rattlesnake, which may result in the snake curling up into a defensive coil and making that distinctive rattling sound with its tail. If you happen to find yourself in this situation, stop, quickly determine the location of the snake, and move deliberately away—do not approach it! Be assured, rattlesnakes are not aggressive and are more afraid of you than you are of them. Like all snakes, rattlers are cold-blooded and will avoid the heat of the day, making the rare encounter on the trail more possible in the early morning or early evening when they are seeking warmth from the sun. Avoid sticking your appendages in crevices or under logs and rocks during the hot part of the day when they prefer the shade. A fatal bite from a rattlesnake is extremely uncommon.

INSECTS

Insects are abundant members of the Tahoe–Reno community. Unfortunately, the species that gets the most attention seems to be the mosquito. Thankfully, depending on elevation and how quickly the previous winter's snowpack melts, the peak of the mosquito season lasts for just a few weeks in the Tahoe backcountry, usually from the last weeks of July into the first week of August.

Ticks would be considered simply nasty bloodsucking pests if not for their potential for causing debilitating diseases. These insects seem to be more prevalent during spring or early summer following a particularly wet winter or early spring. When ticks are troublesome, use plenty of insect repellent and cover up with long-sleeved shirts and long pants with the cuffs tucked into your socks. Self-inspection or examination by a spouse or close friend should be done at least once a day. If a tick burrows into your skin, use tweezers and apply gentle traction to remove the pest, being careful not to leave the head behind. Folk methods, such as applying petroleum jelly or a match so that the tick will back out of the skin are not effective. After complete removal of the tick, thoroughly wash the affected area with antibacterial soap.

The black widow spider is a common insect in the valleys of western Nevada. Only the female, characterized by a red hourglass on her shiny black abdomen, is poisonous. Although her venom is many times more poisonous than a rattlesnake, the amount of venom transmitted in a bite is so small that bites are almost never fatal. Black widows are not aggressive by nature.

Although scorpions are present in Nevada, the species in northern Nevada are not poisonous.

FISH

The lakes and streams of the Tahoe–Reno area teem with fish, where anglers can ply their craft in search of brook, brown, cutthroat, and rainbow trout. Along with these trout, Lake Tahoe itself is home to a couple of additional introduced species—Mackinaw, also known as lake trout, and Kokanee salmon. Although biologists theorize that Mackinaws in Lake Tahoe may reach weights as high as 50 pounds, the record catch so far is 37 pounds, 6 ounces. Landlocked cousins of the sockeye salmon, Kokanee salmon were introduced to Lake Tahoe in 1944. The Taylor Creek Stream Profile Chamber at the Lake Tahoe Visitor Center provides an excellent opportunity for viewing the annual spawning migration of the Kokanee each autumn, usually coinciding with the locally renowned Kokanee Festival that occurs during the first week of October.

Wilderness

On September 3, President Lyndon B. Johnson signed into law the Wilderness Act of 1964. The act defined wilderness as being in contrast with those areas where humans and their own works dominate the landscape, where the earth and its community of life are untrammeled by humans, and where humans themselves are visitors who do not remain. Wilderness retains a primeval character and influence, without permanent improvements or human habitation, which is protected and managed so as to preserve its natural conditions and which generally appears to have been affected primarily by the forces of nature, with the imprint of the work of humans substantially unnoticeable. In addition, wilderness has outstanding opportunities for solitude or a primitive and unconfined type of recreation; has at least 5,000 acres of land or is of sufficient size as to make practicable its preservation and use in an unimpaired condition; and may also contain ecological, geological, or other features of scientific, educational, scenic, or historical value.

The Tahoe–Reno region is blessed with four designated wilderness areas, three in California (Desolation, Granite Chief, and Mokelumne) and one in Nevada (Mt. Rose). In addition to these four, two other areas have been proposed for inclusion in the wilderness system, Castle Peak and Meiss Meadows. The nearly 18,000-acre Castle Peak tract is north of Donner Summit and holds some of the most scenic backcountry in the north Tahoe area. Meiss Meadows is a 31,000-acre parcel 2 miles south of Lake Tahoe, between California Highways 88 and 89. For more information on these proposed wilderness areas, see **calwild.org.**

The preservation of wildlands within the wilderness system is an essential link to our nation's heritage, providing citizens with the opportunity to visit areas unmolested by the permanent presence of humans and development. As stated by President Johnson at the signing of the original Wilderness Act, "If future generations are to remember us with gratitude rather than contempt, we must leave them more than the miracles of technology. We must leave them with a glimpse of the world as it was in the beginning, not just after we got through with it." Proper stewardship of the earth requires that we support the preservation of natural lands for those who follow us.

Wilderness Areas in This Book

WILDERNESS	WHEN DESIGNATED	AREA (ACRES)	TRIPS
Desolation	1969	63,475	Chapter 4: 73; Chapter 5: 78–80, 82–87; Chapter 8: 119–121, 124, 126
Granite Chief	1984	19,048	Chapter 3: 56, 59–61; Chapter 4: 68, 69
Mokelumne	1964	99,161	Chapter 10: 166, 169–171, 174–178, 181
Mt. Rose	1989	28,121	Chapter 9: 129, 131, 133, 136, 139, 142–143, 147

For more information on wilderness areas in the United States, visit **wilderness.net.**

Comfort, Safety, and Etiquette

Trails in the Tahoe–Reno area vary from short, easy strolls in a park, requiring nothing more than a dab of sunscreen and a half-filled water bottle, to full-fledged assaults on high peaks, where extra preparation and a good dose of mountain savvy are prerequisites. By employing some common sense and following some simple guidelines you should be able to experience full enjoyment on the trips described in this guide while minimizing the risks posed by any potential hazards.

Seasons and Weather

Nevada is an arid state—the most arid in the United States. Reno's yearly average for precipitation is a paltry 7.5 inches, more than half of which usually falls between December and March. The massive barrier created by the Sierra Nevada is the principal reason for this lack of precipitation. As Pacific storms move eastward, the moisture-laden clouds rise along the western slope, cool, and drop most of their moisture before spilling over the crest and blowing into Nevada. In contrast to the small amount of precipitation falling in the valleys, Marlette Lake in the Carson Range, a mere 7 miles east of Carson City by air, records more than 27 inches annually. While the bulk of moisture in the mountains falls as winter snow (190 inches at lake level), precipitation in the valleys is mixed, with Reno receiving about 25 total inches of snow over the course of a typical winter. The snowfall from a single storm rarely exceeds more than a few inches and generally remains on the ground for only a few days. Storms reaching western Nevada are usually preceded by high winds. Aside from Pacific storms, a smaller percentage of Reno's precipitation is generated from random summer thunderstorms. Reno can expect measurable precipitation only 51 days of an average year.

Summer conditions tend to be sunny, dry, and hot, with daytime highs typically in the 90s. However, the high desert cools off dramatically at night, with low temperatures above the 60s uncommon. Spring in the Reno area tends to lack the steady progression from winter to summer that more temperate climates experience. Residents often claim that Reno has no spring, simply moving from winter to summer at some unpredictably random date anytime between late April and early July. Fall can perhaps be the most pleasant time of year, with dry conditions prevailing and daytime temperatures in the 60s and 70s.

Like the high desert, the shores of Lake Tahoe enjoy a 93% probability of sunshine on any given day between June and August. However, unlike the high desert, summer daytime temperatures rarely exceed 80°F, thanks in part to the moderating influences of the lake's 193 square miles of surface area and the dense forests carpeting the slopes of the lake's basin. Nighttime temperatures are relatively mild as well, ranging from the 30s in June to the 40s in July and August. Precipitation is light, generally coming in the form of an afternoon thunderstorm, with averages of 0.69 inch in June, 0.26 inch in July, and 0.31 inch in August. Unlike the Rockies, where the locals say they set their watches by the regularity of the afternoon thunderstorms, the Sierra may experience summers of few or no thunderstorms, or a string of days when they're a regular occurrence. Hikers in the Sierra should always be prepared for the potential of an afternoon thunderstorm and beat a hasty retreat when lightning is a threat. Although conditions at lake level may be pleasant, temperatures drop an average of 3.5°F per 1,000 feet of elevation.

Autumn is often an ideal season for enjoying a hike in the Tahoe–Sierra, when most of the tourists have returned home and left the backcountry to the locals and diehards. Warm and dry weather often lingers through the waning days of summer into September and October, before the first major storm of the season blankets the slopes with snow. Temperatures, although cooler, are still pleasant enough for hiking, with daytime highs in October averaging 56°F, and even though the average precipitation for the month climbs to 1.9 inches, there still is an 84% chance of sunny weather on any given day. The autumn color provided by quaking aspens in stream canyons, and willows and grasses in the meadows can be quite spectacular. Usually by early November a Pacific storm has brought a significant snowfall to the higher elevations, encouraging people to put away their hiking boots and start waxing their skis.

Special Hazards

LIGHTNING

There are two aspects of lightning to be avoided: the direct strike and subsequent ground currents. The best place to be out of doors when lightning strikes is in a broad valley, near the shorter trees in a dense stand of timber. This may be a possibility when hiking around Lake Tahoe, but the sparsely timbered valleys around Reno do not offer such havens. The rule of thumb suggests a position lower than nearby projections. If you happen to be on a high ridge

when a thunderstorm develops, beat a hasty retreat to lower ground, avoiding hollows, depressions, overhangs, and small caves, which increase your exposure to ground currents. The following guidelines should help you avoid a lightning strike.

- Keep an eye on the weather, and retreat when thunderstorms are imminent.
- Seek lower ground.
- Avoid metal, hollows, depressions, overhangs, small caves, and solitary projections. Maintain a distance of 15 feet between people.
- Crouch down and cover your ears (to protect from thunder).
- Stay out of narrow drainages that may be prone to flash flooding.

ALTITUDE

Trails in the Tahoe–Reno area range in altitude from 4,500 feet to nearly 11,000 feet, elevations high enough for some flatlanders to experience mountain sickness and its more serious counterpart, acute mountain sickness. Symptoms may include headache, fatigue, loss of appetite, shortness of breath, nausea, vomiting, drowsiness, memory loss, and loss of mental acuity. If such symptoms are present, a quick descent to lower elevations is needed to alleviate the problem. Sufferers of acute mountain sickness may require immediate medical attention.

Although the dynamics of mountain sickness and acute mountain sickness are not fully understood, there are some things you can do to minimize your chances of experiencing these disorders.

- Drink plenty of fluids. Avoid alcohol.
- Eat a diet high in carbohydrates prior to and during your trip.
- Acclimatize slowly.
- People subject to anemia should consult a physician.

SUN

The typically sunny weather that makes the Tahoe–Reno area a desirable place to recreate can become a serious problem for people who are ill prepared for the hazards. Unprotected exposure to the sun at these altitudes for as little as a half hour may be enough for fair-skinned people to develop sunburn. Sunblock with a high UV rating should be applied to exposed areas of the skin, and sunglasses that block out a minimum of 90% of UVA and UVB rays should be worn. Light-colored, loose-fitting, lightweight clothing used in combination with a wide-brimmed hat will offer additional protection.

WATER

Water—either too little or too much can be a problem. Too much water is usually only a problem during spring or early summer in the Tahoe–Reno area, when streams are swollen with runoff from the previous winter's snowpack. Exercise caution at these times when crossing streams.

Water is scarce in some areas—in some places it may be completely unavailable, a condition made worse during drought years. Proper planning may be necessary to assure that rest stops and campsites will have adequate water supplies nearby. Always bring water with you for the start of your trip and replenish your supply in the field as needed. Be sure to drink plenty of fluids during your hike, particularly during hot conditions. And visitors should be aware that the high desert is much drier than areas closer to sea level, making it possible to dehydrate very quickly.

Water quality in the backcountry has become a well-documented concern, especially in high-use areas. Any water acquired in the field should be filtered, treated, or boiled before drinking.

Navigation

No backcountry skill is more important than the ability to find your way to your destination and safely back again. Space does not allow for a detailed dissertation on all of the elements of navigation, orienteering, and route finding, so you will have to gain a more complete understanding of these skills from other sources. The following guidelines are a starting point for learning the necessary skills.

- Study your route carefully before leaving home.
- Give a reliable person a detailed description of your route, expected time of return, and whom to call if you don't return.
- Carry a topographic map of the area, along with a compass or GPS receiver.
- Pay attention to the terrain as you travel, and make mental notes of significant landmarks.
- Hike in a group and keep the group together.
- If you become lost, finding shelter is your first priority.

Trail Etiquette

Public lands belong to everyone and deserve to be respected. Hikers are responsible for leaving the backcountry as it was found, or better, if possible. All recreationists should understand and practice "Leave No Trace" principles in all of their wanderings. The following guidelines should help in keeping the Tahoe–Reno area in pristine condition.

ON THE TRAIL

- Plan ahead and be prepared—know the regulations and concerns of the area and prepare for them.
- Stay on the trail—never cut switchbacks.
- Preserve the serenity of the backcountry for others—avoid making loud noises.
- Yield the right-of-way to uphill hikers.
- Yield the right-of-way to equestrians by stepping off the trail on the downhill side.
- When hiking, stay alert for mountain bikers. Although all signs indicate that mountain bikers should yield to hikers, most bikers seem to expect that hikers will be the ones to step aside.
- Avoid traveling in large groups.

- Leave it there—destruction or removal of plants and animals, or historical, prehistoric, or geological items is unethical and almost always illegal.
- Take it with you—pack out everything, even trash left behind by others.

CAMPING

- Camp a minimum of 100 feet from any water source.
- Select a campsite well away from trails.
- Never build improvements, such as fireplaces, rock walls, drainage swales, and so on.
- Camp on hard surfaces, not on vegetation.
- Use only downed wood for campfires. Never cut trees, dead or alive.
- Use only existing fire rings for campfires.
- Never leave a fire unattended.
- Fully extinguish all campfires by thoroughly soaking with water.

SANITATION

- Bury human waste 6 inches deep and cover with soil, a minimum of 100 feet from trails and 500 feet from water sources.
- Pack out toilet paper, or burn in areas where fires are permissible.
- Cook only the amount of food you can eat to avoid the need to discard leftovers.
- Wash and rinse dishes, clothes, or yourself a minimum of 200 feet from water sources. Never wash in lakes or streams.
- Pack out all trash—do not attempt to burn plastic or foil packaging.
- Filter, boil, or purify all drinking water.

For more information on Leave No Trace principles, see **lnt.org,** or phone 800-332-4100.

DOGS

Dogs are permitted to accompany you on most of the trails described in this guide, noted in the headings for each trip. Consider leaving your pet behind when visiting the more popular trails, as too many dogs and too many people can be a volatile combination. Where bringing along Fido is permitted, make sure your pet is well socialized and is on a leash or under voice control. Uncontrolled dogs can present a hazard to wildlife. Also, make sure to pack along enough water to keep your dog hydrated both while driving to and from the trailhead and on the hike itself. Never leave a dog unattended in a vehicle in sunny or warm conditions.

Campfires should occur only in designated areas.

Using This Book

This guide introduces you to the Lake Tahoe and greater Reno area, with just over 200 possible hikes that run the spectrum from short and easy to long and difficult. Trips are separated into 11 chapters, each covering a loosely defined geographical subregion. Each chapter has an overall map showing the locations of all the trips within the region, and each trip is shown on a map. This section provides explanations of the maps and the trip descriptions that will help you in determining the type of trips that are best suited to your level of interest, skill, and conditioning.

Choosing a Trip

There are three ways to decide which trip is best for you:

- Choose a trip in the area you'd like to visit from the overview maps at the beginning of each chapter.
- Turn to Appendix 1, Best Trips by Theme, on page 430, to choose a hike based on its sights or characteristics, such as geology or autumn color.
- Choose a specific trip from the table of contents.

Explanation of Trip Summaries

Each trip entry includes a capsule summary, highlights, directions to the starting point, information about facilities and/or the trailhead, and the full description of the trail itself. The capsule summary at the beginning includes the following information:

DISTANCE AND TRAIL TYPE
Distances are round-trip, unless specified as one-way. Trail types include loops, semiloops (a trip combining loop and out-and-back segments), out-and-back, and point-to-point hikes. A vehicle shuttle is often recommended for point-to-point hikes; for these hikes, driving directions are provided to the endpoint of the hike as well as the starting point, in the Facilities/Trailhead section of the summary. If a hike looks enticing but its listed distance is longer or shorter than you prefer, don't let it hinder you from extending the hike or turning back sooner.

HIKING TIME
This figure represents an estimate of the time it would take for the average hiker to complete the trip. This estimate may vary depending upon the rate at which you prefer to hike, the number and length of rest stops you prefer, and how much additional time you spend enjoying the surroundings.

ELEVATION
These figures represent the number of vertical feet lost or gained on each trip. Flat trips with minimal elevation gain or loss list elevation as "Negligible."

DIFFICULTY
The difficulty rating takes into consideration the type of trail, terrain, elevation gain, and necessary route finding. The four categories are as follows:

EASY: The trail is well defined and easy to follow, and the terrain is gentle. Easy trails are well suited for hikers of all levels.

MODERATE: Trails are usually well defined, but the terrain has more ups and downs. These trails require hikers to be physically fit.

DIFFICULT: These longer trips have sections of trail that may be in poor condition or require cross-country travel. Terrain is steep and challenging. These trips are suitable for experienced and physically fit hikers only.

VERY DIFFICULT: The longest and most rigorous trips in the book, these may require cross-country or mountaineering skills. Only the most skilled, physically fit, and experienced hikers should attempt these trips.

TRAIL USE

This category describes the uses for which the trail is suited, including backpacking and mountain biking, whether the trail is a good choice for kids, and whether dogs are allowed on the trail. Where this book says "Dogs OK," it is permissible to have your dog off leash.

BEST TIMES

Although conditions may vary from year to year, this entry notes the months when the trail is generally free of snow.

AGENCY

The public agency with jurisdiction over the trail is listed here, with its phone number and website.

The hiker emblem helps keep hikers on track.

RECOMMENDED MAPS

The best maps for successfully navigating the trail are listed here. The abbreviations preceding the map names are the initials of the agency that published the map. Many are from the US Forest Service (USFS) and the U.S. Geological Survey (USGS). Other sources of maps include the Truckee Donner Land Trust (TDLT), Carson Valley Trails Association (CVTA), Washoe County Regional Parks, and the Poedunks.

Map Legend

Symbol	Description	Symbol	Description
------	Main Trail	**S**	Fee Collection
- - - - -	Other Trail	⩎	Picnic Area
········	Cross-Country Route	⚑	Gate
T	Trailhead	■	Structure
28	Trip Number	▲	Peak/Summit
P	Parking	⩛	Marsh
⚠	Campground	80	Interstate Highway
⌂	Ranger Station	395	US Highway
?	Information	41	State Highway

OVERVIEW OF HIKES

HIKE NUMBER	HIKE NAME	DISTANCE (miles)	DIFFICULTY	ELEVATION GAIN (feet)	DOGS ALLOWED	GREAT FOR KIDS	MOUNTAIN BIKING	HORSEBACK RIDING	TRAIL CONFIGURATION
CHAPTER 1: GRAEAGLE AND SIERRA CITY									
1	Madora Lake	1.6	Easy	Neg.		🧍			loop
2	Eureka Peak Loop	4	Moderate	1,275					loop
3	Grass, Rock, Jamison, and Wades Lakes	7.5	Moderate	1,550	🐕				loop
4	Mt. Washington	7	Difficult	1,275	🐕		⚙		out-and-back
5	Gray Eagle Creek	2.2	Moderate	525	🐕	🧍			out-and-back
6	Smith Lake	2	Moderate	350	🐕	🧍			out-and-back
7	Mt. Elwell Loop	7.25	Very difficult	2,025	🐕				loop
8	Long Lake Loop	4.5	Moderate	1,150	🐕				loop
9	Bear Lakes Loop	3.8	Moderate	450	🐕	🧍			loop
10	Frazier Falls	1	Easy	Neg.	🐕	🧍			out-and-back
11	Lower Salmon Lake	1	Easy	Neg.	🐕	🧍			out-and-back
12	Upper Salmon Lake Trail to Deer Lake	4	Moderate	750	🐕				out-and-back
13	Deer Lake Trail and Pacific Crest Trail Loop	8/6	Difficult	1,750	🐕		⚙		loop/out-and-back
14	Tamarack Lakes Road to Sierra Buttes	7	Very difficult	2,250	🐕		⚙		out-and-back
15	Sierra Buttes via Pacific Crest Trail	5	Difficult	1,725	🐕				out-and-back
16	Sardine Overlook	4.6	Moderate	700	🐕		⚙		out-and-back
17	Tamarack Lakes Trail	7.5	Difficult	1,400	🐕		⚙		out-and-back
18	Volcano Lake and Mountain Mine	7	Difficult	1,550	🐕		⚙		out-and-back
19	Loves Falls	0.8	Easy	Neg.	🐕	🧍			out-and-back
20	Wild Plum Loop	2.5	Moderate	550	🐕				loop
21	Haskell Peak	3	Difficult	1,200	🐕		⚙		out-and-back
22	Chapman Creek	4	Moderate	575	🐕				out-and-back
CHAPTER 2: TRUCKEE, DONNER SUMMIT, AND VICINITY									
23	Mt. Lola and White Rock Lake	10.4/ 14.4	Difficult	2,525/ 2,625	🐕		⚙		out-and-back
24	Lacey Valley Trail	3.3/6.6	Easy	225/235	🐕		⚙		out-and-back/point to point
25	Sagehen Creek	5	Easy	Neg.	🐕	🧍	⚙		out-and-back
26	Commemorative Emigrant Trail	7.5	Easy	300	🐕	🧍	⚙		point to point
27	Donner Lake Rim Trail: Gregory Creek to Summit Lake	7	Moderate	1,150	🐕		⚙		out-and-back

Neg. = Negligible elevation gain   ↻ = loop   ◯ = balloon   **8** = figure eight   ↗↙ = out-and-back   ↗ = point to point

HIKE NUMBER	HIKE NAME	DISTANCE (miles)	DIFFICULTY	ELEVATION GAIN (feet)	DOGS ALLOWED	GREAT FOR KIDS	MOUNTAIN BIKING	HORSEBACK RIDING	TRAIL CONFIGURATION
CHAPTER 2: TRUCKEE, DONNER SUMMIT, AND VICINITY *Continued*									
28	Summit Lake Loop	7	Easy to moderate	550	🐕				loop
29	Frog Lake Overlook and Warren Lake	9/15	Very difficult	1,500/2,250	🐕				out-and-back
30	Castle Peak and Basin Peak	9.6	Difficult	1,980	🐕				out-and-back
31	Sand Ridge Lake	12	Moderate	1,025	🐕				out-and-back
32	Castle Valley, Round Valley, and Andesite Peak Loop	9.6	Moderate	1,700	🐕				loop
33	Paradise Lake	15.4	Difficult	1,625	🐕				out-and-back
34	Lola Montez Lakes	7.4	Moderate	1,125	🐕		🚲		out-and-back
35	Loch Leven Lakes	8	Moderate	1,380	🐕		🚲		out-and-back
36	Palisade Creek Trail	14	Difficult	300	🐕		🚲		out-and-back
37	Lyle's Lookout Trail	3	Easy to moderate	250	🐕		🚲		loop
38	Point Mariah	5.5	Moderate	325	🐕		🚲		out-and-back
39	Summit Valley History Trail	4.5	Moderate	Neg.	👪				loop
40	Donner Summit Canyon Trail	3.4/6.8	Moderate	1,000	🐕				out-and-back / point-to-point
41	PCT: Donner Summit to Donner Pass	3.5	Moderate	525	🐕				point-to-point
42	Mt. Judah Loop	5.6	Moderate	1,175	🐕				loop
43	PCT: Donner Pass to Squaw Valley	15	Difficult	3,000	🐕				point-to-point
44	Donner Memorial State Park	0.5/2	Easy	Neg.	👪				loop
45	Coldstream Trail to Tinker Knob	11.5	Difficult	2,675	🐕		🚲		out-and-back
46	Sawtooth Trail	9.5	Moderate	625	🐕		🚲		loop
CHAPTER 3: NORTH TAHOE									
47	Stateline Point	1.8	Moderate	275	🐕				out-and-back
48	TRT: Brockway Summit to Martis Peak	10.4	Moderate	1,750	🐕		🚲		out-and-back
49	TRT: Brockway Summit to Watson Lake	13	Moderate	1,450	🐕		🚲		out-and-back
50	Martis Creek Wildlife Area	4	Easy	Neg.	🐕	👪			loop
51	Martis Creek Lake–Waddell Ranch	7	Moderate	600	🐕		🚲		loop
52	Burton Creek State Park	6.5	Moderate	675	🐕		🚲		loop
53	Western States Trail: CA 89 to Watson Monument	14	Difficult	2,900	🐕		🚲		out-and-back

OVERVIEW OF HIKES

HIKE NUMBER	HIKE NAME	DISTANCE (miles)	DIFFICULTY	ELEVATION GAIN (feet)	DOGS ALLOWED	GREAT FOR KIDS	MOUNTAIN BIKING	HORSEBACK RIDING	TRAIL CONFIGURATION
CHAPTER 3: NORTH TAHOE *Continued*									
54	TRT: Tahoe City to Truckee River Canyon Viewpoint	11.4	Moderate	1,350	🐕		⦿		↗
55	Western States Trail: Painted Rock Loop	11	Moderate	2,500	🐕		⦿		↺
56	Granite Chief Trail to Granite Chief	11.6	Very difficult	2,850	🐕				↗
57	Shirley Lake	4	Moderate	1,325	🐕	🧍			↗
58	Squaw Valley High Camp Trails: High Camp Loop	1.2	Easy	175	🐕	🧍			↺
58	Squaw Valley High Camp Trails: Squaw Peak	4.4	Moderate to difficult	775	🐕				↗
58	Squaw Valley High Camp Trails: Emigrant Peak and Watson Monument	3.4	Moderate	625	🐕				↗
59	Squaw Valley to Alpine Meadows	10.5	Difficult	2,925					↗
60	Five Lakes Trail	4	Moderate	1,000	🐕				↗
61	Alpine Meadows to Twin Peaks	18	Very difficult	3,275	🐕				↗
CHAPTER 4: WEST TAHOE									
62	TRT: Tahoe City to Ward Canyon	4.9	Easy to moderate	800	🐕		⦿		↗
63	TRT: Ward Canyon to Paige Meadows	3	Moderate	450	🐕	🧍	⦿		↗
64	TRT: Ward Canyon to Twin Peaks	12.8	Difficult	2,400	🐕		⦿		↗
65	Blackwood Canyon	3	Easy	Neg.	🐕	🧍	⦿		↺
66	Ellis Peak and Ellis Lake	8.3	Difficult	1,425	🐕		⦿		↗
67	TRT: Barker Pass to Twin Peaks	11.4	Moderate	2,350	🐕				↗
68	Bear Pen	13.5	Moderate	1,650	🐕				↗
69	Powderhorn Trailhead to Alpine Meadows	12	Difficult	1,750					↗
70	Barker Pass to Richardson Lake	13.2	Moderate	600	🐕				↗
71	General Creek Trail to Lost and Duck Lakes	1.8	Moderate	1,500	🐕	🧍	⦿		↗
72	Ed Z'berg-Sugar Pine Point State Park	0.5–1.7	Easy	Neg.		🧍			↗/↺
73	Tahoe–Yosemite Trail: Meeks Bay to Tallant Lakes	16	Difficult	2,100	🐕				↗

Neg. = Negligible elevation gain   ↺ = loop   ◯ = balloon   8 = figure eight   = out-and-back   = point to point

18

OVERVIEW OF HIKES

HIKE NUMBER	HIKE NAME	DISTANCE (miles)	DIFFICULTY	ELEVATION GAIN (feet)	DOGS ALLOWED	GREAT FOR KIDS	MOUNTAIN BIKING	HORSEBACK RIDING	TRAIL CONFIGURATION
CHAPTER 5: SOUTHWEST TAHOE									
74	D. L. Bliss State Park: Rubicon Point and Lighthouse Loop	2	Moderate	550	🐕	👪			loop
75	Emerald Bay and D. L. Bliss State Parks: Rubicon Trail	5	Moderate	375	🐕	👪			point-to-point
76	Emerald Bay State Park: Vikingsholm and Eagle Falls	2.5	Moderate	230	🐕	👪			out-and-back
77	Eagle Lake	2	Moderate	425	🐕	👪			out-and-back
78	Granite Lake	2.2	Moderate	800	🐕	👪			out-and-back
79	Bayview Trail to Velma Lakes	10.5	Moderate	2,725	🐕				loop
80	Cascade Falls	1.5	Moderate	75	🐕				out-and-back
81	Taylor Creek Visitor Center Nature Trails	Varies	Easy	Neg.		👪			loop
82	Floating Island and Cathedral Lakes	5	Moderate	1,200	🐕				out-and-back
83	Mt. Tallac	9.6	Difficult	3,300	🐕				out-and-back
84	Glen Alpine to Susie and Heather Lakes and Lake Aloha	11.8	Moderate	1,850	🐕				out-and-back
85	Glen Alpine to Gilmore Lake	8.4	Moderate	1,750	🐕				out-and-back
86	Glen Alpine to Grass Lake	5	Easy	675	🐕	👪			out-and-back
87	Tamarack Trail: Triangle Lake, Echo Peak, and Angora Lakes Loop	7.2	Very difficult	2,750					loop
CHAPTER 6: SOUTH TAHOE									
88	Big Meadow to Dardanelles Lake	8	Moderate	1,050	🐕		🚲		out-and-back
89	Big Meadow to Carson Pass	10.5	Moderate	2,075	🐕				point-to-point
90	TRT: Grass Lake Meadow to Hell Hole Viewpoint	10	Moderate	1,900	🐕		🚲		out-and-back
91	Armstrong Pass to Freel Peak	10	Difficult	1,650	🐕				out-and-back
92	Armstrong Pass to Star Lake	12	Moderate	1,500	🐕		🚲		out-and-back
93	Armstrong Pass to Hell Hole Viewpoint	8	Moderate	1,400	🐕		🚲		out-and-back
94	Saxon Creek Trail	12	Moderate	2,925	🐕		🚲		out-and-back
95	High Meadows	6.8	Moderate	1,400	🐕		🚲		out-and-back
96	Star Lake	13.6	Moderate	2,650	🐕		🚲		out-and-back
97	Cold Creek Trail	6.6	Moderate	1,425	🐕		🚲		loop
98	Monument Pass–Star Lake Loop	16.8	Difficult	3,000	🐕		🚲		loop
99	TRT: Kingsbury South to Star Lake	17.4	Moderate	2,600	🐕		🚲		point-to-point
100	Van Sickle Trail	7.2	Moderate	1,350	🐕		🚲		out-and-back

OVERVIEW OF HIKES

HIKE NUMBER	HIKE NAME	DISTANCE (miles)	DIFFICULTY	ELEVATION GAIN (feet)	DOGS ALLOWED	GREAT FOR KIDS	MOUNTAIN BIKING	HORSEBACK RIDING	TRAIL CONFIGURATION
CHAPTER 7: EAST TAHOE									
101	Lam Watah Trail to Nevada Beach	2.2	Easy	Neg.		🧍			↗ out-and-back
102	Castle Rock	2	Moderate	300	🐕		⊛		↗ out-and-back
103	Daggett Loop Trail	7	Moderate	1,550	🐕		⊛		◯ loop
104	TRT: Kingsbury North to Genoa Peak	13	Moderate	1,800	🐕		⊛		↗ out-and-back
105	TRT: Kingsbury North to Sierra Canyon	16.1	Difficult	1,750	🐕		⊛		➚ point to point
106	Sierra Canyon Trail to Genoa Peak	19.8	Very difficult	4,800	🐕		⊛		↗ out-and-back
107	Discovery Trail: Eagle Ridge Loop	4/6.2	Moderate	750/1,775	🐕		⊛		↗/◯
108	Discovery Trail: Genoa Loop	7.7/8.7	Moderate	1,325/1,500	🐕		⊛		↗/◯
109	TRT: Spooner Summit to South Camp Peak	10.4	Moderate	1,875	🐕		⊛		↗ out-and-back
110	Clear Creek Trail to Knob Point	13.2	Moderate	1,075	🐕		⊛		↗ out-and-back
111	Spooner Lake	1.8	Easy	Neg.	🐕	🧍			◯ loop
112	Marlette Lake	9	Moderate	1,225	🐕				↗ out-and-back
113	TRT: Spooner Summit to Snow Valley Peak	12.4	Moderate	2,450	🐕				↗ out-and-back
114	Skunk Harbor	3.2	Moderate	150	🐕	🧍			↗ out-and-back
115	Chimney Beach	Up to 2.2	Easy	150	🐕				↗ out-and-back
116	Chimney Beach to Marlette Lake	6	Difficult	1,500	🐕		⊛		↗ out-and-back
117	Flume Trail	13	Moderate	1,850			⊛		➚ point to point
CHAPTER 8: ECHO SUMMIT AND SOUTH FORK AMERICAN RIVER									
118	Becker Peak	2.6	Difficult	800	🐕				↗ out-and-back
119	Echo Lakes to Tamarack, Ralston, and Cagwin Lakes	4/9	Easy/Moderate	450/750	🐕	🧍			↗ out-and-back
120	Echo Lakes to Lake of the Woods and Ropi Lake	8/13	Difficult	990/1,490	🐕				↗ out-and-back
121	Echo Lakes to Lake Aloha	7.6/12.6	Moderate	950/1,225	🐕				↗ out-and-back
122	PCT: Echo Summit to Bryan Meadow	7.6	Moderate	1,475	🐕				↗ out-and-back
123	Pony Express Trail: Sierra-at-Tahoe Road to Echo Summit	3.75	Moderate	825	🐕		⊛		➚ point to point
124	Sayles Canyon–Bryan Meadow Loop	10	Moderate	1,875	🐕		⊛		◯ loop
125	Ralston Peak	6	Difficult	2,775	🐕				↗ out-and-back
126	Lovers Leap	2.5	Easy	500	🐕		⊛		↗ out-and-back
127	Horsetail Falls	3	Moderate	650	🐕				◯ loop

Neg. = Negligible elevation gain   ◯ = loop   ⭕ = balloon   𝟖 = figure eight   ↗ = out-and-back   ➚ = point to point

OVERVIEW OF HIKES

HIKE NUMBER	HIKE NAME	DISTANCE (miles)	DIFFICULTY	ELEVATION GAIN (feet)	DOGS ALLOWED	GREAT FOR KIDS	MOUNTAIN BIKING	HORSEBACK RIDING	TRAIL CONFIGURATION
CHAPTER 9: MT. ROSE AND THE CARSON RANGE									
128	Tom Cooke and Steamboat Ditch Trails to Hole in the Wall	5	Easy	450	🐕		🚲		out-and-back
129	Hunter Creek Trail	7	Moderate	1,450	🐕				out-and-back
130	Hunter Lake	15	Difficult	3,300	🐕		🚲		out-and-back
131	Upper Thomas Creek Loop	16.5/22.9	Difficult	3,375/4,475	🐕				loop
132	Dry Pond Trail	4.5/6.3	Moderate	1,000/1,100	🐕		🚲		out-and-back/loop
133	Upper Whites Creek	7	Moderate	1,300	🐕				out-and-back
134	Galena Creek Visitor Center Nature Trail	0.5	Easy	50		🧍			loop
135	Jones Creek Loop	1.6	Easy	275	🐕	🧍			loop
136	Jones Creek–Whites Creek Loop	9	Difficult	2,525	🐕				loop
137	Galena Creek Regional Park Nature Trail	0.75	Easy	150	🐕	🧍			loop
138	Black's Canyon	4	Difficult	1,300	🐕				out-and-back
139	Southeast Ridge of Mt. Rose	5.4	Very difficult	3,350	🐕				out-and-back
140	Browns Creek Trail	4.9	Moderate	1,000	🐕		🚲		loop
141	Slide Mountain Trail	0.75	Easy to moderate	150	🐕				loop
142	Mt. Rose	9.8	Difficult	2,100	🐕				out-and-back
143	Bronco Creek	11	Moderate	1,400	🐕				out-and-back
144	Rim to Reno Trail	18/20.8	Difficult	2,250	🐕				point-to-point
145	Mt. Houghton	10.6	Moderate	1,800	🐕				loop
146	Relay Peak Loop	10.7	Moderate	1,800	🐕				loop
147	TRT: Mt. Rose Trailhead to Brockway Summit	18	Difficult	2,900	🐕				point-to-point
148	Incline Lake Trail to Gray Lake	8	Moderate to strenuous	2,050	🐕				loop
149	Incline Flume Trail: Mt. Rose Highway to Diamond Peak	3	Moderate	100	🐕		🚲		point-to-point
150	Upper Tahoe Meadows Nature Trail Loops	1.3	Easy	Neg.	🐕	🧍			loop
151	Lower Tahoe Meadows Nature Trail Loops	Up to 3.3	Easy	300	🐕	🧍			loop
152	TRT: Tahoe Meadows to Twin Lakes	19	Difficult	1,325	🐕		🚲		out-and-back
153	Slide Mountain Summit	2.5	Difficult	700	🐕		🚲		out-and-back
154	Ophir Creek Trail	8.1	Difficult	3.875	🐕		🚲		point-to-point
155	Davis Creek Park	0.6	Easy	Neg.	🐕	🧍			loop
156	Hobart Road to Hobart Reservoir	10	Difficult	2,575	🐕		🚲		out-and-back

OVERVIEW OF HIKES

HIKE NUMBER	HIKE NAME	DISTANCE (miles)	DIFFICULTY	ELEVATION GAIN (feet)	DOGS ALLOWED	GREAT FOR KIDS	MOUNTAIN BIKING	HORSEBACK RIDING	TRAIL CONFIGURATION
CHAPTER 10: KIT CARSON COUNTRY									
157	Jobs Peak Ranch Trailhead to Fay-Luther Trailhead	3.5	Moderate	500	🐕				point to point
158	Valley View Loop	3.7	Easy	375	🐕		⚙		loop
159	Fay-Luther Loop Trails: Interpretive Loop	2.2	Easy to moderate	350	🐕		⚙		loop
159	Fay-Luther Loop Trails: Jeffrey Pine Loop	2	Easy to moderate	350	🐕		⚙		loop
159	Fay-Luther Loop Trails: Grand View Loop	3.3	Moderate	600	🐕		⚙		loop
160	Fay Canyon–Luther Creek	8	Moderate	2,575	🐕		⚙		point to point
161	Horsethief Canyon	4	Moderate	1,250	🐕		⚙		point to point
162	Indian Creek Recreation Area Trails: Curtz Lake Interpretive Trail	1.3	Easy to moderate	200	🐕	🧍			loop
162	Indian Creek Recreation Area Trails: Summit Lake Trail	2.4	Easy to moderate	75	🐕	🧍			point to point
162	Indian Creek Recreation Area Trails: Carson River Trail	4.8	Easy to moderate	25	🐕	🧍			out-and-back
163	East Fork Carson River	5	Easy	75	🐕		⚙		out-and-back
164	Charity Valley East to Burnside Lake	5	Difficult	2,400	🐕		⚙		point to point
165	Grover Hot Springs State Park	3/1.8	Easy	200/50	🐕	🧍	⚙		out-and-back
166	Thornburg Canyon	10	Moderate	2,375	🐕				out-and-back
167	Charity Valley West to Burnside Lake	11	Difficult	1,225	🐕		⚙		out-and-back
168	Hope Valley Overlook	5.8	Moderate	1,200	🐕		⚙		out-and-back
169	Granite and Grouse Lakes	12	Moderate	1,575	🐕				out-and-back
170	Upper Blue Lake to Fourth of July Lake	9	Difficult	1,150	🐕				out-and-back
171	PCT: Wet Meadows to Raymond Lake	9	Moderate	1,750	🐕				out-and-back
172	Meiss Meadows Trailhead to Showers Lake	10.2	Moderate	750	🐕				out-and-back
173	Meiss Meadows Trailhead to Round Lake	10.4	Moderate	475	🐕				out-and-back
174	Carson Pass to Forestdale Divide	10.2	Moderate	1,200	🐕				out-and-back
175	Carson Pass to Fourth of July Lake	11	Difficult	1,250	🐕				out-and-back
176	Woods, Winnemucca, and Round Top Lakes Loop	4.8	Moderate	1,200					loop
177	Emigrant Lake	8.2	Moderate	800	🐕				out-and-back
178	Emigrant Pass	10	Difficult	1,175	🐕				out-and-back
179	Lake Margaret	4	Easy	225	🐕		⚙		out-and-back

Neg. = Negligible elevation gain   ⟳ = loop   ◯ = balloon   **8** = figure eight   ↙↗ = out-and-back   ↗ = point to point

22

HIKE NUMBER	HIKE NAME	DISTANCE (miles)	DIFFICULTY	ELEVATION GAIN (feet)	DOGS ALLOWED	GREAT FOR KIDS	MOUNTAIN BIKING	HORSEBACK RIDING	TRAIL CONFIGURATION
CHAPTER 10: KIT CARSON COUNTRY *Continued*									
180	Thunder Mountain Loop	8.5/10.8	Moderate	1,775/2,550	🐕		⚙		⤴/⟳
181	Scout Carson Lake	13	Moderate	1,775	🐕				⤴
182	Granite and Hidden Lakes	6	Easy	475	🐕	👪	⚙		⤴
183	Shealor Lake	3.6	Easy	175	🐕	👪	⚙		⤴
CHAPTER 11: RENO-SPARKS AND CARSON CITY									
184	Swan Lake Nature Study Area	1.5	Easy	150	🐕	👪			⤴
185	Crystal Mine Trail	1.5	Easy	375	🐕	👪			⤴
186	Poeville	6	Moderate	500	🐕		⚙		⤴
187	Peavine Peak	10	Difficult	2,875	🐕		⚙		⤴
188	Rancho San Rafael Park: Nature Trail	0.75	Easy	Neg.	🐕	👪			⟳
189	Evans Canyon	2.2/3.4	Easy	150/200	🐕	👪	⚙		⟳
190	Evans Canyon to Keystone Canyon	6.8	Moderate	700	🐕		⚙		⤴
191	Keystone Canyon	3.4	Moderate	350	🐕	👪	⚙		⤴
192	Oxbow Nature Study Area Nature Trail	1	Easy	Neg.		👪			⤴
193	Huffaker Park Lookout Trail	2	Easy	250	🐕	👪			⟳
194	Huffaker Hills	3.2	Easy	375	🐕	👪	⚙		⟳
195	Hidden Valley Regional Park Trails	2.3	Moderate	650	🐕		⚙		⟳
196	Ballardini Ranch Loop	2.5	Easy	200	🐕		⚙		⟳
197	Lower Whites Creek Trail	3.5	Moderate	925	🐕	👪	⚙		⤴
198	Lower Thomas Creek Trail	2.5	Moderate	750	🐕	👪	⚙		⤴
199	Lower Galena Creek Trail	2.6/5.2	Moderate	750	🐕	👪	⚙		⤴/⤴
200	Little Washoe Lake	1	Easy	Neg.	🐕	👪			⤴
201	Deadman Creek Loop	2.4	Moderate	500	🐕				⟳

Hikers survey Long Lake

Chapter 1

Graeagle and Sierra City

An hour-long drive north from Tahoe–Reno lets hikers leave behind the summertime tourist throngs around the city and the lake, and exchange them for more sedate but no less scenic recreation options. The small communities of Graeagle and Sierra City bookend pockets of splendid northern Sierra forestlands.

The mill town of Graeagle came into existence in the 1800s to support a vigorous logging operation that continued until 1957. A decade or so later, the quaint town, with its row of red company houses lining the main street, became the centerpiece for what is now a thriving resort community complete with upscale homes and golf courses.

Mining around Sierra Buttes was the impetus for the settlement of Sierra City in 1850. A couple of years later, the bawdy town boasted several buildings, including the customary gambling halls and saloons necessary to satisfy the appetites of the scrappy miners. Although the town remains quite small today, several inns, lodges, and bed-and-breakfasts line the banks of the North Yuba River and some of the lakes nearby, offering fine jumping-off points for exploring the surrounding terrain.

Although logging and mining roads crisscross much of this part of the northern Sierra, a number of areas offer the hiker a bounty of opportunities for experiencing some pristine backcountry between Graeagle and Sierra City. Just a few miles west of Graeagle, Plumas-Eureka State Park, harboring artifacts and restored buildings from the Gold Mountain mining days, has a handful of hiking trails within 5,500 acres of prime woodlands. Farther south, numerous interconnecting trails offer abundant routes across the well-named Lakes Basin Recreation Area, managed by Plumas National Forest. Closer to Sierra City and within Tahoe National Forest, the rocky ramparts of Sierra Buttes tower over several trails that lead hikers to picturesque lakes and scenic vistas.

With elevations starting around 4,500 feet, this area does offer some early-season hiking opportunities. However, most of the hiking terrain is between 6,000 and 8,000 feet, which usually limits snow-free travel until sometime after the first part of June. Mild autumn weather typically extends the hiking season in this region into late October, or even through early November in some years.

Access to Graeagle is principally from CA 70, the Feather River Highway. Motorists leave CA 70 near the community of Blairsden and travel south for 2 miles on CA 89 to the center of town. Sierra City is on CA 49, to the west of Yuba Pass. During summer and fall, the Gold Lake Road provides a paved connection between CA 89, just outside Graeagle, and CA 49 at Bassetts, about 5 miles northeast of Sierra City.

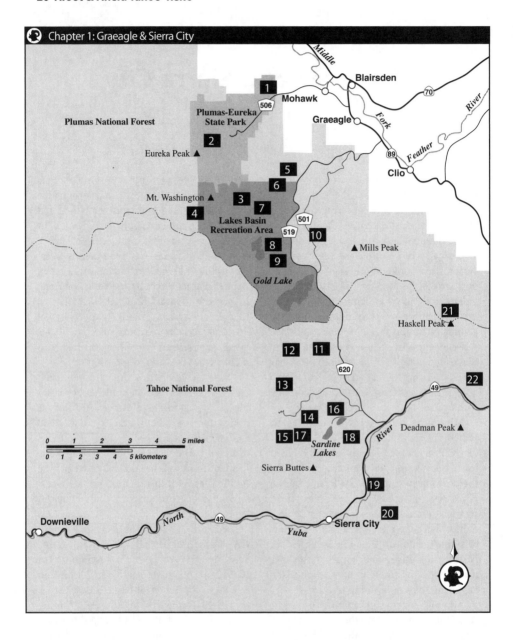

1 Madora Lake

Distance	1.6 miles (semiloop)
Hiking Time	1 hour
Elevation	Negligible
Difficulty	Easy
Trail Use	Good for kids
Best Times	May through October
Agency	Plumas-Eureka State Park at 530-836-2380, parks.ca.gov
Recommended Maps	USFS *Lakes Basin, Sierra Buttes,* and *Plumas-Eureka State Park Recreation Guide*

HIGHLIGHTS The easy 1.6-mile hike around Madora Lake offers hikers of all ages an opportunity to enjoy the tranquil surroundings of a forested lake. Leave the swimsuit at home, however, as Madora Lake is the domestic water supply for one of the nearby communities and therefore swimming is prohibited. Dogs, horses, bicycles, and motorized vehicles are not allowed on this trail.

DIRECTIONS In the town of Graeagle, leave CA 89 and head west on County Road 506, following signs for Plumas-Eureka State Park. About 0.4 mile inside the park boundary, turn right at a sign for Madora Lake, pass through a gate (open from 8 a.m. to sunset), and follow a short paved road to the trailhead.

FACILITIES/TRAILHEAD A pit toilet, picnic table, and colored map of the trail can be found near the trailhead, which is on the north side of the parking area.

Through thick forest composed of incense cedars, ponderosa pines, and red firs, follow the needle-lined path on a mild descent that parallels sometimes-dry Lundy Ditch to your left. After one-third of a mile, near a wood bridge, you reach a junction with the loop trail around the lake. Turn left and cross the bridge over Lundy Ditch and then continue toward Madora Lake. Soon the trees part just enough to

grant you a brief glimpse of the forest-rimmed lake, the water's edge lined with willows and reeds.

An easy stroll leads around to the north side of Madora Lake, where an old picnic table near the shoreline provides an excellent spot to linger, grab a bite, and enjoy the view. Patient bird-watchers should have a good opportunity to spot a wide variety of species. Continuing around the lake, a sign

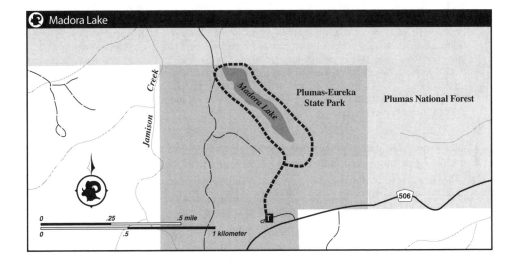

guides you to remain on the trail where an old road angles away to the north.

Stroll away from the lakeshore and follow an elevated-plank walkway across a boggy meadow. The forest thickens again beyond this meadow, and soon the loop closes upon your return to the junction. From there, climb back up the trail one-third of a mile to the parking area.

A shady spot on the shore of Madora Lake

2 Eureka Peak Loop

Distance	4 miles (semiloop)
Hiking Time	2–3 hours
Elevation	+1,275/-1,275 feet
Difficulty	Moderate
Trail Use	None
Best Times	Mid-June through October
Agency	Plumas-Eureka State Park at 530-836-2380, parks.ca.gov
Recommended Maps	USFS *Lakes Basin, Sierra Buttes,* and *Plumas-Eureka State Park Recreation Guide*

HIGHLIGHTS Grand views of the northern Sierra and southern Cascades from the twin summits of Eureka Peak and the connecting ridgecrest will excite hikers who don't object to the initially steep, mile-long climb above Eureka Lake. Those who follow the full loop around the south summit will have a reasonable expectation of solitude, as the limited number of hikers who use this trail usually travel only as far as the north summit.

DIRECTIONS In the town of Graeagle, leave CA 89 and head west on County Road 506, following signs for Plumas-Eureka State Park. Enter the park and continue past park headquarters and through the historic town of Johnsville to the end of the paved road at the Gold Mountain Ski Area parking lot. Durable two-wheel-drive vehicles with reasonable clearance should be able to continue another 1.3 miles on the narrow, steep, rock-and-dirt road to the forest service trailhead near the Eureka Lake dam. If your vehicle or driving skills are not up to the rough road, park in the ski-area lot and walk up the road.

FACILITIES/TRAILHEAD The trailhead has a bear-proof trash can and pit toilet. The trail begins at a steel gate across an old road.

Follow the continuation of the road past a closed gate and over the dam, enjoying the fine view of Eureka Lake backdropped by Eureka Peak. Once across the dam and the overflow channel, climb moderately steeply up an old road through a mixed forest of red firs, Jeffrey pines, and lodgepole pines, soon reaching a three-way junction with a use trail that loops around the lake. Continue up the road, eventually emerging from the trees to ascend across a shrub-covered slope, where the lack of trees permits good views of Eureka Peak and the surrounding terrain. Farther up

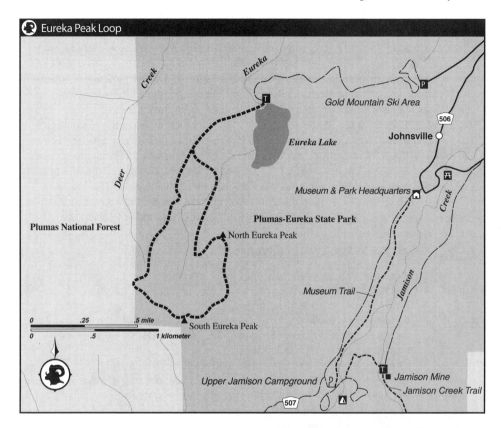

Eureka Peak Loop

Gold Mountain Ski Area

Eureka Lake

Johnsville

Museum & Park Headquarters

Plumas-Eureka State Park

Plumas National Forest

North Eureka Peak

Museum Trail

South Eureka Peak

Upper Jamison Campground

Jamison Mine

Jamison Creek Trail

0   .25   .5 mile
0   .5   1 kilometer

the hillside, reenter forest cover and immediately reach a three-way junction at 1 mile from the trailhead.

Turn left (southeast) onto singletrack trail and continue climbing through the trees to the easy crossing of nascent Eureka Creek, lined with a verdant swath of alders, wildflowers, and small, thirsty plants. Beyond the creek, the grade increases and the conifers thicken, as western white pines and then mountain hemlocks join the mixed forest. Farther up the slope, you pass around a boggy area, where leopard lily and corn lily thrive in the moist soils, to a series of switchbacks that climbs to the crest of the summit ridge, where a fine vista unfolds. Although no maintained trail leads to the top of Eureka Peak, a short, easy rock scramble will take you to the 7,286-foot summit and an expansive view of the surrounding countryside, including Eureka Lake lying directly below the sheer north face.

View from Eureka Peak's summit

After enjoying the dramatic view, resume the loop trip by following the ridge on a gentle climb toward the south summit through pinemat manzanita, chinquapin, tobacco brush, and widely scattered conifers. Just before the trail begins to descend, a little more than 2 miles from the trailhead, a use trail heads toward a very short scramble up the rocks of the 7,447-foot south summit, where you may enjoy additional vistas.

The main trail sweeps around the south side of the peak and makes a sharp descent to the northwest, merging with an old road below the summit. The grade soon eases across a gently sloping meadow rimmed by red firs and filled in early summer with the purple blooms from a plethora of lupines on the way to a signed three-way junction, 2.5 miles from the trailhead.

At the junction, leave the road and follow singletrack trail on a moderate descent through open areas and widely scattered conifers before entering a light forest and closing the loop at 0.4 mile from the previous junction. From there, retrace your steps 1 mile to the trailhead at Eureka Lake.

3 Grass, Rock, Jamison, and Wades Lakes

Distance	7.5 miles (semiloop)
Hiking Time	4–6 hours
Elevation	+1,550/-1,550 feet
Difficulty	Moderate
Trail Use	Backpacking option, leashed dogs OK on Jamison Creek Trail
Best Times	Mid-June through October
Agency	Plumas-Eureka State Park at 530-836-2380, parks.ca.gov; Plumas National Forest at 530-836-2575, www.fs.usda.gov/plumas
Recommended Maps	USFS *Lakes Basin, Sierra Buttes,* and *Plumas-Eureka State Park Recreation Guide*

HIGHLIGHTS A quartet of delightful lakes lures backpackers and hikers alike on this semiloop trip. Grass, Rock, Jamison, and Wades Lakes are among the few lakes around the Lakes Basin Recreation Area where camping is allowed, which explains the lakes' popularity with backpackers. However, camping isn't the only appeal, as the scenery is superb, the fishing is reported to be fair, and the swimming can be quite refreshing on a typically hot summer day. Smith Lake, which is easily accessed by a 1.3-mile lateral from the Jamison Creek Trail, has similar attributes.

Although much of the route is snow-free by mid-June in an average year, Wades Lake may be snowbound until sometime in July—check with Plumas National Forest for current conditions. Early-season hikers should also expect to get their feet wet at some of the stream crossings. While the trails within Plumas-Eureka State Park are not dog friendly, the Jamison Creek Trail is an exception, because, although the trail begins in the park, most of the route is on forest service land.

DIRECTIONS In the town of Graeagle, leave CA 89 and head west on County Road 506, following signs for Plumas-Eureka State Park. Cross the park boundary and continue to a left-hand turn onto a dirt road, 4.6 miles from CA 89, marked JAMISON MINE, GRASS LAKE TRAIL 1.3. Proceed to the end of the dirt road and park in the gravel parking area as space allows.

FACILITIES/TRAILHEAD Although no facilities are available at the trailhead, Upper Jamison Campground is a short distance away. The well-marked trail begins near some restored buildings of the Jamison Mine.

Walk around a closed steel gate and past a junction on the right with a path from Jamison Creek Campground, as you follow an old rocky road on a moderate climb past some of the restored buildings of the Jamison Creek Mine. Beneath the cover of mixed forest, you draw near tumbling Little Jamison Creek, roaring down a narrow canyon just below the trail. Pass by a well-signed, three-way junction with a

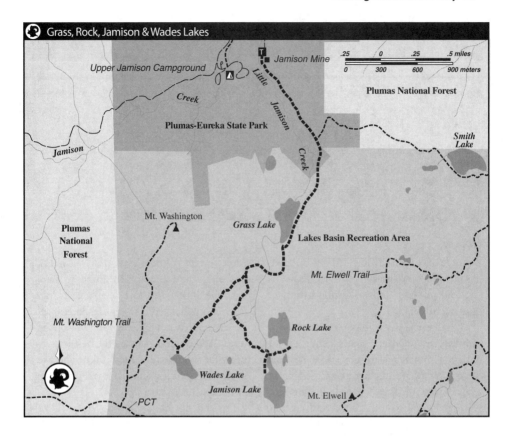

Grass, Rock, Jamison & Wades Lakes

Upper Jamison Campground

Jamison Mine

.25 0 .25 .5 miles

0 300 600 900 meters

Plumas National Forest

Little Jamison Creek

Creek

Plumas-Eureka State Park

Smith Lake

Jamison

Mt. Washington

Grass Lake

Plumas National Forest

Lakes Basin Recreation Area

Mt. Elwell Trail

Mt. Washington Trail

Rock Lake

Wades Lake

Jamison Lake

Mt. Elwell

PCT

1.3-mile lateral to Smith Lake (see Trip 6) at three-quarters of a mile, and proceed up the canyon of Little Jamison Creek. After a quarter mile, you reach another junction, where a short path on the right leads to a fine view of Jamison Falls, a 60-foot-high waterfall that is quite an impressive sight when the creek is flowing at full capacity.

Back on the main trail, make a gentle climb to Grass Lake, 1.3 miles from the trailhead. The trail closely follows the east side of the lake, providing good views of Mt. Washington rising sharply above the far shore. A use trail near the north end of the lake leads across the outlet to a few fair campsites on the west shore before the path dies out in a tangle of thick brush.

Beyond Grass Lake, follow gently graded trail through lush ground cover and light forest, across a small meadow, and then over to a crossing of Little Jamison Creek,

which may present a challenge during high water in late spring or early summer. Slightly rising trail continues to a T-junction between the Jamison Creek and Jamison Lake Trails, 2.25 miles from the trailhead.

Head left (south) from the junction on a mild climb until the grade increases at a series of switchbacks. Shortly after a crossing of the outlet from Wades Lake, reach a junction with the Wades Lake–Jamison Lake Connector, 2.75 miles from the trailhead. Remaining on the Jamison Lake Trail on the left, you soon come to a Y-junction, where the path splits to access Rock Lake to the left and Jamison Lake to the right. A short walk toward Jamison Lake brings you to the old rock dam, where lush foliage surrounding the structure creates the surprising appearance of an ornamental garden. A short scramble up the rocks above the west

Rock Lake

shore leads to a fine view of Jamison Lake, backdropped by the slopes of Mt. Elwell. A handful of fair campsites around the lake lure overnighters.

Windswept Rock Lake is just a few minutes away after backtracking to the junction, but reaching the shoreline does require a ford of Little Jamison Creek on the way. Beyond the ford, a short climb delivers you to the south shore of the aptly named lake, which also has an excellent backdrop from 7,818-foot Mt. Elwell.

After visiting Jamison and Rock Lakes, return to the junction of the Wades Lake–Jamison Lake Connector and begin the steep climb toward Wades Lake. You reach the northeast shore after nearly three-quarters of a mile and 400 vertical feet of climbing. The heavily forested lake reposes in a deep, glacier-scoured bowl below the crest of the range. Wades offers perhaps the best opportunity for solitude of the four lakes, and the north shore has spacious campsites suitable for backpacking parties.

Proceed northbound from Wades Lake to a junction of the Jamison Creek Trail and make a steady descent northeast for 0.9 mile to a junction of the Jamison Lake Trail, thereby closing the loop section. From there, retrace your steps 2.25 miles to the trailhead.

4 Mt. Washington

Distance	7 miles (out-and-back)
Hiking Time	4–6 hours
Elevation	+1,275/-450 feet
Difficulty	Difficult
Trail Use	Dogs OK, mountain biking OK
Best Times	Late June through October
Agency	Plumas National Forest at 530-836-2575, www.fs.usda.gov/plumas
Recommended Maps	USFS *Lakes Basin, Sierra Buttes,* and *Plumas-Eureka State Park Recreation Guide*

HIGHLIGHTS At 7,818 feet, Mt. Washington provides a fine perch from which to view the peaks and ridges of the northern Sierra. Choosing to begin at the A Tree Trailhead minimizes the distance and, perhaps more importantly, the elevation gain. Definitely a high route, the first half of the trip follows a little-used section of the well-graded Pacific Crest Trail (PCT) along the spine of the Sierra, while the second half follows the extension of Mt. Washington's south ridge to the summit. A short rock scramble is necessary to gain the top, but the climb is easily accomplished by all but severe acrophobes.

DIRECTIONS In the town of Graeagle, leave CA 89 and head west on County Road 506, following signs for Plumas-Eureka State Park. Cross the park boundary and continue over the bridge across Jamison Creek to a left-hand turn onto CR 507, signed for the Plumas-Eureka State Park Museum and Upper Jamison Campground.

Follow paved road for 1.1 miles to the campground turnoff, and continue as the surface changes to dirt. Reach a Y-junction at 4.3 miles from the junction with Road 506, and turn left onto Forest Service Road 23N08, following a sign marked A TREE AND EUREKA RIDGE. Drive on 23N08 for 2 miles to a ridgecrest saddle and another road junction, where the Pacific Crest Trail crosses the road nearby. Park along the shoulder as space allows.

FACILITIES/TRAILHEAD There are no facilities at the trailhead. Your route begins on the section of signed Pacific Crest Trail that heads south from the saddle.

Head southbound through fir forest and pockets of lush ground cover along the Pacific Crest Trail, on an uphill climb incorporating an occasional switchback. The forest thins as you progress, parting occasionally to allow filtered views of the surrounding terrain. Reach an unmarked junction at 0.8 mile, where an infrequently used path descends toward Spencer Lakes. Continuing on the PCT, follow the trail as it hugs the hillside directly south of the crest. Eventually, you break out of the forest to cross open slopes carpeted with mule-ears early in the season on the way to the crest of a ridge, where your ascent is well rewarded by fine views of the shimmering Spencer Lakes below and the impressive ramparts of Sierra Buttes to the southeast. Nearing the crest, reach a signed Y-junction with the Mt. Washington Trail, 1.9 miles from the trailhead.

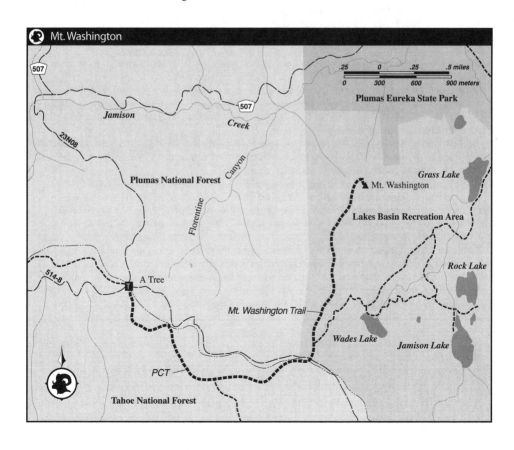

Turn left (north) at the junction and cross an old four-wheel-drive road to the continuation of singletrack trail near a group of trail signs. Briefly stroll through dense shrubs and scattered firs until a short descent leads into thicker forest on the way to a Y-junction with the Jamison Creek Trail. Beyond this junction, the descent bottoms out at a quarter mile from the road, where a steady climb along the crest of Mt. Washington's south ridge begins. Initially, open slopes covered with pinemat manzanita and dotted with widely scattered firs allow good views of the four lakes tucked into the canyon of Little Jamison Creek below and the towering summit of Mt. Elwell above. The views are eventually left behind as the trail reenters a dense forest composed of mountain hemlocks and red firs. After skirting a subsidiary peak, the trail traverses across the west slope of Mt. Washington to the far side of the peak, where maintained trail abruptly ends. A short, easy rock scramble from there leads to the 7,818-foot summit and the expansive view.

5 Gray Eagle Creek

Distance	2.2 miles (point-to-point)
Hiking Time	1–2 hours
Elevation	+525/-100 feet
Difficulty	Moderate
Trail Use	Dogs OK, good for kids
Best Times	June through October
Agency	Plumas National Forest at 530-836-2575, www.fs.usda.gov/plumas
Recommended Maps	USFS *Lakes Basin, Sierra Buttes,* and *Plumas-Eureka State Park Recreation Guide*

HIGHLIGHTS If you're looking for a short, forested stroll accompanied by a serenade from a tumbling stream, the Gray Eagle Creek Trail won't disappoint. Early-summer hikers have the additional blessing of a fine wildflower display, and an après-hike dinner at Gray Eagle Lodge is a fine experience any time during the hiking season.

DIRECTIONS *Start:* Follow CA 89 to the Gold Lake Highway (County Road 519), 1.5 miles southeast of Graeagle. Drive the Gold Lake Highway 3.1 miles to a paved turnout on the right-hand shoulder, and park near the small trail sign for the Gray Eagle Creek Trail.

End: Continue up the Gold Lake Highway another 2 miles from the lower Gray Eagle Creek Trailhead to the access road for Gray Eagle Lodge, which is also signed for the Smith Lake and Gray Eagle Creek Trails. Proceed on the access road, which quickly turns to dirt, for 0.4 mile to a right-hand turn onto a rougher dirt road. Find a parking spot after 0.1 mile as space allows near the signed upper Gray Eagle Creek Trailhead.

FACILITIES/TRAILHEAD There are no facilities at either the lower or upper trailheads. However, dinner at rustic Gray Eagle Lodge's Firewood Restaurant would provide an excellent conclusion to your hike, and an overnight stay at the rustic lodge would be an ideal weekend retreat. Visit the website at **grayeaglelodge.com** or call 800-635-8778 for reservations. The singletrack Gray Eagle Creek Trail begins about 25 feet to the left of the sign at the lower trailhead.

Passing through thick shrubs and a mixed forest of white firs, incense cedars, and lodgepole pines, you walk downhill toward Gray Eagle Creek. After a switchback, the trail heads downstream to a stout bridge spanning the tumbling creek, one-third of a mile from the parking lot. A high percentage of hikers go no farther than the photogenic view of Gray Eagle Creek from the bridge, so you may have the rest of the

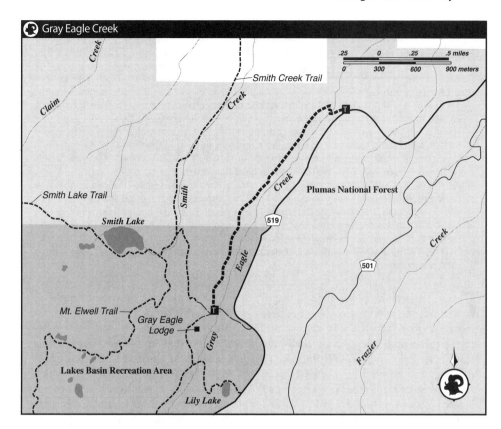

Gray Eagle Creek

Smith Creek Trail

Claim

Creek

Smith Creek Trail

Smith Lake Trail

Smith

Smith Lake

Plumas National Forest

519

Creek

501

Mt. Elwell Trail

Gray Eagle
Lodge

Gray

Eagle

Frazier

Lakes Basin Recreation Area

Lily Lake

.25   0   .25   .5 miles
0   300   600   900 meters

trail pretty much to yourself, at least until approaching the customary hubbub around Gray Eagle Lodge.

A short climb leads away from the bridge to a signed three-way junction. Turn upstream on gravel trail, staying within earshot of the creek but remaining a good distance away for the nearly 2-mile-long journey to the lodge.

About halfway to the lodge, thin rivulets and an abundance of groundwater produce a lush foliage that includes ferns, willows, alders, and young aspens, along with a

healthy population of wildflowers. Mule-ears, lady's slipper, and aster are just a few of the many species in bloom during the early summer. Eventually, the lush vegetation is left behind and you continue along the ascending path through forest and shrubs to the dirt road accessing the Smith Lake Trailhead. Turning right at the road leads shortly to the Smith Lake and Long Lake Trailheads (see Trips 6 and 8). A left turn will get you to the access road that leads a short distance to Gray Eagle Lodge.

6 **Smith Lake**

Distance	2 miles (out-and-back)
Hiking Time	1–2 hours
Elevation	+350/-50 feet
Difficulty	Moderate
Trail Use	Backpacking option, dogs OK, good for kids

see
map on
p. 36

Best Times	June through October
Agency	Plumas National Forest at 530-836-2575, www.fs.usda.gov/plumas
Recommended Maps	USFS *Lakes Basin, Sierra Buttes,* and *Plumas-Eureka State Park Recreation Guide*

HIGHLIGHTS Smith Lake is one of the more popular hikes in the Lakes Basin Recreation Area. The 1-mile hike (one way) puts the lake within striking distance of all but the most out-of-shape bipeds, and the lake is one of only five in the area that allows overnight camping. Despite the popularity, scenic Smith Lake is well worth the short time and little effort necessary for a visit. If the forecast is for high temperatures, consider an early start to beat the heat along the first half of the trip, which climbs across an exposed, south-facing slope. Dinner at Gray Eagle Lodge near the trailhead would be an excellent culinary climax to the hike (see Trip 5 for details).

DIRECTIONS Follow CA 89 to the Gold Lake Highway (County Road 519), 1.5 miles southeast of Graeagle. Drive the Gold Lake Highway for 5.1 miles to the access road for Gray Eagle Lodge, which is also signed for the Smith Lake and Gray Eagle Creek Trails. Proceed on the access road, which quickly turns to dirt, for 0.4 mile to a right-hand turn onto a rougher dirt road. Find a parking spot after 0.1 mile as space allows near the Smith Lake Trailhead.

FACILITIES/TRAILHEAD There are no facilities at the trailhead, although Gray Eagle Lodge is just a short distance away.

From the well-signed trailhead, begin a moderate ascent across a shadeless morainal ridge carpeted with shrubs, primarily manzanita. After a steady, half-mile climb, the trail bends around the nose of the ridge and enters a light, mixed forest. A brief descent leads to an easy crossing of braided Smith Creek at 0.6 mile, followed quickly by a junction with a little-used trail that follows the creek downstream. Proceed upstream on a mild climb for 0.2 mile to a signed junction with the Mt. Elwell Trail (see Trip 7). Veer right at the junction and

continue another 0.2 mile to the outlet of scenic Smith Lake.

Although access to the lake requires just a mile of hiking, Smith Lake is one of only five lakes in the greater Lakes Basin Recreation Area that permits camping, which has resulted in several heavily used campsites spread around the lakeshore. The easy access also enables numerous anglers to ply the waters in search of the resident trout—so if you bring your pole, don't expect to nab any trophy-size fish. The forest-rimmed lake is a relatively deep body

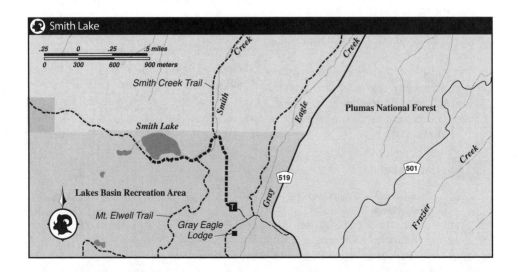

The short distance makes Smith Lake a fine family outing.

of water, which makes for chilly swimming that can actually be quite refreshing on a hot summer day. The trail along the south side of the lake continues west to a junction with the Jamison Creek Trail (see Trip 3).

7 Mt. Elwell Loop

see map on p. 38

see map on p. 38

Distance	7.25 miles (loop)
Hiking Time	4–6 hours
Elevation	+2,025/-2,025 feet
Difficulty	Very difficult
Trail Use	Dogs OK
Best Times	June through October
Agency	Plumas National Forest at 530-836-2575, www.fs.usda.gov/plumas
Recommended Maps	USFS *Lakes Basin, Sierra Buttes,* and *Plumas-Eureka State Park Recreation Guide*

HIGHLIGHTS The Mt. Elwell Loop provides one of the most diverse hikes in the Lakes Basin Recreation Area. Not only do you have the opportunity to stand atop one of the area's highest peaks and enjoy the expansive view, but you also pass by picturesque Long Lake, the largest lake in the Lakes Basin Recreation Area that is accessible by trail. A fine early-season wildflower display, delightful streams, and serene forests further contribute to the scenic diversity found on this trip. To complete the experience, finish off your hike with a meal at nearby Gray Eagle Lodge (see Trip 5 for details).

DIRECTIONS Follow CA 89 to the Gold Lake Highway (County Road 519), 1.5 miles southeast of Graeagle. Drive the Gold Lake Highway for 5.1 miles to the access road for Gray Eagle Lodge, which is also signed for the Smith Lake and Gray Eagle Creek Trails. Proceed on the access road, which quickly turns to dirt, for 0.4 mile to a right-hand turn onto a rougher dirt road. Find a parking spot after 0.1 mile as space allows near the Smith Lake Trailhead.

FACILITIES/TRAILHEAD There are no facilities at the trailhead, although Gray Eagle Lodge is just a short distance away.

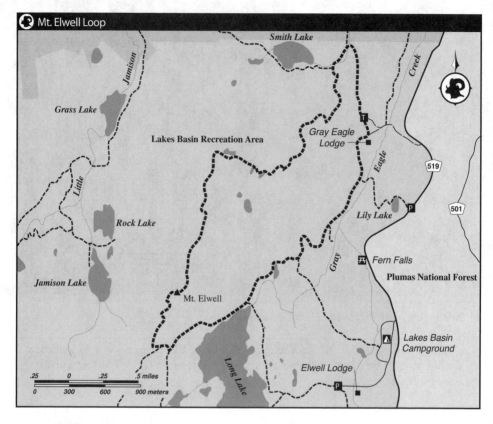

Mt. Elwell Loop

Smith Lake

Jamison

Grass Lake

Lakes Basin Recreation Area

Gray Eagle Lodge

Eagle

519

Little

Rock Lake

Lily Lake

501

Jamison Lake

Gray

Fern Falls

Plumas National Forest

Mt. Elwell

Lakes Basin Campground

Long Lake

Elwell Lodge

.25 0 .25 .5 miles
0 300 600 900 meters

From the well-signed trailhead, begin a moderate ascent across a shadeless morainal ridge carpeted with shrubs, primarily manzanita. After a steady, half-mile climb, the trail bends around the nose of the ridge and enters a light, mixed forest. A brief descent leads to an easy crossing of braided Smith Creek at 0.6 mile, followed quickly by a junction with a little-used trail that follows the creek downstream. Proceed upstream on a mild climb for 0.2 mile to a signed junction of the Mt. Elwell and Smith Lake Trails (see Trip 6 for a side trip to Smith Lake).

Veer left at the junction and immediately cross back over Smith Creek via some well-placed logs and rocks. Climb away from the creek, up a gully through mixed forest, to a junction with a very faint path that leads to an old viewpoint at the edge of a steep hillside. The obscure junction is marked by an old, deteriorating wooden sign nailed to a dead snag that reads OBSERVATION POINT 200

YARDS. At one time, the view must have been quite impressive, but over time the vegetation has grown up and diminished the vista of such notable landmarks as Beckwourth Peak and Mills Peak Lookout.

The stiff climb continues away from the old junction, as after a couple of switchbacks you gain a ridgecrest and follow it through a shady forest of western white pines, red firs, and a smattering of sugar pines. Farther up the ridge, lighter forest allows shrubs such as chinquapin, pinemat manzanita, and green-leaf manzanita to flourish. The grade eases as you reach a pond-dotted bench, where lodge-pole pines and mountain hemlocks join the mixed forest. After the trail passes by three ponds, you reach waist-deep and grass-lined Maiden Lake, the largest of the trio.

Beyond the ponds, a stiff climb resumes for the next half mile, until a mild upward traverse leads you toward the summit of Mt. Elwell, which makes brief appearances along the way through gaps in the trees. Nearing the peak, the grade increases again and the trail follows winding, rocky tread through diminishing trees to a cleft in the ridge between the two low summits. A short scramble from the trail is required to reach the top of the northwest summit, highest of the two at 7,818 feet. Steel rails and sheets of corrugated metal litter the slopes just below the summit, indicating that at some time in the past a lookout must have occupied the top of the peak. Looking a little farther afield, you have a bird's-eye view of the numerous lakes shimmering in the sunlight of the appropriately named Lakes Basin Recreation Area. Sierra Buttes and Mt. Lola dominate the view to the south, while snow-clad Lassen Peak towers over the southern Cascades to the north. Directly east is the broad plain of the Sierra Valley.

A zigzagging descent leads down the shrub-covered south side of Mt. Elwell into widely scattered red firs. Eventually, beautiful Long Lake springs into view on a winding downhill romp to a junction of the Long Lake Trail, 4.4 miles from the trailhead.

From the junction, head northeast on the Long Lake Trail across the steep hillside above the north shore of the well-named lake to a junction near the far end, which does not appear on either the US Forest Service or U.S. Geological Survey maps. Following signed directions for Gray Eagle Creek, continue northeast on the Long Lake Trail through low-growing shrubs and very widely scattered western white

and lodgepole pines. As the shrubs become taller and thicker, you pass a small pond and farther on encounter dense forest shading a lush understory, which is interrupted for a time by a pocket of wet meadow. Just after the crossing of a tributary of Gray Eagle Creek, you reach a three-way junction with the Grassy Lake Trail to Lakes Basin Campground, 6 miles from the trailhead.

Veer left at the junction and follow the trail away from the main branch of Gray Eagle Creek back to the lushly lined tributary. The soft, dirt tread of the forested trail is a welcome change for your feet from the previously rocky tread. Just before a crossing of the tributary, 0.4 mile from the Grassy Lake Trail, is a junction with a short lateral heading southeast to Hawley Falls. Although the falls aren't nearly as dramatic as the area's more notable Frazier Falls, the short diversion is worthwhile to see the swirling pools and turbulent cascades along Gray Eagle Creek and the short plunge of Hawley Falls.

Back on the main trail, you continue through forest and lush foliage to a crossing of another tributary before entering drier surroundings. At 6.9 miles is a three-way junction with the Lily Lake Trail, followed by a moderate climb of a shrub-covered slope dotted with an occasional fir or pine. Soon the trail descends to a junction with a lateral to Gray Eagle Lodge, where you continue north across a pair of diminutive streams and into forest again before returning to the Long Lake Trailhead.

View from the summit of Mt. Elwell

8 Long Lake Loop

Distance	4.5 miles (loop)
Hiking Time	2–3 hours
Elevation	+1,150/-1,150 feet
Difficulty	Moderate
Trail Use	Dogs OK
Best Times	June through October
Agency	Plumas National Forest at 530-836-2575, www.fs.usda.gov/plumas
Recommended Maps	USFS *Lakes Basin, Sierra Buttes,* and *Plumas-Eureka State Park Recreation Guide*

HIGHLIGHTS The extensive network of connecting trails in the Lakes Basin Recreation Area provides multiple options for loop trails of varying lengths. Perhaps none of these prospective trips captures the essence of the area better than this loop around the largest lake accessible by trail in the Lakes Basin. Not only will you pass by picturesque Long Lake and several other fine lakes en route, but the circuit visits many fine vista points as well. Extending the trip to the surrounding lakes is quite possible via a number of connecting trails.

DIRECTIONS Follow CA 89 to the Gold Lake Highway (County Road 519), 1.5 miles southeast of Graeagle. Drive the Gold Lake Highway for 6.8 miles to a right-hand turn onto the road into Lakes Basin Campground. Pass turnoffs for Elwell Lodge and the campground to the trailhead parking area.

FACILITIES/TRAILHEAD No facilities are available at the trailhead. The Lakes Basin Campground is a short distance from the trailhead, offering piped water, vault toilets, and trailer space for the $12 nightly fee. Elwell Lakes Lodge is also nearby, offering weekly rentals during the summer at housekeeping cabins that sleep from two to six people (530-836-2347 or **elwelllakeslodge.com** for more information).

Just beyond the trailhead, you pass over a culvert and follow a moderately rising tread through shrubs and mixed forest. Pass by an unsigned path to the left and continue to a junction at a half mile; the trail heading southwest from the junction and around Long Lake will ultimately provide the return route. Continue ahead (west) from the junction and proceed another 0.1 mile to another junction, where the loop trail heads north around Long Lake, and a short lateral straight ahead leads to the east shore. By following the lateral, in a few minutes you'll reach Long Lake, near a dock

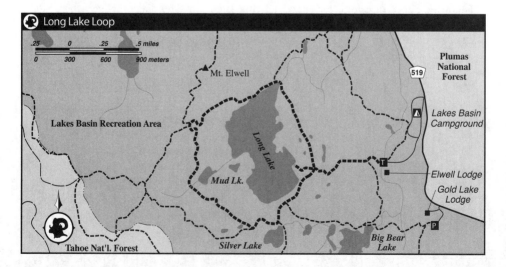

Long Lake in Lakes Basin Recreation Area

and boathouse operated by Elwell Lakes Lodge. Rugged cliffs and steep hillsides, carpeted with shrubs and broken by talus slides, rim the scenic lake.

Back at the loop junction, head north past a trio of seasonal ponds and make a brief climb of a rock outcropping, from which you have excellent views of the lake and the slopes of Mt. Elwell. Proceed across open, rocky terrain toward the northeast corner of the lake. A clearly defined path falters in the rocks at times, but ducks should help guide you until more discernible tread returns prior to your arrival at a small concrete dam across Gray Eagle Creek. Walk across the top of the dam to the resumption of singletrack trail on the far side, and make a very brief climb to a three-way junction with the Long Lake Trail, 1.4 miles from the trailhead.

Turn sharply left (southwest) at the junction and skirt the treeless lower slopes of Mt. Elwell along the brushy north shore of Long Lake. After 0.3 mile, begin a steady climb across a talus slide to a grassy wildflower-covered slope beyond. At 2.3 miles is a junction with the Mt. Elwell Trail (see Trip 7).

From the junction, head steeply downhill on the Mud Lake Trail. Conifers return as you near the floor of the basin, where the trail passes well to the west of Mud Lake. The lake appears to be misnamed, as its clear blue waters appear to be anything but muddy. The soggy soil around the shoreline may explain the name.

The trail climbs out of Mud Lake's basin with the aid of some switchbacks, to a pond-dotted bench holding Helgramite Lake. After passing by the north shore of Helgramite Lake, a very short descent leads to an impressive vista of the lakes below and a T-junction with the Silver Lake Trail, 3.4 miles from the trailhead.

Turn left at the junction and continue a winding descent to the northeast shore of shimmering Silver Lake and a three-way junction with a lateral to Round Lake at 3.7 miles.

Head north from the junction and proceed for 0.2 mile to yet another junction, this one with the Bear Lakes Loop. Veer left (northeast) and head downhill past the southeast shore of Long Lake to the first junction you encountered from the trailhead. From there, turn right and retrace your steps a half mile to the Lakes Basin Trailhead.

9   Bear Lakes Loop

Distance	3.8 miles (loop)
Hiking Time	2–3 hours
Elevation	+450/-450 feet
Difficulty	Moderate
Trail Use	Dogs OK, good for kids
Best Times	June through October
Agency	Plumas National Forest at 530-836-2575, www.fs.usda.gov/plumas
Recommended Maps	USFS *Lakes Basin, Sierra Buttes,* and *Plumas-Eureka State Park Recreation Guide*

HIGHLIGHTS A short loop trail with minimal elevation gain visits several picturesque lakes within the Lakes Basin Recreation Area, including Silver, Big Bear, Little Bear, and Cub Lakes. Hot summer days will lure swimmers into the refreshing waters, and anglers can test their skills on the resident trout. Relics near Round Lake provide a historical glimpse into the mining activity of the past.

DIRECTIONS Follow CA 89 to the Gold Lake Highway (County Road 519), 1.5 miles southeast of Graeagle. Drive the Gold Lake Highway for 7.7 miles to a left-hand turn onto the access road for Gold Lake Lodge, also signed Round Lake Trailhead. Where the road forks, follow the left-hand road to the trailhead.

FACILITIES/TRAILHEAD There are no facilities at the trailhead. Gold Lake Lodge is just a short distance from the trailhead, offering rustic cabins for rent during the summer months with meals included. Nonguests can purchase breakfasts or dinners in the cozy dining room. Call 530-836-2350 or visit **goldlakelodge.com** for more information.

From the Round Lake Trailhead, follow the wide path for 0.2 mile to a Y-junction with a connector trail to the Bear Lakes Loop. Turn right (west) and follow the connector trail, soon crossing a seasonal stream coursing through a meadow. Beyond a low ridge, you walk alongside the outlet from the Bear Lakes for a while before hopping across the outlet and reaching a signed three-way junction near Big Bear Lake, a half mile from the trailhead.

Veer left at the junction, heading above the forested north shore of scenic Big Bear Lake, by far the largest of the Bear Lakes. Shortly after leaving Big Bear Lake behind, you pass just above the north shore of

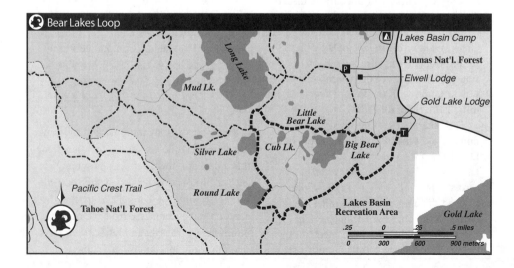

Silver Lake on Bear Lakes Loop

boomerang-shaped Little Bear Lake. A short use trail leads to the shallow lake, which offers less chilly swimming than at deeper Big Bear Lake. Another quarter mile of hiking leads above the north shore of circular Cub Lake, which can also be accessed via a short use trail. Beyond Cub Lake, the Bear Lakes Loop bends northwest toward Long Lake and leads to a signed three-way junction in a small flat, 1.3 miles from the trailhead.

Turn left onto the Silver Lake Trail and make a short climb to a fine view of picturesque Long Lake, backdropped by the southeast slope of 7,818-foot Mt. Elwell. From the viewpoint, the trail drops to a flat and follows a wandering course south to a junction near lovely Silver Lake, 1.5 miles from the trailhead, where a mixed forest of western white pines, red firs, mountain hemlocks, and lodgepole pines rims the shoreline.

Veer left at the junction, hop across Silver Lake's outlet, head south along the east shore of Silver Lake, and then make a short climb to the crest of a broad moraine. As you cross the top of the moraine, Round Lake comes into view well below the trail. A steep but short descent across open terrain

brings you to a crossing of the outlet and then along the east side of cirque-bound Round Lake. From the southeast shore, a very brief climb to the former mill site reveals artifacts from the old mining days, including the foundation of the old stamp mill, a rusted engine block, and a tailings pile. During the early 1900s, miners searched for gold in a nearby quartz vein, fragments of which are strewn about in the tailings. Just past these remains, you reach a three-way junction with a three-quarter-mile connector to the Pacific Crest Trail, 2.25 miles from the trailhead.

Away from Round Lake, follow the Round Lake Trail along the course of an old mining road through scattered trees and shrubs and past a small pond, and then along a lightly forested ridge. Near the 3-mile mark, a short use trail leads to a fine view of Big Bear Lake below, where you'll surely want to have a camera to capture the scene. Back on the main trail, enter a thicker forest of western white pines and red firs on the way to the closing of the loop at 3.6 miles. From there, retrace your steps 0.2 mile to the Round Lake Trailhead.

10 Frazier Falls

Distance	1 mile (out-and-back)
Hiking Time	30 minutes–1 hour
Elevation	Negligible
Difficulty	Easy
Trail Use	Leashed dogs, good for kids
Best Times	Late May through October
Agency	Plumas National Forest at 530-836-2575, www.fs.usda.gov/plumas
Recommended Maps	USFS *Lakes Basin, Sierra Buttes*, and *Plumas-Eureka State Park Recreation Guide*

HIGHLIGHTS Once the access road sheds its snow and Frazier Creek is running at full force, scads of sightseers flock to Frazier Falls on the weekends, with good reason, as a short, nearly flat and wheelchair-accessible half-mile trail leads to an excellent view of the thundering falls. The paved trail is suitable for young and old alike, but make sure you keep an eye on children who may want to leave the safety of the trail, especially where a well-worn path leads to slippery rocks above the falls. During the height of the season, plan a visit to the area on a weekday in order to escape the crowds.

DIRECTIONS Follow CA 89 to the Gold Lake Highway (County Road 519), 1.5 miles southeast of Graeagle. Drive the Gold Lake Highway for 1.6 miles to the signed left-hand turnoff for Frazier Falls—look carefully for this junction, which occurs in the midst of a sharp bend in the highway. Follow the narrow, paved road (CR 501) for 4 miles to the signed trailhead parking lot.

FACILITIES/TRAILHEAD The parking area has modern vault toilets and picnic tables.

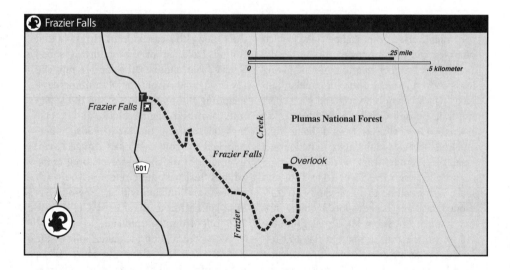

The paved, wheelchair-accessible trail follows a winding course through light forest and past rock slabs to a stout, wooden bridge across Frazier Creek, near the halfway point to the falls. Although a use trail leads from the vicinity of the bridge to the top of the falls, this part of the route is not for children—or adults who aren't surefooted, for that matter—as the wet rocks above the falls can be quite slick. From the bridge, continue along the serpentine path of the paved trail for another quarter mile to a viewing area enclosed by iron railings. Here, you can clearly see the full extent of the 176-foot falls, plunging over the rocky lip and crashing into the dark pool at its base in watery splendor.

Opposite: Frazier Falls

11 Lower Salmon Lake

Distance	1 mile (out-and-back)
Hiking Time	1 hour
Elevation	Negligible
Difficulty	Easy
Trail Use	Backpacking option, dogs OK, good for kids,
Best Times	Late May through October
Agency	Tahoe National Forest at 530-994-3401, www.fs.usda.gov/tahoe
Recommended Maps	USFS *Lakes Basin, Sierra Buttes,* and *Plumas-Eureka State Park Recreation Guide*

HIGHLIGHTS Most hikers bypass the trip to Lower Salmon Lake in favor of the Upper Salmon Lake Trail nearby. However, the fact that the Lower Salmon Lake Trailhead is unsigned may contribute to its relative lack of use. The lake doesn't deserve to be shunned, because the scenery is quite attractive, providing a fine destination for hikers in search of a short, easy trip. Although the elevation gain and loss is minimal, bear in mind that the route from the trailhead to the lake is all downhill, requiring a higher degree of effort on the return trip. An old mine on the far side of the lake can provide hours of interesting exploration.

DIRECTIONS From CA 49 near Bassetts, turn onto Gold Lake Highway (County Road 519) and proceed 4 miles to the signed turnoff for Salmon Lake. Follow paved road east for 0.7 mile to an unmarked jeep road on the left and park in a gravel area near a closed steel gate.

FACILITIES/TRAILHEAD There are no facilities near the trailhead. The trail follows the closed jeep road beyond the steel gate, upon which a sign indicates that the road is open to hikers, fishing enthusiasts, and canoers.

Walk around the closed gate and follow the downhill course of the old jeep road through thick shrubs beneath a scattered, mixed forest of lodgepole pines, red firs, and Jeffrey pines. The decline eases as you pass a seasonal pond that reverts to a meadow as the summer progresses. A moderate descent resumes farther down the trail, as glimpses of the shimmering surface of Lower Salmon Lake appear through gaps in the trees. Soon you arrive at the grass- and forest-rimmed lakeshore, a half mile from the parking area.

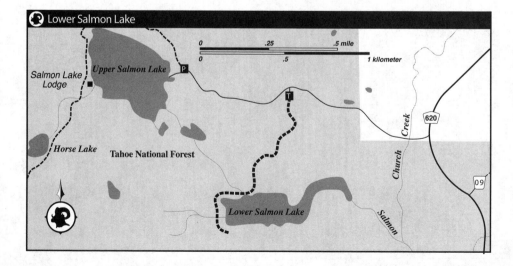

The old road crosses Salmon Creek and continues around the west end of the lake to cross a small inlet stream. Although overnight camping is allowed, early-season campers may have a significant battle with mosquitoes during the morning and evening hours. From a junction just past this second crossing, the middle road leads to the site of the abandoned mine, where processing equipment is strewn about, and the remains of a narrow-gauge railroad track can still be seen entering the closed mine.

12 Upper Salmon Lake Trail to Deer Lake

see map on p. 48

Distance	4 miles (out-and-back)
Hiking Time	2–4 hours
Elevation	+750/-225 feet
Difficulty	Moderate
Trail Use	Backpacking option, dogs OK
Best Times	Mid-June through October
Agency	Tahoe National Forest at 530-994-3401, www.fs.usda.gov/tahoe
Recommended Maps	USFS *Lakes Basin, Sierra Buttes,* and *Plumas-Eureka State Park Recreation Guide*

HIGHLIGHTS Stunningly scenic Deer Lake is a popular destination at the height of summer, particularly on weekends. Good views abound along much of the trail, but the climax occurs at the lake, where the dramatic spires of Sierra Buttes provide a fine complement to the picturesque lake.

DIRECTIONS From CA 49 near Bassetts, turn onto Gold Lake Highway (County Road 519) and proceed 4 miles to the signed turnoff for Salmon Lake. Follow the paved road west for 1 mile to the trailhead on the right-hand side of the road.

FACILITIES/TRAILHEAD There are no facilities at the trailhead. A boat dock is available for launching watercraft into Upper Salmon Lake at the end of the road. Salmon Lake Lodge, on the south shore of Upper Salmon Lake, offers 14 housekeeping units for rent during the summer months (call 530-757-1825 for more information). Avoid the tendency to drive all the way to the end of the parking area near the boat dock at Upper Salmon Lake, as the actual trailhead is approximately 75 yards before the end of the road. Park near the trailhead as conditions allow.

From the edge of the road, the Upper Salmon Lake Trail ascends an open hillside sprinkled with widely scattered Jeffrey pines and firs, which allows for nearly continuous views of Upper Salmon Lake and the surrounding terrain. The slopes are carpeted with a wide array of shrubs, including huckleberry oak, manzanita, snowbush, serviceberry, deer brush, and squaw carpet. After the initial climb, you follow an arcing traverse high above the lake until the trail drops toward the far shoreline to avoid some steep cliffs. Closely following the west shore of the lake, you pass by summer cabins and arrive at an informal junction, where the left-hand path continues along the shoreline to Salmon Lake Lodge. Veer

right at the junction and climb on rocky tread past more summer cabins until you reach a gravel path from the lodge. Follow the gravel path to a wood bridge, cross the bridge, and then immediately turn right onto a dirt trail, where a sign points the way to the Deer Lake Trail and Horse Lake.

Leaving the last remnant of civilization behind, the well-graded trail leads you through a mixed forest of western white pines, lodgepole pines, and white and red firs to Horse Lake, 1.1 miles from the trailhead. The shoreline of the serene lake is graced with willows and a fine display of early-season wildflowers. Beyond Horse Lake, the rate of ascent increases dramatically as you follow a steep, switchbacking,

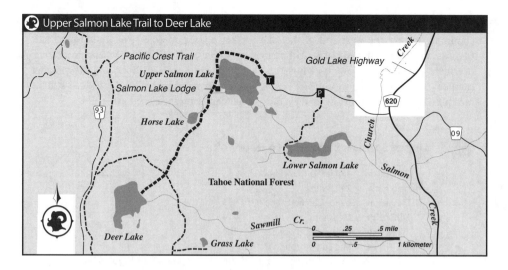

Upper Salmon Lake Trail to Deer Lake

half-mile climb to a saddle and a four-way junction.

Continue straight ahead from the junction; this mildly graded stretch of trail is a welcome relief after the steep ascent from Horse Lake. Scattered forest allows intermittent views of Sierra Buttes to the south and Salmon Lake behind. Pass by a couple of small ponds before you crest a rise, where Deer Lake suddenly springs into view, followed by a brief descent to the northeast shore.

Beautiful Deer Lake is surrounded by picturesque cliffs and is dramatically backdropped by the towering ramparts of Sierra Buttes. A use trail encircles the lake, providing shoreline access for swimmers, picnickers, and sunbathers to the sandy beaches around the lake. Several good campsites are peppered around the shoreline.

13 Deer Lake Trail and Pacific Crest Trail Loop

Distance	8 miles (loop); 6 miles (point-to-point)
Hiking Time	3–5 hours
Elevation	+1,750/-1,750 feet; +1,750/-700 feet
Difficulty	Difficult
Trail Use	Backpacking option, dogs OK, mountain biking OK
Best Times	Mid-June through October
Agency	Tahoe National Forest at 530-994-3401, www.fs.usda.gov/tahoe
Recommended Maps	USFS *Lakes Basin, Sierra Buttes,* and *Plumas-Eureka State Park Recreation Guide*

HIGHLIGHTS Whether you do this route as an 8-mile loop or as a 6-mile shuttle trip, you'll experience great views from a 2.5-mile-long ridge and fine scenery at a picturesque lake. Without the shuttle, a 2-mile, knee-jarring descent on paved road is necessary to return to the trailhead. Deer Lake is one of the more scenic lakes accessible by trail in the region, but the exquisite view of the lake with the rugged Sierra Buttes in the background will more than compensate for the potential crowds.

DIRECTIONS *Start:* From CA 49 near Bassetts, turn onto Gold Lake Highway (County Road 519) and proceed 1.3 miles to the signed turnoff for Sardine and Packer Lakes. Follow paved road (CR S621) west for 0.3 mile to a junction between Packer Lake Road on the right and Sardine Lakes Road on the left. Proceed on Packer Lake Road to the Packsaddle Trailhead parking area on the left, 2.4 miles from the Sardine Lakes Road junction.

End: Continue on Packer Lake Road from the Packsaddle Trailhead and the turnoff for Packer Lake Lodge, beyond which the road designation changes to FS 93. After the Tamarack Lakes Trailhead, the pavement narrows, and the grade becomes quite a bit steeper on a climb to Packer Saddle and a large roadside parking area.

FACILITIES/TRAILHEAD No facilities are available at either trailhead. Packer Lake Road accesses three forest service campsites: Packsaddle, Berger, and Diablo. Nearby Packer Lake has a forest service picnic area. Privately run Packer Lake Lodge offers six cabins, eight housekeeping cabins, and boats for rent, and it has a restaurant and bar that serves breakfast, lunch, and dinner during limited hours in the summer months (call 530-862-1221 for more information). Find the Deer Lake Trail on the opposite side of the road and a short way down from the Packsaddle parking lot. A large Pacific Crest Trail (PCT) emblem marks the trailhead near Packer Saddle.

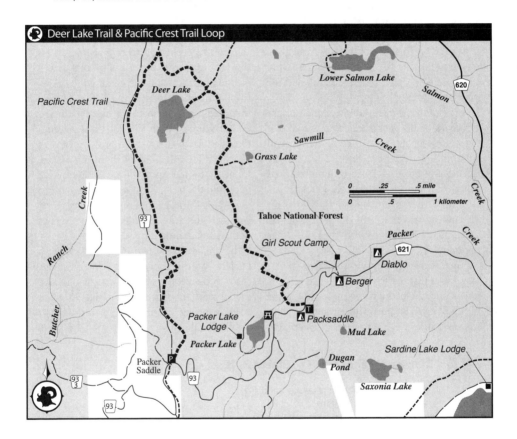

Deer Lake Trail & Pacific Crest Trail Loop

egin hiking on a mildly graded trail through a scattered forest of Jeffrey pines, incense cedars, lodgepole pines, and red firs. Cross over a trio of lushly lined seasonal rivulets and pass below some power lines; next, a moderate climb with a pair of switchbacks leads you across shrub-covered slopes to a T-junction with the lateral to Grass Lake, 1.4 miles from the trailhead. The quarter-mile lateral leads to the grass-lined, shallow, and irregularly shaped lake, which is surrounded by alders and a light forest of western white pines and red firs. A nice display of seasonal wildflowers complements the grassy shoreline in early summer.

Back on the main trail, you climb through scattered forest to the boulder and log crossing of Sawmill Creek. Mountain hemlocks join the mixed forest beyond the crossing on the way to a signed four-way junction at

2.1 miles. A sharp left at the junction leads through scattered forest, past a couple of small ponds and over a rise to Deer Lake. The lake is quite scenic, surrounded by picturesque cliffs and dramatically back-dropped by the towering ramparts of Sierra Buttes. A use trail encircles the lake, provid-ing shoreline access for swimmers, picnick-ers, and sunbathers to the sandy beaches scattered around the lake. Overnighters will find several good campsites scattered around the lakeshore. An unmaintained use trail leaves the north shore of the lake, providing a steep shortcut to the Pacific Crest Trail for those who don't mind the climb and the poor condition of the tread.

Instead of reaching the PCT via the use trail, you could backtrack from the lake to the four-way junction. From there, head west on a moderate ascent across mostly open terrain for 0.4 mile, to the unmarked junction with the use trail from Deer Lake. Continue the climb toward the ridge on an angling traverse into deepening forest and reach a junction with the PCT after another 0.3 mile.

Turn south on the well-graded and well-traveled PCT, which mildly ascends the left-hand side of the ridge through a forest of red firs and western white pines. Gaps in the trees allow excellent views of Deer Lake below, backdropped nicely by Sierra Buttes. Make a pair of crossings over a four-wheel-drive road that closely parallels the PCT for a while before eventually veering away to the west. The location of the jeep road so close to the PCT is most unfortunate, but hopefully your trip won't coincide with its use by noisy off-road machines.

Continue along the ridge across a slope that was clear-cut at some time in the recent past, evidenced by the young trees carpet-ing the slope that have yet to reach the stature of decent-size Christmas trees. But this lack of mature forest is a bit of a mixed blessing, as you are afforded good views to the north. Return to light forest and then begin a switchbacking descent toward Packer Saddle. Eventually, you break out into the open again to a very impressive view of Sierra Buttes and some of the nearby lakes, followed by a lengthy descending traverse back into the trees. Cross an old jeep road to the Wallis Mine, and then walk along nearly level trail to Packer Saddle amid good views of the surrounding terrain.

If you are fortunate enough to have a vehicle waiting for you at Packer Saddle, count your blessings. Otherwise, you'll have to descend the pavement of FS 93 on a steep, winding, 2-mile descent to the Pack-saddle Trailhead.

14 Tamarack Lakes Road to Sierra Buttes

Distance	7 miles (out-and-back)
Hiking Time	4–6 hours
Elevation	+2,250/-200 feet
Difficulty	Very difficult
Trail Use	Backpacking option, dogs OK, mountain biking OK
Best Times	Mid-June through October
Agency	Tahoe National Forest at 530-994-3401, www.fs.usda.gov/tahoe
Recommended Maps	USFS *Lakes Basin, Sierra Buttes,* and *Plumas-Eureka State Park Recreation Guide*

HIGHLIGHTS Just as in the old saying about Rome, all roads (and trails) in this area seem to lead to the lookout atop Sierra Buttes, at least eventually. The unrivaled aerie that provides such an unpar-alleled view is an achievement any physically fit visitor to the region should experience at least once. Although not the shortest way to the top, this route passes a pair of picturesque lakes on the way—fine destinations for a picnic lunch en route, a refreshing dip after the strenuous climb, or an overnight destination well suited for recovering from the steep ascent.

DIRECTIONS From CA 49 near Bassetts, turn onto Gold Lake Highway (County Road 519) and proceed 1.3 miles to the signed turnoff for Sardine and Packer Lakes. Follow paved road (CR S621) west for 0.3 mile to a junction between Packer Lake Road on the right and Sardine Lakes Road on the left. Proceed on Packer Lake Road to the Tamarack Lakes Trailhead parking area on the right, 0.2 mile past the turnoff for Packer Lake Lodge.

FACILITIES/TRAILHEAD No facilities are available at the trailhead. The Packer Lake Road accesses three forest service campsites: Packsaddle, Berger, and Diablo. Nearby Packer Lake has a forest service picnic area. Privately run Packer Lake Lodge offers six cabins, eight housekeeping cabins, and boats for rent, and it has a restaurant and bar that serves breakfast, lunch, and dinner during limited hours in the summer months (call 530-862-1221 for more information).

From the parking lot, cross the road and follow the old jeep road for a quarter mile to a junction, and continue straight ahead. Eventually, you come alongside the outlet from Tamarack Lakes and follow the seasonal creek to a junction of another old jeep road that serves as the route of the Tamarack Lakes Trail (see Trip 17), 0.9 mile from the trailhead.

Walk a short distance from the junction to the north shore of the first of the two Tamarack Lakes, a lovely body of water enhanced by a splendid backdrop provided by the rugged Sierra Buttes. To reach the upper lake, continue up the road briefly to a Y-junction and take the left-hand branch for 0.2 mile. The second lake is equal in beauty to its lower counterpart. Both lakes are rimmed by lodgepole pines, which are also known as tamarack pines—hence the lakes' name.

If you're bound for Sierra Buttes, at some point you'll have to tear yourself away

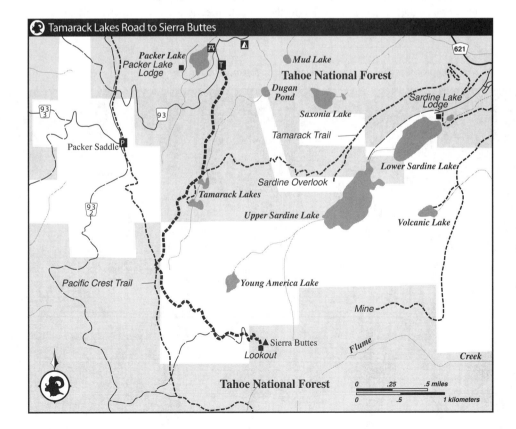

from the lovely surroundings of Tamarack Lakes and head back to the Y-junction. From there, follow the right-hand road on a stiff climb to the crossing of an old jeep road. Beyond the crossing, singletrack trail climbs toward the top of the ridge above the head of the canyon. After a trio of short switchbacks, the trail arcs around to a junction with the Pacific Crest Trail (PCT), 1.9 miles from the trailhead.

Head south on the PCT for a very short distance to a junction, and veer left onto the Sierra Buttes Trail. The steady climb proceeds along the ridge, with excellent views into the canyon below, Sierra Buttes above, and out to distant ridges and peaks parading toward the horizon. Past an old rocky road on the right, the forest starts to thicken, with mountain hemlocks and western white pines now joining the mixed forest.

Breaking out into the open after a while, the towering ramparts of Sierra Buttes burst into view, as the lakes below sparkle in the sunlight. Farther up the ridge, singletrack trail crosses the Sierra Buttes jeep road and then continues toward the top. A short way up this road a closed steel gate blocks further vehicle access, so even the off-road crowd has to walk the final three-quarters of a mile to the base of the stairs below the lookout. Roughly paralleling the access road, the trail winds up the slope through scattered conifers to some switchbacks.

Above the switchbacks, the trail soon merges with the road for good, which snakes its way out of the trees and into the rocky realm near the top of the Buttes. You pass an old water tank and bend around some cliffs to a sudden and imposing view of the series of stairs scaling the nearly sheer face below the lookout. A plaque at the bottom of the stairs provides the history of their construction in 1964. Non-acrophobes can climb the stairs to the airy lookout and its fenced, grated balcony, which juts out into open air. The expansive view spreading out in all directions is more than ample reward for the rugged ascent.

A hiker approaches the stairway to the lookout on top of Sierra Buttes.

15 Sierra Buttes via Pacific Crest Trail

Distance	5 miles (out-and-back)
Hiking Time	3–5 hours
Elevation	+1,725/-400 feet
Difficulty	Difficult
Trail Use	Dogs OK
Best Times	Mid-June through October
Agency	Tahoe National Forest at 530-994-3401, www.fs.usda.gov/tahoe
Recommended Maps	USFS *Lakes Basin, Sierra Buttes,* and *Plumas-Eureka State Park Recreation Guide*

see map on p. 54

HIGHLIGHTS There may not be an easy way to the lookout perched on the knife-edged ridge of Sierra Buttes, but this route is certainly the shortest. The expansive view from the lookout is more than enough reward for the effort required to get there.

DIRECTIONS From CA 49 near Bassetts, turn onto Gold Lake Highway (County Road 519) and proceed 1.3 miles to the signed turnoff for Sardine and Packer Lakes. Follow paved road (CR S621) west for 0.3 mile to a junction between Packer Lake Road on the right and Sardine Lakes Road on the left. Proceed on Packer Lake Road past the Deer Creek Trailhead and the turnoff for Packer Lake Lodge, beyond which the road designation changes to FS 93. After the Tamarack Lakes Trailhead, the pavement narrows and the grade becomes quite a bit steeper on a climb to Packer Saddle. Remain on FS 93 for 0.4 mile past the saddle and then veer left onto FS 93-02. Follow this dirt road, which should be passable for most sedans, for another 0.1 mile or so to a sign marked SIERRA BUTTES 12E06 and park nearby as space allows.

FACILITIES/TRAILHEAD There are no facilities near the trailhead. The trail begins by heading south on the wide track of an old jeep road beyond a closed steel gate.

Proceed on a moderately steep climb that winds up the nose of a ridge through scattered timber. Eventually, you leave the road, following signed directions onto a singletrack trail. Grand views of Sierra Buttes are complemented by a fine display of early-season wildflowers, including mule-ears, Indian paintbrush, pennyroyal, and gilia. The steady climb proceeds to a Y-junction with the Sierra Buttes Trail from Tamarack Lakes, 1 mile from the trailhead.

As the Pacific Crest Trail angles sharply away to the right, travel a very short distance along the Sierra Buttes Trail to a junction with the Tamarack Connection Trail 12E30 coming up from below. The unrelenting ascent continues, as the Sierra Buttes Trail heads southeast following the course of the ridge through thickening forest, which now includes western white pines and mountain hemlocks. The conifers are still spaced widely enough to allow intermittent but grand views of Tamarack, Young America, and Sardine Lakes in the canyons below and the imposing rock buttresses of Sierra Buttes above.

Cross over the Sierra Buttes jeep road at 2 miles from the trailhead, and continue the stiff climb past a set of switchbacks. Above the switchbacks, the trail soon merges with the road for good, which snakes its way out of the trees and into the rocky realm near the top of the Buttes. You pass an old water tank and bend around some cliffs to a sudden and imposing view of the series of stairs scaling the nearly sheer face below the lookout. A plaque at the bottom of the stairs provides the history of their construction in 1964. Non-acrophobes can climb the stairs to the airy lookout and its fenced, grated balcony, which juts out into the open air. The expansive view spreading out in all directions is more than ample reward for all that climbing.

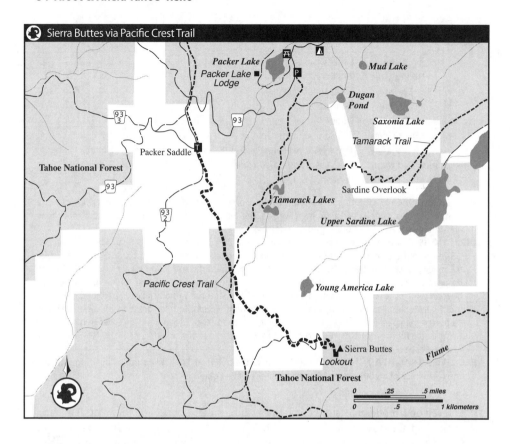

Sierra Buttes via Pacific Crest Trail

16 Sardine Overlook

Distance	4.6 miles (out-and-back)
Hiking Time	3–4 hours
Elevation	+700/-125 feet
Difficulty	Moderate
Trail Use	Dogs OK, mountain biking OK
Best Times	Late May through October
Agency	Tahoe National Forest at 530-994-3401, www.fs.usda.gov/tahoe
Recommended Maps	USFS *Lakes Basin, Sierra Buttes,* and *Plumas-Eureka State Park Recreation Guide*

HIGHLIGHTS The dramatic views of Sierra Buttes and the Sardine Lakes from the Tamarack Lakes Trail and the Sardine Overlook are some of the best views accessible by trail anywhere in the region. Don't forget to pack your camera, as any photographer—professional or amateur—will find the outstanding scenery virtually impossible to ignore. The entire route passes through open terrain, which accounts for the great views, but you'll be faced with constant exposure to the glaring summer sun. Start your journey early in the morning to avoid the heat, and make sure to apply plenty of sunblock.

DIRECTIONS From CA 49 near Bassetts, turn onto Gold Lake Highway (County Road 519) and proceed 1.3 miles to the signed turnoff for Sardine and Packer Lakes. Follow paved road (CR S621) west for a quarter mile to a junction between Packer Lake Road on the right and Sardine Lakes Road on the left. Proceed on Sardine Lakes Road about 75 yards, and locate the Tamarack Lakes Trailhead on the right-hand shoulder, where you'll find very limited parking.

Hiker admires the view of Sierra Buttes and Upper Sardine Lake.

FACILITIES/TRAILHEAD There are no facilities at the trailhead. The Forest Service administrates the nearby Sardine Campground and Sand Pond Picnic Area. Sardine Lake Resort on the north shore of Lower Sardine Lake offers lodging and dining (call 530-862-1196 for more information).

Begin hiking along a closed, rocky jeep road that zigzags somewhat steeply up a manzanita-covered hillside sprinkled with widely scattered pines, firs, and cedars. At 0.6 mile, you reach a three-way junction and bend sharply left (southeast), following the switchbacking road to the crest of a lateral moraine. A steady climb southwest along the shrubby moraine is blessed with outstanding views of the Sardine Lakes and the towering, dominating, northeast face of Sierra Buttes. An occasional Jeffrey pine is all that inhibits the grand vistas en route to a three-way junction of the Tamarack Lakes

and Sardine Overlook Trails, 2 miles from the trailhead.

Veer left at the Tamarack Lakes junction and follow descending trail 0.3 mile to the Sardine Overlook near a switchback. If possible, the view from the overlook is even more impressive than the ones along the moraine, with the Sierra Buttes immediately in front of you and Upper Sardine Lake directly below. Avoid the inclination to continue the descent toward the lake, as the route has long been abandoned, although it looks like the trail continues here.

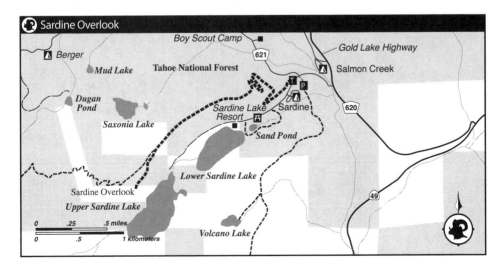

17   Tamarack Lakes Trail

Distance	7.5 miles (out-and-back)
Hiking Time	4–6 hours
Elevation	+1,400/-425 feet
Difficulty	Difficult
Trail Use	Dogs OK, mountain biking OK
Best Times	Mid-June through October
Agency	Tahoe National Forest at 530-994-3401, www.fs.usda.gov/tahoe
Recommended Maps	USFS *Lakes Basin, Sierra Buttes,* and *Plumas-Eureka State Park Recreation Guide*

HIGHLIGHTS Grand views of Sierra Buttes, coupled with a pair of charming lakes, make this trip along the Tamarack Lakes Trail well worth the effort. Strong hikers can accept the additional challenge of reaching the lookout atop Sierra Buttes on a 2.5-mile extension from the lakes, as described in Trip 15. The first 2 miles of trail are fully exposed to the hot summer sun, and a reliable source of water is not available until arriving at the lakes. These potential drawbacks can be minimized by an early start to beat the heat and an extra bottle of water stowed in the pack. Although the Tamarack Lakes are accessible to four-wheel-drive vehicles via a different route, chances are good that you won't see any, as motorized travel to the lakes is generally very light.

DIRECTIONS From CA 49 near Bassetts, turn onto Gold Lake Highway (County Road 519) and proceed 1.3 miles to the signed turnoff for Sardine and Packer Lakes. Follow paved road (CR S621) west for a quarter mile to a junction between the Packer Lake Road on the right and the Sardine Lakes Road on the left. Proceed on Sardine Lakes Road about 75 yards and locate the Tamarack Lakes Trailhead on the right-hand shoulder, where you'll find limited parking.

FACILITIES/TRAILHEAD There are no facilities at the trailhead. The Forest Service manages the nearby Sardine Campground and Sand Pond Picnic Area. Sardine Lake Resort, on the north shore of Lower Sardine Lake, offers lodging and dining (call 530-862-1196 for more information).

Begin hiking along a closed, rocky jeep road that zigzags somewhat steeply up a manzanita-covered hillside sprinkled with widely scattered pines, firs, and cedars. At 0.6 mile, reach a three-way junction and

bend sharply left (southeast), following the switchbacking road to the crest of a lateral moraine. A steady climb southwest along the shrubby moraine is blessed with outstanding views of the Sardine lakes and the towering,

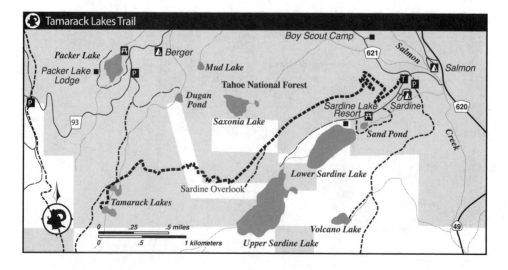

dominating northeast face of Sierra Buttes. An occasional Jeffrey pine is all that inhibits the grand vistas en route to a three-way junction of the Tamarack Lakes and Sardine Overlook Trails, 2 miles from the trailhead.

Proceed straight ahead at the junction, continuing the steady climb along the southeast side of the moraine for a short distance to a series of switchbacks that zigzag up the slope. Scattered stands of mountain hemlock and red fir offer pockets of intermittent shade on the way to the crest of the moraine. Descend away from the top of the ridge via more switchbacks through light forest until breaking out into the open again, near where the trail merges with a rocky jeep road. Follow this winding road downhill to a crossing of the outlet from Tamarack Lakes, which usually dries up by midsummer. Just beyond the crossing is a T-junction with a four-wheel-drive road from Packer Lake, 3.5 miles from the trailhead.

Turn left at the junction and follow the four-wheel-drive road a short distance to the first of the Tamarack Lakes. To reach the upper lake, take the left-hand fork from a Y-junction near the lower lake. Both lakes are quite scenic, thanks to a backdrop from the pinnacled ridgeline of Sierra Buttes. The lakes are rimmed by lodgepole pines, also known as tamarack pines—hence the name.

Hardy hikers can scale Sierra Buttes from Tamarack Lakes by taking the right-hand fork in the road near the lower lake as described in Trip 17.

Lower Tamarack Lake

---

18 **Volcano Lake and Mountain Mine**

see map on p. 58

Distance	7 miles (out-and-back)
Hiking Time	4–6 hours
Elevation	+1,550/-350 feet
Difficulty	Difficult
Trail Use	Dogs OK, mountain biking OK
Best Times	June through October
Agency	Tahoe National Forest at 530-994-3401, www.fs.usda.gov/tahoe
Recommended Maps	USFS *Lakes Basin, Sierra Buttes,* and *Plumas-Eureka State Park Recreation Guide*

HIGHLIGHTS An old mining road leads to a scenic cirque lake and one of the most impressive views of Sierra Buttes in the entire area. A tricky ford, ankle-twisting roadbed, and stiff climb may deter the faint of heart, but hikers who don't mind such adversity will reap big rewards for their efforts on this route.

DIRECTIONS From CA 49 near Bassetts, turn onto Gold Lake Highway (County Road 519) and proceed 1.3 miles to the signed turnoff for Sardine and Packer Lakes. Follow paved road (CR S621) west for 0.3 mile to a junction between the Packer Lake Road on the right and the Sardine Lakes Road on the left, and turn left into the unmarked parking area near the intersection. Parking is very limited, but it seems adequate for the light use the trail receives.

FACILITIES/TRAILHEAD There are no facilities at the trailhead. The Forest Service manages the nearby Sardine Campground and Sand Pond Picnic Area. Sardine Lake Resort, on the north shore of Lower Sardine Lake, offers lodging and dining (call 530-862-1196 for more information). The route follows the closed gravel road away from the parking area.

Walk along a gravel road through the light forest and shrubs around the edge of Sardine Campground to a closed gate near a ford of Sardine Creek, where the most straightforward route across the creek uses a log perched above a pile of rocks. Once over the creek, climb along the rocky road, which has filtered views of the canyon of the North Yuba River. Pass by lesser roads on the way to a junction with the road to Volcano Lake, 1.3 miles from the trailhead.

Veer right and make a steep but short climb through scattered forest up the winding, rock-strewn road to the lake basin, where very short use trails provide access

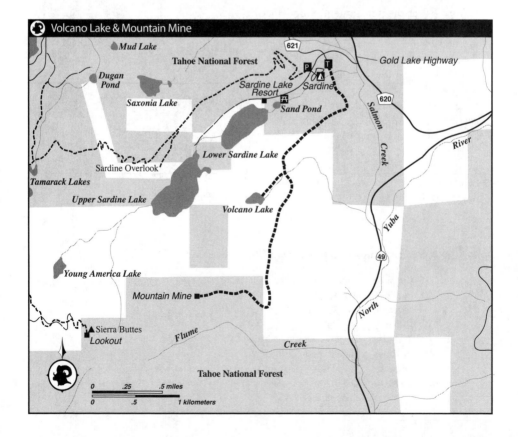

to a rocky shoreline dotted with lodgepole pines, western white pines, and red firs. The lake is cradled in a deep cirque rimmed almost completely by rocky cliffs; these are somewhat dwarfed in appearance by the uppermost pinnacles of Sierra Buttes. Smooth rock slabs dip into the lake at the far end, luring swimmers who don't mind the chilly waters. A few seldom-used campsites are scattered around the lakeshore, as well as a couple of old beat-up picnic tables.

Many hikers will be content with Volcano Lake as their sole destination, but those looking for some fairly remarkable views should plan on extending the trip toward Mountain Mine. Return to the junction and continue climbing up the mining road, gaining gradually improving views into the deep cleft of the North Yuba River's canyon. If you can take your eyes off the scenery for a while, you may notice the extent of the engineering that went into construction of this road, especially where the soil has been washed away around a steel girder used to support the roadbed. The steady ascent leads to the nose of a ridge and a superb vista of the surrounding terrain. However, just a short way up the road, the breathtaking view of the northeast face of Sierra Buttes through the cleft of Flume Canyon will fully capture your attention. Imagining a more spectacular perspective of the Buttes is hard to contemplate.

The rocky road bends west and continues the ascent toward the mine, with views of the Buttes as a constant companion. Near the head of the canyon, you reach the site of Mountain Mine and the obvious pile of tailings nearby. The road continues past the mine, switchbacking to the crest of the ridge, from where you have fine views to the south of Mt. Lola and Castle Peak.

19   Loves Falls

Distance	0.8 mile (out-and-back)	
Hiking Time	30 minutes–1 hour	
Elevation	Negligible	
Difficulty	Easy	
Trail Use	Dogs OK, good for kids	
Best Times	June through October	
Agency	Tahoe National Forest at 530-994-3401, www.fs.usda.gov/tahoe	
Recommended Maps	USFS *Lakes Basin, Sierra Buttes,* and *Plumas-Eureka State Park Recreation Guide*	

see map on p. 60

HIGHLIGHTS While the rest of the Sierra remains buried under snow, early-season hikers can stroll along this low-elevation section of the Pacific Crest Trail (PCT) to a set of dramatic, cascading waterfalls. The short hike provides a pleasant journey for bipeds of all ages. Spring or early summer is the best time to see the falls in all their glory, but stay on the trail at all times, because the rocks along the banks of the North Yuba River are wet and slippery, and a slip into the river almost certainly would be fatal.

DIRECTIONS Follow CA 49 to a small gravel parking area on the north side of the road, 3.5 miles west of Bassetts and about 1.5 miles east of Sierra City.

FACILITIES/TRAILHEAD There are no facilities at the trailhead. Sierra City is a short drive away to the southwest via CA 49. Wild Plum Campground is a mile east from Sierra City via Wild Plum Road. From the parking area on the north side of CA 49, carefully cross the highway to the south side and find the resumption of the marked Pacific Crest Trail.

Start hiking on the Pacific Crest Trail through a mixed forest of Jeffrey pines, oaks, and cedars and a healthy understory of shrubs. Initially, the trail parallels the highway, as you pass by unsightly water tanks and concrete boxes to where the roar from the North Yuba River starts to drown out the vehicle noise from the highway. Douglas

Loves Falls on the North Yuba River

firs and red firs find a haven in the cooler and wetter climes in the cleft of the canyon. Nearing the stout bridge across the river, a side trail heads down the hillside to access control gates for the municipal water supply; warning signs remind you to remain on the PCT. A short distance farther, you stand upon the steel and wood bridge, admiring the power of the river, which thunders down the canyon in a series of short falls, collectively known as Loves Falls, that tumble into swirling pools. Keen eyes will spot a small waterfall coursing down the east side of the rocky gorge early in the season. Although you won't find any feature nearly as dramatic as Loves Falls, you can continue southbound along the PCT for as far as you like—in spring or early summer you'll inevitably hit the snowline.

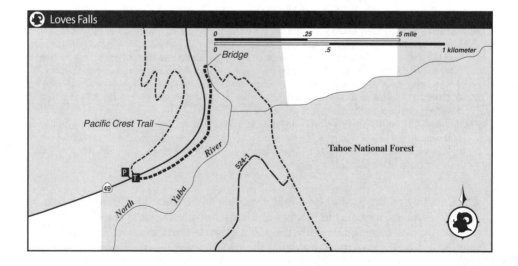

20 Wild Plum Loop

see map on p. 62

Distance	2.5 miles (loop)
Hiking Time	1.5–2 hours
Elevation	+550/-550 feet
Difficulty	Moderate
Trail Use	Dogs OK
Best Times	Late April through mid-November
Agency	Tahoe National Forest at 530-994-3401, www.fs.usda.gov/tahoe
Recommended Maps	USFS *Lakes Basin, Sierra Buttes,* and *Plumas-Eureka State Park Recreation Guide*

HIGHLIGHTS The short distance of the Wild Plum Loop, combined with the relatively low elevation, provides hikers with an early-season opportunity to ply their craft and get in shape while awaiting the disappearance of winter's mantle higher up in the mountains. Spring has the additional bonus of a fine display of wildflowers. Fall, with its mild temperatures, is an equally pleasant time to enjoy the diverse habitats found on this trip. Even during the hot summer, the abundant shade along the loop makes for tolerable conditions. No matter what the season, hikers will be treated to several fine vistas of Sierra Buttes and the deep canyon of the North Fork of the Yuba River.

DIRECTIONS Follow CA 49 to the east end of Sierra City, and turn east onto Wild Plum Road. Follow the road across a bridge over a stream, and proceed on gravel road for 1 mile to the Wild Plum Trailhead parking area on the right.

FACILITIES/TRAILHEAD The trailhead has running water and picnic tables. The Wild Plum Campground, just down the road from the trailhead, has 47 pleasantly forested sites along the banks of Haypress Creek. The trail begins on the far side of the parking area near some trailhead signs, one of which indicates that restrooms are available an eighth of a mile away at the campground.

Stroll through a mixed forest of incense cedars, white firs, Jeffrey pines, and an occasional oak tree alongside Haypress Creek, to the access road near the entrance into Wild Plum Campground, which is just past a bridge over the creek. Cross the road and refind the trail near a group of signs, one of which warns about the possible presence of rattlesnakes (none was seen or heard during my visit). Back on singletrack trail, you follow the left-hand bank of the roaring creek on a mildly rising grade before the trail veers away from the stream and switchbacks more steeply up a hillside. Near the top of the switchbacks is a rock knob just off the trail; a short scamper to the top provides an excellent vista of Sierra Buttes and the canyon of the North Fork of the Yuba River. Back on the trail, a short climb above the knob leads to a junction with the Pacific Crest Trail (PCT), 1.1 mile from the trailhead.

Turn right (southeast) from the junction onto the PCT; you'll soon come to the crossing of an unnamed tributary of Haypress Creek. Past this stream, the Sierra Buttes momentarily return to view through a break in the forest, where a fine assortment of early-season wildflowers lines the trail. About a quarter mile from the stream is an inauspicious junction with the little-used Haypress Creek Trail on the left. Remaining on the PCT, you follow short switchbacks down to a stout bridge across Haypress Creek and a junction immediately beyond the bridge.

Turn right (southwest) at the junction and leave the PCT to continue the loop back toward Wild Plum Campground. The trail follows Haypress Creek before bending away on a mild climb to the crest of a minor ridge, which offers another fine view of Sierra Buttes. Descend away from the ridge into the canyon of a tributary stream, and proceed to where the singletrack trail dead-ends at a gravel road. Turn right onto the road and follow it past a steel gate and across a wooden bridge spanning the stream.

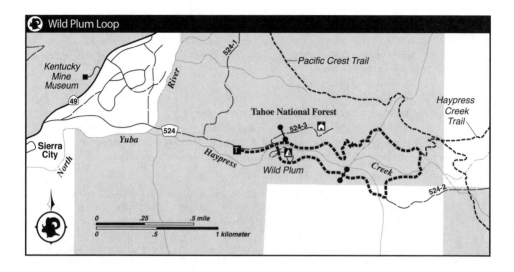

Continue down the road on a steep descent that parallels the creek. A smattering of dogwoods alongside the road offers delightful color from blossoms in spring and blazing leaves in fall. Just past a small powerhouse, concrete tank, and block building, you cross another side stream and soon reach the eastern limits of Wild Plum Campground. Proceed through the campground and over the bridge to the singletrack trail that leads back to the parking area, and then retrace your steps to the car.

21 Haskell Peak

Distance	3 miles (out-and-back)
Hiking Time	1.5–2 hours
Elevation	+1,200/-50 feet
Difficulty	Difficult
Trail Use	Dogs OK, mountain biking OK
Best Times	July through October
Agency	Tahoe National Forest at 530-994-3401, www.fs.usda.gov/tahoe
Recommended Map	USGS 7.5-minute *Clio*

HIGHLIGHTS A short hike along a nearly forgotten trail provides a dose of solitude on the way to an expansive view of the northern Sierra and southern Cascades. At 8,107 feet, Haskell Peak is second in height only to Sierra Buttes, the treeless summit affording one of the best vistas in the region. Unfortunately, the trail is missing from the USGS map.

DIRECTIONS From CA 49 near Bassetts, turn onto Gold Lake Highway (County Road 519) and proceed 3.4 miles to a right-hand turn onto FS 09, signed for Howard Creek and Chapman Creek Saddle. Follow the well-graded gravel road for 8 miles to the marked Haskell Peak Trailhead on the left. Park your vehicle in the large parking area directly east of the trailhead on the opposite shoulder.

FACILITIES/TRAILHEAD There are no facilities near the trailhead. The trail begins across the road from the parking area, near a trail sign.

A mild climb leads away from the trailhead through a mixed forest of Jeffrey pines, western white pines, lodgepole pines, red firs, and incense cedars. Lush areas of the forest floor are carpeted with ferns, and drier areas are graced with a fine display of mule-ears in early summer. Soon the forest thickens and the grade increases, as the trail follows a winding course up the slope. Where the trees thin again, manzanita carpets the hillside on the way to a saddle between Haskell Peak and Peak 7833 directly to the south, 1.1 miles from the trailhead.

From the saddle, the trail veers north toward the dual summits of Haskell Peak. Pass through more open vegetation on the way past the lesser summit and then veer northeast to ascend the main summit ridge. With diminishing conifers and improving views of the surrounding countryside, you continue the climb along a rocky path until the tread completely disappears in the talus field just below the top. From there, you can scramble easily across the treeless, rocky slope to the broad summit of Haskell Peak, where obnoxious cairns and windbreaks have been left by previous visitors. The 360-degree view includes such notable landmarks as Lassen Peak, Sierra Buttes, Mt. Lola, Castle Peak, Mt. Rose, and the broad plain of the Sierra Valley.

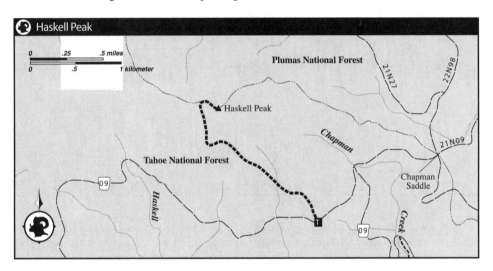

22 Chapman Creek

Distance	4 miles (out-and-back)
Hiking Time	2–3 hours
Elevation	+575/-50 feet
Difficulty	Moderate
Trail Use	Dogs OK
Best Times	Mid-May through October
Agency	Tahoe National Forest at 530-994-3401, www.fs.usda.gov/tahoe
Recommended Map	USGS 7.5-minute *Clio*

see map on p. 64

HIGHLIGHTS The lightly used Chapman Creek Trail offers hikers a pleasant, forested walk along a delightful stream. Unlike many trails named after creeks, this one actually follows the stream for the entire journey, occasionally directly alongside the tumbling brook. The trailhead is within shady Chapman Creek Campground, which is a fine overnight accommodation.

DIRECTIONS Drive on CA 49 to the entrance into Chapman Creek Campground, 4 miles west of Yuba Pass and 3 miles east of Bassetts. Park alongside the campground access road as space allows.

FACILITIES/TRAILHEAD The 29-unit Chapman Creek Campground has picnic tables, grills, vault toilets, and running water. The trailhead is located between campsites 9 and 11.

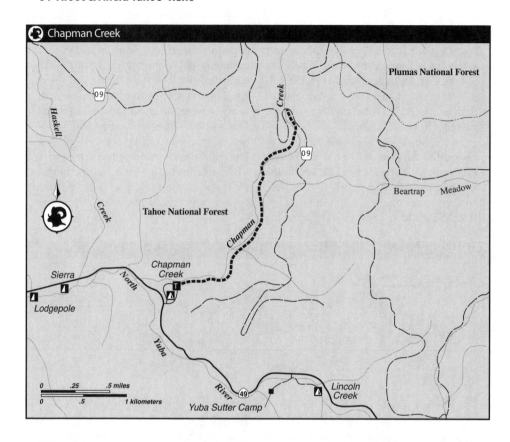

The trail follows an upstream course along the banks of Chapman Creek, a cascading stream lined with a tangle of alders. The red-fir forested path leads through a mixture of shrubs, ferns, and plants, crossing a number of tiny tributaries along the way. At 1.25 miles, you cross the Chapman Creek itself, but this shouldn't present any problems unless you're here at the peak of snowmelt. Continue up the west bank for 0.4 mile before the trail recrosses the creek and quickly ends at a gravel road near a bridge over Chapman Creek. From there, retrace your steps back to the trailhead.

More Hikes

Museum Trail

A short and easy stroll through mixed forest from the museum to Upper Jamison Campground in Plumas-Eureka State Park (1.2 miles).

Spencer Lakes

The A Tree, a section of the Pacific Crest Trail, leads to an unmaintained trail that descends to the lakes (3.6 miles).

Red Fir Nature Trail

From Sierra County Road 822 to Mills Peak Lookout, a loop with interpretive signs travels through cool forest (0.5 mile).

Lily Lake

Just off the Gold Lake Highway, the short hike to the lake is well suited for families (0.2 mile).

Sand Pond Interpretive Trail

This wheelchair-accessible loop between the Sardine Campground and Sand Pond Picnic Grounds has interpretive signs (0.9 mile).

Truckee, Donner Summit, and Vicinity

Truckee was initially settled as a stop on a wagon road that connected the mining districts of Virginia City and Coloma during the mid-1800s. Later the town would become an important waypoint for the transcontinental railroad on its journey over the Sierra Nevada. Along with transportation, thriving lumber and ice industries would keep Truckee bustling into the twentieth century. Saloons, dance halls, and a busy red-light district accompanied this prosperity until shortly after World War I, when decreased demand for Truckee's products sunk the area into a 40-year period of stagnant growth and development.

Although the town had made something of a name for itself in winter recreation during the early 1900s, with an ice rink, ski jump, and toboggan slide, the Tahoe–Truckee area became renowned for winter sports as a result of the 1960 Winter Olympics held at Squaw Valley. Since then, the greater Truckee area has seen a steady increase in tourism and a more recent explosion in population growth and real estate values. While the historic downtown area has been able to hold onto its quaint charm, the same can't be said for the ever-expanding tentacles of development around the town. With more and more people moving into the area, the surrounding recreation lands have experienced increased pressure as well. Thankfully, due to a fairly abundant number of trails, hikers, mountain bikers, and equestrians can be spread out across this portion of the Tahoe National Forest without too much overcrowding.

Straddling the Sierra crest, this region experiences the full brunt of winter storms. Consequently, hiking generally begins at the start of the summer and reaches full swing by mid-July. Areas east of the crest offer a few early-season opportunities for hitting the trails thanks to a drier climate and slightly lower elevations. Pleasant autumns usually see trails staying open well into October or November, before the first major storm blankets the mountains and turns the interest of recreationists toward winter pursuits.

The east–west ribbon of I-80 provides the principal access to the region, topping Donner Summit at an elevation of 7,227 feet. The two-lane Donner Pass Road that parallels the freeway used to be the sole access over the Sierra, which still provides unhurried motorists with exceptional roadside scenery. In addition, a handful of trips in this chapter begin from CA 89, north of Truckee.

Frog Lake perched below the sheer face of Frog Lake Overlook

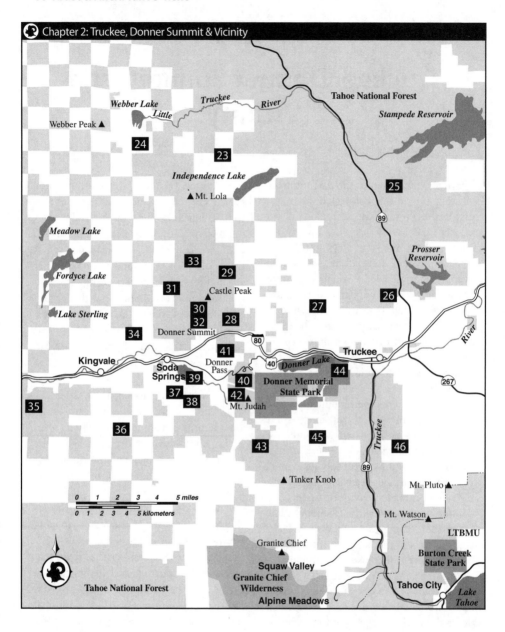

Chapter 2: Truckee, Donner Summit & Vicinity

23   Mt. Lola and White Rock Lake

Distance	10.4 miles to Mt. Lola (out-and-back);
	14.4 miles to White Rock (out-and-back)
Hiking Time	5–6 hours; 8–10 hours
Elevation	+2,525; +2,625/-1,325 feet
Difficulty	Difficult
Trail Use	Backpacking option, dogs OK, mountain biking OK
Best Times	Mid-July through mid-October
Agency	Tahoe National Forest at 530-994-3401, www.fs.usda.gov/tahoe
Recommended Maps	USGS 7.5-minute *Independence Lake* and *Webber Peak*

see map on p. 70

HIGHLIGHTS An infrequently used trail north of Lake Tahoe leads strong hikers to a far-ranging view of the northern Sierra and southern Cascades from the tallest peak between Lassen in the north and Freel to the south. Those with extra time and stamina have the option of a fine extension to picturesque, island-studded White Rock Lake. Backpackers have several campsite choices, either along Cold Stream or around White Rock Lake.

DIRECTIONS From I-80 near Truckee, follow CA 89 north for 14.5 miles; make a left turn onto FS 07, signed INDEPENDENCE LAKE. Proceed on paved road for 1.5 miles and then turn left onto FS 07-10. Follow this gravel road for 0.6 mile across a bridge over the Little Truckee River, to an unsigned junction with Henness Pass Road. Turn right and proceed on Henness Pass Road for 3.1 miles to a short spur road on the left, signed MT. LOLA TRAIL. Drive a short distance to the end of the road and the informal trailhead parking area.

FACILITIES/TRAILHEAD There are no facilities at the trailhead. The general vicinity offers a number of forest service campgrounds. The signed trail begins at the far end of the parking area.

From the trailhead, follow singletrack trail on a moderate climb through a mixed forest of western white pines, lodgepole pines, and white firs. After 0.6 mile, you hop across a small seasonal stream lined with a tangle of alders and young aspens, and then continue the climb toward the mouth of Cold Stream Canyon. Where the trail merges with an old roadbed, head upstream high above the level of the stream, where a light forest allows for an understory of tobacco brush, pinemat manzanita, and currant to flourish. Farther up the canyon, the trail eventually draws near Cold Stream before intersecting a fairly well-traveled road, 2.2 miles from the trailhead.

Follow the road across a substantial wooden bridge that spans the stream and reach a fork in the road. Take the left-hand fork and head upstream a short distance to the resumption of singletrack trail on the left, which is unsigned but marked by a series of metal diamonds. Within a stone's throw of the road to the right and the stream to the left, you continue upstream on a mild grade through mixed forest, breaking out into the open at Cold Stream Meadow. Dotted with clumps of willow and carpeted with a variety of grasses, the meadow lends a pastoral feel to the surroundings. A spur road near the far end of the meadow leads to a campsite in a copse of trees.

Just beyond the campsite spur, the route follows the main road briefly until singletrack trail resumes where the road bends sharply toward a crossing of Cold Stream. Proceed upstream for a while on mildly graded trail, hopping over a pair of rivulets along the way. As the canyon narrows, the grade of ascent increases and the trail draws nearer to the diminishing stream. The trail crosses over Cold Stream to the east bank at 3.8 miles from the trailhead.

Past the stream crossing, the trail adopts a steeper grade and reaches a junction with a faint use trail after a quarter mile. The short use trail leads to a view of a short

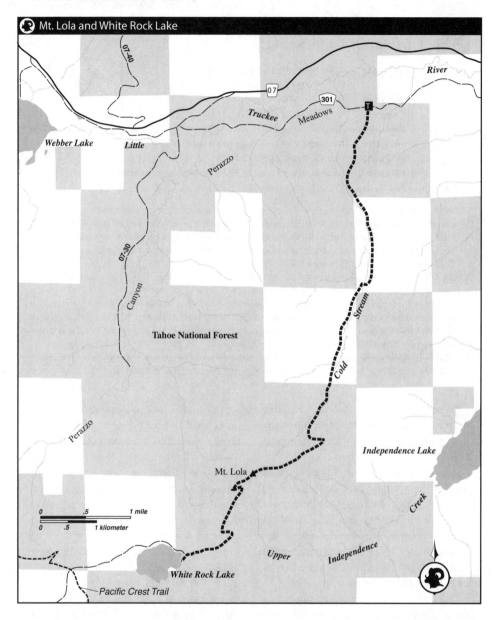

Mt. Lola and White Rock Lake

07-40

River

07

301

T

Truckee   Meadows

Webber Lake   Little

Perazzo

07-30

Canyon

Tahoe National Forest

Cold   Stream

Perazzo

Independence Lake

Mt. Lola

Creek

0   .5   1 mile
0   .5   1 kilometer

Upper   Independence

White Rock Lake

Pacific Crest Trail

waterfall, where the braided stream courses through moss-lined channels and tumbles picturesquely down a slanted rock face. Back on the main trail, you angle away from Cold Stream and ascend into the realm of mountain hemlocks. Beyond a prominent switchback, the forest parts enough to allow a glimpse of the upper slopes of Mt. Lola and, as you follow the winding trail up the northeast ridge of the peak, other landmarks spring into view, including Independence Lake to the east and Castle Peak to the south. Finally gaining the summit, the incredible 360-degree view is more than ample reward for the toil of the ascent. Scores of additional peaks are visible from Mt. Lola, including snow-clad Lassen Peak, Sierra Buttes, Mt. Rose, and Freel Peak. You'll also see verdant plains like Sierra Valley and Martis Valley, and many bodies

White Rock Lake from the lower slopes of Mt. Lola

of water, including Stampede, Boca, and Prosser reservoirs. An old wooden sign reading MT. LOLA, ELEV. 9143 FT. marks the summit, along with some low brick pillars, a few rock enclosures, and a metal army box containing a summit register. A short stroll to the southern lip of the summit area reveals the shimmering surface of White Rock Lake, a mere 1.25 air miles southwest. Hikers satisfied with the journey to the summit should retrace their steps back to the trailhead.

Hardy souls who wish to continue toward White Rock Lake should weave down the trail along the southwest ridge of the volcanic peak, initially through low-growing shrubs, scattered wildflowers, and a few stunted pines farther down the ridge.

After a couple of switchbacks, follow a descending traverse across the head of a canyon through scattered western white pines, mountain hemlocks, and firs. Briefly descend the cleft of a seasonal drainage until the trail merges with a steep, rocky old road that leads down to a junction east of the lake. The left-hand branch heads across a seasonal inlet to pleasant campsites along the stream bank. Veer right at the junction and follow the road past a large meadow to the east shore of White Rock Lake, where shady conifers line the shoreline and dramatic cliffs provide a rugged backdrop. Several decent campsites are spread around the shore, which is unfortunately open to four-wheel-drive vehicles via a road to the west.

24 Lacey Valley Trail

see map on p. 72

Distance	3.3 miles (point-to-point); 6.6 miles (out-and-back)
Hiking Time	1.5–2 hours; 3–4 hours
Elevation	+225 feet/-10 feet; +235 feet/-235 feet
Difficulty	Easy
Trail Use	Dogs OK (voice command), mountain bikes OK
Best Times	June through mid-October
Agency	Truckee Donner Land Trust (TDLT), tdlandtrust.org; Tahoe National Forest at 530-994-3401, www.fs.usda.gov/tahoe
Recommended Maps	USGS *Webber Peak*, TDLT *Webber Lake/Lacey Meadows*

HIGHLIGHTS Lovers of wildlife and wildflowers should find plenty to admire on this easy and relatively short stroll through Lacey Valley. Thanks to the work of several conservation organizations of the Northern Sierra Partnership, the public now has access to these beautiful lands holding the headwaters of the Little Truckee River and acres of verdant meadowlands in Lower and Upper Lacey Meadows. The trail also visits stands of lush lodgepole-pine forest and an old homestead.

Since sheep occasionally graze in this area, and a substantial amount of wildlife use the meadows, you must have dogs under strict voice control. Otherwise, leave Fido at home. Also note that the southern lakeshore of nearby Webber Lake is closed to the public until 2017. Please respect the private property of Webber Lake Ranch on the way to the trailhead and on the hike. Mosquitoes may be a nuisance when the flowers are at their peak—don't forget the repellent.

DIRECTIONS From I-80 just east of Truckee, follow CA 89 north toward Sierraville for about 14 miles to a left-hand turn onto Cottonwood Lake following signed directions to Webber Lake. Bear immediately left onto Jackson Meadows Road and continue for another 8 miles, and then turn left at a sign for Webber Lake. After 0.3 mile, bear right at the access road for private Webber Ranch and proceed 0.5 mile to the trailhead access road, which should be signed for Lacey Valley Trail. Continue another 0.5 mile to the trailhead parking area to the right of a closed steel gate.

With a second vehicle, rather than turning left onto the trailhead access road, continue ahead for not quite a half mile to the junction with Meadow Lake Road and turn left. Follow gravel Meadow Lake Road for about 4.75 miles to the south trailhead.

FACILITIES/TRAILHEAD Other than some signboards about the history of the area and the preservation of Lacey Meadows there are currently no facilities at the trailhead.

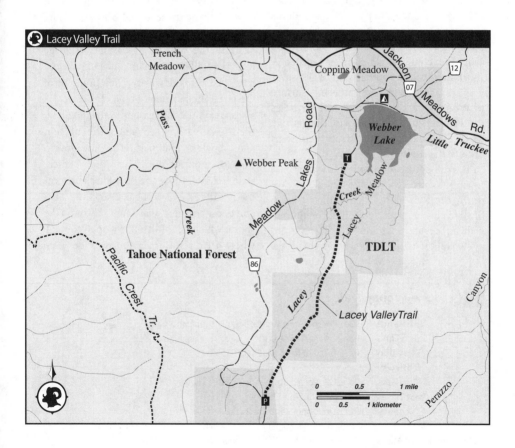

Lacey Valley Trail

The Lacey Valley Trail follows the course of a closed road, initially on a gentle grade through a mostly lodgepole-pine forest to the southwest of Webber Lake. Soon you break out of the trees along the west edge of expansive Lower Lacey Meadow. From early to midsummer, the meadow is carpeted with colorful wildflowers and is host to numerous bird species. Make sure you turn around for a view of the shimmering waters of Webber Lake. At 0.6 mile from the parking area, a metal sign indicates the old Johnson Family homestead lies just west of the trail on a low rise, where a number of outbuildings and artifacts are visible.

Away from the homestead, the old road heads south across the heart of the meadow to a usually easy ford of the shallow Lacey Creek. To the right of the trail near the south edge of the meadow is a lone picnic table beneath some lodgepole pines, a fine spot to enjoy a snack and watch the wildlife.

About a mile into the hike, the road exits the lower meadow and heads into the forest on a short (quarter-mile) and gentle ascent. The groundcover remains quite lush on the way through the trees, and if the day is hot you'll appreciate the shade. The grade soon eases again on the way to the long and narrow upper meadow. Near the 1.5-mile mark, you emerge from the forest and follow the east edge of the upper meadow for the next 0.75 mile. Along the way are fine views of the mountains at the head of the valley.

The remainder of the route away from the upper meadow follows the old road through the trees on a mild to moderate climb. Eventually you reach a closed metal gate and informational signboard at the south trailhead, just a short distance from the gravel Meadow Lake Road. Without a vehicle at the upper trailhead, retrace your steps 3.3 miles back to the Webber Lake Trailhead.

25   Sagehen Creek

Distance	5 miles (out-and-back)
Hiking Time	2–3.5 hours
Elevation	Negligible
Difficulty	Easy
Trail Use	Dogs OK, good for kids, mountain biking OK
Best Times	May through October
Agency	Tahoe National Forest at 530-994-3401, www.fs.usda.gov/tahoe
Recommended Map	USGS 7.5-minute *Hobart Mills* (trail not shown)

HIGHLIGHTS Wildflower season reaches a dramatic crescendo in early to midsummer along Sagehen Creek, where a short, easy trail provides access to the area for flower lovers young and old. Fall is a delightful time for a visit as well, when autumn colors are at their height. No matter what the season, hikers who travel all the way to the end of the trail have the added bonus of a fine view of Stampede Reservoir, although it develops a somewhat unsightly bathtub ring late in the season as the water level drops.

DIRECTIONS Follow CA 89 north from I-80 near Truckee for 6.8 miles to a dirt parking area on the right-hand side of the highway. The turnout is just past a highway bridge over Sagehen Creek.

FACILITIES/TRAILHEAD There are no facilities at the trailhead. Although the trailhead is not marked, the start of the well-worn trail on the northeast bank of Sagehen Creek should not be difficult to locate.

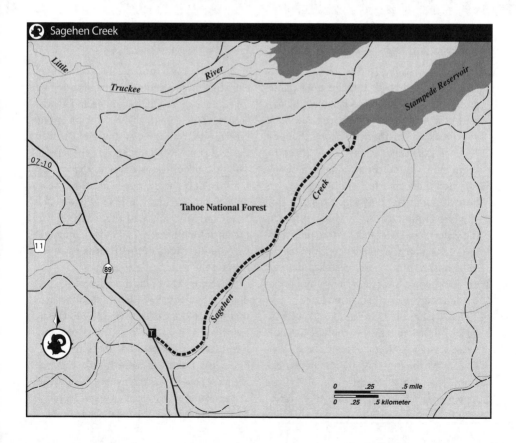

Head downstream along Sagehen Creek through a mixed forest of lodgepole pines, Jeffrey pines, white firs, incense cedars, and junipers. Lush riparian foliage carpets the creek bottom to your right, along with a diverse variety of wildflowers, including lupine, aster, penstemon, and buttercup. Wild rosebushes alongside the trail provide delicate pink blossoms and a sweet fragrance in midsummer. Meadowlands farther downstream beckon amateur botanists and curious youngsters alike to leave the trail and carefully explore the lush surroundings.

Eventually, the trail veers northeast and moves a little farther away from the creek. Now you stroll through a forest consisting mostly of lodgepole pines, where, in early summer, a bounty of mule-ears covers the sandy slopes with a stunning display of yellow flowers. Careful observation of the hillside above the trail reveals that this area has seen past logging and at least one forest fire.

About 2 miles from the trailhead, you traverse a grassy clearing, cross a small rivulet, and emerge into a broad, sagebrush- and grass-filled meadow bordering the southeast arm of Stampede Reservoir. The trail navigates the sometimes-boggy meadow on a raised finger of ground to a small copse of pines, where an old timber beam provides passage across the main channel of Sagehen Creek. The trail continues alongside the creek for a short distance before disappearing for good in the meadowland. Despite the lack of trail, reaching the shore of the reservoir is straightforward across the open terrain. Rimmed by pine-dotted hills, the sapphire-blue waters of the reservoir stretch out before you.

Sagehen Creek and the broad meadows near Stampede Reservoir

26 Commemorative Emigrant Trail

Distance	7.5 miles (point-to-point)
Hiking Time	4 hours
Elevation	+300/-600 feet
Difficulty	Easy
Trail Use	Dogs OK, good for kids, mountain biking OK
Best Times	May through October
Agency	Tahoe National Forest at 530-994-3401, www.fs.usda.gov/tahoe
Recommended Map	USGS 7.5-minute *Truckee, Hobart Mills*

HIGHLIGHTS Follow in the steps of history along the Overland Emigrant Trail, which roughly parallels a route used by emigrants in the 1800s. A popular mountain-biking route, the trail travels a portion of the Tahoe National Forest between the Tahoe Donner community and Stampede Reservoir. Easy access from a handful of sedan-worthy roads allows the trail to be broken into smaller chunks for those not up to the full distance. At the start of the trail, a 3-mile stroll along lushly lined Alder Creek leads to a crossing of CA 89 and the Donner Camp Picnic Ground. From there, the trail turns north, traverses the northwest arm of Prosser Reservoir, fords Prosser Creek, and proceeds through stands of forest and open clearings to crossings of the Old Reno and East Pasture roads, before ending at Stampede Reservoir.

The minimal elevation gain and loss promises that your conditioning won't be overly taxed, even if you decide to complete the whole 15-mile route. The general ease of the route, combined with the relatively early snowmelt at this elevation and the colorful spring wildflower display, makes this a fine choice for an early-season trip. Expect high temperatures in summer, with more pleasant conditions returning in autumn.

Hikers should be alert for encounters with mountain bikers and equestrians, as the trail is quite popular with both groups. While mountain bikers and strong hikers may be interested in completing the entire trail, the following description only goes about halfway, covering the most interesting topography along the route.

DIRECTIONS *Start:* Follow CA 89 north from I-80 near Truckee for almost 2.5 miles to Alder Creek Road. Turn left and proceed for 3 miles to a dirt road on the left-hand side that angles sharply downhill away from the pavement. Turn down this road and park as space allows.

End: From the junction of Alder Creek Road, continue northbound on CA 89 for 2.2 miles to a right-hand turn onto Nevada County Road 886, signed for Hobart Mills. Veer left after 0.2 mile, remaining on 886, and travel another 0.3 mile to a junction with Old Highway 89. Turn right, still on 886, and continue 0.2 mile to a junction with the Old Reno Road. Here, turn right and follow 886E for 1 mile to where the signed trail crosses the road. Park off the road as space allows.

FACILITIES/TRAILHEAD There are no facilities at either trailhead. The beginning of the trail follows the continuation of the dirt road.

Head downstream along Alder Creek through mixed forest. Lush riparian foliage lines the creek bottom, along with a diverse variety of wildflowers in early summer. Some beaver activity will be seen through the creek section. The trail fords Alder Creek four times en route to CA 89, and these may be wet fords in early to mid-summer—packing along a pair of sandals or old tennis shoes might be a wise idea at those times. At 1.25 miles, you cross Schussing Road and continue downstream for another mile or so before the trail leaves the creek bottom and crosses Alder Creek Road.

Away from the lush environs of the creek, the trail enters a pine forest with an understory of sagebrush. Soon the sound of traffic heralds the approach to CA 89. Signs lead across the highway to the entrance into Donner Camp Picnic Ground. A short stroll down the access road leads to the picnic area, complete with vault toilets and shady picnic sites equipped with barbecue

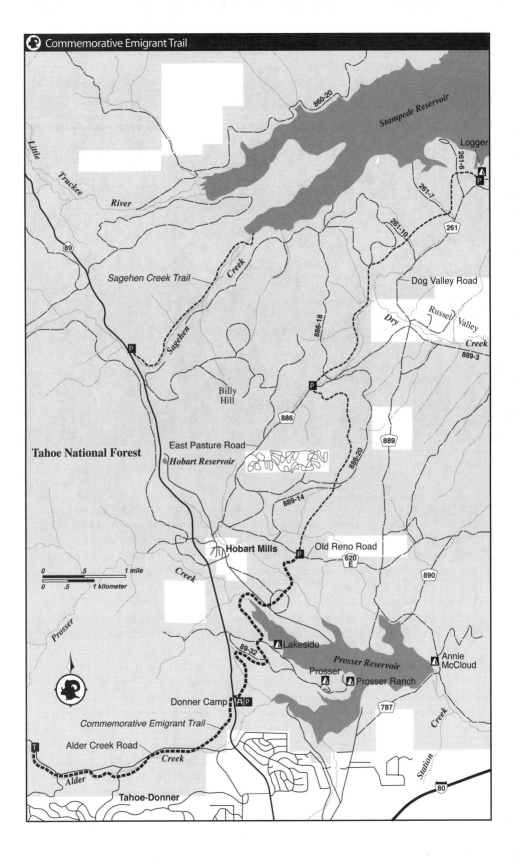

Hiker on the Commemorative Emigrant Trail

grills. Historical signs and an interpretive loop trail offer additional interesting diversions. Some groups, especially those with young children in tow, will want to end their trip at the picnic area after the straightforward 3-mile hike.

If you're continuing, find the resumption of the Commemorative Emigrant Trail at the north end of the picnic grounds, just left of the start of the interpretive trail. Alongside the beginning of the trail are several birdhouses attached to lodgepole and Jeffrey pines. Proceed on an elevated section of trail that spans a grassy meadow. Away from the meadow, the trail travels through alternating sections of previously logged forest and open areas carpeted with a mixture of drought-tolerant shrubs, including sagebrush and bitterbrush. Mule-ears add a splash of yellow in early summer. About

a half mile from the picnic ground, cross a well-traveled road and then switchback to the southeast. Soon the trail veers north again and crosses FS 89-32, which provides access to campgrounds and a boat launch at Prosser Reservoir.

With glimpses of the reservoir through the trees, drop down to a dirt road and then follow singletrack trail around the northwest arm of Prosser Reservoir. After crossing another dirt road, a short descent leads to a signed Y-junction with the lateral to the highway bridge over Prosser Creek. Except during times of high water, you can continue on the main trail on the right to the ford. (When the water is high, you can follow the lateral to the highway, cross the bridge, and return on a lateral along the north bank of the creek back to a junction with the main trail.) Cross the broad creek bottom past head-high willows and grassy meadow to the far side of the drainage and the ford of Prosser Creek. Even in late season, you should plan on getting your feet wet, so packing along those sandals or old tennis shoes for the fords of Alder Creek will come in handy here.

A very short climb up the north bank leads to a junction with the trail to the bridge. Veer right at the junction and head southeast above the arm of Prosser Reservoir for about a half mile until the trail turns northeast and merges briefly with Forest Road 886-2, which provides access to the north shore of the reservoir. After approximately 40 yards, singletrack trail resumes and proceeds through mostly open terrain, crossing a trio of old roads along the way. The lack of forest in this section allows good views to the east of Mt. Rose and the Carson Range. Reach a grassy meadow, where an elevated section of boardwalk leads to the crossing of a tributary of Prosser Creek trickling toward the reservoir.

Away from the creek, the trail passes through open terrain before entering a Jeffrey pine forest. A winding climb up a forested slope leads to a signed crossing of the Old Reno Road at the halfway point of the trail.

27 Donner Lake Rim Trail: Gregory Creek to Summit Lake

see map on p. 80

Distance	7 miles (out-and-back)
Hiking Time	3.5–5 hours
Elevation	+1,150/-150 feet
Difficulty	Moderate
Trail Use	Backpacking option, dogs OK, mountain biking OK
Best Times	Mid-May through October
Agency	Tahoe National Forest at 530-587-3558, www.fs.usda.gov/tahoe
Recommended Map	USGS 7.5-minute *Norden* (trail not shown)

HIGHLIGHTS Ultimately, the Donner Lake Rim Trail (DLRT) will be what its name suggests—a 23-mile trail around the rim of the picturesque lake. Presently, only about half of the trail exists, with the segment described here being one of the latest additions. By incorporating this new segment of trail with existing trails through Tahoe Donner and sections of the Pacific Crest and Summit Lake Trails, a continuous 13-mile trip from a trailhead near Skislope Way in Tahoe Donner to the saddle between Donner Peak and Mt. Judah is now possible.

The remaining part of the DLRT is realistically many years away from completion, with extensive trail building required eastward around Tahoe Donner and south to Donner Memorial State Park, as well as west along Schallenberger Ridge over to the Donner Peak–Mt. Judah saddle. Those interested in assisting the project with donations of labor or funds should contact the Truckee Donner Land Trust office at 530-582-4711 or visit the website at **tdlandtrust.org.**

This section of the trail described here incorporates a short lateral from the Donner Lake interchange up Gregory Creek (in politically incorrect Negro Canyon) to a connection with the DLRT below Donner Ridge. From there, hikers head west on a combination of new trail and existing roads to forest-rimmed Summit Lake. Most of the route is south facing, providing an early-season opportunity to get out on the trail, but by midsummer much of the trip can be a scorcher until encountering forest shade prior to the lake. Summit Lake is a pleasant body of water that's well suited for either an afternoon swim or a bit of fishing. A number of campsites may attract backpackers. From the lake, numerous trip extensions are possible.

This section of the DLRT is a multiuse trail open to hikers, bikers, and equestrians. Unfortunately, sections of the trail that coincide with the Summit Lake Road are also open to off-road vehicles, including access to the lake.

DIRECTIONS Drive I-80 to the Donner Lake interchange, between Donner Summit and Truckee, and travel to the north side of the freeway, where a gravel road splits off to the west. Follow this road a short distance to an informal parking area marked with DONNER LAKE RIM TRAIL signs.

FACILITIES/TRAILHEAD There are no facilities near the trailhead. The trail begins up the right-hand road, which may be marked by temporary signs for the Donner Lake Rim Trail.

Head up an old road through scattered, mixed forest and thick shrubs on a moderate to moderately steep climb that roughly parallels Gregory Creek. In early season, the sound of the tumbling creek helps to diminish the persistent traffic noise rising from the freeway. Gazing upstream, a power line further detracts from any sense of being completely out in the wilderness. Farther up the canyon, hop across a vibrant side stream flowing through lush foliage and wildflowers and then reach a three-way junction with the Donner Lake Rim Trail. (By continuing straight ahead, you can follow the singletrack DLRT on a switchbacking climb to the top

of Donner Ridge and then connect to the extensive network of trails in Tahoe Donner).

Turn left at the junction and descend on singletrack trail to a stout bridge spanning Gregory Creek. Once across the bridge, the trail heads in a downstream direction for a while, climbing steadily above the creek to a union with the Summit Lake Road. Follow the road for about 0.1 mile to where singletrack trail resumes, arcing above the road to make a rising traverse around the nose of a shrub-covered ridge dotted with an occasional Jeffrey pine. Curving into the next ravine, you hop over a seasonal stream, pass below the power lines, and continue the ascent around the head of the canyon,

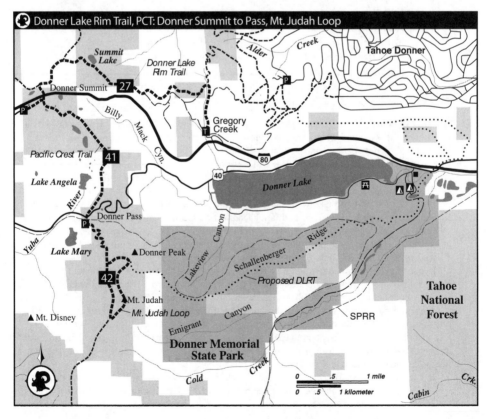

View from the Donner Lake Rim Trail

crossing more seasonal swales along the way, one via a short, wooden bridge. Good views of Donner Lake below and the Sierra crest above are nearly constant companions along this open stretch of trail. Following a switchback, the trail gains the crest of a subridge, peppered with a smattering of conifers, and then merges with the Summit Lake Road again just past a 4-by-4-inch post. About 25 yards farther is a Y-junction marked by another post, 2.25 miles from the trailhead.

Veer right and traverse northwest through moderate forest cover on the Summit Lake Road with the din of freeway noise rising up from I-80 below. After the half-mile traverse, you pass a gated road branching off to the right and soon reach a Y-junction, where your route veers right following a marker designating the road as an off-highway vehicle (OHV) route. Follow the dusty road on a moderately steep climb through the forest to a field of mule-ears, where the grade eases. Returning to forest cover, an easy stroll leads to the southeast shore of alder- and forest-rimmed Summit Lake.

The Summit Lake Road terminates near the southwest side of the lake, where the Summit Lake Trail heads west three-quarters of a mile to a junction with the Warren Lake Trail and then another 0.4 mile southwest to a junction with the Pacific Crest Trail (PCT). You could avoid backtracking to the Gregory Creek Trailhead by leaving a car at the Pacific Crest Trailhead, which is accessible from the Castle Peak/Boreal exit from I-80 (see the directions for Trip 28), creating a one-way, 5.75-mile shuttle trip. (Mountain bikers will have to follow a lateral to Castle Valley Road, as mountain bikes are prohibited from traveling on the PCT.)

28   Summit Lake Loop

Distance	7 miles (partial loop)
Hiking Time	3 hours
Elevation	+550/-550 feet
Difficulty	Easy to moderate
Trail Use	Dogs OK
Best Times	July through mid-October
Agency	Tahoe National Forest at 530-587-3558, www.fs.usda.gov/tahoe
Recommended Map	USGS 7.5-minute *Norden* (trail not shown)

HIGHLIGHTS The hike to Summit Lake is an easy 2-mile-plus, mostly forested stroll to a quiet lake quite suitable for an afternoon swim on a hot summer day, or for plunking a line in search of the resident trout. Camping around the lake is permissible, but the area is accessible to the four-wheel-drive crowd via a dirt road to the east.

    With recent completion of a section of the Donner Lake Rim Trail, you can now extend the trip beyond a simple out-and-back to the lake by traveling west through serene forest to a connection with the Pacific Crest Trail (PCT) in Castle Valley and then back to the Donner Summit trailhead.

DIRECTIONS West of Donner Summit, take the Castle Peak/Boreal Ridge exit from I-80 and drive to the frontage road on the south side of the freeway. Head east on this road 0.3 mile to the Pacific Crest Trail parking area.

FACILITIES/TRAILHEAD The trailhead has vault toilets, picnic tables, running water in season, and equestrian facilities. The well-marked trail begins on the east side of the parking area.

Follow a gravel path across a stone bridge over a seasonal stream and continue on dirt tread through a mixed forest of lodgepole pines, western white pines, and white firs, soon reaching the first junction with the Glacier Meadow Loop on the left. Continue eastbound toward the Pacific Crest Trail, soon reaching the second junction with the loop trail on the left. Remain on the right-hand trail and pass by a shallow pond, where mountain hemlocks join the mixed forest, and proceed on a short, mild descent to a junction with the PCT near the edge of a grass- and willow-filled meadow, a half mile from the trailhead.

Turn left and head north on the PCT around the fringe of the meadow and pass through a pair of culverts beneath the eastbound and then westbound lanes of I-80. Beyond the culverts, you make a moderate climb to the crossing of a seasonal stream and then reach a well-signed, four-way junction, 1 mile from the trailhead.

Following signed directions for Summit Lake, turn right and proceed on a mild to moderate climb through alternating stretches of mixed forest and open areas sprinkled with granite slabs, boulders, and seasonal wildflowers. At 1.7 miles, just past a small meadow carpeted in early season with corn lilies, you reach a four-way junction with the Warren Lake (see Trip 29) and Donner Lake Rim trails.

Veer right at the junction and leave the forest to cross a granite ridge carpeted with pinemat manzanita, where views of the Donner Summit region temporarily open up. The trail eventually returns to forest cover and continues to the shoreline of serene Summit Lake. Except for some cliffs at the north end, trees surround the lake and alders ring the shoreline. After thoroughly enjoying the lake, retrace your steps a half mile to the four-way junction.

Head northwest from the junction on a newly constructed section of the Donner Lake Rim Trail on a winding course through mixed forest. The route generally follows the topography on a rolling traverse toward Castle Valley, crossing a few seasonal streams along the way, lushly lined with wildflowers and other foliage

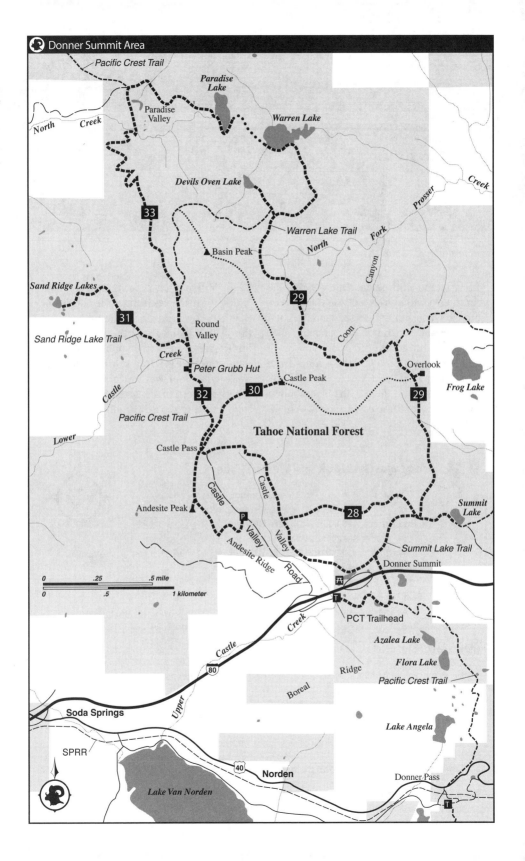

Forest-rimmed Summit Lake

in early and midseason. Openings in the forest cover allow views of the Castle Peak area to the north and to the lands beyond the freeway to the south. Shortly after merging with an old dirt road, you reach a junction with the PCT at 4.4 miles from the trailhead.

Turn left and follow the southbound PCT just beyond the east fringe of verdant Castle Valley. After drawing near to Castle Creek, the trail veers into the forest and then bends east, passing an unmarked junction with a path toward the Donner Summit Rest Area and a small pond. Beyond the pond, the trail makes a short climb to the well-signed, four-way junction at the close of the loop section. From there, retrace your steps 1 mile to the PCT trailhead.

29 Frog Lake Overlook and Warren Lake

see map on p. 83

Distance	9 miles to Frog Lake Overlook (out-and-back); 15 miles to Warren Lake (out-and-back)
Hiking Time	4–6 hours (Frog Lake Overlook); 8–12 hours (Warren Lake)
Elevation	+1,500/-100 (Frog Lake Overlook); +2,250/-2,125 feet (Warren Lake)
Difficulty	Very difficult
Trail Use	Backpacking option, dogs OK
Best Times	Mid-July through mid-October
Agency	Tahoe National Forest at 530-587-3558, www.fs.usda.gov/tahoe
Recommended Maps	USGS 7.5-minute *Norden* and *Independence Lake*

HIGHLIGHTS Strong hikers who don't shy away from a challenge will find the 7.5-mile trip to Warren Lake (and back) a worthy undertaking. The trail gains and loses nearly 4,500 feet of elevation along the way, which makes for a very long day of hiking—most parties will want to do this trip as a two- to three-day backpack. Although a strenuous trip, the rewards are many, including a dramatic view of Frog Lake from Frog Lake Overlook as described in Trip 30, a scenic traverse of North Fork Prosser Creek's sweeping basin, and the pleasant surroundings of cirque-bound Warren Lake. Hikers with cross-country experience can create an excellent loop trip by following an off-trail route between Warren and Paradise Lakes and then reversing the description in Trip 33 from Paradise Lake.

DIRECTIONS West of Donner Summit, take the Castle Peak/Boreal Ridge exit from I-80 and drive to the frontage road on the south side of the freeway. Head east on this road 0.3 mile to the Pacific Crest Trail (PCT) parking area.

FACILITIES/TRAILHEAD The trailhead has vault toilets, picnic tables, running water in season, and equestrian facilities. The well-marked trail begins on the east side of the parking area.

Follow a gravel path across a stone bridge over a seasonal stream, and continue on dirt tread through a mixed forest of lodgepole pines, western white pines, and white firs, soon reaching the first junction with the Glacier Meadow Loop on the left. Continue eastbound toward the Pacific Crest Trail, shortly reaching the second junction with the loop trail on the left. Remain on the right-hand trail and pass by a shallow pond where mountain hemlocks join the mixed forest, then proceed on a short, mild descent to a junction with the PCT near the edge of a grass- and willow-filled meadow, a half mile from the trailhead.

Turn left and head north on the PCT around the fringe of the meadow and pass through a pair of culverts beneath the eastbound and westbound lanes of I-80. Beyond the culverts, you make a moderate climb to the crossing of a seasonal stream and then reach a well-signed, four-way junction, 1 mile from the trailhead.

Following signed directions for Summit Lake, turn right and proceed on a mild to moderate climb through alternating stretches of mixed forest and open areas sprinkled with granite slabs and boulders. At 1.7 miles, just past a small meadow carpeted with corn lilies, you reach a junction between the Warren Lake and Donner Lake Rim Trails (see Trip 27).

From the junction, take the left-hand trail and head north on a steep climb of a forested hill toward the top of a volcanic ridge directly west of Peak 7888. Before reaching the top, the forest gives way to shrub-covered slopes that allow for fine views of the surrounding terrain. Beyond this point, the grade temporarily abates as you stroll through a clearing and drop to cross a tributary of South Fork Prosser Creek. All too soon, the steep climb resumes on the way to a saddle just west of Peak 8653, hopping over several more seasonal streams en route. Acres and acres of mule-ears carpet the upper slopes, a particularly stirring sight during early summer when covered with yellow blooms. Nearing

the saddle, a short use trail branches away from the main trail to make a rocky ascent of the peak. Standing at the edge of Frog Lake Cliff, you have dramatic views straight down the face to privately owned Frog Lake, as well as west toward the volcanic battlements of Castle Peak and east toward Mt. Rose and the Carson Range.

A steep winding descent leads down from the saddle and across a stream on the way to a flat spot on a ridge, where an old, little-used trail heads east to privately owned Frog Lake. Here the trail veers west and drops moderately steeply into Coon Canyon, to cross numerous flower-lined rivulets draining the north side of rugged Castle Peak. Following the steep descent, the trail begins an undulating 2.5-mile traverse across the head of North Fork Prosser Creek's upper basin, encountering more flower-filled slopes and willow-lined streams along the way. Near the conclusion of the 2.5-mile traverse, you climb up to a junction with a trail to Devils Oven Lake, 6.2 miles from the trailhead.

All but superhuman hikers will not have the time to visit both Devils Oven and Paradise Lakes, as they each require steep climbs on the return trip. However, if you plan to do this trip as a backpack, you may have time to visit remote Devils Oven Lake. Be forewarned that the tread is not very well defined on the half-mile trail to the lake: This should be viewed as more of a cross-country route, albeit a short one. To reach Devils Oven Lake, veer left at the junction and climb the trail up to a level area on the crest of a ridge. Close attention must be paid here, as the more obvious route on the ground leads not to the lake but on an arcing traverse around the north and east sides of Basin Peak, eventually connecting with the PCT well southwest of the summit. The deteriorating route to the lake heads north from the level area on a curving descent that bends northeast before arriving at the southeast shore. Campsites are more limited here than at the neighboring lakes, perhaps a testament to the fact that

Warren Lake

most backpackers are unwilling to make the steep climbs out of both Devils Oven and Warren Lakes.

From the Devils Oven junction, proceed along an open, flower- and view-rich slope eastward along a ridge to a saddle, where the Warren Lake Trail turns left and a use trail continues along the ridge before petering out just before reaching an exposed overlook of the canyon below. The sweeping view from the saddle of North Fork Prosser Creek's basin, which arcs past Basin and Castle peaks to Frog Lake Cliff and out to Carpenter Valley, is most impressive.

Leave the saddle and follow the trail on a moderate descent through widely scattered mountain hemlocks and western white pines. The moderate grade soon becomes a thing of the past, as the trail plunges extremely steeply down a rocky gully on a tightly winding descent before eventually leveling off at the south shore of Warren Lake—the mile-long drop may represent the steepest section of maintained trail in the Tahoe National Forest. A number of good campsites line the south shore of the picturesque lake.

Off-trail enthusiasts could accept the challenge of reaching Paradise Lake via a short but difficult route that climbs from the southwest shore, across the cirque wall, to a saddle above the west shore. It then follows an easy, short descent to Paradise Lake. From there, a loop trip could be followed back to the trailhead by reversing the description in Trip 33.

30 Castle Peak and Basin Peak

Distance	9.6 miles (out-and-back)
Hiking Time	5–7 hours
Elevation	+1,980/-225 feet
Difficulty	Difficult
Trail Use	Dogs OK
Best Times	Mid-July through September
Agency	Tahoe National Forest at 530-587-3558, www.fs.usda.gov/tahoe
Recommended Map	USGS 7.5-minute *Norden*

see map on p. 83

HIGHLIGHTS A climb to one of North Tahoe's highest summits gives summiteers an expansive view of the northern Sierra, which on clear days includes distant Lassen Peak in the north and the coastal hills of California to the west. Castle Peak and the neighboring mountains are mostly volcanic in nature, offering an abundance of interesting-looking ramparts, turrets, and "castles." Unlike much of the Tahoe Sierra to the south, where glacier-scoured granitic rocks hold a bevy of lakes, the relatively porous volcanic rocks in this area offer relatively few lakes.

DIRECTIONS West of Donner Summit, take the Castle Peak/Boreal Ridge Road exit from I-80. Drive to the frontage road on the south side of the freeway and proceed east 0.3 mile to the Pacific Crest Trail (PCT) parking area.

Two alternatives will shorten the trip. The first option is to park near the start of the Castle Valley Road, just north of the I-80 ramps, and walk the road to Castle Pass. With a high-clearance vehicle you can take the second option, which is to drive the Castle Valley Road to a parking area near the Hole in the Wall Trailhead. From there, a shorter hike along the road leads to Castle Pass.

FACILITIES/TRAILHEAD The large parking lot has trailer parking, pit toilets, picnic tables, and running water in season. The well-marked trail begins on the northwest side of the parking lot.

From the parking lot, follow a well-signed gravel path to a stone bridge over a seasonal stream and continue on dirt track through lodgepole pines, western white pines, and white firs. You'll soon encounter a junction with the Glacier Meadow Loop, where you veer right and continue eastbound toward the Pacific Crest Trail. After a short distance, you come to a second junction with the Glacier Meadow Loop, where you veer to the right again. Pass by a shallow pond, where mountain hemlocks join the mixed forest, and then make a short descent to the Pacific Crest Trail junction near the edge of a grassy, willow-filled meadow, a half mile from the trailhead.

Ridge to Castle Peak

Head north on the PCT around the fringe of the meadow, and pass through a pair of large culverts underneath the eastbound and westbound lanes of I-80. Beyond the culverts, you make a moderate climb to the crossing of a seasonal creek, and then come to a well-signed, four-way junction, 1 mile from the trailhead.

Remaining on the Pacific Crest Trail, proceed straight ahead at the four-way junction, following signed directions to Castle Pass. The PCT rises and then drops to the north shore of a small pond, where you should veer right at an unmarked Y-junction with a path bound for the Donner Summit Rest Area.

Beyond the unmarked junction, you follow mildly graded trail through mixed forest toward Castle Valley. Eventually, the trail brings you alongside the creek for a bit, and then travels just east of the verdant meadows of Castle Valley. Use trails branch away from the PCT at various points, headed toward the creek and meadows. At 2.3 miles from the trailhead, you come to a junction with the Donner Lake Rim Trail on the left, and then continue upstream through Castle Valley, hopping over a number of lushly lined tributaries along the way. Nearing the head of the valley, the PCT bends to the west on an ascending traverse to a signed three-way junction with a trail from the Castle Valley Road. From there, a short but stiff climb brings you to Castle Pass and a junction with a trio of paths, 3.3 miles from the trailhead.

At Castle Pass, take the use trail to the right that ascends the west ridge of Castle Peak. As you climb the rocky ridge, the conifers diminish, allowing you increasingly good views of Castle Peak ahead, as well as other peaks and landmarks scattered around the Donner Pass region. A steep, zigzagging ascent heads around to the north side of the mountain, where switchbacks then lead you toward the summit. After a rocky stretch of climbing, a splendid view greets you at the top of the 9,103-foot peak. Clear days offer a 360-degree view all the way to Lassen Peak in the north, Mt. Diablo and the coastal hills to the west, the peaks of Desolation Wilderness to the south, and the Carson Range to the east. Don't forget to pack a map of the area to help you identify the numerous landmarks visible from the summit.

Ambitious peak baggers can double-summit by following a boot-beaten path from Castle Peak along the north ridge, 1.75 miles to the top of 9,017-foot Basin Peak. On the way back, you can skip climbing Castle Peak again by dropping west from the ridge about halfway between Castle and Basin Peaks to head cross-country to a connection with the PCT in Round Valley. From there, simply follow the PCT southbound back to the Donner Summit Trailhead.

31 Sand Ridge Lake

Distance	12 miles (out-and-back)
Hiking Time	6–8 hours
Elevation	+1,025/-425 feet
Difficulty	Moderate
Trail Use	Backpacking option, dogs OK
Best Times	July through mid-October
Agency	Tahoe National Forest at 530-587-3558, www.fs.usda.gov/tahoe
Recommended Maps	USGS 7.5-minute *Norden, Soda Springs,* and *Webber Peak*

HIGHLIGHTS The Pacific Crest Trail north of I-80 is a relatively popular path, leading to a variety of attractive destinations, including scenic lakes, lush meadows, and high summits. This trip heads to one of the least-visited spots in the general area—Sand Ridge Lake. While the shallow body of water won't make anyone's top-ten list of scenic wonders, the serene lake does provide pleasant surroundings along with the potential for seclusion.

DIRECTIONS West of Donner Summit, take the Castle Peak/Boreal Ridge Road exit from I-80. Drive to the frontage road on the south side of the freeway and proceed east 0.3 mile to the Pacific Crest Trail (PCT) parking area.

Two alternatives will shorten the trip. The first option is to park near the start of the Castle Valley Road, just north of the I-80 ramps, and walk the road to Castle Pass. With a high-clearance vehicle, you can take the second option, which is to drive the Castle Valley Road to a parking area near the Hole in the Wall Trailhead. From there, a shorter hike along the road leads to Castle Pass.

FACILITIES/TRAILHEAD The large parking lot has trailer parking, pit toilets, picnic tables, and running water in season. The well-marked trail begins on the northwest side of the parking lot.

From the parking lot, follow a well-signed gravel path to a stone bridge over a seasonal stream and continue on dirt track through lodgepole pines, western white pines, and white firs. You'll soon encounter a junction with the Glacier Meadow Loop, where you veer right and continue eastbound toward the Pacific Crest Trail. After a short distance, you come to a second junction with the Glacier Meadow Loop, where you veer to the right again. Pass by a shallow pond, where mountain hemlocks join the mixed forest, and then make a short descent to the Pacific Crest Trail junction near the edge of a grassy, willow-filled meadow, a half mile from the trailhead.

Head north on the PCT around the fringe of the meadow, and pass through a pair of large culverts underneath the eastbound and westbound lanes of I-80.

Beyond the culverts, you make a moderate climb to the crossing of a seasonal creek, and then come to a well-signed, four-way junction, 1 mile from the trailhead.

Remaining on the Pacific Crest Trail, you proceed straight ahead at the four-way junction, following signed directions to Castle Pass. The PCT rises and then drops to the north shore of a small pond, where you should veer right at an unmarked Y-junction with a path bound for the Donner Summit Rest Area.

Beyond the unmarked junction, you follow mildly graded trail through mixed forest toward Castle Valley. Eventually, the trail brings you alongside the creek for a brief time and then travels just east of the verdant meadows of Castle Valley. Use trails branch away from the PCT at various points headed toward the creek and meadows. At

Sand Ridge Lake

2.3 miles from the trailhead, you come to a junction with the Donner Lake Rim Trail on the left, and then continue upstream through Castle Valley, hopping over a number of lushly lined tributaries along the way. Nearing the head of the valley, the PCT bends to the west on an ascending traverse to a signed, three-way junction with a trail from the Castle Valley Road. From there, a short but stiff climb brings you to Castle Pass and a junction with a trio of paths, 3.3 miles from the trailhead.

At Castle Pass, proceed north on the Pacific Crest Trail on a traverse across a lightly forested slope. After about a half mile, you begin a moderate, switchbacking descent toward Round Valley. Nearing the floor of the valley, a short use trail leads to Peter Grubb Hut, 4.2 miles from the Pacific Crest Trailhead. The hut is complete with a wood-burning stove and firewood, gas stove and cooking utensils, table and chairs, a loft with sleeping platforms, and a detached outhouse. Interesting old photos and memorabilia cover the walls and provide a sample of the area's history.

The PCT crosses Lower Castle Creek north of the hut and leads to a Y-junction with the Sand Ridge Trail a short way farther, where you leave the PCT and turn left (east). A winding descent through a mixed forest of western white pines, red firs, and lodgepole pines follows, leading across some lushly lined streams and

below a striking granite cliff before reaching another Y-junction, 0.6 mile from the previous one.

Turn right (northwest) at the junction onto the Hole in the Ground Trail, and follow mildly graded trail through forest groves and past areas pocked with granite slabs and boulders. Hop over a seasonal stream, then walk along an elevated section of trail across a thin pocket of meadow that's filled with grasses and tinged with colorful wildflowers. Next, you head back into forest to make a winding climb up a hillside. At the top of the hill is a junction, where the Hole in the Ground Trail continues straight ahead, but you turn right (west) toward Sand Ridge Lake, following a sign marked SAND RIDGE LAKE.

Continue climbing up the hillside through a diminishing cover of forest, to the top of a ridge peppered with granite slabs and boulders. As the grade eases, the sparkling waters of Sand Ridge Lake spring into view near a sign that forbids bikers to proceed any farther. The path continues a short distance past a campsite and onto a point of land that juts into the shallow lake. Tall grasses, granite humps and slabs, pockets of meadow, and stands of forest rim the picturesque lake. Additional campsites are spread around the lakeshore, but early-season campers may have to fend off a healthy population of mosquitoes.

32 Castle Valley, Round Valley, and Andesite Peak Loop

see map on p. 83

Distance	9.6 miles (loop)
Hiking Time	5–7 hours
Elevation	+1,700/-1,700 feet
Difficulty	Moderate
Trail Use	Backpacking option, dogs OK
Best Times	June through mid-October
Agency	Tahoe National Forest at 530-587-3558, www.fs.usda.gov/tahoe
Recommended Map	USGS 7.5-minute *Norden*

HIGHLIGHTS Although most of this route travels outside the proposed Castle Peak Wilderness, plenty of pleasant terrain is encountered along the way, including two picturesque meadows and an excellent view from atop Andesite Peak. Both Castle and Round Valley meadows offer the chance to see raptors in search of prey or deer browsing the tender foliage. Throw in Peter Grubb Hut for a bit of Tahoe Sierra history, and you have the makings for a fine adventure. A shuttle option described below shortens the hike by 1.6 miles.

DIRECTIONS West of Donner Summit, take the Castle Peak/Boreal Ridge Road exit from I-80. Drive to the frontage road on the south side of the freeway and proceed east 0.3 mile to the Pacific Crest Trail (PCT) parking area.

Two alternatives will shorten the trip. The first option is to park near the start of the Castle Valley Road, just north of the I-80 ramps, and walk the road to Castle Pass. With a high-clearance vehicle, you can take the second option, which is to drive the Castle Valley Road to a parking area near the Hole in the Wall Trailhead. From there, a shorter hike along the road leads to Castle Pass.

FACILITIES/TRAILHEAD The large parking lot has trailer parking, pit toilets, picnic tables, and running water in season. The well-marked trail begins on the northwest side of the parking lot.

From the parking lot, follow a well-signed gravel path to a stone bridge over a seasonal stream and continue on dirt track through lodgepole pines, western white pines, and white firs. You'll soon encounter a junction with the Glacier Meadow Loop, where you veer right and continue eastbound toward the Pacific Crest Trail. After a short distance, you come to a second junction with the Glacier Meadow Loop, where you veer to the right again. Pass by a shallow pond, where mountain hemlocks join the mixed forest, and then make a short descent to the Pacific Crest Trail junction near the edge of a grassy, willow-filled meadow, a half mile from the trailhead.

Head north on the PCT around the fringe of the meadow, and pass through a pair of large culverts, underneath the eastbound and westbound lanes of I-80. Beyond the culverts, you make a moderate climb to the crossing of a seasonal creek, and then come to a well-signed, four-way junction, 1 mile from the trailhead.

Remaining on the Pacific Crest Trail, you proceed straight ahead at the four-way junction, following signed directions to Castle Pass. The PCT rises and then drops to the north shore of a small pond, where you should veer right at an unmarked Y-junction with a path bound for the Donner Summit Rest Area.

Beyond the unmarked junction, you follow mildly graded trail through mixed forest toward Castle Valley. Eventually, the trail brings you alongside the creek for a bit and then travels just east of the verdant meadows of Castle Valley. Use trails branch away from the PCT at various points, headed toward the creek and meadows. At 2.3 miles from the trailhead, you come to a junction with the Donner Lake Rim Trail on the left, and then continue upstream through Castle Valley, hopping over a number of lushly lined tributaries along the way. Nearing the head of the valley, the PCT bends to the west on an ascending traverse to a signed, three-way junction with a trail from the Castle Valley Road. From there, a short but stiff climb brings you to Castle Pass and a junction with a trio of paths, 3.3 miles from the trailhead.

At Castle Pass, proceed north on the Pacific Crest Trail on a traverse across a lightly forested slope. After about a half mile, you begin a moderate, switchbacking descent toward Round Valley. Nearing the floor of the valley, a short use trail leads to Peter Grubb Hut, 4.2 miles from the Pacific Crest Trailhead.

The PCT crosses Lower Castle Creek north of the hut and leads to a Y-junction with the Sand Ridge Trail a short way farther, where you leave the PCT and turn left (east). Next, you make a winding descent through a mixed forest of western white pines, red firs, and lodgepole pines; this takes you across some lushly lined streams and below a striking granite cliff to another Y-junction, this one with the Hole in the Ground Trail, 0.6 mile from the previous junction.

Turn left (south) at the junction on a moderately graded, winding descent through mixed forest to a small, willow-filled meadow bordered with wildflowers, and proceed to a crossing of Lower Castle Creek. Beyond the crossing, you make a moderately steep winding climb toward the crest of a hill, and then follow the gently rising trail toward the vicinity of Castle Pass, where you reach a junction with a short connecting trail to the PCT, 6 miles from the trailhead.

Continue to climb toward the north ridge of Andesite Peak. As you gain the crest of the ridge, Castle Peak and Valley burst into view. Follow the crest toward Andesite Peak, reaching a Y-junction with the 0.1-mile spur to the summit. The short climb to the top of Andesite Peak is rewarded by a fine, 360-degree view.

From the summit, return to the junction and follow the Hole in the Wall Trail on a switchbacking descent across a forested hillside toward Castle Valley below. The trees part temporarily to allow one more view of Castle Peak and the Carson Range in the distant east. Soon back in the forest, a series of switchbacks leads down the hillside to the floor of the valley and a junction with the Castle Valley Road, at 7.9 miles. Near a couple of trailhead signs, a small patch of dirt provides parking for any high-clearance vehicles that have traveled this far up the road.

Head southeast, following a rough and rocky section of the road for about 0.1 mile to a second parking area that's suitable for sedans less roadworthy than their high-clearance counterparts. Without a vehicle parked here, you must continue to walk the road down the valley all the way to the end of the Castle Valley Road, and then beneath I-80 to the frontage road on the south side of the freeway that leads to the PCT Trailhead parking area.

PETER GRUBB HUT

Patterned after hut systems in the Swiss Alps, Peter Grubb Hut was the northernmost in a series of six huts planned for the Tahoe Sierra along the crest between Donner and Echo passes. Although only four of the six were eventually built, overnight shelter at a nominal cost has been provided for backcountry skiers and hikers for several decades. For more information or to make a reservation, visit **clairtappaanlodge.com /peter-grubb-hut** or call 530-426-3632.

The hut has a wood-burning stove and firewood, solar lights, gas stove and cooking utensils, table and chairs, a loft with sleeping platforms, and a detached outhouse. Interesting old photos and memorabilia line the walls, providing a sample of the area's history.

33	**Paradise Lake**

see map on p. 83

Distance	15.4 miles (out-and-back)
Hiking Time	8–12 hours
Elevation	+1,625/-1,100 feet
Difficulty	Difficult
Trail Use	Backpacking option, dogs OK
Best Times	Mid-July through mid-October
Agency	Tahoe National Forest at 530-587-3558, www.fs.usda.gov/tahoe
Recommended Maps	USGS 7.5-minute *Norden, Webber Peak,* and *Independence Lake*

HIGHLIGHTS Paradise Lake is one of the prettiest lakes in the north Tahoe region. The trip all the way to the lake is a bit much for all but the strongest dayhikers, but hardy backpackers will find it well suited for a weekend, or longer, adventure. Those with extra time can add in technically easy ascents of Castle and Basin Peaks, and cross-country enthusiasts can create an excellent loop trip by following a short off-trail route to Warren Lake and then reversing the trail description in Trip 29. Many other diversions are possible by taking other trails in the area.

DIRECTIONS West of Donner Summit, take the Castle Peak/Boreal Ridge Road exit from I-80. Drive to the frontage road on the south side of the freeway and proceed east 0.3 mile to the Pacific Crest Trail (PCT) parking area.

Two alternatives will shorten the trip. The first option is to park near the start of the Castle Valley Road, just north of the I-80 ramps, and walk the road to Castle Pass. With a high-clearance vehicle, you can take the second option, which is to drive the Castle Valley Road to a parking area near the Hole in the Wall Trailhead. From there, a shorter hike along the road leads to Castle Pass.

FACILITIES/TRAILHEAD The large parking lot has trailer parking, pit toilets, picnic tables, and running water in season. The well-marked trail begins on the northwest side of the parking lot.

From the parking lot, follow a well-signed gravel path to a stone bridge over a seasonal stream and continue on dirt track through lodgepole pines, western white pines, and white firs. You'll soon encounter a junction with the Glacier Meadow Loop, where you veer right and continue eastbound toward the Pacific Crest Trail. After a short distance, you come to a second junction with the Glacier Meadow Loop, where you veer to the right again. Pass by a shallow pond, where mountain hemlocks join the mixed forest, and then make a short descent to the Pacific Crest Trail junction near the edge of a grassy, willow-filled meadow, a half mile from the trailhead.

Head north on the PCT around the fringe of the meadow and pass through a pair of large culverts underneath the eastbound and westbound lanes of I-80. Beyond the culverts, you make a moderate climb to the crossing of a seasonal creek and then come to a well-signed, four-way junction, 1 mile from the trailhead.

Remaining on the Pacific Crest Trail, you proceed straight ahead at the four-way junction, following signed directions to Castle Pass. The PCT rises and then drops to the north shore of a small pond, where you should veer right at an unmarked Y-junction with a path bound for the Donner Summit Rest Area.

Beyond the unmarked junction, you follow mildly graded trail through mixed forest toward Castle Valley. Eventually, the trail brings you alongside the creek for a bit and then travels just east of the verdant meadows of Castle Valley. Use trails branch away from the PCT at various points, headed toward the creek and meadows. At 2.3 miles from the trailhead, you come to a junction with the Donner Lake Rim Trail on the left, and then continue upstream through Castle Valley, hopping over a number of lushly lined tributaries along the way. Nearing the head of the valley, the PCT bends to the west on an ascending traverse to a signed, three-way junction with a trail from the

Castle Valley Road. From there, a short but stiff climb brings you to Castle Pass and a junction with a trio of paths, 3.3 miles from the trailhead.

At Castle Pass, proceed north on the Pacific Crest Trail on a traverse across a lightly forested slope. After about a half mile, you begin a moderate, switchbacking descent toward Round Valley. Nearing the floor of the valley, a short use trail leads to Peter Grubb Hut, 4.2 miles from the Pacific Crest Trailhead.

The PCT crosses Lower Castle Creek north of the hut and leads to a Y-junction with the Sand Ridge Trail a short way farther. Remaining on the PCT, proceed straight ahead on a stroll through mixed forest, skirting the west edge of Round Valley's extensive meadow. Soon you begin a moderate climb that takes a number of switchbacks before the grade eases to more of an ascending traverse across the west slope of Basin Peak. Here, periodic breaks in the forest allow fine views to the south and west. Pass through a pair of lush swales filled with wildflowers and willows on the way to the crest of Basin Peak's shoulder, and follow a mellow traverse across flower-filled slopes that are sure to thrill the amateur botanist within. Peak baggers wishing to add Basin Peak to their list can leave the trail at any convenient point and ascend easy, open slopes to the summit.

Eventually, the trail leads back into forest and begins a pronounced, switchbacking descent toward the floor of Paradise Valley. After the 700-foot descent, you follow winding trail across a forest floor carpeted with lush plants and flowers to a wide and stout wood-plank bridge over a lazy stretch of North Creek, which cuts a serpentine path through small pockets of meadow. A mild, winding ascent leads past a pond surrounded by meadow to a junction with an old road, 6.6 miles from the trailhead. Nailed to a lodgepole pine just before the road is an old wooden sign simply marked PARADISE LK, with an arrow to the right.

Turn right (east) and leave the PCT to follow the nearly level road around the lush meadowlands of Paradise Valley. Past the meadows, the trail starts climbing through the forest and ultimately weaves around granite boulders and small slabs toward the lake. Ducks should help guide you in the spots where the tread falters, but the location of the lake is fairly obvious, tucked into a granite cirque basin at the head of the canyon. Soon you reach the sparsely forested west shore of the beautiful lake, surrounded by slabs and low cliffs. Plenty of somewhat secluded campsites can be found on dirt patches, in between low humps of granite bedrock.

Experienced cross-country travelers can access the off-trail route to Warren Lake by heading around the south side of Paradise Lake, where a short climb above some bedrock cliffs will be necessary. Once past the cliffs, briefly follow the lakeshore and then ascend toward the saddle directly east of the lake. Look for a large cairn at the head of a rock slot that signifies the beginning of the ducked cross-country route down to Warren Lake.

Head south from the saddle on an angling descent across the headwall of Warren Lake's cirque, which changes to a slightly rising traverse below the base of some steep cliffs. Drop down some steep rocks, and then follow a rocky swale through shrubs to easier terrain below, where the route bends left to avoid some talus. Continue the descent over rock slabs interspersed with sandy patches, and through waist-high shrubs toward the tree-lined southwest shore. Nearing the lake, very briefly follow an alder-lined stream to a secluded campsite and proceed a very short distance to the use trail that hugs the shoreline. From there, a fine loop back to the trailhead is possible by reversing the description in Trip 29.

34   Lola Montez Lakes

Distance	7.4 miles (out-and-back)
Hiking Time	3.5–5 hours
Elevation	+1,125/-225 feet
Difficulty	Moderate
Trail Use	Backpacking option, dogs OK, mountain biking OK
Best Times	June through October
Agency	Tahoe National Forest at 530-587-3558, www.fs.usda.gov/tahoe
Recommended Map	USGS 7.5-minute *Soda Springs*

HIGHLIGHTS A mostly forested walk on stretches of road and trail lead to two fine lakes, both well suited for a bit of swimming on a hot summer day or some angling for the resident trout.

DIRECTIONS Take the Soda Springs exit from I-80, approximately 3 miles west of Donner Summit, and drive to the frontage road on the north side of the freeway. Turn east and drive 0.3 mile to the trailhead on the north side of the road.

FACILITIES/TRAILHEAD There are no facilities near the trailhead. The beginning of the trail is well marked. Signs indicate that parts of the trail cross private land and that hikers should respect the rights of property owners.

With the roar of traffic behind you, begin hiking on singletrack trail through moderate forest cover of lodgepole pines and white firs. Soon the trail passes below a power line and then descends to a gravel road. Turn right and follow the gravel road on a mildly descending course that eventually leads to the crossing of Lower Castle Creek at 0.9 mile from the trailhead. About 0.2 mile past the creek, singletrack trail resumes at a marked junction.

Leave the road behind and climb up a forested hillside. After a pair of switchbacks, the forest parts enough to allow views east of the area around Castle Peak. At 1.75 miles from the trailhead, you intersect another road and turn uphill to follow the road to a Y-junction a quarter mile farther. No-trespassing signs and a cable across the left-hand road make it clear which way to proceed.

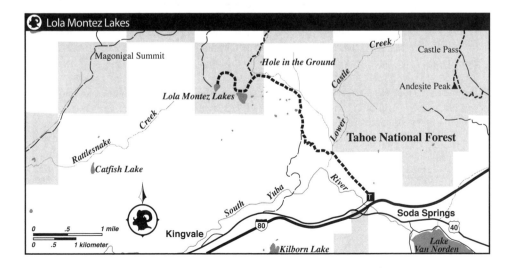

Upper Lola Montez Lake

The mildly graded road makes for a pleasant walk through the forest. Past signs for an area closed to vehicles, the tread narrows back to a singletrack trail again, which you follow to a fair-size meadow carpeted with lush grasses and rimmed by lodgepole pines. The path quickly veers away and crosses the small stream that drains the meadow. Just a little farther along, you reach a signed Y-junction with a lateral to the Hole in the Ground Trail, 3 miles from the trailhead.

From the junction, an easy, forested stroll leads to Lower Lola Montez Lake, rimmed by a dense forest that shades several passable campsites. Granite humps and low buttes provide a pleasant backdrop to the dark waters of the lake.

Near the northwest shore, a ducked route leads away from the lower lake over granite boulders and slabs to the upper lake, where a bit of scrambling may be necessary in order to successfully negotiate the route. A granite knoll partway up the climb allows fine views of the surrounding terrain. From the knoll, an ascending traverse beneath some cliffs leads to more climbing around boulders and over slabs to lovely and picturesque Upper Lola Montez Lake.

Granite slabs and patches of flower-filled meadow rim the upper lake, which is smaller than its lower counterpart. A lighter forest of western white pines, lodgepole pines, mountain hemlock, and white fir shelters some well-developed campsites above the west shore. Although Upper Lola Montez Lake is perhaps the more attractive of the two, most backpacking parties may prefer to camp at the lower lake, as the upper lake is unfortunately accessible to off-road vehicles.

35   Loch Leven Lakes

Distance	8 miles (out-and-back)
Hiking Time	4–6 hours
Elevation	+1,380/-330 feet
Difficulty	Moderate
Trail Use	Backpacking option, dogs OK, mountain biking OK
Best Times	June through October
Agency	Tahoe National Forest at 530-288-3231, www.fs.usda.gov/tahoe
Recommended Maps	USGS 7.5-minute *Cisco Grove* and *Soda Springs*

see map on p. 98

HIGHLIGHTS The Loch Leven Lakes provide hikers who are itching for summer to begin an early-season opportunity to reach a trio of picturesque lakes nestled into a granite basin. A pleasant side trip to Salmon Lake increases the total possible lakes to four. Swimmers will appreciate the relatively warm waters and scads of slabs and islands for sunbathing, while anglers can test their skills on the stocked trout that inhabit the lakes.

DIRECTIONS Take the Rainbow Road/Big Bend exit from I-80 and follow Hampshire Rocks Road westbound for 0.9 mile to the trailhead parking area on the right-hand shoulder. The trail begins on the opposite side of the road from the parking lot.

FACILITIES/TRAILHEAD The trailhead parking area has a vault toilet. The Hampshire Rocks Picnic Area, Rainbow Campground, and Big Bend Visitor Center are nearby. The trail begins on the opposite side of the road from the parking area. Be aware that the alignment of the Loch Leven Lakes Trail is incorrectly shown on the old USGS *Cisco Grove* quadrangle.

An old wooden sign marked LOCH LEVEN TRAIL is all that delineates the start of the trail, which climbs over a shrub- and boulder-covered hillside of exposed granite slabs beneath widely scattered conifers. A short, winding descent takes you briefly into a stand of white firs and lodgepole pines with a lush understory. The climbing resumes across mostly open terrain, with nice views of Cisco Butte and the South Yuba River canyon. Soon the trail leads back into a grove of trees with a small pond, which turns into little more than a quagmire by late summer. Beyond the pond, cross another stretch of shrubs and granite slabs before dropping through more forest to a bridge across an alder-lined tributary of the river. Beyond the bridge, a steep, quarter-mile climb leads to the twin tracks of the Union Pacific Railroad, 1.25 miles from the trailhead. As you cross the tracks, pay close attention to oncoming traffic, especially from the downhill direction, as trains descending from Donner Pass move swiftly and relatively quietly.

Refind the trail on the far side of the tracks, and resume climbing through a mixed forest of incense cedars, white firs, and Jeffrey, lodgepole, and western white pines. Soon you reach the first of many switchbacks that will eventually transport you out of the South Yuba River canyon and into the lakes basin. Approaching Loch Leven Summit, the high point of the climb, the grade mercifully eases and you follow a slight descent into the lakes basin until a steep, short, and rocky section of trail brings you alongside the first lake. An old sign heralds your arrival at the west shore of Loch Leven Lake, 2.75 miles from the trailhead. Passable campsites are scattered around the lake, and gently sloping granite slabs are sure to lure swimmers and sunbathers. Continue along the west side of Lower Loch Leven Lake to an unsigned junction with a lateral to Salmon Lake.

From the Salmon Lake junction, a brief descent followed by a short climb leads to Middle Loch Leven Lake, where a number of pleasant campsites will lure overnighters. At the far end of the lake is a junction with the Cherry Point Trail, which heads southwest toward the North Fork of the American River.

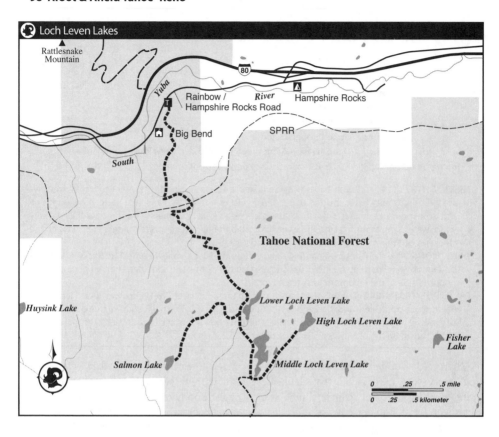

Loch Leven Lakes

Rattlesnake Mountain

80

Rainbow / Hampshire Rocks Road

Hampshire Rocks

Yuba

River

Big Bend

SPRR

South

Tahoe National Forest

Huysink Lake

Lower Loch Leven Lake

High Loch Leven Lake

Fisher Lake

Salmon Lake

Middle Loch Leven Lake

0   .25   .5 mile
0   .25   .5 kilometer

Turn left at the junction and follow the trail around the lower end of the middle lake. Ascend a rock cleft, and then climb over granite slabs to the upper lake. High Loch Leven Lake is perhaps the most picturesque of the lakes, with heather-rimmed shores bordered by granite cliffs and stands of conifers. Fine campsites above the southeast shore will certainly appeal to those backpackers willing to hike all the way to the last lake in the chain.

Rainbow Lodge, halfway between the trailhead and the freeway, provides an excellent watering hole or eatery after a trip to the lakes. Bed-and-breakfast packages are available for those looking for an overnight adventure. Call 530-562-5061 or visit **the rainbowlodge.com** for more information.

Lower Loch Leven Lake

see
map on
p. 100

SIDE TRIP TO SALMON LAKE

(1 mile, +150/-250) From the junction, follow the trail on a rising and winding climb across slopes covered with grass and flowers for 0.3 mile, followed by a gradual descent through alternating sections of granite slabs and light forest. Just before the lake, you reach a junction with a trail heading west to the Salmon Lake Trailhead on Huysink Lake Road. Veer left at the junction and continue another 0.2 mile to Salmon Lake. Although smaller and perhaps not as scenic as the Loch Leven Lakes, elliptically shaped Salmon Lake is rimmed by low granite humps, scattered trees, and clumps of shrubs and grasses. Backpackers will find more solitude than at Loch Leven Lakes, but far fewer campsites.

36 Palisade Creek Trail

Distance	14 miles (out-and-back)
Hiking Time	7–9 hours
Elevation	+300/-2,450 feet
Difficulty	Difficult
Trail Use	Backpacking option, dogs OK, mountain biking OK
Best Times	July through October
Agency	Tahoe National Forest at 530-587-3558, www.fs.usda.gov/tahoe
Recommended Maps	USGS 7.5-minute *Soda Springs* and *Royal Gorge*

HIGHLIGHTS Most hikers prefer attacking a steep elevation gain at the beginning of a trip rather than at the end when they may be tired and spent, but the Palisade Creek Trail defies the norm by starting out fairly mildly for the first couple of miles or so before plunging steeply toward a terminus at the bottom of North Fork American River's canyon, just upstream from Royal Gorge. The route begins amid glacier-polished granite basins that hold tarns shaded by white firs and western white and lodgepole pines, but it passes through a number of vegetative zones on its nearly half mile of vertical descent en route to the river. Water is a bit scarce along the route, usually available only at Palisade Creek, 5 miles into the journey, and at the river. Backpackers will find modest campsites at both of those locations as well. Horses are not allowed on the trail.

DIRECTIONS Take the Soda Springs exit from I-80 and proceed eastbound 0.8 mile to a right-hand turn onto Soda Springs Road, following a sign marked SERENE LAKES. Follow Soda Springs Road over railroad tracks and past the Soda Springs ski area for 0.9 mile, and turn right at Pahasti Road. After a half mile, the road narrows and the surface turns to dirt and gravel, as it generally follows a set of power lines past turnoffs to a number of summer camps. After 3 miles on the dirt-and-gravel surface, the road leads across the spillway of Kidd Lake and then climbs to the top of a hill near Royal Gorge's Devils Lookout warming hut. Continue ahead for another 0.3 mile to the marked trailhead. The trail begins on the continuation of the closed road.

FACILITIES/TRAILHEAD There are no facilities at the trailhead.

From the parking area, the designated trail follows the continuation of the road down a steep embankment and across a rock dam that separates the two Cascade Lakes. Past trail signs on the far side of the dam, you proceed through a mixed forest of firs, western white pines, and lodgepole pines on a gently graded trail to a three-way junction with a path to a summer camp near Long Lake. Following signs for Palisade Creek Trail, turn right at the junction and follow

mildly rising trail through an open terrain of shrubs and boulders to the top of a low granite knoll, which offers views of imposing Devils Peak in the foreground and more distant views of Castle Peak and Granite Chief. With Devils Peak continually looming above, you pass by several ponds and continue through open granite terrain occasionally broken by small groves of conifers.

About 1.5 miles from the trailhead, nearing the head of a side canyon that carries a

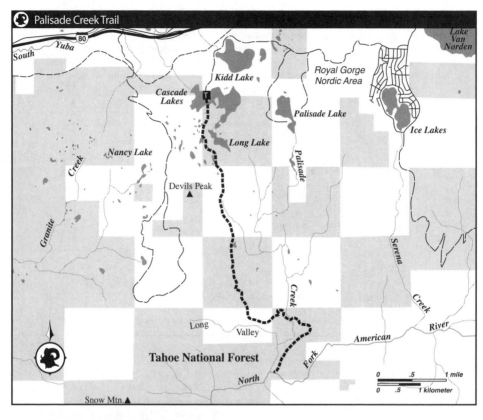

Palisade Creek Trail

North Fork American River from bridge

tributary of Palisade Creek, the trail begins a several-mile descent that won't end until reaching the bridge in the bottom of the North Fork American River canyon. Initially, mildly descending trail passes through areas of dense forest and lush trailside vegetation on the way to a pond just to the left of the trail near the 2.5-mile mark. Another mile of mild descent leads through mixed forest, which now includes incense cedars, Jeffrey pines, and a smattering of sugar pines.

With a corresponding drop in elevation, oaks begin to intermix with the conifers and the trail uses several sets of switchbacks on the way down to Palisade Creek. The path briefly follows a lazy section of the creek past a campsite, before the stream resumes its tumbling ways toward a union with the North Fork of the American River in the canyon below. A short, moderately steep, and winding descent leads to a forested flat before you reach a stout bridge across Palisade Creek, at 5 miles from the trailhead.

Beyond the bridge, a short, gently graded stroll through the forest is followed by a lengthy, steep, rocky, switchbacking descent that passes in and out of forest cover on the way toward the bottom of the canyon. Nearing the river, the trail crisscrosses an open slope of manzanita before reaching a bridge that spans a narrow slot of rock through which the nascent North Fork American River swiftly courses. A few passable campsites are tucked into the trees on sandy soil near where the creek merges with the river. Downstream, many inviting pools will tempt even the most casual of swimmers in your group.

37 Lyle's Lookout Trail

see map on p. 102

Distance	3 miles (loop)
Hiking Time	1.5 hours
Elevation	+250/-250 feet
Difficulty	Easy to moderate
Trail Use	Dogs OK, mountain biking OK
Best Times	June through mid-October
Agency	Truckee Donner Land Trust at 530-582-4711, tdlandtrust.org
Recommended Maps	TDLT Lyle's Lookout Trail, USGS 7.5-minute *Soda Springs* (trail not shown)

HIGHLIGHTS A pleasant walk through the woods leads to a fine vista of Devils Peak, Snow Mountain, and the surrounding terrain. Utilizing some of the old logging roads that become Royal Gorge's cross-country ski trails in the winter, this loop travels through lands now under the protection of the Truckee Donner Land Trust.

DIRECTIONS From the Soda Springs exit from I-80, drive east on Donner Pass Road for 0.75 mile to a right-hand turn onto Soda Springs Road.

FACILITIES/TRAILHEAD There are no facilities at the trailhead. The trail heads southwest away from the parking area on an old road. Drive 0.8 mile and turn right onto Pahasti Road and drive 0.5 mile to the trailhead opposite Royal Gorge Ski Area's Summit Station.

Drop shortly away from the wood chip–covered parking area past some signs about Royal Gorge and the work of the Truckee Donner Land Trust and follow the course of an old logging road, which now serves as the Big Ben cross-country ski trail in the winter. Immediately pass a picnic table on the right and continue along the gently graded road through a mixed forest of lodgepole pines, western white pines, and red firs. Initially, the sight of private homes around Ice Lakes diminishes the sense of being away from it all. Pass below a power line running through a clearing and reach a log landing just before the half-mile mark. Pass by a marshy area on the way to a large clearing at the base of 7,559-foot Palisade Peak, 0.75 mile from the trailhead. Rather than continue ahead (south) on the road, which is the Reindeer ski trail, curve west and follow the right-hand edge of the clearing and descend briefly for 0.1 mile to signs marking junctions with the Mountain's Hideout, James Joys, Rodney's Run, and Killy's Cruise ski trails.

Take the Killy's Cruise ski trail heading uphill to the left, which is a more primitive trail than Big Ben. Follow a gently rolling route to junctions with Crosscut on the right and Mountain's Hideout on the left, noting the location of Crosscut ski trail, because that will be your return route. Continue ahead on Killy's Cruise, crossing a seasonal swale and proceeding to a

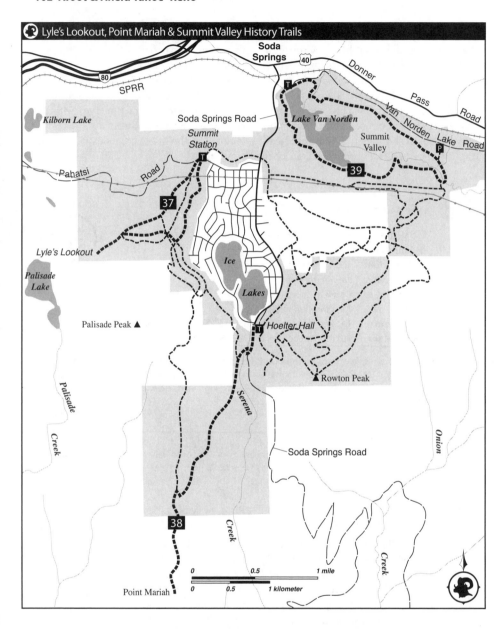

Lyle's Lookout, Point Mariah & Summit Valley History Trails

Soda Springs

Kilborn Lake

Soda Springs Road

Summit Station

Lake Van Norden

Summit Valley

Pahatsi

Road

37

Lyle's Lookout

Palisade Lake

Ice

Lakes

Palisade Peak ▲

Hoelter Hall

▲ Rowton Peak

Palisade

Serena

Creek

Soda Springs Road

Onion

38

Creek

Creek

Point Mariah

Y-junction with the ski trail to Lyle's Lookout on the left, 1.3 miles from the trailhead.

Leaving Killy's Cruise, turn left (southwest) and climb more steeply up the hillside, crossing another seasonal swale. Where the grade eases, you stroll to the end of the road and reach Lyle's Lookout at 1.6 miles. Moving about a tad will improve the view through the trees of Devils Peak to the

southwest and Snow Mountain above Royal Gorge. After enjoying the view, retrace your steps 0.3 mile to the junction of Crosscut ski trail. On the initial stretch, you have a fine view of Castle Peak to the northeast.

At the Y-junction with the signed Crosscut ski trail, head downhill briefly to where the trail bottoms out and reaches a 3-way junction with the Gold Rush ski trail on the

Devils Peak from Lyle's Lookout

left. Remaining on the Crosscut ski trail, turn right and soon come to the next junction with the Palisade ski trail. Turn right again and follow the Palisade ski trail on a steady climb through the trees, passing by an unmarked road on the right and continuing to the signed junction with Rodney's Run, 0.3 mile from Y-junction. Keep climbing another 0.4 mile to a power line clearing. Immediately prior to the clearing is a junction between the James Joys ski trail on the right and the Little Dipper ski trail behind and to the left.

Cross the power line clearing and pick up the continuation of the route on the far side and slightly to the left. From there, a steady climb leads back to Kidd Lakes Road (which Pahasti Road becomes beyond Summit Station). Turn right and follow dirt road back to where the surface returns to pavement and then reach the trailhead just beyond.

38   Point Mariah

see map on p. 102

Distance	5.5 miles (out-and-back)
Hiking Time	3 hours
Elevation	+325/-425 feet
Difficulty	Moderate
Trail Use	Dogs OK, mountain biking OK
Best Times	June through mid-October
Agency	Truckee Donner Land Trust at 530-582-4711, tdlandtrust.org
Recommended Maps	TDLT Point Mariah Trail, USGS 7.5-minute *Soda Springs* (trail not shown)

HIGHLIGHTS Following some of Royal Gorge's cross-country ski trails, this trip leads to an impressive view of the Sierra crest and the Royal Gorge of North Fork American River. Thanks to the Truckee Donner Land Trust and its partners, the area has been saved from development.

DIRECTIONS From the Soda Springs exit from I-80, drive east on Donner Pass Road for 0.75 mile to a right-hand turn onto Soda Springs Road. Head south for 2 miles, turn left onto a wood chip–covered road marked by a trailhead sign, and drive another 0.2 mile to the parking area.

FACILITIES/TRAILHEAD There are no facilities at the trailhead. The trail follows an old road from the far end of the parking area.

From the south side of the parking area, follow a dirt road around a cable and down to the dirt surface of Soda Springs Road beyond Ice Lakes Lodge and the intersection of Serene Road. Proceed along Soda Springs Road for 0.3 mile and turn right on a road heading downhill to a bridge over Serena Creek.

Away from the bridge, the route follows above the creek for a while before veering away on a rolling course across the west side of the canyon through a mixed forest. About a half mile from the parking area, the Reindeer ski trail heads uphill to the right, where you continue ahead on the Sterling's Canyon ski trail. At 1 mile, crest a rise at an open area offering a fine viewpoint just to the left of the road of Serena Creek canyon and the upper reaches of North Fork American River. Continue along the rolling road, reaching the next junction at 1.4 miles, where the Whitney's Bowl ski trail angles away to the right. Proceed ahead through lighter forest to the vicinity of the Hellman warming hut sitting on the top of the ridge above the road, 1.8 miles from the trailhead. A short way farther, the road curves to the right across the crest of the ridge and over to an unmarked junction. The right-hand road heads north on the Hellman's Way ski trail back toward the warming hut, while the twin-tracked road on the left heads south toward Point Mariah.

Follow the Point Mariah ski trail, initially on a descent along the lightly forested ridge. The trees part on occasion to allow fine views to the west of Devils Peak and Snow Mountain. Farther on, the road merges with a section of singletrack trail that weaves through the trees and climbs up into the open at Point Mariah. Cross the rocky point carpeted with patches of pinemat manzanita to the edge of the cliff and an excellent view. To the east lies the Sierra crest, including the summits from north to south of Crows Nest, Mt. Disney, Mt. Lincoln, Anderson Peak, Tinker Knob, Billys Peak, and Granite Chief. The deep cleft to the south is a section of Royal Gorge on the North Fork American River backdropped by Forest Hill Divide. After thoroughly appreciating the stunning vista, retrace your steps to the trailhead.

Deep Cleft Royal Gorge from Point Mariah

39   Summit Valley History Trail

Distance	4.5 miles (loop)
Hiking Time	2 hours
Elevation	Negligible
Difficulty	Moderate
Trail Use	Good for kids
Best Times	Late June through mid-October
Agency	Truckee Donner Land Trust at 530-582-4711, tdlandtrust.org
Recommended Maps	TDLT Summit Valley History Trail, USGS 7.5-minute *Soda Springs* (trail not shown)

see map on p. 102

HIGHLIGHTS   Lake Van Norden once covered more than half of Summit Valley before Pacific Gas and Electric began lowering the water level in 1976 due to fears of the dam's potential failure following an earthquake. A coalition spearheaded by the Truckee Donner Land Trust (TDLT) recently purchased the land, and efforts to restore the area to a more natural condition are ongoing. Following the course of one of Royal Gorge's cross-country ski trails, the Summit Valley History Trail loops around the meadows of the namesake valley, providing opportunities to experience some of the human and natural history along the way. Midsummer visitors should enjoy a fine wildflower display, and wildlife enthusiasts should be well rewarded by the variety of birds.

Referring to this loop as a "trail" is a bit generous, as a defined path rarely exists on the ground for very long; old roads and wagon trails routinely disappear in the verdant vegetation carpeting the meadow. While getting lost would be exceedingly difficult to accomplish in such open terrain bordered on nearly every side by high peaks, losing the actual track is relatively easy in places. Hopefully, the excellent record of the TDLT with other projects indicates improvements to make the trail more hiker friendly will be made in the future.

DIRECTIONS   From the Soda Springs exit from I-80, drive east on Donner Pass Road for 0.75 mile to a right-hand turn onto Soda Springs Road. Head south across the railroad tracks and turn left into the large dirt parking area near the Lake Van Norden dam.

FACILITIES/TRAILHEAD   There are no facilities at the trailhead. The trip begins at the spillway adjacent to the Lake Van Norden dam.

The trip description for the Summit Valley History Trail on the TDLT website recommends climbing up the left-hand side of the spillway and then crossing the top of the dam. This is certainly a viable route and one that offers a fine view of Lake Van Norden and the valley from a slightly higher vantage. However, the traverse across the top of the dam is through an encroaching stand of forest, primarily young lodgepole pines, which produces a rather claustrophobic effect. Perhaps a better start to the trip is to walk around the base of the dam to Lake Van Norden Road. Either way, once you arrive at the road, head generally east to where the road bends and crosses Castle Creek on a concrete bridge. About 100 yards past the bridge and 0.5 mile from the parking area, look for a very faint old track heading south-southwest toward the lake.

A cable may be stretched across the start of this track.

You head into the lush grasses and sedges of the meadow along the indistinct track of the old road. Shortly a sign marked SUBARU appears atop a pair of poles off to the left—obviously left over from some winter ski event. In that same direction but a little farther on, keep your eyes peeled for the West Van Norden warming hut. Once in sight, veer toward the hut and the signs for the Bill Paterson Loop ski trail. Continue away from the vicinity of the hut toward a sign farther out in the meadow. Near the sign is a Y-junction with a slightly more distinct track, 0.9 mile from the parking area.

Turn left (southeast) onto this track, which is a section of the old Overland Emigrant Trail used by pioneers on their journeys to the western valleys of California.

As you follow the trail eastward, you have fine views across the meadow of Donner Peak, Mount Judah, Mt. Disney, Crows Nest, and the slopes of Sugar Bowl Ski Area. The track disappears for a while where the route draws nearer to Lake Van Norden Road, but continue in the same general direction until the twin tracks of the old wagon road reappear. Eventually, the top of the East Van Norden warming hut comes into view, which provides a landmark to head toward if the track is lost in the thick vegetation. At 1.8 miles, pass a picnic table on the right and proceed to a T-junction with the very distinct track of a dirt road. A left turn on the road leads very shortly past the old posts of a former sheep corral to an alternate trailhead with a pair of signs about the acquisition of the Royal Gorge property and a plaque with a list of donors attached to a large boulder.

Retrace your steps away from the alternate trailhead and head initially south on the continuation of the road. The road winds around past a junction on the left with Snoop's Loop and another picnic table on the right on the way to a bridge across nascent South Yuba River. Immediately after the bridge, 2.2 miles from the parking area, an extremely faint track heads northwest across the meadow away from the road toward a stand of trees. A ski trail sign atop a tall pole is all that marks this otherwise nonexistent junction (if you reach the power line via the road, you've gone too far).

On the continuation of the Bill Paterson Loop, head generally west into the trees and along the South Yuba River. If you lose the track, just continue to follow the south bank of the river for a half mile to a forested rise. Reportedly, Native Americans used this area, and a little exploration may reveal evidence of where they used the rocks in the vicinity to grind seeds into flour (a list of GPS coordinates is on the TDLT website).

Away from the forested rise, the track continues along the river for about a half mile before veering away toward the gash in the forest through which passes the power line. If you lose the route, which is highly possible, the lake will ultimately force you to the south. Look for a gap in the line of trees immediately north of the power line. Pass through this gap and then follow the unsightly cut in the forest toward the west end of the lake. After about a half mile, reach a ski trail sign and veer to the right away from this eyesore back into the forest. Follow a faint track to the left of the mostly unseen shoreline back to the spillway and the parking area just beyond.

Lake Van Norden

40 Donner Summit Canyon Trail

Distance	3.4 miles (point-to-point); 6.8 miles (out-and-back)
Hiking Time	1.5–2 hours; 3–4 hours
Elevation	+1,000 feet/-100 feet
Difficulty	Moderate
Trail Use	Dogs OK
Best Times	Mid-June through mid-October
Agency	Truckee Donner Land Trust at 530-582-4711, tdlandtrust.org; Tahoe National Forest at 530-587-3558, www.fs.usda.gov/tahoe
Recommended Map	TDLT Donner Summit Canyon

see map on p. 108

HIGHLIGHTS A relatively new addition to the area, the Donner Summit Canyon Trail traces a historical route from the vicinity of Donner Lake to Donner Summit. Along the way, you'll encounter lush foliage and early-season wildflowers, a beaver pond, serene forest, and scenic views across slopes of classic Sierra granite. The presence of man also will be seen, as much of the route follows an old wagon road used to supply workers on the transcontinental railroad. The upper section is never too far from the old Lincoln Highway (Donner Pass Road: the main trans-Sierra road before the four-lane thoroughfare of I-80 was constructed) and the old railroad grade, with snow sheds and stone retaining walls visible from many spots along the trail. While nowadays the old road transports only light traffic and the railroad grade has long been abandoned in favor of a tunnel to the south, the modern-day scene includes climbers scaling the vertical rock faces near the summit. Casual hikers interested in an easier hike can follow shorter sections of trail to a couple of picnic areas.

DIRECTIONS Head westbound on Donner Pass Road to the west end of Donner Lake and continue 0.5 mile past South Shore Drive to the dirt parking area on the left-hand shoulder.

FACILITIES/TRAILHEAD There are signs at the trailhead with a map, historical information, and details about the Truckee Donner Land Trust (TDLT), but no other facilities.

The trail passes around a closed steel gate and drops away from the trailhead onto the forest floor via an old dirt road and immediately comes to a Y-junction. The right-hand road travels shortly to a picnic area and then loops around a beaver pond back to the main trail. Following directions on a metal sign, veer left, cross a bridge over perennial Donner Creek, and soon reach another junction with the loop, 0.2 mile from the trailhead.

Proceed ahead and soon emerge from the forest to follow a raised section of roadbed across the beaver pond, where early-season hikers may find the mosquitoes to be quite a nuisance. The inconvenience may be balanced somewhat by the presence of lush vegetation and a healthy assortment of colorful wildflowers away from the pond. The mellow stroll continues into a mixed forest on the way to a four-way junction of the loop at 0.5 mile.

Continue ahead across a usually dry swale, and then follow the old road as it bends to the north. Soon after, the inevitable ascent to Donner Summit begins. While climbing moderately, slim gaps in the forest reveal the rocky summit of Donner Peak to the southwest, hints of grander scenery to come. At 1.25 miles, you reach another junction marked by a metal sign. Here a 0.2-mile lateral leads east to an overlook of Donner Lake and vicinity, where a lone picnic table at the Kathy Polucha Kessler Picnic Area offers a memorial to a Truckee skier killed with six others by an avalanche in the Canadian Rockies in 2003. The picnic area is a good turnaround point for hikers desiring a short and relatively easy journey.

Take the right-hand path from the junction and continue climbing through the forest for a while, eventually passing out of Truckee Donner Land Trust property and onto forest service land. Where the tread turns rocky, the trail breaks out of the trees to open views of the granite summits surrounding the upper part of the canyon and the usual array of boats cutting wakes across the surface of Donner Lake to the east. Visible on the northeast face of Donner Peak above are some of the snowsheds along the abandoned railroad grade. Heading toward the old highway, you dip down to cross the creek and then clamber up the far side onto an old roadbed.

Although not particularly obvious at first glance, the correct route turns upstream for a while and then parallels the curve of the old highway on a horseshoe bend. Despite the appearance of a trail on the TDLT map, finding a defined and easily followed route on the ground beyond the curve through the dense vegetation along the upper creek is a bit tricky. Perhaps the best alternative is to work your way up to the parking area next to the old highway and simply walk along the edge of the parking lot to the west end. Primarily rock climbers park

here, along with sightseers interested in the petroglyphs nearby and the old China Wall above. If you want to shorten your hike by about 0.75 mile, a second vehicle could be parked at this spot instead of the Pacific Crest trailhead above.

From the far end of the parking area the next landmark is clearly visible—the old railroad grade between two snowsheds directly west of the China Wall. Drop away from the parking area and follow a sometimes-faint path through a marsh. Early season hikers may need to improvise a way around a low spot in the trail that often is covered by a few inches of water. More defined tread can be seen beyond the marsh and across granite slabs angling up to an old roadbed. Follow the road to the 1913 underpass below the old railroad grade and then turn north. Soon the trail

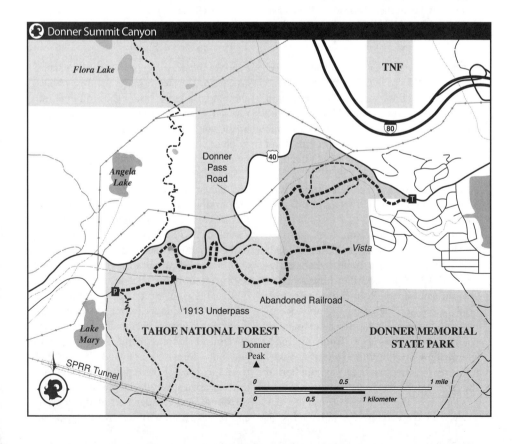

Donner Lake from Donner Summit Canyon Trail

enters a lush grove of vegetation, where a prolific display of early-season wildflowers graces the 0.4-mile, slightly ascending stroll to the dirt road of the route of the Pacific Crest Trail (PCT). To reach the PCT trailhead, turn right and follow the road a short distance to the trailhead. Out-and-back hikers must retrace their steps 3.4 miles back to the lower trailhead.

41   PCT: Donner Summit to Donner Pass

see map on p. 80

Distance	3.5 miles (point-to-point)
Hiking Time	2–3 hours
Elevation	+525/-625 feet
Difficulty	Moderate
Trail Use	Dogs OK
Best Times	July through October
Agency	Tahoe National Forest at 530-587-3558, www.fs.usda.gov/tahoe
Recommended Map	USGS 7.5-minute *Norden*

HIGHLIGHTS The 3.5-mile section of the Pacific Crest Trail (PCT) between Donner Summit (I-80) and Donner Pass (Old Highway 40) isn't the most stupendous stretch of the famous trail, but hikers looking for a nice picnic spot with decent views won't be disappointed with the scenery. Wildflowers lift the spirits of passersby until midseason, and rock climbers will find plenty of challenging bouldering routes all summer long.

DIRECTIONS *Start:* West of Donner Summit, take the Castle Peak/Boreal Ridge Road exit from I-80. Drive to the frontage road on the south side of the freeway and proceed east 0.3 mile to the Pacific Crest Trail parking area.

Donner Lake and the old Donner Pass Road from the PCT

End: From I-80, take the Soda Springs/Norden exit and travel 3.7 miles east on the old Donner Pass Road to Donner Pass; make a right-hand turn onto a narrow paved road. Travel south 0.2 mile to a dirt road branching west, which is the start of the trail. Park your vehicle along the side of the road as space allows, paying close attention to the signed no-parking areas in the vicinity.

FACILITIES/TRAILHEAD ***Start:*** The large PCT–Donner Summit parking lot has trailer parking, pit toilets, picnic tables, and running water in season. The well-marked trail begins on the northwest side of the parking lot.

End: In recent years, there has been a portable toilet near the trailhead. Parking is extremely limited. If space is not available in the vicinity, you may have to park closer to the highway. The trail begins at the start of the dirt road near a series of trail signs.

From the parking lot, follow a well-signed gravel path to a stone bridge over a seasonal stream and continue on dirt track through lodgepole pines, western white pines, and white firs. You'll soon encounter a junction with the Glacier Meadow Loop, where you veer right and continue eastbound toward the Pacific Crest Trail. After a short distance, you come to a second junction with the Glacier Meadow Loop, where you veer to the right again. Pass by a shallow pond, where mountain hemlocks join the mixed forest, and then make a short descent to the Pacific Crest Trail junction near the edge of a grassy, willow-filled meadow, a half mile from the trailhead.

Turn right and proceed southbound on the PCT, on a mild climb through mixed forest. You'll pass a low, open knoll to the left and then a small pond to the right before emerging from the forest to cross an open area filled with granite humps and pinemat manzanita. After a moderate descent through light forest, the trail passes below some power lines and then begins a half-mile, switchbacking climb that leads to gentler terrain across the crest of a knoll harboring a small pond. Past the pond, a short, winding ascent leads to the trail's high point and a good, open view of Donner Peak and the surrounding terrain.

A moderately steep, zigzagging descent leads down shrub-covered slopes with good views of the Donner Pass region. Along the way, you pass by a couple of boot-beaten paths that lead to popular rock-climbing areas. The trail wanders around a bit, passes below more power lines, and then follows just above Donner Pass Road to the edge of the highway at Donner Pass.

42 Mt. Judah Loop

Distance	5.6 miles (semiloop)
Hiking Time	2.5–3 hours
Elevation	+1,175/-1,175 feet
Difficulty	Moderate
Trail Use	Dogs OK
Best Times	Mid-July through mid-October
Agency	Tahoe National Forest at 530-587-3558, www.fs.usda.gov/tahoe
Recommended Map	USGS 7.5-minute *Norden*

see map on p. 80

HIGHLIGHTS With a minimal effort, hikers can reach some of the grandest views available in the northern Tahoe Sierra via the 4.6-mile Mt. Judah Loop. The rugged terrain around Donner Pass is quite impressive, and the loop affords many excellent vista points on the way to the awe-inspiring view from the summit of Mt. Judah. The section of the loop that connects with the Pacific Crest Trail (PCT) is relatively new, constructed in the 1990s, but despite its newness, the Mt. Judah Loop has justifiably become a very popular hike; don't anticipate a lot of solitude. Be sure to pack plenty of water, as none is available en route.

DIRECTIONS From I-80, take the Soda Springs/Norden exit and travel 3.7 miles east on the old Donner Pass Road to Donner Pass; make a right-hand turn onto a narrow paved road. Travel south for 0.2 mile to a dirt road branching west, which is the start of the trail. Park your vehicle along the side of the road as space allows, paying close attention to the signed no-parking areas in the vicinity.

FACILITIES/TRAILHEAD In recent years there has been a portable toilet near the trailhead. Parking is extremely limited. If space is not available in the vicinity, you may have to park closer to the highway. The trail begins at the start of the dirt road near a series of trail signs.

Follow the Pacific Crest Trail south-bound, past a narrow swath of lush foliage sprinkled with wildflowers and ferns, to a series of short switchbacks leading up a pine- and fir-dotted granite headwall. Beyond the switchbacks, the trail angles across a mostly open hillside carpeted with huckleberry oak that allows improving views of Lake Mary below. Farther up the trail, pass through a stand of red firs before breaking back out into the open at the crossing of a ski slope. In this clearing, 1 mile from the trailhead, you reach a junction between the continuation of the PCT ahead and your route along the north end of the Mt. Judah Loop.

Remaining on the PCT, you pass below a chairlift for the Sugar Bowl Ski Area, and then cross a dirt road, 0.1 mile from the junction. Reenter forest beyond the road, where mountain hemlocks begin to intermix with the red firs, and mule-ears provide bursts of color in early summer. Reach the south junction of the Mt. Judah Loop at 2 miles from the trailhead.

Leave the PCT and follow the loop trail on a winding ascent of Mt. Judah's southwest ridge, reaching the top of the peak at 0.75 mile from the junction. The marvelous view includes such notable landmarks as Donner Lake, Martis Valley, and the Carson Range to the east; Castle Peak, Mt. Lola, and Sierra Buttes to the north; Sugar Bowl, Summit Valley, and Lake Van Norden to the west; and the continuation of the Sierra crest weaving toward the south.

From the top of Mt. Judah, descend a bare ridge to a saddle and then start climbing again toward the north summit. The trail veers east away from this slightly lower peak, although a short use trail branching away from the main trail provides an easy way to the top. Traverse along the east side of the ridge, then descend through mixed forest around the nose of the ridge, to a three-way junction at a saddle between Mt. Judah and Donner Peak, 3.8 miles from the trailhead.

For additional views, leave the maintained trail at the saddle and proceed on

The view from the summit of Mt. Judah

a use trail toward the multispired summit of Donner Peak. Follow the boot-beaten path to a short scramble up some exfoliated granite slabs, after which you'll reach the top and an expansive view. Unless you're an expert climber, avoid the highest pinnacle, as the climbing is difficult and the exposure is significant.

From the junction, bend left and follow the course of an old road for 0.4 mile on a steady descent around the north side of the mountain to the resumption of singletrack trail. Heading southwest, you continue the descent into a thickening forest until reaching the ski slope and the north junction of the PCT, 4.6 miles from the trailhead.

From there, retrace your steps 1 mile along the PCT to the trailhead.

43   PCT: Donner Pass to Squaw Valley

Distance	15 miles (point-to-point)
Hiking Time	8–10 hours
Elevation	+3,000/-3,800 feet
Difficulty	Difficult
Trail Use	Backpacking option, dogs OK
Best Times	Mid-July through mid-October
Agency	Tahoe National Forest at 530-587-3558, www.fs.usda.gov/tahoe
Recommended Maps	USGS 7.5-minute *Norden, Granite Chief,* and *Tahoe City*

HIGHLIGHTS This section of the Pacific Crest Trail (PCT) lives up to its name, offering some of the finest views in the Tahoe area from a several-mile stretch of trail that stays on or near the actual crest of

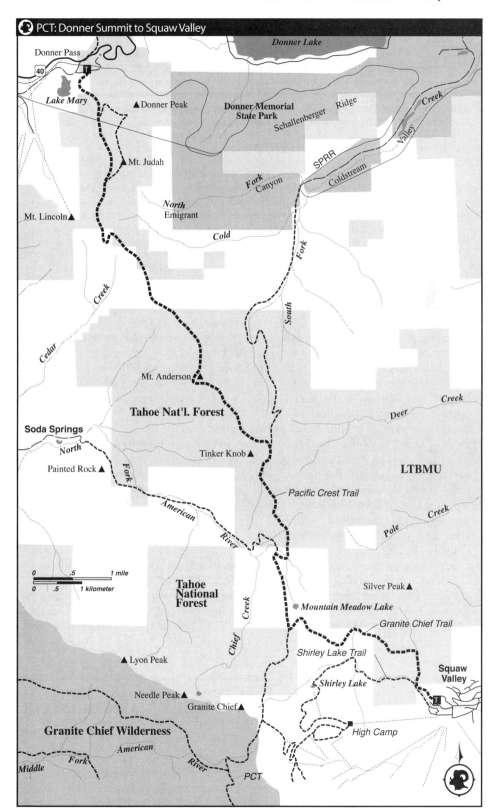

the range. This hike is very challenging for the average hiker, especially when considering the plunge into and the climb out of the North Fork American River's canyon, but experienced hikers in good condition will find the well-maintained PCT a rewarding challenge. Backpackers can break the trip into two days by camping along tributaries of North Fork, or by making arrangements to stay in the Sierra Club's Benson Hut.

DIRECTIONS *Start:* From I-80, take the Soda Springs/Norden exit and travel 3.7 miles east on the old Donner Pass Road to Donner Pass; make a right-hand turn onto a narrow paved road. Travel south 0.2 mile to a dirt road branching west, which is the start of the trail. Park your vehicle along the side of the road as space allows, paying close attention to the signed no-parking areas in the vicinity.

End: From CA 89, approximately 8.5 miles south of Truckee and 5 miles north of Tahoe City, turn west onto Squaw Valley Road and proceed toward Squaw Valley. Rather than following the main road as it bends sharply left toward the center of the village, veer right, proceed to the large north parking lot, and park near the fire station.

FACILITIES/TRAILHEAD In recent years, there has been a portable toilet near the trailhead. Parking is extremely limited. If space is not available in the vicinity, you may have to park closer to the highway. The trail begins at the start of the dirt road near a series of trail signs.

Although there are no facilities per se at the Squaw Valley Trailhead, the trip begins in the resort community, where a wide array of upscale amenities is available. The hike ends at the Granite Chief Trailhead, in the spacious north parking lot near the Olympic Village Inn.

Follow the Pacific Crest Trail southbound, past a narrow swath of lush foliage sprinkled with wildflowers and ferns to a series of short switchbacks leading up a pine- and fir-dotted granite headwall. Beyond the switchbacks, the trail angles across a mostly open hillside carpeted with huckleberry oak that allows improving views of Lake Mary below. Farther up the trail, pass through a stand of red firs before breaking back out into the open at the crossing of a ski slope. In this clearing, 1 mile from the trailhead, you reach a junction between the continuation of the PCT ahead and your route along the north end of the Mt. Judah Loop.

Remaining on the PCT, you pass below a chairlift for the Sugar Bowl Ski Area, and then cross a dirt road, 0.1 mile from the junction. Reenter forest beyond the road, where mountain hemlocks begin to intermix with the red firs, and mule-ears provide bursts of color in early summer. Reach the south junction of the Mt. Judah Loop at 2 miles from the trailhead.

Remaining on the Pacific Crest Trail, continue south from the junction for a short distance, to a hemlock-shaded saddle known as Roller Pass.

Away from Roller Pass, the PCT closely follows the Sierra crest through light forest. Soon the trees diminish, and the first of a nearly continuous stream of awesome views begins as you traverse the east slope of Mt. Lincoln. Seemingly in the middle of nowhere, an old wooden sign marked MT. LINCOLN points toward the summit, but all evidence of a former trail has vanished. If you want to scale this peak, you can take an easier way to the summit, which is farther south, where a use trail leaves the PCT to follow the southeast ridge to the top.

ROLLER PASS

At the pass, a metal post bears a historical marker with a plaque and a quotation from Nicholas Carriter, a member of the ill-fated Donner Party. In September 1846, pioneers winched their wagons up to this spot from the east using oxen. A short path leads from the saddle to the lip above the steep wall of Emigrant Canyon. The unfolding vista here will certainly increase your admiration for these rugged pioneers and their dogged determination to get their wagons out of the deep canyon below and up to the pass.

View toward Castle Peak from the PCT

Continuing, the Sierra crest seems to stretch out ahead of you forever, while to the west the gash created by the North Fork American River seems too deep to be real. For the next several miles, this section of the PCT is the prototypical model for crest trails, as the path stays high, either directly on or very near the apex of the range. Heading away from Mt. Lincoln, the PCT descends across an open volcanic slope that is covered in a sea of yellow during midsummer from multitudinous mule-ears. A pair of long-legged switchbacks takes you through a stand of western white pines, red firs, and mountain hemlocks before you emerge back out into the open across shrub-covered slopes. You reach the bottom of the three-quarter-mile descent from Mt. Lincoln at a 7,500-foot saddle overlooking Coldstream Valley to the east and Cedar Creek Canyon to the west.

From the saddle, ascend lunar-looking slopes, where only small tufts of vegetation and a few mule-ears seem capable of taking root in the porous volcanic soils. Eventually, tobacco brush, currant, and sagebrush regain a foothold as you progress toward the next high point, Anderson Peak, which presents a dramatic foreground profile as viewed from the trail. Cross a hillside covered with muddy-looking lava flows, follow a pair of switchbacks, and then pass below Peak 8374 on the way to the base of Anderson Peak, where you'll encounter a use trail branching away from the PCT, 5.3 miles from the trailhead.

Following this unsigned path away from the PCT will take you up the north ridge of Anderson Peak in 10 minutes or so to Benson Hut, one of four historic huts operated by the Sierra Club. Unless you're caught in a life-threatening storm, advance reservations are required to use the hut. Peak baggers can continue on a use trail beyond the hut, which leads across a talus slope and then climbs steeply to the summit of Anderson Peak, offering another superb vista.

BENSON HUT

Backpackers won't find many campsites along this route: The only reasonable sites are in a pair of basins just north of the North Fork American River crossing. But overnighters may be able to reserve the no-frills Benson Hut by visiting **clairtappaanlodge.com/benson-hut** or calling 530-426-3632.

Away from the spur trail to Benson Hut, the PCT skirts the west side of Anderson Peak well below the summit, and follows a mile-long, gently ascending course southeast toward Tinker Knob, as tiny, drought-tolerant wildflowers cheer you onward. Just below Tinker Knob, where the PCT veers sharply east, you reach the high point of the route between Donner Pass and Squaw Valley. If you wish to reach the summit, leave the trail at this point and make the easy scramble over fractured rock to the top of the 8,949-foot peak. Once again, an impressive vista awaits you at the summit.

Begin your 2-mile descent from Tinker Knob to the North Fork of the American River by turning east on a descending trail below the north face of Tinker Knob. After a quarter mile, reach the junction with the Coldstream Trail near Tinker Knob Saddle, 8.2 miles from the trailhead. The 6-mile Coldstream Trail offers an alternate route to a remote trailhead in Coldstream Valley, but access through Donner Memorial State Park and across private land is sometimes problematic (see Trip 44).

From Tinker Knob Saddle, you drop steeply via switchbacks into the canyon of a tributary of the North Fork American River. After 0.6 mile, the grade eases as you follow a descending traverse well below the crest, hopping over a pair of spring-fed streams along the way. Enter a basin where waterless campsites are available, and continue to a smaller basin with both water and at least one campsite, 0.3 mile farther. Beyond the second basin, a steeper descent takes you past rock outcrops to a crossing of the North Fork American River and a junction with Painted Rock Trail, at 10.7 miles from the trailhead.

From the Painted Rock junction, a series of switchbacks leads you up to the crest of a ridge to good views of Granite Chief to the south and Needle and Lyon Peaks to the southwest. The USGS Granite Chief quad shows the old trail route, which used to follow the headwaters of the North Fork upstream to Mountain Meadow Lake. The PCT was subsequently rerouted, as the land around the lake is privately owned and also is used by the University of California as an ecological study area. Follow this newer section of trail to a junction, about 0.4 mile directly southwest of the lake and 12.2 miles from the trailhead, where the Granite Chief Trail heads northeast.

Leave the PCT at the junction and head northeast on the Granite Chief Trail, following a winding descent through a thick forest of mountain hemlocks and red firs. Switchbacks lead into a tributary canyon of Squaw Creek, where patches of flower-filled meadow periodically interrupt the forest. Break out into the open as you leave the trees and descend a series of sloping, granite benches that afford fine views of the Squaw Valley area. Locating the route of the trail over these granite benches may be difficult at times, but ducks and old paint marks on rocks may help guide you.

About 1.5 miles from the PCT junction, you make an easy crossing of a perennial stream and continue the descent through alternating stretches of light forest and granite slabs. Cross a marshy hillside fed by seeps and then follow switchbacks to the easy crossing of another Squaw Creek tributary, which you then follow downstream through thickening vegetation. Nearing the valley floor, a number of intersecting paths combined with a lack of signs creates a mildly confusing conclusion to your journey, but, fortunately, all paths lead to the large parking lot at Squaw Valley.

44 Donner Memorial State Park

Distance	0.5 mile (loop, Nature Trail); 2 miles (semiloop, Lakeshore Trail)
Hiking Time	30 minutes; 1–2 hours
Elevation	Negligible
Difficulty	Easy
Trail Use	Good for kids
Best Times	July through mid-October
Agency	Donner Memorial State Park at 530-582-7892, parks.ca.gov
Recommended Map	*CSP Donner Memorial State Park* brochure map

HIGHLIGHTS Donner Memorial Park has enough diversions to fill a couple of hours or an entire week. The park boasts two trails: a short nature-trail loop that takes 30 minutes to complete, and a 2-mile semiloop that mostly parallels the lakeshore but also goes through the forest. With swimming areas, boat rentals, picnic areas, campgrounds, and a museum dedicated to the ill-fated Donner Party, the park offers plenty of family activities in addition to hiking. So many fun adventures await park visitors that a trip to the museum is necessary to understand the tragedy for which the park is named.

DIRECTIONS Leave I-80 at the Donner Pass Road exit (exit 184) and follow the signs for Donner Memorial State Park. Head westbound on Donner Pass Road for 0.3 mile to the park entrance, and turn left into the park. To access the Nature Trail, veer left and park in the museum parking lot. To access the Lakeshore Trail, veer right and pass through the entrance station (day-use fee required); proceed a short distance to a junction. Turn right and drive 0.1 mile to a gravel turnout on the right and park.

FACILITIES/TRAILHEAD Donner Memorial State Park offers a picnic area, campground, visitor center, restrooms, swimming, and nonmotorized boating. The short Nature Trail begins directly south of the museum. The Lakeshore Trail starts 0.2 mile southwest of the entrance station. Portable toilets and picnic tables are nearby.

Nature Trail: The half-mile, self-guided trail follows a wide, gently graded dirt and gravel path away from the museum past post 1 and into a mixed forest. The numbered posts correspond to descriptions in a park brochure, available from the museum, that provide insights into some of the natural history of the immediate area. Near post 7, the trail bends alongside Donner Creek and follows the stream to a bridge. Once across the bridge, you hike downstream along the east bank within sight of Creek Campground on your right, and proceed to a second bridge. From there, the trail follows a raised boardwalk across a boggy

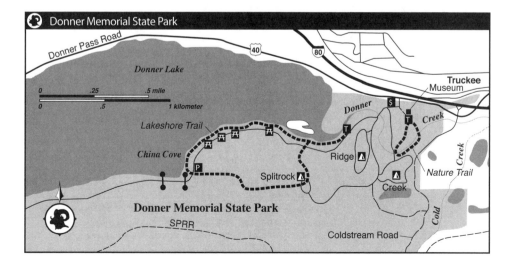

meadow before reentering forest shade. Soon after, you arrive at the close of the loop near the museum.

Lakeshore Trail: Begin upstream from the dam across Donner Creek, and head through a picnic area on a gently graded dirt path about halfway between the access road and the lakeshore. You pass through a mixed forest of lodgepole pines, Jeffrey pines, and white firs; eventually you'll see willows, alders, small plants, and wildflowers lining the shore. Near a short bridge across a narrow finger of the lake is the first of several interpretive placards about the ecology and history of the area. Reach a junction with a trail on the left, a quarter mile from the start of the trail that will ultimately provide your return route. In the opposite direction is Donner Lake Water Sports, near the lakeshore. The trail continues around the lake, passing by several picnic tables and a couple of restroom buildings on the way to the China Cove swimming area.

Near a large parking area at the end of the road, cross the paved access road and follow the China Cove Trail along the course of an old road through scattered, mixed forest. Early-summer wildflowers here include mule-ears, lupine, gentian, and false Solomon's seal. Follow the gently graded road toward Splitrock Campground, where the roadbed turns from dirt to gravel. Near campsite 138, you reach paved road and turn left to follow it toward campsite 124, where the route resumes. Now headed north, follow the path across a bridge and then across the paved access road to a junction with the Lakeshore Trail. Turn right and retrace your steps a quarter mile back to the parking area.

---

45 Coldstream Trail to Tinker Knob

see map on p. 120

Distance	11.5 miles (out-and-back)
Hiking Time	5–7 hours
Elevation	+2,675 feet
Difficulty	Difficult
Trail Use	Dogs OK, mountain biking OK (no bikes allowed on PCT)
Best Times	Mid-July through mid-October
Agency	Donner Memorial State Park at 530-582-7892, parks.ca.gov; Tahoe National Forest at 530-587-3558, www.fs.usda.gov/tahoe
Recommended Maps	USGS 7.5-minute *Truckee, Norden,* and *Granite Chief*

HIGHLIGHTS This route is so seldom used that a nearby resort owner has dubbed it the "Lost Trail," and the path provides tranquil passage to the Pacific Crest Trail via Coldstream Valley. The first half of the route follows a section of the Coldstream Road that's open to off-road traffic; later, singletrack trail that's closed to motor vehicles leads through the upper part of the canyon to the Sierra crest. Views from the uppermost part of Coldstream Canyon, the Sierra crest, and atop Tinker Knob are as good as they come in the Tahoe Sierra.

DIRECTIONS Leave I-80 at the Donner Pass Road exit (exit 184) and head south from the four-way stop onto Coldstream Road. Follow good, paved road for 0.3 mile to the vicinity of a closed gate at the entrance to a gravel pit. Veer to the left onto a dirt road circumventing the gravel pit, soon passing through an open steel gate and coming to the intersection of a road on the right from Donner Memorial State Park. Proceed up Coldstream Valley, following signed directions for Lost Trail Lodge, Pacific Crest Trail (PCT), Coldstream Road, and Tinker Knob at a Y-junction, and then proceed to a crossing of the stream from Emigrant Canyon. Just past the stream, you come below the Union Pacific Railroad tracks at Horseshoe Bend. Park your vehicle in the signed, small dirt clearing just off the road.

Vehicular access to Horseshoe Bend is day-use only. If the steel gate on Coldstream Road is closed, you can access the trailhead via a route through Donner Memorial State Park. However, doing so will require you to pay the park admission fee. From the four-way stop at exit 184, head westbound on Donner Pass Road for 0.3 mile to the park entrance and turn left into the park. Drive a short distance into the park and pass through the entrance station, paying the $8 day-use fee. Proceed on the access road toward the campgrounds and continue past the entrance to Ridge Campground. Just past the entrance into Creek Campground, turn left at a signed junction for Coldstream Valley, 0.4 mile from the park entrance. Follow the dirt road 0.4-mile to a T-junction, and turn right onto Coldstream Road. From there, follow the directions above.

FACILITIES/TRAILHEAD There are no facilities at the trailhead. Nearby Donner Memorial State Park offers swimming and boating opportunities on the lake, picnic facilities, campgrounds, and the Emigrant Trail Museum, which documents the travails of the ill-fated Donner Party. The trail begins across the railroad tracks at Horseshoe Bend, along the dirt road heading up Coldstream Valley.

Walk across the twin set of railroad tracks at Horseshoe Bend and then head up the road on the far side through a forest of Jeffrey pines, white firs, lodgepole pines, and western white pines. Side roads appear to the left and right from time to time, but the route of the Coldstream Trail follows the obvious main road to a Y-junction at 0.3 mile from the parking area. Veer left at the junction and proceed to a crossing of Cold Creek, where a makeshift bridge of logs and planks provides an easy way across the stream. Shortly after the creek, you reach the grounds of Lost Trail Lodge.

LOST TRAIL LODGE

Built primarily as a winter retreat for backcountry skiers and snowshoers, the lodge has been in operation for only a short time. Summer visitors interested in accommodations can check the website at **losttraillodge.com.**

Pass quickly through the lodge grounds and continue on the dirt road, which soon becomes steeper. Tobacco brush lines the roadbed, along with a fine display of wildflowers in early summer, including paintbrush, delphinium, mule-ears, lupine, penstemon, and yarrow. Proceed upstream to a T-junction at 1.2 miles, where a road veers left to cross the creek. Continue straight ahead from the junction on a moderate to moderately steep climb for another three-quarters of a mile to the end of the road and the beginning of singletrack trail. A number of trail signs appear nearby, some of which indicate that the trail beyond is closed to motor vehicles.

Now on trail, you soon hop over a trio of side streams spilling across the trail. Proceed through thickening forest to cross the first channel of South Fork Cold Creek on logs, just below a short cascade that spills into a small pool. This is immediately followed by a boulder hop of the alder-lined second channel.

Climb away from Cold Creek to a switchback and then break out into the open momentarily across a slope carpeted with pinemat manzanita and tobacco brush, and sprinkled with lupine, penstemon, mule-ears, mariposa lily, and paintbrush. Back in light forest, the trail climbs along a ridge below Tinker Knob with improving views of the Sierra crest above, more distant peaks and ridges to the north and east, and Deep Creek Canyon below. Farther up the slope, you head back into the forest, which now includes mountain hemlocks, and come alongside and then cross a thin stream while following an old roadbed

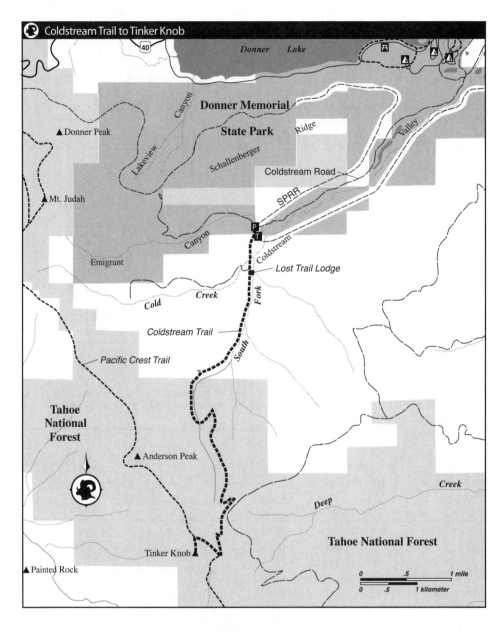

Coldstream Trail to Tinker Knob

to a junction with an off-highway vehicle (OHV) road.

Turn right onto the OHV road, and make a moderately easy climb to the top of a ridge, where singletrack trail resumes. Climb up the trail across a slope sprinkled with dwarf firs, hemlocks, and whitebark pines, switchbacking a couple of times before reaching the signed PCT junction.

Stunning views spread out in all directions, as you turn right and follow the north-bound PCT through an extensive field of mule-ears. Pass a sign noting Tinker Knob and its elevation on the way to the crest of the north ridge.

From there, leave the PCT to follow a use trail to the base of the peak, and then wind up through the rocks to the

Junction of Pacific Crest and Coldstream Trails

8,945-foot summit, where a number of large cairns and low windbreaks greets you. To say that views are quite impressive in all directions seems a bit understated. Some of the more notable landmarks visible from the top include Devils Peak; the canyon of the North Fork American River winding through Royal Gorge; numerous peaks within Desolation Wilderness; a good slice of Lake Tahoe; Freel Peak, Mt. Rose, and the rest of the Carson Range; the community of Truckee; Boca, Prosser, and Stampede reservoirs; and Sierra Buttes in the northern distance.

46 Sawtooth Trail

Distance	9.5 miles (semiloop)
Hiking Time	5–7 hours
Elevation	+625/-625 feet
Difficulty	Moderate
Trail Use	Dogs OK, mountain biking OK
Best Times	June through October
Agency	Tahoe National Forest at 530-587-3558, www.fs.usda.gov/tahoe
Recommended Map	USGS 7.5-minute *Truckee*

see map on p. 122

HIGHLIGHTS Built in 2002, the Sawtooth Trail provides an excellent opportunity for hikers, joggers, bikers, and dog walkers to squeeze in a trip to the woods on the outskirts of Truckee. The curving nature of the well-graded trail certainly seems to have been built with mountain bikers in mind, so be prepared for numerous encounters while on the trail. The mostly forested route does lead to several vista points that offer good views of the Truckee River canyon and peaks around Donner Summit—excellent spots for runners to catch their breath or for hikers to enjoy the surroundings. The Sawtooth Road leads to several trail access points, which allow trail users to tailor their visits according to their schedules. The description below uses a 1.6-mile connection to the loop, creating a nearly 10-mile-long hike. By parking farther up the road, those pressed for time could follow just the 6.3-mile loop section.

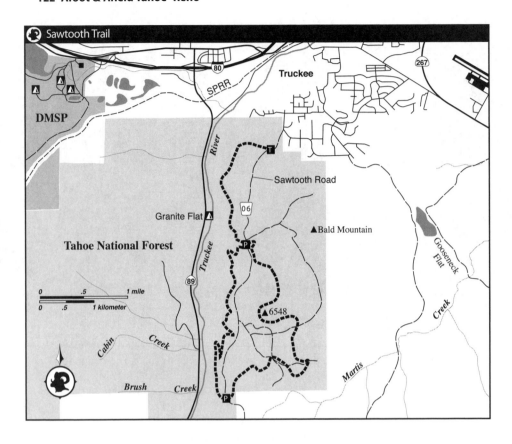

DIRECTIONS From I-80, take the Highway 267 exit and head south toward Lake Tahoe, crossing a bridge high over the Truckee River on the way to a traffic signal at Brockway Road. Turn right at Brockway Road and proceed for 1.2 miles to a traffic signal; turn left onto Palisades Drive. Drive on Palisades Drive for 0.4 mile and veer left onto Ponderosa at a signed 15-mile-per-hour curve. After 0.8 mile, make a right turn onto Silver Fir and continue another 0.4 mile to a left turn onto Thieland. Follow Thieland for 0.1 mile and then turn onto FS 06, passing through an open steel gate and proceeding 0.2 mile to the end of paved road and the gravel trailhead parking lot on the right.

FACILITIES/TRAILHEAD There are no facilities at the trailhead. The trail begins on the west side of the parking area near a trailhead signboard.

Follow gently graded, singletrack trail away from the parking area through a scattered-to-light, previously logged Jeffrey pine and white fir forest above a smattering of shrubs, including bitterbrush, manzanita, currant, sagebrush, and tobacco brush. Soon you cross a dirt road and stroll along a winding trail through an area sprinkled with boulders and mule-ears. Proceed to the edge of the hillside well above the Truckee River canyon, where you have limited views of the river, CA 89 running alongside, and the ridges across the canyon. Castle Peak, Mt. Lincoln, and Anderson Peak also make brief appearances from viewpoints. The slightly rising trail bends away from the canyon and leads to a junction near a parking area, 1.6 miles from the trailhead.

Turn right (south) at the junction and follow curving trail through the trees back toward the edge of the canyon, where rocky viewpoints give you another look at the peaks mentioned above. At 2.75 miles, you reach a T-junction with a short loop trail that heads to an overlook of the Truckee River canyon.

After a visit to the overlook, head south on the main trail, enjoying fine views. Eventually, the trail bends away from the canyon momentarily, and proceeds to a couple of long-legged switchbacks that lead back to the rim of the canyon for a while. The trail eventually veers away from the canyon again and then makes a moderate climb to the crest of a minor ridge on the way to a crossing of Sawtooth Road near a parking area, 4.5 miles from the trailhead.

Walk across the road to where the trail resumes and pass beneath some power lines; follow the trail generally northeast. At 0.8 mile from Sawtooth Road, you walk across a well-traveled dirt road and then come to the crossing of a less-traveled road a quarter mile farther. About 0.1 mile later is an unmarked four-way junction, where your route proceeds straight ahead to merge with the road that was previously crossed. Turn left, following a sign marked SAWTOOTH TRAIL, and walk a short distance along the road to the resumption of singletrack trail on the right. Continue through light forest across an old logging road and beneath a set of power lines. A moderate climb leads to another road crossing on the way to an arcing ascent around Peak 6548, as shown on the USGS map. The shrub-covered slopes of the peak afford good views of the surrounding countryside, including Castle Peak to the northwest.

Descend away from the peak and pass by a low rock formation before the trail angles toward Sawtooth Road. Walk across the road and past the parking area, and follow a short section of winding trail to the close of the loop, at the first trail junction you encountered from the trailhead. From there, retrace your steps 1.6 miles to the trailhead.

More Hikes

Cottonwood Botanical and Overlook Trails

The Cottonwood Campground off CA 89, just south of Sierraville, offers a short interpretive loop along Cottonwood Creek and a longer climb to an overlook of Coldstream Canyon (0.6 and 2 miles).

Kyburz Interpretive Trail

An extremely short, wheelchair-accessible boardwalk off County Road 450 explores the human and natural history of the Kyburz Flat area.

Rowton Peak

The view from Rowton Peak helps to make this loop Royal Gorge's "signature hike." Unfortunately, much of the route is open to motorized vehicles. Consult the Truckee Donner Land Trust website at **tdlandtrust .org** for more information.

Truckee River Canyon from the Sawtooth Trail

Wildflowers along the Western States Trail

Chapter 3

North Tahoe

For the purposes of this guide, North Tahoe is loosely defined as the area between the lakeshore communities of Tahoe City and Kings Beach, north to the outskirts of Truckee. Tahoe City was established in the mid-1860s, primarily by miners after mines in Squaw Valley were shut down. Kings Beach, named after a bootlegger and speakeasy operator, grew into a popular resort area in the early 1900s. Since the successful Winter Olympics of 1960, held at Squaw Valley, the region has seen steady growth.

Two state highways (CA 89 and CA 267) provide the principal access to this area, connecting Tahoe City, Kings Beach, and Truckee. CA 89 follows the course of the Truckee River canyon from the river's outlet gates at Tahoe City to the town of Truckee, providing access to the resort communities of Squaw Valley and Alpine Meadows along the way. CA 267 travels between Kings Beach and Truckee over 7,199-foot Brockway Summit.

The Sierra crest runs along the western edge of this area, with significant mountains such as Squaw Peak, Granite Chief, and Silver Peak reaching the highest heights. Away from the crest, forested Mt. Watson and Martis Peak are two prominent peaks in the North Tahoe region. Undeveloped lands within this area are mostly forested, the result of second growth after most of the Tahoe Basin was denuded in the mid-1800s to supply lumber for the mines of the Comstock Lode and supporting infrastructure for the nearby communities of Virginia City and Gold Hill.

With numerous logging roads crisscrossing the landscape, the North Tahoe region has become a popular mountain-biking haven. Northstar California operates a mountain-bike park in the summer months, and several commercial biking establishments within north-shore communities offer bike rentals, sales, and service. Except for trails in Granite Chief Wilderness, most of the hiking trails in the area are open to mountain biking as well. Consequently, hikers must be alert for possible encounters with mountain bikes while using the trail network at this end of the lake.

Although most of the trails are open to equestrians also, the Western States Trail sees the heaviest equine use, as the path follows a historic emigrant and mail route. The annual Tevis Cup 100-mile ride is held every August, following the Western States Trail from Lake Tahoe to Auburn. Riders who cover the 100 miles within 24 hours are awarded a coveted belt buckle, provided their horses are "fit to continue."

Lake-level trails are usually snow-free sometime in May, but the bulk of the trails in this section travel through shady forest at higher elevations. Consequently, the hiking season doesn't usually hit full stride until the beginning of summer.

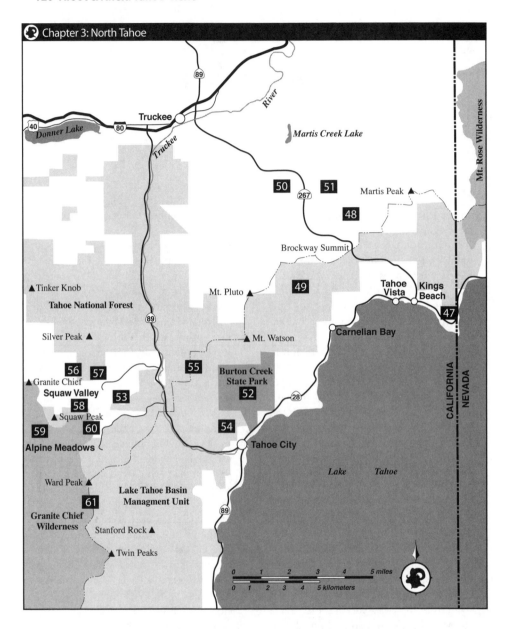

47 Stateline Point

Distance	1.8 miles (out-and-back)
Hiking Time	1 hour
Elevation	+275/-275 feet
Difficulty	Moderate
Trail Use	Dogs OK
Best Times	April through October
Agency	Lake Tahoe Basin Management Unit at 530-543-2600, www.fs.usda.gov/ltbmu
Recommended Map	USGS 7.5-minute *Kings Beach*

HIGHLIGHTS Although some tourists would quibble with the notion, most hikers would agree that the stunning Lake Tahoe vista from the old Stateline Peak fire lookout is one of the most easily accessible grand views of the lake in the area. While not a soul can argue with the quality of the view, the half-mile-plus climb does gain a significant amount of elevation in a short distance. Interpretive signs and benches at the top enhance the visually stunning experience.

DIRECTIONS Follow CA 28 to Crystal Bay. Immediately north of the Tahoe Biltmore Lodge, turn west onto Reservoir Road, drive two blocks, and then turn right onto Lakeview Avenue. Follow Lakeview for a half mile to the vicinity of a steel gate on the left, which marks the beginning of the hike up a closed fire road. Park your vehicle in the vicinity as space allows.

FACILITIES/TRAILHEAD There are no facilities at the trailhead. At the site of the old fire lookout, there are vault toilets, picnic tables, and interpretive signs.

The route to the top of Stateline Peak follows the course of a paved road closed to vehicles that leads to the site of an old fire lookout. From the closed gate, follow the road on a stiff uphill climb to where the road curves to the southwest and continue the ascent to the top. A short loop trail circles the upper slopes of the peak, with periodically placed interpretive signs providing information about the natural and human history of the area. Park benches along the way encourage visitors to sit and enjoy the views. At the end of the loop, retrace your steps back down the road to the closed gate.

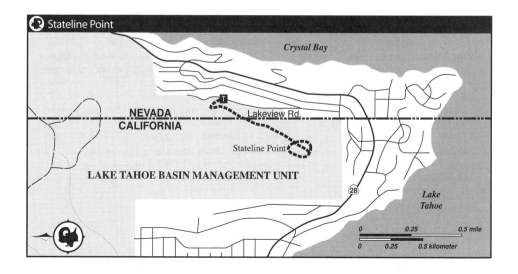

Lake Tahoe as seen from Stateline Point

48   TRT: Brockway Summit to Martis Peak

Distance	10.4 miles (out-and-back)
Hiking Time	5–7 hours
Elevation	+1,750/-100 feet
Difficulty	Moderate
Trail Use	Dogs OK, mountain biking OK
Best Times	July through October
Agency	Lake Tahoe Basin Management Unit at 530-543-2600, www.fs.usda.gov/ltbmu
Recommended Map	USGS 7.5-minute *Martis Peak* (trail not shown)

HIGHLIGHTS Supreme views of Lake Tahoe from the Martis Peak lookout are the chief goal of this trip. For less committed hikers, a viewpoint 1.5 miles from the trailhead offers a fine vista of the lake, although it's not nearly as impressive as the view from the lookout. The majority of the route is along a mostly forested section of the Tahoe Rim Trail (TRT), but the last three-quarters of a mile to the lookout shares the course with the paved Martis Peak Road, a byway passable to the average sedan.

DIRECTIONS Drive CA 267 between Truckee and Kings Beach to the turnoff for Forest Service Road 16N56 on the north side of the highway, 2.75 miles northwest of Kings Beach and a half mile southeast of Brockway Summit. The Tahoe Rim Trail parking area is a short distance up the road.

FACILITIES/TRAILHEAD There are no facilities at the trailhead. The trail begins near the trailhead signboard.

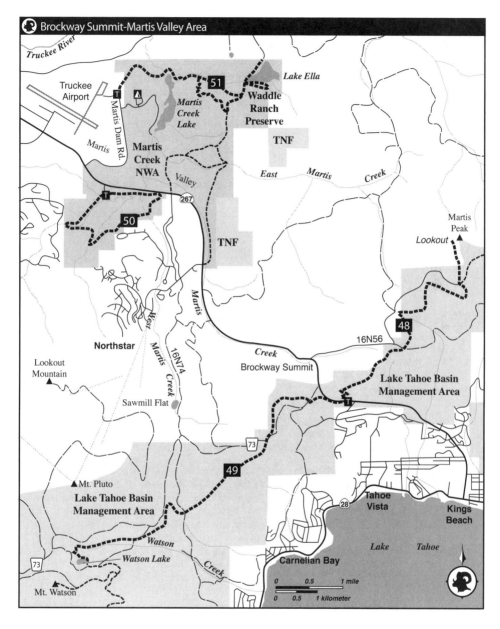

Brockway Summit-Martis Valley Area

ike away from the road on a moderate climb of a hillside covered with a light forest of Jeffrey pine and white fir. After a trio of switchbacks, the trail heads northeast to ascend the slopes below Peak 7766. The steady climb brings you to a junction, 1.2 miles from the trailhead, with a short lateral to the rocky summit of Peak 7766,

where you'll have good views of Lake Tahoe and some of the surrounding mountains.

Back on the main trail, the path descends a bit and then levels out across the top of a ridge. At 0.7 mile from the lateral, you cross gravel FS 16N33 and make a moderate climb through a selectively logged forest. Past the crossing of an old abandoned road, the grade eases and then follows a mild decline to a willow- and flower-lined rivulet.

A moderate climb through an extensive section of tobacco brush amid a light forest of red firs and lodgepole pines leads to an open hillside, carpeted in early summer with a bounty of mule-ears. Travel back into forest for a while before emerging onto an open, rocky, south-facing slope with superb views of Lake Tahoe and the mountains rimming the basin, including the Freel peak group above the southeast shore and the Crystal Range above the southwest shore. Arcing around the rocky slope, the trail returns to the trees momentarily before you

skirt another meadow covered with mule-ears. Reach a well-traveled dirt road farther on, 4.3 miles from the trailhead. The TRT continues along the road to the right for 0.3 mile before singletrack trail resumes.

Turn left (west) onto the road and proceed a short distance to a junction with FS 16N92B (Martis Peak Road). Turn right (north) and follow the paved road on a steady 0.7-mile climb toward the lookout. The restored lookout sits atop a windblown ridge below the actual summit of Martis Peak. At one time the structure was the last staffed fire lookout in the Tahoe basin. Nearby are picnic tables and an outhouse.

---

49 TRT: Brockway Summit to Watson Lake

see map on p. 129

Distance	13 miles (out-and-back)
Hiking Time	6.6–8 hours
Elevation	+1,450/-675 feet
Difficulty	Moderate
Trail Use	Backpacking option, dogs OK, mountain biking OK
Best Times	June through October
Agency	Tahoe National Forest at 530-587-3558, www.fs.usda.gov/ltbmu
Recommended Maps	USGS 7.5-minute *Martis Peak* and *Kings Beach* (trail not shown)

HIGHLIGHTS This section of the Tahoe Rim Trail (TRT) has only one decent view of Lake Tahoe, and the destination is easily reached by passenger cars. Despite these obvious drawbacks to getting away from it all, the 6.5-mile hike is a fine journey through the mostly forested terrain commonly found in the north Tahoe basin.

DIRECTIONS Take CA 267 between Truckee and Kings Beach to the small parking area on the south shoulder of the highway, 2.75 miles northwest of Kings Beach and a half mile southeast of Brockway Summit, where a small hiker emblem and TRT symbol are all that mark the trail.

FACILITIES/TRAILHEAD There are no facilities at the trailhead. The trail begins next to the parking area, down a closed road.

Begin your hike by following sandy tread that descends away from the highway through mixed forest and thick trailside foliage, soon passing a TRT signboard. Initially the road follows the highway, then singletrack trail veers away on a mild to moderate climb. At a half mile from the trailhead, you cross a road, and then follow a switchback up to a crossing of a prominent paved road, FS 73, also known locally

to mountain bikers as the Fiberboard Freeway. Locate the continuation of the trail on the far side of the road, and continue climbing through light fir forest and a more open area sprinkled with seasonal wildflowers on the way to the crossing of an old logging road, 1 mile from the trailhead. A half mile farther, you cross another old road and proceed on more gently graded trail for a while, before a short descent leads back to a second crossing of the Fiberboard Freeway at 1.9 miles.

From the road, continue a moderate, slightly winding descent along a shrubby path, headed south and then southwest. Near the 3-mile mark, you traverse an extensive field of mule-ears and follow a gently graded path across FS 16N77, and then across a seasonal stream near a pocket meadow filled with an extensive array of grasses and wildflowers. Away from the stream, the trail makes a rising ascent back over FS 16N77 and then across FS 16N74 a short distance farther. A more moderate climb ensues, which switchbacks up to the crest of a hill, 4.6 miles from the trailhead. Here you can leave the trail to make a short climb up some rocks to a wonderful view of Lake Tahoe.

A gentle descent leads to the crossing of FS 16N49. Mt. Watson appears through gaps in the mixed forest and across small clearings carpeted with mule-ears. After walking across another old logging road, the trail parallels willow-lined Watson Creek. Nearby, a meadow supplies splashes of early to midsummer color from a profusion of wildflowers that includes lupine, paintbrush, daisy, corn lily, monkey flower, aster, and columbine. Follow a moderate, curving climb until the grade eases where the trail merges with an old roadbed and reaches a three-way junction, 6 miles from the trailhead.

Bend left at the junction and head south across a flower-filled vale; then ascend a low hill covered with mountain hemlocks, white firs, and lodgepole pines. From the crest of the hill, Watson Lake comes into view. A short descent leads to the forested lakeshore and a junction with a path that circles the shallow lake. Watson Lake is the only natural lake in the north part of the Tahoe basin, making it a worthy goal for hikers and mountain bikers. Unfortunately, the lake is easily accessible by passenger car, diminishing the wilderness ambience. You could create a shuttle trip by leaving a second vehicle at the lake, and avoid retracing your steps the 6.5 miles back to CA 267.

The Tahoe Rim Trail passes by serene Watson Lake.

50 Martis Creek Wildlife Area

Distance	4 miles (loop)
Hiking Time	2–3 hours
Elevation	Negligible
Difficulty	Easy
Trail Use	Good for kids, leashed dogs
Best Times	May through October
Agency	U.S. Army Corps of Engineers at 530-587-8113, www.spk.usace.army.mil /Locations/SacramentoDistrictParks/MartisCreekLake.aspx
Recommended Maps	USGS 7.5-minute *Truckee* and *Martis Peak* (trail not shown)

see map on p. 129

HIGHLIGHTS In 1972, the Corps of Engineers dammed Martis Creek, creating Martis Creek Lake, a reservoir that at full capacity holds 20,400 acre-feet of water with a surface area of 770 acres. Across CA 267 to the south, in the open plain of Martis Valley adjacent to the Northstar California resort community, the Corps manages a wildlife area that has a fine network of trails suitable for hikers, joggers, dog walkers, and amateur biologists. With so many connecting paths, trail users can easily customize their trips. The trip described below is a 4-mile loop around the fringe of the wildlife area. Wildlife sightings may include mule deer, coyote, golden-mantled ground squirrel, pocket mouse, chipmunk, and raccoon. Birds common to the area include red-tailed hawk, killdeer, mountain quail, and the Canada goose.

DIRECTIONS Follow CA 267 to the turnoff for Martis Creek Wildlife Area, on the south side of the highway, 3.1 miles from I-80 near Truckee. Drive a short distance on a dirt road to the gravel parking area.

FACILITIES/TRAILHEAD The trailhead has a portable toilet, garbage can, picnic table, and plastic bags for picking up after your dog. Paths head east and southwest from the trailhead.

Start walking eastbound away from the trailhead parking area, along the toe of the slope that's below the highway and roughly parallel to Middle Martis Creek, enjoying the views across the verdant meadows south of the highway as you go. After 0.6 mile, cross Frank's Fish Bridge and continue eastward toward a junction near the Northstar California Golf Course, 0.9 mile from the parking area. The path straight ahead eventually circles around Porcupine Hill, but this route turns south and travels over Goomba's Crossing, a log-and-plank bridge that spans one of the creek's braided tributaries.

Beyond the bridge, the trail bisects a boggy section of meadow, where early in the season you may not be able to avoid getting your feet wet. A fine assortment of wildflowers provides a splash of color, including purple larkspur and yellow buttercups. Following a dry area of sagebrush, short, elevated bridges pass over a pair of tiny rivulets that course through the

meadow on the way to a third bridge over West Martis Creek.

Beyond the creek, the trail veers south through more sagebrush, passes below a set of power lines, and reaches a fence at the edge of the golf course, where signs indicate that the golf course is private property. For the next 250 yards, you walk through a 10-foot-wide passageway between a green, wood-rail fence to the left and a barbed-wire fence to the right. Follow the trail to a 90-degree bend to the south, and proceed to a three-way junction.

Turn right (west) at the junction and cross Ron's Webb Bridge. The path wanders through alternating pockets of meadow and sagebrush toward a light forest of Jeffrey pines, white firs, and lodgepole pines. Wind around to Michael Cousin's Bridge and along the fringe of the forest to Squeak's Bridge and a three-way junction with a path headed into one of Northstar's subdivisions. Proceed straight ahead at the junction and continue a very short distance to a second junction. From there, proceed

Martis Creek Lake with Northstar ski resort in the background

straight ahead on a shrub-lined course through light forest on mildly descending trail. At the bottom of the descent, 0.3 mile from the previous junction, is yet another junction. Veer southwest and briefly follow an unnamed creek to Jakes Bridge and a T-junction on the opposite bank, 2.6 miles from the trailhead.

Follow the creekside trail downstream, eventually merging with the course of an old road that leads out of the trees and onto the open plain of Martis Valley. Head west on the old road until the trail curves northwest to the crossing of the main branch of willow-lined Martis Creek at Pappe's Bridge.

Just past the bridge is an indistinct junction that provides two choices for the return to the parking area. The left-hand trail crosses a meadow, climbs a pine-dotted hill, and then follows a gravel road along a low rise back to the parking area access road. The right-hand trail, perhaps the more scenic route, follows Martis Creek 0.8 mile back to the parking area.

51   Martis Creek Lake–Waddell Ranch

Distance	7 miles (semiloop)
Hiking Time	2.5–3 hours
Elevation	+600/-600 feet
Difficulty	Moderate
Trail Use	Leashed dogs OK, mountain biking OK
Best Times	May through October

see map on p. 129

Agency   U.S. Army Corps of Engineers at 530-587-8113, www.spk.usace.army.mil
/Locations/SacramentoDistrictParks/MartisCreekLake.aspx;
Truckee Donner Land Trust at 530-582-4711, tdlandtrust.org
Recommended Maps   TDLT Martis Valley Trails

HIGHLIGHTS Once past a rather mundane, mile-plus walk along a paved road to and then across Martis Dam, the route to the Waddle Ranch Preserve becomes a pleasant hike through serene forest to Ella Lake. The seasonal lake is a wildlife sanctuary for a host of birds and mammals, especially pleasant in early season when water is typically most abundant and wildflowers adorn the shore. Originally slated for development, the nearly 1,500-acre tract was acquired through the efforts of the Truckee Donner Land Trust and the Trust for Public Land in 2007 for 23.5 million dollars. Nowadays, recreationists can enjoy the area via a fine network of trails.

DIRECTONS From CA 267 in Martis Valley, turn northeast onto Martis Dam Road and continue to the small trailhead parking area near the intersection of Glider Port Road.

FACILITIES/TRAILHEAD The trailhead has a portable toilet. The trail follows the extension of Martis Dam Road.

Continue on the paved road away from the trailhead, crossing a bridge over a spillway and passing by a side road on the way toward the dam. Cross the top of the dam to the far side, 1.2 miles from the trailhead.

Follow dirt tread away from the dam and into the canyon of a tributary of Martis Creek. At a three-way junction, follow signed directions toward Waddle Ranch Preserve. Soon the trail bends around and crosses the lushly lined stream and comes to another junction with a path descending to the shoreline. Head uphill through light forest on a moderate climb up the canyon into the lands of the Waddle Ranch Preserve. Reach a signed three-way junction with Erika's Trail on the right, which leads to a scenic overlook, 2 miles from the trailhead.

Continue ahead on Matt's Trail, passing through a quiet stretch of forest on a half-mile ascent up the course of an old roadbed. Eventually the grade eases, as you reach a junction with Sawmill Road at 2.5 miles. Nearby attached to a large boulder is a memorial plaque.

Turn left onto the road and head north on gently graded Sawmill Road for 0.3 mile to the southwest shore of seasonal Lake Ella. Immediately before the lake, the road splits; the road ahead is named Megan's Trail and follows the northwest shore to

the edge of private property. The right-hand road heads east well above the south shore to a junction with Katy's Walk and continues to the end of the preserve near a seasonal inlet.

Dry Lake was renamed Lake Ella in the 1960s for the wife of the property owner at the time. The water level fluctuates from season to season and year to year, but it is an important home for numerous birds and mammals, many of which are mentioned on a sign near the southwest shore. Picnic tables along the shoreline offer pleasant spots from which to sit and enjoy the surroundings. Nearby, you can follow Katy's Walk through the forest fringe above the south shore to where it merges with a dirt road and then follow the road back to Sawmill Road.

From the southwest shore of Lake Ella, retrace your steps on Sawmill Road 0.3 mile to the junction with Matt's Trail. Rather than simply retracing your steps back to the trailhead, continue ahead on Sawmill Road for 0.25 mile to Beacon Meadow and a junction with Erika's Trail on the right. Nearby is another picnic table and a dedication plaque for the preserve on a large boulder.

Leaving Sawmill Road, you head northwest on Erika's Trail on a moderately rising, somewhat winding climb. Pass a picnic table after a while and then follow the edge of a forested rise to a viewpoint and another picnic table, where a piece of Martis Valley and the hills beyond are visible. Away from the viewpoint, the trail snakes down the hillside to a junction with Matt's Trail. From there, retrace your steps 2 miles to the parking area.

52 Burton Creek State Park

Distance	6.5 miles (loop)
Hiking Time	3–5 hours
Elevation	+675/-675 feet
Difficulty	Moderate
Trail Use	Dogs OK, mountain biking OK
Best Times	Mid-May through October
Agency	Burton Creek State Park at 530-525-7232, parks.ca.gov
Recommended Maps	USGS 7.5-minute *Kings Beach* and *Tahoe City, CSP Burton Creek State Park* brochure map

HIGHLIGHTS A pleasant forest walk with minimal elevation gain in Burton Creek State Park, this delightful morning or afternoon excursion should be a crowd pleaser. But there's no prominent signage, so the slightly obscure locale remains relatively undiscovered, promising an uncrowded and serene hiking experience. Numerous side trails come and go along this route, providing an array of options for trip extensions and alternate starting points. Make sure you pack the *CSP Burton Creek State Park*

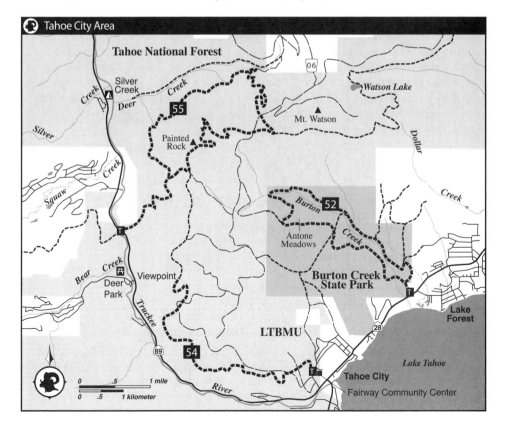

brochure map, as the intersecting trails and roads can be quite confusing at times. You can download it from the park web page; just click on "Brochures."

DIRECTIONS The unsigned trailhead is a bit difficult to locate: From the junction of CA 28 and CA 89 in Tahoe City, travel 1.7 miles northwest on CA 28; make a left turn onto a paved road on the west side of the Tamarack Lodge property. Continue a short distance to a wood-chip parking area on the left.

FACILITIES/TRAILHEAD There are no facilities at the trailhead. The trip begins up the road, past a sign reading ENTERING STATE PARK PROPERTY.

Walk up the road to a steel gate and turn to your right; soon you reach a Y-junction with gated roads to the right and left. Take the right-hand fork and continue up a moderately steep and rocky road through mixed forest. At a half mile from the trailhead, a lesser road veers right to North Tahoe High School. Stay on the main road to the left and continue the climb, as you eventually draw nearer to lushly lined Burton Creek. Cross over a side stream and continue to a junction near the 2-mile mark, where a number of different paths converge. (The main road curves left here, providing a shorter, 4.5-mile loop option.)

From the junction, proceed straight ahead on singletrack trail that follows a nearly level course past a pocket of shrubs and grasses lining Burton Creek. A half mile from the previous junction, you reach another junction with a trail on the right and, veering left, continue another 0.2 mile to a substantial wood-plank bridge spanning a rivulet. Follow the trail as it arcs around Antone Meadows, carpeted with willows, alders, and tall grasses, to a bridge over Burton Creek, 3 miles from the trailhead.

On the far side of the bridge, a path angles away from the main trail to follow the creek upstream. However, you stick to the main trail, which curves around the edge of the meadows and into the forest on a mild to moderate ascent. Through the trees, you have periodic glimpses of forested Mt. Watson to the north. Eventually, the trail starts its descent toward the trailhead, at 4.5 miles passing a shortcut back to the return route. Over the next 1.5 miles, you should ignore a few lesser roads that intersect the obvious main road on the way to a bridge across Burton Creek. From the bridge, the trail soon reaches the conclusion of the loop at the first Y-junction. From there, retrace your steps back to the parking area.

53 Western States Trail: CA 89 to Watson Monument

Distance	14 miles (out-and-back)
Hiking Time	7–9 hours
Elevation	+2,900/-375 feet
Difficulty	Difficult
Trail Use	Dogs OK, mountain biking OK
Best Times	Mid-July through mid-October
Agency	Tahoe National Forest at 530-587-3558, www.fs.usda.gov/tahoe
Recommended Maps	USGS 7.5-minute *Tahoe City* and *Granite Chief*

HIGHLIGHTS The Western States Trail was one of three principal routes used by emigrants across the Tahoe Sierra (along with the Pony Express and Donner Pass routes). The most direct of the three, it certainly was not the easiest, gaining 18,000 feet and losing 23,000 feet on a typically narrow track impassable to wagons. At one time, the route connected Salt Lake City to Sacramento, but only sections of the route still exist today.

Few modern-day travelers seem to accept the challenge of this section of the trail, from CA 89 to the ridgecrest between Squaw Peak and Granite Chief, so those who do take it on can expect to have the trail mostly to themselves. The 7-mile, moderate climb travels through forest before crossing the mostly open terrain surrounding Squaw Valley Resort. The ski lifts, maintenance roads, and structures associated with the resort might diminish the backcountry ambience for most hikers, but the midsummer wildflower displays and sweeping views should more than compensate for the intrusion of civilization. With a shuttle, hikers can avoid most of the backtracking by descending via the cable car from High Camp to the parking lot at Squaw Valley. With enough greenbacks, the utterly decadent could relax in the pool or grab a cocktail or a meal at High Camp before the descent.

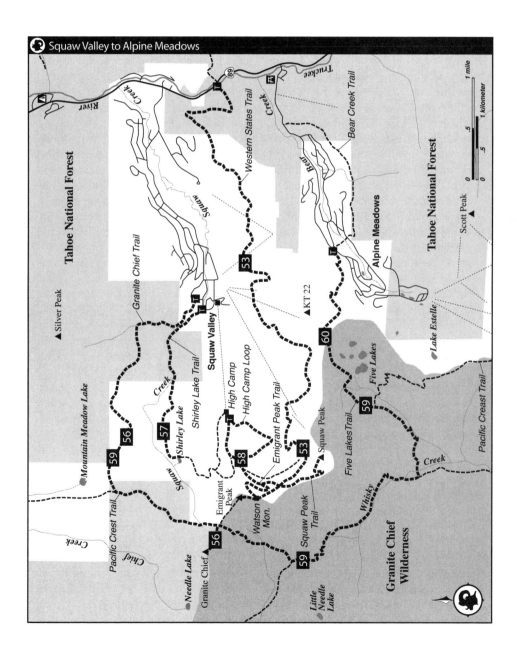

DIRECTIONS On CA 89, 0.7 mile south of the turnoff for Squaw Valley and 0.7 mile north of the turnoff for Alpine Meadows, look for the signed Western States Trail on the west shoulder of the highway near the north side of a highway bridge over the Truckee River. Parking is available on the gravel shoulder.

FACILITIES/TRAILHEAD There are no facilities at the trailhead. The westbound trail begins near the north side of the highway bridge over the Truckee River.

Angle up the hillside to a switchback, and climb into pine and fir forest where clearings are carpeted with yellow mule-ears in early summer. Proceed straight ahead on singletrack trail at each of the following junctions: with an old road branching left, a trail angling from behind on the right, and another trail splitting off to the left. Farther on, in a large clearing 0.4 mile from the trailhead, you encounter yet another junction—this time turn right and proceed a short way to a pair of switchbacks. Beyond the switchbacks, the trail turns north and continues a steady climb, passing an old road on the left before the grade moderates. Swing around the nose of the ridge that divides the Bear Creek and Squaw Creek drainages and proceed to a crest, where a set of signs provides directions and warnings about entering private property, 0.8 mile from the trailhead.

Now headed generally southwest, follow a couple of switchbacks as the trail proceeds along the north side of the ridge. Occasional gaps in the trees allow brief glimpses of Squaw Valley and Squaw Peak. Cross an old logging road and continue to a signed Y-junction, where another road veers left and the trail angles slightly downhill to the right.

A mildly undulating traverse leads across ski slope clearings, where a fine array of wildflowers provides vibrant color through midsummer. Near a chairlift, the trail intersects a road and follows it uphill very briefly to the resumption of singletrack trail. Step across a shrub- and wildflower-lined rivulet and enter light forest on the way to a Y-junction with a road, where you turn downhill and follow the road to meet a well-used trail. Wrap around the hillside and contour south into a side canyon, to a union with a well-traveled ski resort maintenance road, 3 miles from the trailhead.

Climb to a Y-junction in the road and follow the bend to the right, to arc around the bottom of the Olympic Lady chairlift. Singletrack trail resumes after a very brief, downstream stint along the road, as you angle up the hillside on a moderate ascent above the descending road. Climbing through shrub-covered terrain dotted with conifers, you pass below more chairlifts and some cliffs, generally following the course of a canyon containing an unnamed tributary of Squaw Creek. Beyond a pair of seeps, the trail starts to switchback up the open slope through pockets of wildflowers and widely scattered trees, which now include mountain hemlocks.

You climb across the head of the canyon to the northeast slopes of Squaw Peak, which become more and more rocky with the gain in altitude. Signs and roadside markers should help guide you toward Watson Monument, as higher up the mountain the route follows alternating stretches of road and trail. Switchbacks lead below the northeast ridge of Squaw Peak to an X-junction near the 6-mile mark.

Here you have the choice of following the uphill road on the left to the summit of Squaw Peak, or the uphill road on the right, to continue on the Western States Trail to Watson Monument. To reach the monument, begin a long upward traverse on rocky trail below the ridge to a set of short switchbacks. Then cross the road (which is the designated Siberia Ridge hiking route) to the top of Squaw Peak, and continue the climb to the ridgecrest and the Watson Monument, and a fine view.

54 TRT: Tahoe City to Truckee River Canyon Viewpoint

Distance	11.4 miles (out-and-back)
Hiking Time	4–6 hours
Elevation	+1,350/-50 feet
Difficulty	Moderate
Trail Use	Dogs OK, mountain biking OK
Best Times	June through October
Agency	Lake Tahoe Basin Management Unit at 530-543-2600, www.fs.usda.gov/ltbmu
Recommended Map	USGS 7.5-minute *Tahoe City* (trail not shown)

see map on p. 135

HIGHLIGHTS A sometimes-stiff climb leads away from Tahoe City to excellent views of the Lake Tahoe Basin from a volcanic knob and the Truckee River canyon from the Cinder Cone viewpoint. Along the way, you'll cross several old logging roads, evidence of the extensive logging that once took place here. The logging roads are frequently used by mountain bikers, so be prepared for possible encounters.

DIRECTIONS From the junction of CA 28 and CA 89 in Tahoe City, proceed northbound on CA 89 for 0.1 mile and turn right onto Fairway Drive. Travel a quarter mile to the Fairway Community Center and park in the parking lot.

FACILITIES/TRAILHEAD There are no facilities at the trailhead. This segment of the Tahoe Rim Trail (TRT) begins across the road from the community center.

Climb steeply away from the trailhead, as a few short switchbacks lead up the slope amid manzanita and bitterbrush, beneath a scattered to light forest of incense cedars, white firs, sugar pines, and Jeffrey pines. Thankfully, the steep climb abates soon after this section of short switchbacks and continues at a more moderate grade. Here, Lake Tahoe makes a brief appearance through the trees. After a while the trail

A fine view of Lake Tahoe from a vista point on the Tahoe Rim Trail

switchbacks, ascends to the crossing of an old logging road, and then continues to a crossing of FS 73, 0.3 mile from the trailhead. This road is referred to as the Fiberboard Freeway by locals, so named for the former major landowner in the area.

The TRT continues climbing moderately through mixed forest until you reach the edge of the rim of the Truckee River Canyon above Twin Crags, about a mile from the trailhead. Here fine views open up of Lake Tahoe and the Granlibakken ski runs across the canyon. Eventually, the trail leaves the views behind, entering the forest again on an ascent over a low rise. Recent logging activity has created some unsightly areas along this stretch, but they're quickly forgotten where you come back along the edge of the canyon above Thunder Cliff. Excellent views of the Truckee River accompany this romp along the top of the cliff for the next half mile.

The trail veers away from the canyon edge and heads back into fir forest on a moderate, occasionally switchbacking climb. A mile or so from Thunder Cliff, the TRT traverses around the west slope of the volcanic Cinder Cone, where a grand view of the Truckee River canyon unfolds, including Alpine Meadows, as well as a part of Lake Tahoe and Twin Peaks, a more than suitable reward for the 5-plus-mile climb. A short walk farther reveals a second vista point, where a piece of Squaw Valley joins the Alpine Meadows view. Plenty of rocks at both locations offer excellent perches to sit upon and enjoy the views. After thoroughly enjoying the surroundings, retrace your steps 5.7 miles to the trailhead.

55 Western States Trail: Painted Rock Loop

see map on p. 135

Distance	11 miles (semiloop)
Hiking Time	5–6 hours
Elevation	+2,500/-2,500 feet
Difficulty	Moderate
Trail Use	Dogs OK, mountain biking OK
Best Times	July through October
Agency	Tahoe National Forest at 530-587-3558, www.fs.usda.gov/tahoe
Recommended Map	USGS 7.5-minute *Tahoe City*

HIGHLIGHTS By combining a part of the Western States Trail eastbound from CA 89, a section of the Tahoe Rim Trail (TRT), and old logging roads, hikers can follow a mostly forested route on a partial loop with a fine view from vista points atop Painted Rock. Although generally well marked, the route uses several trail and road segments, which requires trail users to exercise some route-finding skill. Much of the Tahoe National Forest at this end of the lake is prime mountain-biking country, and these trails and roads are no exception, so be alert.

DIRECTIONS On CA 89, 0.7 mile south of the turnoff for Squaw Valley and 0.7 mile north of the turnoff for Alpine Meadows, look for the signed Western States Trail on the west shoulder of the highway, near the north side of a highway bridge over the Truckee River. Parking is available on the gravel shoulder.

FACILITIES/TRAILHEAD There are no facilities at the trailhead. The eastbound trail begins near the north side of the highway bridge over the Truckee River.

Squaw Valley from the Western States Trail

Carefully cross CA 89 from the parking area, and head past trailhead signs on the east side of the road onto singletrack trail into a mixed forest of Jeffrey pines, white firs, and lodgepole pines. A weaving ascent leads to the crossing of a dirt road and the beginning of some switchbacks that zigzag up the hillside. Cross a twin-branched, tiny stream lined with cow parsnip, monkey flower, columbine, and thimbleberry on a pair of wood-beam bridges; continue a short distance to a thin, shallow rivulet spilling across the trail. Away from these freshets, the winding climb up the forested slope continues to a junction with an old logging road marked by an American Discovery Trail marker.

Turn left (north) and follow the road around a grassy meadow on the right, and then climb to a three-way junction. Turn left (north) and ascend past an alder-rimmed meadow to a crossing of a road marked 62842 and continue a short distance to a T-intersection at 1.5 miles from the trailhead (the right-hand road will be your return route).

Veer left (north) and head downhill briefly as you pass above a shrub-filled drainage, before the road starts on an undulating course to the northwest and then north to a tight Y-junction, where a less-used road veers uphill. Remaining on the better-traveled route to the left, you begin a gradual descent through previously logged forest before breaking out into the open across a shrub-covered slope filled with chinquapin and pinemat and greenleaf manzanita. A short climb of a hill leads to a newer section of singletrack trail marked by a trail adoption sign, 2 miles from the trailhead.

Descend off the hill via a couple of switchbacks and then begin a general traverse through thick forest across the south side of Deer Creek canyon, stepping across a number of lushly lined freshets along the way. After a mile, the trail merges with the road again and proceeds through open forest with good views of the surrounding terrain, soon passing a lesser road angling downhill to the left. Make a moderate climb through thick forest again, across a piped stream to a steel barricade erected to block motor vehicles from the section of road you were just on.

Continue climbing along the road to the crest of a hill, and then descend toward the bottom of Deer Creek canyon. Reach a junction with a section of newly constructed singletrack trail angling uphill to the right, which is marked as a connector to the Tahoe Rim Trail, 4.5 miles from the trailhead.

Leave the road and follow the connector trail on a switchbacking climb of a mostly open, sunny slope carpeted with patches of pinemat manzanita. Higher up the slope, cross an open ridge dotted with shrubs and large boulders before continuing a winding ascent in light forest. Pass below some power lines and then traverse a saddle past low rock outcrops. This area offers good views across the Truckee River canyon, with Silver Peak above and Castle Peak in the distance. Pass below the power lines again on the way to a paved road near a junction with a dirt road to the right.

Head down the dirt road that angles away from the paved road marked TAHOE RIM TRAIL. Follow the dirt road around a hairpin turn, beneath some more power lines, and around a big, sweeping bend to a signed crossing of the Tahoe Rim Trail.

Leave the road and head right (west) onto the TRT at the TAHOE CITY 8 sign and make a winding climb followed by a rising traverse across a lightly forested hillside consisting mainly of white firs. Gain the crest of the ridge and angle sharply toward the top of Painted Rock, where a short lateral leads to a viewpoint with a fine vista across the Truckee River canyon of the Sierra crest.

Gently graded trail leads away from the viewpoint, across Painted Rock to the edge of a bluff, from where you have a partial lake view to the southwest. A moderate, winding descent heads downslope from Painted Rock to a short side trail, which leads to a dirt road near a metal barricade that's lying on the ground next to a pair of posts. Turn right and descend along this dirt road, which starts with views of the Squaw Valley area that are eventually obscured by thickening forest. Reach the close of the loop at the T-junction you first arrived at, 1.5 miles from the trailhead. From there, retrace your steps to the trailhead.

---

56 Granite Chief Trail to Granite Chief

Distance	11.6 miles (out-and-back)
Hiking Time	4.5–6 hours
Elevation	+2,850/-100 feet
Difficulty	Very difficult
Trail Use	Dogs OK
Best Times	Mid-July through mid-October
Agency	Tahoe National Forest at 530-587-3558, www.fs.usda.gov/tahoe
Recommended Maps	USGS 7.5-minute *Tahoe City* and *Granite Chief*

see map on p. 137

HIGHLIGHTS If you don't mind the effort of a 5.8-mile climb and an elevation gain of nearly 3,000 feet, this route offers bountiful rewards, no matter how discriminating you are. Views are plentiful, not only from the airy summit of Granite Chief but also from various points along the Granite Chief and Pacific Crest Trails as well. From early to midseason, you'll have the added treat of a fine assortment of wildflowers and dancing streams along the way. If your goal is mainly to summit Granite Chief, you can shorten the trip by taking the $39 aerial tram ride from Squaw Valley to High Camp (see Trip 58).

DIRECTIONS From CA 89, approximately 8.5 miles south of Truckee and 5 miles north of Tahoe City, turn west onto Squaw Valley Road and proceed toward Squaw Valley. Rather than following the main road as it bends sharply left toward the center of the village, veer right, proceed to the large north parking lot, and park near the fire station.

FACILITIES/TRAILHEAD Although there are no facilities at the trailhead, the trip begins in the resort community of Squaw Valley, where a wide array of upscale amenities is available. To begin the hike on the Granite Chief Trail, park your vehicle in the spacious north parking lot and walk to the trailhead near the Olympic Village Inn.

The start of the trail is not marked. Across from Olympic Village Inn, look for a dirt road near the adventure course and follow it uphill a short distance to the crossing of the singletrack tread of the Granite Chief Trail. Turn left (northwest) onto the trail and make a moderate ascent up the forested hillside, which has an understory of thimbleberry and bracken fern. Several paths intersect your trail, but the main course should be obvious if you keep climbing, as a trail crew rerouted the path out of some sensitive drainage areas and made the correct route more defined in 2014. The trail bears generally northwest for one-third of a mile before drawing near to gurgling Squaw Creek.

Soon the trail turns north to follow one of Squaw Creek's tributaries upslope, where periodic gaps in the forest allow improving views of the Squaw Valley area. After a steady half-mile climb, you cross the tributary stream, switchback a couple of times, and follow the trail on a westerly climb across the north wall of Squaw Creek canyon. Passing through alternating pockets of mixed forest and clearing, a number of seeps and springs are crossed along this traverse, and open slopes are graced with a fine display of wildflowers through midsummer.

Farther up the canyon wall, the terrain is composed of granite benches and cliffs, interspersed with thick shrubs and an occasional conifer. Here the views of Squaw Valley below and the complex of High Camp to the south are quite impressive. Eventually a sliver of Lake Tahoe joins the splendid vista.

Approaching Granite Chief along the PCT

The trail bends northwest and climbs into a hanging side canyon blessed with a few small, flower-filled meadows; at this point you head back into forest cover and bid farewell to the fine views. A series of switchbacks leads to a signed Y-junction with the Pacific Crest Trail (PCT), 3.8 miles from the trailhead.

Turn left (south) and follow the PCT briefly through the trees, across a sloping meadow, and then on a switchbacking climb below the northeast ridge of Granite Chief. Continue on sandy tread through scattered, mixed forest to a small meadow near the headwaters of Squaw Creek. Hop across the creek, and continue the winding climb across a boulder-studded slope. You'll go past rugged cliffs and beneath a chairlift, to the crest of Granite Chief's southwest ridge. A short descent from the crest leads to a junction, 5.4 miles from the trailhead, just before the signed Granite Chief Wilderness boundary. The seldom-used path on your left ascends southeast along the ridge toward Emigrant Pass and Watson Monument. (After the climb to Granite Chief, you could shorten the return trip by following this route across the crest and down to High Camp, where the aerial tram descends back to Squaw Valley.)

Peak baggers can make a straightforward ascent of Granite Chief by leaving the PCT at the junction and turning right (northwest) to follow a use trail along the west ridge that leads toward the summit. After 0.4 mile, you arrive at the 9,006-foot summit and a wonderful view.

57 Shirley Lake

see map on p. 137

Distance	4 miles (out-and-back)
Hiking Time	2–3 hours
Elevation	+1,325 feet
Difficulty	Moderate
Trail Use	Dogs OK, good for kids
Best Times	July through October
Agency	Tahoe National Forest at 530-587-3558, www.fs.usda.gov/tahoe; Squaw Valley Resort at 530-583-6985, squawalpine.com/homepage?season=summer
Recommended Map	USGS 7.5-minute *Tahoe City* and *Granite Chief* (trail not shown)

HIGHLIGHTS Although the tread of the Shirley Lake Trail evolved from the repeated boot prints of hikers rather than planned design and construction, the informal path that follows alongside Squaw Creek for much of the distance is a delightful route for young and old alike. Families with young children will find plenty of enjoyment frolicking in the creek or picnicking along the banks, even without traveling all the way to the lake. Big people who successfully manage the moderate climb to Shirley Lake will appreciate the pastoral surroundings. With the extra effort of a steep 1.5-mile climb from the lake, hikers can enjoy the pleasures of High Camp before returning to Squaw Valley via a ride on the cable car.

DIRECTIONS From CA 89, about 8.5 miles south of Truckee or 5 miles north of Tahoe City, head west on Squaw Valley Road for 2.25 miles into the center of Squaw Valley. Turn right on Squaw Peak Road and continue to the lower intersection with Squaw Peak Way; park on the wide shoulder. (Parking is not available at the Shirley Lake Trailhead, near the upper intersection between Squaw Peak Road and Squaw Peak Way.) If you opt for the cable-car route for the return, you will have to make the short walk from the cable-car building to your car.

FACILITIES/TRAILHEAD Although there are no facilities at the trailhead, the trail begins in the resort community of Squaw Valley, where a wide array of upscale amenities is available.

Shirley Lake

From the parking area, follow a short dirt path that leads to the actual trailhead near the upper intersection of Squaw Peak Road and Squaw Peak Way. Pick up the path again along the left-hand bank of Squaw Creek, which is sheltered by red firs and lodgepole and Jeffrey pines. Lacking a single designated route, multiple paths follow a moderately steep course upstream, past shrubs and around boulders. Entering a shady forest, thimbleberry and bracken fern carpet the canyon floor, while the tumbling creek drops over short rock steps and into picturesque pools.

Leave the forest cover to climb steeply over boulders and slabs, where blue paint marks help to keep you on the route. After hopping across a side stream, you reenter mixed forest as western white pines join the mix of conifers. Continue the stiff climb alongside the creek, which is lined with lush vegetation and wildflowers in season. The grade temporarily abates as you reach the top of an open bench and enjoy a limited view of the surroundings before returning to a climb through the trees. Eventually the trail veers away from Squaw Creek and leads to a log crossing of an alder-lined tributary stream, 1.25 miles from the trailhead.

Beyond the stream crossing, you climb over an extensive area of granite slabs and boulders with intermittent stretches of dirt trail. The open terrain allows views of the canyon and Squaw Valley below, as well as the supports and cables for the passing cable cars on your left. The grade eases a bit above the slabs, and you follow a mild ascent through scattered forest and around granite humps. A short descent then leads to the shoreline of diminutive, shallow Shirley Lake, 2.2 miles from the trailhead. Lodgepole pines and mountain hemlocks on the near shore and meadows and shrubs on the far shore rim the lake. An area of granite cliffs lends an alpine ambience to the lake.

The tram option from High Camp lets hikers avoid retracing their steps back to the trailhead. While taking the cable car will save a couple of miles of backtracking, you'll have to make the steep but short climb from Shirley Lake to High Camp. However, riding the cable car from High Camp down to Squaw Valley for free may be possible, since in previous years paid tickets were collected only at the lower terminal. (However, be prepared to cough up the $10 fee just in case.)

To reach High Camp, head south from the lake and make a steep climb, via switchbacks beneath a chairlift and across wildflower-carpeted slopes, to Shirley Lake Road. Proceed along this road past the junction of the Solitude Trail, 2.8 miles into your trip. Continue on a steep climb that zigzags underneath the Shirley Lake Express chairlift for 0.4 mile, to a signed junction with the High Camp Loop Trail. From there, walk the north side of the loop trail 0.3 mile to High Camp. See Trip 56 for more information on hikes around High Camp.

58 Squaw Valley High Camp Trails

HIGHLIGHTS For those who don't mind coughing up $39 per person for the cable-car ride to High Camp, Squaw Valley's upper resort at 8,200 feet, a number of trails beckon the casual hiker to walk the wide, well-graded maintenance roads of Squaw Valley Resort to a variety of destinations. The trails vary from an easy, 1-mile loop around flower-filled meadows to more rigorous walks to peak tops with extraordinary views of the north Tahoe countryside. The routes starting from High Camp are well signed at every junction, providing directions and mileages that make getting lost virtually impossible. The resort offers an extensive array of amenities for getting the most out of the experience.

DIRECTIONS From CA 89, about 8.5 miles south of Truckee or 5 miles north of Tahoe City, head west on Squaw Valley Road for 2.25 miles into the center of Squaw Valley, and park in the large parking lot.

FACILITIES/TRAILHEAD All trips begin in the resort community of Squaw Valley, where a wide array of upscale amenities is available. From the parking lot, walk to the cable-car terminal, purchase tickets, and proceed to the boarding area. The cable-car ride to High Camp features floor-to-ceiling panoramic views on a 2,000-foot, view-packed climb. At the top, travelers can avail themselves of the many amenities available at High Camp, including swimming or soaking in the Swimming Lagoon and Spa, ice skating at the Olympic Ice Pavilion, enjoying a meal or beverage at one of the three cafés, or reviewing Olympic glory at the Olympic Museum. Those who prefer a guided trip can choose from weekend hikes, nature hikes, sunset hikes, and full-moon hikes. For more information visit the website at squawalpine.com.

High Camp Loop

Distance	1.2 miles (loop)
Hiking Time	30 minutes–1 hour
Elevation	+175/-175 feet
Difficulty	Easy
Trail Use	Leashed dogs, good for kids
Best Times	July through mid-October
Agency	Squaw Valley Resort at 530-583-6985, squawalpine.com
Recommended Map	*Squaw Valley USA Hiking Trails*

see map on p. 137

The easiest and most popular trip from High Camp follows a mile-long loop around the sloping meadows directly above the facilities of High Camp Bath and Tennis Club. The route follows the wide, well-graded course of the maintenance roads that provide access to the ski area's lifts and equipment. From the cable-car terminal, follow the right-hand road on a counter-clockwise loop that rises gently and traverses open terrain. In early to midsummer, a profusion of wildflowers carpets the slopes, including yellow mule-ears, purple lupines, and bright red paintbrush. At 0.4 mile, you reach a junction with the route that descends toward Shirley Lake (see Trip 57).

Veer left at the junction and continue climbing along the High Camp Loop,

reaching another junction after 0.1 mile, with routes branching right to the top of Newport Chairlift and to the summits of Squaw and Emigrant Peaks.

Just beyond the second junction, you reach the high point of the loop and begin the mild descent back to High Camp, enjoying sweeping views of Squaw Peak immediately above and the northern Tahoe Sierra farther afield.

Squaw Peak

Distance	4.4 miles (out-and-back)
Hiking Time	2–4 hours
Elevation	+775 feet
Difficulty	Moderate to difficult
Trail Use	Leashed dogs
Best Times	Mid-July through mid-October
Agency	Squaw Valley Resort at 530-583-6985, squawalpine.com
Recommended Map	*Squaw Valley USA Hiking Trails*

see map on p. 137

Follow the High Camp Loop to the second junction, a half mile from High Camp, and turn right. Pass the Shirley Express Chairlift and make a moderate climb up the wide roadbed to another junction, where the Newport route heads left, and the route toward Squaw Peak and Emigrant Peak turns right; a short distance farther upslope the routes to the peaks separate. Here you veer left and ascend to the crest of Siberia Ridge, then follow a long, upward traverse along the ridge toward the summit. Nearing Squaw Peak, the route climbs across the west side of the peak before winding to the summit. You'll see outstanding views of the Lake Tahoe Basin to the southeast and the Granite Chief Wilderness to the west.

Emigrant Peak and Watson Monument

Distance	3.4 miles (out-and-back)
Hiking Time	2–3 hours
Elevation	+625 feet
Difficulty	Moderate
Trail Use	Leashed dogs
Best Times	Mid-July through mid-October
Agency	Squaw Valley Resort at 530-583-6985, squawalpine.com
Recommended Map	*Squaw Valley USA Hiking Trails*

see map on p. 137

Follow the High Camp Loop to the second junction, a half mile from High Camp, and turn right. Pass the Shirley Express Chairlift and make a moderate climb up the wide roadbed to another junction, where the Newport route heads left, and the route toward Squaw Peak and Emigrant Peak turns right; a short distance

View from Squaw Valley's High Camp

farther upslope, the routes to the peaks separate. Here you turn right and ascend toward the ridge above, switchbacking once before reaching the crest, where a faint path heads south a short distance to Watson Monument. The monument honors Robert M. Watson, who, among other accomplishments, in 1931 helped mark the route of the Western States Trail, from Auburn to Lake Tahoe. From the monument, the summit of Emigrant Peak is an easy 0.2-mile climb, where you'll have views nearly as impressive as those from Squaw Peak, 111 feet higher.

59   Squaw Valley to Alpine Meadows

see map on p. 137

Distance	10.5 miles (point-to-point, shuttle)
Hiking Time	5.5–7 hours
Elevation	+2,925/-2,625 feet
Difficulty	Difficult
Trail Use	Backpacking option
Best Times	Mid-July through mid-October
Agency	Tahoe National Forest at 530-587-3558, www.fs.usda.gov/tahoe
Recommended Maps	USGS 7.5-minute *Tahoe City* and *Granite Chief*

HIGHLIGHTS Starting near one major Tahoe ski resort and ending near another, hikers along this trip will experience some beautiful scenery and perhaps a healthy dose of solitude. Away from the resorts and the extremely popular Five Lakes Basin, the middle section of this route sees limited foot traffic, despite the close proximity to population centers and the easy access. With only a 6-mile car shuttle between trailheads, avoiding the backtracking of the typical out-and-back trip is fairly pain-less. Pleasant campsites near the headwaters of Middle Fork American River and along Whisky Creek make this trip well suited for a weekend backpack; several trip extensions are also possible.

DIRECTIONS *Start:* From CA 89, approximately 8.5 miles south of Truckee and 5 miles north of Tahoe City, turn west onto Squaw Valley Road and proceed toward Squaw Valley. Rather than following the main road as it bends sharply left toward the center of the village, veer right, proceed to the large north parking lot, and park near the fire station.

    End: From CA 89, approximately 9.5 miles south of Truckee or 4 miles north of Tahoe City, turn onto Alpine Meadows Road and proceed for 2.1 miles to the well-signed Five Lakes Trailhead, on the right-hand shoulder. Park on the shoulder as space allows.

FACILITIES/TRAILHEAD There are no facilities at either trailhead, although the trip begins in the resort community of Squaw Valley, where a wide array of upscale amenities is available. To begin the hike on the Granite Chief Trail, park your vehicle in the spacious north parking lot and walk to the trailhead near the Olympic Village Inn. You can drastically shorten the trip to Granite Chief by purchasing a $39 ticket and riding the tram from the valley to High Camp (see Trip 58).

The start of the trail is not marked. Across from Olympic Village Inn, look for a dirt road near the adventure course and follow it uphill a short distance to the crossing of the singletrack tread of the Granite Chief Trail. Turn left (northwest) onto the trail and make a moderate ascent up the forested hillside, which has an understory of thimbleberry and bracken fern. Several paths intersect your trail, but the main course should be obvious if you keep climbing, as a trail crew rerouted the path out of some sensitive drainage areas and made the correct route more defined in 2014. The trail bears generally northwest for one-third of a mile before drawing near to gurgling Squaw Creek.

Soon the trail turns north to follow one of Squaw Creek's tributaries upslope, where periodic gaps in the forest allow improving views of the Squaw Valley area. After a steady half-mile climb, you cross the tributary stream, switchback a couple of times, and follow the trail on a westerly climb across the north wall of Squaw Creek canyon. Passing through alternating pockets of mixed forest and clearing, a number of seeps and springs are crossed along this traverse, and open slopes are graced with a fine display of wildflowers through midsummer.

Farther up the canyon wall, the terrain is composed of granite benches and cliffs interspersed with thick shrubs and an occasional conifer. Here the views of Squaw Valley below and the complex of High Camp to the south are quite impressive. Eventually a piece of Lake Tahoe joins the splendid vista.

The trail bends northwest and climbs into a hanging side canyon blessed with a few small, flower-filled meadows; at this point you head back into forest cover and bid farewell to the fine views. A series of switchbacks leads to a signed Y-junction with the Pacific Crest Trail (PCT), 3.8 miles from the trailhead.

Turn left (south) and follow the PCT briefly through the trees, across a sloping meadow, and then on a switchbacking climb below the northeast ridge of Granite Chief. Continue on sandy tread through scattered, mixed forest to a small meadow near the headwaters of Squaw Creek. Hop across the creek and continue the winding climb across a boulder-studded slope. You'll go past rugged cliffs and beneath a chairlift, to the crest of Granite Chief's southwest ridge. A short descent from the crest leads to a junction, 5.4 miles from the trailhead, just before the signed Granite Chief Wilderness boundary. The seldom-used path on your left ascends southeast along the ridge toward Emigrant Pass and Watson Monument.

From the junction, the PCT descends past a seasonal rivulet and soon arrives at a more pronounced junction, this one with the Western States Trail, which heads east to Emigrant Pass and west to a junction with the Tevis Cup Trail. On descending trail, you switchback down an open slope to the crossing of the headwaters of Middle Fork American River, where overnighters will find a nearby campsite. Just past the

The "back side" of Squaw Peak from the Pacific Crest Trail

crossing is a junction with the Tevis Cup Trail headed east toward Emigrant Pass.

Through light forest, you wind down to a saddle on a ridge that separates the drainages of Middle Fork American River and Whisky Creek. The Tevis Cup Trail, which has shared the course of the PCT for the last 0.4 mile, now heads west away from the PCT, bound for an eventual union with the Western States Trail.

Continue the descent along the PCT, crossing a flower-filled meadow before returning to forest cover and coming alongside nascent Whisky Creek. Near the 6-mile mark, you emerge from the forest into a hanging valley, where views open up down the canyon and the floor is covered with a very extensive field of mule-ears. Away from this colorful flat, the descent down the canyon resumes through mixed forest and occasional small clearings. After a mile-long descent, you reach a signed junction with the Whisky Creek Trail, 7.2 miles from the trailhead. Campsites can be found near Whisky Creek Camp, 0.4 mile down this trail, and across Whisky Creek, but you'll have to camp at least 250 feet away from the historical structures at the site.

From the junction, follow the PCT on a moderate climb through gradually thinning forest and pockets of shrubs and wildflowers in season. The trail swings around the hillside into the Five Lakes Creek drainage, to head generally northeast as most of the trees are left behind. The occasionally switchbacking trail ascends upstream well above the creek, past wet hillsides covered with willows and wildflowers, before approaching the level of the creek near the head of the canyon. In a stand of conifers, 8 miles from the trailhead, you reach a minimally signed T-junction with the Five Lakes Trail, which is simply marked FIVE LKS with an arrow pointing left.

Leave the PCT at the junction and follow the Five Lakes Trail on a moderate ascent that passes in and out of light forest to a junction with an unmarked lateral to Five Lakes, 0.2 mile from the T-junction. Proceed straight ahead at the junction, eventually coming alongside and then crossing a branch of flower-lined Five Lakes Creek, 0.3 mile from the lateral. Stroll across the forested flat of Five Lakes Basin to the north of the lakes—if you want to visit any of the lakes you'll have to leave the main trail and follow unmarked use trails or simply head cross-country. At the far side of the basin, you almost simultaneously exit Granite Chief Wilderness and leave the red-fir forest behind.

On a moderate descent you cross open granitic slopes, where only an occasional western white pine or Jeffrey pine can gain a foothold; here, excellent views abound of the Alpine Meadows area. The path arcs around to the crest of a granite ridge and then proceeds across slopes densely matted with shrubs, principally huckleberry oak. As you near the floor of the canyon, a light forest of Jeffrey pines and white firs provides the south-facing slope with some intermittent shade. Reach the well-signed trailhead near the north shoulder of Alpine Meadows Road.

60 Five Lakes Trail

Distance	4 miles (out-and-back)
Hiking Time	2–3 hours
Elevation	+1,000 feet
Difficulty	Moderate
Trail Use	Dogs OK
Best Times	July through October
Agency	Tahoe National Forest at 530-587-3558, www.fs.usda.gov/tahoe
Recommended Map	USGS 7.5-minute *Tahoe City*

see map on p. 137

HIGHLIGHTS Although the climb to Five Lakes basin is fairly stiff, the shores of the five lakes on the forested flat require only an hour's worth of hiking to reach, leaving plenty of time to fish, swim, or simply relax. The only drawback is the area's popularity, no doubt a direct result of the relatively short access. The overuse has resulted in a ban on camping, campfires, and the use of stoves within 600 feet of the lakes—backpackers can find decent campsites near a junction with the Pacific Crest Trail (PCT) or better sites 1.5 miles away at Whisky Creek Camp.

DIRECTIONS From CA 89, approximately 9.5 miles south of Truckee or 4 miles north of Tahoe City, turn onto Alpine Meadows Road and proceed for 2.1 miles to the well-signed Five Lakes Trailhead, on the right-hand shoulder. Park on the shoulder as space allows.

FACILITIES/TRAILHEAD There are no facilities at the trailhead. The Five Lakes Trail begins on the hillside above the north shoulder of Alpine Meadows Road.

Most of the trail to Five Lakes lies on private property, and hikers are reminded to stay on the trail until entering Granite Chief Wilderness near the eastern edge of the basin. An unrelenting ascent across the north wall of the Bear Creek canyon begins at the trailhead, and it doesn't cease until you pass into the wilderness and reach the nearly flat floor of the Five Lakes basin. Initially the trail climbs through a light forest of Jeffrey pines and white firs, but farther up the hillside the trees begin to thin, as a healthy population of shrubs, principally huckleberry oak, takes over. The open terrain allows improving views of Alpine Meadows Ski Resort and the surrounding terrain.

The shrub-covered slopes continue as the trail follows a couple of switchbacks higher up the slope and then curves around to the crest of a granitic ridge. With only a few Jeffrey and western white pines able to gain a foothold in the grainy soils, sweeping views of the canyon are nearly constant companions along this section of trail. From the ridge, the trail veers northwest and follows a rising arc toward Five Lakes. A healthy forest of red firs heralds your arrival into Granite Chief Wilderness and the gentler terrain of the Five Lakes basin.

The ban on camping, campfires, and the use of stoves within 600 feet of the lakes effectively makes it illegal to camp anywhere in the basin. Even with the overnight ban, the lakes are still heavily used by day hikers during the summer months. A short distance from the wilderness boundary, a faint use trail leads 75 yards south to the northernmost lake, which is visible through the trees from the main trail. Farther up the trail is a signed three-way junction, where the path straight ahead proceeds a half mile to a junction with the PCT. Turn left and stroll to the largest of the Five Lakes. From there, use trails access the remaining lakes.

Camping option: Backpackers in search of a campsite must proceed westbound on the main path from the largest lake, to a crossing of Five Lakes Creek and then a three-way junction. Turn left (southwest), and traverse a patchily forested hillside for a quarter mile, to a T-junction with the PCT. By turning left on the southbound PCT, you can quickly reach a passable campsite near the crossing of Five Lakes Creek. A right turn on the northbound PCT leads out of the forest and across shrub-covered slopes, down the canyon of Five Lakes Creek until the trail returns to forest cover and arcs around the lower slopes of Squaw Peak to a well-signed junction. Following directions for Whisky Creek Camp, turn left and follow switchbacking trail to a crossing of Whisky Creek. Just up from the crossing is the forested flat of Whisky Creek Camp, where three historic structures occupy the south side. Camping is not allowed within 250 feet of the structures, so look for shady campsites at the north end.

61   Alpine Meadows to Twin Peaks

see map on p. 154

Distance	18 miles (out-and-back)
Hiking Time	9–12 hours
Elevation	+3,275/-1,000 feet
Difficulty	Very difficult
Trail Use	Backpacking option, dogs OK
Best Times	Mid-July through October
Agency	Tahoe National Forest at 530-587-3558, www.fs.usda.gov/tahoe; Lake Tahoe Basin Management Unit at 530-543-2600, www.fs.usda.gov/ltbmu
Recommended Maps	USGS 7.5-minute *Tahoe City, Granite Chief,* and *Homewood*

HIGHLIGHTS The 9-mile journey from Alpine Meadows to Twin Peaks is a rigorous undertaking by anyone's standards, but the incomparable views from the ridgecrest section of the Pacific Crest Trail (PCT) and the Twin Peaks summit are hard to beat. The trade-off for such magnificent scenery is a 2-mile climb from Alpine Meadows to the Five Lakes basin, followed by another, almost-2-mile, switchbacking climb to the Sierra crest. Once the crest is gained, the hiking is much less difficult and the marvelous views are nearly unremitting.

Be sure to pack plenty of water, as after the crossing of Five Lakes Creek, 2.5 miles into the trip, water is not available en route to Twin Peaks, at least not without a serious detour off the trail. Once past the creek, backpackers also will have a hard time finding a decent place to pitch a tent. Difficulties aside, the seldom-trodden section of the PCT offers a reasonable dose of solitude along with the gorgeous vistas.

DIRECTIONS From CA 89, approximately 9.5 miles south of Truckee or 4 miles north of Tahoe City, turn onto Alpine Meadows Road and proceed for 2.1 miles to the well-signed Five Lakes Trailhead, on the right-hand shoulder. Park on the shoulder as space allows.

FACILITIES/TRAILHEAD There are no facilities at the trailhead. The Five Lakes Trail begins on the hillside above the north shoulder of Alpine Meadows Road.

Most of the trail to Five Lakes lies on private property, and hikers are reminded to stay on the trail until entering Granite Chief Wilderness near the eastern edge of the basin. An unrelenting ascent across the north wall of the Bear Creek canyon begins at the trailhead, and it doesn't cease until you pass into the wilderness and reach the nearly flat floor of the Five Lakes basin. Initially, the trail climbs through a light forest of Jeffrey pines and white firs, but farther up the hillside the trees begin to thin, as a healthy population of shrubs, principally huckleberry oak, takes over. The open terrain allows improving views of Alpine Meadows Ski Resort and the surrounding terrain.

The shrub-covered slopes continue as the trail follows a couple of switchbacks higher up the slope and then curves around to the crest of a granitic ridge. With only a few Jeffrey and western white pines able to gain a foothold in the grainy soils, sweeping views of the canyon are nearly constant companions along this section of trail. From the ridge, the trail veers northwest and follows a rising arc toward Five Lakes. A healthy forest of red firs heralds your arrival into Granite Chief Wilderness and the gentler terrain of the Five Lakes basin.

The Five Lakes area is extremely popular, and the severe overuse the lakes previously received has resulted in a ban on camping, campfires, and the use of stoves within 600 feet of the lakes. The regulation effectively makes camping anywhere in the basin an illegal activity. Even with the overnight ban, the lakes are still heavily used by day hikers during the summer months. A short distance from the wilderness boundary, a faint use trail leads 75 yards south to the northernmost lake, which is visible through the trees from the main trail. Farther up the trail is a signed three-way junction, where the path to the left heads to the largest of the Five Lakes. From there, use trails access the remaining lakes.

Proceed straight ahead at the junction to a crossing of Five Lakes Creek, and then traverse forested slopes to a junction with the previously mentioned trail to the lakes. Continue straight ahead on the traverse of the forested hillside with occasional clearings for another quarter mile to a T-junction with the PCT.

Turn left on the southbound PCT, soon passing a decent campsite near the Five Lakes Creek crossing. Away from the creek, the trail ascends a meadow-covered hillside, where willows, alders, and wildflowers flourish until late summer, including delphinium, paintbrush, yarrow, corn lily, aster, and daisy. Following the first in a long series of switchbacks, climb past the upper limits of the meadow and then wind back and forth across a forested hillside. Farther up the slope, the trail emerges from the trees onto open slopes carpeted with grasses, sagebrush, and an assortment of drier-habitat wildflowers that includes mule-ears, lupines, pennyroyal, and paintbrush. Across the open slopes, laboring hikers at least have improving views of Squaw Peak and the Granite Chief Wilderness to console them on the seemingly endless climb. Nearing the crest of the ridge, the trail passes just below a small peak, where the views expand to include Ward Peak in the immediate foreground and a part of the Crystal Range within Desolation Wilderness in the distance.

Thankfully, the switchbacking climb is left behind once you gain the crest and proceed along its north–south trending spine. Ward Peak, whose east slope is home to Alpine Meadows Ski Area, lies ahead, its summit littered with communications antennas and ski lifts. In a saddle between Peaks 8468 and 8474, you have your first view to the east of Lake

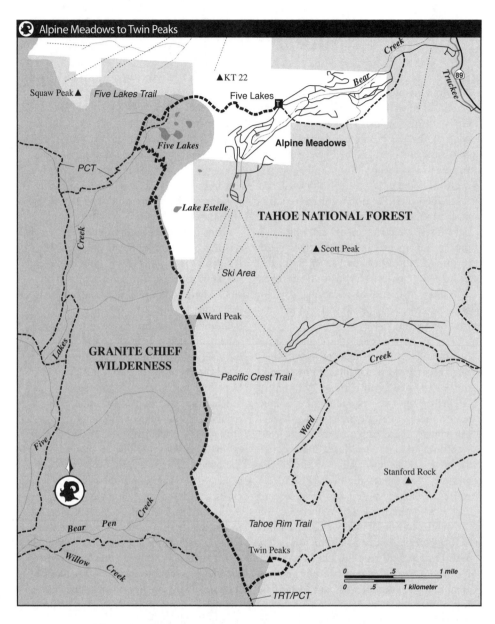

Alpine Meadows to Twin Peaks

Squaw Peak ▲   Five Lakes Trail

▲ KT 22

Five Lakes

Bear   Creek

Truckee 89

Five Lakes

PCT

Alpine Meadows

Lake Estelle

TAHOE NATIONAL FOREST

▲ Scott Peak

Ski Area

Creek

▲ Ward Peak

GRANITE CHIEF
WILDERNESS

Creek

Lakes

Pacific Crest Trail

Ward

Five

Stanford Rock
▲

Bear   Pen   Creek

Tahoe Rim Trail

Willow   Creek

Twin Peaks
▲

0   .5   1 mile
0   .5   1 kilometer

TRT/PCT

Tahoe and the surrounding peaks and ridges of the Tahoe basin. With continuous views of Granite Chief Wilderness across mule-ears–covered slopes, you follow the ridge-running trail past a snow fence and into a saddle. Apparently in the middle of nowhere, a sign in this saddle gives mileages back to the Five Lakes Trail and Whisky Creek Camp. Downslope to the east, a ski-area maintenance road provides a possible escape route to Alpine Meadows.

Proceed around the west side of Ward Peak to another saddle with perhaps the best lake views so far. From here, the trail arcs around a rock outcrop, passes through a saddle, and dips below the crest to avoid some impressive-looking rock cliffs above.

The moist hillside below these cliffs harbors a luxuriant display of shrubs and wildflowers. Beyond the cliffs, the trail passes through the first grove of conifers along the ridge, a small pocket of forest composed of western white pines, white firs, and mountain hemlocks.

The trail soon leaves the trees as it passes above Grouse Canyon and then meets a satellite ridge. Briefly back in the trees, follow a few switchbacks up this ridge and back to the treeless main ridge, where Lake Tahoe returns to view. Through prodigious amounts of tobacco brush that threaten to overgrow the trail in spots, you continue the southbound excursion on or near the ridgeline. Nearing the northwest ridge of Twin Peaks, you reenter forest for the duration of the trip until nearing the summit of Twin Peaks.

The trees thin enough in places to allow pockets of vibrant wildflowers to flourish until midsummer. Reach the Tahoe Rim Trail–Pacific Crest Trail junction at 8 miles from the trailhead.

Turn left (east) at the junction and follow the Tahoe Rim Trail on a traverse of the south slopes of Twin Peaks toward the east ridge. After a half mile, you reach an unmarked junction with a use trail to the top of the easternmost peak. Veer left at this junction and climb steeply up the east ridge of Twin Peaks, where you'll be treated to stunning views across flower-covered slopes of Lake Tahoe and the surrounding terrain. Continue the steep ascent up the ridge to a short scramble on the rocks directly below the summit. A stunning, 360-degree view awaits you from the top.

More Hikes

Bear Creek

A short, forested stroll through the valley of Alpine Meadows between the Loch Leven Trailhead and Alpine Meadows Stables (2 miles).

Truckee River Bike Path

A paved path follows a pleasant stretch of the Truckee River from Tahoe City to Squaw Valley Road (5.5 miles).

West Tahoe

West Tahoe covers the lands above the west shore of Lake Tahoe, bounded roughly on the north by Tahoe City, and going south along CA 89 to Meeks Bay. The area is characterized by gentle, forested terrain bisected by a number of lively creeks that wind their way toward the lake. Although lakeside communities on the west shore see plenty of activity in the summer, the woodlands beyond the shoreline seem to have a more sedate feeling than other areas around Lake Tahoe.

Unlike much of the popular backcountry in the Lake Tahoe Basin, the lands within and surrounding Granite Chief Wilderness, created by Congress in 1984, offer a modicum of solitude in one of the region's least-used wilderness areas. While fees are charged for overnight permits, and trailhead quotas are in effect for Desolation Wilderness, currently neither is required for entry into Granite Chief Wilderness. Despite the name, most of the rock within Granite Chief is volcanic. Due to the porous nature of volcanic soils, the west side of the Lake Tahoe Basin has few lakes that are possible trip destinations, especially compared with the many lakes found just to the south, in the predominantly granitic Desolation Wilderness.

While many of the area's trails follow streams up wooded valleys, a few paths do lead to high points with excellent vistas— don't forget the camera. Lake Tahoe views from Twin Peaks, Ellis Peak, and Eagle Rock are particularly stunning. Early to midsummer visitors will be treated to some fine wildflower displays as well, especially along streams and on well-watered hillsides.

Ed Z'berg-Sugar Pine Point State Park offers a trio of easy nature hikes, and the majority of the General Creek Trail to Lost and Duck Lakes lies within the park. The park's full-service campground makes an excellent base camp. Along with the trails, campground, and picnic areas, the park also is blessed with a 2-mile stretch of picturesque shoreline along Lake Tahoe, well suited for contemplating a dip in Tahoe's refreshing waters. The historic Hellman-Erhman Mansion is available for tours at a nominal fee.

At the southernmost limit of this section, the renowned Tahoe–Yosemite Trail begins at Meeks Bay and travels into the northern limits of Desolation Wilderness.

Since many of the hikes in this section begin at elevations near lake level, the season generally begins a smidgen earlier than elsewhere around the lake, with a few trails opening up as early as May. The initial sections of some of the other trips described in this chapter could also offer snow-free travel for early-season hikers itching to get out into the woods. While summer is the height of the season, autumn offers some delightful opportunities to enjoy these trails after the crush of tourists has departed.

Administration of these lands is divided among the Lake Tahoe Basin Management Unit, Tahoe National Forest, and Eldorado National Forest.

Lake Tahoe vista from Eagle Rock

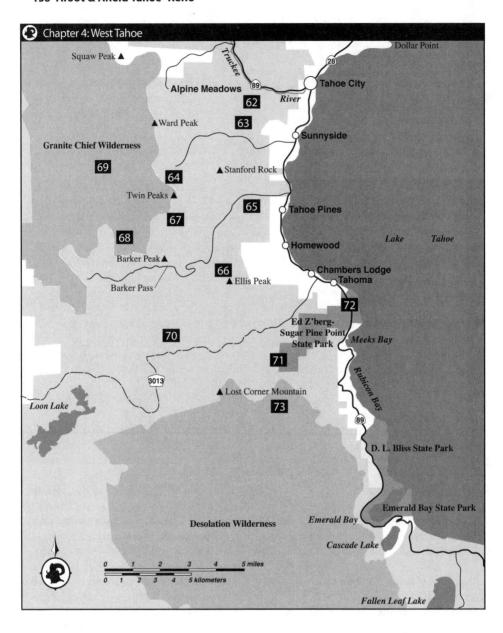

Chapter 4: West Tahoe

62 TRT: Tahoe City to Ward Canyon

Distance	4.9 miles (point-to-point)
Hiking Time	2.5 hours
Elevation	+800/-475 feet
Difficulty	Easy to moderate
Trail Use	Dogs OK, mountain biking OK
Best Times	Late May through October
Agency	Lake Tahoe Basin Management Unit at 530-543-2600, www.fs.usda.gov/ltbmu
Recommended Map	USGS 7.5-minute *Tahoe City* (trail not shown)

see map on p. 160

HIGHLIGHTS This 5-mile section of the Tahoe Rim Trail (TRT) probably won't make anyone's top-ten-trails-of-Lake-Tahoe list, but you do experience a stretch of quiet forest on the way to Paige Meadows, where colorful wildflowers provide visual treats in early season.

DIRECTIONS *Start:* Drive to Tahoe City and turn into 64 Acre Park just south of the CA 28 junction. The park is on the west side of CA 89, on the south side of the Truckee River, and just behind the Tahoe City Transit Center. Watch for a sign marked TRAIL AND RIVER ACCESS.

    End: Drive south on CA 89 approximately 2 miles from the junction of CA 28 in Tahoe City to Pineland Drive and turn right (west). Veer left after 0.4 mile as the road becomes Twin Peaks Road. Continue to the TRT Trailhead and park your vehicle as space allows.

FACILITIES/TRAILHEAD 64 Acre Park has park benches, picnic tables, barbecue grills, and restrooms. The Ward Canyon trailhead has no facilities. The trail begins on the bike path next to the river.

A way from the parking area at 64 Acres Park, this section of the Tahoe Rim Trail follows the Truckee River on a paved road, which will eventually turn to dirt. Past a steel gate, cross gravel road and then follow singletrack tread for 0.1 mile to a junction. Veer left at the junction, leaving the river behind to climb a forested hillside of red firs and sugar pines. After a while the grade increases up a narrow and rocky canyon of an unnamed creek on the way to a junction on the left with a mountain bike connector to Rawhide Drive and Tahoe City. Beyond the junction, gently graded tread heads through light forest for 1.3 miles to the next junction, where another mountain bike connector heads west toward Alpine Meadows.

Turn left at the junction and pass through fir forest and a grove of aspens to the first of the clearings known collectively as Page Meadows. Partway through the meadow, you pass a junction with a trail heading east to some of the other meadows and a route back to Tahoe City. On built-up trail, you proceed ahead through the meadow for a while before heading back under the trees. The trail merges with an old road near a set of low posts, where a path on the right travels toward the lowest of Page Meadows and the Alpine Peaks residential area.

Continue on the road through the trees for 0.4 mile to another junction and veer right. Descend steeply down the road through white firs and Jeffrey pines for a little more than a half mile to where single-track trail on the right angles downhill toward Ward Creek Boulevard. Following the singletrack, you reach the edge of the road at 4.9 miles from the South Tahoe City Trailhead in 64 Acres Park.

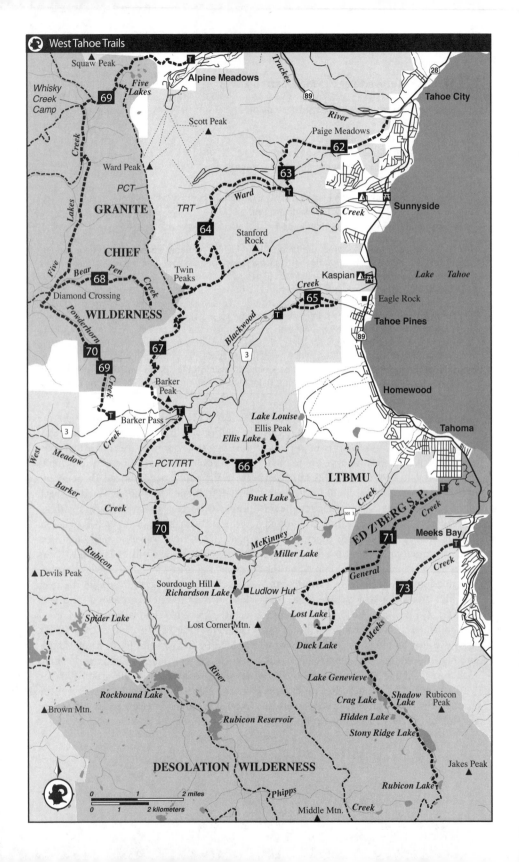

Squaw Peak

Five Lakes

69

Whisky Creek Camp

Five Lakes Creek

Alpine Meadows

Truckee

River

28

Tahoe City

89

Scott Peak

Paige Meadows

62

Ward Peak

PCT

GRANITE

63

TRT

Ward

Creek

Sunnyside

CHIEF

64

Stanford Rock

Five

Bear Pen Creek

68

Lake   Tahoe

Twin Peaks

Kaspian

Diamond Crossing

Creek

WILDERNESS

Powderhorn

Eagle Rock

65

Tahoe Pines

70

67

Blackwood

3

69

Creek

Barker Peak

89

Homewood

Barker Pass

T

Lake Louise

Ellis Peak

Tahoma

T

West

Creek

PCT/TRT

Ellis Lake

66

Meadow

Barker

Buck Lake

LTBMU

Creek

301

3

Creek

70

Rubicon

McKinney

Miller Lake

ED Z'BERG S. P.

71

Meeks Bay

▲ Devils Peak

Sourdough Hill ▲

■ *Ludlow Hut*

General

Creek

Richardson Lake

73

Meeks

Spider Lake

Lost Corner Mtn. ▲

Lost Lake

▲ Brown Mtn.

River

Duck Lake

Lake Genevieve

Rockbound Lake

Crag Lake

Shadow Lake

Rubicon Peak

Rubicon Reservoir

Hidden Lake

Stony Ridge Lake

DESOLATION   WILDERNESS

Jakes Peak

Rubicon Lake

Phipps

Creek

Middle Mtn. ▲

0   1   2 miles

0   1   2 kilometers

63 **TRT: Ward Canyon to Paige Meadows**

Distance	3 miles (out-and-back)
Hiking Time	1.5–2 hours
Elevation	+450 feet
Difficulty	Moderate
Trail Use	Dogs OK, good for kids, mountain biking OK
Best Times	June through October
Agency	Lake Tahoe Basin Management Unit at 530-543-2600, www.fs.usda.gov/ltbmu
Recommended Map	USGS 7.5-minute *Tahoe City* (trail not shown)

see map on p. 160

HIGHLIGHTS Paige Meadows is a series of five interconnecting grasslands, rimmed by aspens and carpeted with a showy display of wildflowers from early to midsummer. After the first half mile of stiff climbing on a rocky jeep road, which has the potential for encounters with off-road vehicles, the grade eases to a gentle stroll, and without the noisy vehicles the surroundings become serene. The meadows are well suited for wandering about and for exploring the interesting ecosystem. Whether on foot, horseback, or bike, a number of additional roads and trails in the area provide plenty of opportunities for extending your trip.

DIRECTIONS Drive south on CA 89 approximately 2 miles from the junction with CA 28 in Tahoe City to Pineland Drive and turn right (west). Veer left after 0.4 mile as the road becomes Twin Peaks Road. Continue to the Tahoe Rim Trail (TRT) on the right-hand shoulder, 1.8 miles from CA 89. Park on the opposite shoulder as space allows.

FACILITIES/TRAILHEAD There are no facilities at the trailhead. The trail begins on the north side of the road.

Follow singletrack trail up a forested hillside for a about 0.25 mile to a dirt road (FS 15N60), turn left, and make a stiffer climb up the rocky road. Continue climbing through a forest of Jeffrey pines and white firs to a curve in the road, where the forest momentarily opens to allow a view of the canyon, Ward Peak, and one of the chairlifts servicing the Alpine Meadows Ski Area. Head back into the trees and proceed to a three-way junction, a half mile from the trailhead, where motorized traffic turns right, and foot and bike traffic continues straight ahead on the TRT, following signed directions for Paige Meadows.

The road assumes a gentler grade, passing over a couple of culverts carrying small streams that drain Paige Meadows, on the way to the end of the road near the 1-mile

mark, where low posts block further vehicular progress. Nearby, a use trail provides quick access to the lower meadow.

Following TRT emblems, proceed toward Paige Meadows, a series of adjoining meadows covered with lush grasses and vibrantly colored wildflowers in season. A mixed forest of pines, firs, and aspens borders the meadows. The tread narrows to singletrack as you follow well-graded path around the fringe of the meadow before angling directly across it on an elevated section of trail. A use trail branches away from the main route to the right, leading to potential campsites and three additional sections of meadow. Farther on is a signed T-junction, where a right turn on the continuation of the TRT will lead 3 miles to Tahoe City. A left turn heads west 2 miles to Alpine Meadows.

64   TRT: Ward Canyon to Twin Peaks

Distance	12.8 miles (out-and-back)
Hiking Time	4.5–6.5 hours
Elevation	+2,400 feet
Difficulty	Difficult
Trail Use	Dogs OK, mountain biking OK
Best Times	July through October
Agency	Lake Tahoe Basin Management Unit at 530-543-2600, www.fs.usda.gov/ltbmu
Recommended Maps	USGS 7.5-minute *Tahoe City* and *Homewood* (trail not shown)

see map on p. 160

HIGHLIGHTS This trip combines one of the best wildflower gardens with one of the best summit views found anywhere in the Tahoe Basin. Despite the natural beauty, this section of the Tahoe Rim Trail (TRT) is not as heavily used as might be expected. The last quarter mile to the top of Twin Peaks is off-trail, requiring a short scramble over rocky terrain.

DIRECTIONS Drive south on CA 89 approximately 2 miles from the junction with CA 28 in Tahoe City to Pineland Drive, and turn right (west). Veer left after 0.4 mile as the road becomes Twin Peaks Road and then Ward Peak Boulevard. Head toward the Alpine Peaks subdivision, and continue another 0.2 mile, past the Tahoe Rim Trail on the right-hand shoulder, to a small turnout on the left-hand side of the road, 2 miles from CA 89.

FACILITIES/TRAILHEAD There are no facilities at the trailhead. This section of the TRT begins near a 6-by-6-inch post and a small trailhead signboard, heading northwest on the closed Forest Service Road 15N62.

From Ward Peak Boulevard, the TRT follows an easy stroll along the old road on the nearly level floor of Ward Canyon through a light forest of Jeffrey pines, red firs, and quaking aspens not far from gurgling Ward Creek. Recently, the Forest Service has installed boulders, split rail fences, and shrubs to try to restrict traffic across the meadows and improve the stream's fisheries. Of course, you should help by staying on the trail. The floor of the canyon is filled with luxuriant foliage and trailside shrubs, including currant, bitterbrush, and pinemat manzanita.

The road moves farther away from the creek and continues upstream. Periodic gaps in the forest provide fine views up the canyon to the rim and of such notable peaks as Grouse Rock. Proceed through lush grasses, shrubs, and colorful seasonal wildflowers to the crossing of a tributary stream, 1.75 miles from the trailhead. Another half-mile stroll leads to a steel bridge placed in 2007 across the main branch of Ward Creek.

Beyond the crossing, head upstream, making a gentle climb alongside the dancing creek amid more lush flower gardens. The profuse variety of wildflowers you're apt to see along Ward Canyon include aster, columbine, daisy, lupine, paintbrush, elephant head, corn lily, arnica, and mariposa lily. At its height, this area is one of the best wildflower displays in the Tahoe Basin. Continuing up the canyon, you encounter a thicker, mixed forest of lodgepole pines, western white pines, red firs, Jeffrey pines, and aspens, interspersed with pockets of lush foliage.

Eventually, the trail bends away from the main channel of Ward Creek and follows a steeper route up the canyon of a side stream. Soon the sound of tumbling water heralds your approach to a 30-foot-high waterfall, 3.3 miles from the trailhead. Locals call the falls McLoud Falls, although the stream does not appear on the USGS map.

Continue a switchbacking climb across flower-filled slopes and pockets of light forest, with improving views of the surrounding topography. At 4.75 miles from the trailhead, you reach the crest of the ridge and encounter a signed three-way junction with a path to your left that heads toward the summit of Stanford Rock. Peak baggers wishing to add Stanford Rock to their list of accomplishments can opt to follow this 0.9-mile, one-way route to the top.

Turn right (west) at the junction and follow a rising trail along the ridge through western white pines and mountain hemlocks, with pinemat manzanita as the principal ground cover. Soon a steeper, switchbacking climb leads past a rock knob to an unmarked Y-junction at 6.1 miles.

(The TRT veers left and continues on a 0.5-mile traverse below Twin Peaks to a junction with the Pacific Crest Trail).

Veer right at the junction and climb steeply up the east ridge of Twin Peaks, where you'll be treated to stunning views across wildflower-covered slopes of Lake Tahoe, the summits of Desolation Wilderness, and the surrounding canyons. Continue the steep ascent of the ridge and scramble over rocks to the east summit of Twin Peaks and an awe-inspiring, 360-degree view. Be sure to pack along a map of the Tahoe area to help you identify all the landmarks visible from this vantage point.

65 Blackwood Canyon

Distance	3 miles (semiloop)
Hiking Time	1.5–2 hours
Elevation	Negligible
Difficulty	Easy
Trail Use	Dogs OK, good for kids, mountain biking OK
Best Times	May through October
Agency	Lake Tahoe Basin Management Unit at 530-543-2600, www.fs.usda.gov/ltbmu
Recommended Map	USGS 7.5-minute *Homewood*

see map on p. 160

HIGHLIGHTS An easy semiloop trip awaits hikers of all ages and conditioning in the nearly flat area on the south side of Blackwood Creek. The short trip offers opportunities to wander over to the lazy creek, where hikers could enjoy a picnic lunch or while away the hours skipping rocks across the surface. Early-season visitors will enjoy a nice display of wildflowers along the banks of the creek and numerous side streams.

DIRECTIONS Drive on CA 89 to Blackwood Canyon Road, 8 miles south of the junction of CA 28 in Tahoe City, and turn west. Follow paved road for 2.25 miles to where the road bends and crosses Blackwood Creek. On the far side of the creek, the road bends upstream. Park on the shoulder near the bend in the road as space allows.

FACILITIES/TRAILHEAD There are no facilities at the trailhead. The trail heads east from the bend in the Blackwood Canyon Road on the south side of Blackwood Creek. Only a trailside marker signed NO VEHICLES marks the start of the trail.

Climb up the hillside amid thick vegetation and mixed forest along the fringe of the meadow carpeting the floor of Blackwood Canyon. Once past the short climb, the trail assumes a gently descending grade along the course of an old roadbed. Past a steep, momentary drop, you reach a social trail heading toward the north bank of the creek. Farther on, a half mile from the trailhead, is a Y-junction where the loop section of the trip begins.

Veer to the right and follow gently graded, singletrack trail through a mixed forest broken by small clearings. You soon cross a flower-lined tributary that drains the slopes of Blackwood Ridge. Just beyond the tributary, the trail enters a stand of quaking aspen, where a number of boggy rivulets and seasonal streams create the damp soil necessary for sustaining these deciduous trees. Briefly break out into the open, cross another seasonal stream, and head back into coniferous forest for a while until you pass through a small, willow-covered meadow. Immediately following the meadow, the trail intersects a road and comes to a Y-junction.

Turn left and follow the wide roadbed, eventually past a closed road on the right that heads toward the stream. The mostly forested walk leads to a set of 8-by-8-inch posts blocking vehicle access to the wide and rocky crossing of the tributary stream. Continue in an upstream direction through a T-junction with a trail on the right, and soon come to the close of the loop. From there, retrace your steps a half mile to the trailhead.

66 Ellis Peak and Ellis Lake

Distance	8.3 miles (out-and-back)
Hiking Time	4–6 hours
Elevation	+1,425/-400 feet
Difficulty	Difficult
Trail Use	Backpacking option, dogs OK, mountain biking OK
Best Times	June through October
Agency	Lake Tahoe Basin Management Unit at 530-543-2600, www.fs.usda.gov/ltbmu
Recommended Map	USGS 7.5-minute *Homewood*

see map on p. 160

HIGHLIGHTS This trip starts with a brutal, half-mile climb, but the remainder is a pleasant hike through alternating groves of serene forest and open stretches of view-packed ridgeline, which ultimately leads to the shores of a beautiful lake and the apex of a lofty summit with even more fantastic vistas. Until fairly recently, this trail was open to motorcycles, but the Forest Service wisely banned them. With both a lake and a mountain as destinations, this trip is sure to please even the most discriminating hiker.

DIRECTIONS Near the community of Tahoe Pines, approximately 4.3 miles south of Tahoe City, turn west from CA 89 onto Barker Pass Road (the junction is marked by signs for Sno-Park and Kaspian Campground). Follow paved road up Blackwood Canyon for 2.3 miles and bend left at a junction with FS 15N38, which continues straight ahead to an off-highway vehicle staging area. Head across a bridge over Blackwood Creek, and start the long climb toward the pass on the left side of the canyon. At 4.7 miles from the creek, reach the end of paved road near the rough dirt parking area for the Ellis Peak Trailhead on the left. A short section of steep, rocky, dirt road leads up to the parking area.

FACILITIES/TRAILHEAD There are no facilities at the trailhead. The trail begins near a set of signs.

The Ellis Peak Trail doesn't mess around, attacking the steep hillside with a vengeance on a stiff, winding climb that leads through a scattered-to-light fir forest. Survivors who reach the top of the ridge after three-quarters of a mile will find the less sadistic grade ahead a welcome respite.

Once atop the ridge, the trees diminish and the widely scattered lodgepole pines, junipers, western white pines, and white firs allow splendid views of Blackwood Canyon, Twin Peaks, Hell Hole Reservoir, and the peaks of Desolation Wilderness—something to enjoy while catching your breath after the steep ascent. Head south-west across the open ridge carpeted with arid shrubs such as bitterbrush, sagebrush, and tobacco brush, along with a splendid display of yellow-flowered mule-ears in early to midsummer. The old jeep road passes to the south of Peak 8614 and then begins a three-quarter-mile descent into a thickening forest of mountain hemlocks, firs, and pines.

Reach a small meadow at the bottom of the descent and start climbing through selectively logged forest on the way to an unmarked T-junction with a faint path heading left, 2.6 miles from the trailhead. Veer right and continue a very short distance on the roadbed to a second junction, where signs direct you left onto a road to Ellis Lake and right on a road to Ellis Peak. Also, a boot-beaten path straight ahead takes a more direct approach to the peak.

To reach Ellis Lake, turn left from the junction and follow the track of the old jeep road generally south on a mild to moderate descent through the trees for a half mile to the northeast shore. Just before the lake is a damp hillside at the base of a talus slope, where a garden of wildflowers provides a burst of color in midsummer. The lake is quite attractive, backdropped by rugged cliffs that form the east face of Ellis Peak. A light forest of white firs, mountain hemlocks, lodgepole, and western white pines shelters a few pleasant campsites, and pockets of willow line the shore. Without a permanent inlet or outlet, the level of the lake tends to diminish by late summer.

To reach Ellis Peak, proceed straight ahead from the junction on the boot-beaten path that climbs directly up the hillside, roughly paralleling the route of the road. After 0.3 mile, the trail rejoins the old jeep road and then climbs, steeply at times, toward the base of the rocks below the summit. Before reaching the rocks, watch for a cairn marking a path that ascends the west side of the peak, and follow that path to the top of the ridge and then shortly to the summit. A fine view unfolds from the top of Ellis Peak, which includes such notable landmarks as Lake Tahoe, Desolation Wilderness, Ellis Lake and Lake Louise, the deep green gash of Blackwood Canyon, and Hell Hole Reservoir.

Ellis Lake

67 TRT: Barker Pass to Twin Peaks

see map on p. 160

Distance	11.4 miles (out-and-back)
Hiking Time	5–7 hours
Elevation	+2,350/-1,200 feet
Difficulty	Moderate
Trail Use	Backpacking option, dogs OK
Best Times	Mid-July through mid-October
Agency	Lake Tahoe Basin Management Unit at 530-543-2600, www.fs.usda.gov/ltbmu
Recommended Map	USGS 7.5-minute *Homewood*

HIGHLIGHTS Follow a segment of the Pacific Crest (PCT) and Tahoe Rim (TRT) Trails to the east summit of Twin Peaks, from where hikers experience a fine view of Lake Tahoe and the surrounding terrain. From an open ridge along the Sierra crest, you'll have additional views into the heart of Granite Chief Wilderness and the peaks of the more distant Desolation Wilderness.

DIRECTIONS Near the community of Tahoe Pines, approximately 4.3 miles south of Tahoe City, turn west from CA 89 onto Barker Pass Road (the junction is marked by signs for Sno-Park and Kaspian Campground). Follow paved road up Blackwood Canyon for 2.3 miles and bend left at a junction with FS 15N38, which continues straight ahead to an off-highway-vehicle staging area. Head over Blackwood Creek and start the long climb toward the pass on the left side of the canyon. At 4.7 miles from the creek, reach the end of paved road near the rough dirt parking area for the Ellis Peak Trailhead on the left. Continue on the well-graded dirt road another 0.4 mile to Barker Pass and the signed PCT parking area on the right.

FACILITIES/TRAILHEAD The trailhead has pit toilets and picnic tables. The trail begins near the trailhead signboard.

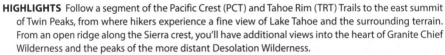

Follow the wide, well-graded, and heavily used PCT–TRT around the slopes of Barker Peak, to an open hillside carpeted with scattered shrubs and mule-ears. Here you'll have fine views to the north of a pair of unnamed volcanic knobs along the Sierra crest. Continue in and out of light forest, crossing over an old road about a mile from the trailhead. A short distance beyond the road, a path branches away from the trail and quickly leads to the edge of the ridge for a view of Blackwood Canyon. On rising trail, head northeast to a 4-by-4-inch post below the easternmost volcanic knob, 1.7 miles from the trailhead, where a short path followed by an easy scramble leads to a partial lake view atop the knob. The knob makes a good turnaround point for an easy, half-day trip.

Away from the knob, you drop off the ridge and follow a switchbacking, 1.7-mile descent across the head of the canyon of Blackwood Creek's North Fork. You'll see mountain hemlocks, western white pines, and red firs and cross numerous lushly lined streams and seeps along the way.

After bottoming out, you'll make a switchbacking, mile-long climb through alternating sections of light forest and shrub-covered slopes that leads toward a rocky ridge. Approaching the crest, follow the trail around the nose of the ridge to a dramatic view of your ultimate goal, Twin Peaks. Continue climbing toward the Sierra crest, crossing the signed boundary of Granite Chief Wilderness on the way. From the exposed ridge, you have a fine view down into the canyon of Bear Pen Creek. Proceed toward a junction between the PCT and TRT at 4.9 miles from the trailhead.

Turn right and follow the TRT for a half mile across the south side of Twin Peaks, to an unsigned junction with a use trail to the top of the eastern peak. Veer left at the junction and climb steeply up the east ridge of Twin Peaks, where, across wildflower-covered slopes, you'll be treated to stunning vistas of Lake Tahoe, the summits of Desolation Wilderness, and the surrounding canyons. Continue the steep ascent of the ridge, and scramble over rocks to the east summit of Twin Peaks and an awe-inspiring, 360-degree view. Be sure to pack along a map of the Tahoe area to help identify all the landmarks visible from this vantage point.

68 Bear Pen

see map on p. 160

Distance	13.5 miles (out-and-back)
Hiking Time	7–9 hours
Elevation	+1,650/-1,775 feet
Difficulty	Moderate
Trail Use	Backpacking option, dogs OK
Best Times	July through October
Agency	Tahoe National Forest at 530-587-3558, www.fs.usda.gov/tahoe
Recommended Maps	USGS 7.5-minute *Homewood* and *Wentworth Springs*

HIGHLIGHTS Although it's located in the popular Lake Tahoe region, Granite Chief Wilderness is extremely lightly used compared with other areas around the lake, particularly the popular Desolation Wilderness to the south. Instead of permits and quotas, backpackers will experience deep forests, rushing streams, seasonal wildflowers, excellent views, and a definite lack of fellow humans. This trip follows a pair of delightful streams to Bear Pen, a secluded basin rimmed by granite cliffs on the eastern fringe of the wilderness.

DIRECTIONS From CA 89, about 4.25 miles south of the junction with CA 28 in Tahoe City, turn west onto Barker Pass Road (FS 03), marked SNO-PARK and KASPIAN CAMPGROUND. Follow FS 03 along the north side of the valley, bend left to cross Blackwood Creek near the 2-mile mark, and then continue up the south side of Blackwood Canyon to the Pacific Crest Trailhead parking area near Barker Pass, 7 miles from CA 89. Continue downhill from Barker Pass for 1.3 miles to a four-way junction and then continue ahead another 0.3 mile to the Powderhorn Trailhead on the right (trailhead sign was missing in 2015, but NO BIKES and NO MOTORCYCLES signs were nailed to a tree). Very limited parking is available for two to three vehicles.

FACILITIES/TRAILHEAD There are no facilities at the trailhead. Vault toilets and picnic tables are available at the Barker Pass Trailhead, 1.5 miles east. The trail begins on the right-hand side of the road near a trail sign.

From the trailhead, climb across the hillside through selectively logged fir forest to a switchback and continue to where you merge briefly with a dirt road on the way to the top of the hill. Where the road bends to the left, proceed straight toward a cairn, where singletrack trail begins a protracted drop into the canyon of Powderhorn Creek. Follow this steep, winding descent into the trees, soon crossing the nascent creek and then following it downstream.

Continue the descent past the signed Granite Chief Wilderness boundary, down Powderhorn Creek Canyon. Along the descent, avalanche swaths have thinned the forest enough in spots to allow a profusion of wildflowers, plants, and shrubs to flourish. Amid a thickening forest, cross a narrow stream flowing through a tangle of alders and colorful wildflowers, and proceed on a mild to moderate descent down the canyon. The grade eventually eases where the trail crosses a wildflower-carpeted meadow. Next, the trail takes you across a boulder hop of Powderhorn Creek (early-season hikers may find the crossing to be a bit more difficult than a simple boulder hop). A marginal campsite is near the crossing.

Heading northeast, the trail proceeds through the trees for approximately 300 yards, to the open meadow known as

The verdant meadowlands of Bear Pen in Granite Chief Wilderness

Diamond Crossing. Pass by a marked three-way junction in this meadow, where a very faint trail heads southwest toward a trail-head near Hell Hole Reservoir. Continue through the meadow and then reenter forest on the way to a second junction, this one with a slightly more distinct trail heading up the canyon of Bear Pen Creek.

Turn right and head east on the Bear Pen Creek Trail on a moderate climb up a canyon filled with thick forest. The trail to Bear Pen is infrequently used, and the tread tends to falter where it crosses a small meadow. After 2.75 miles of mostly forested trail, reach a willow- and grass-filled meadow known as Bear Pen, an opening in the thick forest backdropped by a dramatic amphitheater of cliffs. Little-used, hemlock-shaded campsites around the meadow's perimeter offer secluded camping to solitude seekers. With a little luck, visitors may also see a namesake critter or two.

69 Powderhorn Trailhead to Alpine Meadows

see map on p. 160

Distance	12 miles (point-to-point)
Hiking Time	6–8 hours
Elevation	+1,750/-2,850 feet
Difficulty	Difficult
Trail Use	Backpacking option, maps and compass
Best Times	July through October
Agency	Tahoe National Forest at 530-587-3558, www.fs.usda.gov/tahoe; Lake Tahoe Basin Management Unit at 530-543-2600, www.fs.usda.gov/ltbmu
Recommended Maps	USGS 7.5-minute *Wentworth Springs, Granite Chief,* and *Tahoe City*

HIGHLIGHTS This shuttle trip allows experienced day hikers and backpackers to experience a sense of remoteness that's uncommon to much of the Lake Tahoe backcountry, in the heart of Granite Chief Wilderness. Most of the trail passes alongside tumbling creeks through serene forest, at least until views of the greater Alpine Meadows area open up near trail's end. The area within the wilderness is a lonely parcel of land where little-used trails can disappear in grassy meadows—make sure you carry a map and compass, or GPS receiver, and know how to use them.

DIRECTIONS *Start:* From CA 89, about 4.25 miles south of the junction of CA 28 in Tahoe City, turn west onto Barker Pass Road (FS 03), marked SNO-PARK and KASPIAN CAMPGROUND. Follow FS 03 along the north side of the valley, bend left to cross Blackwood Creek near the 2-mile mark, and then continue up the south side of Blackwood Canyon to the Pacific Crest Trailhead parking area near Barker Pass, 7 miles from CA 89. Continue downhill from Barker Pass for 1.3 miles to a four-way junction and then continue ahead another 0.3 mile to the Powderhorn Trailhead on the right (trailhead sign was missing in 2015, but NO BIKES and NO MOTORCYCLES signs were nailed to a tree). Very limited parking is available for two to three vehicles.

    End: From CA 89, approximately 9.5 miles south of Truckee or 4 miles north of Tahoe City, turn onto Alpine Meadows Road and proceed for 2.1 miles to the well-signed Five Lakes Trailhead on the right-hand shoulder. Park on the shoulder as space allows.

FACILITIES/TRAILHEAD There are no facilities at either trailhead. Vault toilets and picnic tables are available at the Barker Pass Trailhead, 1.5 miles east of the Powderhorn Trailhead. The trail begins on the right-hand side of the road near a trail sign.

From the trailhead, climb across the hillside through selectively logged fir forest to a switchback and continue to where you merge briefly with a dirt road on the way to the top of the hill. Where the road bends to the left, proceed straight toward a cairn, where singletrack trail begins a protracted drop into the canyon of Powderhorn Creek. Follow this steep, winding descent into the trees, soon crossing the nascent creek and then following it downstream.

Continue the descent past the signed Granite Chief Wilderness boundary, down Powderhorn Creek Canyon. Along the descent, avalanche swaths have thinned the forest enough in spots to allow a profusion of wildflowers, plants, and shrubs to flourish. Amid a thickening forest, cross a narrow stream flowing through a tangle of alders and colorful wildflowers, and proceed on a mild-to-moderate descent down the canyon. The grade eventually eases where the trail crosses a wildflower-carpeted meadow. Next, the trail takes you across a boulder hop of Powderhorn Creek (early-season hikers may find the crossing to be a bit more difficult than a simple boulder hop). A marginal campsite is near the crossing.

Heading northeast, the trail proceeds through the trees for approximately 300 yards to the open meadow known as Diamond Crossing. Pass by a marked three-way junction in this meadow, where a very faint trail heads southwest toward a trailhead near Hell Hole Reservoir. Continue through the meadow and then reenter forest on the way to a second junction, this one with a slightly more distinct trail heading up the canyon of Bear Pen Creek.

From the junction, head northbound on the Five Lakes Creek Trail through a mixed forest of incense cedar, Jeffrey pine, and red and white firs, immediately encountering the crossing of Bear Pen Creek. Beyond the crossing, briefly parallel the alder-lined course of Bear Pen Creek until it bends eastward, and then proceed up the trail on a gentle ascent of forested Five Lakes Creek canyon. About a mile from the junction, damp soils allow a sprinkling of aspens to join the forest, a few specimens with trunks as massive as 2 feet in diameter. A half mile farther, the trail crosses the rocky channel of the seasonal outlet from Grouse Canyon and then continues another quarter mile to a trickling, spring-fed rivulet lined with grasses and wildflowers.

Another half mile of gently graded trail from the spring-fed rivulet leads to a signed junction just before a good-size meadow. Despite directions on a sign for Whisky Creek Camp to the left, any indication of a trail on the ground has almost completely disappeared and is virtually impossible to follow. Therefore, continue straight ahead (north), following signed directions for Big Spring.

Crossing the meadow north of the junction, the tread may be difficult to follow through the tall grasses, but a distinct path reappears ahead where the trail reenters the forest. From the meadow, a shady half mile of easy walking leads to Big Spring, a gurgling eruption of water surrounded by alders at the south end of a large meadow, where a nearby grove of conifers harbors a couple of decent campsites. Although defined trail disappears in the meadow grass beyond the spring and the campsites, the key to continuing the route is to find the resumption of trail at the west edge of the meadow, about midway through the clearing. This path soon leads down to a ford of Five Lakes Creek and just as quickly up to a junction with a faint trail heading south toward Shanks Cove, and more pronounced tread heading north toward Whisky Creek Camp.

Turn right (north) at the junction and follow gently graded trail on the west side of alder-lined Five Lakes Creek for 0.3 mile, to the crossing of a side stream. Beyond this stream, the grade of the ascent increases to moderate, until you experience a momentary respite upon reaching the forested flat that harbors Whisky Creek Camp. A metal-roofed log cabin, a smaller shed, and a cooking fireplace are the three historic structures that occupy the south side of the flat. (Camping is not allowed inside the cabin or within 250 feet of the structures.) Nearby is a three-way junction with a trail that heads west toward the Greyhorse Valley Trailhead. Overnighters will find a couple of shady campsites on the north side of the flat. Water is easily obtained from nearby Five Lakes Creek.

From Whisky Creek Camp, head east a short distance to the crossing of Five Lakes Creek, and then make a 0.3-mile switchbacking climb through the trees to a T-junction with the Pacific Crest Trail (PCT). Turn right at the junction, following signed directions for the Alpine Meadows Trailhead, and proceed on the PCT on a moderate climb through a gradually lightening forest, where shrubs and wildflowers become increasingly prominent. Follow occasional switchbacks up the left-hand side of Five Lakes Creek canyon across initially dry slopes, followed by a moist hillside of flourishing wildflowers and willows. Beyond this incredibly verdant hillside, where conifers start to reappear, is a signed junction with a lateral to Five Lakes. (Backpackers will have to choose a campsite at least 600 feet away from any of the lakes in the Five Lakes basin.)

From the three-way junction with the Five Lakes lateral, veer left and make a moderate climb across a hillside that passes in and out of light forest, to a junction with an unmarked lateral to Five Lakes, 0.2 mile from the T-junction. Proceed straight ahead at the junction, eventually coming alongside and then crossing a branch of flower-lined Five Lakes Creek, 0.3 mile from the lateral. Stroll across the forested flat of Five Lakes Basin to the north of the lakes—if you want to visit any of the lakes, you'll have to leave the main trail and follow unmarked use trails or simply head cross-country. At the far side of the basin, you nearly simultaneously exit Granite Chief Wilderness and leave the red fir forest behind.

On a moderate descent, you cross open granitic slopes, where only an occasional western white or Jeffrey pine can gain a foothold; here, excellent views abound of the Alpine Meadows area. The path arcs around to the crest of a granite ridge and then proceeds across slopes densely matted with shrubs, principally huckleberry oak. As you near the floor of the canyon, a light forest of Jeffrey pines and white firs provides the south-facing slope with some intermittent shade. Reach the well-signed trailhead near the north shoulder of Alpine Meadows Road.

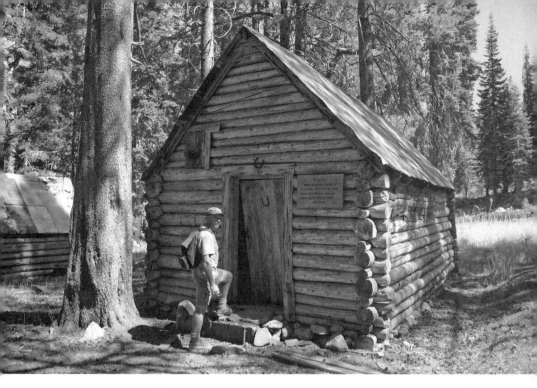

Historic structure at Whiskey Creek Camp

70   **Barker Pass to Richardson Lake**

see map on p. 160

Distance	13.2 miles (out-and-back)
Hiking Time	6–8 hours
Elevation	+600/-850 feet
Difficulty	Moderate
Trail Use	Dogs OK, backpacking option
Best Times	Mid-July through October
Agency	Tahoe National Forest at 530-587-3558, www.fs.usda.gov/tahoe
Recommended Map	USGS 7.5-min. *Homewood*

HIGHLIGHTS Above the west shore of Lake Tahoe is a wedge of land between Granite Chief Wilderness to the north and Desolation Wilderness to the south that is primarily the domain of off-highway vehicles. This trip uses a section of the Pacific Crest and Tahoe Rim Trails to pass through this region on a nonmotorized, mostly forested romp between Barker Pass and forest-rimmed Richardson Lake. Several flower-lined streams and small meadows provide diversions along the way.

DIRECTIONS Near the community of Tahoe Pines, approximately 4.3 miles south of Tahoe City, turn west from CA 89 onto Barker Pass Road (the junction is marked by signs for SNO-PARK and KASPIAN CAMPGROUND). Follow paved road up Blackwood Canyon for 2.3 miles, and bend left at a junction with FS 15N38, which continues straight ahead to an off-highway-vehicle staging area. Head over Blackwood Creek, and start the long climb toward the pass on the left side of the canyon. At 4.7 miles from the creek, reach the end of paved road near the rough dirt parking area for the Ellis Peak Trailhead on the left. Continue on the well-graded dirt road another 0.4 mile to Barker Pass and the signed Pacific Crest Trail (PCT) parking area on the right.

FACILITIES/TRAILHEAD The trailhead has pit toilets and picnic tables. The trail begins across the main road, south of the trailhead, near a number of trail signs.

Proceed from the south side of the road on singletrack trail across an open, shrubby hillside covered with early-season wildflowers, including mule-ears and lupines. Soon you stroll into shady forest on the wide and well-maintained tread of the Pacific Crest and Tahoe Rim trails, and proceed on a descending 2.5-mile traverse to the stream that drains Bear Lake. Along the way, you pass through a few clearings and over several rivulets and seeps that trickle across the trail, characteristically lined with lush foliage and brilliant wildflowers, including tall parsnip, lupine, delphinium, corn lily, buttercup, paintbrush, and daisies. Walk across a jeep road at 1.25 miles from the trailhead, and continue another mile to a diagonal crossing of a more traveled off-highway-vehicle (OHV) road from Barker Pass, which provides motorized access to Bear Lake and, later, a connection to the McKinney-Rubicon Road. A quarter mile farther, the trail bottoms out at alder-lined and boulder-strewn Bear Creek.

Follow gently graded trail for the next 1.5 miles, as you traverse a mixed forest of white firs, lodgepole pines, western white pines, and Jeffrey pines. Sourdough Hill appears through occasional breaks in the forest, before a 4-by-4-inch post heralds your arrival at a major road crossing with the McKinney-Rubicon OHV road. This frequently traveled road links the west shore of Lake Tahoe and the Loon Lake area.

Beyond the McKinney-Rubicon Road, you soon traverse a jeep road, cross Miller Creek, and then walk across another jeep road as the trail veers east and starts to climb. Extensive Miller Meadows appears through the gaps in the previously logged forest as the grade eases for a while. Soon the trail resumes climbing, arcing east and then south around Sourdough Hill. Along the way, you cross a slope carpeted with wildflowers and lush plants before returning to forest. Eventually, Richardson Lake appears through the trees and you proceed to a junction with a road near the north shore. The PCT continues along the west side of the lake, but by following the road around the northeast side of the lake and across the outlet, you can access a short path that climbs to Ludlow Hut, owned and operated by the Sierra Club. Several well-developed campsites are scattered around the lake, no doubt a direct result of the vehicle access.

71 General Creek Trail to Lost and Duck Lakes

see map on p. 160

Distance	10.8 miles (out-and-back)
Hiking Time	4–6 hours
Elevation	+1,500/-100 feet
Difficulty	Moderate
Trail Use	Backpacking option, leashed dogs, good for kids, mountain biking OK
Best Times	July through October
Agency	Ed Z'berg-Sugar Pine Point State Park at 530-525-7982, parks.ca.gov; Lake Tahoe Basin Management Unit at 530-543-2600, www.fs.usda.gov/ltbmu
Recommended Map	USGS 7.5-minute *Homewood*

HIGHLIGHTS Two quiet lakes that are far enough off the beaten path to ensure a peaceful visit are the goals of this trip. The first 2.75 miles follow a cool and shady course up the wide, forested valley of General Creek, gaining only 200 feet of elevation along the way to the Lily Pond junction. After a short climb, Lily Pond is a good turnaround point for groups with young children, or anyone else who wants to take it easy. Past the junction, the General Creek Trail climbs more steeply to the lakes, which let swimmers take a refreshing afternoon dip and where anglers can dangle a line.

DIRECTIONS Drive CA 89 to the west entrance into Ed Z'berg-Sugar Pine Point State Park, approximately 9 miles south of Tahoe City and 18 miles north of the junction of CA 50 and CA 89 in South Lake Tahoe. Following signs for General Creek Campground, head past the entrance station (fee required) and continue to the day-use parking lot.

FACILITIES/TRAILHEAD Ed Z'berg-Sugar Pine Point State Park offers running water, restrooms, picnic areas, beach access, campgrounds, a visitor center, and guided tours of the historic Hellman-Erhman Mansion. To find the trailhead, follow paved paths from the day-use parking area to the start of the North Fire Road, near campsite 150.

Head southwest on the wide dirt track of the old road, on a gentle grade amid shady, mixed forest composed of red and white firs, Jeffrey pines, incense cedars, and sugar pines, the park's namesake tree. Eventually, you find yourself on a single-track trail that makes a virtually imperceptible climb up from the broad floor of the canyon, a good distance away from the placid, meandering creek and bordering meadowlands. Continue the gentle stroll through the serenity of a dense forest. Beyond a bridge over a diminutive side stream, you reach a junction marked by a 4-by-4-inch post, 2.75 miles from the parking lot. The right-hand path follows a short climb to Lily Pond (no bikes allowed here). Although not the most scenic body of water on this trip, shallow Lily Pond will provide amateur botanists with a few interesting plant species, including pond lilies and bulrushes. Lily Pond is a good destination for those interested in a short, easy hike.

To continue to Duck and Lost Lakes, veer left at the Lily Pond junction and proceed upstream along the General Creek Trail through dense forest and lush trailside vegetation. Eventually, the gentle terrain comes to an end, where the canyon walls narrow and the grade increases, forcing the trail away from the valley floor on a moderate climb across the right-hand side of the gorge. The steady climb is briefly interrupted at a 4-by-4-inch post, where, following signage for Lost Lake, you turn left and drop to a crossing of General Creek at 3.2 miles from the trailhead. Short cascades drop into lovely pools along this section of the creek, providing a fine opportunity for a rest stop, lunch break, or perhaps a refreshing dip.

Beyond the creek crossing, make a 0.3-mile climb over granite slabs and around granite humps and boulders, to a T-junction marked with a 6-by-6-inch post, 3.6 miles from the trailhead. (The route ahead continues 0.75 mile to a junction with the Genevieve Trail.) Following signed directions for Lost Lake, you turn left and proceed on the wide track of an old dirt road on a short, steep climb to the crest of a minor ridge. A forested descent from the ridge offers a brief respite beneath the shade of lodgepole pines and firs. Soon you start climbing again on rocky road. After a while, a thick tangle of alders, grasses, and wildflowers heralds your arrival at a crossing of the creek draining Lost and Duck Lakes, 4.4 miles from the trailhead. Continue climbing for another 0.6 mile, to a second crossing of the creek. Here the road bends west and follows a gentle 0.4-mile course to a peninsula at the south shore of forest-rimmed Lost Lake. Although no defined path exists, Duck Lake is an easy 250-yard trek south from Lost Lake.

72   Ed Z'berg-Sugar Pine Point State Park

Distance	0.5 mile, out-and-back (Lakefront Interpretive Trail)
	1 mile, out-and-back (Rod Beaudry Trail)
	1.7 miles, loop (Dolder Nature Trail)
Hiking Time	15 minutes (Lakefront Interpretive Trail)
	30 minutes (Rod Beaudry Trail)
	1 hour (Dolder Nature Trail)
Difficulty	Easy
Trail Use	Good for kids
Best Times	May through October
Agency	Ed Z'berg-Sugar Pine Point State Park at 530-525-7982, parks.ca.gov
Recommended Maps	*CSP Sugar Pine Point State Park* and USGS 7.5-minute *Meeks Bay*

HIGHLIGHTS Ed Z'berg-Sugar Pine Point State Park has three easy trails that are sure to please the most discriminating sightseer. History abounds on the quarter-mile Lakefront Interpretive Trail, including the opportunity to tour one of Tahoe's splendid architectural wonders, the Hellman-Erhman Mansion. Tours of the mansion are conducted twice daily from July to Labor Day. The Rod Beaudry Trail connects the mansion grounds and the General Creek Campground via the Edwin L. Z'berg Natural Preserve. The 1.7-mile loop along the Dolder Nature Trail offers a serene stroll past a sandy beach with beautiful lake views to the Sugar Pine Point Lighthouse, with a return through quiet forest to the day-use parking area. Be sure to pack a lunch to enjoy from any of the several excellent picnic spots sprinkled around the park.

DIRECTIONS Drive CA 89 to the east entrance into Sugar Pine Point State Park, approximately 10 miles south of Tahoe City and 17 miles north of the junction of CA 50 and CA 89 in South Lake Tahoe.

FACILITIES/TRAILHEAD Ed Z'berg-Sugar Pine Point State Park offers running water, restrooms, picnic areas, beach access, campgrounds, a visitor center, and guided tours of the historic Hellman-Erhman Mansion in the summer. To find the trailhead, follow the short access road to the day-use parking lot (fee required) near the nature center and the Hellman-Erhman Mansion.

Lakefront Interpretive Trail: From the day-use parking lot, acquire a printed guide from the nature center (and tickets for the mansion tour, if so inclined) and then wander down a dirt road toward the shoreline of Lake Tahoe to the start of the paved Lakefront Interpretive Trail. Begin your stroll near the South Boathouse and proceed northbound along the picturesque shore of Lake Tahoe. From the shoreline, you have excellent views across the sapphire-blue waters of the lake to a number of significant Tahoe landmarks, including several Carson Range peaks above the far shore. Occasional picnic tables and park benches invite you to relax, linger, and enjoy the beautiful scenery. Nearing the end of the quarter-mile trail, you pass below the expansive, manicured lawn rising up to the striking Hellman-Ehrman Mansion, also known as Pine Lodge. The mansion was built in 1903 and was sold to California State Parks in 1965. The Lakefront Interpretive Trail ends near a cluster of buildings at the north end. From there, you can retrace your steps back to the parking lot, or follow the road behind the mansion and past the nature center to the day-use area.

Rod Beaudry Trail: From the day-use parking lot, follow paved road past the nature center and tennis courts to the beginning of the trail near the public restroom. Turn left, leave the mansion grounds, and follow a paved path on a short descent to a wooden bridge over lushly lined General Creek. Beyond the bridge, you enter the Edwin L. Z'berg Natural Preserve, named for a legislator in the California State Assembly who championed many environmental protections for Lake Tahoe. Reach a Y-junction just beyond the bridge, where the dirt path of the Dolder Nature Trail veers left.

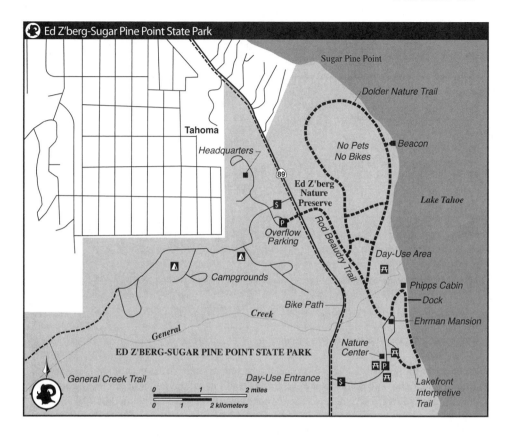

Continue on paved trail, passing through mixed forest typical of the west shore, including incense cedars, red and white firs, Jeffrey pine, and an occasional sugar pine. Soon a grassy clearing appears, which allows filtered glimpses of Lake Tahoe through the trees on the far side of the clearing. After a short while, you reach another junction with a dirt path that provides an alternate connection to the Dolder Nature Trail and access to a small stretch of beach in the opposite direction. Back in forest, a mildly rising climb leads to a crossing of CA 89 and the bike path just beyond the far shoulder. A short walk from there brings you to the day-use parking lot near General Creek Campground. Without arrangements for pickup, you'll have to retrace your steps to the day-use parking area near the nature center.

Dolder Nature Trail: From the day-use parking lot, follow the Rod Beaudry Trail described earlier to the junction with the Dolder Nature Trail (bicycles and dogs are not permitted).

Head north on a dirt, singletrack trail through light forest and verdant ground cover to a grassy clearing sprinkled with lupine and penstemon in early summer. Veering toward the lakeshore, you cross a couple of connecting trails that provide access from the Rod Beaudry Trail to a section of sandy beach and a fine lake view. Back in forest, parallel the now-rocky shoreline of Lake Tahoe until you reach a three-way junction, 0.6 mile from the day-use parking lot.

A short walk down the path toward the lake leads to the Sugar Pine Point Lighthouse, which in modern times is simply a blinking light atop a steel pole mounted on a wood deck, supported by four concrete pillars. Although less than noteworthy in appearance, the 6,200-foot elevation makes this "lighthouse" the world's highest operational navigational light.

Hellman-Ehrman Mansion at Ed Z'berg-Sugar Pine Point State Park

Back on the main trail, you continue the secluded forest stroll, eventually arcing away from the shoreline and following a mildly rising trail toward the trailhead. Ignore a couple of seldom-used paths from General Creek Campground and proceed to a junction in a clearing. A right turn takes you to the Rod Beaudry Trail, while a left turn connects to the beginning section of the Dolder Nature Trail. You can return to the day-use parking area via either trail.

73 Tahoe–Yosemite Trail: Meeks Bay to Tallant Lakes

see map on p. 160

Distance	16 miles (out-and-back)
Hiking Time	8–10 hours
Elevation	+2,100/-100 feet
Difficulty	Difficult
Trail Use	Backpacking option, dogs OK
Best Times	Mid-July through October
Agency	Lake Tahoe Basin Management Unit at 530-543-2600, www.fs.usda.gov/ltbmu
Recommended Maps	USGS 7.5-minute *Homewood* and *Rockbound Valley*; ENF and LTBMU *A Guide to the Desolation Wilderness*
Notes	Overnight visitors must obtain a valid wilderness permit. The closest location to the trailhead is the Taylor Creek Visitor Center.

HIGHLIGHTS Along the northernmost section of the famed Tahoe–Yosemite Trail (TYT), hikers follow Meeks Creek from its placid terminus at Meeks Bay upstream into Desolation Wilderness, along a raucous course to its headwaters below Phipps Pass. The upper canyon boasts a string of seven picturesque lakes, precious jewels known locally as the Tallant Lakes, offering excellent opportunities for fishing, swimming, camping, or simply relaxing. Backpackers and equestrians with extra time will find connecting trails providing several options for longer journeys into the heart of the backcountry. Wildflowers are generally at their peak from late July to mid-August, but so are the mosquitoes. September offers mild weather, fewer people, and fewer blood-sucking pests.

DIRECTIONS Follow CA 89 to Meeks Bay, and park on the west side of the highway, 0.1 mile north of the entrance to Meeks Bay Campground. The trailhead is approximately 16.5 miles north of the CA 50–CA 89 junction in South Lake Tahoe, or 11 miles south of Tahoe City.

FACILITIES/TRAILHEAD There are no facilities at the trailhead. Find the trailhead near a closed gate.

Follow the gentle incline of an old dirt road across the north side of the broad, lush valley of Meeks Creek, through a mixed forest of incense cedars, white firs, lodgepole pines, ponderosa pines, and sugar pines. After an easy 1.5 miles, the grade increases, as you forsake the old road at a well-marked junction and follow singletrack trail past verdant foliage near a seeping spring, to the signed wilderness boundary at 2.5 miles.

Beyond the wilderness boundary, the trail roughly parallels the creek, which is within earshot but remains mostly out of sight. Through alternating groves of conifers and pocket meadows, you continue up the canyon to a log-and-timber bridge across the creek at 3.3 miles.

A moderate climb follows an arcing path around a red-fir-forested side canyon filled with thimbleberry, fireweed, vine maple, and currant. Climbing out of this canyon, you circle around the nose of a minor ridge with a partial view of Lake Tahoe to rejoin Meeks Creek. A steady climb alongside the tumbling creek leads to a three-way junction marked by a 6-by-6-inch post, 4.6 miles from the trailhead. The old Lake Genevieve Trail to the right is a seldom-used lateral that connects to the General Creek and Pacific Crest Trails. Just beyond the junction is Lake Genevieve, a greenish, shallow lake rimmed by pines. A number of fair campsites are spread around the far shoreline, but more appealing sites with better scenery are just a short distance up the trail, at Crag Lake.

Follow the TYT around the east shore of Lake Genevieve, and make a short, steady climb through western white pines, red firs, and Jeffrey pines, to Crag Lake. The lake has a splendid backdrop in the granitic slopes of 9,054-foot Crag Peak to the south. Overnighters should look for good campsites above the northeast shore.

Pass around the long east shore of Crag Lake, and ascend rocky trail to a boulder hop of Meeks Creek. Just past the creek, an unmarked use trail travels southwest to Hidden Lake, a shallow, irregularly shaped pond near the base of Crag Peak. A steeper climb through thick forest ascends some morainal ridges above the west shore of meadow-rimmed Shadow Lake, whose shallow waters are sprinkled with numerous lily pads. A moderate climb follows the course of Meeks Creek, tumbling and plunging its way down the rocky canyon. At 6.3 miles, you reach the north shore of Stony Ridge Lake, the largest of the Tallant Lakes. Except for the steep east shore, the lake is bordered by lodgepole pines. A number of excellent campsites will lure overnighters.

Follow the TYT on a gentle grade around the west shore of Stony Ridge Lake, hopping over the outlet from isolated Cliff Lake along the way. Near the far end of the lake, a mildly rising ascent leads above the verdant meadow and then past a well-watered hillside carpeted with wildflowers. Eventually, the trail resumes its climbing ways, switchbacking between the two upper tributaries of Meeks Creek, on the way to the last of the Tallant Lakes. At 8 miles from the trailhead, you reach the east shore of Rubicon Lake. Rubicon is perhaps the prettiest of the lakes, rimmed by mountain hemlocks and lodgepole pines that shelter several excellent campsites.

More Hikes

Eagle Rock and Blackwood Creek

From a small parking area on the west side of CA 89, 0.4 mile south of Blackwood Canyon Road, very short paths lead to a scramble to the top of Eagle Rock, which offers views of Tahoe and a pleasant stretch of Blackwood Creek.

Quiet Triangle Lake in Desolation Wilderness

Southwest Tahoe

The terrain above the southwest shore of Lake Tahoe is perhaps the most well-known backcountry among hikers and backpackers in the area, where sparkling granite basins hold azure-blue lakes, towered over by serrated granite peaks. Set aside in 1969, the 63,960-acre Desolation Wilderness, typically the most heavily used wilderness area in the United States, draws a horde of visitors during the summer months from around the country and even from around the globe. Visitation is so frequent that the Forest Service long ago instituted trailhead quotas and more recently devised a plan to charge each backpacker for overnight stays within the wilderness. Parking at a few of the area's trailheads is also subject to a nominal fee. Even day hikers are required to obtain a free, day-use permit (usually available by self-registration at trailheads). On weekends, backpackers should plan ahead when attempting to secure a wilderness permit, and day hikers should plan on arriving early at popular trailheads in order to find a parking place.

In addition to the ruggedly beautiful subalpine and alpine terrain found within Desolation Wilderness, southwest Tahoe is also home to some of California's most picturesque state parks, D. L. Bliss and Emerald Bay. Like Desolation, these parks do not lack for visitors during the summer. Tourists, campers, boaters, swimmers, picnickers, and hikers flock to the shoreline parks, with the heaviest visitation occurring between the Fourth of July and Labor Day, when parking spaces and campsites are often at a premium.

Despite the large number of visitors, trails in the area have much to offer, including high peaks with sweeping vistas, lakeshore hikes with stunning Tahoe views, forested walks, and journeys to alpine lakes. Make sure you pack along a camera and a swimsuit.

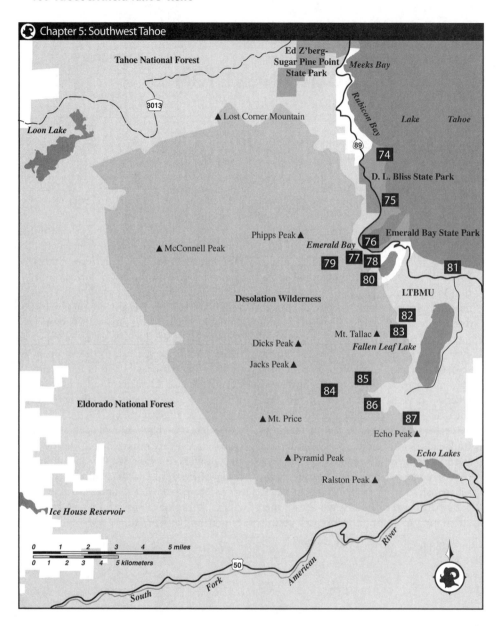

Chapter 5: Southwest Tahoe

Tahoe National Forest

Ed Z'berg-
Sugar Pine Point
State Park

Meeks Bay

3013

▲ Lost Corner Mountain

Rubicon Bay

Loon Lake

Lake   *Tahoe*

89

74

D. L. Bliss State Park

75

Phipps Peak ▲

▲ McConnell Peak

Emerald Bay

Emerald Bay State Park

76

79   77 78

80

LTBMU

Desolation Wilderness

81

82

Mt. Tallac ▲   83

Dicks Peak ▲

Fallen Leaf Lake

Jacks Peak ▲

85

84

Eldorado National Forest

86

87

▲ Mt. Price

Echo Peak ▲

▲ Pyramid Peak

Echo Lakes

Ralston Peak ▲

Ice House Reservoir

0   1   2   3   4   5 miles
0   1   2   3   4   5 kilometers

River

50

South   *Fork*   *American*

74 D. L. Bliss State Park: Rubicon Point and Lighthouse Loop

Distance	2 miles (loop)
Hiking Time	1–2 hours
Elevation	+550/-550 feet
Difficulty	Moderate
Trail Use	Leashed dogs, good for kids
Best Times	Mid-May through September
Agency	D. L. Bliss State Park at 530-525-7277, parks.ca.gov
Recommended Map	*CSP D. L. Bliss and Emerald Bay State Parks Trail System*

see map on p. 182

HIGHLIGHTS For good reasons, the Rubicon Trail is very popular with hikers and tourists alike. Tracing the southwest shore of Lake Tahoe, the trail treats travelers to incredible lake views throughout a mile-long section to Calawee Cove, where diversions include a refreshing dip in Lake Tahoe or lunch on the picturesque shore. By returning on the Lighthouse Trail, additional treats include a bit of history at old Rubicon Point Lighthouse.

DIRECTIONS Drive CA 89 to the entrance of D. L. Bliss State Park, approximately 11 miles north of the CA 50–CA 89 junction in South Lake Tahoe and 16 miles south of Tahoe City. Proceed on paved road to the campground entrance station (fee required) and continue to the small parking lot on the left-hand shoulder, 1.1 miles from the highway.

FACILITIES/TRAILHEAD Although there are no facilities right at the trailhead, D. L. Bliss State Park offers campgrounds, picnic areas, restrooms, and access to Lake Tahoe at Calawee Cove for swimmers, boaters, and anglers. Both the Rubicon and Lighthouse trails begin across the road from the parking area.

Follow signs for the Rubicon Trail, to the right of the Lighthouse Trail, which will be your return route. Walk on a wide, gently graded old roadbed through mostly fir forest, soon encountering a loop at the end of the old road. Find the beginning of the singletrack Rubicon Trail on the far side of the loop and turn left, obeying a sign for Calawee Cove.

Proceed on well-maintained trail with filtered views through the trees of Lake Tahoe and the peaks above the far shore. Soon scattered Jeffrey pines and firs allow better lake views, which improve even more where you reach open, shrub-covered slopes of chinquapin, manzanita, and tobacco brush. The excellent lake views continue to a junction with a lateral on the left, which climbs steeply up the hillside to the lighthouse.

Past the lateral junction, you descend granite stairs to an unmarked path that travels a short distance to a vista point offering a supreme Lake Tahoe view. Beyond the vista point, the main trail continues to the edge of a sheer cliff that's negotiated

with the aid of a narrow boardwalk lined with a chain fence. This area can be quite a logjam on busy summer weekends, as tourists queue up waiting for their turn at the single-file passage. Once the crux of the route is safely negotiated, easier trail leads to the parking lot at Rubicon Point-Calawee Cove, 1 mile from the trailhead.

To continue the loop, follow the Lighthouse Trail from the parking lot on a mild to moderate climb across a forested hillside to a switchback. As you climb away from the switchback, you may notice evidence of a previous fire. Eventually, the grade eases where the trail nears the top of the ridge. Then the trail meets a short path that leads down granite steps to the edge of the hillside and the restored Rubicon Point Lighthouse. If you're familiar with seacoast lighthouses, you may be a bit surprised at the scale of this lighthouse, which appears to be about outhouse size. However, what the structure lacks in appearance is more than made up for by the stunning view of Lake Tahoe (you'll have to enjoy the view from outside the lighthouse), and by the claim of having held the highest elevation of any lighthouse on a navigable body of water in the world. Renovation and stabilization of the Rubicon Point Lighthouse was completed in 2001.

Away from the lighthouse junction, you continue to ascend the ridge for a brief time before the trail leaves the boulder-studded ridge and follows a moderate descent through mixed forest back to the trailhead.

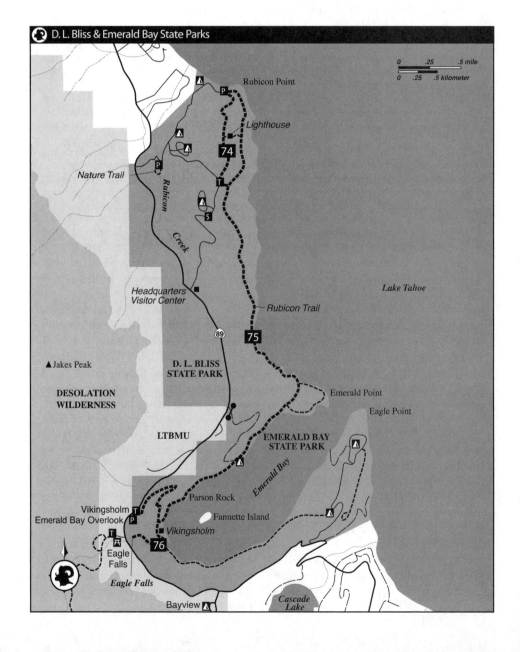

75 Emerald Bay and D. L. Bliss State Parks: Rubicon Trail

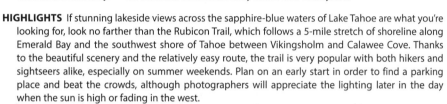

see map on p. 182

Distance	5 miles (point-to-point)
Hiking Time	2.5 hours
Elevation	+375/-700 feet
Difficulty	Moderate
Trail Use	Leashed dogs, good for kids
Best Times	Mid-May through September
Agency	D. L. Bliss State Park at 530-525-7277, parks.ca.gov
Recommended Map	*CSP D. L. Bliss and Emerald Bay State Parks Trail System*

HIGHLIGHTS If stunning lakeside views across the sapphire-blue waters of Lake Tahoe are what you're looking for, look no farther than the Rubicon Trail, which follows a 5-mile stretch of shoreline along Emerald Bay and the southwest shore of Tahoe between Vikingsholm and Calawee Cove. Thanks to the beautiful scenery and the relatively easy route, the trail is very popular with both hikers and sightseers alike, especially on summer weekends. Plan on an early start in order to find a parking place and beat the crowds, although photographers will appreciate the lighting later in the day when the sun is high or fading in the west.

DIRECTIONS *Start:* Drive CA 89 to the Vikingsholm parking lot above Emerald Bay on the west side of the highway, approximately 9 miles from the CA 50–CA 89 junction in South Lake Tahoe and 18 miles south of Tahoe City. The parking lot is a quarter mile north of the Eagle Falls parking lot. If your hike is planned for a weekend between Memorial Day and Labor Day, make sure you arrive early, as the Vikingsholm parking lot fills up fast.

End: Drive CA 89 to the entrance into D. L. Bliss State Park, approximately 11 miles north of the CA 50–CA 89 junction in South Lake Tahoe and 16 miles south of Tahoe City. Proceed on paved road past the campground entrance station (fee required) and past the small parking lot on the left-hand shoulder, 1.1 miles from the highway, where the Rubicon and Lighthouse trails begin on the opposite side of the road. Continue on paved road another a half mile to a stop sign at a T-junction and turn right, reaching the large parking lot at the end of the road near Calawee Cove, 2.4 miles from CA 89.

FACILITIES/TRAILHEAD Both the Vikingsholm and Rubicon Point parking areas have restrooms. A viewpoint near the Vikingsholm parking area offers superb views of Emerald Bay and Lake Tahoe. Calawee Cove near the Rubicon Point Trailhead offers lakeshore access for swimmers, boaters, and anglers. Both D. L. Bliss and Emerald Bay state parks offer most of the amenities tourists expect: campgrounds; restrooms (some with hot showers); picnic areas; access to Lake Tahoe for swimmers, boaters, and anglers; visitor centers; and tours of Vikingsholm castle (see Trip 76). The trail to Vikingsholm begins on the northeast side of the parking area. The Rubicon Point Trailhead at the end of the description is on the east side of the Calawee Cove parking lot.

Find a paved road at the northwest end of the parking lot and descend steeply along this road that in bygone days provided residents and guests access to the Vikingsholm mansion and grounds below. Follow the road as it switchbacks 400 feet down the hillside toward the mansion grounds at the bottom, where the Rubicon Trail begins near the lakeshore.

Head north from the beach area, passing outbuildings and picnic tables on the way to a number of bridges spanning small creeks and seeps that trickle down shady nooks filled with lush foliage. Proceed through a mixed forest of incense cedars, Jeffrey pines, white firs, and sugar pines along the shoreline of Emerald Bay past Parson Rock, a hump of granite that offers shutterbugs a supreme Tahoe view and swimmers an excellent diving spot.

Past the last of the bridges, you pass through the Emerald Bay Boat-in Campground and continue along the shoreline trail, past tall willows toward Emerald Point. At the start of this peninsula, 2.2 miles from the parking lot, a lightly used path veers right to follow the shoreline around Emerald Point, reconnecting with the Rubicon Trail 0.2 mile farther. If you're not in a hurry, Emerald Point provides an excellent view of Emerald Bay and the surrounding terrain, including Maggies Peaks.

The Rubicon Trail climbs over a low moraine to the north junction with the Emerald Point Trail at a picturesque cove. Nearby, a small stretch of sandy beach provides the last easily accessible piece of lakeshore between here and the end of the

Lake Tahoe from the Rubicon Trail

trail at Calawee Cove. Climbing away from the cove, you reach a vista point at a pile of large boulders that provides a vantage point for a grand view of the lake. Follow a short, zigzagging climb and continue above the lakeshore before a short descent leads to a thimbleberry-lined stream spilling across the path. Farther on, after a pair of switchbacks, the trail leaves the picturesque lake views and veers into dense forest.

For the next mile, you make a steady climb through shady forest to the trail's high point, followed by a short decline to a signed junction with the old road from D. L. Bliss State Park, 4.2 miles from the parking lot. If time is of the essence, a pickup could be arranged 0.1 mile away along this closed road at the Rubicon-Lighthouse Trailhead (see Trip 74), rather than at Calawee Cove.

From the junction, continue descending on well-maintained trail with filtered views through the trees of Lake Tahoe and the peaks above the far shore. Soon scattered Jeffrey pines and firs allow better lake views, which improve even more where you reach open shrub-covered slopes of chinquapin, manzanita, and tobacco brush. The excellent lake views continue to a junction with a lateral on the left, which climbs the steep hillside to the Rubicon Point Lighthouse (see Trip 74).

Past the lighthouse lateral, you descend granite stairs to an unmarked path that travels a short distance to a vista point offering a supreme Lake Tahoe view. Beyond the vista point, the main trail continues to the edge of a sheer cliff that you negotiate with the aid of a narrow boardwalk lined with a chain fence. This area can be quite a logjam on busy summer weekends, as tourists queue waiting for their turn at the single-file passage. Once the crux of the route is safely negotiated, easier trail leads to the parking lot near Rubicon Point at Calawee Cove, where Lester Beach offers hot and tired hikers a fine opportunity for a refreshing dip in the chilly waters of Lake Tahoe.

76   Emerald Bay State Park: Vikingsholm and Eagle Falls

see map on p. 182

Distance	2.5 miles (out-and-back)
Hiking Time	1.5–2 hours
Elevation	+230/-500 feet
Difficulty	Moderate
Trail Use	Leashed dogs, good for kids
Best Times	Mid-May through September
Agency	Emerald Bay State Park at 530-541-3030; D. L. Bliss State Park at 530-525-7277, parks.ca.gov
Recommended Map	*CSP D. L. Bliss and Emerald Bay State Parks Trail System*
Notes	Although there are campgrounds on the west and east shores of Emerald Bay, the Vikingsholm area, including Eagle Falls, is day-use only, open from 6 a.m. to 9 p.m.

HIGHLIGHTS Purchased by the state of California in 1953, designated a National Natural Landmark in 1969, and designated an underwater state park in 1994, Emerald Bay is Lake Tahoe's crown jewel. Along with a plethora of spectacular views, visitors to Emerald Bay State Park, who come by boat or descend the 1.25-mile trail, will find many diversions, including sandy beaches for sunbathing, excellent picnic spots, a vibrant waterfall, and the architectural wonder of Vikingsholm mansion. A tour of Vikingsholm (mid-June through September) is an absolute must for any first-time visitor to Emerald Bay State Park. Eagle Falls provides the height of drama when the creek is swollen with snowmelt from the mountains above, usually throughout the month of June.

DIRECTIONS Drive CA 89 to the Vikingsholm parking lot above Emerald Bay on the west side of the highway, approximately 9 miles from the CA 50–CA 89 junction in South Lake Tahoe and 18 miles south of Tahoe City. The parking lot is a quarter mile north of the Eagle Falls parking lot. If your hike is planned for a weekend between Memorial Day and Labor Day, make sure you arrive early, as the Vikingsholm parking lot fills up quickly.

FACILITIES/TRAILHEAD The trailhead parking area has restrooms. A nearby viewpoint offers superb views of Emerald Bay and Lake Tahoe. Emerald Bay State Park offers most of the amenities tourists expect: campgrounds; restrooms (some with hot showers); picnic areas; access to Lake Tahoe for swimmers, boaters, and anglers; visitor centers; and tours of Vikingsholm castle. The trail to Vikingsholm begins on the northeast side of the parking area.

Before heading down to Vikingsholm, take in the view of Emerald Bay and Lake Tahoe from the nearby overlook. The vista is a Tahoe classic, but you will definitely want your camera if your timing happens to coincide with a visit of the *Tahoe Queen* or the *M. S. Dixie* to Emerald Bay. Tiny Fannette Island, near the west end of the bay, is the only island in Lake Tahoe.

After enjoying the view from the overlook, find a paved road at the northwest end of the parking lot and descend steeply along this road, which used to provide residents and guests vehicular access to the Vikingsholm mansion below. Follow the road as it switchbacks 400 feet down the wall of the canyon above Emerald Bay, toward the shady mansion grounds at the bottom. By following all signs for Vikingsholm, you'll reach the front of the magnificent mansion 0.9 mile from the parking lot. To tour the mansion, walk a short distance south to the visitor center and purchase nominally priced tickets. Guided tours are conducted every half hour between 10 a.m. and 4 p.m.

To visit Eagle Falls, find the start of the signed trail near the visitor center. Head west on singletrack trail paralleling lushly lined Eagle Creek through cool forest. Soon the grade increases, and you climb shrub-covered slabs to a fenced viewing area near the base of the falls, 0.2 mile from the visitor center.

VIKINGSHOLM

Mrs. Lora Josephine Knight of Santa Barbara purchased the property around Emerald Bay, including Fannette Island, in 1928 for a price of $250,000. With her nephew by marriage, Lennart Palme, a Swedish-born architect, Knight set out to design and build a structure that would be one of the finest examples of Scandinavian architecture in the western hemisphere.

At great expense, the 38-room mansion was completed in September of 1929 by employing 200 craftsmen using old-world techniques, such as hand-hewing large timbers, making intricate carvings, and making hinges and latches. Following Knight's wishes, not a single large tree was disturbed in the construction of her magnificent residence.

Vikingsholm Mansion

Most of the materials used in construction of the mansion came from the Tahoe basin, including the granite stones in the foundation and walls. However, the furnishings inside Vikingsholm were either imported from Scandinavia or meticulously reproduced after priceless treasures from Norwegian and Swedish museums. A handful of less spectacular outbuildings also were built on the grounds, including the stone Tea House on Fannette Island.

Servants would boat Knight and her guests out to the island each summer day for afternoon tea. Knight spent her summers at Vikingsholm until her death in 1945. The property was generously sold to the State of California for half its appraised value in 1953.

see map on p. 188

77 Eagle Lake

Distance	2 miles (out-and-back)
Hiking Time	1–2 hours
Elevation	+425/-25 feet
Difficulty	Moderate
Trail Use	Dogs OK, good for kids
Best Times	Mid-June through October
Agency	Lake Tahoe Basin Management Unit at 530-543-2600, www.fs.usda.gov/ltbmu
Recommended Map	*ENF and LTBMU A Guide to the Desolation Wilderness*
Notes	Wilderness permits are required for both day hikes and overnight backpacks. Day hikers may self-register at the trailhead. Backpackers bound for the Velma Lakes and points beyond can obtain their permits from the Lake Tahoe Visitor Center, 5.5 miles south on CA 89.

HIGHLIGHTS The short but steep 1-mile climb to Eagle Lake along the Eagle Falls Trail is one of Tahoe's most popular hikes, and for good reason. Where else can one visit such a picturesque lake tucked into an alpine-like granite cirque with such little effort? There is also a short nature trail close to the trailhead, providing hikers and sightseers with an interesting and informative loop diversion.

DIRECTIONS Follow CA 89 to Emerald Bay, and locate the popular Eagle Falls Trailhead on the east side of the highway, approximately 9 miles north of the CA 50–CA 89 junction and 19 miles south of Tahoe City. The Forest Service charges a $5-per-day fee for parking. Very limited free parking is available along the highway just outside of the trailhead parking area. Parking at the Eagle Lake Trailhead is at a premium all summer long, so arrive early if you expect to snag a parking space, especially on weekends.

FACILITIES/TRAILHEAD The trailhead has picnic tables, barbecue pits, toilets, and running water. The well-signed trail begins at the far end of the parking area.

Climb away from the well-signed trailhead and follow wood-beam steps to a junction with the Eagle Loop Nature Trail, marked by a 6-by-6-inch post. Veer left at the junction and proceed through shrubs and scattered conifers past a vertical cliff to the Eagle Creek Bridge, 0.2 mile from the trailhead.

From the bridge, follow granite steps across a field of blocky talus, soon crossing the signed Desolation Wilderness boundary. Past a patch of dense shrubs and lush trailside vegetation, you break out into the open across granite slabs, with grand views of Lake Tahoe and the towering cliffs rimming the canyon. Continue past scattered Jeffrey pines and junipers on a gentler grade, eventually encountering a denser forest of primarily lodgepole pines where the trail nears Eagle Creek. A short, stiff climb leads to a junction with the lateral to Eagle Lake, 0.8 mile from the trailhead.

Take the lateral on the right and climb across shrubby slopes to the northwest shore of Eagle Lake. The scenic lake reposes serenely in an impressive granite cirque composed of steep cliffs. The shrub-covered slopes dotted with Jeffrey pines and white firs surrounding the lake offer limited access to the abrupt shoreline, providing something of a challenge for both swimmers interested in a chilly dip and anglers plying the waters for the resident trout.

You can vary the route of your return slightly by following the Eagle Loop Nature Trail. Immediately after crossing the Eagle Creek Bridge, veer left at a junction with the Eagle Loop. Just past an informational sign about the first sighting of Lake Tahoe by John C. Fremont and Charles Preuss, you reach another junction. The left-hand

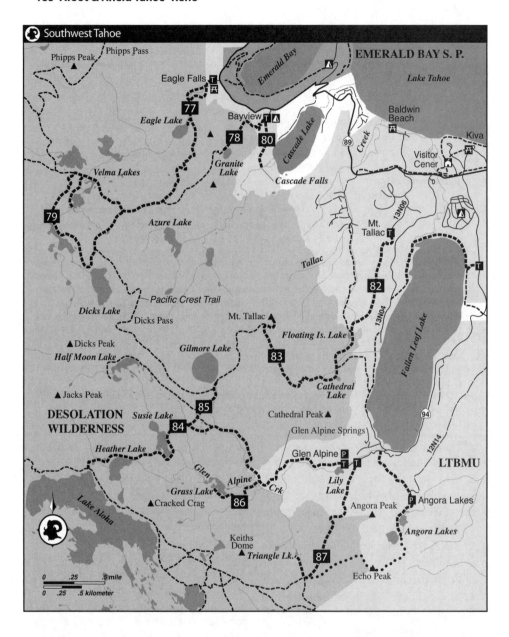

trail climbs granite steps and slabs to a viewpoint of Emerald Bay and Lake Tahoe, complete with benches and informational signs. The right-hand trail descends open slopes past more signs, to the lower junction with the Eagle Falls Trail. From there, follow the main trail back to the trailhead.

| 78 | **Granite Lake** |

Distance	2.2 miles (out-and-back)
Hiking Time	1–1.5 hours
Elevation	+800 feet
Difficulty	Moderate
Trail Use	Dogs OK, good for kids
Best Times	July through mid-October
Agency	Lake Tahoe Basin Management Unit at 530-543-2600, www.fs.usda.gov/ltbmu
Recommended Map	*ENF and LTBMU A Guide to the Desolation Wilderness*
Notes	Wilderness permits are required for both day hikes and overnight backpacking trips. Day hikers may self-register at the trailhead. Backpackers bound for the Velma Lakes and points beyond can obtain their permits from the Lake Tahoe Visitor Center, 4.5 miles south on CA 89.

see map on p. 188

HIGHLIGHTS The 1.1-mile hike to Granite Lake gains a significant amount of elevation along the way, but the effort is well rewarded once you arrive at the forest-rimmed lake. Towered over by the twin summits of Maggies Peaks, Granite Lake is a picturesque spot for swimming in the chilly waters, angling for the resident trout, or for simply relaxing along the lakeshore.

DIRECTIONS Drive CA 89 to Emerald Bay and locate the Bayview Trailhead on the south side of the highway, approximately 7.5 miles from the CA 50–CA 89 junction and 19.5 miles south of Tahoe City. Parking is at a premium on summer weekends, so plan on an early arrival to secure a parking space.

FACILITIES/TRAILHEAD The Bayview Trailhead has equestrian facilities. The adjacent Bayview Campground is a primitive forest service campground. The trail begins at the south end of the parking area near a Desolation Wilderness signboard.

Just past the trailhead, you reach a junction with the trail to Cascade Falls (see Trip 80). Following a sign for Desolation Wilderness, turn right at the junction and make a stiff, switchbacking climb through mixed forest of primarily white fir with a chinquapin understory. Beyond the wilderness boundary, you follow the crest of a ridge, where the forest parts enough to allow good views of Emerald Bay and Lake Tahoe. Leaving the ridge, the trail follows Granite Lake's alder-lined outlet on a gentler ascent through bracken ferns, thimbleberry, wildflowers, and a mixture of shrubs, including chinquapin, tobacco brush, and greenleaf and pinemat manzanita. As you progress up the trail, lodgepole pines and western white pines join the forest on the way to serene Granite Lake, 1 mile from the trailhead. The Bayview Trail stays well above Granite Lake, so you'll have to descend to the forest-rimmed lakeshore via one of the use trails on the northwest side of the lake.

Granite Lake

79 Bayview Trail to Velma Lakes

see map on p. 188

Distance	10.5 miles (semiloop)
Hiking Time	5–7 hours
Elevation	+2,725/-2,725 feet
Difficulty	Moderate
Trail Use	Backpacking option, dogs OK
Best Times	Mid-July through mid-October
Agency	Lake Tahoe Basin Management Unit at 530-543-2600, www.fs.usda.gov/ltbmu
Recommended Map	*ENF and LTBMU A Guide to the Desolation Wilderness*
Notes	Wilderness permits are required for both day hikes and overnight backpacks. Day hikers may self-register at the trailhead. Backpackers bound for the Velma Lakes and points beyond can obtain their permits from the Lake Tahoe Visitor Center, 4.5 miles south on CA 89.

HIGHLIGHTS This 10.5-mile semiloop trip through the heart of the Desolation Wilderness samples several cirque-bound lakes amid the characteristic granite terrain that makes the area so picturesque. Whether you're just out for the day or on an overnight backpack, the lakes provide great scenery, along with fine swimming and fishing opportunities. Desolation's backcountry usually frees itself from snow by mid-July, and wildflowers bloom from then until late August, when swimmers will find the water in the lakes to be the least chilly.

DIRECTIONS Drive CA 89 to Emerald Bay and locate the Bayview Trailhead on the south side of the highway, approximately 7.5 miles from the CA 50–CA 89 junction and 19.5 miles south of Tahoe City. Parking is at a premium on summer weekends, so plan on an early arrival to secure a parking space.

FACILITIES/TRAILHEAD The Bayview Trailhead has equestrian facilities. The adjacent Bayview Campground is a primitive forest service campground. The trail begins at the south end of the parking area near a Desolation Wilderness signboard.

Just past the trailhead, you reach a junction with the trail to Cascade Falls (see Trip 80). Following a sign for Desolation Wilderness, turn right at the junction and make a stiff, switchbacking climb through mixed forest of primarily white fir with a chinquapin understory. Beyond the wilderness boundary, you follow the crest of a ridge, where the forest parts enough to allow good views of Emerald Bay and Lake Tahoe. Leaving the ridge, the trail follows Granite Lake's alder-lined outlet on a gentler ascent through bracken ferns, thimbleberry, wildflowers, and a mixture of shrubs, including chinquapin, tobacco brush, and greenleaf and pinemat manzanita. As you progress up the trail, lodgepole pines and western white pines join the forest on the way to serene Granite Lake, 1 mile from the trailhead. The Bayview Trail stays well above Granite Lake, so if you wish to visit the shoreline, you'll have to descend via one of the use trails on the northwest side.

Near the far end of Granite Lake, the trail begins a switchbacking climb across the south-facing slope below the twin summits of Maggies Peaks. After a three-quarter-mile climb, you bid farewell to the lake basin and follow mildly graded trail along the backside of South Maggies Peak to a gentle descent along the forested southwest ridge. At 2.7 miles from the trailhead, you reach a saddle and a signed, three-way junction with the Eagle Lake Trail.

Veer right at the junction and follow sandy trail on a mildly undulating route through widely scattered mixed forest and around granite boulders and slabs. At 0.6 mile from the junction, you intersect the Velma Lakes Trail. Bear right and follow the Velma Lakes Trail on a downhill course through acres of granite slabs, boulders, and rocks interspersed with widely scattered pines. Along the way, you have occasional glimpses of the unnamed pond directly north of Upper Velma Lake. Reach the floor of the lakes basin and walk along the north shore of the pond, ford the outlet, and come to a three-way junction marked with a 6-by-6-inch post, 4.1 miles from the trailhead. Upper Velma Lake is reached via the half-mile trail to the left (south), which dead-ends near the inlet.

Continue straight ahead at the junction and make a short climb to intersect the Pacific Crest Trail (PCT), 4.25 miles from the trailhead. A short walk northbound on the PCT leads to an unobstructed view of Middle Velma Lake. Backpackers wishing to stay at Middle Velma can leave the PCT and head cross-country to campsites scattered around the lakeshore.

Turn left at the junction and head southbound on the PCT on a moderate, winding climb above Upper Velma Lake. Where the rate of ascent eases, Dicks Pass and Fontanillis Lake pop into view, and then you make a short drop to the crossing of the outlet from Fontanillis Lake. Cross the lake's multihued rock basin along the east shore, shadowed by towering Dicks Peak. With a location on the popular PCT, several campsites sheltered in groves of lodgepole pines and mountain hemlocks offer fine overnight accommodations.

At the far end of the lake, a brief ascent across boulder-covered slopes leads to the top of a rise and the short lateral to Dicks Lake, where backpackers will find additional campsites. From the lateral, the PCT bends away from the cirque of Dicks Lake on a mild ascent to a junction with the Eagle Lake Trail, 6.4 miles from the trailhead.

A steep 0.3-mile descent from the PCT leads to milder trail that traverses a pond-dotted basin. You reach the three-way junction of the Eagle Falls and Velma Lakes trails at 7.2 miles, closing the loop section. From there, retrace your steps 0.6 mile to the Bayview–Eagle Falls junction and then 2.7 miles to the Bayview Trailhead.

Upper Velma Lake

80 Cascade Falls

see map on p. 188

Distance	1.5 miles (out-and-back)
Hiking Time	1–1.5 hours
Elevation	+75/-125 feet
Difficulty	Moderate
Trail Use	Dogs OK
Best Times	June through mid-October
Agency	Lake Tahoe Basin Management Unit at 530-543-2600, www.fs.usda.gov/ltbmu
Recommended Map	*ENF and LTBMU A Guide to the Desolation Wilderness*
Notes	Wilderness permits are required for both day hikes and overnight backpacks. Day hikers may self-register at the trailhead.

HIGHLIGHTS During the height of snowmelt, Cascade Falls is a turbulent display of raucous watery splendor tumbling 200 feet down a granite cliff into Cascade Lake. The maintained trail ends before the falls, requiring that hikers scramble over granite slabs and boulders to reach the brink of the falls, where adults should keep a watchful eye on children at all times. Above the falls are several delightful picnic spots near swirling pools and cascades, along appropriately named Cascade Creek.

DIRECTIONS Drive CA 89 to Emerald Bay and locate the Bayview Trailhead on the south side of the highway, approximately 7.5 miles from the CA 50–CA 89 junction and 19.5 miles south of Tahoe City. Parking is at a premium on summer weekends, so plan on an early arrival to secure a parking space.

FACILITIES/TRAILHEAD The Bayview Trailhead has equestrian facilities. The adjacent Bayview Campground is a primitive forest service campground. The trail begins at the south end of the parking area near a Desolation Wilderness signboard.

Cascade Lake from the trail to Cascade Falls

Just past the trailhead, you reach a junction with the trail to Granite and Velma Lakes (see Trips 78 and 79). Following signed directions to Cascade Falls, turn left and climb over a low hill, then follow a gently graded path through a light covering of mixed forest and an understory of shrubs, including greenleaf manzanita, mountain chinquapin, and huckleberry oak. After a short climb over rock steps, pretty Cascade Lake springs into view below, cradled into a glacier-scoured cirque basin. Unfortunately, all but a slim portion of the eastern side of this lake is privately owned.

Follow the trail on a descending traverse across the west side of the lake's basin toward the far end of the lake, and then start to climb over granite slabs and rocky sections of trail. Although maintained trail ends before the falls, use trails branch left toward the falls—simply follow the sound of the tumbling water. Exercise caution here, as loose rocks, slippery slabs, and overhangs could be potentially hazardous.

The tread deteriorates a bit past the slabs, but a series of cairns marks the course of a faint path that cuts through dense foliage and loops around through the forest for those who wish to continue beyond the falls.

---

81   Taylor Creek Visitor Center Nature Trails

see map on p. 194

Distance	Varies (semiloop)
Hiking Time	15 minutes–1 hour
Elevation	Negligible
Difficulty	Easy
Trail Use	Good for kids
Best Times	May through October
Agency	Lake Tahoe Basin Management Unit at 530-543-2600; www.fs.usda.gov/ltbmu
Recommended Map	ENF and LTBMU A Guide to the Desolation Wilderness

HIGHLIGHTS Backpackers will know the Taylor Creek Visitor Center as the place on the east side of Desolation Wilderness to acquire a wilderness permit. More casual hikers and tourists flock to the area to stroll along one of the several gently graded nature trails that travel through a variety of habitats and past a number of diverse points of interest. The area is a hub of activity for young and old alike throughout the summer and again in the fall, when the Kokanee salmon spawn in Taylor Creek.

DIRECTIONS The Taylor Creek Visitor Center is located just off of CA 89, 0.1 mile west of Fallen Leaf Road. The well-signed turnoff into the visitor center is about 3.5 miles north of the Y-junction with CA 50 in South Lake Tahoe.

FACILITIES/TRAILHEAD Forest service rangers staff the visitor center on a daily basis during the summer months. The visitor center has restrooms with running water and flush toilets. Picnic areas and beaches are nearby. Fallen Leaf Campground is a half mile away to the south of CA 89. Camp Richardson Resort is a short drive to the east. All trails can be accessed from the vicinity of the visitor center.

Rainbow Trail: A paved, wheelchair-accessible trail with interpretive signs heads away from the visitor center past an aspen grove and to a meadow carpeted with wildflowers in early summer. Boardwalks guide you across boggy sections while providing needed protection of the sensitive plant species that inhabit the wet soils in the meadow. Park benches placed around the loop and an overlook of the marsh, near where Taylor Creek empties into Lake Tahoe, offer peaceful spots to pause and ponder the natural surroundings. After a quarter mile, the trail reaches the Stream Profile Chamber, where 12-foot-high, floor-to-ceiling windows provide a below-water view of the creek. From there, the path loops back to the visitor center through aspens and meadows.

Forest Tree Trail: The Forest Tree Trail, an extremely short nature trail that sees very little use, begins on the north side of the visitor center. The loop trail passes several interpretive signs about the Jeffrey pine and its relationship with other plants and animals in the forest.

Lake of the Sky Trail: Head south from the visitor center on paved trail to a junction with a paved path on the left that heads to the amphitheater. Veer left and follow a wide gravel path through scattered Jeffrey pines and shrubby foliage, then come alongside a three-pole log fence next to a lush meadow bisected by Taylor Creek. An elevated wood viewing deck provides an opportunity to perhaps spot a bald eagle if you happen to be here in the off-season. Summer visitors can search for some of the 31 different species of animal pictured on the nearby placard.

Pass more interpretive signs on the way to a four-way junction, where a lateral on the right heads west to a parking lot. Continue straight ahead and proceed toward Tallac Point, with Taylor Creek Marsh directly west of the trail and Baldwin Beach just beyond the marsh.

Reaching Tallac Point, the trail bends to the east and follows the edge of the forest above the sandy beach along the shoreline of Lake Tahoe. Proceed through a scattered forest of firs, pines, and aspens to a Y-junction. Turn right for an immediate return to the visitor center, or proceed straight ahead toward the Tallac Historic Site. Near the junction, a set of stairs provides access to the beach.

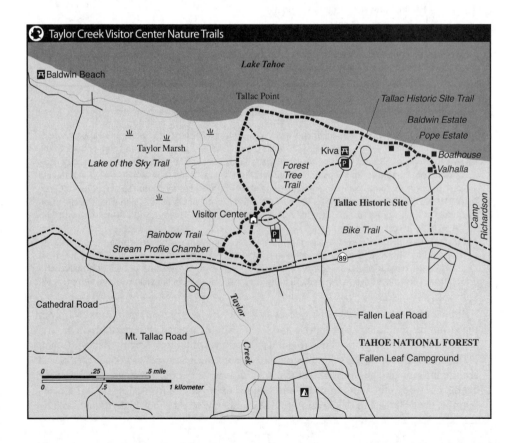

Tallac Historic Site Trail: The Tallac Historic Site Trail can be accessed from either the Lake of the Sky Trail at Tallac Point as described above, or from the Kiva Picnic Area parking lot. Continuing west from the Lake of the Sky Trail, you pass an interpretive display about the history of Lucky Baldwin's Tallac Resort. A concrete foundation is all that remains of the elaborate structures that made up the resort. Heading away from the site of the resort, you reach the Kiva Picnic Area, complete with barbecue pits, picnic tables, and restrooms. A set of wooden stairs nearby provides access to the sandy beach.

Beyond the picnic area, the trail continues eastward to a grape-stake fence near the boundary of the Baldwin Estate. Inside the fence, the trail passes the Baldwin Estate guest cabins and some larger structures, as interpretive placards provide historical information along the way. Nowadays the Baldwin House is home to the Tallac Museum.

Past the Washoe Gardens and some park benches, you walk through a gate into the Pope Estate and pass through an arboretum created in 1902 by the Lloyd Tevis family, the second owners of the property. The Pope Estate is the largest and oldest estate at the site, currently housing the interpretive center. At the far end of the estate, the trail passes the boathouse, the boathouse theater, and the Valhalla pier as it meets the Tallac Bike Trail. The restored Valhalla Estate is just a short walk away, currently used for community events.

82   Floating Island and Cathedral Lakes

see map on p. 188

Distance	5 miles (out-and-back)
Hiking Time	2.5–3 hours
Elevation	+1,200 feet
Difficulty	Moderate
Trail Use	Backpacking option, dogs OK
Best Times	July through mid-October
Agency	Lake Tahoe Basin Management Unit at 530-543-2600, www.fs.usda.gov/ltbmu
Recommended Map	*ENF and LTBMU A Guide to the Desolation Wilderness*
Notes	Since part of the Mt. Tallac Trail lies within Desolation Wilderness, you will need a permit for both day hikes and backpacks. Day hikers may self-register at the trailhead, but backpackers will need to get their permit from the Lake Tahoe Visitor Center.

HIGHLIGHTS For those who desire something easier than the climb to the summit of Mt. Tallac (see Trip 83), the 2.5-mile hike to the Floating Island and Cathedral Lakes on the Mt. Tallac Trail is a fine option. The lakes are both scenic but look very different: Floating Island is a forest-rimmed lake named for mats of sod that periodically break away from the shore and float around the lake, while Cathedral exudes much more of a subalpine ambience. While overnight camping is allowed at the lakes, campsites are nearly nonexistent at Floating Island and of marginal quality at Cathedral.

DIRECTIONS Drive CA 89 to Forest Service Road 13N06, which is across from the road to the Lake Tahoe Visitor Center; turn south on 13N06, following a sign reading TALLAC TRAILHEAD. Follow paved road for 0.3 mile to an intersection, turn left, and proceed 0.2 mile to a junction with a road on the left to Camp Concord. Continue straight ahead at the junction, reaching the trailhead parking area at 1 mile from the highway.

FACILITIES/TRAILHEAD There are no facilities at the trailhead. The Taylor Creek Visitor Center, with picnic areas, beach access, and restrooms, is just a short drive away. Fallen Leaf Campground is nearby as well. The trail begins near some trail signs.

From the trailhead, follow an old gravel roadbed on a mild climb through scattered Jeffrey pines and white firs. Beyond some backcountry signs, the grade increases, the forest thickens, and on singletrack trail, you gain the crest of a morainal ridge. As you steadily climb along the ridge, Fallen Leaf Lake dramatically springs into view across a hillside carpeted with huckleberry oak and greenleaf manzanita, but as fine as these views are, even better ones await farther up the trail. About 1.25 miles from the trailhead, the trail forsakes the ridgecrest, briefly drops into a gully, and then on a steep ascent comes alongside the outlet from Floating Island Lake. Eventually, the grade eases and you reach the northeast shore of the serene, forest-rimmed lake soon after crossing the Desolation Wilderness boundary, 1.7 miles from the trailhead.

Five-acre Floating Island Lake was named in the late 1800s for a 20-foot-diameter, grass- and shrub-covered natural island that at one time sported a thriving conifer. Since that time, several more grassy mats have sloughed off from the lakeshore and floated about the lake, although when I recently visited the lake, the surface was devoid of floating islands. The quiet lake, bordered by dense, mostly red fir forest, is a fine destination for an easy two-hour hike.

Mild trail follows the shoreline past the lake and leads to a winding climb over rocky terrain through thinning trees. Return to dense forest and thick shrubs while strolling alongside Floating Island Lake's inlet. Soon you break out of the trees and climb across an open slope carpeted with sagebrush, serviceberry, currant, and wildflowers, which allows fine views of Mt. Tallac. Back into the trees, the trail drops to a crossing of Cathedral Creek, lined with a luxuriant swath of vegetation, and then climbs to a junction with Trail 17E05. This trail provides a steep, exposed, 1-mile connection to Trail 17E05A above the southwest shore of Fallen Leaf Lake. (By following this trail to the north, you'll reach a tiny parking area in the Fallen Leaf Tract of summer homes. By heading south, you'll encounter Stanford Camp, the private university's extension campus, where there is absolutely no public parking and therefore no shortcut to Tallac's summit.)

Continue climbing from the junction to shortly reach Cathedral Lake, 2.5 miles from the trailhead. The diminutive lake sits in a steep rock basin, surrounded by talus and sheltered by a few clumps of pines. Although reasonably attractive, the lake fails to exude the reverential awe its appellation would suggest, having received the name from the nearby cliff on Tallac's southeast ridge.

83 Mt. Tallac

Distance	9.6 miles (out-and-back)
Hiking Time	5–7 hours
Elevation	+3,300/-100 feet
Difficulty	Difficult
Trail Use	Backpacking option, dogs OK
Best Times	Mid-July through mid-October
Agency	Lake Tahoe Basin Management Unit at 530-543-2600, www.fs.usda.gov/ltbmu
Recommended Map	*ENF and LTBMU A Guide to the Desolation Wilderness*
Notes	Since part of the Mt. Tallac Trail lies within Desolation Wilderness, you will need a permit for both day hikes and multiday backpacking trips. Day hikers may self-register at the trailhead, but backpackers will need to get their permit from the Lake Tahoe Visitor Center.

see map on p. 188

HIGHLIGHTS Many regard Mt. Tallac as the quintessential Tahoe peak. The dark, metamorphic hulk looms over the south end of the lake in dominant fashion, casting a long shadow over the surrounding terrain. "Tallac" is a Native American word meaning "Great Mountain," a particularly appropriate moniker for this stately peak. Not only is the mountain an imposing sight when viewed from various points around the basin, but the vista from the summit is equally stunning. Prospective peak baggers don't need specialized mountaineering skills in order to reach the incredible view, as a maintained trail can be followed all the way to the top of the peak.

At 9,735 feet, Mt. Tallac holds onto its winter mantle well into midsummer—don't expect snow-free trails until after mid-July. The potential for high winds and winter weather at this altitude usually signals an end to the hiking season on Mt. Tallac during early to mid-October.

DIRECTIONS Drive CA 89 to Forest Service Road 13N06, which is across from the road to the Lake Tahoe Visitor Center; turn south on 13N06, following a sign reading TALLAC TRAILHEAD. Follow paved road for 0.3 mile to an intersection, turn left, and proceed 0.2 mile to a junction with a road on the left to Camp Concord. Continue straight ahead at the junction, reaching the trailhead parking area at 1 mile from the highway.

FACILITIES/TRAILHEAD There are no facilities at the trailhead. The Taylor Creek Visitor Center, with picnic areas, beach access, and restrooms, is just a short drive away. Fallen Leaf Campground is nearby as well. The trail begins near some signs.

From the trailhead, follow an old gravel roadbed on a mild climb through scattered Jeffrey pines and white firs. Beyond some backcountry signs, the grade increases, the forest thickens, and on singletrack trail, you gain the crest of a morainal ridge. As you steadily climb along the ridge, Fallen Leaf Lake dramatically springs into view across a hillside carpeted with huckleberry oak and greenleaf manzanita, but as fine as these views are, even better ones await farther up the trail. About 1.25 miles from the trailhead, the trail forsakes the ridgecrest, briefly drops into a gully, and then, on a steep ascent, comes alongside the outlet from Floating Island Lake. Eventually, the grade eases and you reach the northeast shore of the serene, forest-rimmed lake, soon after crossing the Desolation Wilderness boundary, 1.7 miles from the trailhead. The lake makes a fine destination for an easy two-hour hike (see Trip 82).

Mild trail follows the shoreline past the lake and leads to a winding climb over rocky terrain and through thinning trees before returning to dense forest and thick shrubs alongside Floating Island Lake's inlet. Soon you break out of the trees and climb across an open slope carpeted with sagebrush, serviceberry, currant, and wildflowers, which allows fine views of Mt. Tallac. Back into the trees, the trail drops to a crossing of Cathedral Creek, lined with a luxuriant swath of vegetation, and then climbs to a junction with Trail 17E05. This trail provides a steep, exposed, 1-mile connection to Trail 17E05A above the southwest shore of Fallen Leaf Lake. (By following this trail to the north, you'll reach a tiny parking area in the Fallen Leaf Tract of summer homes. By heading south, you'll encounter Stanford Camp, the private university's extension campus, where there is absolutely no public parking and therefore no shortcut to Tallac's summit.) Continue climbing from the junction to shortly reach diminutive Cathedral Lake, 2.5 miles from the trailhead, which sits in a steep rock basin, surrounded by talus and sheltered by a few clumps of pines.

Beyond Cathedral Lake, the trail leaves the dense forest behind and attacks the hillside with a vengeance. On steep, rocky trail, you climb across shrub-covered slopes with increasingly fine views of Lake Tahoe and the peaks rimming the southeast shore. A small brook adorned with flowers, including monkey flower, fireweed, larkspur, forget-me-not, and thimbleberry, provides the last reliable water for the remainder of the ascent. Long-legged switchbacks lead across slopes covered with tobacco brush,

View of Fallen Leaf Lake and Lake Tahoe from the Tallac Trail

sagebrush, and bitterbrush to the crest of Mt. Tallac's southeast ridge.

Now heading northwest, you follow the ridge through wildflowers, shrubs, and groves of stunted conifers, including western white pines, mountain hemlocks, whitebark pines, and lodgepole pines. Improving views to the west of the Crystal Range and the canyons of Desolation Wilderness become quite impressive. The steep ascent eventually leads to a marked junction at 4.4 miles with Trail 17E33 to

Gilmore Lake, where backpackers can find decent campsites.

Veer to the right at the junction and continue the ascent over rocky slopes through diminishing pines around the south side of Mt. Tallac. Regaining the southeast ridge, Lake Tahoe springs back into view, and you follow the ridge the last 150 vertical feet to the summit. Situated a mere 3.5 miles from the lakeshore, the view from the top of Mt. Tallac is one of the Tahoe Basin's finest vistas.

84   Glen Alpine to Susie and Heather Lakes and Lake Aloha

Distance	11.8 miles (out-and-back)
Hiking Time	6–8 hours
Elevation	+1,850/-275 feet
Difficulty	Moderate
Trail Use	Backpacking option, dogs OK
Best Times	Mid-July through early October
Agency	Lake Tahoe Basin Management Unit at 530-543-2600, www.fs.usda.gov/ltbmu
Recommended Map	*ENF and LTBMU A Guide to the Desolation Wilderness*

see map on p. 188

Notes   Since this trail lies within Desolation Wilderness, you will need a permit for both day hikes and backpacking trips. Day hikers may self-register at the trailhead, but backpackers will need to get their permit from the Lake Tahoe Visitor Center.

HIGHLIGHTS   This trip provides a fine example of the classic Desolation Wilderness experience, visiting the granite country for which the area is noted. An easy section of trail takes visitors to the historical setting of Glen Alpine Springs, before a moderate climb leads to three picturesque lakes in the shadow of Jacks Peak. John Muir's endorsement of the area reads, "The Glen Alpine Springs tourist resort seems to me one of the delightful places in all the famous Tahoe region. From no other valley, as far as I know, may excursions be made in a single day to so many peaks, wild gardens, glacier lakes, glacier meadows and alpine groves, cascades, etc." Don't anticipate huge doses of solitude, as this area is deservedly popular with both hikers and backpackers alike.

DIRECTIONS   Follow CA 89 to Fallen Leaf Road, approximately 3 miles northwest of the Y-junction with CA 50 in South Lake Tahoe. Turn south and follow Fallen Leaf Road for 4.6 miles to the far end of Fallen Leaf Lake and a signed junction for Glen Alpine. Turn left at the junction and proceed on a very narrow paved road for a half mile to the trailhead parking area just past a bridge over Glen Alpine Creek.

FACILITIES/TRAILHEAD   The trailhead has modern vault toilets. Plan on an early arrival on weekends, as parking is at a premium.

Begin hiking on a closed gravel road past private cabins and alongside lush riparian vegetation on the left that obscures views of neighboring Lily Lake. The hillside to the right is covered with a mixed forest of junipers, Jeffrey pines, incense cedars, lodgepole pines, firs, and aspens. Continue along the road past Lily Lake to a scenic waterfall on Glen Alpine Creek, and then proceed to Glen Alpine Springs, 1 mile from the trailhead.

Dirt road continues beyond Glen Alpine Springs for a short distance, until single-track trail climbs through mixed forest, followed by open, shrub-covered terrain with good views of the surrounding peaks and ridges. You enter the signed Desolation Wilderness and soon encounter a junction with the Grass Lake Trail, 1.6 miles from the trailhead (see Trip 86).

Turn right (north) and follow an extended, switchbacking climb over open granite slopes up the canyon of Gilmore Lake's outlet. Back under forest cover, you hop across an alder-lined rivulet, continue climbing to a ford of the outlet, and soon encounter a junction at 3 miles.

Veer left at the junction and follow Trail 17E32 toward Susie Lake. A short climb continues through the trees and leads to a westward traverse past a quartet of shallow ponds covered with lily pads. Beyond the four serene ponds, the path descends to a junction with the Pacific Crest Trail (PCT) near a wildflower-covered meadow, 3.5 miles from the trailhead.

Turn left and follow the PCT past two more ponds and over a ridge to an overlook of rockbound Susie Lake. A mild descent leads to a ford of the outlet near the southeast shore, a potentially difficult crossing early in the season. Named either for Nathan Gilmore's oldest daughter, or for the matriarch of the Washoe Indian squaws, Susie Lake is enchanting, cradled in the sort of rocky bowl that characterizes the heart of Desolation Wilderness. The metamorphic hulk of Jacks Peak provides a fine backdrop to the long, irregularly shaped lake, bordered by clumps of heather.

To continue to Heather Lake, follow the trail around the south shore of Susie Lake and make a steady climb toward the V-shaped notch of the outlet. Climb over the low, barren ridge to drop into Heather Lake's basin, well above the shore and continue toward the far end of the lake.

Rocky trail climbs to a nice view of a waterfall and across Heather Lake's inlet. Continue the ascent past a placid tarn and to the crest of a ridge between the basins of Heather Lake and Lake Aloha. Here you have a marvelous view of the jagged Crystal Range beyond the island-dotted surface of sizable Lake Aloha. Dropping off the crest, you reach a junction with the Rubicon Trail at the northeast corner of Lake Aloha. The lake is most attractive in midsummer, before the level of the lake drops to the point where it appears to be a series of interconnected ponds.

GLEN ALPINE SPRINGS

While searching for stray cattle in 1863, Nathan Gilmore discovered the mineral springs that his wife would name Glen Alpine Springs for a verse in a romantic poem by Sir Walter Scott. Gilmore built a wagon road to the springs from Fallen Leaf Lake, bottled and sold the carbonated water, and developed a first-class resort that attracted several noteworthy figures over the years. A summer camp was established in 1878 and a post office in 1904, both of which were later relocated to Fallen Leaf Lake. Several structures remain from the bygone days, including the resort's social hall, an edifice of steel, redwood, stone, and glass designed by Bernard Maybeck, the noted architect of the San Francisco Palace of Fine Art. Nowadays, in conjunction with the Forest Service, Glen Alpine Springs is under the care of a nonprofit corporation with a mission of preserving, restoring, and interpreting the site's resources. The old social hall houses an interpretive center, with guided tours and docents available from mid-June to mid-September. Glen Alpine Springs also sponsors special events throughout the summer. For more information, call 530-573-2405.

Waterfall near Glen Alpine Springs

85 Glen Alpine to Gilmore Lake

see map on p. 188

Distance	8.4 miles (out-and-back)
Hiking Time	4–6 hours
Elevation	+1,750 feet
Difficulty	Moderate
Trail Use	Backpacking option, dogs OK
Best Times	Mid-July through early October
Agency	Lake Tahoe Basin Management Unit at 530-543-2600, www.fs.usda.gov/ltbmu
Recommended Map	*ENF and LTBMU A Guide to the Desolation Wilderness*
Notes	Since this trail lies within Desolation Wilderness, you will need a permit for both day hikes and backpacks. Day hikers may self-register at the trailhead, but backpackers will need to get their permit from the Lake Tahoe Visitor Center.

HIGHLIGHTS Perhaps the most symmetrically round lake in the Tahoe area, lodgepole-rimmed Gilmore Lake is an excellent destination for day hikers and backpackers alike. The lake is named for

Nathan Gilmore, perhaps the original pioneer of the area around Fallen Leaf Lake and also one of the first proponents of preserving lands around Lake Tahoe for the public.

DIRECTIONS Follow CA 89 to Fallen Leaf Road, approximately 3 miles northwest of the Y-junction with CA 50 in South Lake Tahoe. Turn south and follow Fallen Leaf Road for 4.6 miles to the far end of Fallen Leaf Lake and a signed junction for Glen Alpine. Turn left at the junction and proceed on a very narrow paved road for a half mile to the trailhead parking area just past a bridge over Glen Alpine Creek.

FACILITIES/TRAILHEAD The trailhead has modern vault toilets. Plan on an early arrival on weekends, as parking is at a premium.

Begin hiking on a closed gravel road past private cabins and alongside lush riparian vegetation on the left that obscures views of neighboring Lily Lake. The hillside to the right is covered with a mixed forest of junipers, Jeffrey pines, incense cedars, lodgepole pines, firs, and aspens. Continue along the road past Lily Lake to a scenic waterfall on Glen Alpine Creek and proceed to Glen Alpine Springs, 1 mile from the trailhead.

Dirt road continues beyond Glen Alpine Springs for a short distance until singletrack trail climbs through mixed forest, followed by open, shrub-covered terrain with good views of the surrounding peaks and ridges. You enter the signed Desolation Wilderness and soon encounter a junction with the Grass Lake Trail (see Trip 86), 1.6 miles from the trailhead.

Turn right (north) and follow an extended, switchbacking climb over open granite slopes up the canyon of Gilmore Lake's outlet. Back under forest cover, you hop across an alder-lined rivulet, continue climbing to a ford of the outlet, and soon encounter a junction at 3 miles.

Turn right at the junction and make a quarter-mile climb to a juniper-covered flat and a four-way junction with the Pacific Crest Trail (PCT), Tahoe–Yosemite Trail (TYT), and Trail 17E31 to Half Moon and Alta Morris Lakes.

Head north along the PCT–TYT on a switchbacking climb through mostly open terrain with good views along the way of Grass Lake to the south and Susie Lake to the southwest. The trail draws near to Gilmore Lake's outlet and then veers slightly away from the cascading stream before you reach another junction amid a scattered lodgepole-pine forest.

At the junction, leave the PCT–TYT, which continues climbing toward Dicks Pass, and continue northbound on Trail 17E33. Just before reaching Gilmore Lake, hop across the outlet and then proceed a short distance to the southeast shore of the oval-shaped lake. Backpackers will find decent campsites on both the south and east sides.

86 **Glen Alpine to Grass Lake**

Distance	5 miles (out-and-back)
Hiking Time	2.5–3 hours
Elevation	+675 feet
Difficulty	Easy
Trail Use	Backpacking option, dogs OK, good for kids
Best Times	July through mid-October
Agency	Lake Tahoe Basin Management Unit at 530-543-2600, www.fs.usda.gov/ltbmu
Recommended Map	ENF and LTBMU A Guide to the Desolation Wilderness

see map on p. 188

Notes Since this trail lies within Desolation Wilderness, you will need a permit for both day hikes and multiday backpacking trips. Day hikers may self-register at the trailhead, but backpackers will need to get their permit from the Lake Tahoe Visitor Center.

HIGHLIGHTS The short, easy hike to Grass Lake is a great way to spend a morning or afternoon enjoying some of the southeastern fringe of Desolation Wilderness. The lake is surrounded by the characteristic Desolation granite and has a pretty cascade that tumbles down cliffs on the west side. Since the lake is only 2.5 miles from a trailhead, don't expect to be alone.

DIRECTIONS Follow CA 89 to Fallen Leaf Road, approximately 3 miles northwest of the Y-junction with CA 50 in South Lake Tahoe. Turn south and follow Fallen Leaf Road for 4.6 miles, to the far end of Fallen Leaf Lake and a signed junction for Glen Alpine. Turn left at the junction, and proceed on a very narrow paved road for a half mile to the trailhead parking area just past a bridge over Glen Alpine Creek.

FACILITIES/TRAILHEAD The trailhead has modern vault toilets. Plan on an early arrival on weekends, as parking is at a premium.

Begin hiking on a closed gravel road, past private cabins and alongside lush riparian vegetation on the left, which obscures views of neighboring Lily Lake. The hillside to the right is covered with a mixed forest of junipers, Jeffrey pines, incense cedars, lodgepole pines, firs, and aspens. Continue along the road past Lily Lake to a scenic waterfall on Glen Alpine Creek and proceed to Glen Alpine Springs, 1 mile from the trailhead.

Dirt road continues beyond Glen Alpine Springs for a short distance, until single-track trail climbs through mixed forest, followed by open, shrub-covered terrain with good views of the surrounding peaks and ridges. You enter the signed Desolation Wilderness and soon encounter a junction with the Grass Lake Trail, 1.6 miles from the trailhead.

Turn left (west) from the junction and after a few yards, come to a ford of the outlet from Gilmore Lake. If the water is high, you may be able to boulder-hop the creek downstream of a picturesque cascade. Gently graded trail leads out of the forest into more open terrain. In early season, you'll soon encounter a grassy pond filled with overflow from Glen Alpine Creek, requiring a tricky log crossing in order to circumvent this seasonal obstacle. Proceed through light and then scattered forest to a rock-and-log crossing of the main branch of Glen Alpine Creek at 1.75 miles.

Beyond the creek crossing, you reach a switchback and then make a moderate climb up the canyon. The trail almost reaches the north bank of Lake Lucille's outlet before veering northwest and continuing to climb through alternating sections of forest and clearing. As the grade eases, you get your first glimpse of the lake through the trees and then stroll over to the southeast shore.

87 Tamarack Trail: Triangle Lake, Echo Peak, and Angora Lakes Loop

Distance	7.2 miles (loop)
Hiking Time	4–6 hours
Elevation	+2,750/-2,750 feet
Difficulty	Very difficult
Trail Use	Map and compass
Best Times	Mid-July through September
Agency	Lake Tahoe Basin Management Unit at 530-543-2600, www.fs.usda.gov/ltbmu
Recommended Map	*ENF and LTBMU A Guide to the Desolation Wilderness*

see map on p. 188

HIGHLIGHTS Hikers searching for a more challenging adventure will find this loop trip to be right up their alley. Just locating the trailhead can be a daunting task for first-timers. From there, an unmaintained, primitive trail follows a stiff ascent up the canyon of the south fork of Glen Alpine Creek before gentler terrain leads to Triangle Lake and the summit of Echo Peak. The steep, off-trail descent from Echo Peak to Angora Lakes is the crux of the route, but a refreshing dip in the upper lake followed by a glass of world-famous, fresh-squeezed lemonade at Angora Lakes Resort are worthy rewards. An easy hike along roads and trail completes the return to the trailhead. The views throughout the trip of Lake Tahoe and the surrounding terrain are worth the trip alone.

DIRECTIONS Finding the start of the trail may be the most difficult part of the trip. Follow CA 89 to Fallen Leaf Road, approximately 3 miles northwest of the Y-junction with CA 50 in South Lake Tahoe. Turn south and follow Fallen Leaf Road for 4.6 miles, to the far end of Fallen Leaf Lake and a signed junction for Glen Alpine. Turn left at the junction and proceed on a very narrow paved road for one-third of a mile to the cryptic start of the Tamarack Trail. Without a defined parking area or any signs marking the trailhead, a discernible path is almost impossible to spot from your car. The best plan may be to first park your vehicle in one of the very few spaces that exist along the road, and then walk along the road until you see the defined track of the trail on the south side. If parking spots are not available along the road, you will have to park your car at the Glen Alpine Trailhead at the end of the road.

FACILITIES/TRAILHEAD There are no facilities at the trailhead. The Glen Alpine Trailhead, a quarter mile farther up the road, has modern vault toilets.

A short section of primitive trail leads away from the road through open terrain, to a 6-by-6-inch post and a sign that would have been much more helpful located next to the road. After a small grove of Jeffrey pines, junipers, white firs, and lodgepole pines, you emerge into an open area of shrubs with nice views of the surrounding terrain, including Angora Peak and Indian Rock high above. Soon back in forest, you start a steep climb on rocky tread through dense foliage. Aspen, thimbleberry, bracken fern, spirea, vine maple, alder, willow, currant, and tobacco brush crowd the trail, along with a colorful display of wildflowers, which includes columbine, leopard lily, lady slipper, and monk's hood. Eventually, the jungle-like vegetation is left behind, as the stiff ascent continues across shrub-covered and boulder-dotted slopes with very widely scattered conifers that allow improving views of Lake Tahoe, Fallen Leaf Lake, and the nearby topography. As you continue the climb up the canyon, you make several crossings of the thin, lushly lined stream, as mountain hemlocks and western white pines join the scattered forest.

Eventually, the stiff climb abates as you reach the top of the canyon and follow gently graded trail through scattered timber and drier vegetation of grasses, sedges, sagebrush, and assorted wildflowers, mainly lupines. At 2.2 miles, you pass an unmarked trail on the left, angling sharply away from the main trail, which will soon be your route to Echo Peak. Continue on the main trail about 100 yards farther to the signed, four-way junction with a lateral to Triangle Lake on the right.

To visit Triangle Lake, head north on a mild descent through mixed forest and past small, flower-filled meadows. After a quarter mile, the descent becomes steeper, eventually leading across a boggy meadow to the south shore of secluded Triangle Lake. The serene lake is sandwiched between low rock hummocks and surrounded by scattered conifers.

Retrace your steps 0.3 mile to the four-way junction and then 100 yards to the unmarked junction of the route to Echo Peak. Head northeast on a mild to moderate climb through a mixed forest of lodgepole pines, western white pines, mountain hemlocks, whitebark pines, and white firs.

After 0.8 mile, you emerge from the forest and reach the low point of a ridgecrest between Indian Rock and Echo Peak. From the brink of the ridge, you gaze straight down a nearly vertical cliff to shimmering Angora Lakes, 1,300 feet below. Turn right and follow a ducked route along the crest toward the granite blocks that form the summit of Echo Peak, where you'll enjoy a marvelous 360-degree view. Some of the more notable Tahoe landmarks visible from the summit include Mt. Tallac, the Crystal Range, and the peaks near Carson Pass.

After reveling in the summit view, follow a well-defined path along the southeast ridge of Echo Peak for a short distance and then descend steeply down the northeast ridge toward the east side of Upper Angora Lake. Several descent routes seem to come and go, but the general route is easy to determine. Around 7,775 feet, you reach a small flat southeast of the lake, where your knees will enjoy the temporary reprieve from the steep descent. Away from the flat,

descend a steep hillside, cross a talus field, and reach the east shore of the upper lake.

On a typical summer day, you're apt to have plenty of company here, as the family-run Angora Lakes Resort manages a large sandy beach, boat rentals, a snack shop, and eight housekeeping cabins, all of which make Upper Angora Lake a popular destination for swimmers, sunbathers, boaters, and sightseers. Both lakes are stocked with trout, attracting many anglers as well. High granite ledges above the south shore lure adventurous divers, but every year or so there seems to be a related fatality at the upper lake.

From the upper lake, follow the wide road above the west shore of Lower Angora Lake, which, despite the presence of several summer cabins along the far shore, has a much more subdued atmosphere than the upper lake. Remain on the road for a quarter mile past the lower lake to the Angora Lakes parking lot and continue to the far end, where the trail to Fallen Leaf Lake

Angora Lakes lie at the base of Echo Peak.

begins. Although unmarked at the start of the trail, a marked 6-by-6-inch post a short distance down the path provides assurance that you're on the right route.

Leaving the hustle and bustle of Angora Lakes behind, a slightly rising trail amid white firs and lodgepole pines leads to a short and steep climb to the crest of a ridge, where you have filtered views through the trees of Fallen Leaf Lake below and Mt. Tallac above. A long, angling descent incorporating a few switchbacks cuts across the hillside above the south shore of Fallen Leaf Lake. Farther down the slope, you encounter pockets of dense, head-high foliage alternating with open areas that provide excellent views across the lake. A final series of short switchbacks takes you back into the trees and down to Fallen Leaf Road, near the fire station and a chapel. From there, walk the road toward Glen Alpine 0.3 mile back to the start of the Tamarack Trail.

More Hikes

Balancing Rock Nature Trail

In the north part of D. L. Bliss State Park, a short, self-guided nature trail loop examines the diverse ecology around Rubicon Creek (0.5 mile).

Fallen Leaf Lake

A virtually flat path arcs around the north shore of the lake to a picnic spot at Sawmill Cove (4 miles).

Angora Lakes

Drive past Angora Lookout on FS 12N14 to a short hike to Upper Angora Lake, where scads of sunbathers, swimmers, and picnickers enjoy the warm sunshine and cool waters.

Chapter 6

South Tahoe

Bounded by CA 50 in the north and CA 88 in the south and bisected by CA 89, which tops out at 7,735-foot Luther Pass, the south Tahoe area comprises a fine section of backcountry, with trails suitable for hikers, backpackers, mountain bikers, and equestrians alike. In the midst of this area, 31,000 acres have been suggested for wilderness protection as the Meiss Meadow Wilderness, harboring the headwaters of the Upper Truckee River, the only stream in the entire Lake Tahoe Basin with a genetically pure strain of Lahontan cutthroat trout. In addition to the proposed wilderness, south Tahoe claims the basin's highest mountain, 10,881-foot Freel Peak, and highest lake, 9,125-foot Star Lake (technically, Mud Lake near Mt. Rose is higher at 9,239 feet, but without an inlet or outlet it's more of a shrinking, muddy pond than a bona fide lake). A long section of the Tahoe Rim Trail travels through south Tahoe as well, providing access to Freel Peak, Star Lake, Meiss Meadows, and many more interesting features.

This end of Lake Tahoe is without doubt the most developed area in the basin, with Stateline's towering casinos and South Lake Tahoe's sprawling commercial and residential districts. Between the Fourth of July and Labor Day, traffic on the major thoroughfares can seem gridlocked at times, and space on the beaches oftentimes appears to be elbow to elbow. Despite the summer hordes jockeying for space in the more developed areas of south Tahoe, the backcountry is far from crowded. While some of the trails receive considerable use, especially by mountain bikers, many trails offer a good dose of peaceful and serene hiking. The generally fair weather during late summer and early autumn offers even more opportunities for quiet forays into the backcountry, when many of the tourists have returned home for the season. With plenty of shady forests, sparkling lakes, high peaks, and flower-covered meadows, the south Tahoe area is sure to please the most discriminating hiker.

Lake Tahoe vista from Heavenly Valley's observation deck

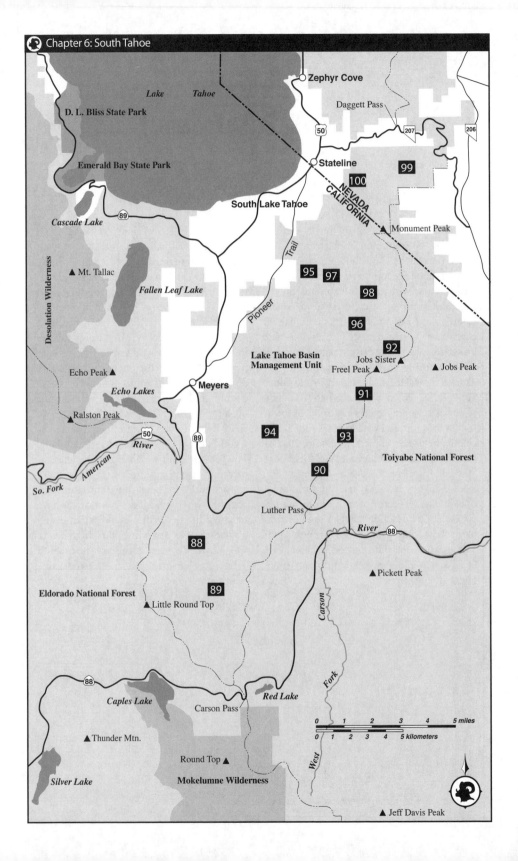

88   Big Meadow to Dardanelles Lake

see map on p. 210

Distance	8 miles (out-and-back)
Hiking Time	4–5 hours
Elevation	+1,050/-550 feet
Difficulty	Moderate
Trail Use	Backpacking option, dogs OK, mountain biking OK
Best Times	Mid-July through mid-October
Agency	Lake Tahoe Basin Management Unit at 530-543-2600, www.fs.usda.gov/ltbmu
Recommended Maps	USGS 7.5-minute *Freel Peak* and *Echo Lake*

HIGHLIGHTS Dardanelles Lake is a scenic lake backdropped by impressive granodiorite cliffs that offers decent fishing and relatively warm water for swimming. Far enough off the thoroughfare of the Tahoe Rim Trail, hikers should be able to enjoy some relative seclusion at this lake. The lakeshore is shaded by light forest and dotted with boulders and slabs, and the picturesque cliffs of the Dardanelles loom above the south shore.

DIRECTIONS Drive on CA 89 to the well-signed Tahoe Rim Trail parking lot, 6 miles from the CA 88 junction in Hope Valley, and 5 miles from the CA 50 junction near Myers.

FACILITIES/TRAILHEAD The Big Meadow Trailhead parking area has modern vault toilets, horse-loading facilities, and a campground nearby. The trailhead is well marked.

Leave the parking area and follow the singletrack Tahoe Rim Trail a short distance south to a crossing of CA 89. Carefully cross the highway and start a winding, moderate climb through a forest of Jeffrey pines, lodgepole pines, and red firs. At a switchback, you have a fine view of the aspen-lined, rocky channel of Big Meadow Creek, which is vibrantly alive with snowmelt in early July and a swath of golden color in autumn. Following more switchbacks, the grade eases just before reaching a three-way junction, a half mile from the trailhead, where a trail to Scotts Lake branches left.

Veer right at the junction and quickly leave the trees behind, as you emerge into the grassy, flower-covered clearing of Big Meadow. Follow the trail through the meadow to a wood plank bridge that spans the gurgling creek and then proceed to the far edge of the meadow, where a lightly forested ascent resumes. Sagebrush, currant, and drought-tolerant wildflowers, principally mule-ears, line the path. Farther up the trail, wood beam reinforced steps ameliorate the steeper sections of trail, alongside a diminishing tributary of Big Meadow

Creek, a sprightly watercourse lined with luxuriant foliage. Continue climbing to a densely forested saddle, and then follow a switchbacking descent into the next canyon, through which flows an Upper Truckee River tributary. Reach the floor of the canyon and a three-way junction marked by an 8-by-8-inch post, where you intersect the Meiss Meadow Trail, 2.2 miles from the trailhead.

From the Meiss Meadow Trail junction, head northwest briefly for 0.2 mile to another three-way junction. Turn left (west) here, make a very brief descent to a boulder hop of the Upper Truckee River tributary, and soon reach a ford of a wider branch of the stream. Early in the season, you may need to search for logs upstream in order to make the second crossing without getting your feet wet. Away from the streams, stroll across a bench holding a small meadow and seasonal ponds. Descend off the bench through a dense forest of western white pines, red firs, and lodgepole pines and follow an alder- and willow-lined stream down a canyon. The grade eases as you pass through meadow-like vegetation of grasses, wildflowers, and willows to the boulder hop

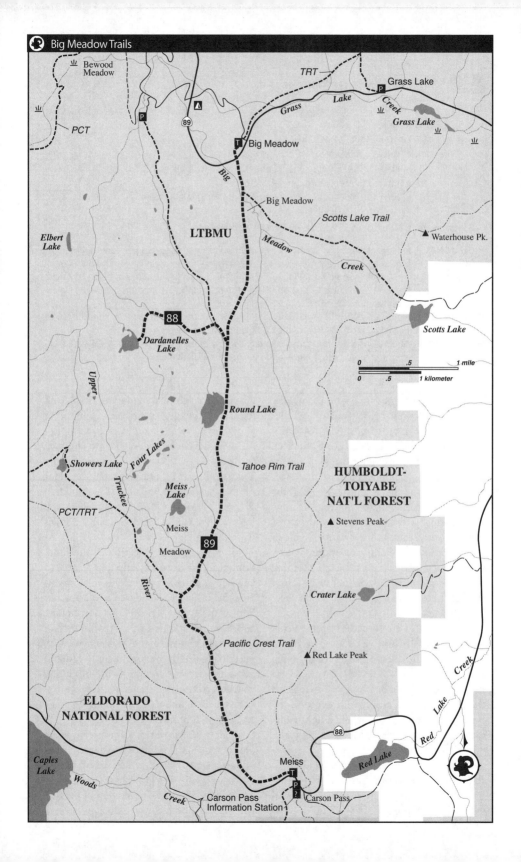

A hiker suns on a rock at Dardanelles Lake.

of Round Lake's outlet. A short climb amid boulders and granite slabs leads to the west shore of Dardanelles Lake, 1.3 miles from the Tahoe Rim Trail junction.

From sunny slabs of polished granite, hikers can admire the striking cliffs above the south shore, contemplate a refreshing dip in the relatively warm waters, or dip a line in search of the elusive trout. Overnighters will find passable campsites beneath junipers and lodgepole pines above the east and northwest shores.

89 Big Meadow to Carson Pass

see map on p. 210

Distance	10.5 miles (point-to-point, shuttle)
Hiking Time	5–6 hours
Elevation	+2,075/-1,000 feet
Difficulty	Moderate
Trail Use	Backpacking option, dogs OK
Best Times	Mid-July through mid-October
Agency	Lake Tahoe Basin Management Unit at 530-543-2600, www.fs.usda.gov/ltbmu
Recommended Maps	USGS 7.5-minute *Freel Peak, Echo Lake, Caples Lake, Carson Pass*

HIGHLIGHTS With arrangements for a shuttle, a 10.5-mile trip travels through the heart of the proposed 31,100-acre Meiss Meadow Wilderness. Following sections of the Tahoe Rim (TRT) and Pacific Crest (PCT) Trails, recreationists can travel from CA 89 to CA 88, visiting Big Meadows, Round Lake, and Meiss Meadows along the way. An optional 1.3-mile side trip to scenic Dardanelles Lake (see Trip 88) provides a fine diversion. Peak baggers with extra time and energy could accept the challenge of climbing Red Lake Peak from a saddle, 1.2 miles northwest of the Meiss Meadow Trailhead. The peak is known for a bit of history, as John C. Fremont and Charles Pruess reached the summit on Valentine's Day in 1844 and made the first sighting of Lake Tahoe by Europeans.

DIRECTIONS The drive between the trailheads is approximately 16 miles long.

Start: Drive on CA 89 to the well-signed Tahoe Rim Trail parking lot, 6 miles from the CA 88 junction in Hope Valley and 5 miles from the CA 50 junction near Myers.

End: Follow CA 88 to the Meiss Meadow Trailhead parking lot, 0.2 mile westbound of Carson Pass.

FACILITIES/TRAILHEAD The Big Meadows Trailhead parking area has modern vault toilets, horse-loading facilities, and a campground nearby. The Meiss Meadows Trailhead parking area has portable toilets, but the Carson Pass Information Station, 0.2 mile to the east at Carson Pass, is staffed during daylight hours in the summer and has vault toilets nearby. Along with wilderness permits, a limited selection of books and maps is available. Both trailheads are well marked.

L eave the parking area and follow the singletrack Tahoe Rim Trail a short distance south to a crossing of CA 89. Once across the highway, start a winding, moderate climb through a forest of Jeffrey pines, lodgepole pines, and red firs. At a switchback you have a fine view of the aspen-lined, rocky channel of Big Meadow Creek, which is vibrantly alive with snowmelt in early July and a golden swath of color in autumn. Following more switchbacks, the grade eases just before reaching a three-way junction, a half mile from the trailhead, where a trail to Scotts Lake branches left.

Veer right at the junction and quickly leave the trees behind, as you emerge into the grassy, flower-covered clearing of Big Meadow. Follow the trail through the meadow to a wood plank bridge that spans the gurgling creek and proceed to the far edge, where a lightly forested ascent resumes. Sagebrush, currant, and drought-tolerant wildflowers, principally mule-ears, line the path. Farther up the trail, wood beam reinforced steps ameliorate the steeper sections of trail, alongside a diminishing tributary of Big Meadow Creek, a sprightly watercourse lined with luxuriant foliage. Continue climbing to a densely forested saddle, and then follow a switchbacking descent into the next canyon, through which flows an Upper Truckee River tributary. Reach the floor of the canyon and a three-way junction marked by an 8-by-8-inch post, where you intersect the Meiss Meadow Trail, 2.2 miles from the trailhead. (To visit Dardanelles Lake, follow the description in Trip 88.)

From the junction to Dardanelles Lake, the route of the TRT follows a steady climb through dense forest on sections of newly rerouted trail. After 0.6 mile, you reach an informal junction at the lip of Round Lake's basin above the northeast shore. From there, a use trail wraps around the lake's west shore, which is lined with rock outcrops and scattered forest, and then follows a popular cross-country route to Meiss Lake. Continue on the TRT, which skirts the east shore of Round Lake through thick forest away from the lush meadows and thick willows that border the inlet at the south end.

Beyond the lake, the TRT resumes its climbing ways, soon reaching an extensive sloping meadow carpeted with willows, wildflowers, and other lush foliage, well watered by a thin, rock-lined rivulet spilling across the trail. Away from the meadow, reenter forest cover and hop across a pair of trickling rivulets. Eventually the grade eases to a mellow stroll as you break out into an open forest sprinkled with stands of aspen and swaths of drier ground cover, including sagebrush, currant, grasses, and drought-tolerant wildflowers. A part of the extensive network of Meiss Meadow appears through scattered lodgepole pines to the right of the trail, with Meiss Lake lying just one-third mile to the west.

Leaving the meadow behind, you hop across Round Lake's inlet and proceed to the crossing of a creek coursing through a rocky channel, 0.4 mile farther, where open terrain allows views of the rugged slopes leading up to 10,059-foot Stevens

Hiker in Meiss Meadows

Peak. Continue on gently graded trail through lodgepole pines to the heart of Meiss Meadow and a well-signed junction with the Pacific Crest Trail, 7.7 miles from the trailhead.

Near the junction, an old cabin hearkens back to the days, not so long ago, when cattle were allowed to graze the lush grasses of picturesque and pastoral Meiss Meadow. Fortunately, the cows are gone, the trampling of the meadows is over, the cow pies have decomposed, and the trails have been left to the bipeds.

Heading south on the PCT from the junction, stroll across the pleasant meadowlands to a crossing of the Upper Truckee River and follow it upstream to a second crossing. Soon afterward, the terrain gets steeper as you start a moderate climb up a narrowing gorge to a saddle at the head of the canyon just beyond a seasonal pond, 9.2 miles from the trailhead. A fine view from the saddle unfolds to the south of the jagged peaks of the Carson Pass region.

Leaving the saddle, a steep descent takes you across a stream and into light forest, followed by an arcing traverse across the hillside above CA 88. At 10.5 miles, reach the Meiss Meadows Trailhead parking lot.

90   TRT: Grass Lake Meadow to Hell Hole Viewpoint

see map on p. 214

Distance	10 miles (out-and-back)
Hiking Time	5–6 hours
Elevation	+1,900/-250 feet
Difficulty	Moderate
Trail Use	Backpacking option, dogs OK, mountain biking OK
Best Times	Mid-July through mid-October
Agency	Lake Tahoe Basin Management Unit at 530-543-2600, www.fs.usda.gov/ltbmu; Humboldt-Toiyabe National Forest at 775-882-2766, www.fs.usda.gov/htnf
Recommended Map	USGS 7.5-minute *Freel Peak* (trail not shown)

HIGHLIGHTS Although this section of the Tahoe Rim Trail is lightly used, you're apt to see as many mountain bikers as hikers. The trail follows a mild to moderate ascent to Freel Meadows, a verdant series of meadowlands sprinkled with vibrantly colored wildflowers through midsummer. Beyond the meadows, the climb continues to a ridge overlooking the Trout Creek drainage, which provides dramatic views of Freel Peak, Lake Tahoe, Hell Hole, and the surrounding terrain.

DIRECTIONS Drive on CA 89 to the vicinity of Grass Lake, 1.7 miles west of Luther Pass. Park along the highway shoulder as space allows.

FACILITIES/TRAILHEAD There are no facilities at the trailhead. The trail begins on the north side of CA 89 near an old Tahoe Rim Trail sign.

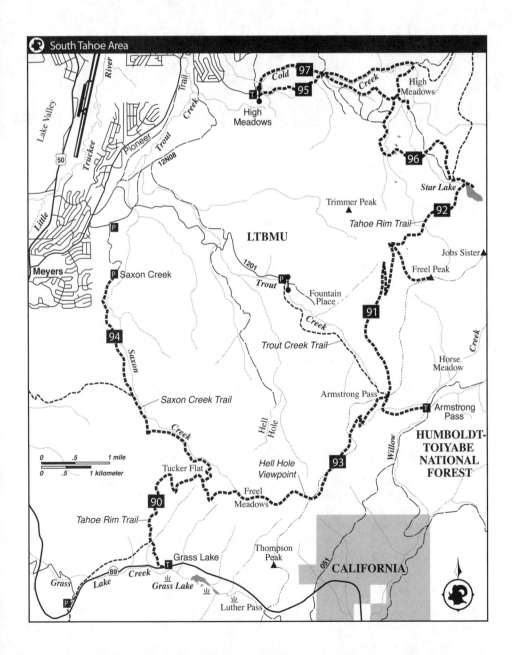

egin hiking away from the highway and up the hillside through a scattered, mixed forest of red firs, junipers, and Jeffrey pines. Soon the trail turns away from the highway entering thicker forest and switchbacking a couple of times on the way to a bridged crossing of a Grass Lake Creek tributary and a signed T-junction on the far side, a half mile from the highway. From the junction, the left-hand trail descends 1.4 miles to the Big Meadow Trailhead.

Turn right at the junction and follow a moderate, winding climb through alternating sections of coniferous forest, aspen stands, and open, boulder-studded slopes with limited views to the south of Hawkins and Pickett Peaks. Pass alongside a small meadow covered with grasses and wildflowers and edged by tall shrubs before gaining the top of a minor ridge. Follow a mildly rising course along the pinemat manzanita–covered ridge, before leaving the ridge to climb more steeply through lodgepole and western white pines. The

grade eases south of Peak 9078, and then the path descends to a saddle and a junction with the Saxon Creek Trail (see Trip 94), 2.75 miles from the highway.

Away from the junction, make a mild to moderate climb south and then east to Freel Meadows, where a series of lush, grassy meadows carpeted with wildflowers through midsummer lines the headwaters of Saxon Creek. Soon the trail bends east to cross the stream and proceeds across a finger of lodgepole pines to the north side of the upper meadow. The trail passes above the lush meadow across a slope carpeted with mule-ears, lupines, and paintbrush. Marginal campsites can be found along the fringe of both the upper and lower meadows.

Past the meadow the trail climbs to the top of a crest saddle. By walking a few yards north of the trail, you reach Hell Hole Viewpoint, with views northeast of the Freel Peak group, northwest of Lake Tahoe, and below to the namesake feature.

91   Armstrong Pass to Freel Peak

see map on p. 214

Distance	10 miles (out-and-back)
Hiking Time	5–8 hours
Elevation	+1,650/-700 feet
Difficulty	Difficult
Trail Use	Dogs OK
Best Times	Mid-July through mid-October
Agency	Humboldt-Toiyabe National Forest at 775-882-2766, www.fs.usda.gov/htnf; Lake Tahoe Basin Management Unit at 530-543-2600, www.fs.usda.gov/ltbmu
Recommended Map	USGS 7.5-minute *Freel Peak* (trail not shown); TAMBA *South Tahoe Trail Map*

HIGHLIGHTS Freel Peak, at 10,881 feet, is the Tahoe Basin's highest summit. The maintained tread of the Tahoe Rim Trail (TRT) leads to within a mile and 1,100 feet of the summit, where a recently improved path following the former climbing route will take you the rest of the way. The climb is not technical, except when lingering snowfields cover the path and some hikers may desire an ice axe, but the ascent is strenuous. Successful summiteers will enjoy a far-ranging view; on clear days the vista extends from Lassen Peak in the north to Yosemite-area peaks in the south. From Freel Peak's summit, peak baggers can add Jobs Sister (10,823 feet) and/or Jobs Peak (10,633 feet) to their lists, the second- and fourth-highest Tahoe peaks, respectively. Nearby Star Lake (see Trip 92) would make an excellent base camp for a weekend or longer adventure.

Tahoe view from Freel Peak

DIRECTIONS From CA 89, turn north onto Forest Service Road 051, 1.8 miles from the CA 88 junction in Hope Valley and 0.8 mile from Luther Pass. Follow the dirt road roughly northwest for nearly 3.5 miles to FS 051F on your left, which is blocked to traffic by large boulders. This junction immediately follows the second bridge crossing over Willow Creek. Park on the shoulder of the main road as space allows.

FACILITIES/TRAILHEAD There are no facilities at the trailhead. Undeveloped campsites may be available near Horse Meadows. The trail begins down the closed road.

From the informal trailhead, proceed on dirt road for a short distance to a flat area just before the rough road makes a steep climb up a hill. Follow the road for a half mile to a wide turnaround, where a TRT sign marks the start of singletrack trail.

Climb moderately steeply, soon crossing a small tributary of Willow Creek. Beyond the crossing, switchbacks attack a hillside carpeted with sagebrush, currant, and tobacco brush and dotted with an occasional western white pine or juniper. At 1 mile from the trailhead, the stiff climb ends at a four-way junction at Armstrong Pass amid scattered red firs.

Turn right and follow the pleasantly graded Tahoe Rim Trail on a rising traverse below the west slope of the Carson Range

crest. You quickly emerge from the scattered forest and walk across mostly open slopes past an occasional western white pine or juniper. Past a rock cliff known as Fountain Face, you enjoy good views across the Trout Creek drainage of the meadows in Hell Hole and Fountain Place, and across Lake Tahoe to the Crystal Range. Continue the steadily rising traverse, hopping over a few tiny rivulets along the way. Farther on, the trail angles across the slope via the first of a pair of long-legged switchbacks. At 4.5 miles, amid scattered whitebark pines, the climb culminates at the crest of an auxiliary ridge of Freel Peak, at 9,730 feet the high point of the trail to Star Lake.

Turning right, you leave the TRT at the high point and follow the improved tread of the former scramble trail along the side of the ridge to where the trail zigzags stiffly via rock steps and sandy soils to the crest. Continue climbing steeply up mostly open slopes with improving views of the surrounding terrain, including behind you to the Sierra crest across the shimmering surface of Lake Tahoe. Along the way, a sign encourages you to remain on the trail to prevent damage to the Tahoe Draba, a low-growing alpine plant with yellow flowers found only in three locations within the Tahoe Basin. Eventually the trail leaves the ridge and veers eastward to make an angling ascent across the northwest face. A final climb leads to the summit.

In former days, an array of communications equipment littered Freel Peak's summit, producing an annoying electronic hum that would irritate the ears of successful climbers. Thankfully, almost all of the equipment has been removed except for a noiseless rectangular foundation. From the top of the Tahoe Basin's highest summit is a 360-degree, unobstructed view of the lake and surrounding terrain. Peak baggers can easily add Jobs Sister to their list of accomplishments by following a mile-long traverse along the ridge between Freel Peak and Jobs Sister. Experienced cross-county hikers bound for Star Lake need not retrace their steps to the TRT, but rather can descend the stream gully between Freel Peak and Jobs Sister to the TRT, or the north ridge of Jobs Sister directly to the lake.

92 Armstrong Pass to Star Lake

see map on p. 214

Distance	12 miles (out-and-back)
Hiking Time	6–8 hours
Elevation	+1,500/-700 feet
Difficulty	Moderate
Trail Use	Backpacking option, dogs OK, mountain biking OK
Best Times	July through October
Agency	Humboldt-Toiyabe National Forest at 775-882-2766, www.fs.usda.gov/htnf; Lake Tahoe Basin Management Unit at 530-543-2600, www.fs.usda.gov/ltbmu
Recommended Map	USGS 7.5-minute *Freel Peak* (trail not shown); TAMBA *South Tahoe Trail Map*

HIGHLIGHTS This trip leads to Star Lake, one of the Tahoe basin's highest lakes. After a mile-long climb to Armstrong Pass, a lightly used section of the Tahoe Rim Trail (TRT) takes you the rest of the way to the lake. Backdropped by the volcanic slopes of rugged Jobs Sister, the lake's setting is quite picturesque, luring both day hikers and backpackers to the serene shores. The high elevation of Star Lake ensures chilly swimming throughout the season, but the relatively warmer temperatures from mid-July through August will make the possibility of a lake dip seem a bit more palatable. Although cooler temperatures prevail in autumn, you'll find much less traffic on the trail.

DIRECTIONS From CA 89, turn north onto Forest Service Road 051, 1.8 miles from the CA 88 junction in Hope Valley and 0.8 mile from Luther Pass. Follow the dirt road roughly northwest for nearly 3.5 miles to FS 051F on your left, which is blocked to traffic by large boulders. This junction immediately follows the second bridge crossing over Willow Creek. Park on the shoulder of the main road as space allows.

FACILITIES/TRAILHEAD There are no facilities at the trailhead. Undeveloped campsites may be available near Horse Meadows. The trail begins down the closed road.

From the informal trailhead, proceed on dirt road for a short distance to a flat area just before the rough road makes a steep climb up a hill. Follow the road for a half mile to a wide turnaround, where a TRT sign marks the start of singletrack trail.

Climb moderately steeply, soon crossing a small tributary of Willow Creek. Beyond the crossing, switchbacks attack a hillside carpeted with sagebrush, currant, and tobacco brush and dotted with an occasional western white pine or juniper. At 1 mile from the trailhead, the stiff climb ends at a four-way junction at Armstrong Pass amid scattered red firs.

Turn right and follow the pleasantly graded Tahoe Rim Trail on a rising traverse below the west slope of the Carson Range crest. You quickly emerge from the scattered forest and walk across mostly open slopes past an occasional western white pine or juniper. Past a rock cliff known as Fountain Face, you enjoy good views across the Trout Creek drainage of the meadows in Hell Hole and Fountain Place, and across Lake Tahoe to the Crystal Range. Continue the steadily rising traverse, hopping over a few tiny rivulets along the way. Farther on, the trail angles across the slope via the first of a pair

of long-legged switchbacks. At 4.5 miles, amid scattered whitebark pines, the climb culminates at the crest of an auxiliary ridge of Freel Peak, at 9,730 feet the high point of the trail to Star Lake.

Remaining on the TRT, descend from the ridge via some switchbacks to the floor of a cirque basin on the northwest side of Freel Peak. A short moderate descent leads through open forest to the crossing of a thin ribbon of water from a tributary of Cold Creek. Beyond the stream, follow a nearly mile-long traverse to the north ridge of Jobs Sister, and then make a short drop along the ridge to Star Lake.

At 9,100 feet, Star Lake is one of the highest lakes in the Tahoe basin, and therefore not one of the warmest. Before construction of the Tahoe Rim Trail, this picturesque cirque-bound gem beneath the towering north flank of Jobs Sister was virtually inaccessible, as the only viable route to the lake crossed private property. Nowadays, while relaxing along the serene lakeshore, not having a trail to this delightful spot is hard to imagine. Backpackers will find a number of passable campsites along the north shore with a nice view across the lake of Jobs Sister.

93 Armstrong Pass to Hell Hole Viewpoint

see map on p. 214

Distance	8 miles (out-and-back)
Hiking Time	4–5 hours
Elevation	+1,400/-300 feet
Difficulty	Moderate
Trail Use	Mountain biking OK, dogs OK
Best Times	July through October
Agency	Humboldt-Toiyabe National Forest at 775-882-2766, www.fs.usda.gov/htnf; Lake Tahoe Basin Management Unit at 530-543-2600, www.fs.usda.gov/ltbmu
Recommended Map	USGS 7.5-minute *Freel Peak* (trail not shown); TAMBA *South Tahoe Trail Map*

HIGHLIGHTS After climbing to Armstrong Pass, this trip follows a ridgecrest section of the Tahoe Rim Trail (TRT) to Hell Hole Viewpoint. Along the way are partial views of Lake Tahoe and full views of Hope Valley and the peaks of the Carson Pass region.

DIRECTIONS From CA 89, turn north onto Forest Service Road 051, 1.8 miles from the CA 88 junction in Hope Valley and 0.8 miles from Luther Pass. Follow the dirt road roughly northwest for nearly 3.5 miles to FS 051F on your left, which is blocked to traffic by large boulders. This junction immediately follows the second bridge crossing over Willow Creek. Park on the shoulder of the main road as space allows.

FACILITIES/TRAILHEAD There are no facilities at the trailhead. Undeveloped campsites may be available near Horse Meadows. The trail begins down the closed road.

From the informal trailhead, proceed on a dirt road for a short distance to a flat area just before the rough road makes a steep climb up a hill. Follow the road for a half mile to a wide turnaround, where a Tahoe Rim Trail sign marks the start of singletrack trail.

Climb moderately steeply, soon crossing a small tributary of Willow Creek. Beyond the crossing, switchbacks attack a hillside carpeted with sagebrush, currant, and tobacco brush and dotted with an occasional western white pine or juniper. At 1 mile from the trailhead, the stiff climb ends at a four-way junction at Armstrong Pass amid scattered red firs.

Turn left and follow the TRT away from the junction with the Trout Creek Trail. Proceed to a switchback and then swing around the southeast side of Peak 9638 across a scrubby slope dotted with widely scattered conifers. After a pair of long legged switchbacks, you cross over the crest to the west side and continue climbing through scattered lodgepole and western white pines. Gain the crest and follow the boulder-studded ridge for a while, with good views to the south of Hope Valley and the surrounding peaks. Drop down the east side of the ridge, arc around Peak 9587, and head west to a saddle and the Hell Hole Viewpoint, with views northeast of the Freel Peak group, northwest of Lake Tahoe, and below to the namesake feature.

94 Saxon Creek Trail

see map on p. 214

Distance	12 miles (out-and-back)
Hiking Time	6–7 hours
Elevation	+2,925/-100 feet
Difficulty	Moderate
Trail Use	Backpacking option, dogs OK, mountain biking OK
Best Times	June through October
Agency	Lake Tahoe Basin Management Unit at 530-543-2600, www.fs.usda.gov/ltbmu
Recommended Map	USGS 7.5-minute *Freel Peak*

HIGHLIGHTS Most of the traffic on the Saxon Creek Trail is from mountain bikers attempting to complete the route locals refer to as Mr. Toad's Wild Ride. Hikers should find the trail to be quite enjoyable as well, especially beyond the first couple of miles, where the route becomes off limits to motorized vehicles. The mostly forested trail travels upstream through the drainage of Saxon Creek to meet the Tahoe Rim Trail, continues climbing to flower-covered Freel Meadows, and then eventually reaches scenic Hell Hole Viewpoint.

DIRECTIONS From CA 50 in South Lake Tahoe, follow Pioneer Trail 6.5 miles to Oneidas Street (this intersection is 1.2 miles from CA 50 in Meyers). Follow Oneidas Street to the end, where it becomes Forest Service Road 1201, and proceed on paved road to the trailhead parking area on the right, 0.5 mile from Pioneer Trail.

FACILITIES/TRAILHEAD There are no facilities near the trailhead. The trail begins on a dirt road heading south.

Following the course of Saxon Creek, you walk along the road through a mixed forest of Jeffrey pines, white firs, lodgepole pines, western white pines, and a few incense cedars on a gentle up and down stroll until the road starts climbing more steeply. Pass a lightly used trail marked for foot traffic and continue a mild to moderate climb on a narrowing section of road. Cross a side stream on a log plank bridge and proceed through thick forest past another singletrack section of trail on the right to a second bridge over an alder-lined rivulet, 1.25 miles from the trailhead.

Away from the stream crossing, the trail makes a steeper, winding climb up the Saxon Creek drainage to the top of a lightly forested ridge, where a short stroll to the edge reveals a nice view of Lake Tahoe and such geographical features as Cave Rock and Mt. Rose. Here a number of markers indicate the end of motorized travel.

Climb away from the ridgetop and soon reach a delightful little stream flowing down rocks and across the trail toward a union with Saxon Creek in the bottom of the deep canyon below. The trail beyond the stream is steep at times, because a number of well-placed wood beam and granite steps aid the ascent and attempt to curb any potential erosion of the tread. After a stretch of more open forest that allows an understory of pinemat manzanita, the grade eases a bit on the way to a rock bridge spanning a side stream. Light forest shades a sprinkling of boulders on the way to the easy crossings of a pair of thin side streams lined with alders before a steady ascent eventually leads to a junction with the Tahoe Rim Trail near Tucker Flat, 4.25 miles from the trailhead.

Away from the junction, make a mild to moderate climb south and then east to Freel Meadows, where a series of grassy meadows, carpeted with wildflowers through midsummer, lines the headwaters of Saxon Creek. Soon the trail bends east to cross the stream and proceeds across a finger of lodgepole pines to the north side of the upper meadow. The trail passes above the lush meadow across a slope carpeted with mule-ears, lupines, and paintbrush. Marginal campsites can be found along the fringe of both the upper and lower meadows.

Past the meadow, the trail climbs to the top of a crest saddle. Hell Hole Viewpoint is a few yards north of the trail, with views northeast of the Freel Peak group, northwest of Lake Tahoe, and below to Hell Hole.

95 High Meadows

Distance	6.8 miles (out-and-back)
Hiking Time	3–4 hours
Elevation	+1,400/-200 feet
Difficulty	Moderate
Trail Use	Dogs OK, mountain biking OK
Best Times	July through October
Agency	Lake Tahoe Basin Management Unit at 530-543-2600, www.fs.usda.gov/ltbmu
Recommended Map	USGS 7.5-minute *South Lake Tahoe*

see map on p. 214

HIGHLIGHTS High Meadows is a picturesque series of clearings above the south shore of Lake Tahoe in the shadow of the first and third highest mountains in the basin, Freel Peak (10,881 feet) and Jobs Sister (10,823 feet). Before the relatively recent construction of the Tahoe Rim Trail, the road to High Meadows and beyond provided the sole access to one of the highest lakes in the basin, Star Lake (9,100 feet). Unfortunately, that road crossed private property, making it technically off-limits to recreationists. Fortunately, the Giovachinni family of Carson Valley agreed to sell a 1,790-acre tract of their land to the Forest Service through the American Land Conservancy in 2003, allowing legal access from the west to both High Meadows and Star Lake.

The road to High Meadows climbs, steeply at times, through mixed forest all the way to a series of broad clearings along the tumbling waters of Cold Creek. The verdant meadows provide a fine setting for a picnic lunch, particularly in midsummer when the grass is green and the wildflowers are blooming.

DIRECTIONS From CA 50 in South Lake Tahoe, follow Pioneer Trail 3.2 miles to High Meadows Trail near Sierra House Elementary School (this intersection is 4.5 miles from CA 50 in Meyers). Drive to the end of the pavement at three-quarters of a mile and continue on a dirt road to the trailhead at 1.3 miles from Pioneer Trail.

FACILITIES/TRAILHEAD There are no facilities at the trailhead. The route begins along the continuation of the dirt road.

Follow the road down to a bridge over a tributary of Cold Creek and pass by some private property on the right that holds a ramshackle cabin. Beyond the creek the road climbs at a moderate to moderately steep grade through a mixed forest of white firs, incense cedars, and Jeffrey pines with a patchy understory of manzanita, tobacco brush, and chinquapin. After topping a minor ridge, the dirt road descends to a straightforward crossing of a thin Cold Creek tributary lined with verdant foliage, followed by a short climb to a second crossing of another Cold Creek tributary spilling across the road.

Beyond the stream crossings, the road closely follows the main channel of Cold Creek upstream past a junction on the left with the short Cold Creek Trail, which leads back to the trailhead. Continue climbing on the main road up the canyon of Cold Creek past several junctions with lesser roads and below a set of power lines. Along the way, infrequent gaps in the trees allow filtered views of the Crystal Range to the west and south to the Freel Peak area. As lodgepole pines join the mixed forest, you reach a marked Y-junction, 2.6 miles from the trailhead, between the route to Star Lake on the right (see Trip 96) and your route straight ahead to High Meadows.

From the junction at the high point of the trip to the meadows, descend to a crossing of Cold Creek and proceed to the western fringe of High Meadows.

96 Star Lake

see map on p. 214

Distance	13.6 miles (out-and-back)
Hiking Time	5–6 hours
Elevation	+2,650/-150 feet
Difficulty	Moderate
Trail Use	Backpacking option, dogs OK, mountain biking OK
Best Times	Mid-July through October
Agency	Lake Tahoe Basin Management Unit at 530-543-2600, www.fs.usda.gov/ltbmu
Recommended Map	USGS 7.5-minute *South Lake Tahoe* (trail not shown); TAMBA *South Tahoe Trail Map*

HIGHLIGHTS There used to be only one way to scenic Star Lake, and that route was over private land. Since the construction of the Tahoe Rim Trail and purchase of the property around High Meadows, the lake can now be accessed by a variety of routes. Using road and trail segments, this trip follows the shortest route to the lake, which has become a bonanza for hikers, backpackers, mountain bikers, and equestrians.

Discounting Mud Lake in the Mt. Rose Wilderness, which is really nothing more than a stagnant pond, at 9,100 feet Star Lake is the highest lake in the Tahoe Basin. Cradled into a steep-walled cirque below the rugged north face of Jobs Sister, the lake is also one of the region's prettiest sights. Backpackers will find campsites along the northeast shore to be quite attractive, with views across the surface of towering Jobs Sister.

DIRECTIONS From CA 50 in South Lake Tahoe, follow Pioneer Trail 3.2 miles to High Meadows Trail near Sierra House Elementary School (this intersection is 4.5 miles from CA 50 in Meyers). Drive to the end of the pavement at three-quarters of a mile and continue on a dirt road to the trailhead at 1.3 miles from Pioneer Trail.

FACILITIES/TRAILHEAD There are no facilities at the trailhead. The route begins along the continuation of the dirt road.

Follow the road down to a bridge over a tributary of Cold Creek and pass by some private property on the right that holds a cabin. Beyond the creek, the road climbs at a moderate to moderately steep grade through a mixed forest of white fir, incense cedar, and Jeffrey pine with a patchy understory of manzanita, tobacco brush, and chinquapin. After topping a minor ridge, the road descends to a crossing of a thin Cold Creek tributary lined with verdant foliage, followed by a short climb to a second crossing of a tributary spilling across the road.

Beyond the stream crossings, the road closely follows the main channel of Cold Creek upstream past a junction on the left with the short Cold Creek Trail, which leads back to the trailhead. Continue climbing on the main road up the canyon of Cold Creek past several junctions with lesser roads and below a set of power lines. Along the way, infrequent gaps in the trees allow filtered views of the Crystal Range to the west and south to the Freel Peak area. As lodgepole pines join the mixed forest, you reach a marked Y-junction, 2.5 miles from the trailhead, between your route to Star Lake on the right and a route straight ahead to High Meadows (see Trip 95).

From the junction, turn right and proceed generally south along a road through scattered forest with filtered views of the south end of Lake Tahoe for 0.4 mile to a signed junction.

Leave the road at the junction and follow singletrack trail on a moderate, switchbacking climb into thicker forest on the west side of a canyon above a branch of Cold Creek. After a mile, you make the first of a pair of stream crossings over a well-placed granite slab; the second crossing is a straightforward boulder hop. Beyond the streams, the trail goes east on a milder climb for about 0.75 mile before the grade increases again. Hop over the main branch of Cold Creek and follow switchbacks steeply up the slope. Eventually the path draws near Cold Creek once more and makes a stiff, winding ascent up the canyon, reaching a junction with the Tahoe Rim Trail near the northwest shore of beautiful Star Lake.

97 **Cold Creek Trail**

Distance	6.6 miles (loop)
Hiking Time	2–3 hours
Elevation	+1,425/-1425 feet
Difficulty	Moderate
Trail Use	Dogs OK, mountain biking OK
Best Times	July through October
Agency	Lake Tahoe Basin Management Unit at 530-543-2600, www.fs.usda.gov/ltbmu
Recommended Map	USGS 7.5-minute *South Lake Tahoe* (some trails not shown); TAMBA *South Tahoe Trail Map*

see map on p. 214

HIGHLIGHTS With recent trail construction, recreationists may now enjoy a shady, creekside route on the Cold Creek Trail to High Meadows and then a return on the old High Meadows Road. The verdant meadows offer a fine wildflower display in early summer and excellent views of towering Freel Peak and neighboring Jobs Sister and Jobs Peak year-round. Other trails and roads in the area offer additional extensions to this trip especially well suited to mountain bikers.

DIRECTIONS From CA 50 in South Lake Tahoe, follow Pioneer Trail 3.2 miles to High Meadows Trail near Sierra House Elementary School (this intersection is 4.5 miles from CA 50 in Meyers). Drive to the end of the pavement at three-quarters of a mile and continue on a dirt road to the trailhead at 1.3 miles from Pioneer Trail.

FACILITIES/TRAILHEAD There are no facilities at the trailhead. The route begins on singletrack trail heading north away from the trailhead signboard.

Following a sign marked POWERLINE TRAIL, head south away from High Meadows Road on singletrack tread and old road through mixed forest, eventually dropping to a bridged crossing of Cold Creek at 0.25 mile and reaching a four-way junction with the Cold Creek Trail on the far bank.

Turn right (east) and follow a gently graded stretch of trail along Cold Creek through shady, mixed forest. Come to an unmarked junction with a connector on the left headed toward a union with the Powerline Trail. Beyond the junction, the grade soon increases to a moderate climb. Hop over a thin rivulet and continue the moderate ascent through the trees. After a switchback, you come to a junction with a short trail on the right that drops to the creek and immediately reaches the High Meadows Road on the far side.

The moderate climb continues with moderately steep stretches at times, soon crossing another tributary stream. Farther on, the canyon narrows and the trail follows a more winding route that leads to the crossing of one more little side stream. Reach a power line clearing, where aspens and shrubs thrive in the additional sunlight. The canyon narrows and bends slightly to the north-northeast, eventually crossing another tributary on a short wood-plank bridge. Pass alongside another large stand of aspen and keep climbing through Jeffrey and lodgepole pines beyond. A stretch of more open forest coincides with a welcome easing of the grade on the approach to the north lobe of High Meadows, as Cold Creek takes on a correspondingly slower, slightly meandering course. Continue the gentle stroll to the fringe of the meadows, where you reach a junction between the Monument Pass Trail and a connection along an old road back to the Cold Creek Trail, 3.9 miles from the trailhead.

Views open up across the clearing of High Meadows, where Freel Peak, Jobs Sister, and Jobs Peak tower to the south. Although the lake itself is not visible, keen eyes may locate the vicinity of Star Lake's basin tucked below the north face of Jobs

Sister. The general position of your next destination, Monument Pass, is also in view to the northeast. The verdant plain of High Meadows presents a pretty picture, although the power line running across the west side and some dead timber along the fringe mars the scene a tad.

From the junction, turn right (south) and follow a road around High Meadows along the fringe of a widely scattered forest with filtered views of the surrounding terrain, soon passing below a power line. Continue the gentle stroll for 0.7 mile to the next junction, where the road ahead to the left is part of the Star Lake Trail.

Veer to the right at the junction and begin the oftentimes-steep descent on the gravel surface of High Meadows Road through mixed forest. Occasional gaps in the trees permit filtered views to the west of the Crystal Range in Desolation Wilderness

and to the south of the Freel Peak area. About a mile from the junction, you cross beneath the power line again and continue the descent for a short while to a junction with a short connector across the creek to the Cold Creek Trail.

Remaining on High Meadows Road, you continue the descent for another half mile to the first of a pair of stream crossings, neither of which should present any difficulties after the peak of snowmelt. Beyond the second crossing, a short stiff climb provides a good reminder that roads weren't built with hikers in mind. Beyond this momentary insult, the stiff descent resumes. With less than a mile to the High Meadows Trailhead, the road continues to drop through a mixed forest of white firs, Jeffrey pines, and incense cedars. Pass by a cabin and cross a bridge over a Cold Creek tributary on the way back to the trailhead.

98 Monument Pass–Star Lake Loop

Distance	16.8 miles (loop)
Hiking Time	6–8 hours
Elevation	+3,000/-3,000 feet
Difficulty	Difficult
Trail Use	Backpacking option, dogs OK, mountain biking OK
Best Times	July through mid-October
Agency	Lake Tahoe Basin Management Unit at 530-543-2600, www.fs.usda.gov/ltbmu
Recommended Map	USGS 7.5-minute *South Lake Tahoe* (trail not shown); TAMBA *South Tahoe Trail Map*

HIGHLIGHTS Mountain bikers and strong hikers will revel in this extended loop trip utilizing the Cold Creek, Monument Pass, Tahoe Rim, and Star Lake trails. Along the way are shady stretches along vigorous Cold Creek, wide-ranging views at the upper elevations, and an opportunity to visit beautiful Star Lake at the base of rugged Jobs Sister. The lake offers wonderful spots for campsites for those who wish to stay overnight. The 16.8-mile distance and 3,000-foot elevation gain make for a long day hike, and the final 2.5-mile descent on oftentimes-steep High Meadows Road can create a tedious end to the trip.

DIRECTIONS From CA 50 in South Lake Tahoe, follow Pioneer Trail 3.2 miles to High Meadows Trail near Sierra House Elementary School (this intersection is 4.5 miles from CA 50 in Meyers). Drive to the end of the pavement at three-quarters of a mile and continue on a dirt road to the trailhead at 1.3 miles from Pioneer Trail.

FACILITIES/TRAILHEAD There are no facilities at the trailhead. The route begins on singletrack trail heading north away from the trailhead signboard.

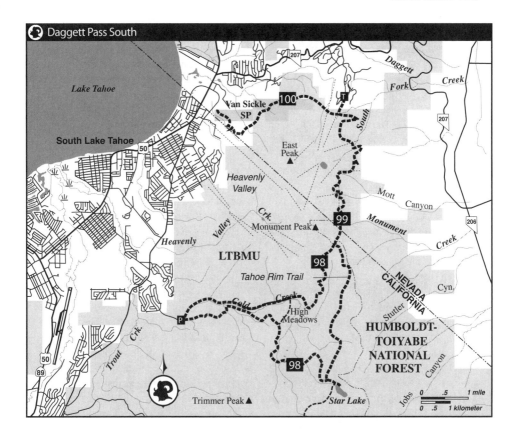

Following a sign marked POWERLINE TRAIL, head south away from High Meadows Road on singletrack tread and old road through mixed forest, eventually dropping to a bridged crossing of Cold Creek at 0.25 mile and reaching a four-way junction with the Cold Creek Trail on the far bank.

Turn right (east) and follow a gently graded stretch of trail along Cold Creek through shady, mixed forest. Come to an unmarked junction with a connector on the left headed toward a union with the Powerline Trail. Beyond the junction, the grade soon increases to a moderate climb. Hop over a thin rivulet and continue the moderate ascent through the trees. After a switchback, you come to a junction with a short trail on the right that drops to the creek and immediately reaches the High Meadows Road on the far side.

The moderate climb continues with moderately steep stretches at times, soon crossing another tributary stream. Farther on, the canyon narrows and the trail follows a more winding route that leads to the crossing of one more little side stream. Reach a power line clearing, where aspens and shrubs thrive in the additional sunlight. The canyon narrows and bends slightly to the north-northeast, eventually crossing another tributary on a short wood-plank bridge. Pass alongside another large stand of aspen and keep climbing through Jeffrey and lodgepole pines beyond. A stretch of more open forest coincides with a welcome easing of the grade on the approach to the north lobe of High Meadows, as Cold Creek takes on a correspondingly slower, slightly meandering course. Continue the gentle stroll to the fringe of the meadows, where you reach a junction between the

Monument Pass Trail and a connection along an old road back to the Cold Creek Trail, 3.9 miles from the trailhead.

Views open up across the clearing of High Meadows, where Freel Peak, Jobs Sister, and Jobs Peak tower to the south. Although the lake itself is not visible, keen eyes may locate the vicinity of Star Lake's basin tucked below the north face of Jobs Sister. The general position of your next destination, Monument Pass, is also in view to the northeast. The verdant plain of High Meadows presents a pretty picture, although the power line running across the west side and some dead timber along the fringe mars the scene a tad.

From the junction, veer left and follow the Monument Pass Trail on a short section of dirt road to where singletrack tread resumes, passing below the power line on the way. The first mile is a gently rising ascent that arcs around the nose of a ridge and then slices across the west slope of an aspen-filled Cold Creek tributary. Fine views of the surrounding terrain propel you onward, as the grade increases to moderate. Switchbacks lead you farther up the canyon, where a drier stretch of forest is composed mainly of scattered western junipers. The trail bends northeast momentarily to pass below some cliffs and then continues north-northeast toward the head of the canyon through western white pines and white firs with an understory of pinemat manzanita. By the time you reach Monument Pass and a junction with the Tahoe Rim Trail (TRT) at 6.3 miles, the sandy surroundings include an understory of widely scattered clumps of sagebrush and pinemat manzanita sprinkled with dwarf mountain mahogany and multi-trunked clusters of stressed whitebark pines. At 10,067 feet, Monument Peak looms immediately to the northwest.

Turn right (south) onto the TRT and begin a gently descending traverse on sandy tread through mostly open terrain, which allows for continuous views ahead of the Freel group of peaks. To the west, views extend to the Crystal Range peaks in Desolation Wilderness and a portion of Lake Tahoe. Where the trail swings around the nose of the west ridge of Peak 9546 the gentle descent ends and a moderate climb bends into the canyon of a Cold Creek tributary. After crossing this stream, the ascent continues through a mixed forest of mountain hemlocks, western white pines, and lodgepole pines. Eventually the path veers into the canyon of the main stem of Cold Creek, which also serves as the outlet of Star Lake. Reach the northwest tip of the lake and the junction with the Star Lake Trail at 10 miles.

Discounting Mud Lake in the Mt. Rose Wilderness, which is really nothing more than a stagnant pond, at 9,100 feet Star Lake is the highest lake in the Tahoe Basin. Cradled in a steep-walled cirque below the rugged north face of Jobs Sister, the lake is also one of the region's prettiest sights. Backpackers will find campsites along the northeast shore to be quite attractive, with views across the surface of towering Jobs Sister. Anglers may find the fishing to be fairly good as well.

After thoroughly enjoying Star Lake, head westerly down the canyon of Cold Creek on a moderately steep, switchbacking descent through mixed forest. After about 0.4 mile, the trail veers north away from the creek and plunges across the hillside before resuming its switchbacking ways. Eventually the path heads back toward Cold Creek on a less steep descent, winds down the canyon for a while, and then crosses the vigorous stream. From the creek, the trail winds around to the west to a pair of crossings of Cold Creek tributaries, one with the aid of a very well placed slab of granite. From the second stream crossing, the trail turns north and drops gently down the canyon to a set of steeper switchbacks leading down the west rim. Traveling through more open forest, you eventually merge with an old road, 13.9 miles from the trailhead.

Walk along the road for 0.4 mile to a three-way junction with the well-graded surface of the High Meadows Road and turn west (the road ahead provides a connection to the Cold Creek and Monument Pass Trails). The descent along the gravel road is steep at times and can be tiring at the end of a long day. After a mile, you pass beneath the power line and continue the stiff descent to a pair of crossings of branches of Cold Creek. Beyond the second crossing, a short stiff climb provides a good reminder that roads weren't built with hikers in mind. Beyond this momentary insult, the stiff descent resumes for not quite 2 miles to the High Meadows Trailhead.

99   TRT: Kingsbury South to Star Lake

Distance	17.4 miles (out-and-back)
Hiking Time	6–8 hours
Elevation	+2,600/-900 feet
Difficulty	Moderate
Trail Use	Backpacking option, dogs OK, mountain biking OK
Best Times	July through October
Agency	Humboldt-Toiyabe National Forest at 775-882-2766, www.fs.usda.gov/htnf; Lake Tahoe Basin Management Unit at 530-543-2600, www.fs.usda.gov/ltbmu
Recommended Map	USGS 7.5-minute *Freel Peak* (trail not shown); TAMBA *South Tahoe Trail Map*

see map on p. 225

HIGHLIGHTS Although not the shortest route to lovely Star Lake, this trip offers fine views along the way of Carson Valley and Lake Tahoe. The 18-mile round trip distance makes for a long day but helps in reducing the number of people you're apt to meet along the trail. Once you surmount the first half mile of steep trail, the remainder is one of the most pleasantly graded sections along the entire 165-mile Tahoe Rim Trail.

DIRECTIONS Drive on NV 207, also known as Kingsbury Grade, to Daggett Pass and turn south onto Tramway Drive, which eventually becomes a one-way road that circles through the Nevada side of Heavenly Valley Ski Resort. Park your vehicle in the parking lot near the base of the Stagecoach Express ski lift, 1.5 miles from NV 207.

FACILITIES/TRAILHEAD There are no facilities at the trailhead. Amid towering condominiums and ski-area development, the route of the Tahoe Rim Trail begins on the southwest side of the parking area up a set of stairs and onto a dirt road.

Walk briefly along the road and follow an equally brief stretch of singletrack trail to the Tahoe Rim Trail kiosk near a switchback. Pass below the elevated rails for the Skier Express connecting the Stagecoach Chairlift with the Ridge Tahoe resort. More switchbacks lead steeply up the lightly forested slope past the Ridge Tahoe and a junction with a lateral to the resort on the left. The grade eases to a moderate climb, passes below a set of power lines, and then swings into the canyon of a tributary to South Fork Daggett Creek. Cross the seasonal stream and continue to a junction with the Tahoe Rim Trail, 0.6 mile from the trailhead.

Following an upward traverse through Jeffrey pines, western white pines, lodgepole pines, and white firs, you reach a switchback, where there is a partial view through the trees of Carson Valley to the east backdropped by the Pine Nut Mountains, the spine of the Carson Range to the north, and part of Lake Tahoe to the west. More switchbacks lead to a saddle, about 1.5 miles from the trailhead and directly southeast of Peak 8331.

Now through lighter forest, which allows a flourishing ground cover of pinemat manzanita, tobacco brush, and chinquapin, you follow mildly graded trail past an informal junction with a short spur to a ski-area road and then pass below another chairlift while crossing a ski-slope clearing. Shortly past the ski slope, hop across the narrow channel of South Fork Daggett Creek, 1.7 miles from the trailhead.

A short, mildly rising traverse leads to a jeep road crossing and more eastward views of Carson Valley. Back into the forest, a mile-long, switchbacking climb climaxes at a saddle near Peak 8611, 3 miles from the trailhead. In this saddle, the trail merges with a ski-area road from East Peak Lake. Just before the saddle, you have a fine vista across an open slope of 10,057-foot Monument Peak, a mile south-southwest, and the more distant Freel Peak, Jobs Peak, and Jobs Sister.

Descend very steeply along the road toward the bottom of Mott Canyon and curve around to where a well-graded, singletrack trail gratefully resumes. A short way after the resumption of trail, step over trickling Mott Canyon Creek, which usually is dry at this elevation by late summer, and pass below another Heavenly Valley chairlift. A moderate climb leads out of the canyon, followed by a rising traverse that follows the folds and creases along the east side of the Carson Range before angling directly across a mostly open slope. Along the traverse, you have expansive eastward views of the Carson Valley and views to the south of Jobs Peak. Cross the unmarked and inconspicuous Nevada–California border and then continue the ascent to the crest of the Carson Range at Monument Pass, 4.75 miles from the trailhead. Aside from the power lines that run through the pass, the view of Freel Peak and Jobs Sister is quite dramatic, made even more so by a short scramble to the top of a neighboring rock outcrop.

Now on the west side of the crest, follow sandy trail on an open, 2-mile traverse through widely scattered trees with good views down into High Meadows and across the lake to the Crystal Range peaks in Desolation Wilderness. On a nearly imperceptible descent, you eventually enter a light forest that obscures most of the views.

At 7.7 miles, you encounter the flower-lined, refreshing brook of a Cold Creek tributary. From there, slightly rising trail proceeds through western white pines, mountain hemlocks, and lodgepole pines toward Star Lake. Just before the lake, the trail curves east and then drops to a crossing of the lake's outlet.

At 9,100 feet, Star Lake is one of the highest lakes in the Tahoe Basin, and therefore not one of the warmest. Before construction of the Tahoe Rim Trail, this picturesque cirque-bound gem beneath the north flank of Jobs Sister was virtually inaccessible, as the only viable route to the lake crossed private property. Nowadays, while relaxing along the serene lakeshore, not having a trail to this delightful spot is hard to imagine. A number of good campsites along the north shore backdropped by Jobs Sister will surely appeal to overnighters.

100 Van Sickle Trail

Distance	7.2 miles (out-and-back)
Hiking Time	3–4 hours
Elevation	+1,350/-50 feet
Difficulty	Moderate
Trail Use	Dogs OK, mountain biking OK
Best Times	June through October
Agency	California and Nevada State Parks, Lake Tahoe Basin Management Unit at 530-543-2600, www.fs.usda.gov/ltbmu
Recommended Map	USGS 7.5-minute *South Lake Tahoe* (trail not shown); TAMBA *South Tahoe Trail Map*

see map on p. 225

HIGHLIGHTS A new connection to the Tahoe Rim Trail, the Van Sickle Trail offers features of its own, including wonderful views of Lake Tahoe and a pretty waterfall. The trail climbs stiffly for the entire way, but those who don't mind the physical challenge will be well rewarded with some fine scenery. Van Sickle Bi-State Park has the distinction of being the only state park straddling the border of two states in the country.

DIRECTIONS Follow US 50 to the casino district of Stateline, Nevada, on the south shore of Lake Tahoe. Westbound motorists should turn left onto Lake Parkway East and drive 0.8 mile to a four-way stop at the intersection of Montreal Road and Heavenly Village Way. Turn left at the intersection into Van Sickle Bi-State Park and follow the access road to the trailhead parking lot near the end of the pavement. Eastbound motorists should turn right from US 50 onto Heavenly Village Way, proceed to the four-way stop, and then continue into the park.

FACILITIES/TRAILHEAD Vault toilets and picnic tables are at the equestrian trailhead. Nearby, the park has some recently restored historic buildings. The trail begins from the first parking area on the right side of the access road.

A steep but short climb leads away from the parking area and then eases on the way through mixed forest before dropping slightly and then ascending mildly. At 0.2 mile, you cross an old road, pass by a mileage sign, and then cross over a second road. A more moderate climb leads to a junction with a lateral to a visit point at 0.5 mile. A stiff but short climb leads to a clamber over some rocks to the viewpoint, where the south end of Lake Tahoe springs into sight. Across the water, the dark hulk of Mt. Tallac towers over the surrounding peaks.

Return to the junction and continue the climb for 0.1 mile to the crossing of another old road and an interpretive sign about the 2002 Gondola Fire on the far side. Another stretch of climbing leads to a junction at a switchback marked by a 6-by-6-inch post, 0.9 mile from the trailhead. Veer left here and climb for another 0.1 mile to a marked junction with the Cal Neva Loop.

Switchback to the left and climb across a slope thinned by the Gondola Fire, which allows good views of the lake and the Crystal Range in Desolation Wilderness. After more than a decade, shrubs such as chinquapin, tobacco brush, and manzanita have begun the process of regeneration after the fire. In early season, you should have the added bonus of a smattering of drought-tolerant wildflowers as well. A long ascending traverse leads into a canyon and a lovely waterfall at 1.5 mile. A good percentage of hikers go no farther than this landmark, so you may have the rest of the trail to yourself.

Beyond the waterfall, the trail continues the rising traverse following the folds and creases across the northwest slope of East Peak. Along the way, you hop over a few streams and pass through stands of intact forest. Although the trees diminish the views, the shady forest will be appreciated on a hot summer day. A set of short-legged switchbacks interrupts the otherwise continuous upward traverse, beyond which the forest lightens. After exiting the park and entering forest service land at 3.2 miles, the trail crosses an abandoned road and heads into thicker forest again. Reach a marked junction with the Tahoe Rim Trail (TRT) at 3.6 miles. A short walk north on the TRT leads to a short lateral up to a vista point, although the view is inferior to those you enjoyed on the lower section of the Van Sickle Trail.

Waterfall on the Van Sickle Trail

More Hikes

Big Meadow to Scotts Lake

Branching away from the more popular route to Round Lake, this trail ends at Scotts Lake, which is accessible to motor vehicles from the east (6 miles).

Heavenly Valley Trails

Like Squaw Valley, the ski resort offers multiple hikes along service roads to viewpoints and points of interest. However, the highlight is the supreme Lake Tahoe view from the gondola's observation deck, en route to the trails (varies).

Armstrong Trail

Popular with mountain bikers in combination with other trails, this path ascends the canyon of Trout Creek to Armstrong Path, where several alternatives offer trip extensions (5.8 miles).

Meiss Meadow Trail

This seldom-used (and longer) alternate route to Dardanelles Lake begins at the South Upper Truckee River Road (8 miles).

Powerline Trail, Railroad Grade Trail, Cedar Trail, Corral Trail, Sidewinder Trail, and Connector Trail

Along with a number of dirt and paved roads and backcountry trails, these routes carpet the South Tahoe front country with a bounty of opportunities for mountain bikers, offering rides of varying lengths for all levels of technical abilities. Although open to hikers as well, the terrain is not particularly impressive and much better suited to the two-wheeled crowd.

Skunk Harbor

East Tahoe

In contrast to the neighboring south Tahoe region, this area is perhaps the least developed side of the lake. Located on the west flank of the linear Carson Range, the topography rises quickly from the lakeshore to the crest of the range in just a few miles. Along with the Forest Service, the state of Nevada administers a large portion of this land within Lake Tahoe Nevada State Park, which has become a mountain bikers' haven over the last couple of decades. The park's Flume Trail is perhaps the best-known mountain bike route in the Tahoe region. The east shore of Lake Tahoe is also home to some of the best beaches around the lake, a couple of which can only be accessed by boat or trail.

Situated east of the Sierra crest, east Tahoe experiences a rain-shadow effect, as Pacific storms dump the majority of their moisture on the journey up the west side of the Sierra, leaving a smaller amount for areas on the east side of the lake. The difference between the amounts of precipitation dropped on the west side of the Sierra compared to the east shore of the lake and the adjoining Carson Range is quite dramatic—about half as much. Consequently, glaciers had a minimal impact in the formation of the area's topography. While Desolation Wilderness across the lake is peppered with an inordinate number of glacier-scoured

lakes, tarns, and ponds, most of the handful of lakes on the east side are human-made. The relative lack of moisture is also evidenced by the drier vegetation that carpets the east-side slopes, although riparian areas around streams can be quite luxuriant. With half the moisture, there's less snow to melt on the east side of the lake, resulting in trails opening up a full month before the paths on the west side.

Trails in this area will appeal to a wide range of recreationists. As previously mentioned, mountain bikers flock to the area, mainly to ride the popular Flume Trail, with its gentle grade and supreme lake views. A number of short, easy trails provides straightforward access to sandy beaches along Tahoe's east shore, a supreme lake view atop Castle Rocks, and a pleasant loop around Spooner Lake. More challenging routes lead to Marlette Lake and to sweeping views of Lake Tahoe from sections of the Tahoe Rim Trail.

This area has benefitted greatly with the addition of several new trails built primarily by volunteers in conjunction with the Tahoe Rim Trail Association and Carson Valley Trails Association, including Trips 103, 105–108, and 110, which has increased the number of trips from 11 in the first edition to 17.

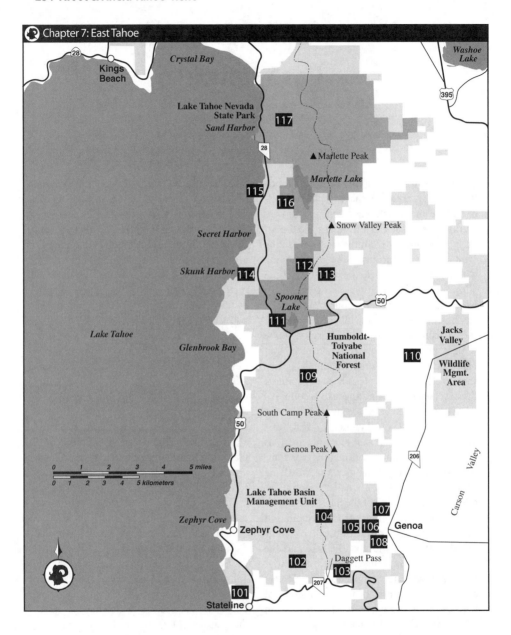

Chapter 7: East Tahoe

101 Lam Watah Trail to Nevada Beach

Distance	2.2 miles (out-and-back)
Hiking Time	1 hour
Elevation	Negligible
Difficulty	Easy
Trail Use	Good for kids
Best Times	May through October
Agency	Lake Tahoe Basin Management Unit at 530-543-2600, www.fs.usda.gov/ltbmu
Recommended Map	USGS 7.5-minute *South Lake Tahoe* (trail not shown)

HIGHLIGHTS The Lam Watah Trail, with a name derived from a Washoe Indian phrase meaning "permanent mortar by the stream," crosses an area that once was slated for casino development. Fortunately, the land was purchased by the Nature Conservancy and then donated to the Forest Service. Along with such features as a willow-lined pond, flower-covered meadows, a sprightly stream, and stands of pine forest, several interpretive signs placed alongside the trail provide insights into the natural and human history of the area. The path ultimately leads to Nevada Beach, a sandy stretch of shoreline well suited to soaking in the sun or a refreshing dip in Tahoe's chilly waters. An additional bonus to hiking the Lam Watah Trail is not having to pay the nominal per-vehicle fee at the Nevada Beach area.

DIRECTIONS Follow NV 50 to Tahoe Village and the intersection of Kahle Drive, which is 0.2 mile north of the NV 207 junction. Turn northwest and park along the shoulder of Kahle Drive as space allows.

FACILITIES/TRAILHEAD There are no facilities at the trailhead. The trail terminates at Nevada Beach, site of a popular campground and day-use area (no pets), complete with restrooms with running water and picnic tables. Vehicle access to Nevada Beach is from Elk Point Road, 1 mile north of Kahle Drive.

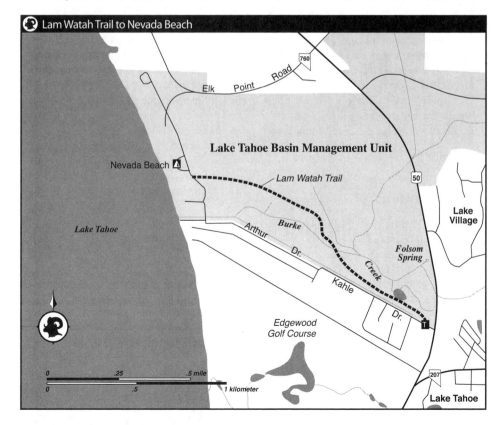

Pond near the Lam Watah Trail

ead away from the road through a meadow carpeted with tall grasses and verdant foliage. Just past an interpretive sign about rubber rabbitbrush, you pass a willow-lined pond and a small stand of quaking aspen. Past more signs, the trail veers over to cross the thin stream that drains the pond and bisects the meadow on a log-plank bridge. Farther on, the trail briefly enters a light stand of Jeffrey pines and then crosses a strip of meadow on the course of a twin-tracked old road. A number of social paths intersect the main trail, some of which you can use to extend your trip through forested areas to the north. Continue through additional forest groves and pockets of meadow on the way toward Nevada Beach. The trail ends at the campground access road, where the sandy beach and deep blue waters of Lake Tahoe are a short stroll away.

102 Castle Rock

Distance	2 miles (out-and-back)
Hiking Time	1 hour
Elevation	+300/-200 feet
Difficulty	Moderate
Trail Use	Dogs OK, mountain biking OK
Best Times	June through October
Agency	Lake Tahoe Basin Management Unit at 530-543-2600, www.fs.usda.gov/ltbmu
Recommended Map	USGS 7.5-minute *South Lake Tahoe* (trail not shown)

HIGHLIGHTS Wonderful views of Lake Tahoe from the top of Castle Rock requiring a short hike and a little bit of rock climbing will reward hikers grandly for a minimal investment of time and energy.

Although technical climbing skills are necessary to scale the fourth-class rock and reach the actual summit, a slightly lower pinnacle nearby offers similar views with just a bit of easy scrambling required. If not for the climbing and the exposed aerie of the summit, the trip would be well suited for families with young children.

DIRECTIONS Follow Kingsbury Grade (NV 207) to North Benjamin Drive, which is 0.3 mile west of Daggett Pass and 2.9 miles east of the NV 50 junction. Turn north and drive through the Upper Kingsbury subdivision, as Benjamin becomes Andria Drive. Proceed nearly 2 miles from the highway almost to the end of the pavement and park on the left-hand shoulder.

FACILITIES/TRAILHEAD There are no facilities at the trailhead. The trail begins south of the Tahoe Rim Trail Trailhead on an old road closed by a green steel gate and marked by a brown forest service marker.

Head down the closed road through a light covering of mixed forest of Jeffrey pines, white firs, lodgepole pines, and western white pines, with an understory of sagebrush, currant, chinquapin, and greenleaf and pinemat manzanita. After leaving behind a row of houses from the adjacent subdivision visible from the road, the atmosphere becomes a bit wilder, as you descend into the forest. Along the way, drought-tolerant wildflowers line the roadbed in early summer. A quarter mile into the journey, the road veers left and your route follows single-track trail ahead to the right on a slightly descending traverse that arcs around a hillside to reach a T-junction with the Tahoe Rim Trail marked by a 6-by-6-inch post.

Turn right (north) onto gently graded tread, followed by a short moderate ascent up a usually dry gully to another junction marked by a 6-by-6-inch post.

Here the Castle Rock Trail turns left (southwest) and proceeds through open forest toward the base of Castle Rock. The forest thickens where the grade increases and the trail arcs around to the west face. Although reaching the true summit requires fourth-class rock-climbing skills, you can scramble up one of the slightly lower pinnacles fairly easily for a fine view of the Tahoe Basin. The unobstructed lake view from the top is sweeping, with a vista encompassing the south shore casino district all the way along the west side of the lake to the distant north shore. After thoroughly enjoying the magnificent view, retrace your steps 1 mile to the trailhead.

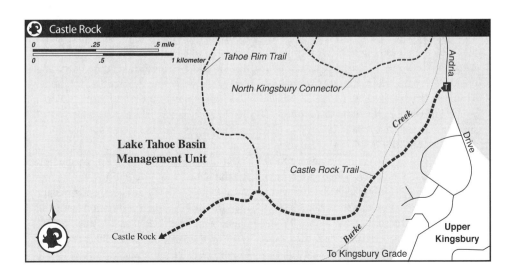

103 Daggett Loop Trail

Distance	7 miles (loop); plus 0.4-mile out-and-back to vista and 0.6-mile out-and-back to Castle Rock
Hiking Time	2.5–4 hours
Elevation	+1,550/-1,550 feet
Difficulty	Moderate
Trail Use	Dogs OK, mountain biking OK
Agency	Lake Tahoe Basin Management Unit at 530-543-2600, www.fs.usda.gov/ltbmu
Best Times	June through October
Recommended Map	USGS 7.5-minute *South Lake Tahoe* (trail not shown)

HIGHLIGHTS Recent work performed by the Tahoe Rim Trail Association has created this fine loop on the west flank of the Carson Range from the North Kingsbury Trailhead. Along the way are good Lake Tahoe views, including some of the higher peaks around the south end of the basin. Side trails to a vista point and Castle Rock lead to additional views.

DIRECTIONS Follow Kingsbury Grade (NV 207) to North Benjamin Drive, which is 0.3 mile west of Daggett Pass and 2.9 miles east of the NV 50 junction. Turn north and drive through the Upper Kingsbury subdivision, as Benjamin becomes Andria Drive. Proceed nearly 2 miles from the highway almost to the end of the pavement and park on the left-hand or right-hand shoulder as space allows.

FACILITIES/TRAILHEAD There are no facilities at the trailhead. The trail begins on the east side of the road near a trail sign.

The hike begins on a stiff, switchbacking climb away from the road across a hillside covered with a light mixed forest. After the 0.7-mile climb, the grade eases and views open up across the south end of Lake Tahoe to the dark hulk of Mt. Tallac and the granite peaks of the Crystal Range in Desolation Wilderness. Also briefly visible is the trio of high summits to the south, Freel Peak, Jobs Peak, and Jobs Sister. Farther on, after crossing over a minor ridge, these peaks come back into view, along with much of the Nevada side of Heavenly Ski Area on the slopes of East Peak. A gently graded descent leads to the dirt surface of Kimberly Brooke Lane at 1.1 miles, which you follow very briefly to the resumption of singletrack trail on the far side.

Away from the road, the trail heads deeper into forest cover, dropping and then climbing to a T-junction, where a 0.2-mile lateral heading southwest leads to a vista point on top of a boulder-strewn knob. The view includes the south end of Lake Tahoe to the southwest, Heavenly Ski Area and the Freel group to the south, and the closer landmarks of Castle Rock and Round Hill immediately west.

Back on the main trail, you begin an extended descent toward Kingsbury Grade through light forest. Views of the Heavenly area open up near a rock knob, where the highway also comes into view below. Eventually, a series of switchbacks leads down the steep slope above the highway. After crossing beneath a power line, a short climb takes you to a Y-junction, 3.1 miles from the trailhead, where a 0.2-mile lateral heads southeast to Tramway Drive. Continue ahead on a pleasantly graded, winding descent toward the residential neighborhood of Upper Kingsbury, reaching North Benjamin Drive at 3.5 miles.

Veer right onto the paved surface of the road and walk a short distance to where the trail resumes down an old roadbed on the far side. Soon singletrack trail veers away from the road and descends deeper into the forest. Reach a junction with the Tahoe Rim Trail (TRT) at 3.7 miles.

From the junction, turn right (north) and follow the TRT on a short descent to the

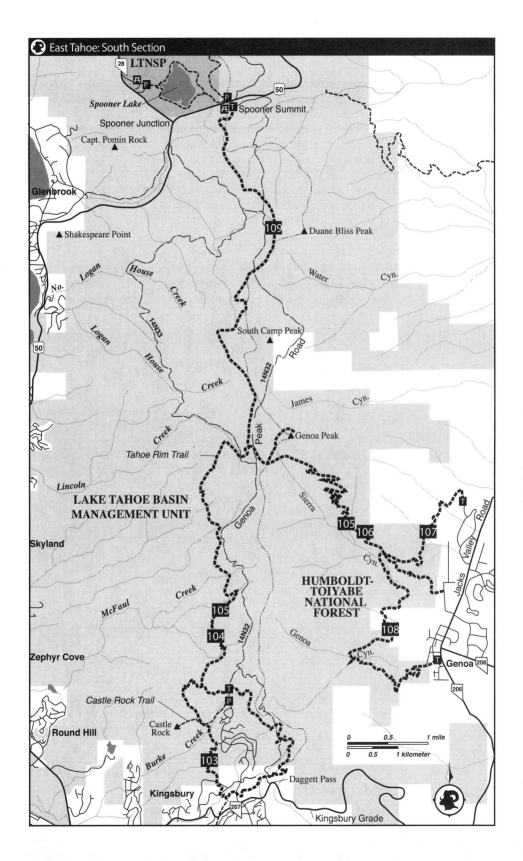

28 **LTNSP**

50

Spooner Lake

Spooner Junction

P

Spooner Summit

Capt. Pomin Rock

Glenbrook

▲ Shakespeare Point

109 ▲Duane Bliss Peak

Logan

House Creek

No.

Water Cyn.

Cyn.

14N33

Logan

House

South Camp Peak ▲

Creek

Road

14N32

James Cyn.

Cyn.

Creek

Genoa Peak ▲

Tahoe Rim Trail

Peak

Lincoln

**LAKE TAHOE BASIN
MANAGEMENT UNIT**

Genoa

Sierra

105 106 107

Skyland

Cyn.

**HUMBOLDT-
TOIYABE
NATIONAL
FOREST**

Jacks Valley Road

Creek

McFaul

105

104 14N32

Genoa

108

Zephyr Cove

Cyn.

Genoa 206

P

Castle Rock Trail

Castle
Rock

Round Hill

Creek

103

206

0   0.5   1 mile

0   0.5   1 kilometer

Burke Creek

Kingsbury

207

Daggett Pass

Kingsbury Grade

crossing of a seasonal tributary of Edgewood Creek. Merge briefly with an old road on the far side of the aspen- and willow-lined creek before singletrack trail veers away on a stiff climb to the north. At 4 miles, you cross an old road and continue the moderate ascent for another 0.2 mile to cross a power line road. Above the road, a scattered forest allows filtered views on the way to a pile of boulders offering an unobstructed vista of Lake Tahoe and the surrounding mountains. Back into the trees, eventually the climb abates where the trail makes a gentle descent around the drainage of Burke Creek. Along the way, the trail nears a few houses, the first signs of civilization in quite a while.

Just beyond a tall rock that looks suitable for some bouldering, an unmarked path from the neighborhood merges with the TRT. Beyond Burke Creek, a moderate climb heads up a usually dry drainage on the way to a junction marked by a 6-by-6-inch post with the Castle Rock Trail on the right (if interested in a shortcut, you can follow this trail 0.6 mile back to Andria Drive and then walk 0.1 mile up the road to the Kingsbury North Trailhead).

Continue climbing northwest on the TRT for another 0.1 mile to a second junction marked with a 6-by-6-inch post, 5.6 miles from the trailhead, with the Castle Rock Trail.

Castle Rocks and Lake Tahoe as seen from the Daggett Loop Trail

SIDE TRIP TO CASTLE ROCK: At the junction, the Castle Rock Trail turns left (southwest) and proceeds through open forest toward the base of Castle Rock. The forest thickens where the grade increases and the trail arcs around to the west face. Although reaching the true summit requires fourth-class rock-climbing skills, you can scramble up one of the slightly lower pinnacles fairly easily for a fine view of the Tahoe Basin. The unobstructed lake view from the top is sweeping, with a vista encompassing the south-shore casino district all the way along the west side of the lake to the distant north shore. After thoroughly enjoying the magnificent view, retrace your steps 0.3 mile to the junction.

From the Castle Rock junction, the TRT continues climbing moderately through light mixed forest. At 6 miles, you reach a three-way junction with the Stinger Trail on the left, primarily a mountain bike route leading to the Stateline area. Keep climbing away from the junction to the top of a rock knoll and then drop shortly to another three-way junction at 6.5 miles.

Leaving the TRT, you continue ahead on the lateral to the Kingsbury North Trailhead, following an arcing descent around the south side of Peak 8204. Filtered views of Castle Rock, the south end of Lake Tahoe, and Freel Peak cheer you onward before a final stretch of descent leads to the end of the loop at the parking area along Andria Drive.

104 TRT: Kingsbury North to Genoa Peak

see map on p. 239

Distance	13 miles (out-and-back)
Hiking Time	6.5–7.5 hours
Elevation	+1,800/-525 feet
Difficulty	Moderate
Trail Use	Mountain biking OK, dogs OK
Best Times	July through October
Agency	Lake Tahoe Basin Management Unit at 530-543-2600, www.fs.usda.gov/ltbmu
Recommended Maps	USGS 7.5-minute *South Lake Tahoe, Glenbrook* (trail not shown), CVTA *Genoa Trail System*

HIGHLIGHTS The 13-mile section of the Tahoe Rim Trail (TRT) between the Kingsbury North Trailhead and Spooner Summit is one of the more recently built and lightly used sections of the 176-mile trail. Despite the lack of popularity, some of the best views of Lake Tahoe can be had from various locations near the midpoint. One of those locations is the summit of Genoa Peak, which offers impressive views to the east of Carson Valley backdropped by the Pine Nut Mountains as well. Bring plenty of water, because after early summer the trail is dry between the trailhead and the peak despite the appearance of year-round streams on the USGS map.

DIRECTIONS Follow Kingsbury Grade (NV 207) to North Benjamin Drive, which is 0.3 mile west of Daggett Pass and 2.9 miles east of the NV 50 junction. Turn north and drive through the Upper Kingsbury subdivision, as Benjamin becomes Andria Drive. Proceed nearly 2 miles from the highway to the end of the pavement and park on the left-hand shoulder.

FACILITIES/TRAILHEAD There are no facilities at the trailhead. The trail begins near a Tahoe Rim Trail signboard.

Begin the hike by ascending a slope dotted with firs and Jeffrey pines and covered with chinquapin, currant, bitterbrush, and pinemat and greenleaf manzanita.

On a moderate climb, wrap around Peak 8204 with filtered views of Castle Rock immediately to the southwest, Freel Peak to the south, and Lake Tahoe to the west.

At 0.5 mile, you reach a signed junction with the TRT.

Turn north at the junction and proceed on gently graded tread lined with patches of lupines carpeting the forest floor until midseason. After 0.5 mile is a three-way junction with the Stinger Trail, primarily a mountain bike route headed to the Stateline area.

Remain on the TRT by heading northeast, winding around and dropping to the crossing of a well-used four-wheel-drive road before continuing across two lesser-used old roads. The trees lighten a bit beyond the middle road, which allows for partial lake views and more shrubs along the forest floor. The generally mildly rising trail continues a northbound course that follows the contours of the topography through a scattered to light forest of red firs, western white pines, and Jeffrey pines.

Near the 5-mile mark, the trail arcs to the east around the nose of a ridge and comes above the upper part of Lincoln Creek canyon. Head southeast for a short time and curve onto the floor of the canyon and a crossing of Forest Service Road 14N33. From the road, wind up a tree-covered slope to a three-way junction with the Sierra Canyon Trail.

Leaving the TRT, turn right and follow this relatively new trail through dense forest to the crossing of an old road, beyond which the forest lightens on the way to a crossing of the more distinct and well-traveled Genoa Peak Road.

Turn left onto the road and follow a moderate, half-mile climb to a T-junction. Turn right here and climb generally southeast toward Genoa Peak. The grade increases as you eventually break out of the trees and draw near to the peak. Follow a path across open slopes and then wind steeply up to the summit. Good views of both the Carson Valley to the east and Lake Tahoe to the west greet you from the top. The only drawbacks are the buzzing communication equipment littering the peak and the possibility of stiff afternoon breezes.

Lake Tahoe from near Daggett Pass

105   TRT: Kingsbury North to Sierra Canyon

see map on p. 239

Distance	16.1 miles (point-to-point)
Hiking Time	6–9 hours
Elevation	+1,750/-4,750 feet
Difficulty	Difficult
Trail Use	Mountain biking OK, dogs OK
Best Times	Early to mid-July through early October
Agency	Lake Tahoe Basin Management Unit at 530-543-2600, www.fs.usda.gov/ltbmu; Humboldt Toiyabe National Forest at 775-882-2766, www.fs.usda.gov/htnf
Recommended Maps	USGS 7.5-minute *South Lake Tahoe, Glenbrook, Genoa* (trail not shown), CVTA *Genoa Trail System*

HIGHLIGHTS Mountain bikers should love a trip with so much singletrack downhill, but strong hikers up for a 16-mile jaunt should find plenty to like as well on this rolling route along a section of the Tahoe Rim Trail (TRT) followed by the extended, zigzagging descent down Sierra Canyon to the town of Genoa. Occasional views of Lake Tahoe from the TRT and sweeping vistas across Carson Valley to the Pine Nut Mountains down Sierra Canyon provide visual highlights. Water is extremely scarce along almost the entire route, so be sure to pack plenty for the long day's journey.

DIRECTIONS *Start:* Follow Kingsbury Grade (NV 207) to North Benjamin Drive, which is 0.3 mile west of Daggett Pass and 2.9 miles east of the NV 50 junction. Turn north and drive through the Upper Kingsbury subdivision, as Benjamin becomes Andria Drive. Proceed nearly 2 miles from the highway almost to the end of the pavement and park on the left-hand or right-hand shoulder as space allows.

End: From the center of Genoa, drive northeast on Main Street (Jacks Valley Road) for 0.5 mile and turn left (west) onto Centennial Drive. Follow Centennial around a bend to the north to an intersection with Snowshoe Lane. Park your vehicle on the east side of Centennial Drive across from Snowshoe Lane.

FACILITIES/TRAILHEAD There are no facilities at either the North Kingsbury or Sierra Canyon Trailheads. Mormon Station State Historic Park in Genoa has restrooms with running water, picnic tables with grills, and a visitor center. The trail begins on the west side of the road near a trail sign at the North Kingsbury Trailhead.

Begin the hike by ascending a slope dotted with firs and Jeffrey pines and covered with chinquapin, currant, bitterbrush, and pinemat and greenleaf manzanita. On a moderate climb, wrap around Peak 8204 with filtered views of Castle Rock immediately to the southwest, Freel Peak to the south, and Lake Tahoe to the west. At 0.5 mile, you reach a signed junction with the TRT.

Turn north at the junction and proceed on gently graded tread lined with extensive patches of lupines carpeting the forest floor until midseason. After 0.5 mile is a three-way junction with the Stinger Trail, primarily a mountain bike route headed to the Stateline area.

Remain on the TRT by heading northeast, winding around and dropping to the crossing of a well-used four-wheel-drive road before continuing across two more lesser-used old roads. The trees lighten a bit beyond the middle road, which allows for partial lake views and more shrubs along the forest floor. The generally mildly rising trail continues a northbound course that follows the contours of the topography through a scattered to light forest of red firs, western white pines, and Jeffrey pines.

Near the 5-mile mark, the trail arcs to the east around the nose of a ridge and comes above the upper part of Lincoln Creek canyon. Head southeast for a short time and curve onto the floor of the

Sierra Canyon and Carson Valley

canyon and a crossing of Forest Service Road 14N33. From the road, wind up a tree-covered slope to a three-way junction with the Sierra Canyon Trail.

Leaving the TRT, you turn right and follow this relatively new trail through dense forest to the crossing of an old road, beyond which the forest lightens on the way to a crossing of the more distinct and well-traveled Genoa Peak Road.

Beyond the Genoa Peak Road, the forest opens up to stunning views down Sierra Canyon and out to verdant Carson Valley

backdropped by the spine of the Pine Nut Mountains. After a few short switchbacks, a long and rocky descending traverse leads across the north wall of the canyon. Despite the 3,600-foot difference in elevation between the head and the bottom of the canyon, one aspect of the Sierra Canyon Trail soon becomes apparent, as the trail makes periodic rises. While having to repeatedly regain a portion of this lost elevation may frustrate hikers, these rises are designed to slow the speed of mountain bikers along the extended descent. Near the 7.5-mile mark, the previously continuous vista starts to become obscured for stretches by a scattered forest. Also not far from this spot, the trail starts to follow numerous long-legged switchbacks toward the bottom of the canyon. Continue the seemingly interminable zigzagging descent down Sierra Canyon.

At about 11 miles, you reach the first water source along the route so far, where a spring-fed seep gurgles through a slim patch of lush vegetation. Further evidence of the slightly wetter environment of the lower canyon is seen in widely scattered incense cedars intermixing with the more common pines and firs. Proceed through shady forest past another seep and continue to where the trail bends over and briefly follows above the steep defile of the main branch of the creek. The path moves away and then bends back toward the creek one more time, reaching the crossing of a more vigorous tributary at 13.2 miles. Shortly after this refreshing brook, you break out of the forest for a bit and angle across the north wall of the canyon. After a short return to the trees, continue across a more exposed slope dotted with mountain mahoganies, eventually reaching a four-way junction with the Discovery Trail, 14.1 miles from the North Kingsbury Trailhead.

Veer to the right at the junction and head northwest back toward Sierra Canyon, reaching a second junction with the Discovery Trail after 0.2 mile.

You turn left at the junction and follow the Sierra Canyon Trail angling sharply down the canyon on the north side of the creek, enjoying the intermittent shade from a mixed forest of Jeffrey pines, white firs, and incense cedars. Soon the trail follows a zigzagging course down the canyon via a series of switchbacks. Farther down the canyon, you cross the creek on a stout wood bridge and continue downstream. After briefly merging with a section of old road, singletrack tread veers away from the creek and descends across a lightly forested hillside via occasional switchbacks. Reach the Sierra Canyon Trailhead signboard and then follow the gravel surface of Snowshoe Lane out to the intersection with Centennial Drive.

106 Sierra Canyon Trail to Genoa Peak

see map on p. 239

Distance	19.8 miles (out-and-back)
Hiking Time	7–10 hours
Elevation	+4,800/-200 feet
Difficulty	Very difficult
Trail Use	Dogs OK, mountain biking OK
Best Times	Mid-June through mid-October
Agency	Lake Tahoe Basin Management Unit at 530-543-2600, www.fs.usda.gov/ltbmu; Humboldt Toiyabe National Forest at 775-882-2766, www.fs.usda.gov/htnf
Recommended Maps	USGS 7.5-minute *Genoa, Glenbrook* (trail not shown), CVTA *Genoa Trail System*

HIGHLIGHTS Some may consider the long grunt from the historic town of Genoa to the top of Genoa Peak a bit masochistic, but for strong hikers and mountain bikers, the almost 10-mile, nearly 5,000-foot climb and corresponding descent might present a significant fitness challenge. This is definitely not a trip for the faint of heart. Along with bragging rights for completing such a feat, the views from upper Genoa Canyon and Genoa Peak are a worthy reward for all the toil and suffering.

DIRECTIONS From the intersection of Main Street (Jacks Valley Road) and Genoa Lane (NV 206) in the center of Genoa, drive north-northeast on Main Street for 0.9 mile and turn left onto Eagle Ridge

Road. Bear left after 0.5 mile to remain on Eagle Ridge Road and travel another 0.6 mile to Timberline Drive. Turn left onto Timberline and continue to the end at the trailhead parking area, just beyond a water tank.

FACILITIES/TRAILHEAD There are no facilities at the trailhead. Mormon Station State Historic Park in Genoa has restrooms with running water, picnic tables with grills, and a visitor center. The trail begins on the continuation of a dirt road.

Climb away from the Eagle Ridge Trailhead on gravel road a short distance to a horseshoe bend near a trailhead kiosk and a sign with various destinations and mileages. Continue climbing along a dirt road for 0.3 mile to a switchback, where a sign directs you onto singletrack tread. After a while, the trail switchbacks again, where the grade eases on a rising traverse across sagebrush-covered slopes dotted with widely scattered Jeffrey pines. Merge with the old road again and turn steeply up the seasonal drainage of Adams Canyon. Bend away from canyon and proceed on singletrack into slightly denser forest, where the intermittent shade will be quite welcome on a hot summer day. Traverse in and out of a few side drainages, crossing the thin ribbon of a perennial stream at 1 mile from the trailhead.

Past the stream, the forest eventually becomes more scattered again on the way to the edge of Sierra Canyon. Here, a series of short, steep switchbacks leads up the nose of the ridge above this steep defile. Mountain mahoganies provide little shade on the steep and exposed climb up a dozen switchbacks, followed by a rising traverse over to a junction with the Sierra Canyon Trail at 2.1 miles.

Turn right and follow the Sierra Canyon Trail on what may come to feel like an interminable, switchbacking climb up the canyon. Initially, the trail crosses an open slope dotted with mountain mahoganies but, after a while, enters shady, mixed forest where the path moves closer to the creek. Farther along but still in the lower part of the canyon, the trail crosses spring-fed rivulets three times before long-legged switchbacks lead away from the creek and into a more open forest of Jeffrey pines. Eventually you climb high enough into the upper canyon in order to break out of the trees, where a sweeping view of Carson Valley and the Pine Nut Mountains unfolds. Beyond the last switchback, a long, ascending traverse leads across the head of Sierra Canyon and, where the grade at last eases, you intersect the fairly well traveled surface of Genoa Peak Road, 9.1 miles from the parking area along Centennial Drive.

Turn right (north-northeast) and follow Genoa Peak Road for 0.5 mile on a steep climb to a T-junction. Turn right at the junction and climb moderately steeply southeast toward the top of Genoa Peak. The grade increases where the trees are left behind, and you follow a winding path up shrub-covered slopes to the top for fine views of Carson Valley backdropped by the Pine Nut Mountains to the east and the Lake Tahoe basin to the west. The incredible scenery is marred slightly by the constant electronic hum from the communication equipment that litters the summit.

After thoroughly enjoying the hard-earned view, retrace your steps 9.9 miles back to the Eagle Ridge Trailhead.

107 **Discovery Trail: Eagle Ridge Loop**

see map on p. 239

Distance	4 miles (point-to-point), 6.2 miles (loop)
Hiking Time	1.5–2 hours, 2–3 hours
Elevation	+750/-1,750 feet, +1,775/-1,775 feet
Difficulty	Moderate
Trail Use	Dogs OK, mountain biking OK
Best Times	Late March through November
Agency	Humboldt Toiyabe National Forest at 775-882-2766, www.fs.usda.gov/htnf/
Recommended Maps	USGS 7.5-minute *Genoa* (trail not shown), CVTA *Genoa Trail System*

HIGHLIGHTS Especially when the trails higher up in the mountains are buried under snow, the Genoa Trail System has a couple of lower-elevation loop options for hikers, mountain bikers, and equestrians. The Eagle Ridge Loop offers sweeping views of Carson Valley and the Pine Nut Mountains, as well as a pair of perennial little streams along the way. The trip is best done as a point-to-point hike, shuttling between the Eagle Ridge and Sierra Canyon Trailheads. Otherwise, you'll have to walk a couple of miles along roads in order to get back to either trailhead. When hiking here in the summer, start early in the day to avoid the hot afternoon temperatures.

DIRECTIONS From the intersection of Main Street (Jacks Valley Road) and Genoa Lane (NV 206) in the center of Genoa, drive north-northeast on Main Street for 0.9 mile and turn left onto Eagle Ridge Road. Bear left after 0.5 mile to remain on Eagle Ridge Road and travel another 0.6 mile to Timberline Drive. Turn left onto Timberline and continue to the end at the trailhead parking area, just beyond a water tank.

For the point-to-point option, you will need to leave a second vehicle at the Sierra Canyon Trailhead. From the center of Genoa, head northeast from the intersection of Main Street (Jacks Valley Road) and Genoa Lane (NV 206) and drive on Main Street for 0.5 mile to a left-hand turn onto Centennial Drive. Follow Centennial around a bend to the intersection of Snowshoe Lane. Park your vehicle along the east side of Centennial Drive.

FACILITIES/TRAILHEAD There are no facilities at either trailhead. Mormon Station State Historic Park in Genoa has restrooms with running water, picnic tables with grills, and a visitor center. The trail begins on the continuation of a dirt road.

Climb away from the Eagle Ridge Trailhead on gravel road a short distance to a horseshoe bend near a trailhead kiosk and a sign with various destinations and mileages. Continue climbing along a dirt road for 0.3 mile to a switchback, where a sign directs you onto singletrack tread. After a while the trail switchbacks again, where the grade eases on a rising traverse across sagebrush-covered slopes dotted with widely scattered Jeffrey pines. Merge with the old road again and turn steeply up the seasonal drainage of Adams Canyon. Bend away from canyon and proceed on singletrack into slightly denser forest, where the intermittent shade will be quite welcome on a hot summer day. Traverse in and out of a few side drainages, crossing the thin ribbon of a perennial stream at 1 mile from the trailhead.

Past the stream, the forest eventually becomes more scattered again on the way to the edge of Sierra Canyon, where a series of short, steep switchbacks lead up the nose of the ridge above this steep defile. Mountain mahoganies provide little shade on the steep and exposed climb up a dozen switchbacks, followed by a rising traverse over to a junction with the Sierra Canyon Trail at 2.1 miles.

A descending traverse from the junction leads shortly to the next junction, where the Discovery Trail continues across the stream draining Sierra Canyon and continues a southbound course. You turn left and follow the Sierra Canyon Trail angling sharply down the canyon on the north side of the creek, enjoying the intermittent shade from a mixed forest of Jeffrey pines, white firs, and incense cedars. Soon the trail follows a zigzagging course down the canyon via a series of switchbacks. Farther down the canyon, you cross the creek on a stout wood bridge and continue downstream. After briefly merging with a section of old road, singletrack tread veers away from the creek and descends across a lightly forested hillside

via occasional switchbacks. Reach the Sierra Canyon Trailhead signboard and follow the gravel surface of Snowshoe Lane out to the intersection with Centennial Drive.

For the loop option, head south and then east on Centennial Drive to Jacks Valley Road. Proceed north-northeast on Jacks Valley Road to Eagle Ridge Road and ascend to the intersection of Timberline Road. Climb steeply up the pavement to the trailhead just beyond the water tank.

108 Discovery Trail: Genoa Loop

see map on p. 239

Distance	7.7 miles (point-to-point), 8.7 miles (loop)
Hiking Time	2.5–4 hours, 3–4 hours
Elevation	+1,325/-1,325 feet, +1,500/-1,500 feet
Difficulty	Moderate
Trail Use	Dogs OK, mountain biking OK (not recommended in lower Genoa Canyon)
Best Times	Late March through November
Agency	Humboldt Toiyabe National Forest at 775-882-2766, www.fs.usda.gov/htnf
Recommended Maps	USGS 7.5-minute *Genoa* (trail not shown), CVTA *Genoa Trail System*

HIGHLIGHTS Similar to the Eagle Ridge Loop, the longer Genoa Loop offers superb views of Carson Valley backdropped by the Pine Nut Mountains to the east. In addition to the sweeping vistas, the trail leads to a pretty, short waterfall near the midpoint. This is an excellent spring and fall hike. Summertime visitors should plan on an early start to avoid the afternoon heat. Passing through the quaint, historic town of Genoa offers the possibility of grabbing a meal or enjoying a libation at Nevada's oldest bar after the hike.

DIRECTIONS From the intersection of Main Street (Jacks Valley Road) and Genoa Lane (NV 206) in the center of Genoa, drive north-northeast on Main Street for 0.5 mile and turn left onto Centennial Drive. Follow Centennial around a bend to the intersection of Snowshoe Lane. Park your vehicle along the east side of Centennial Drive.

For the point-to-point option you will need to leave a second vehicle at the Genoa Canyon Trailhead. From the center of Genoa, head southwest on Main Street for 0.2 mile and then turn right onto Carson Street. Follow this gravel road to a turnaround at the end and park your vehicle along the side without blocking access to the private homes in the vicinity.

FACILITIES/TRAILHEAD There are no facilities at either trailhead. Mormon Station State Historic Park in Genoa has restrooms with running water, picnic tables with grills, and a visitor center. The trail begins at the far end of Snowshoe Lane.

Walk up Snowshoe Lane to the Sierra Canyon Trailhead signboard and then very briefly follow an old dirt road to a switchback, where singletrack trail slices across the hillside. Continue through Jeffrey pine forest to the next switchback and then

head north toward Sierra Canyon. After a few more switchbacks, the trail merges with an old road above the creek and proceeds up the canyon into riparian foliage and a crossing of the stream on a stout wood bridge. Follow the old road shortly to where singletrack trail switchbacks up above the north bank through open, predominantly Jeffrey pine forest with lesser amounts of white firs and incense cedars. Just after meeting a section of the old road angling in from behind and below on the left, a stiffer climb leads to a signed junction with the Discovery Trail, 1.9 miles from the parking area on Centennial Drive.

Veer to the left and follow the Discovery Trail farther up Sierra Canyon back into riparian vegetation and to a boulder hop of the creek. From there, climb away from the stream via three switchbacks, followed by an ascending, rolling traverse across the south wall of the canyon into more open forest, which now includes mountain mahogany. Through breaks in the trees, you have expanding views across the ranches of Carson Valley to the distant Pine Nut Mountains. Exiting Sierra Canyon, the trail follows the folds and creases of the topography, dipping into usually dry Slaughterhouse Canyon on the way. Continue this pattern to the high point of the journey (6,140 feet) at the north lip of Genoa Canyon.

As the trail cuts across the north side of Genoa Canyon, keen eyes will see the trail

Genoa Falls

on the opposite side and a few of the many switchbacks leading toward the bottom of the canyon. Enter into shady forest on the way to a crossing of the north branch of Genoa Creek, 4.25 miles from the parking area. A very short path leads up to the base of Genoa Falls, a short but picturesque waterfall spilling down a black rock face.

The trail climbs moderately away from the north branch into the canyon of the south branch of Genoa Creek, where you can usually jump the narrow stream. A mellow, rolling stroll leads away from the second crossing to the top of the switchbacks, where the trail begins a steep, 2-mile, zigzagging plunge toward town. The descent is not recommended for mountain bikers and equestrians due to exposure, falling rock potential, tight switchbacks, and poor visibility. After a few switchbacks, a long-legged switchback leads over to and away from a narrow side canyon before a series of very short switchbacks wind downslope. After crossing a gully, the trail follows the crest of a narrow ridge with steep drop-offs on either side. Beyond the ridge, more switchbacks lead down the hillside and back into Genoa Canyon, where you follow the creek through shady forest on the way to a boulder hop over to the north bank. Continue downstream to the vicinity of Sierra Shadows water tank and merge with a dirt road. Veer to the right and follow the road down into town and a kiosk at the Genoa Canyon Trailhead.

For the loop option, head down Carson Street to Main Street, turn left, and follow Main Street through the center of town. At Centennial Drive, turn left and follow the road around a curve and up to the intersection of Snowshoe Lane.

109 TRT: Spooner Summit to South Camp Peak

see map on p. 239

Distance	10.4 miles (out-and-back)
Hiking Time	5–6 hours
Elevation	+1,875/-225 feet
Difficulty	Moderate
Trail Use	Backpacking option, dogs OK, mountain biking OK
Best Times	Mid-June through October
Agency	Humboldt-Toiyabe National Forest at 775-882-2766, www.fs.usda.gov/htnf; Lake Tahoe Basin Management Unit at 530-543-2600, www.fs.usda.gov/ltbmu
Recommended Map	USGS 7.5-minute *Glenbrook* (trail not shown)

HIGHLIGHTS Lake Tahoe is considered to be the premier natural wonder in northern Nevada, and this trip to South Camp Peak may provide the quintessential view. Don't forget your camera, as even the most jaded photographer will be impressed by the vistas from the open slopes along the mile-long traverse of the broad mesa that tops the peak. Getting there does require a 5-mile, 1,875-foot climb along a stretch of the Tahoe Rim Trail (TRT), but the scenic rewards are definitely worth the effort. Water is not available along the entire route of the trail—make sure you're carrying a sufficient amount for both the hike in and the hike out.

DIRECTIONS Follow NV 50 to Spooner Summit, three-quarters of a mile east of the junction of NV 28. Park your vehicle south of the highway in the Spooner Summit picnic area.

FACILITIES/TRAILHEAD The Spooner Summit picnic area has picnic tables and vault toilets. The well-signed trail begins at the south end of the picnic area.

Leave the trailhead parking lot and make a stiff, switchbacking climb on sandy trail up the hillside south of NV 50 through sagebrush, tobacco brush, currant, chinquapin, and manzanita, beneath scattered Jeffrey pines and quaking aspens that dot the slope. Eventually the roar of traffic from the highway is left behind, as you gain a ridge and follow a milder climb along the crest. Farther on, keen eyes will reveal that this area was selectively logged at some time in the past, the result of a bark beetle infestation that killed a number of trees in the early 1990s. This scattered forest of Jeffrey pines and red firs provides partial views of Carson Valley to the east and Lake Tahoe to the west, and allows enough sunlight to reach the forest floor to produce a fine array of early summer wildflowers, including mule-ears, lupine, and paintbrush. Near the 1.5-mile mark, you climb a knoll, where a very short use trail leads to impressive views.

A stretch of mild descent, followed by a mild climb brings you to a crossing of a dirt road, 2.5 miles from the trailhead. Then a mildly rising traverse leads across a selectively logged slope below Duane Bliss Peak. At a quarter mile past the first road crossing, you cross an abandoned road and climb to the crest again. A moderate climb along the ridge takes you just below a rocky knob, where a short use trail leads up the knob to good views to the east of Carson Valley backdropped by the Pine Nut Range. You eventually leave the views behind, following a mildly graded descent into a mixed forest of western white pines, Jeffrey pines, and red firs to the signed crossing of the Genoa Peak Road (FS 14N32), 3 miles from the trailhead, a major backcountry thoroughfare not only

for the four-wheel-drive crowd but heavily used by mountain bikers as well.

A moderate climb away from Genoa Peak Road passes through an area of selective logging and slash burning that is a bit unsightly, although this clearing activity has produced a fine wildflower display in early summer. The long steady climb reaches a switchback, beyond which the trail bends east before curving back toward the southwest. As you gain elevation, mountain hemlocks and lodgepole pines join the dense, mixed forest. Nearing the crest at the north end of South Camp Peak, approximately 1.3 miles from Genoa Peak Road, you suddenly break out of the forest into a sublime Tahoe vista. A short climb takes you up to the top of a rocky knoll, where an even better view awaits. Be sure you pack along a detailed map of the Tahoe Basin to help identify the bounty of landmarks visible from this exceptional viewpoint, from where a finer view of the lake is hard to imagine.

The essentially flat-topped plateau of South Camp Peak stretches south for another mile, providing nearly continuous, stupendous lake views. The true summit is actually 0.7 mile east of the trail, hardly worth the extra effort of a cross-country journey. The high point along the trail is another 0.8 mile south, near where a conveniently placed log bench offers an excellent seat for perhaps Tahoe's best show.

By continuing south on the TRT, you could make a short connection to the Genoa Peak Road and follow it to a jeep road that ascends to the summit of Genoa Peak for additional views of Freel Peak, Jobs Peak and Jobs Sister, and the Carson Valley. With arrangements for a shuttle, continuing all the way to the Daggett Pass Trailhead (13 miles total distance) is possible.

110 **Clear Creek Trail to Knob Point**

Distance	13.2 miles (out-and-back)
Hiking Time	5–6 hours
Elevation	+1,075/-100 feet
Difficulty	Moderate
Trail Use	Dogs OK, mountain biking OK
Best Times	March through November
Agency	Humboldt Toiyabe National Forest at 775-882-2766, www.fs.usda.gov/htnf
Recommended Maps	USGS 7.5-minute *Genoa* (trail not shown), CVTA *Clear Creek Trail*

HIGHLIGHTS The Clear Creek Trail is a bit of a misnomer, as the path is nowhere close to the stream until near the 8-mile mark, where it crosses a perennial tributary and then the main branch a half mile farther. Unfortunately, after crossing Clear Creek the trail dead ends at 10.5 miles, not far from a proposed upper trailhead at Lake Tahoe Golf Course Drive. Hopefully, negotiations for an easement across this section of private property will be secured in the future, allowing recreationists to utilize an 11-mile shuttle option versus a 21-mile out-and-back trip.

In the meantime, the 6.6-mile hike to Knob Point is a fine destination until, if and when, the upper trailhead becomes a reality. The trail starts out on the floor of Jacks Valley and climbs for 2.5 miles through sagebrush scrub, enjoying fine views of Jacks and Carson Valleys on the way, as well as some interesting looking rock formations on the hills above. The remainder of the trip passes through Jeffrey pine forest, weaving in and out of some canyons before angling across the slope on the way to the point. Knob Point affords recreationists an excellent view and a fine lunch spot, as well as a good turnaround point. As the trail passes across a large tract of private land, staying on the trail at all times is imperative for the continued use of the trail.

DIRECTIONS From US 395 in south Carson City, turn southwest onto Jacks Valley Road (NV 206) and drive 1.8 miles to the trailhead on the right-hand shoulder.

FACILITIES/TRAILHEAD There are no facilities at the trailhead. The trail begins at a closed steel gate on the north shoulder of Jacks Valley Road.

The Clear Creek Trail briefly follows the course of an old dirt road away from the trailhead before a couple of signs direct you onto singletrack trail on a steady, winding climb that heads north up the hillside through sagebrush scrub. Continuing the ascent, the trail passes to the left of a water tank, reaches the crest of the hill, and then turns west. Along the way, you will cross a number of old jeep roads, but the crossings are clearly marked by trail signs. Beyond the 1.5-mile mark, the trail passes below some interesting looking rock formations and dips briefly into a couple of shallow side canyons. Around 2 miles is a rock knob offering a fine view of Jacks and Carson Valleys backdropped to the east by the Pine Nut Range—a fine turnaround point for anyone just interested in a short hike. The trail drops across the hillside away from

the viewpoint before resuming the ascent. At 2.5 miles, you cross out of forest service land and onto private property. Respecting the rights of the owners, remaining on the trail at all times is essential to be able to continue to use this trail in the future. In this vicinity, the environment shifts from sagebrush scrub to Jeffrey pine forest.

Traversing across the slope, the trail dips into another side canyon, arcs around an open hillside, and then proceeds into the forested canyon of a seasonal stream. Early-season hikers may find water here, but later in the year, the stream is generally dry. Cross the creek on a short wood bridge and begin a more pronounced ascent through the trees. Above some switchbacks, you reach Bennett Canyon and climb above the east rim for a while. Higher up the canyon, the winding trail crosses the usually dry gully a few times before curving around to the south. The stiff climb continues to a junction, where you turn left and follow a short lateral to Knob Point at 6,050 feet. The wide-ranging view covers a large part of Carson Valley bordered on the east by the Pine Nut Mountains. Once you've taken in the fine vista, retrace your steps 6.6 miles to the trailhead.

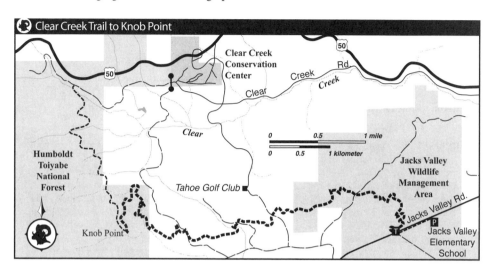

Clear Creek Trail to Knob Point

Carson Valley from Clear Creek Trail

111 Spooner Lake

Distance	1.8 miles (loop)
Hiking Time	1 hour
Elevation	Negligible
Difficulty	Easy
Trail Use	Good for kids, leashed dogs OK
Best Times	May through October
Agency	Humboldt Toiyabe National Forest at 775-882-2766, www.fs.usda.gov/htnf; Lake Tahoe Basin Management Unit at 530-548-2600, www.fs.usda.gov/ltbmu
Recommended Maps	LTNSP *Marlette-Hobart Backcountry,* USGS 7.5-minute *Glenbrook* (trail not shown)

HIGHLIGHTS Spooner Lake was created in the 1850s for use as a millpond when a timber company constructed a dam across Spooner Creek. The dam was rebuilt in 1929 for irrigation purposes. Nowadays, within Lake Tahoe Nevada State Park, recreation has replaced logging and irrigation as the principal use around Spooner Lake, with hikers, naturalists, picnickers, and anglers flocking to the pleasant surroundings. A nearly level, 1.6-mile path encircles the lake, providing an easy hike complete with interpretive displays, park benches, and superb scenery. The trail passes through diverse plant communities, including Jeffrey pine forest, aspen groves, flower-filled meadows, and sagebrush scrub. The area is also home to a wide range of wildlife.

Although mountain biking is perhaps the most popular form of recreation within the park, the Spooner Lake trail is open to pedestrians only. Pets must be leashed. Fishing is catch-and-release only, with mandatory use of barbless artificial lures.

DIRECTIONS Drive on NV 28 to the entrance into the Spooner Lake section of Lake Tahoe Nevada State Park, 1 mile northwest of the junction of NV 50. Follow the park access road to the visitor center parking lot. A fee is charged for entry into the park.

To avoid paying the entrance fee, you could drive on NV 50 to Spooner Summit, three-quarters of a mile east from the junction with NV 28, and park on the north side of the road in the Tahoe Rim Trail (TRT) parking lot. Follow the TRT north for approximately 50 yards to an informal junction. Turn left, leaving the TRT, and descend on a lateral, initially paralleling NV 50. After three-quarters of a mile from the TRT trailhead, you reach a junction with the Spooner Lake Trail on the east side of the lake.

FACILITIES/TRAILHEAD The Spooner Lake section of Lake Tahoe Nevada State Park offers a picnic area with tables and barbecue grills, restrooms, mountain bike rentals and equipment sales, rental cabins, and ranger-led nature programs.

A short walk from the parking lot leads to a signed, four-way junction. Following directions to Spooner Lake, you stroll past a signboard and begin a clockwise loop around the lake by passing over the dam. Interpretive signs placed around the loop provide opportunities to learn tidbits about the human and natural history of the area. Conveniently placed park benches provide ample opportunities to relax and survey the lake views. Circling around the lake, you encounter a variety of vegetation. Large clearings are filled with sagebrush, bitterbrush, and mule-ears. Where the soil is able to hold onto more moisture, pockets of willow flourish. Away from the lakeshore, thick stands of Jeffrey pine forest intermix with a smattering of white fir. Near the inlet, dense aspen groves shimmer with a splash of grayish green in summer and a blaze of yellow-gold in fall.

On the southeast side of the lake, you reach a junction with the lateral on the left that climbs up to the Tahoe Rim Trail Trailhead near Spooner Summit. Veer right here and proceed to a wood bridge across Spooner Creek. Beyond the bridge, the trail draws closer to the lakeshore and passes through a flower-filled meadow, which provides a fine habitat for several species of

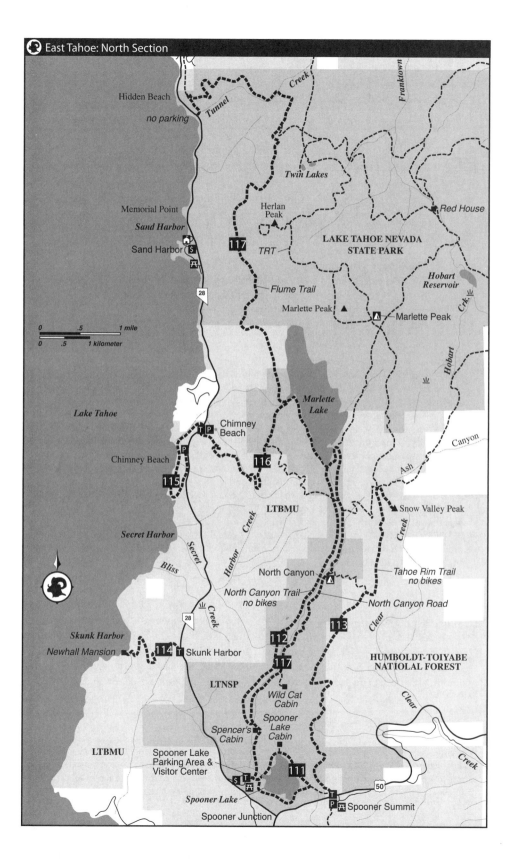

birds, including osprey, bald eagle, and kill-deer. Continue around the lake to close the loop at the junction. From there, follow the short lateral back to the parking lot.

---

112   Marlette Lake

Distance	9 miles (out-and-back)
Hiking Time	4.5–5 hours
Elevation	+1,225/-400 feet
Difficulty	Moderate
Trail Use	Leashed dogs
Best Times	June through October
Agency	Humboldt Toiyabe National Forest at 775-882-2766, www.fs.usda.gov/htnf; Lake Tahoe Basin Management Unit at 530-548-2600, www.fs.usda.gov/ltbmu
Recommended Maps	LTNSP *Marlette-Hobart Backcountry,* USGS 7.5-minute *Glenbrook* (trail not shown)

see map on p. 255

HIGHLIGHTS As the initial segment of the legendary Flume Trail ride, the 5-mile trip to Marlette Lake along the North Canyon Road has been very popular with mountain bikers for quite some time. With recent completion of the North Canyon Trail, hikers and equestrians can now journey to the lake on a segment of singletrack trail that is closed to bikes. The 4.5-mile journey starts at one artificial lake, Spooner, and ends at another, Marlette. In between, you stroll through mixed forest up North Canyon before a short descent leads to the scenic lakeshore. Recreationists with extra time and energy have additional opportunities to reach fine Lake Tahoe views, colorful wildflower displays, and extensive aspen stands. The route to Marlette Lake is generally open for snow-free travel by June. Fall is an especially fine time for a visit, when the extensive aspen groves in North Canyon and along Marlette's west shore are ablaze in autumnal splendor.

DIRECTIONS Drive on NV 28 to the entrance into the Spooner Lake section of Lake Tahoe Nevada State Park, 1 mile northwest of the junction with NV 50. Follow the access road to the second parking lot near the visitor center.

FACILITIES/TRAILHEAD The Spooner Lake section of Lake Tahoe Nevada State Park offers a picnic area with tables and barbecue grills, restrooms, mountain bike rentals and equipment sales, rental cabins, and ranger-led nature programs.

From the parking lot, follow a wide path for 0.1 mile to a junction with North Canyon Road, just west of Spooner Lake's dam. Head north on the road across Spooner Lake's outlet and proceed across an open area of sagebrush scrub before entering a mixed forest of lodgepole pines, white firs, and Jeffrey pines. Soon after entering the forest, you pass a quarter-mile lateral on the right to Spooner Lake Cabin.

SPOONER LAKE CABIN

A hand-hewn, Scandinavian-style structure that sleeps four adults, Spooner Lake Cabin is complete with cooking and heating stoves, kitchen supplies, and an odor-free composting toilet. The Wildcat Cabin is a similar structure accessible farther north from the North Canyon Road. For more information, or to make reservations, consult the Zephyr Cove website at **zephyrcove.com/spoonercabins** or call 775-749-1120.

Not far past the lateral, you stroll by rustic Spencer's Cabin on the left, follow the road over the creek, and meet the junction with the new North Canyon Trail near a closed gate, three-quarters of a mile from the parking lot.

The new trail follows the west bank of North Canyon Creek all the way from Spencer's Cabin to Marlette Lake. For the next 3 miles, you make a steady climb up North Canyon through mixed forest. Near the 2-mile mark, the trail crosses a tributary of Secret Harbor Creek, which diverts the majority of North Canyon Creek's stream flow away from Spooner Creek on a shortcut west to Lake Tahoe. At 3.2 miles from the parking lot, the North Canyon Campground lies directly east and may be accessible by a short lateral. Near the vicinity of the campground, a steep 1.2-mile trail provides a connection to the Tahoe Rim Trail.

Along the creek, stands of quaking aspen and pockets of meadow contrast nicely with the conifers. At 4 miles from the trailhead, in a saddle separating North Canyon from Marlette Lake's basin, you encounter an old closed road on the right, which follows a steep westbound course down to Chimney Beach (see Trip 116).

From the high point, a half-mile descent leads to a road along the south shore of picturesque Marlette Lake. Nearby is a Nevada Division of Wildlife trout hatchery built in 1987 (fishing is not allowed in Marlette Lake). Since the lake is a domestic water source for Carson City, camping is not allowed, but swimming is permissible, and the temperature of the water can be quite refreshing on a hot summer day.

From Marlette Lake, several options exist for extending your trip: From where the trail meets the road at the south end of Marlette Lake, a left turn (northwest) leads to the dam and the beginning of the Flume Trail (see Trip 117). A 0.3-mile stroll to the right (northeast) will take you to a junction near a restroom. From there, a 1-mile climb northeast past dense stands of aspen and luxuriant flower gardens leads to a wonderful view of Marlette Lake and Lake Tahoe from Marlette Overlook. By continuing on the road another 0.7 mile, you will intersect the Tahoe Rim Trail, which leads north toward Marlette Peak and Marlette Peak Campground, or south to the Spooner Lake Trailhead.

Marlette Lake

113   TRT: Spooner Summit to Snow Valley Peak

see map on p. 255

Distance	12.4 miles (out-and-back)
Hiking Time	6–7 hours
Elevation	+2,450/-450 feet
Difficulty	Moderate
Trail Use	Backpacking option, dogs OK
Best Times	Mid-June through October
Agency	Humboldt Toiyabe National Forest at 775-882-2766, www.fs.usda.gov/htnf; Lake Tahoe Basin Management Unit at 530-548-2600, www.fs.usda.gov/ltbmu
Recommended Maps	LTNSP *Marlette Hobart Backcountry*, USGS 7.5-minute *Glenbrook* (trail not shown)

HIGHLIGHTS Views of Lake Tahoe from Snow Valley Peak are stunning. However, you'll have to journey through 4 miles of dense forest before the lake is revealed in all its glory. A trio of vista points within the first 2.25 miles offers limited views for those who prefer a shorter hike, but they fail to compare to the awesome grandeur at the trip's climax atop Snow Valley Peak.

Considering the shady forest this section of the Tahoe Rim Trail (TRT) passes through, one might get the impression that the previous winter's snowpack would hang around well into summer. However, since considerably less snow falls on the Carson Range than the Sierra crest to the west, this trail opens up sooner than might be expected. In most years, hikers can anticipate snow-free hiking beginning in June. The downside is that by midsummer very little water, if any, will be available en route to Snow Valley Peak. The cooler climes of autumn make for pleasant hiking, particularly when the aspens in North Canyon below the trail are ablaze with color.

DIRECTIONS Drive on NV 50 to Spooner Summit, three-quarters of a mile east of the junction of NV 28. Parking is available in the well-signed TRT parking lot on the north side of the highway.

TRAILHEAD/FACILITIES There are no facilities at the trailhead. TRT signs clearly indicate the start of the trail adjacent to the parking lot.

A short, mild climb from the parking lot leads into light Jeffrey-pine and red-fir forest past a junction with a lateral to Spooner Lake. Beyond this junction, the grade of ascent becomes moderate and the forest cover increases. Sporadic gaps in the trees allow brief, partial glimpses of Spooner Lake below, but the majority of the first 4 miles of trail passes through thick, viewless forest. At 1.3 miles from the trailhead, a 4-by-4-inch post marks a short lateral leading to a vista point, which offers a view to the east of NV 50 winding down Clear Creek canyon.

Continue the steady ascent, curving around minor hills and ridges. At 0.6 mile from the previous junction, you reach a second junction with a lateral to a viewpoint, marked by a 4-by-4-inch post. The short path leads to a boulder-covered knoll and

views of Carson Valley to the east and tops of the peaks in Desolation Wilderness to the southwest.

Back on the TRT, proceed on a northbound course through moderate forest cover. After a while, the trail veers west and climbs to the crest of a ridge, where another 4-by-4-inch post signals a junction with another lateral to a viewpoint, 2.25 miles from the trailhead. Follow the lateral for a few hundred feet and then scramble over boulders to a hilltop view of Lake Tahoe.

From the lateral junction, the TRT loosely follows the crest of the Carson Range for the next 1.75 miles on a more gently graded ascent through mixed forest cover. At 4 miles from the trailhead, you encounter a junction with a 1.2-mile-long trail connecting with the North Canyon Road and Marlette Lake Trail, 700 vertical

Lake Tahoe from the Tahoe Rim Trail

feet below, where backpackers can access an overnight campground.

Proceeding toward Snow Valley Peak, a mild climb leads away from the junction, passing through open terrain on the east side of the ridge that allows views of Carson Valley and the Pine Nut Mountains. After a switchback, the trail shifts to the west side of the ridge, where Lake Tahoe and the surrounding peaks spring into view, an ample reward for the previous miles of viewless hiking. A few groves of conifers interrupt the views temporarily, but soon you break out into the open for good, following an angling ascent across a hillside carpeted with tobacco brush, sagebrush, and bitterbrush. The views of the Lake Tahoe Basin are quite impressive. Rather than head directly toward the summit, the TRT climbs steadily toward a saddle directly northwest of the peak. In this saddle, 5.8 miles from the trailhead, you reach a junction with the old Snow Valley Peak jeep road.

Turn right, briefly follow the old road, and then soon turn right again onto an old

track heading toward the summit of Snow Valley Peak. After a winding 0.4-mile climb, you reach the 9,214-foot summit. Despite the communication towers and accompanying equipment that occupy the summit, the views are stunning, although the broad topography of Snow Valley Peak requires that you move about to get the best views in all directions. Lake Tahoe is the preeminent gem, with Marlette Lake shimmering in the foreground below. Visible peaks are too numerous to list (be sure to pack along a map to help identify them). To the east are Carson City and Eagle Valley, and to the northeast, Washoe Lake, Washoe Valley, and the Truckee Meadows.

On the return from Snow Valley Peak, a loop trip can be created by descending the 1.2-mile lateral from the junction to the Marlette Lake Trail. Head south to Spooner Lake, follow the trail around the lake to a junction near the southeast shore, and then climb a three-quarter-mile lateral back up to the Spooner Summit Trailhead.

114 Skunk Harbor

see map on p. 255

Distance	3.2 miles (out-and-back)
Hiking Time	1.5–2 hours
Elevation	+150/-775 feet
Difficulty	Moderate
Trail Use	Good for kids, leashed dogs
Best Times	April through November
Agency	Humboldt Toiyabe National Forest at 775-882-2766, www.fs.usda.gov/htnf; Lake Tahoe Basin Management Unit at 530-548-2600, www.fs.usda.gov/ltbmu
Recommended Map	USGS 7.5-minute *Marlette Lake*

HIGHLIGHTS Lake Tahoe is world renowned for the beauty of its exceptionally clear waters and sparkling sand beaches. Despite the name, Skunk Harbor confirms that reputation, beckoning swimmers, sunbathers, picnickers, and sightseers to visit the scenic, crescent-shaped shoreline. Along with the natural beauty, visitors will experience a bit of history from the Newhall Mansion, a preserved relic from Tahoe's resort period of the early 1900s. The 1.6-mile hike and limited parking at the trailhead ensure that Skunk Harbor won't be as crowded as other Tahoe beaches. Nevertheless, don't expect to be alone.

The lake-level elevation ensures a long hiking season, from April to November, but unless you're a card-carrying member of the polar bear club, don't plan on swimming in the typically frigid waters of Lake Tahoe except in summer.

DIRECTIONS Reaching the trailhead may be the most formidable challenge of this trip, as it's unsigned, parking is extremely limited, and there is no mass transit service available. The trailhead is on the west shoulder of NV 28 at a closed steel gate, 2.4 miles north of the junction with NV 50.

FACILITIES/TRAILHEAD There are no facilities at the trailhead. The trail begins near the closed steel gate that bars vehicle access to the road that serves as the route to Skunk Harbor.

Historic Newhall Mansion near Skunk Harbor

From the highway, descend northwest on a paved road that quickly turns to dirt amid Jeffrey pines and white firs, with an understory of manzanita, sagebrush, chinquapin, rabbitbrush, buckwheat, tobacco brush, and wild rose. Lupines and mule-ears brighten the slopes early in the season. Soon the road curves above the head of Slaughterhouse Canyon and proceeds in a more westerly direction. Keen eyes may spy the old railroad grade hugging the hillside below the road. Built in 1875, the narrow-gauge railroad hauled timber to sawmills near Glenbrook. The resulting lumber was used primarily in the town of Virginia City and the mines of the Comstock Lode nearby. A half mile from the highway, the trail intersects the railroad grade. The old railroad grade provides a gently descending route to Prey Meadows, a fine destination in late spring when copious wildflowers are blooming.

Continue on the main road on a steeper, curving descent toward the lake. Nearing the shoreline, cedars join the increasingly dense forest and the underbrush thickens as well. At 1.5 miles, you reach a three-way junction, where the right-hand road leads to the north side of Skunk Harbor's crescent-shaped, sandy beach bordered by a pile of large boulders.

Turning left, you cross a tiny stream and parallel the creek toward the lakeshore. Soon the roof and rear walls of the Newhall Mansion appear, along with a patio complete with outdoor fireplace. Granite steps lead down to the structure.

NEWHALL MANSION

The mansion was built in 1923 as a wedding present from George Newhall to his wife, Caroline, and served as a retreat and entertainment center for family and friends until its sale in 1937, to George Whitthell. Eventually the property was acquired by the Forest Service and made accessible for public enjoyment. The front porch of the mansion overlooks the sandy beach and the sparkling clear waters of Skunk Harbor. Although the doors are locked, visitors can peer through iron screens over the windows for a dark view of the inside. A number of plaques with photographs provide insights into the history of the area.

115 Chimney Beach

see map on p. 255

Distance	Up to 2.2 miles (out-and-back)
Hiking Time	1–1.5 hours
Elevation	+150/-350 feet
Difficulty	Easy
Trail Use	Dogs OK
Best Times	April through November
Agency	Humboldt Toiyabe National Forest at 775-882-2766, www.fs.usda.gov/htnf; Lake Tahoe Basin Management Unit at 530-548-2600, www.fs.usda.gov/ltbmu
Recommended Map	USGS 7.5-minute *Marlette Lake*

HIGHLIGHTS Chimney Beach is a favorite eastside beach for Tahoe locals, but the parking is extremely limited, especially on weekends. A half-mile hike leads down to the sandy shoreline, where nearby picnic tables and restrooms provide some civilized amenities. The trail continues south from Chimney Beach nearly a mile to more secluded stretches of shoreline, but be prepared for the possibility of encountering nude sunbathers—families may wish to limit their visits to the immediate surroundings of Chimney Beach.

DIRECTIONS Drive on NV 28 to a signed forest service parking lot on the east side of the highway, approximately 2.25 miles south of Sand Harbor. Parking is at a premium, especially on summer weekends—arrive early to beat the hordes. Another parking lot is one-third of a mile south on the west side of the highway.

FACILITIES/TRAILHEAD The trailhead has vault toilets and garbage cans. The trail begins across the highway near a signboard.

From the edge of the highway, you follow a mildly descending trail through a light forest of Jeffrey pines and firs, a sprinkling of granite boulders, and a scattered understory of shrubs, including tobacco brush, chinquapin, bitterbrush and manzanita. Farther downslope, you experience more of a mixed forest, with incense cedars and a variety of deciduous trees joining the firs and pines. With the aid of wood beam stairs, you head down to the crossing of Marlette Creek on a wood bridge.

Once across the bridge, follow the creek downstream toward the shore. As you approach the lake, informal paths veer toward Chimney Beach, so named for the remains of a chimney that can still be seen above the shoreline.

To continue on the main trail, cross back over the creek on a bridge and head south through scattered forest and shrubs with good views of Lake Tahoe and the peaks rimming the far shore. At 0.6 mile is a Y-junction, where the left-hand trail climbs steeply up the slope to the south parking lot on the west side of the highway. The path ahead continues another 0.6 mile to more secluded areas of shoreline, where signs warn about the possibility of encountering nude sunbathers.

---

116 Chimney Beach to Marlette Lake

see map on p. 255

Distance	6 miles (out-and-back)
Hiking Time	3–4 hours
Elevation	+1,500/-175 feet
Difficulty	Difficult
Trail Use	Dogs OK, mountain biking OK
Best Times	June through October
Agency	Humboldt Toiyabe National Forest at 775-882-2766, www.fs.usda.gov/htnf; Lake Tahoe Basin Management Unit at 530-548-2600, www.fs.usda.gov/ltbmu
Recommended Map	USGS 7.5-minute *Marlette Lake*

HIGHLIGHTS This trip is definitely the road less traveled to Marlette Lake. While hordes of hikers and mountain bikers reach the lake every summer weekend from the south along the Marlette Lake Trail and the North Canyon Road, very few take on the challenge of the shorter but much steeper route from the Chimney Beach parking area. Not only does the route demand plenty of stamina, it also requires a bit of route finding, as the junction between the infrequently maintained Chimney

Beach–North Canyon Trail and the unmaintained use trail to Marlette Lake's dam is unmarked and ill defined. However, the positives definitely outweigh the negatives, as the trail offers fine views of Lake Tahoe and delightful stretches of luxuriant foliage on the way to picturesque Marlette Lake. The lake is a fine place to swim, and the shoreline makes an excellent picnic spot, but fishing is not allowed, as the south end of the lake is the site of a Nevada Division of Wildlife trout-spawning station.

DIRECTIONS Drive on NV 28 to a signed forest service parking lot on the east side of the highway, approximately 2.25 miles south of Sand Harbor. Parking is at a premium, especially on summer weekends—arrive early to beat the hordes. Another parking lot is one-third of a mile south on the west side of the highway.

FACILITIES/TRAILHEAD The trailhead has vault toilets and garbage cans. The trail begins on the south side of the parking area, where a closed steel gate blocks vehicle access to an old road.

The road starts climbing steeply, soon doubling back and narrowing. Continue the stiff climb, as you pass through a light Jeffrey pine and fir forest with filtered views of the lake that seem to improve with the gain in elevation. After three quarters of a mile, the grade eases momentarily, as the trail wraps around the hillside and then travels above the drainage of a tributary of Marlette Creek. Moist soils in this section allow a lush assemblage of foliage to flourish, including ferns, alders, and thimbleberry, as western white pines join the mixed forest. Follow alongside the stream on a moderate climb with occasional switchbacks and then cross the trickling stream on a short, wood-plank bridge.

Away from the stream, the trail follows a rising traverse across a Jeffrey pine–dotted hillside with an understory of tobacco brush, bitterbrush, and manzanita. Soon the grade increases to a moderately steep climb that leads to the top of a minor ridge, 2.25 miles from the trailhead. On this ridgetop is an unmarked and somewhat obscure junction between the continuation of the Chimney Beach to North Canyon Trail that trends generally southeast to connections with the North Canyon Trail and the North Canyon Road, and your route to the north that leads to the Marlette Lake dam and the beginning of the Flume Trail (see Trip 117).

Head north-northeast from the ridgetop on a short, mild descent to an area of lush foliage, where aspens, grasses, small plants, and wildflowers flourish and nearly overgrow the trail in spots. Soon exiting this verdant dell, a moderate climb resumes, leading across more open slopes carpeted with pinemat manzanita, tobacco brush, chinquapin, bitterbrush, and currant. As the grade increases, vistas of Lake Tahoe and peaks in Desolation Wilderness improve on the way to the trail's high point, where through the scattered trees the sapphire-blue waters of Marlette Lake spring into view.

After a short traverse across the hillside, you make a steep, winding descent toward the narrow, V-shaped canyon of Marlette Creek. Cross the stream and intersect the Flume Trail just below the dam. Turn upstream and travel a short distance to the dam and walk across the top to access the lake's shoreline.

From the dam, you can follow the well-traveled road around the southwest shore toward the south end of the lake, where several trip options are available. You could create a semiloop trip back to the trailhead by heading south on the North Canyon Trail for a half mile to a junction with the Chimney Beach to North Canyon Trail. From there, head northwest for 1.75 miles along an old roadbed to the junction with the route you previously hiked to Marlette Lake.

From the south end of the lake, a 0.3-mile stroll northeast will take you to a junction near a restroom. From there, a 1-mile climb northeast past dense stands of aspen and luxuriant flower gardens leads to a wonderful view of Marlette Lake and Lake Tahoe from Marlette Overlook.

Lake Tahoe from the Chimney Beach Trail

117 Flume Trail

see map on p. 255

Distance	13 miles (point-to-point)
Hiking Time	6.5–7 hours
Elevation	+1,850/-2,625 feet
Difficulty	Moderate
Trail Use	Mountain biking OK
Best Times	June through October
Agency	Humboldt Toiyabe National Forest at 775-882-2766, www.fs.usda.gov/htnf; Lake Tahoe Basin Management Unit at 530-548-2600, www.fs.usda.gov/ltbmu
Recommended Maps	*LTNSP Marlette-Hobart Backcountry*, USGS 7.5-minute *Marlette Lake*

HIGHLIGHTS The Flume Trail is one of the West's most renowned mountain bike trails, with great views of Lake Tahoe and an easy, graded section of singletrack trail combining for Tahoe's ultimate fat-tire excursion. While a stiff climb makes up the first five miles, once the incredible views begin, the effort is quickly forgotten for the remainder of the downhill romp. All this grandeur does have one drawback—the trail can be quite crowded on sunny summer weekends. Hikers are allowed to use the trail, but they must stay alert for mountain bikers at all times. Horses are not permitted on the Flume Trail.

DIRECTIONS *Start:* Drive on NV 28 to the entrance into the Spooner Lake section of Lake Tahoe Nevada State Park, 1 mile northwest of the junction with NV 50. Follow the access road to the second parking lot near the visitor center.

End: Parking is nonexistent anywhere near where the Tunnel Creek Road meets NV 28. Parking along the shoulder of the highway is not allowed in the immediate vicinity, and beach users usually occupy legal spaces farther along the highway, especially on summer weekends. Two shuttle and bike rental operations serve the Flume Trail and Tahoe Meadows routes: Zephyr Cove Resort (775-749-5349, **zephyrcove.com/flumetrail**) and Flume Trail (775-298-2501, **flumetrailtahoe@gmail.com**). Shuttle cost is $15 for both services.

FACILITIES/TRAILHEAD Not only are mountain bikes available for rent, but reservations can be made for a pair of backcountry cabins. Both the Spooner Lake Cabin and Wild Cat Cabin are hand-hewn Scandinavian-style structures that sleep two to four adults. The cabins are complete with cooking and heating stoves, kitchen supplies, and odor-free composting toilets. Check out the website at **zephyrcove.com/spoonercabins** or phone 775-749-1120 to make reservations or for more information. The Spooner Lake section of Lake Tahoe Nevada State Park offers a picnic area with tables and barbecue grills, restrooms, mountain bike rentals and equipment sales, and ranger-led nature programs. The trip begins on the course of an old road.

From the parking lot follow a wide path for 0.1 mile to a junction with North Canyon Road. Head north on a gentle climb across an open area of sagebrush scrub into a mixed forest of lodgepole pines, white firs, and Jeffrey pines, where the grade of ascent increases. Soon after entering the forest, you pass a quarter-mile lateral on the right to Spooner Lake Cabin. Not far past the lateral, you stroll by rustic Spencer's Cabin on the left, follow the road over the creek, and pass the junction with the new Marlette Lake Trail near a closed gate, 0.75 mile from the parking lot. (Hikers should leave the road here to follow the trail as described in Trip 112).

Mountain bikers continue a stiff climb on the road through the rolling terrain of North Canyon, amid conifers and aspen groves. At 3.25 miles from the parking lot, a steeper 0.75-mile climb leads to the top of a saddle and the high point of your journey, where roads branch off to Chimney Beach on the left and Snow Valley Peak on the right.

With the last of the climbing behind, you head downhill toward a well-signed junction of the Hobart Road on the southeast side of scenic Marlette Lake. The lake may provide an inviting swim if you're still hot from the climb. Turn left and follow the flat road around the south and west sides of the lake. During periods of high water, you may have to carry your bike across some boulders and then across the outlet in order to reach the start of the Flume Trail proper near the dam.

Now on the Flume Trail, you ride pleasantly graded singletrack that makes a mild drop of 40 feet per mile. The trail is narrow and exposed in spots, and you may feel the need to walk your bike across some rockslides, but the stupendous views of Lake Tahoe along the way make the Flume Trail a world-famous ride. The mellow 4.5-mile ride along the Flume Trail ends where the trail merges with Tunnel Creek Road.

Continue the northbound descent on the road for 0.4 mile to Tunnel Creek Station. From there, the steep, sandy road bends west and drops 1,300 feet in 2 miles to NV 28.

MARLETTE LAKE

Marlette Lake was created in the summer of 1872 when D.L. Bliss and H.M. Yerington, co-owners of the Carson and Tahoe Lumber and Fluming Co., constructed a dam of dirt fill and stone across Marlette Creek. The lake was later named for Seneca Hunt Marlette, a New York native who obtained a civil-engineering degree, migrated west, and eventually served as the Surveyor General for both California and Nevada. From the dam, water from Marlette Lake was diverted into a flume and traveled 4.75 miles north to Tunnel Creek Station, where it entered a 4,500-foot tunnel descending southeast, carved out of the bedrock below the crest of the Carson Range. From there, the water dropped into a second flume, sinuously traveling to a terminus on a ridge near Lakeview, near the south end of Washoe Valley. Here the water entered a pipe, and after a nearly 2-mile descent, was then propelled 5 miles uphill to another flume, which delivered Gold Hill and Virginia City's water supply to a reservoir near the crest of the Virginia Range.

The design and construction of this water system was quite an engineering feat at the time, a testament not only to the engineers and builders but also to the incredible bonanza generated by the Comstock Lode. Although the mines were played out long ago, a more recent bonanza has swept the area. With the aid of volunteers, the Flume Trail was cleaned up and repaired, and nowadays is considered to be one of the premier mountain-bike trails in the nation.

View from the top of Lovers Leap

Echo Summit and South Fork American River

This area has long been a getaway destination for Sacramento-area residents. A mostly two-lane section of CA 50, climbing toward 7,377-foot Echo Summit, provides the principal access to an area sprinkled with rustic cabins and quaint resorts. Beyond this bucolic corridor alongside the highway, a mostly forested landscape beckons recreationists into the backcountry.

Echo Lakes is perhaps the busiest jumping-off point for hikers, backpackers, and equestrians, providing the southern gateway into the glacier-polished lands of Desolation Wilderness. A ride across the lakes on Echo Chalet's water taxi saves 2.5 miles of hiking along the shoreline, depositing riders at the very edge of the wilderness. Along with Echo Lakes, Horsetail Falls is another extremely popular trailhead, where day-use parking is subject to a $5-per-day fee (an annual pass is $20). The large parking lot fills up fast on weekends, particularly during early summer when the falls are at their peak.

Aside from Echo Lakes and Horsetail Falls, the trails in this area see far less use, especially those on the south side of CA 50, heading away from the ever-popular Desolation Wilderness. While these trails may lack some of the jaw-dropping terrain associated with Desolation, the mostly forested routes follow serene paths alongside rambunctious creeks and visit flower-covered meadows.

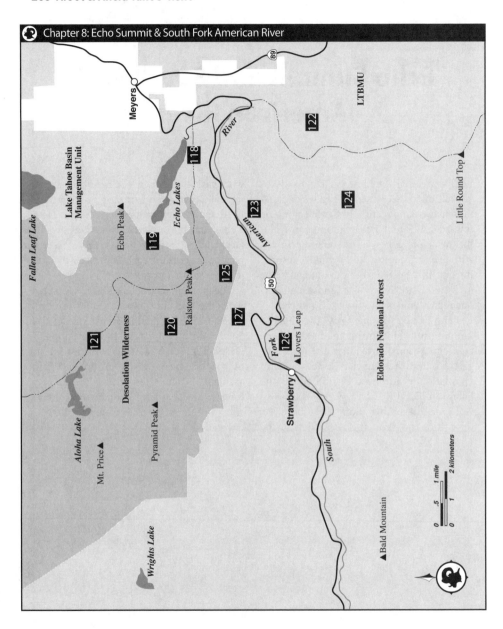

Chapter 8: Echo Summit & South Fork American River

118   Becker Peak

see map on p. 270

Distance	2.6 miles (out-and-back)
Hiking Time	1.5–2 hours
Elevation	+800 feet
Difficulty	Difficult
Trail Use	Dogs OK
Best Times	July through October
Agency	Lake Tahoe Basin Management Unit at 530-543-2600, www.fs.usda.gov/ltbmu
Recommended Map	ENF and LTBMU A Guide to the Desolation Wilderness

HIGHLIGHTS Although the distance is short, this trip requires navigating along a mostly cross-country route to the base of some summit rocks, and some basic climbing skills from there are required to reach the top of Becker Peak. Once atop the tiny aerie, successful summiteers are treated to dramatic views straight down to Echo Lakes and more distant vistas of the stunning topography at the south end of Lake Tahoe.

DIRECTIONS From CA 50, about 1.25 miles west of Echo Summit and 1.8 miles east of the road to Sierra-at-Tahoe Ski Resort, turn east onto Johnson Pass Road, following a sign for Berkeley Camp and Echo Lakes. Drive a half mile to a left turn onto Echo Lakes Road, and proceed another 0.9 mile to the large trailhead parking area above the south shore of Lower Echo Lake.

FACILITIES/TRAILHEAD The large trailhead parking area has modern vault toilets. The Echo Lake Chalet near the trailhead offers nine housekeeping cabins for rent, a small grocery store, deli, soda fountain, boat rentals, and post office. See **echochalet.com** for more details. The well-marked Pacific Crest Trail (PCT) continues southbound at the south edge of the parking lot.

From the parking lot, follow the southbound PCT as it climbs moderately across a hillside covered with firs and hemlocks to a switchback. Leave the trail at the switchback and follow a faint path on a moderately steep ascent to the crest of a ridge. Eventually, the grade eases a bit, as you follow a swale between the main ridge to the right and a low rise to the left. As you approach the top of the ridge, the grade gets steeper again and the forest lightens enough to allow filtered views of Becker Peak ahead and Echo Lakes below. Approaching a low saddle just left of the main peak, the path becomes more distinct as it leads toward the base of the summit rocks. A short scramble over boulders and high-angle slabs leads to the narrow and airy summit.

Peering down at Echo Lakes from the summit of Becker Peak

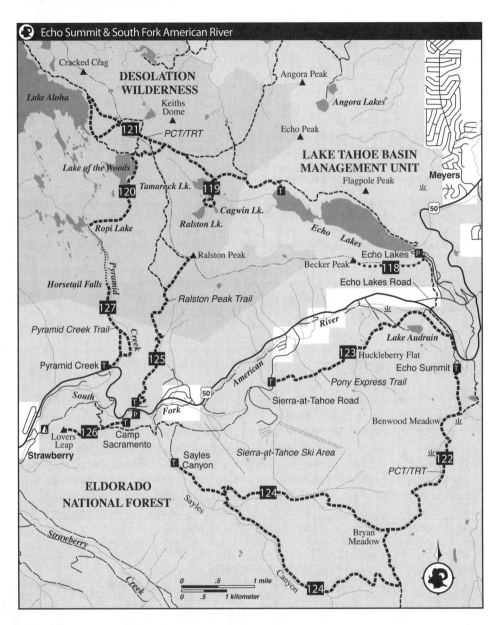

Echo Summit & South Fork American River

Cracked Crag

DESOLATION
WILDERNESS

Lake Aloha

Keiths
Dome

121

PCT/TRT

Angora Peak

Angora Lakes

Echo Peak

LAKE TAHOE BASIN
MANAGEMENT UNIT

Flagpole Peak

Meyers

Lake of the Woods

120 Tamarack Lk. 119

Cagwin Lk.

Ralston Lk.

50

Ropi Lake

Echo   Lakes

Echo Lakes

Ralston Peak

Becker Peak 118

Horsetail Falls

127

Ralston Peak Trail

Echo Lakes Road

Pyramid Creek Trail

Pyramid

Creek

River

Lake Audrain

125

123 Huckleberry Flat

Pyramid Creek

American

Echo Summit

South

50

Pony Express Trail

Fork

Sierra-at-Tahoe Road

Benwood Meadow

Lovers
Leap 126 Camp
Sacramento

Strawberry

Sayles
Canyon

Sierra-at-Tahoe Ski Area

122

PCT/TRT

ELDORADO
NATIONAL FOREST

Sayles

124

Bryan
Meadow

Strawberry

Creek

Canyon 124

0   .5   1 mile
0   .5   1 kilometer

119   Echo Lakes to Tamarack, Ralston, and Cagwin Lakes

Distance	4 miles (water taxi); 9 miles (no taxi); out-and-back
Hiking Time	2–3 hours; 3–4 hours
Elevation	+450/-125 feet; +750/-375 feet
Difficulty	Easy; Moderate
Trail Use	Dogs OK, good for kids
Best Times	Mid-July through mid-October

see
map
above

Agency	Lake Tahoe Basin Management Unit at 530-543-2600, www.fs.usda.gov/ltbmu
Recommended Map	*ENF and LTBMU A Guide to the Desolation Wilderness*
Notes	Since this trail lies within Desolation Wilderness, you will need a permit for both day hikes and overnight backpacks. Day hikers may self-register at the trailhead, but backpackers will need to get their permit from the Lake Tahoe Visitor Center. (Camping is not allowed at any of these lakes.)

HIGHLIGHTS With a boat ride on Echo Lakes Chalet's water taxi across Lower and Upper Echo Lakes, you can easily access a cozy basin holding three delightful lakes tucked into the southeast corner of Desolation Wilderness. Without the water taxi, the round-trip distance increases by 5 miles. Tamarack, Ralston, and Cagwin Lakes are distinctively different from one another, each with its own unique charm and appeal. Due to the lakes' close proximity to a trailhead and the resulting popularity, camping at the lakes is not allowed.

DIRECTIONS From CA 50, about 1.25 miles west of Echo Summit and 1.8 miles east of Sierra-at-Tahoe Ski Resort, following a sign for Berkeley Camp and Echo Lakes, turn east onto Johnson Pass Road. Travel a half mile and then turn left at Echo Lakes Road. Continue up this road for 0.9 mile to the large trailhead parking area above the south shore of Lower Echo Lake.

FACILITIES/TRAILHEAD The large trailhead parking area has modern vault toilets. The Echo Lake Chalet near the trailhead offers nine housekeeping cabins for rent, a small grocery store, deli, soda fountain, boat rentals, and post office. See **echochalet.com** for more details.

Without water-taxi service, you'll have to walk the extra 2.5 miles (each way) around the north shore of Echo Lakes and add that distance to your mileage. From the water-taxi pier, climb a lateral to the junction with the Pacific Crest Trail (PCT). Turn left (west) and proceed on rocky tread across open slopes on a westbound course away from the Echo Lakes. Near the Desolation Wilderness boundary, meet a junction with a lightly used trail to Triangle Lake, 0.7 mile from the pier. Another 0.4 mile of hiking leads to a second junction, this one with the lateral to Tamarack, Ralston, and Cagwin Lakes.

ECHO LAKE WATER TAXI

The Echo Lake Chalet offers water-taxi service, from the resort's dock at the south end of Lower Echo Lake to the public dock at the far end of Upper Echo Lake, reducing the total hiking distance by 5 miles. The normal season runs from the Fourth of July through Labor Day weekend, although service usually extends through September, depending on weather conditions and lake levels. The fee in 2014 was $12 one-way with a $36 minimum (dogs are $5 each). A credit-card phone at the upper dock can be used for pickup. When the channel to the upper lake is no longer navigable, usually by mid-September, passengers are dropped at the end of the lower lake for a reduced fee with a four-person minimum. Call 530-659-7207 (8 a.m.–6 p.m., summer only) for more information. To use the water taxi, buy your ticket at the Echo Lake Chalet and then proceed to the boat dock. To hike the 2.5 miles around Echo Lakes, cross over the dam and proceed northbound on the Pacific Crest Trail.

Leave the PCT and head southwest over open granite slopes 0.1 mile on ducked trail to the west shore of Tamarack Lake, largest of the three lakes in this basin. A light forest of mountain hemlocks, western white pines, and lodgepole pines rings the shoreline. A small, tree-covered island near the south end adds a bit of character to the scenic lake.

The trail follows the east shore to the south end of shallow Tamarack Lake and a junction with the short loop that accesses Ralston and Cagwin Lakes. To reach Ralston Lake, bear right and climb over a low ridge to the north shore of the deep lake, which is cradled into a cavernous, rocky basin. From there, the trail continues along the course of Ralston Lake's outlet for 0.1 mile to the northern tip of forest-rimmed Cagwin Lake, smallest of the three lakes. To return to Tamarack Lake from Cagwin Lake, head north on a short climb over the low ridge and back to the junction. From there, retrace your steps to the water-taxi pier, or follow the PCT around Echo Lakes back to the trailhead.

120 Echo Lakes to Lake of the Woods and Ropi Lake

see map on p. 270

Distance	8 miles (water taxi); 13 miles (no taxi); out-and-back
Hiking Time	2–3 hours; 3–4 hours
Elevation	+990/-200 feet; +1,490/-600 feet
Difficulty	Difficult
Trail Use	Backpacking option, dogs OK, map and compass
Best Times	Mid-July through mid-October
Agency	Lake Tahoe Basin Management Unit at 530-543-2600, www.fs.usda.gov/ltbmu; Eldorado National Forest at 530-644-2349, www.fs.usda.gov/eldorado
Recommended Map	ENF and LTBMU A Guide to the Desolation Wilderness
Notes	Since this trail lies within Desolation Wilderness, you will need a permit for both day hikes and overnight backpacks. Day hikers may self-register at the trailhead, but backpackers will need to get their permit from the Lake Tahoe Visitor Center.

HIGHLIGHTS Lake of the Woods, with numerous coves, islands, and campsites, is a popular hiking destination accessible by maintained trail. The rest of Desolation Valley beyond Lake of the Woods is one of the most picturesque corners of Desolation Wilderness. Beneath the rugged east face of majestic Pyramid Peak, the granite, glacier-scoured basin holds a plethora of lakes and ponds, most of which are not accessible by developed and maintained trail. Hikers and backpackers with rudimentary cross-country skills have a fantastic playground for exploration of the nooks and crannies of this alpine-like basin.

DIRECTIONS From CA 50, about 1.25 miles west of Echo Summit and 1.8 miles east of Sierra-at-Tahoe Ski Resort, following a sign for Berkeley Camp and Echo Lakes, turn east onto Johnson Pass Road, travel a half mile, and then turn left at Echo Lakes Road. Continue on this road for 0.9 mile to the large trailhead parking area above the south shore of Lower Echo Lake.

FACILITIES/TRAILHEAD The large trailhead parking area has modern vault toilets. The Echo Lake Chalet, near the trailhead, offers nine housekeeping cabins for rent, a small grocery store, deli, soda fountain, boat rentals, and post office. See **echochalet.com** for more details. The Echo Lake Chalet offers water-taxi service from the resort's dock at the south end of Lower Echo Lake to the public dock at the far end of Upper Echo Lake, reducing the total hiking distance by 5 miles (see sidebar in Trip 119).

Without water-taxi service, you'll have to walk the extra 2.5 miles (both out and back) around the north shore of Echo Lakes and add that distance to your mileage. From the water-taxi pier, climb a lateral to the junction with the Pacific Crest Trail (PCT). Turn left (west) and proceed on rocky tread across open slopes on a westbound course away from the lakes. Near the Desolation Wilderness boundary, you meet a junction with a lightly used trail to Triangle Lake, 0.7 mile from the pier. Another 0.4 mile of hiking leads to a second junction, this one with a lateral to Tamarack, Ralston, and Cagwin Lakes. These three picturesque lakes are worth a visit if you have the extra time and energy (see Trip 119).

Beyond the junction, the PCT follows a moderate climb to a diminutive rivulet coursing through a ravine and then continues the ascent via a pair of switchbacks to an open bench and a junction with the Tamarack Trail, 1.1 miles from the pier.

Gently ascending trail brings you along the northern fringe of the broad expanse of grass-covered Haypress Meadows, where early to midsummer wildflowers put on a fine floral display. Near the far end of the meadows, at 2 miles, is the junction with Trail 17E40 to Lake of the Woods.

Leave the PCT and head southwest, skirting the edge of Haypress Meadows

and climbing to the crest of a low ridge, where you cross the Ralston Peak Trail. From the ridge, follow a moderately steep switchbacking descent to a junction near the northeast shore of Lake of the Woods, 2.6 miles from the pier.

To reach Ropi Lake, head south along the east shore of Lake of the Woods and make a brief climb over the lip of the basin. On descending trail, you head down the canyon of the outlet to a crossing of the stream at 3.5 miles. Follow the trail as it bends west and descends around a knob to the east shore of Ropi Lake. From there, the trailless backcountry is your oyster, but make sure you're packing a good topographic map and possess the requisite cross-country skills necessary for off-trail travel.

Lake-dotted terrain of Desolation Wilderness

121   Echo Lakes to Lake Aloha

Distance	7.6 miles (water taxi); 12.6 miles (no taxi); out-and-back
Hiking Time	2–3 hours; 3–4 hours
Elevation	+950/-225 feet; +1,225/-500 feet
Difficulty	Moderate
Trail Use	Backpacking option, dogs OK
Best Times	Mid-July through mid-October
Agency	Lake Tahoe Basin Management Unit at 530-543-2600, www.fs.usda.gov/ltbmu; Eldorado National Forest at 530-644-2349, www.fs.usda.gov/eldorado
Recommended Map	*ENF and LTBMU A Guide to the Desolation Wilderness*
Notes	Since this trail lies within Desolation Wilderness, you will need a permit for both day hikes and overnight backpacks. Day hikers may self-register at the trailhead, but backpackers will need to get their permit from the Lake Tahoe Visitor Center.

see map on p. 270

HIGHLIGHTS This section of the famed Pacific Crest Trail (PCT) is one of the most popular routes into the heart of Desolation Wilderness. The relatively high-elevation start, coupled with the ability to shave off 2.5 miles of hiking (each way) by taking the water taxi across Echo Lakes, makes this a highly desirable entry point for backcountry enthusiasts. With a bounty of scenic lakes and plenty of dramatic mountain scenery so easily accessible, the area's popularity is no mystery. While backpackers contend for a limited number of wilderness permits, hikers are free to roam the backcountry within a day's journey at will—just don't expect to be alone.

DIRECTIONS From CA 50, about 1.25 miles west of Echo Summit and 1.8 miles east of Sierra-at-Tahoe Ski Resort, following a sign for Berkeley Camp and Echo Lakes, turn east onto Johnson Pass Road and travel a half mile and then turn left at Echo Lakes Road. Continue up this road for 0.9 mile to the large trailhead parking area above the south shore of Lower Echo Lake.

FACILITIES/TRAILHEAD The large trailhead parking area has modern vault toilets. The Echo Lake Chalet near the trailhead offers nine housekeeping cabins for rent, a small grocery store, deli, soda fountain, boat rentals, and post office. See **echochalet.com** for more details. The Echo Lake Chalet offers water-taxi service from the resort's dock at the south end of Lower Echo Lake to the public dock at the far end of Upper Echo Lake, reducing the total hiking distance by 5 miles (see sidebar in Trip 119).

Without water-taxi service, you'll have to walk the extra 2.5 miles (each way) around the north shore of Echo Lakes and add that distance to your mileage. From the water-taxi pier, climb a lateral to the junction with the PCT. Turn left (west) and proceed on rocky tread across open slopes on a westbound course away from the lakes. Near the Desolation Wilderness boundary, you meet a junction with a lightly used trail to Triangle Lake, 0.7 mile from the pier. Another 0.4 mile of hiking leads to a junction with a lateral to Tamarack, Ralston, and Cagwin Lakes. These three picturesque lakes are worth a visit if you have the extra time and energy (see Trip 119).

Beyond the junction, the PCT follows a moderate climb to a diminutive rivulet coursing through a ravine and then continues the ascent via a pair of switchbacks to an open bench and a junction with the Tamarack Trail, 1.1 miles from the pier.

Gently ascending trail brings you along the northern fringe of the broad expanse of grass-covered Haypress Meadows, where early to midsummer wildflowers put on a fine floral display. Near the far end of the meadows, at 2 miles, is the junction with Trail 17E40 to Lake of the Woods (see Trip 120).

After a quarter-mile stroll from the Lake of the Woods junction, you pass the lightly used Ralston Peak Trail near the high point of the journey and continue toward Lake Aloha. Reach another junction after a mere 0.1 mile with east end of Trail 17E09 to Lake Margery and Lake Lucille on the right. The 0.7-mile trail makes a fine diversion for a slight variation on the return trip. Proceed along the gently graded PCT to the Lake Aloha Trail, at 2.75 miles from the pier.

Leave the PCT and turn left onto the Lake Aloha Trail, heading southwest toward the sprawling lake. After 0.4 mile, pass a lateral heading southeast to Lake of the Woods. A short distance later, you'll encounter an unmarked path on the left that leads to Lake Aloha's dam, where swimming can be quite pleasant when the water level is accommodating. Continuing north on the main trail will take you along the east shore of Lake Aloha to a reunion with the PCT at 3.8 miles. Turn right (southeast), follow the PCT back to the pier at Upper Echo Lake, and call for the water taxi.

---

122 PCT: Echo Summit to Bryan Meadow

Distance	7.6 miles (out-and-back)
Hiking Time	3–4 hours
Elevation	+1,475/-335 feet
Difficulty	Moderate
Trail Use	Backpacking option, dogs OK
Best Times	July through October
Agency	Eldorado National Forest at 530-644-2349, www.fs.usda.gov/eldorado
Recommended Map	USGS 7.5-minute *Echo Lake*

see map on p. 270

HIGHLIGHTS This trip follows a seldom-used section of the Pacific Crest (PCT) and Tahoe Rim (TRT) Trails. What little traffic this section does receive, other than from thru-hikers bound for Canada, is from day-trippers headed to Benwood Meadow, which is only three-quarters of a mile from the trailhead. Beyond there, the serene forest beckons the solitude seeker who doesn't wilt at the thought of a moderately steep climb. Bryan Meadow, at the conclusion of the trip, is a half-mile-long clearing along a tributary of Sayles Canyon Creek that will delight botanists from early to midsummer.

DIRECTIONS From CA 50, about a quarter mile westbound of Echo Summit, turn west onto an access road marked SNO-PARK and CALIFORNIA CONSERVATION CORPS. Drive to the end of the road and the large trailhead parking area.

FACILITIES/TRAILHEAD The parking area, which doubles as a California Sno-Park in the winter, has modern vault toilets. The trail begins on the south side of the parking area near a TRT sign.

Begin hiking on singletrack trail through the open terrain of a former ski area, immediately crossing an old section of paving and finding the trail on the far side. Climb across grass- and shrub-covered slopes, with a nice array of wildflowers early in the season, toward the edge of the forest. Just before the trees, the trail merges with an old road that you follow for about 40 yards to the resumption of singletrack trail. Continue across the former ski slope, carpeted with manzanita and tobacco brush and sprinkled with young lodgepole pines, to another stretch of road that is followed briefly until trail veers away to the left. Fortunately, the route is well marked at all of these junctions by 4-by-4-inch posts with TRT and PCT emblems.

Now on singletrack trail for good, make a mild ascent through a forest composed of western white pines, white firs, Jeffrey pines, and lodgepole pines. Just before you reach the northern fringe of Benwood Meadow, a 4-by-4-inch post marks a junction with a lateral on the left that heads northeast to an unnamed pond.

Continuing on the PCT–TRT, you pass well to the west of Benwood Meadow, which is just visible through the trees on the left. A use trail provides access to the environmentally sensitive meadow—if you choose to visit the area, please keep your impact on the fragile flora and soil to a minimum.

Leaving the vicinity of the meadow, you climb across a hillside past boulders and slabs and a pocket of lush vegetation to the crossing of a rivulet, soon followed by a bridged crossing of the stream that flows into Benwood Meadow.

Beyond the bridge, a steeper, winding climb with occasional switchbacks takes you upslope into a lightening forest punctuated with granite outcrops and large boulders. Along the way, you have brief, sporadic views of the south end of Lake Tahoe. About three-quarters of a mile from the bridge, you reach a tiny saddle in between two low hills, from where some of the peaks around Carson Pass are visible.

From the saddle, a mildly rising traverse leads over to a steep, rocky canyon that carries the headwaters of the stream flowing into Benwood Meadow. After a couple of switchbacks, you hop over the stream to the north bank and continue the switchbacking climb up the cleft. Near one of the switchbacks is a rock outcrop that provides a stunning view of the south end of Tahoe. Proceed upstream to an open hillside covered with grasses, wildflowers, and willows before crossing back over the stream and heading into forest cover. More switchbacks lead you out of the canyon and across a meadowy hillside to the crest of a forested ridge, the high point of your journey.

Leaving the climbing behind, you follow a mild to moderate descent around Peak 8905, through open forest sprinkled with yellow mule-ears and purple lupines in season. The grade eases where the trail crosses a forested saddle east of Bryan Meadow. A short distance farther is a junction with the Bryan Meadow Trail near the eastern fringe of the meadow.

123 Pony Express Trail: Sierra-at-Tahoe Road to Echo Summit

Distance	3.75 miles (point-to-point)
Hiking Time	2–3 hours
Elevation	+825/-475 feet
Difficulty	Moderate
Trail Use	Mountain biking OK, dogs OK
Best Times	July through October
Agency	Eldorado National Forest at 530-644-2324, www.fs.usda.gov/eldorado
Recommended Map	USGS 7.5-minute *Echo Lake* (trail not shown)

see map on p. 270

HIGHLIGHTS This trip follows a section of the Pony Express National Historic Trail from Sierra-at-Tahoe Road to Echo Summit, a trail new enough not to appear on any maps. The relatively undiscovered route offers quiet serenity on a mostly forested journey that visits aptly named Huckleberry Flat and offers a short side trip to Lake Audrain.

DIRECTIONS *Start:* From CA 50, about 2.6 miles westbound of Echo Summit, turn southeast onto Sierra-at-Tahoe Road and drive 0.9 mile to a dirt pullout on the right-hand shoulder. Park your vehicle as conditions allow.

End: From CA 50, about a quarter mile westbound of Echo Summit, turn west onto an access road marked SNO-PARK and CALIFORNIA CONSERVATION CORPS. Park on the shoulder of the road just down from the highway, or continue a short distance to the Echo Summit Trailhead at the end of the road.

FACILITIES/TRAILHEAD There are no facilities at the Sierra-at-Tahoe Road Trailhead. The Echo Summit Trailhead has a large parking area with modern vault toilets. The trail begins on the opposite side of Sierra-at-Tahoe Road from the parking area near a plastic trail marker.

Angle across a hillside through a mixed forest of lodgepole pine and white firs to an old logging road, which is followed uphill for 0.2 mile to the resumption of singletrack trail. Soon you crest the top of a ridge, where shrubby vegetation allows partial views of Mt. Ralston across the canyon of South Fork American River. Follow an ascending arc around the ridge back into forest cover, and then head east, stepping over a couple of rivulets that should be flowing through late summer. Just past the second rivulet, you traverse the nose of a ridge and soon encounter an alder- and fern-lined stream. Beyond the stream, the trail leads up a shrub-covered ridge studded with boulders. The open ridge provides views of peaks beyond Echo Summit. Directly below is Huckleberry Flat.

Descend from the crest of the ridge via a trio of switchbacks across an open slope to the floor of forested Huckleberry Flat. Gently graded trail leads across the flat through plenty of the namesake shrub, along with ferns, alders, and wildflowers, to a bridged crossing of an unnamed stream. Beyond the stream, level terrain continues for a short distance to the eastern edge of the flat.

From the flat, the trail makes a short climb over another ridge and then merges with a well-traveled road at a hairpin turn. Turn left and follow the road, which is marked by blue diamonds as a winter cross-country ski route. Stick to the obvious main road at junctions with side roads. Just after crossing a South Fork American River tributary, a path heads southeast upstream to Lake Audrain, a forest-rimmed body of water that appears to be more of a large pond than a bona fide lake. Rather than continuing on the dusty road, an alternate route proceeds on this trail to the north shore of Lake Audrain and then follows a crude use trail north across a ridge and down the far side, where it rejoins the road. The designated route of the Pony Express Trail continues ahead along the road as it curves around a hill separating Lake Audrain from the north branch of South Fork American River.

Just past the obscure junction with the use trail mentioned above from Lake Audrain, singletrack trail veers away from the dusty road at a marked junction and makes a mildly rising ascent through scattered forest and shrubs. Farther on, the grade of the ascent increases, as you ascend a narrow ridge with improving views of the area around Echo Summit. Follow the trail as it descends off the ridge and drops down to intersect the Pacific Crest Trail, where you turn right and then parallel CA 50 to the trailhead near the junction with the Echo Summit access road.

Monk's Rock, along the Pony Express Trail

124 Sayles Canyon–Bryan Meadow Loop

see map on p. 270

Distance	10 miles (semiloop)
Hiking Time	5–7 hours
Elevation	+1,875/-1,875 feet
Difficulty	Moderate
Trail Use	Backpacking option, dogs OK, mountain biking OK
Best Times	July through October
Agency	Eldorado National Forest at 530-644-2324, www.fs.usda.gov/eldorado
Recommended Map	USGS 7.5-minute *Echo Lake*

HIGHLIGHTS Early to midsummer hikers will experience a burst of color from a bounty of wildflowers along this route that follows the Sayles Canyon and Bryan Meadow trails and a short section of the Pacific Crest Trail (PCT) to form the 8-mile loop portion of a 10-mile trip. Although the route is mostly forested, Round and Bryan Meadows provide two picturesque clearings along the way with passable campsites nearby for overnighters.

DIRECTIONS Leave CA 50 about 2.6 miles westbound of Echo Summit and turn southeast onto Sierra-at-Tahoe Road. Proceed on paved road for 1.4 miles to a junction and turn right onto a dirt road. Continue on this dirt road through the Sierra-at-Tahoe ski area to a loop at the end of the road, 1.8 miles from the junction.

FACILITIES/TRAILHEAD There are no developed facilities at the trailhead, although primitive camp-sites have been established. The well-marked trail begins at the upper end of the loop road.

Follow the trail past several trailhead signs and begin climbing near Sayles Canyon Creek through a mixed forest with an understory of ferns and seasonal wildflowers. Hop over a thin rivulet and climb well above the creek through diminishing forest. Views open up behind you of Pyramid Peak across the chasm of the South Fork American River canyon until the forest thickens again. Gain the top of a minor ridge and proceed on mildly rising trail to a signed Y-junction, 1 mile from the trailhead.

Turn right at the junction (the left-hand trail will be your return route) and proceed through the forest and across a boulder field sprinkled with aspens to a crossing of Bryan Meadow Creek. Beyond the crossing, you make a continuous climb up Sayles Canyon on a mostly forested journey with occasional stretches of lush ground cover and tiny clearings. At times, the trail closely follows the creek and at others it stays a good distance away. Near the 2.5-mile mark, you spy a small meadow through the trees on your right covered with grasses, wildflowers, and willows. A couple of passable campsites can be found near the fringe of this meadow. Another 0.4 mile of forested hiking brings you to Round Meadow, a grass-covered meadowland backdropped by steep granite cliffs, a much more attractive setting for an overnight stay than the previous meadow.

Beyond Round Meadow, somewhat indistinct tread marked by ducks climbs more steeply toward the head of the canyon. Along the way, you pass through areas of lush vegetation that are ablaze with color during the height of wildflower season. A lengthy upward traverse leads to the crest of the ridge and a marked junction with the PCT, 5 miles from the trailhead.

Turn left (north) and follow the PCT along the ridgetop through lodgepole pines, mountain hemlocks, red firs, and western white pines on a short climb to the high point of the journey. A mild descent that soon becomes moderate leads away from the high point and continues three-quarters of a mile to the floor of Bryan Meadow, where a 6-by-6-inch post marks a junction with the Bryan Meadow Trail.

Turn left (west) at the junction and follow gently graded trail along the fringe of the meadow, a veritable garden of wildflowers through midsummer. At the far end of the half-mile-long meadow, you head back into

Pyramid Peak from Sayles Canyon Trail

the forest on mildly descending tread that eventually becomes rocky and moderately steep. Switchbacks lead down the hillside to a creek canyon and into thickening forest with intermittent swaths of lush ground cover. At 1.4 miles from the PCT junction, you cross Bryan Meadow Creek and continue down the canyon above the alder-choked and grass-lined stream for another 0.4 mile to a crossing of the creek on a flat-topped log.

Shortly after the creek crossing, apparently in the middle of nowhere, you pass a sign giving directions ahead to CA 50 and back to Bryan Meadow and the PCT. Farther on, where the creek drops more steeply, the trail remains high on the hillside until switchbacks take you down to the floor of the canyon and the close of the loop at the junction with the Sayles Canyon Trail. From there, retrace your steps 1 mile to the trailhead.

125 Ralston Peak

see map on p. 270

Distance	6 miles (out-and-back)
Hiking Time	3–5 hours
Elevation	+2,775/-100 feet
Difficulty	Difficult
Trail Use	Dogs OK
Best Times	Mid-July through mid-October
Agency	Eldorado National Forest at 530-644-2324, www.fs.usda.gov/eldorado
Recommended Map	*ENF and LTBMU A Guide to the Desolation Wilderness*
Notes	Since this trail lies within Desolation Wilderness, you will need a permit for both day hikes and overnight backpacks. Day hikers may self-register at the trailhead, but backpackers will need to get their permit from the Lake Tahoe Visitor Center.

HIGHLIGHTS Although the climb is steady and stiff, where else in the Tahoe Basin can you achieve such a lofty view with only a 3-mile hike in? Most hikers seem to favor the route to Ralston Peak from Echo Lakes, which is a mile longer via the water taxi (3.5 miles longer without) but requires 800 less feet of elevation gain. With this being the case, you may not have to share the serenity of the route described below with too many other hikers.

DIRECTIONS Drive CA 50 to Sayles Flat and turn north onto a gravel-and-dirt road opposite the entrance into Camp Sacramento (about 5.75 miles west of Echo Summit and 1.25 miles east of Twin Bridges). Follow this road past the Chapel of Our Lady of the Sierra to the small parking area, 250 yards from the highway. If parking is not available at the trailhead, park along the broad shoulder of the highway at Sayles Flat.

FACILITIES/TRAILHEAD There are no facilities at the trailhead. The trail begins on the uphill side of the small parking area near some trail signs.

The Ralston Peak Trail starts climbing right off the bat through the cool shade of a dense fir forest, where an occasional chinquapin shrub steals enough sunlight to eke out an existence on the forest floor. The trail snakes up the hillside on a steady climb toward the huge moraine that forms the east lip of Pyramid Creek Canyon, flirting with the possibility of a view into the deep gorge but failing to deliver until you've logged the first mile. At that point, a short use trail wanders to the brink of the canyon, where a fine vista of the deep, granite canyon unfolds.

Soon the trail makes a very brief descent to follow alongside a lushly lined stretch of Tamarack Creek, where alders, ferns, and scattered wildflowers interrupt the otherwise dry vegetation. All too soon, the trail forsakes the creek and returns to a winding ascent of the morainal ridge, as a lighter forest allows chinquapin, manzanita, and huckleberry oak to flourish. Near the 1.5-mile mark, you uneventfully cross the unsigned boundary into Desolation Wilderness and follow a switchbacking climb into more open forest, where shrubs and boulders dot the slope. Views of the surrounding terrain improve with the gain in elevation, including glimpses of Pyramid Peak, Lovers Leap, and the ski runs of Sierra-at-Tahoe Ski Resort. After stepping over a boggy stretch of trail from a tiny seep spilling across the path, you continue the ascent across dry, meadow-like slopes, carpeted with lupines, asters, and mule-ears through midsummer, to an unsigned junction, 2.25 miles from the trailhead.

Leave the Ralston Peak Trail here and follow the faint track of a ducked path that climbs steeply along the southwest ridge of Ralston Peak through scattered western white pines and red firs. Higher up the slope, pass a colorful, spring-fed patch of grasses and wildflowers before a final climb over fractured rocks leads to the summit. A splendid view of Desolation Wilderness is at your feet. More distant views include a part of Lake Tahoe and the Freel Peak group to the east.

Echo Lakes as seen from Ralston Peak

126 Lovers Leap

see map on p. 270

Distance	2.5 miles (out-and-back)
Hiking Time	1–2 hours
Elevation	+500 feet
Difficulty	Easy
Trail Use	Mountain biking OK, dogs OK
Best Times	June through October
Agency	Eldorado National Forest at 530-644-2324, www.fs.usda.gov/eldorado
Recommended Maps	USGS 7.5-minute *Echo Summit, Pyramid Peak*

HIGHLIGHTS Lovers Leap is a picturesque granite dome that tops out at almost 7,000 feet and has a nearly 600-foot face that is the envy of technical climbers from far and wide. For nonclimbers, a 1.25-mile trail beginning in Camp Sacramento is the easiest route to the top of Lovers Leap and the dramatic view across the chasm of South Fork American River to the peaks of Desolation Wilderness.

DIRECTIONS Drive CA 50 to Sayles Flat and turn south onto the access road into Camp Sacramento (about 5.75 miles west of Echo Summit and 1.25 miles east of Twin Bridges). Immediately after a bridge over South Fork American River is the signed Lovers Leap Trail parking area on the left. Parking is available for about six to eight vehicles.

FACILITIES/TRAILHEAD There are no facilities at the trailhead. Lovers Leap Campground nearby is a no-fee, first-come, first-serve campground with vault toilets and running water. Strawberry Lodge has a café. A separately owned general store is nearby. The trail begins at the west end of Camp Sacramento, near a pair of low 4-by-4-inch posts and a telephone pole.

To access the start of the Lovers Leap Trail, you must walk up the road into Camp Sacramento and proceed past the meeting room and several cabins to the far end of the camp. Within earshot of the traffic on CA 50, you traverse a mostly open slope well watered by seeps and covered with wildflowers and grasses and then proceed on gently graded trail through a mixed forest of firs and pines, with a sprinkling of aspens. Soon reach a junction with the Pony Express Trail, which shares the path for a short distance before angling downhill away from the Lovers Leap Trail.

Continue the easy stroll through mostly fir forest on a mildly undulating course with occasional views through the trees of Pyramid Creek Canyon, Horsetail Falls, and Pyramid Peak across the canyon of South Fork American River. The road noise from the highway diminishes as you pass behind a hill and the road bends away to the north. Past the hill, you start a moderate climb toward the summit of Lovers Leap. After a pair of short switchbacks, views start to open up of Mt. Ralston and the area around Echo Summit. Continue climbing through

widely scattered pines and shrubs to where the trail bends sharply left and merges with a jeep road. Near an old sign and a cairn, you leave the road and make a short ascent to the top of Lovers Leap.

Lovers Leap from the Pony Express Trail

127 Horsetail Falls

see map on p. 270

Distance	3 miles (semiloop)
Hiking Time	1.5–2 hours
Elevation	+650/-25 feet
Difficulty	Moderate
Trail Use	Dogs OK
Best Times	June through October
Agency	Eldorado National Forest at 530-644-2324, www.fs.usda.gov/eldorado
Recommended Map	*ENF and LTBMU A Guide to the Desolation Wilderness*
Notes	Since this trail lies within Desolation Wilderness, you will need a permit for both day hikes and overnight backpacks. Day hikers may self-register at the trailhead, but backpackers will need to get their permit from the Lake Tahoe Visitor Center.

HIGHLIGHTS Tumbling down the head of the deep, ice-sculpted, granite cleft of Pyramid Creek Canyon, the thin ribbon of Horsetail Falls is dramatically scenic at any time of year, but especially spectacular during the height of snowmelt. Located a mere 1.5 miles from a major highway linking the Sacramento Valley with Lake Tahoe, conditions are ripe for this area to be very popular with both recreationists and sightseers alike. Recent parking improvements and construction of a short loop trail have made the area even more attractive.

Horsetail Falls is most magnificent during the height of snowmelt, usually mid-June to mid-July. However, several deaths have occurred here over the years, and extreme caution should be exercised, especially when the rocks along Pyramid Creek at the end of maintained trail are slick from spray. Families should keep a constant watch over young children in this area.

DIRECTIONS Drive CA 50 to Twin Bridges, approximately 6.75 miles west of Echo Summit, and park in the well-marked Pyramid Creek parking lot ($5 day-use fee).

FACILITIES/TRAILHEAD The trailhead area is complete with flush toilets and running water. The well-marked trailhead begins at the northeast edge of the parking lot.

From the parking lot, follow singletrack trail through oaks, incense cedars, white firs, and Jeffrey pines with an understory of chinquapin, huckleberry oak, and manzanita to a trail junction near an area of large, sloping granite slabs. Turn right (east), obeying a sign marked PYRAMID CREEK LOOP TRAIL, CASCADE VISTA 1/4 and follow hiker emblem signs attached to widely spaced conifers, as you hike over granite slabs alongside the twisting and turning course of Pyramid Creek, which tumbles over steps and swirls through cataracts. Continue climbing up the canyon with occasional views of Horsetail Falls,

following an alternating route over rock slabs and sections of dirt trail in and out of scattered forest. You veer away from the creek slightly and reach a junction, three-quarters of a mile from the trailhead.

To continue toward the falls, turn right (northwest) at the junction and hike over more slabs and sandy sections of trail to the signed Desolation Wilderness boundary and a day hikers' trail register just beyond. Proceed up the canyon a fair distance away from the roaring creek through sparse stands of junipers and pines and patches of shrubs. Nearing the falls, the canyon narrows and the terrain becomes much steeper,

View of Lovers Leap and Highway 50 from Horsetail Falls Trail

forcing the rocky trail closer to the creek. Eventually, defined tread falters altogether as granite slabs and boulders bar the way. A short climb leads to a pool near the base of the lower falls, which should be the turnaround point for most parties, especially early in the season when the water-polished bedrock above is wet and slippery.

Although a well-known cross-country route continues up the canyon toward Desolation Valley, only skilled off-trail enthusiasts should contemplate this route.

You can streamline your return to the trailhead by following the Pyramid Creek Trail past the junctions with the Pyramid Creek Loop directly back to the parking lot.

Mt. Rose and the Carson Range

Named for famed guide Kit Carson, the Carson Range is a north–south-trending, linear mountain range to the east of Lake Tahoe, considered to be a subrange of the Sierra Nevada lying to the west. More than 50 miles in length, the range extends from near Carson Pass (CA 88) to the Truckee River (I-80). The northern and southern ends of the range contain rocks of principally volcanic origin, while the center of the range is made up of mostly granitic rocks.

A transition zone between the Great Basin to the east and the Sierra Nevada to the west, the Carson Range harbors a unique plant community, with species from both areas. Elevations ranging from 5,000 to near 11,000 feet have aided this biological diversity; a small alpine zone occupies the summits of some of the highest peaks. The range actually contains the most diverse collection of trees in the entire state of Nevada, despite the fact that the area was almost completely denuded in the mid-1800s to fuel the frenzy created by the Comstock Lode. Most of the trees that visitors see today are from a second-growth forest. The animal population is equally diverse, with 11 species found nowhere else within the state.

Blocked by the massive wall of the Sierra crest to the west, the Carson Range receives about half of the moisture from Pacific storms that falls on the Sierra. Due in part to the relative lack of precipitation, glaciers had little impact on the composition of the mountains. Consequently, the area is nearly devoid of natural lakes. However, several streams have gouged out canyons on the east front, which plummet steeply toward the valley floors below. With significantly less snow to melt, the Carson Range is open for recreation about a month before the neighboring Sierra.

Situated in Reno's backyard, the 28,000-acre Mt. Rose Wilderness is the highly prized centerpiece of the Carson Range. Recent improvements to the trails and trailheads in and around the wilderness have greatly enhanced the access to and the condition of the trails in this area. Trailheads have been improved at Thomas Creek, Whites Creek, Browns Creek, Mt. Rose Summit, and the new Galena Creek Visitor Center. New trails include the Rim to Reno, Browns Creek, Mt. Houghton, and Thomas Creek Loop Trails. In addition, realignments and upgrades have been made to many sections of the Tahoe Rim, Tahoe Meadows, Jones Creek-Whites Creek, and Mt. Rose Trails. The Mt. Rose Highway (NV 431), connecting Reno with Incline Village over 8,933-foot Mt. Rose Summit, provides the main access for trails in and around the Mt. Rose area.

South of Mt. Rose, between NV 431 and CA 50, much of the Carson Range falls within Lake Tahoe Nevada State Park. From the east side, a number of routes follow steep ascents to a network of old roads within the park that have seen increased use in recent years, especially among mountain bikers. The Tahoe Rim Trail travels along or near the crest of the Carson Range for a good portion of the journey between Tahoe Meadows and Luther Pass. Recreational access from Carson Valley into the range from the east is extremely limited.

Waterfall along the Mt. Rose Trail

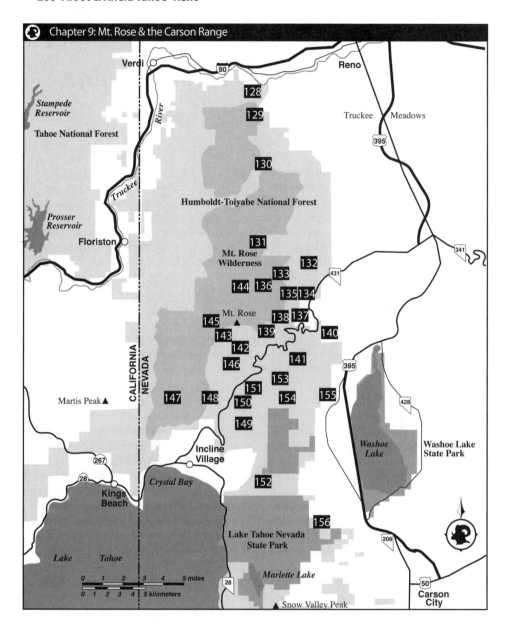

Chapter 9: Mt. Rose & the Carson Range

128 Tom Cooke and Steamboat Ditch Trails to Hole in the Wall

Distance	5 miles (out-and-back)
Hiking Time	2.5–3 hours
Elevation	+450/-150 feet
Difficulty	Easy
Trail Use	Dogs OK, mountain biking OK
Best Times	March through November
Agency	Humboldt-Toiyabe National Forest at 775-882-2766, www.fs.usda.gov/htnf
Recommended Maps	USGS 7.5-minute *Verdi, Mt. Rose NW*

see map on p. 288

HIGHLIGHTS The Tom Cooke Trail climbs away from the Truckee River to a connection with the Steamboat Ditch Trail, which has been the source of a heated controversy over public access in the past. With straightforward and legal egress to the ditch trail, dog walkers, joggers, hikers, mountain bikers, and horse lovers flock to the trail just about every day. By heading west on the ditch trail, trail users can follow the mellow grade of the wide path to Hole in the Wall, a tunnel that carries the ditch through a hill.

   Summer users should opt for an early-morning or early-evening visit, as the route is virtually devoid of shade. Families with young children must keep a constant eye on the little ones along the ditch trail section, as the unfenced Steamboat Ditch carries irrigation water usually from spring to late summer.

DIRECTIONS From the West McCarran Boulevard and West Fourth Street intersection, drive west on Fourth Street 1.9 miles to a left-hand turn onto Woodland. Follow Woodland 0.1 mile and turn right at White Fir. Proceed for 0.3 mile to the Patagonia Outlet and park on the shoulder as space allows.

FACILITIES/TRAILHEAD A greenbelt along the Truckee River has picnic tables. The trail begins on the far side of a bridge over the river, a short distance down a closed gravel road on the left-hand side of White Fir. Signs mark the beginning of singletrack trail.

Start climbing away from the river, immediately reaching a short bridge across the Last Chance Ditch. Continue a moderate climb up the hillside amid scattered sagebrush and grasses, as the trail makes several switchbacks. Wildflowers add color in early spring, including paintbrush, phlox, lupine, and California poppy. The grade eases as you approach a saddle. Head southwest from the saddle across gentle terrain, soon intersecting the course of a twin-tracked old road. A very short climb along the road leads to a junction with the Steamboat Ditch Trail, three-quarters of a mile from the trailhead.

Turn right and follow the nearly level grade of the wide path, as it follows alongside the winding course of the Steamboat Ditch. Surrounded by acres and acres of high desert flora, the banks of the ditch are lined with an oasis of vegetation, including willows, wild rose, and other moisture-loving plants. At 0.4 mile from the junction, you swing into a seasonal stream canyon filled with a profuse assemblage of tall vegetation. A trio of logs provides passage across the stream when it's flowing; otherwise you can dip down and cross the dry gully to the far bank.

Proceed along the pleasant grade of the ditch trail through typical foothills terrain. As you walk along, you can't help but notice the striking contrast between the sprawling development below the trail and the undeveloped land above. Nearly a mile from the previous canyon is another seasonal drainage, lined with willows and shaded by cottonwoods. A concrete channel above the stream carries the ditch water across this gully.

Beyond the drainage, the ditch trail turns north and passes by a lone Jeffrey pine

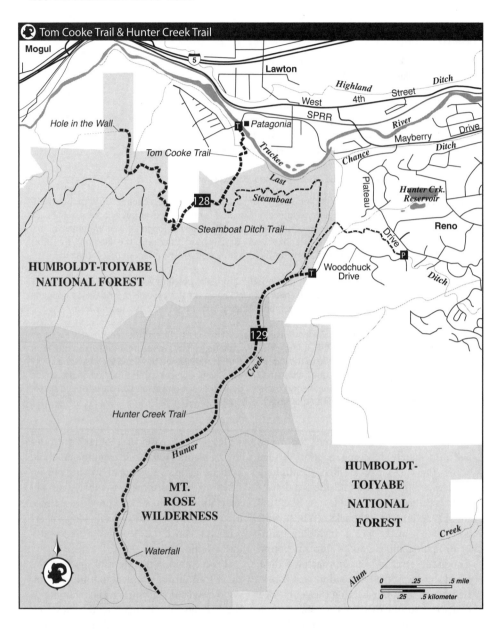

Tom Cooke Trail & Hunter Creek Trail

before turning west again to arrive at Hole in the Wall. Here the ditch trail technically ends, where the ditch water exits a tunnel through the hillside. Dirt roads continue both over and around the hill. Depending on the extent of future development, a network of old roads and use trails between the ditch and the river makes looping back to the trailhead a distinct possibility.

129 Hunter Creek Trail

Distance	7 miles (out-and-back)
Hiking Time	3.5–4 hours
Elevation	+1,450/-150 feet
Difficulty	Moderate
Trail Use	Dogs OK
Best Times	Mid-April through October
Agency	Humboldt-Toiyabe National Forest at 775-882-2766, www.fs.usda.gov/htnf
Recommended Map	USGS 7.5-minute *Mount Rose* (trail not shown), HTNF *Mount Rose Wilderness*

HIGHLIGHTS A once-undiscovered hike on the very edge of Reno leads to some surprises for first-time visitors, including a significant waterfall, lush meadows, and a forest grotto more reminiscent of a coastal hike than a foray into the eastern Sierra. Although the first couple of miles are shadeless, the tread is rough in spots, and rumors of rattlesnakes persist, numerous treasures await those who persevere beyond the initial stretch of trail.

Due to the low elevation, the trail is usually snow-free six months out of the year, providing a rare early-season opportunity for eastern Sierra hikers to shake off the cobwebs and stretch out the legs, as they wait for winter's snowpack to melt in the higher elevations. Spring is the best time to view the fall and witness the tumbling creek, while autumn can be equally enjoyable when brilliant colors adorn the canyon. Summers tend to be quite hot, so plan on an early start to help beat the heat.

Hardly the best example of trail building and maintenance in the Mt. Rose Wilderness, the Hunter Creek Trail is rough, indistinct for stretches, poorly graded in spots, rocky in parts, and severely eroded in others. Families with small children may find that keeping track of their progeny is a bit nerve-racking on the more precarious sections of trail. Despite these drawbacks, the trip is well worth the effort for larger folk, rewarding diligent hikers with some unexpected delights.

DIRECTIONS From the McCarran Boulevard/Plumb Lane–Caughlin Parkway intersection, head west on Caughlin Parkway for 1.2 miles and then turn right onto Plateau Road. Continue on Plateau for 0.6 mile, turn left onto Woodchuck Circle, and then proceed for 0.6 mile to the access road for the Michael D. Thompson Trailhead on the right.

FACILITIES/TRAILHEAD The trailhead is equipped with vault toilets, picnic tables, and interpretive signs.

Begin hiking along the course of an old road that heads toward the mouth of Hunter Creek Canyon. After 0.3 mile, you reach a ford of the creek. If the water is high, find a wood plank over the creek immediately upstream of the ford and make the crossing over to the west side.

Continue upstream on the jeep road for 0.2 mile to a sharp bend opposite a diversion structure on the far side of Hunter Creek. Proceed straight ahead, past a short path leading to a gauging station on the far side of the creek, to the start of singletrack trail, where a brown vinyl marker heralds your passage into the Mt. Rose Wilderness.

Follow the primitive trail up the narrowing canyon on an undulating course across the steep, sagebrush-covered hillside, well above the level of the stream, where precipitous cliffs and periodic washouts plague the initial section. As you progress up the canyon, mountain mahogany and ponderosa pines appear, lending a subtle hint that a light forest awaits farther up the canyon. Typical eastern Sierra riparian vegetation chokes the banks of Hunter Creek, including aspen, willow, cottonwood, and elderberry.

Around 2 miles from the trailhead, you enter a forested grove that seems totally out of place this far east of the Sierra crest.

A canopy of mixed conifers, including ponderosa pines, white firs, and incense cedars, shades a lush understory of ferns and other shade-loving plants. Following the trail through the grove, you hop across a trio of tiny rivulets along the way. The path may be a bit hard to follow in this section, but more distinct trail appears as you leave the woodland and emerge into a small clearing.

Beyond the clearing, the trail descends to a crossing of the main branch of Hunter Creek, where a large tree has conveniently fallen across the stream, providing a relatively easy way over the tumbling creek.

Nearby is a waterfall, which puts on quite a display during peak flow. At one time, a more distinct trail climbed the hillside above the waterfall to a large meadow. Unfortunately, this path fell into disuse after a recent forest fire and is now hard to follow. For those willing to make the short climb without aid of a decent trail, the meadow is quite picturesque. Past the meadow, the trail disappears completely and progress farther up the narrowing, brush-choked canyon is extremely difficult. Further complicating matters, a 2014 fire charred the forest in the upper part of Hunter Creek Canyon.

130 Hunter Lake

Distance	15 miles (out-and-back)
Hiking Time	7.5–8.5 hours
Elevation	+3,300/-350 feet
Difficulty	Difficult
Trail Use	Backpacking option, dogs OK, mountain biking OK, maps and compass
Best Times	Mid-April through November
Agency	Humboldt-Toiyabe National Forest at 775-882-2766, www.fs.usda.gov/htnf
Recommended Maps	USGS 7.5-minute *Mt. Rose NE, Mt. Rose NW*, HTNF *Mount Rose Wilderness*

HIGHLIGHTS A cursory glance at maps of the Carson Range reveals a curious division of the Mt. Rose Wilderness into two unequal parcels of land separated by a thin, winding corridor of nonwilderness land corresponding to the route of the Hunter Lake Road. This strip of land is the result of a concession to off-roaders in order to secure passage of the 1989 Nevada Wilderness Bill that in part set aside the Mt. Rose Wilderness. Many years later, the condition of the road has deteriorated so much that mountain bikes seem to be much more common than motorized vehicles. Today, human-powered recreationists can follow the rough, rocky, and steep road to Hunter Lake, a shallow pond nestled into a willow-fringed meadow below the crest of the Carson Range.

Perhaps the most challenging part of the trip is at the beginning—attempting to ascertain which one of the several roads to follow. Be sure to pack along a topographic map and compass or GPS unit. The road cuts a swath through the eastern hills of the Carson Range on a generally southwest course to the lake.

DIRECTIONS From the intersection with McCarran Boulevard, head westbound on Caughlin Parkway past the shopping center and turn left onto Village Green Parkway. Proceed on Village Green for 0.7 mile and turn left at Pine Bluff. Drive to a turnaround at the end of the road and park as space allows.

FACILITIES/TRAILHEAD There are no facilities at the trailhead. The route begins near a Hunter Lake Road access sign.

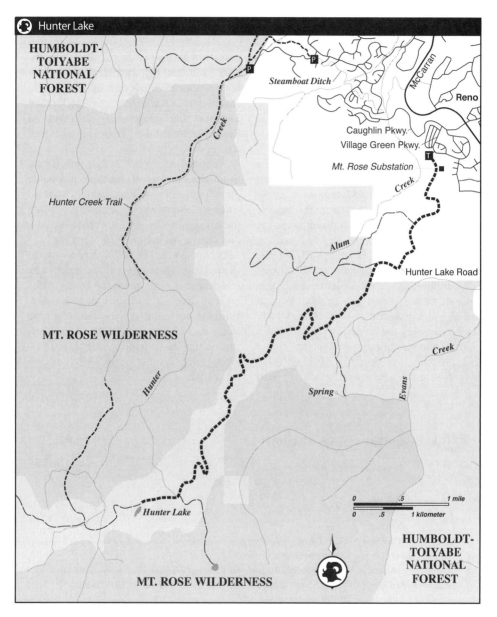

From the edge of the pavement, follow dirt and rock road past the Mt. Rose Substation and around the cyclone fence of a storage facility to a flat, which could be an alternate parking area for high-clearance vehicles. Along the first half of the trip, jeep roads and dirt bike trails come and go, but the wide tread of the Hunter Lake Road is plainly obvious. Follow the main road around a bend heading east and then south and come above the canyon of a seasonal stream. Pass through open sagebrush-covered slopes dotted with mountain mahogany and then climb steeply on rocky tread. Continue on the main road as it skirts the base of a hill and climbs to a level spot with good views behind of the Truckee Meadows. A steeper ascent leads toward a light forest of Jeffrey pines, some of which show signs of a previous fire. Reach a Y-junction in a saddle, 1.9 miles from the trailhead, where the right-hand road drops into the canyon of Alum Creek.

Veer left at the junction and make a steady ascent up a lightly forested canyon of a tributary of Evans Creek. After a half mile of stiff climbing, you encounter another junction with a road on the right opposite a national forest signboard. Continue ahead on more gently graded tread, soon breaking out of the trees to a view up the canyon, particularly attractive in autumn when the aspens and willows lining the drainage have turned golden. Heading back into the pines, you wind around and reach a trio of roads splitting off to the left and heading down to the creek. The middle road, at 2.75 miles, is Forest Road 41392A, which, after crossing the stream, wraps around a hillside to meadow-rimmed springs.

From the junction, the road continues up the canyon before switchbacking across a sage-covered slope and climbing to a forested saddle. More climbing awaits, as you pass through alternating stands of conifers, pockets of quaking aspen and willow, and open slopes of sagebrush, tobacco brush, and currant. Excellent views of the Truckee Meadows backdropped by the Virginia Range are plentiful on the way to a crest of a ridge at 6.75 miles.

After the lengthy 6.75-mile climb, a mild to moderate descent through lodgepole pines is a welcome and pleasant change. After three-quarters of a mile, you reach the fringe of the meadow that harbors diminutive, willow-lined Hunter Lake.

Backpackers will be lured to pine-shaded campsites near the edge of the meadow and near where the road crosses Hunter Creek, a half mile past the lake. Hardy riders and hikers can continue along the road over the crest of the Carson Range to expansive Big Meadows. From there, a route north to Boomtown is possible.

---

131   Upper Thomas Creek Loop

see map on p. 294

Distance	16.5 miles (partial loop); 22.9 miles from lower trailhead
Hiking Time	6–9 hours; 7.5–12 hours from lower trailhead
Elevation	+3,375/-3,375 feet; +4,475/-4,475 feet from lower trailhead
Difficulty	Difficult
Trail Use	Dogs OK (on leash first mile)
Best Times	July through mid-October
Agency	Humboldt Toiyabe National Forest at 775-882-2766, www.fs.usda.gov/htnf
Recommended Maps	USGS 7.5-minute *Mt. Rose, NW* (trail not shown), CVTA *Rim to Reno Regional Trail System*

HIGHLIGHTS A lonely and delightful canyon, minutes away from the hubbub of the nearby city, beckons hikers and equestrians to explore a prime section of the Mt. Rose Wilderness. Initially, the route follows the tumbling waters of perennial Thomas Creek up a broad canyon, which is ablaze with gold in autumn. A dramatic rock formation jutting out from the south canyon wall considerably enhances the picturesque scenery. From the head of the canyon, a relatively new section of trail provides an extended, pleasantly graded loop around the far side of the Carson Range before returning to Thomas Creek canyon. A few rocky promontories offer occasional, far-reaching views along the way.

The 16.5-mile distance may deter casual hikers, especially when coupled with the steep climb out of Thomas Creek Canyon. However, for those hikers, trail runners, and equestrians up to the task, the quiet wilderness beckons. While scads of hikers struggle up the nearby Mt. Rose Trail and plenty of others use the lower Thomas Creek Trail to connect with the Dry Pond Trail, those who opt to follow the route described here may be rewarded with high doses of solitude and serenity. Away from Thomas Creek, water is typically unavailable for the majority of the trip—make sure you have plenty of water stowed in your pack.

DIRECTIONS Upper Trailhead: (High-clearance vehicle recommended) From the I-580 off-ramp (Exit 56) at Mt. Rose Highway (NV 431), head westbound toward Incline Village for 2 miles and then turn right onto Timberline Drive. Proceed on Timberline, crossing a short bridge over Whites Creek and continue past where the pavement ends. Immediately after a second bridge over Thomas Creek, 1.1 miles from the highway, turn left onto Thomas Creek Road (FS 049). Proceed on dirt road for 2.2 miles to the top of a hill and a junction with gated, private roads accessing homes around Thomas Meadows. Veer left and drop down to a ford of Thomas Creek and then follow rougher road another 0.3 mile to a closed steel gate. Park off the road as space allows.

Lower Trailhead: Without a vehicle with adequate clearance, you can park at the developed lower trailhead and begin the hike from there (however, doing so adds an extra 6.4 total miles to an already long trip). From the I-580 off-ramp (Exit 56) at Mt. Rose Highway (NV 431), head westbound toward Incline Village for 2 miles and then turn right onto Timberline Drive. Proceed on Timberline, crossing a short bridge over Whites Creek, and continue past where the pavement ends. Proceed on Timberline across a second bridge over Thomas Creek and continue past Thomas Creek Road on the left to the Thomas Creek Trailhead parking area, 0.1 mile beyond Thomas Creek.

FACIITIES/TRAILHEAD There are no facilities at the upper trailhead. The trail begins to the left of the road near a trailhead sign.

The lower trailhead has vault toilets, equestrian facilities, picnic tables, and interpretive signs. The trail begins at a trailhead signboard near the southwest corner of the parking area.

From the lower Thomas Creek Trailhead, follow a short section of trail heading south away from the parking area to a crossing of Thomas Creek Road. Walk up the canyon through an informal parking area on the north bank of Thomas Creek to where singletrack resumes near some trail signs. Wind around to a crossing of the creek and continue upstream along the edge of the riparian zone lining the tumbling stream through a mixed forest of cottonwoods, aspens, Jeffrey pines, and white firs. Sagebrush and Jeffrey pines dominate the drier environment on the slopes above the creek. Small, intermittent clearings on the canyon floor harbor sagebrush, bitterbrush, and a splash of early-season color from a host of lupines. At 1.5 miles from the trailhead, you reach a junction with the Dry Pond Trail marked by a 4-by-4-inch post.

Continue upstream from the junction through similar vegetation, drawing closer to and moving away from the creek a number of times along the way before you veer over to cross Thomas Creek on a plank bridge. Just beyond the crossing, the trail merges with the dirt surface of Thomas Creek Road for approximately 100 yards before the resumption of singletrack trail. A short, steep climb is followed by a moderate ascent through more open terrain, which reveals a view of some interesting cliffs above the far bank of the creek, which is now lined by an extensive stand of aspens. Farther on, a narrow stretch of the canyon forces the trail to merge with the old road once again for approximately 150 yards. Follow the road to a twin-channel ford of Thomas Creek, the first of which is usually an easy traverse of a seasonal flow across arranged stones. The second is a sometimes-wet ford of the main branch that can usually be a dry crossing by midsummer with some deft boulder hopping.

Climb away from the creek to where singletrack snakes away and then above the road, which you follow for to the upper trailhead, 0.3 mile from the creek crossing.

From the upper Thomas Creek Trailhead, the trail begins by switchbacking up the south wall of Thomas Creek Canyon to avoid crossing private property. Climb through predominantly Jeffrey pine forest to the top of the switchbacks and then follow a rising traverse across the shady, pine-studded hillside. After about 0.5 mile, the

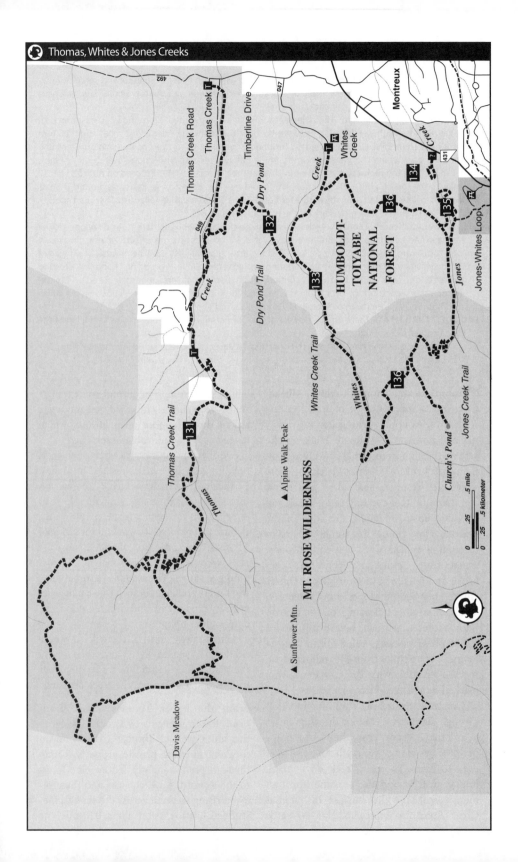

Thomas Creek Road

Thomas Creek

492

Timberline Drive

047

Montreux

Whites Creek

Creek

431

134

049

Dry Pond

135

132

Jones-Whites Loop

Creek

133

HUMBOLDT-
TOIYABE
NATIONAL
FOREST

136

Dry Pond Trail

Whites Creek Trail

Thomas Creek Trail

131

Whites

Jones

Creek

Thomas

136

Alpine Walk Peak

Jones Creek Trail

Church's Pond

MT. ROSE WILDERNESS

.5 mile

.25

0

.5 kilometer

.25

0

Sunflower Mtn.

Davis Meadow

trail bends around a side drainage, crossing an old jeep road along the way. A stretch of descent leads back around toward the creek, where you meet the old Thomas Creek Road, and then ascend up the dirt and rock surface for a while to where singletrack trail veers away to the left (the road continues as the equestrian route). Proceed shortly to a ford of Thomas Creek, 1.6 miles from the parking area, which should be an easy crossing except when the creek is running high during peak snowmelt.

Continue on the north side of the creek through more open forest, soon merging with the equestrian route and the old road again and then crossing the signed Mt. Rose Wilderness boundary. Farther up, quaking aspens lining the stream bank become the dominant tree, soaking up the ample groundwater along this stretch of creek bottom. Just before the 2-mile mark, singletrack trail veers away from the old road and the vicinity of the creek to ascend north into the forest. Soon the trail bends back to the west and then crosses a small but usually vigorous side stream, where once again the equestrian and hiker routes diverge. Eventually singletrack trail nears the main branch of the creek again, where open terrain allows good views up the canyon, including a prominent rock face above the south side of Thomas Creek. Farther on, a few short-legged switchbacks provide a warm-up for the stiff climb lurking ahead, as a moderate ascent leads up a manzanita-covered hillside toward a series of longer-legged switchbacks.

Follow the zigzagging climb up a steep slope carpeted with rabbitbrush, sagebrush, mountain mahogany, and an occasional Jeffrey pine, enjoying a fine upper-canyon view along the way. After a dozen switchbacks, you stand on the crest of the north ridge of the canyon, where the view expands to include the Truckee Meadows to the northeast and Sunflower Mountain, Alpine Walk Peak, Church Peak, Chocolate Peak, and Mt. Rose to the south. Climb along the top of the ridge a short distance to the loop junction, 4.4 miles from the trailhead.

Veer onto the right-hand trail to follow a counterclockwise circuit, continuing to climb through mostly open terrain until entering a mostly lodgepole-pine forest. A couple of switchbacks lead higher up the slope and then across a usually dry tributary of Thomas Creek. Not far beyond this streambed, you reach a saddle between Peaks 9487 and 9246 and then begin a gentle, moderately forested, somewhat-winding descent to the north-northwest, which, after the stiff climb out of Thomas Creek Canyon, is a welcome respite. The almost complete lack of groundcover in this area stands in stark contrast to the lush vegetation previously seen along Thomas Creek. Aside from passing around a couple of boulder fields, the predominantly lodgepole-pine forest remains constant, sprinkled with an occasional whitebark pine or mountain hemlock. Just beyond the 6-mile mark, the gentle descent ends, replaced by a general ascent that will more or less be a constant companion until you reach the crest of the Carson Range in another 4 miles.

Shortly after the climb begins and just beyond some switchbacks is a rock point offering a view of the distant Truckee Meadows. Rising tread leads to another rock knob after a while, with views north toward Peavine Peak and the much closer upper canyon of a Hunter Creek tributary below. Continue the ascent, soon walking over rocky tread beneath an interesting-looking rock outcrop before reentering lodgepole-pine forest. After a long, gently rising stretch of forested trail, you come to another rock knob at 7.5 miles, offering a fine view of Big Meadow and Deep Canyon in the immediate foreground. More distant landmarks seen from this promontory include Peavine Peak, the Verdi Range, Stampede Reservoir, Mt. Lola, and Sierra Buttes. Following a short climb over a saddle near Peak 9436, the grade eases a tad and wanders through the forest for quite a while. Beyond, the grade

Rock outcrop in Upper Thomas Creek Canyon

increases as the trail makes an angling, mile-long, ascending traverse below the west side of the Carson Range crest. Farther on, views open up temporarily where the path crosses a rockslide. Proceed to a junction near a 4-by-4-inch post, 10.6 miles from the trailhead, where the Rim to Reno Trail continues ahead (south).

Turn left (northeast) at the junction and follow a half-mile, moderate, switchbacking climb to the crest of the Carson Range. From the crest, a scramble along the ridge to the top of either Peak 9996 (north) or 9890 (south) offers superb views of the surrounding terrain for anyone with the requisite energy.

The trail drops rather steeply away from the crest back into the Thomas Creek drainage (you'll more than likely be glad not to have climbed up this way), switchbacking down the steep hillside for nearly a mile before reaching a more pleasantly graded traverse across the upper canyon. The mile-long traverse eventually leads back to the loop junction at 12.3 miles. From there, retrace your steps 4.2 miles to the parking area at the upper trailhead, or 7.4 miles to the lower trailhead.

132 Dry Pond Trail

Distance	4.5 miles (point-to-point); 6.3 miles (loop)
Hiking Time	2–3 hours (point-to-point); 2.5–4 hours (loop)
Elevation	+1,000/-750 feet (point-to-point);
	+1,100/-1,100 feet (loop)
Difficulty	Moderate
Trail Use	Dogs OK (on leash first mile), mountain biking OK
Best Times	May through October
Agency	Humboldt Toiyabe National Forest at 775-882-2766, www.fs.usda.gov/htnf
Recommended Maps	USGS 7.5-minute *Mt. Rose NE*, HTNF *Mount Rose Wilderness*

HIGHLIGHTS The Dry Pond Trail is a fairly new trail that provides a connection between trails in Thomas Creek and Whites Creek Canyons. With that connection, hikers can now experience both canyons on a single hike with the added bonus of good views and a seasonal pond in a grassy meadow on top of the ridge in between. The 4.5-mile distance, combined with the proximity to Reno, makes this trip a fine outing for a morning or afternoon romp in the mountains. The meadow near the midpoint of the hike provides a fine setting for a picnic.

DIRECTIONS From the I-580 off-ramp at Mt. Rose Highway (NV 431), head westbound 2 miles on the Mt. Rose Highway to Timberline Drive and turn right. Proceed on Timberline for 0.6 mile to a left-hand turn marked for Whites Creek Trail, just before a short bridge over Whites Creek. Proceed a half mile to the trailhead and park your first vehicle there.

Backtrack the half mile to Timberline and turn left, immediately crossing a bridge over Whites Creek, and then continue to a second bridge over Thomas Creek and an immediate junction with the Thomas Creek Road (FS 049). Proceed another 0.1 mile straight ahead to the Thomas Creek Trailhead parking area on the left.

FACILITIES/TRAILHEAD The trailhead has vault toilets, picnic tables, interpretive signs, and equestrian facilities. The well-signed trail begins on the southwest side of the parking area.

Follow a short section of trail that heads south away from the parking area to the Thomas Creek Road, cross the road, and walk up the canyon through an informal parking area on the north bank of Thomas Creek. Pick up the resumption of singletrack trail on the far side of the parking area and then wind down toward the creek, where a trio of stream branch crossings must be negotiated in order to reach the south bank. Once across, the trail heads upstream along the edge of the riparian zone that lines the tumbling creek through a mixed forest of cottonwoods, aspens, Jeffrey pines, and white firs. Sagebrush and Jeffrey pines dominate the drier environment on the slopes of the canyon farther away from the stream. Small clearings harbor sagebrush, bitterbrush, and a splash of color in early summer from a host of lupines. At 1.5 miles from the trailhead, you reach a trail junction marked by a 4-by-4-inch post.

Turn left (south) at the junction and head away from the creek on a moderate climb that switchbacks up the hillside toward the crest of the ridge that divides the Thomas Creek and Whites Creek drainages. On top of the ridge, a mile from the junction, you reach a grassy meadow with a fine view of Slide Mountain and Mt. Rose. Dry Pond, a small, seasonal, spring-fed pond at the far side of the meadow, is a delight early in the season but is typically dry by midsummer.

The trail skirts the western fringe of the meadow before beginning a moderate descent across the south-facing slopes of Whites Creek Canyon. A series of switchbacks leads down to the floor of the canyon and a crossing of Whites Creek. Just after the crossing, the trail intersects the old Whites Creek Road at 3.5 miles from the trailhead.

Turn left (northeast) and follow the road for a short distance to where singletrack veers away to the left on a moderate descent down the canyon. After three-quarters of a mile, you reach a marked junction with a trail on your right that heads toward Jones Creek and Galena Creek Park. From the junction, continue down the canyon, as mountain mahogany trees join the mixed forest. After about a half mile, you reach a point where the trail splits into two paths. Take the right-hand path, soon encountering a junction marked by a 4-by-4-inch post.

If you're using the shuttle option, follow the right-hand path a short distance over to the Whites Creek Trailhead parking area.

With only one vehicle, proceed ahead on the left-hand trail, heading downstream farther away from Whites Creek through more drought-tolerant vegetation. The trail bends over to cross Whites Creek Road and then continues down the canyon just to the right of the road. The trail ends a short way before reaching Timberline Drive, which forces you to briefly walk the last section of Whites Creek Road.

Once at Timberline Drive, head north (left) and cross bridges over Whites Creek and Thomas Creek, and then continue another 0.1 mile to the Thomas Creek Trailhead parking area.

133   Upper Whites Creek

see map on p. 294

Distance	7 miles (out-and-back)
Hiking Time	3.5–4 hours
Elevation	+1,300 feet
Difficulty	Moderate
Trail Use	Dogs OK (on leash first mile)
Best Times	April through November
Agency	Humboldt-Toiyabe National Forest at 775-882-2766, www.fs.usda.gov/htnf
Recommended Maps	USGS 7.5-minute Mt. Rose NE, Mt. Rose NW, Mount Rose, HTNF Mount Rose Wilderness

HIGHLIGHTS The Forest Service has built new trailheads for the Whites Creek and neighboring Thomas Creek trails, as well as a new trail that connects the two (see Trip 132). The rapidly growing population of the Reno area, coupled with the improved access to these trails, will certainly mean an increase in future traffic, but the paths still have much to offer recreationists searching for a retreat from the rigors of civilization that doesn't require a lengthy drive to reach a trailhead. The Whites Creek Trail follows the course of an old road up the canyon of a tumbling stream into the eastern limits of the Mt. Rose Wilderness. Connecting trails offer additional options for a number of trip extensions.

DIRECTIONS From the I-580 off-ramp at Mt. Rose Highway (NV 431), head westbound 2 miles on the Mt. Rose Highway to Timberline Drive and turn right. Proceed on Timberline 0.6 mile to a left-hand turn marked for Whites Creek Trail, just before a short bridge over Whites Creek. Proceed a half mile to the trailhead parking area.

FACILITIES/TRAILHEAD The trailhead has vault toilets and a couple of picnic tables. The trail begins on the north side of the old road.

Follow a short section of singletrack trail toward Whites Creek and a junction marked by a 4-by-4-inch post. Turn left and head upstream through forest cover of mostly Jeffrey pine, with a sprinkling of white fir and mountain mahogany. Occasionally, the banks are lined with pockets of aspen. Merge with a less-used trail on the right and continue ahead. At 0.4 mile from the trailhead, you reach another junction marked by a 4-by-4-inch post, this one with a connector trail on the left headed toward Jones Creek and part of the Jones Creek–Whites Creek Loop.

Continue ahead, following pleasant Whites Creek through a shady, mixed forest. At 1.2 miles from the trailhead and 0.8 mile from the previous junction, you reach the marked junction of the Dry Pond Trail (see Trip 132) on the right.

Remain on the Whites Creek Trail, following the south bank through the forested canyon. After a half mile or so, the trail merges with a section of the old Whites Creek jeep road. Follow the road for a short while to the signed Mt. Rose Wilderness boundary, beyond which mountain bikers are not allowed. Follow the trail as it bends sharply down to a crossing of Whites Creek, usually a straightforward boulder hop except during periods of peak runoff.

Now on the north bank, you continue the upstream journey on a steady climb through similar vegetation. At 3.5 miles from the trailhead, the Whites Creek Trail up the canyon ends. From there, maintained trail continues across the creek via some logs and then continues up the south wall of the canyon on a stiff climb to the ridge crest as part of the Jones Creek–Whites Creek Loop (see Trip 136). Unless you're feeling more adventurous, retrace your steps back to the Whites Creek Trailhead.

134 Galena Creek Visitor Center Nature Trail

see map on p. 294

Distance	0.4 mile (loop)
Hiking Time	30 minutes
Elevation	+50/-50 feet
Difficulty	Easy
Trail Use	Good for kids, wheelchair accessible
Best Times	May through October
Agency	Humboldt Toiyabe National Forest at 775-882-2766, www.fs.usda.gov/htnf
Recommended Map	None

HIGHLIGHTS This short, paved, wheelchair-accessible path offers a good introduction to the ecosystem of the Carson Range through several interpretive signs placed along the trail.

DIRECTIONS From the I-580 off-ramp at Mt. Rose Highway (NV 431), head westbound 5.6 miles to a left-hand turn into the Galena Creek Visitor Center. Park your vehicle in the visitor center parking lot.

FACILITIES/TRAILHEAD The visitor center is open every day but Monday during the summer season and Friday through Sunday during the winter season. Along with exhibits and naturalists to answer questions, facilities include restrooms and picnic areas. The nature trail begins near the visitor center.

From the visitor center, head west on paved path, avoiding the dirt Jones Creek Trail on the left. You soon reach the first interpretive sign and continue across a bridge over Jones Creek. Depending on the previous winter's snowfall and the time of your visit, the creek may be dry later in the season. Continue away from the bridge through a widely scattered, young forest of Jeffrey pines to the start of the loop near a park bench.

Turn left at the loop junction and head uphill enjoying fine views of Mt. Rose across open slopes composed of tobacco brush, bitterbrush, manzanita, and sagebrush, encountering more interpretive signs along the way. Soon the trail reaches the high point and descends back toward the visitor center above Jones Creek. At the close of the loop, walk across the bridge and retrace your steps back to the visitor center.

see map on p. 294

135 Jones Creek Loop

Distance	1.6 miles (loop)
Hiking Time	30 minutes–1 hour
Elevation	+275/-275 feet
Difficulty	Easy
Trail Use	Good for kids, Dogs OK (leashed)
Best Times	May through October
Agency	Humboldt Toiyabe National Forest at 775-882-2766, www.fs.usda.gov/htnf
Recommended Map	CVTA *Rim to Reno Regional Trail System*

HIGHLIGHTS A relatively short and easy loop through the Jeffrey pine forest typical of the east side of the Carson Range.

DIRECTIONS From the I-580 off-ramp at Mt. Rose Highway (NV 431), head westbound 5.6 miles to a left-hand turn into the Galena Creek Visitor Center. Follow the access road past the visitor center and picnic areas and turn right into the Jones Creek Trailhead parking area.

FACILITIES/TRAILHEAD The visitor center is open every day but Monday during the summer season and Friday through Sunday during the winter season. Along with exhibits and naturalists to answer questions, facilities include restrooms and picnic areas. The trailhead has vault toilets, equestrian facilities, and picnic tables. The trail begins on the west side of the gravel parking lot near a trail sign.

Climb moderately through a light Jeffrey pine forest with an understory of bitterbrush, manzanita, and tobacco brush. After 0.3 mile, you come to a marked junction with a connector to Galena Creek Regional Park.

Veer right at the junction and climb more stiffly on the way to a crossing of Jones Creek. Immediately after the easy crossing, you reach a loop and the high point of the loop, 0.5 mile from the trailhead.

Turn right (east) to begin a moderate, 0.3-mile descent through Jeffrey pine forest to the next junction.

Veer left at the junction and continue downhill. Eventually the trail switchbacks and comes alongside a white fir–shaded section of Jones Creek. Farther downstream, the forest opens up a bit, allowing enough sunlight for alders to flourish along the banks. At 0.5 mile from the previous junction, the trail crosses the creek above a culvert and comes to a junction with the lateral continuing downstream to the Galena Creek Visitor Center.

Proceed ahead (south) on the Jones Creek Loop, heading 0.1 mile past picnic tables to the trailhead.

136   Jones Creek–Whites Creek Loop

see map on p. 294

Distance	9 miles (loop), plus 1.4-mile round-trip to Church's Pond
Hiking Time	3–4.5 hours
Elevation	+2,525/-2,525 feet
Difficulty	Difficult
Trail Use	Dogs OK (on leash first mile)
Best Times	Late May through November
Agency	Humboldt-Toiyabe National Forest at 775-882-2766, www.fs.usda.gov/htnf
Recommended Maps	USGS 7.5-minute *Washoe City, Mount Rose, Mt. Rose NW, Mt. Rose NE;* HTNF *Mount Rose Wilderness*

HIGHLIGHTS On this trip, a 9-mile loop and a 1.4-mile out-and-back journey lead from low elevation forest up to high, open terrain with grand views of the east flank of the Carson Range, particularly Mt. Rose and Slide Mountain. At various spots along the way, the trail offers good views to the east of Washoe Valley, the Virginia Range, and the south part of the Truckee Meadows as well. The loop visits two tumbling creeks, Jones and Whites, where prolific aspen groves douse the canyons with silvery green in summer and brilliant gold in autumn. A half-mile-plus lateral leads to Church's Pond, a diminutive pool near the high point of the trip with a grand view of the volcanic gray slopes of Mt. Rose. Despite the proximity to Reno and a beginning in a popular county park, the Jones–Whites Loop is not as heavily used as you might expect.

DIRECTIONS From the I-580 off-ramp at Mt. Rose Highway (NV 431), head westbound 5.6 miles to a right-hand turn into the Galena Creek Visitor Center. Follow the access road past the visitor center and picnic areas and turn right into the Jones Creek Trailhead parking area.

FACILITIES/TRAILHEAD The trailhead has vault toilets and picnic tables. The trail begins on the west side of the gravel parking lot near a trail sign.

Climb moderately through a light Jeffrey pine forest with an understory of bitterbrush, manzanita, and tobacco brush. After 0.3 mile, you come to a marked junction with a connector to Galena Creek Regional Park.

Veer right at the junction and climb more stiffly on the way to a crossing of Jones Creek. Immediately after the easy crossing, you reach the loop junction, 0.5 mile from the trailhead.

Head up the canyon of Jones Creek, reaching the signed Mt. Rose Wilderness boundary at 0.8 mile from the trailhead. The trailside vegetation beneath a light canopy of Jeffrey pine is composed primarily of manzanita, with an assortment of wildflowers, including lupine and paintbrush. Prolific stands of quaking aspen lining the creek provide an excellent display of autumn color. Climbing moderately steeply upstream, views open up toward the head of the canyon, and you get a glimpse of the ridge high above that the trail must ascend to get out of Jones Creek Canyon.

Soon a series of long-legged switchbacks begins that leads to the top of the ridge separating the drainages of Jones and Whites Creeks. Along the way, views improve of the Virginia Range and Little Washoe Lake to the east, and Mt. Rose and Slide Mountain to the south. At the end of seven switchbacks, you stand atop the ridge with unobstructed views and reach a junction between the lateral to Church's Pond ahead (southwest) and the continuation of the loop toward Whites Creek to the right (northwest).

To visit Church's Pond, continue climbing along the ridge for 0.5 mile and then drop into the basin for another 0.2 mile to the shoreline. Church's Pond is a shallow pool of water with no inlet or outlet that tends to shrink in size as the summer progresses. Gently sloping, sagebrush-covered slopes rise up from the shoreline and continue nearly 2,500 feet to the volcanic-rock summit of Mt. Rose. An assortment of scattered pines and small aspen groves rims the far shore. The lakeshore makes an excellent lunch spot while enjoying the splendid scenery. At the conclusion of your visit, retrace your steps 0.7 mile to the junction.

From the junction, descend off the ridge into the drainage of Whites Creek. You should instantly detect a change in the vegetation from the southern exposure of Jones Creek to the northern exposure of Whites Creek, as aspens, grasses, and wildflowers grace the upper part of the canyon and a dense forest of white firs farther downslope provides a stark contrast to the drier slopes seen previously. The trail winds down the hillside toward a bridged crossing of a tributary stream, a mile from the junction. After a very brief climb away from the stream and a short, level stretch of trail, you continue the descent toward the floor of the canyon. At the bottom, 5 miles from the trailhead, is a ford of the main channel of Whites Creek, which should be a fairly straightforward crossing across some logs, except perhaps during peak runoff.

Now heading downstream, drier vegetation greets you on the south-facing hillside, as tall grasses, sagebrush, and Jeffrey pines carpet the slope. The sandy trail descends mildly through the upper part of the canyon, with the gracefully flowing creek as a constant companion. Farther downstream, white fir, aspen, and small, water-loving plants thrive in the moist soils along the creek on the downhill side of the trail, while the drier vegetation continues on the uphill side. The descent along the north side of the creek continues until the trail makes a log crossing of Whites Creek at 6.25 miles.

Shortly after the crossing, you leave the Mt. Rose Wilderness and continue along the road for 0.8 mile to the Dry Pond junction on the left.

A short distance beyond the junction, singletrack trail diverges from the old road, which now serves as the equestrian route. Another 0.7-mile descent leads to a three-way junction between the Whites Creek Trail ahead and the continuation of the loop on the right.

Turning right, you head south across Whites Creek Road, and then climb stiffly up the pine-dotted slope separating the Whites Creek and Jones Creek drainages to a saddle, where the pines thin and sagebrush, grasses, and wildflowers are prevalent. Once again, Slide Mountain, Mt. Rose, and Washoe Valley pop into view. Beyond the saddle, the trail follows an angling, sidehill traverse across open sagebrush-covered slopes. Nearing the canyon floor, Jeffrey pines reappear, some with scorched trunks from a recent brush fire. A short climb over a minor ridge lined with mountain mahogany is followed by a general descent through Jeffrey pine forest on the way to a junction with the Jones Creek Loop, 1.5 miles from the Whites Creek Trail junction.

Leaving the official loop, veer left at the junction and continue downhill. Eventually the trail switchbacks and comes alongside a white fir–shaded section of Jones Creek. Farther downstream, the forest opens up a bit, allowing enough sunlight for alders to flourish along the banks. At 0.5 mile from the previous junction, the trail crosses the creek above a culvert and comes to a junction, with the lateral continuing downstream to the Galena Creek Visitor Center.

Proceed ahead (south) on a section of the Jones Creek Loop, heading 0.1 mile past picnic tables to the ending trailhead.

137 Galena Creek Regional Park Nature Trail

see map on p. 304

Distance	0.75 mile (loop)
Hiking Time	30 minutes
Elevation	+150/-150 feet
Difficulty	Easy
Trail Use	Good for kids, Dogs OK (leashed)
Best Times	May through October
Agency	Washoe County Regional Parks and Open Space at 775-328-3600, washoecounty.us/parks
Recommended Map	CVTA *Rim to Reno Regional Trail System*

HIGHLIGHTS A forested loop journey with 18 stops keyed to a free brochure about eastern Sierra ecology. The short walk is a fine complement to a picnic in the park.

DIRECTIONS From the I-580 off-ramp at Mt. Rose Highway (NV 431), head westbound 7.2 miles to a right-hand turn into south entrance for Galena Creek Regional Park and proceed a short distance to the parking lot.

FACILITIES/TRAILHEAD Galena Creek Park offers picnic areas and restrooms with running water. The trail begins at a bridge over Galena Creek.

Walk across the bridge over Galena Creek and soon reach the signed junction between the Nature and Bitterbrush trails. Turn left onto the Galena Creek Nature Trail and proceed a short distance to the start of the loop.

Veer left to begin a clockwise loop that initially follows alongside tumbling Galena Creek for about 0.2 mile and then bends north toward the top of a low hill. From the hill, make a short descent to an unmarked junction with the unmaintained path up Black's Canyon.

Away from the creek, the north side of the loop meanders through light forest with an understory dotted with glacial erratics and greenleaf manzanita. Reach an obscure junction near a large, split boulder at Post 14, about 0.6 mile from the trailhead, where the loop corresponding to the numbered posts turns right above the boulder. (If you miss this trail and continue ahead, you'll eventually reach the wide track of the Bitterbrush Trail, where a right turn will lead back to the trailhead.) From the boulder, the trail winds through the trees on the way back toward Galena Creek and the close of the loop near Post 5. From there, turn left, retrace your steps down the Nature Trail to the Bitterbrush junction, and then head across the bridge to the parking area.

138 Black's Canyon

see map on p. 304

Distance	4 miles (out-and-back)
Hiking Time	2–3 hours
Elevation	+1,300 feet
Difficulty	Difficult
Trail Use	Dogs OK
Best Times	May through November
Agency	Humboldt-Toiyabe National Forest at 775-882-2766, www.fs.usda.gov/htnf
Recommended Maps	USGS 7.5-minute *Washoe City, Mount Rose*; HTNF *Mount Rose Wilderness*

HIGHLIGHTS Hikers who have been searching for an off-the-beaten-path route into the Mt. Rose Wilderness should look no farther than the unmaintained trail up Black's Canyon. The path is infrequently used and seemingly few even know of its existence. The trail has several steep sections, parts are washed out, and the tread virtually disappears in spots. Despite these drawbacks, experienced hikers will have excellent views of Mt. Rose along the way, as well as a high likelihood for bountiful amounts of solitude. Cross-country enthusiasts have the option of continuing beyond the end of the trail all the way to the summit of Mt. Rose via Contact Pass.

DIRECTIONS From the I-580 off-ramp at Mt. Rose Highway (NV 431), head westbound 7.2 miles to a right-hand turn into south entrance for Galena Creek Regional Park and proceed a short distance to the parking lot.

FACILITIES/TRAILHEAD Galena Creek County Park offers picnic areas, restrooms with running water, and hiking trails. The trail begins at a bridge over Galena Creek.

Walk across a bridge over Galena Creek and soon reach a signed junction, where the Bitterbrush Trail continues ahead toward the north entrance of the park and a connection with the Jones Creek–Whites Creek Loop Trail. Turn left onto the Galena Creek Nature Trail and proceed a short distance to trail marker 4, where the loop portion of the nature trail begins. Veer left and begin a clockwise loop that initially follows alongside the creek for about 0.2 mile and then bends north on the way to the top of a low hill. From the hill, you make a short descent to an unmarked junction.

Turn left (west) and leave the nature trail to follow the Black's Canyon path on a moderate climb through a light forest of scattered Jeffrey pines and mountain mahogany with an understory of manzanita and sagebrush. Periodic openings in the forest allow good views toward the looming hulk of Mt. Rose. Because this trail is not maintained, some sections are overly steep for short stretches and several deadfalls may need to be crossed on the way up the canyon. Eventually, you reach a narrow and steep side canyon holding a small tributary stream that requires some nimble footwork to negotiate the partially washed-out tread.

Beyond the crossing of the side stream, a short, steep climb leads up to the top of a minor ridge. From there, a stiff climb continues, aided by a few switchbacks, across a hillside well above the level of the main creek. Farther on, the grade eases a bit to more of an ascending traverse that leads

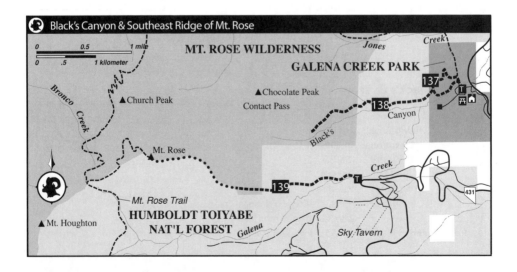

Black's Canyon & Southeast Ridge of Mt. Rose

into the open, with grand views of Mt. Rose up the canyon above an extensive stand of aspen. Approaching the aspens, the tread falters and quickly disappears altogether. Progress beyond here toward Contact Pass and Mt. Rose will require cross-country skills. If you do choose to go farther, follow the right-hand edge of the aspen grove uphill and pass above it—traveling through the tangle of aspens is not a good idea.

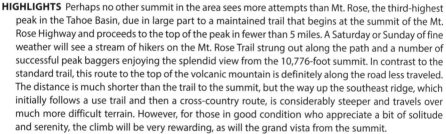

139 Southeast Ridge of Mt. Rose

Distance	5.4 miles (out-and-back)
Hiking Time	3–5 hours
Elevation	+3,350/-100 feet
Difficulty	Very difficult
Trail Use	Dogs OK
Best Times	Mid-July through early October
Agency	Humboldt-Toiyabe National Forest at 775-882-2766, www.fs.usda.gov/htnf
Recommended Map	USGS 7.5-minute *Mount Rose,* HTNF *Mount Rose Wilderness*

see map on p. 304

HIGHLIGHTS Perhaps no other summit in the area sees more attempts than Mt. Rose, the third-highest peak in the Tahoe Basin, due in large part to a maintained trail that begins at the summit of the Mt. Rose Highway and proceeds to the top of the peak in fewer than 5 miles. A Saturday or Sunday of fine weather will see a stream of hikers on the Mt. Rose Trail strung out along the path and a number of successful peak baggers enjoying the splendid view from the 10,776-foot summit. In contrast to the standard trail, this route to the top of the volcanic mountain is definitely along the road less traveled. The distance is much shorter than the trail to the summit, but the way up the southeast ridge, which initially follows a use trail and then a cross-country route, is considerably steeper and travels over much more difficult terrain. However, for those in good condition who appreciate a bit of solitude and serenity, the climb will be very rewarding, as will the grand vista from the summit.

DIRECTIONS Drive on the Mt. Rose Highway (NV 431) to a hairpin turn, 0.3 mile eastbound of the Sky Tavern Ski Area, opposite and slightly down from a highway maintenance building that's on the downhill side of the highway. From the hairpin turn, head briefly west on a dirt road and park among the trees as space allows.

FACILITIES/TRAILHEAD There are no facilities at the trailhead. The trail begins on an old road near a sign reading CLOSED TO MOTOR VEHICLES.

Proceed on a moderate climb up the old roadbed directly above Galena Creek through principally lodgepole-pine forest, with a smattering of white fir and aspen. Clumps of tobacco brush and a sprinkling of lupine make up the scattered ground cover, as you follow the path down to a crossing of Galena Creek, where a pair of logs provides an easy traverse of the tumbling waters. Head up the north bank of the creek on a singletrack use trail that climbs moderately steeply up the canyon. The path wanders away from the creek and up the hillside on a stiff climb through Jeffrey pines and scattered pinemat and greenleaf manzanita. Farther up the trail, the trees thin enough to allow fine views of the surrounding peaks and ridges, including Slide Mountain to the south.

The grade mercifully eases for a time, as you make a mild ascent over an aspen-lined drainage. Soon the path turns sharply uphill again across open slopes carpeted with sagebrush, tobacco brush, and an assortment of drought-tolerant wildflowers in early summer. Since many paths branch off through this section of thick shrubs, look for the route that seems to be the most direct and least overgrown—sometimes a challenging task. Wind up the nose of a ridge through the thick vegetation toward point 10005, as shown on the *Mount Rose* topo map.

A quarter mile of nearly flat terrain along the ridgecrest allows you to catch your breath before the final assault up the southeast ridge of Mt. Rose. A moderately steep climb over volcanic soils leads to the summit ridge, where gentler terrain can be followed to the true summit. If your trip coincides with a weekend, chances are good that you will have plenty of company at the top with hikers who have made the ascent via the maintained Mt. Rose Trail (see Trip 142). However, while you may have to share the summit with others, your party most likely will be the only one on the route described here.

Views from the summit are sublime in all directions. Sierra Buttes is the prominent peak to the north, although exceptionally clear skies will allow glimpses of the distant Cascade volcanoes of Lassen Peak and Mt. Shasta. The Tahoe Basin is stunningly revealed with the azure blue surface of Lake Tahoe reflecting a bounty of picturesque peaks, including Pyramid Peak and Mt. Tallac to the southwest and the Freel Peak group toward the south end of the Carson Range. The sprawling development of the Truckee Meadows is clearly seen to the northeast.

Peering over Galena Creek Canyon from the southeast ridge of Mt. Rose

140   Browns Creek Trail

see map on p. 308

Distance	4.9 miles (semiloop)
Hiking Time	2–4 hours
Elevation	+1,000/-1,000 feet
Difficulty	Moderate
Trail Use	Dogs OK (on leash first mile), mountain biking OK
Best Times	May through October
Agency	Washoe County Regional Parks and Open Space at 775-328-3600, washoecounty.us/parks
Recommended Map	Washoe County Truckee Meadows Trails

HIGHLIGHTS In spring, Browns Creek Trail offers hikers an opportunity to explore the lower forest of the Carson Range when the higher elevations may still be covered in snow. Early season also catches perennial Browns Creek and its seasonal south branch at peak flows, and offers the chance to enjoy the scattered wildflowers as well. At any time of the hiking season, the semiloop trail offers sweeping vistas that include Pleasant and Washoe Valleys backdropped by the Virginia Range. A trail branching away from the southernmost part of the loop provides access to forest service land for those interested in extending the hike.

DIRECTIONS From the I-580 off-ramp at Mt. Rose Highway (NV 431), head westbound 6 miles to a left-hand turn onto Joy Lake Road. Drive 1.5 miles to the trailhead parking area on the left side of the road.

FACILITIES/TRAILHEAD There are no facilities at the trailhead. The trail begins across the road from the parking area near a small sign.

Climb moderately away from the trailhead, switchbacking and wrapping around a hillside into the side canyon of a typically dry swale. A light forest of Jeffrey pine and mountain mahogany provides filtered sunlight for a scattered groundcover of bitterbrush and manzanita. As the steady climb continues, you cross a pair of old jeep roads before approaching the lip of the canyon near the first of two water tanks passed along the way. Near the second tank, the trail makes a switchbacking ascent and then winds across a broad ridge. Reach a junction at the far side of the crest, 1.25 miles from the trailhead, where a short lateral leads to a fine vista of the Virginia Range and Steamboat Hills, where a park bench and interpretive sign provide an opportunity to sit and enjoy the surroundings. If you're interested in a relatively short and easy hike, this vista is a good turnaround point.

Head away from the vista junction, drop off the ridge, and shortly reach another junction, this one with the loop portion of the trip, 1.3 miles from the trailhead.

Turn right at the junction and begin a counterclockwise loop around the drainage of Browns Creek. Initially, the trail descends across a dry, south-facing slope carpeted with shrubs, which permits good views up the gorge of Browns Creek toward Slide Mountain. Reach the floor of the canyon and follow the trail upstream briefly through riparian foliage to the crossing of the creek on a short wood bridge.

Beyond the crossing, the trail makes a gently rising, 0.4-mile traverse through Jeffrey-pine forest and a vibrant understory of manzanita below Peak 6450. At the end of the traverse, you round the nose of a ridge and continue toward the floor of a side canyon carrying a seasonal tributary of Browns Creek. Reach a signed junction, where the trail meets the stream, 0.6 mile from the bridge over the main branch. The trail continuing upstream passes through forest service land on the way to a dirt fire road, used primarily by mountain bikers. (Turning north on this road leads to a junction with singletrack trail climbing up the main channel of Browns Creek to the access road to the Slide side of Mt. Rose Ski Tahoe. Remaining on the fire road eventually leads north to the Mt. Rose Highway.)

Angle sharply left at the junction and descend along the north bank of the tributary for 0.6 mile, where two short-legged switchbacks lead back toward the main stem of Browns Creek. A pair of bridges provides easy crossings of the twin-channeled stream, and then the trail soon comes to an unmarked junction. While the path headed downstream crosses the private land of the upscale community of St. James Village, the

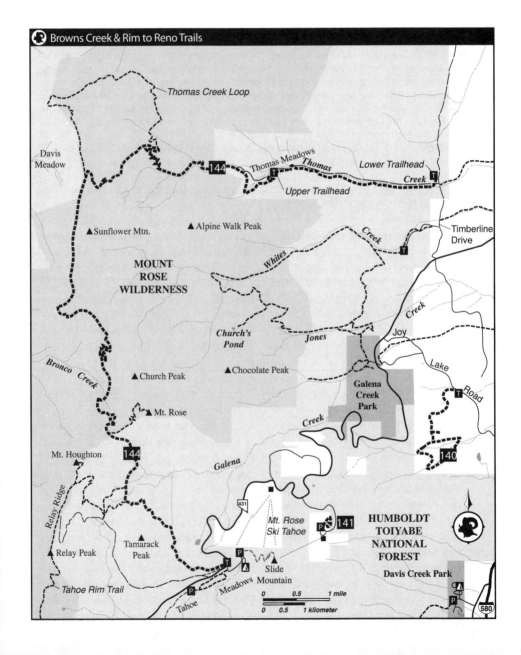

Browns Creek & Rim to Reno Trails

route of the Browns Creek Trail veers left and shortly begins a stiff climb back toward the loop junction. The trail follows an angling ascent across an open, sagebrush-covered slope with good views of the Browns Creek drainage and Slide Mountain above. Upon reaching the loop junction, retrace your steps 1.3 miles back to the trailhead.

141 Slide Mountain Trail

see map on p. 308

Distance	0.75 mile (partial loop)
Hiking Time	30 minutes
Elevation	+150/-150 feet
Difficulty	Easy to moderate
Trail Use	Dogs OK (leashed)
Best Times	Mid-June through mid-October
Agency	Humboldt Toiyabe National Forest at 775-882-2766, www.fs.usda.gov/htnf
Recommended Maps	USGS 7.5-minute *Mount Rose* (trail not shown)

HIGHLIGHTS Aside from the short climb up to the start of the loop section, the Slide Mountain Trail provides an easy jaunt around an unnamed peak with excellent views of the valleys below and Slide Mountain above. Early risers may be able to see hang gliders launching nearby into the usually calm air after first light.

DIRECTIONS From the I-580 off-ramp at Mt. Rose Highway (NV 431), head westbound toward Incline Village for 12.5 miles and turn left onto East Bowl Road (NV 878). Continue to the end of the road at the large ski-area parking lot.

FACILITIES/TRAILHEAD The trailhead has picnic tables. The trail begins near the northeast corner of the parking lot.

Leaving the parking lot, the trail makes an angling ascent across a lightly forested slope composed of Jeffrey pines, mountain mahoganies, western white pines, and white firs toward the north ridge of Peak 8448. At the ridge, the path turns south and continues the ascent to the loop junction. Along the way, a drier forest of principally mountain mahogany allows for good views of Washoe Valley and the Truckee Meadows backed by the Virginia Range.

Continue ahead from the junction and arc around the south and west slopes of the mountain. Well-placed interpretive signs and a park bench offer interesting tidbits of information about the area and a convenient place to sit and enjoy the fine vista, which includes the hulk of Slide Mountain and the ski runs of Mt. Rose Ski Tahoe. A short way beyond the bench is the close of the loop. From there, retrace your steps to the trailhead.

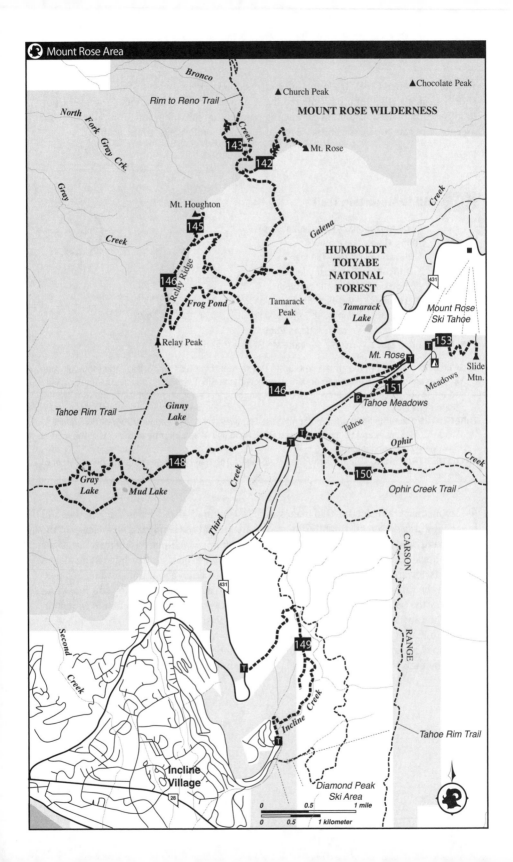

see map on p. 310

142 Mt. Rose

Distance	9.8 miles (out-and-back)
Hiking Time	5–6 hours
Elevation	+2,100/-325 feet
Difficulty	Difficult
Trail Use	Dogs OK
Best Times	Early July through mid-October
Agency	Humboldt-Toiyabe National Forest at 775-882-2766, www.fs.usda.gov/htnf
Recommended Map	USGS 7.5-minute *Mount Rose* (part of trail not shown), HTNF *Mount Rose Wilderness*

HIGHLIGHTS The route to the summit of Mt. Rose may be the most popular trail in the state of Nevada, as evidenced by the full trailhead parking lot on summer weekends. The attractions of this trip are many, including spectacular views of Lake Tahoe from the summit, a significant waterfall near the midpoint, a delightful display of wildflowers in the Galena Creek drainage, and a chance to scale the third-highest peak in the Tahoe Basin.

Although the trail is usually snow free in early July, mid-July to mid-August is the best time to view the wildflower display along Galena Creek. Generally, the trail stays open through October, but autumn days may see an inversion layer over the Truckee Meadows that produces a hazy vista of Reno–Sparks.

DIRECTIONS From Reno, take I-580 to the Mt. Rose Highway (NV 431) and travel southwest to the Mt. Rose Summit (8,911 feet) and the large trailhead parking lot on the right. From Incline Village, the parking area is 8 miles east of the NV 28–NV 431 junction.

FACILITIES/TRAILHEAD The large parking lot has a restroom building and interpretive signs at the southeast end. Signs clearly mark the beginning of the trail. The entrance to the Mt. Rose Campground is directly across the highway from the trailhead parking area.

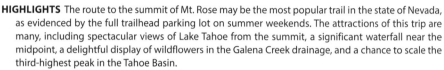

From the parking lot at Mt. Rose Summit, follow the trail on an ascending traverse above the Mt. Rose Highway across a sagebrush- and grass-covered hillside dotted with boulders and sprinkled with lodgepole and whitebark pines. Mule-ears and lupines add dashes of purple and yellow to the slopes in early to midsummer. As you continue the climb, the pines become even more widely scattered, allowing for fine views of the upper end of Tahoe Meadows below and Lake Tahoe to the southwest, rimmed on the far shore by towering peaks. Eventually, the trail veers away from the highway and enters light forest on the way to a saddle between Tamarack Peak on your left and Peak 9201 on your right.

Beyond the saddle, the gently rising trail slices across the eastern flank of Tamarack Peak, where mountain hemlocks begin to intermix with the pines. Gaps in the trees permit periodic glimpses of meadow-rimmed Tamarack Lake 400 feet below, and the reddish-gray, volcanic summit of Mt. Rose looming above the treetops.

Near the 1.5-mile mark, the climbing ends and a mild descent begins across the steep slopes on the northeast side of Tamarack Peak. After the crossing of a seasonal stream, proceed across a forested bench before continuing the descent across another steep hillside. Soon the pleasant sound of running water propels you onward toward a significant waterfall. Reach the floor of Galena Creek canyon at 2.3 miles from the trailhead and stand below this scenic gem, where multiple ribbons of water spill picturesquely down dark rock walls. Downstream, an expansive meadow, sprinkled with wildflowers in midsummer, provides a fine foreground view of the massive hulk of Mt. Rose. Immediately prior to the waterfall is a signed junction, where the Tahoe Rim Trail zigzags up the slope to the left of the fall.

Continuing ahead away from the fall, you cross the creek and skirt the base of a rock-strewn hill opposite a willow- and flower-lined creek bordered by a lush meadow to the right. A moderate climb leads away from the creek and meadow and winds uphill to the crossing of a small tributary stream. A short walk from the stream brings you to a junction with the older section of the Mt. Rose Trail, 2.5 miles from the trailhead.

From the junction, curve around and cross another tributary of Galena Creek, where an uninterrupted climb to the summit begins. During peak season, a lush assemblage of shrubs near the creek is mixed with a brilliant display of wildflowers, including lupine, paintbrush, angelica, larkspur, and mule-ears. Leaving this luxuriant patch of vegetation behind, the trail makes a moderate ascent of a dry hillside until turning into a narrow and steep side canyon. Climb this slender cleft, twice crossing the bed of a seasonal creek, to the wilderness boundary, 150 yards below a saddle southwest of Mt. Rose. A short climb from the boundary leads up to the saddle, where you reach a trail junction amid some weather-beaten whitebark pines, 3.6 miles from the trailhead. The trail straight ahead, the newly built Rim to Reno Trail, drops off the ridge into the Bronco Creek drainage (see Trips 143 and 144).

To reach the summit of Mt. Rose, turn right (east) and head through scattered whitebark pines along a narrow ridge toward the gray volcanic mass of Mt. Rose. At the end of the ridge, the grade increases and you begin the first of five switchbacks up the west slope of the peak, where views of the surrounding countryside improve with each step. From the switchbacks, the trail makes an ascending traverse around to the northwest side of the mountain, where low-growing alpine plants soon replace the stunted pines. Another series of switchbacks climbs up rocky slopes that keep the actual summit just out of view. As you approach what seems to be the top, one more set of three short switchbacks leads to the summit ridge, from where a short and easy jaunt leads to the top.

Various human-made improvements at the summit consist of a trail register and rock walls piled high to restrain the notorious winds that frequent the area. If you happen to arrive under calm conditions, count your blessings. Views are quite impressive in all directions. On extremely clear days, you can see north all the way to the Cascade volcanoes of Lassen Peak and Mt. Shasta. On normal days, Sierra Buttes are visible in that same general direction above and beyond the Little Truckee River reservoirs of Prosser, Boca, and Stampede. Lake Tahoe is the preeminent gem, encircled by an impressive ring of peaks, including Pyramid Peak and Mt. Tallac above the southwest shore, and Jobs Peak, Jobs Sister, and Freel Peak in the Carson Range. Reno–Sparks and the rest of the Truckee Meadows are clearly visible from the summit as well.

143 Bronco Creek

see map on p. 310

Distance	11 miles (out-and-back)
Hiking Time	5.5–6.5 hours
Elevation	+1,400/-1,500 feet
Difficulty	Moderate
Trail Use	Backpacking option, dogs OK
Best Times	Early July through mid-October
Agency	Humboldt-Toiyabe National Forest at 775-882-2766, www.fs.usda.gov/htnf
Recommended Map	USGS 7.5-minute *Mt. Rose* (part of trail not shown), HTNF *Mount Rose Wilderness*

HIGHLIGHTS Although the trail to Bronco Creek shares the route of the Mt. Rose Trail for the first 3.6 miles, the remainder is the antithesis to the much more heavily used trail to the summit, as described in the previous trip. If hundreds travel along the Mt. Rose Trail each summer weekend day, you may have to wait a decade or more to see that many souls along the path to Bronco Creek. Rather than excellent views from the summit of Mt. Rose, this trip offers excellent views of the summit from 2,000 feet below. Primitive campsites along Bronco Creek will lure backpackers in search of an overnight haven away from the crowds.

DIRECTIONS From Reno, take I-580 to the Mt. Rose Highway (NV 431) and travel southwest to the Mt. Rose Summit (8,911 feet) and the large trailhead parking lot on the right. From Incline Village, the parking area is 8 miles east of the NV 28–NV 431 junction.

FACILITIES/TRAILHEAD The large parking lot has a restroom building and interpretive signs at the southeast end. Signs clearly mark the beginning of the trail. The entrance to the Mt. Rose Campground is directly across the highway from the trailhead parking area.

From the parking lot at Mt. Rose Summit, follow the trail on an ascending traverse above the Mt. Rose Highway across a sagebrush- and grass-covered hillside dotted with boulders and sprinkled with lodgepole and whitebark pines. Mule-ears and lupines add dashes of purple and yellow to the slopes in early to midsummer. As you continue the climb, the pines become even more widely scattered, allowing for fine views of the upper end of Tahoe Meadows below and Lake Tahoe to the southwest, rimmed on the far shore by towering peaks. Eventually, the trail veers away from the highway and enters light forest on the way to a saddle between Tamarack Peak on your left and Peak 9201 on your right.

Beyond the saddle, the gently rising trail slices across the eastern flank of Tamarack Peak, where mountain hemlocks begin to intermix with the pines. Gaps in the trees permit periodic glimpses of meadow-rimmed Tamarack Lake, 400 feet below, and the reddish-gray, volcanic summit of Mt. Rose looming above the treetops.

Near the 1.5-mile mark, the climbing ends and a mild descent begins across the steep slopes on the northeast side of Tamarack Peak. After the crossing of a seasonal stream, proceed across a forested bench before continuing the descent across another steep hillside. Soon the pleasant sound of running water propels you onward toward a significant waterfall. Reach the floor of Galena Creek canyon at 2.3 miles from the trailhead and stand below this scenic gem, where multiple ribbons of water spill picturesquely down dark rock walls. Downstream, an expansive meadow, sprinkled with wildflowers in midsummer, provides a fine foreground view of the massive hulk of Mt. Rose. Immediately prior to the waterfall is a signed junction, where the Tahoe Rim Trail zigzags up the slope to the left of the fall.

Continuing ahead away from the fall, you cross the creek and skirt the base of a rock-strewn hill opposite a creek lined with willows and flowers, which is bordered by a lush meadow on the right. A moderate climb leads away from the creek and meadow and winds uphill to the crossing of a small tributary stream. A short walk from the stream brings you to a junction with the older section of the Mt. Rose Trail, 2.5 miles from the trailhead.

From the junction, curve around and cross another tributary of Galena Creek, where an uninterrupted climb to the summit begins. During peak season, a lush assemblage of shrubs near the creek is mixed with a brilliant display of wildflowers, including lupine, paintbrush, angelica, larkspur, and mule-ears. Leaving this luxuriant patch of vegetation behind, the trail makes a moderate ascent of a dry hillside until turning into a narrow and steep side canyon. Climb this slender cleft, twice crossing the bed of a seasonal creek, to the wilderness boundary, 150 yards below a saddle southwest of Mt. Rose. A short climb from the boundary leads up to the saddle, where you reach a trail junction amid some weather-beaten whitebark pines, 3.6 miles from the trailhead.

Continue straight ahead from the junction, dropping away from the saddle through open meadows alternating with stands of conifers. The trail switchbacks across nascent Bronco Creek a couple of times, which may be dry here in late season, before winding down the slope into light forest. The grade eventually eases and the trail heads across a perennial stretch of Bronco Creek, the only reliable source of water for the next several miles, and over to a forested flat, suitable for campsites.

Bronco Creek offers a good dose of solitude in the midst of a tremendous amount of activity nearby. Fewer than 10 miles away, gamblers are cavorting in North Shore casinos. Much closer, hundreds of weekenders may be struggling toward the summit of Mt. Rose along the much more popular Mt. Rose Trail. However, along Bronco Creek, your party should have the run of the basin, where the rock faces of Church Peak and Mt. Rose provide a dramatic backdrop to the verdant grasses of the green meadow. Opportunities for further exploration abound, including traveling farther north along the newly constructed Rim to Reno Trail (see Trip 144).

Galena Creek Meadows below Mt. Rose

see map on p. 308

144   Rim to Reno Trail

Distance	18 miles (point-to-point);
	20.8 miles to lower Thomas Creek Trailhead
Hiking Time	6–9 hours;
	7–10.5 hours to lower Thomas Creek Trailhead
Elevation	+2,250/-4,075 feet; +2,250/-5,200 feet to lower Thomas Creek Trailhead)
Difficulty	Difficult
Trail Use	Dogs OK (leashed first and last mile)
Best Times	Mid-July through early October
Agency	Humboldt Toiyabe National Forest at 775-882-2766, www.fs.usda.gov/htnf
Recommended Maps	USGS 7.5-minute *Mount Rose, Mt. Rose NW* (part of trail not shown);
	HTNF *Mount Rose Wilderness* (part of trail not shown);
	CVTA *Rim to Reno Regional Trail System*

HIGHLIGHTS One of the newer trails built by volunteers in association with the Tahoe Rim Trail Association, this challenging route offers an extended journey through a remote section of the Mt. Rose Wilderness. After following a section of the highly popular Mt. Rose and Tahoe Rim Trails, the route leaves the masses behind and dives into and climbs out of the Bronco Creek drainage before embarking on a long traverse across the west flank of the Carson Range, enjoying some fantastic views along the way. After gaining the crest, the trail drops into lush Thomas Creek Canyon and then follows the tumbling stream down to the upper and lower ending trailheads.

At 18 miles to the upper trailhead (high-clearance vehicle recommended), or nearly 21 to the lower trailhead, the distance alone should deter casual hikers from attempting this trip. Steep climbs to the Mt. Rose saddle, out of Bronco Creek, and up to the Carson Range crest above Thomas Creek Canyon add to the strenuous nature of the route. Providing an additional obstacle, the section between Bronco and Thomas Creeks is without water, requiring hikers to carry an adequate supply for several miles. Backpackers wishing to camp overnight will only find decent sites near Bronco Creek. However, for those up to the task, the scenic rewards and potential for solitude should be adequate compensation for the effort expended.

DIRECTIONS *Start:* From the I-580 off-ramp (Exit 56) at Mt. Rose Highway (NV 431), head southwest toward Incline Village for 15 miles to the Mt. Rose Summit (8,911 feet) and turn right into the Mt. Rose Trailhead parking lot. From Incline Village, the parking area is 8 miles northeast of the NV 28–NV 431 junction.

End: Upper Trailhead: (High-clearance vehicle recommended) From the I-580 off-ramp (Exit 56) at Mt. Rose Highway (NV 431), head westbound toward Incline Village for 2 miles and then turn right onto Timberline Drive. Proceed on Timberline, crossing a short bridge over Whites Creek and continue past where the pavement ends. Immediately after a second bridge over Thomas Creek, 1.1 miles from the highway, turn left onto Thomas Creek Road (FS 049). Proceed on dirt road for 2.2 miles to the top of a hill and a junction with gated, private roads accessing homes around Thomas Meadows. Veer left and drop down to a ford of Thomas Creek, and then follow rougher road another 0.3 mile to a closed steel gate. Park off the road as space allows.

Lower Trailhead: Without a vehicle with adequate clearance, you can park at the developed lower trailhead and begin the hike from there (however, doing so adds an extra 2.8 total miles to an already long trip). From the I-580 off-ramp (Exit 56) at Mt. Rose Highway (NV 431), head westbound toward Incline Village for 2 miles and then turn right onto Timberline Drive. Proceed on Timberline, crossing a short bridge over Whites Creek and continue past where the pavement ends. Proceed on Timberline across a second bridge over Thomas Creek and continue past Thomas Creek Road on the left to the Thomas Creek Trailhead parking area, 0.1 mile beyond Thomas Creek.

FACILITIES/TRAILHEAD The large parking lot at Mt. Rose Summit has a restroom building and interpretive signs at the southeast end. Signs clearly mark the beginning of the trail. The entrance to the Mt. Rose Campground is directly across the highway from the trailhead parking area.

There are no facilities at the upper Thomas Creek Trailhead. The trail ends to the left of the road near a trailhead sign.

The lower Thomas Creek Trailhead has vault toilets, equestrian facilities, picnic tables, and interpretive signs. The trail ends at a trailhead signboard near the southwest corner of the parking area.

From the parking lot at Mt. Rose Summit, follow dirt trail on an ascending traverse above the highway, across a sagebrush- and grass-covered hillside dotted with boulders and sprinkled with lodgepole and whitebark pines. Mule-ears and lupine add dashes of yellow and purple to the slopes from early to midsummer. As you continue the climb, the pines become even more widely scattered, which allows for fine views of the upper end of Tahoe Meadows and more distant Lake Tahoe rimmed by towering peaks. Eventually the trail veers away from above the highway and enters light forest on the way to a saddle between Tamarack Peak on your left and Peak 9201 on your right.

Beyond the saddle, the gently rising trail slices across the eastern flank of Tamarack Peak, where mountain hemlocks begin to intermix with the pines. Gaps in the forest permit periodic glimpses of meadow-rimmed Tamarack Lake, 400 feet below, and the reddish-gray volcanic summit of Mt. Rose looming above the treetops.

Near the 1.5-mile mark, the easy climbing ends and you begin a mild descent across steep slopes on the northeast side of Tamarack Peak. After the crossing of a usually dry seasonal swale, proceed across a forested bench before resuming the descent across another steep hillside. Soon the pleasant sound of running water propels you onward toward a waterfall. Reach the floor of Galena Creek Canyon and a junction between the Tahoe Rim Trail on the left and the Mt. Rose Trail ahead, 2.4 miles from the trailhead. A few steps away, you stand beneath the scenic gem of the waterfall, where multiple ribbons of crystal-clear water spill picturesquely down a wall of dark rock. Downstream, an expansive meadow provides a fine foreground view for the massive hulk of Mt. Rose.

Continuing ahead on the Mt. Rose Trail, you cross the creek below the waterfall and skirt the base of a rock-strewn hill, opposite a willow- and flower-lined creek and lush meadow to the right. Soon a moderate climb leads away from the creek, winding uphill to the crossing of a small tributary stream. A short walk from there leads to a junction with a jeep road, formerly a section of the old Mt. Rose Trail, 2.6 miles from the trailhead.

Veering right at the junction, you curve around to a crossing of another Galena Creek tributary, where a stiffer climb begins. During peak season, a brilliant wildflower display mixes with a lush assemblage of shrubs near the stream, where the variety of flowers includes angelica, columbine, larkspur, lupine, mule-ears, and paintbrush. Leaving the luxuriant vegetation behind, the tail climbs moderately across a dry hillside before turning into a narrow and steep side canyon. Climb steeply up the slender defile, crossing the seasonal stream twice on the way to the Mt. Rose Wilderness boundary. Amid some scattered, weather-beaten whitebark pines, you reach a junction in a broad saddle between Mt. Houghton on your left and Mt. Rose on your right, 3.8 miles from the trailhead.

Continue straight ahead from the junction, dropping away from the saddle through open meadows alternating with stands of conifers. The trail switchbacks across nascent Bronco Creek a couple of times, which may be dry here in late season, before winding down the slope into light forest. The grade eventually eases and the trail heads across a perennial stretch of Bronco Creek, the only reliable source of water for the next several miles, and over to a forested flat, suitable for campsites.

Beyond the flat, the trail arcs around the east side of the canyon and soon begins an extended, steady, switchbacking climb below steep, rocky cliffs to a bench directly east of Peak 9610. The long, stiff climb is eventually rewarded by fine views down the canyon of Bronco Creek and up to Church Peak and Mt. Houghton. The beautiful scenery continues for a while, as the trail follows a gentle, arcing traverse below Peak

10083 to a forested promontory, which offers occasional viewpoints of the surrounding terrain.

The trail curves around the fringe of the promontory before turning north and embarking on a 2-mile, gently graded romp through the trees below the peaks of the Carson Range, including 10,243-foot Sunflower Mountain. Although the views are limited along this stretch of trail, the nearly level grade of the trail makes for very easy hiking. Eventually, you reach a junction with the North Loop of the upper Thomas Creek Trail.

Turn right at the junction and follow the trail on a moderate, switchbacking, half-mile climb to a saddle on the crest of the range; at 9,780 feet, it's the high point of your journey. From the crest, a scramble along the ridge to the top of either Peak 9996 (north) or 9890 (south) offers superb views of the surrounding terrain for anyone with the requisite energy.

The trail drops rather steeply away from the crest into the Thomas Creek drainage (you'll more than likely be glad not to have climbed up this way), switchbacking down the steep hillside for nearly a mile before reaching a more pleasantly graded traverse across the upper canyon. The mile-long traverse eventually leads to the Thomas Creek Loop junction at 12.3 miles.

Proceed along the north ridge above the canyon shortly to the top of a series of switchbacks zigzagging down the open slope toward the creek below. Upon reaching the canyon floor, singletrack trail descends along the stream through aspens

and lush foliage for a while before veering away into Jeffrey pine forest and the crossing of a usually vigorous tributary. Returning to the vicinity of the creek, the trail merges with a section of the old Thomas Creek Road and continues to a crossing of the main branch of Thomas Creek. Back on singletrack, you climb away from the creek through a forest of Jeffrey pine, white fir, and mountain mahogany with occasional stands of aspen. Resuming the descent, you cross an old road and continue to a set of four switchbacks, which leads down the hillside to the upper parking area near a closed steel gate.

To lower trailhead: Without a vehicle at the upper trailhead or shuttle arrangements, you must continue down the Thomas Creek Trail, merging with the Thomas Creek Road and immediately reaching a ford of Thomas Creek after 0.3 mile. Boulder-hop over the main branch and a seasonal tributary, and then continue down Thomas Creek Road for approximately 150 yards to the resumption of singletrack trail. Proceed downstream for a while to another stretch where the narrowness of the canyon forces the trail to merge with a section of road again. Follow the road to where a sign marks the resumption of singletrack and continue to a junction with the Dry Pond Trail on the right. Proceed ahead from the junction, following the creek downstream for a little over a mile to where the route crosses over to the north bank. After a brief walk, you stroll across an informal parking area, cross Thomas Creek Road, and then follow a short section of trail to the lower trailhead.

see
map on
p. 310

145 Mt. Houghton

Distance	10.6 miles (loop)
Hiking Time	4–5 hours
Elevation	+1,800/-225 feet
Difficulty	Moderate
Trail Use	Dogs OK (leashed first and last mile)
Best Times	July through mid-October
Agency	Humboldt Toiyabe National Forest at 775-882-2766, www.fs.usda.gov/htnf
Recommended Maps	USGS 7.5-minute *Mt. Rose* (part of trail not shown),
	HTNF *Mount Rose Wilderness* (part of trail not shown)

HIGHLIGHTS A new section of trail offers an alternative to the popular route to the top of Mt. Rose, requiring about the same effort but with far fewer people. The first couple of miles share the same route to the waterfall on Galena Creek on the way toward Mt. Rose, but then this trip follows the Tahoe Rim Trail (TRT) to Relay Ridge. From there, a recently constructed 0.7-mile lateral makes a switchbacking climb along a ridge to the summit of Mt. Houghton and a wide-ranging view of the northern Sierra.

DIRECTIONS From the I-580 off-ramp (Exit 56) at Mt. Rose Highway (NV 431), head southwest toward Incline Village for 15 miles to the Mt. Rose Summit (8,911 feet) and turn right into the Mt. Rose Trailhead parking lot. From Incline Village, the parking area is 8 miles northeast of the NV 28–NV 431 junction.

FACILITIES/TRAILHEAD The large parking lot at Mt. Rose Summit has a restroom building and interpretive signs at the southeast end. Signs clearly mark the beginning of the trail. The entrance to the Mt. Rose Campground is directly across the highway from the trailhead parking area.

From the parking lot at Mt. Rose Summit, follow dirt trail on an ascending traverse above the highway, across a sagebrush- and grass-covered hillside dotted with boulders and sprinkled with lodgepole and whitebark pines. Mule-ears and lupine add dashes of yellow and purple to the slopes from early to midsummer. As you continue the climb, the pines become even more widely scattered, which allows for fine views of the upper end of Tahoe Meadows and more distant Lake Tahoe rimmed by towering peaks. Eventually the trail veers away from above the highway and enters light forest on the way to a saddle between Tamarack Peak on your left and Peak 9201 on your right.

Beyond the saddle, the gently rising trail slices across the eastern flank of Tamarack Peak, where mountain hemlocks begin to intermix with the pines. Gaps in the forest permit periodic glimpses of meadow-rimmed Tamarack Lake, 400 feet below, and the reddish-gray volcanic summit of Mt. Rose looming above the treetops.

Near the 1.5-mile mark, the easy climbing ends and you begin a mild descent across steep slopes on the northeast side of Tamarack Peak. After the crossing of a usually dry seasonal swale, proceed across a forested bench before resuming the descent across another steep hillside. Soon the pleasant sound of running water propels you onward toward a waterfall. Reach the floor of Galena Creek Canyon and a junction between the Tahoe Rim Trail on the left and the Mt. Rose Trail ahead, 2.4 miles from the trailhead. A few steps away, you can stand beneath the scenic gem of the waterfall, where multiple ribbons of crystal-clear water spill picturesquely down a wall of dark rock. Downstream, an expansive meadow provides a fine foreground view for the massive hulk of Mt. Rose.

Turn left onto the TRT and zigzag up the slope to the left of the waterfall, soon reaching the top of the fall and a fine view down the Galena Creek drainage. Continue climbing away from the waterfall through scattered forest to the crossing of an old jeep road. Before the construction of the new section of the Mt. Rose Trail in 2004, this rocky old road was part of the previous route to the summit.

Across the road, keep climbing through scattered lodgepole pines, passing below a power line and continuing up the slope. Farther above, whitebark pines replace the lodgepoles of below, heralding your entry into the upper elevations of the Mt. Rose Wilderness. Cross the wilderness boundary

at the top of the ridge, where you encounter a junction with the 0.7-mile lateral to 10,490-foot Mt. Houghton.

Turn right (north) and climb moderately along the south ridge of Mt. Houghton. A number of switchbacks leads you along the east and west sides and occasionally right on top of the ridge through dwarf whitebark pines. A final set of three short-legged switchbacks gets you to the top and a superb view.

146 Relay Peak Loop

Distance	10.7 miles (loop)
Hiking Time	4–6 hours
Elevation	+1,800/-1,800 feet
Difficulty	Moderate
Trail Use	Dogs OK (leashed first and last mile)
Best Times	July through mid-October
Agency	Humboldt Toiyabe National Forest at 775-882-2766, www.fs.usda.gov/htnf
Recommended Maps	USGS 7.5-minute *Mt. Rose* (part of trail not shown), HTNF *Mount Rose Wilderness* (part of trail not shown)

see map on p. 310

HIGHLIGHTS Similar to the more popular Mt. Rose Trail, this loop trip takes you to the top of one of the Tahoe Basin's highest peaks while enjoying a picturesque waterfall, wildflower displays, and fantastic views along the way. While not quite as high as Mt. Rose, Relay Peak at 10,338 feet is the highest point along the Tahoe Rim Trail (TRT) circuit around Lake Tahoe. By incorporating a descent along the Relay Ridge Road, a portion of which used to be the route of the Mt. Rose Trail, the trip can be done as a loop instead of an out-and-back hike.

DIRECTIONS From the I-580 off-ramp (Exit 56) at Mt. Rose Highway (NV 431), head southwest toward Incline Village for 15 miles to the Mt. Rose Summit (8,911 feet) and turn right into the Mt. Rose Trailhead parking lot. From Incline Village, the parking area is 8 miles northeast of the NV 28–NV 431 junction.

FACILITIES/TRAILHEAD The large parking lot at Mt. Rose Summit has a restroom building and interpretive signs at the southeast end. Signs clearly mark the beginning of the trail. The entrance to the Mt. Rose Campground is directly across the highway from the trailhead parking area.

From the parking lot at Mt. Rose Summit, follow dirt trail on an ascending traverse above the highway, across a sagebrush- and grass-covered hillside dotted with boulders and sprinkled with lodgepole and whitebark pines. Mule-ears and lupine add dashes of yellow and purple to the slopes from early to midsummer. As you continue the climb, the pines become even more widely scattered,

which allows for fine views of the upper end of Tahoe Meadows and more distant Lake Tahoe rimmed by towering peaks. Eventually the trail veers away from above the highway and enters light forest on the way to a saddle between Tamarack Peak on your left and Peak 9201 on your right.

Beyond the saddle, the gently rising trail slices across the eastern flank of Tamarack

Peak, where mountain hemlocks begin to intermix with the pines. Gaps in the forest permit periodic glimpses of meadow-rimmed Tamarack Lake, 400 feet below, and the reddish-gray volcanic summit of Mt. Rose looming above the treetops.

Near the 1.5-mile mark, the easy climbing ends and you begin a mild descent across steep slopes on the northeast side of Tamarack Peak. After the crossing of a usually dry seasonal swale, proceed across a forested bench before resuming the descent across another steep hillside. Soon the pleasant sound of running water propels you onward toward a waterfall. Reach the floor of Galena Creek Canyon and a junction between the Tahoe Rim Trail on the left and the Mt. Rose Trail ahead, 2.4 miles from the trailhead. A few steps away, you can stand beneath the scenic gem of the waterfall, where multiple ribbons of crystal-clear water spill picturesquely down a wall of dark rock. Downstream, an expansive meadow provides a fine foreground view for the massive hulk of Mt. Rose.

Turn left onto the TRT and zigzag up the slope to the left of the waterfall, soon reaching to top of the fall and a fine view down the Galena Creek drainage. Continue climbing away from the waterfall through scattered forest to the crossing of an old jeep road. Before the construction of the new section of the Mt. Rose Trail in 2004, this rocky old road was part of the previous route to the summit.

Across the road, keep climbing through scattered lodgepole pines, passing below a power line and continuing up the slope. Farther above, whitebark pines replace the lodgepoles of below, heralding your entry into the upper elevations of the Mt. Rose Wilderness. Cross the wilderness boundary at the top of the ridge, where you encounter a junction with the 0.7-mile lateral to 10,490-foot Mt. Houghton to the north.

Now on the west side of Relay Ridge, you follow an ascending traverse below the crest of Relay Ridge, which is littered with an array of communication towers and structures. Once past the man-made equipment, the trail returns to the crest of the ridge and reaches a junction with a very short lateral over to Relay Peak Road (your return route). From there, a moderate climb leads up the steep north ridge of Relay Peak to the 10,338-foot summit—the highest point on the Tahoe Rim Trail. The stunning vista includes a good portion of the Lake Tahoe Basin, Tahoe Meadows, and a piece of Washoe Lake through the gash of Ophir Creek canyon that is backdropped by a parade of distant ranges extending east into the Great Basin. The Sierra Buttes dominate the northern skyline, but on clear days, you may be able to make out Lassen Peak beyond, and on the clearest of days, Mt. Shasta. Unfortunately, the view is not all good, as immediately to the northwest are the results of the extensive Martis Fire of 2001, sparked by an illegal campfire at the hands of careless campers.

Retrace your steps back to the lateral junction to the Relay Peak Road and turn right, very soon reaching the well-graded surface of the service road. Follow the moderately descending road to a switchback and then continue northwest to the base of the old tramway, which used to ferry equipment to the top of Relay Ridge. From there, the road winds around past a spring and reaches the old Mt. Rose Trail junction near Frog Pond.

Continue down the old road into thicker lodgepole-pine forest above the Third Creek drainage. Eventually the road veers away from the creek and follows a descending traverse around the south flank of Tamarack Peak, where the trees part enough on occasion to permit fine views across verdant Tahoe Meadows to the deep blue waters of Lake Tahoe. Before the Relay Ridge Road reaches the Mt. Rose Highway, you come to a junction with a section of singletrack trail on the left. Leave the road and follow this trail 0.5 mile back to the trailhead parking lot.

147 TRT: Mt. Rose Trailhead to Brockway Summit

Distance	18 miles (point-to-point)
Hiking Time	9–11 hours
Elevation	+2,900/-4,850 feet
Difficulty	Difficult
Trail Use	Backpacking option, dogs OK
Best Times	July through mid-October
Agency	Humboldt-Toiyabe National Forest at 775-882-2766, www.fs.usda.gov/htnf; Lake Tahoe Basin Management Unit at 530-543-2600, www.fs.usda.gov/ltbmu
Recommended Maps	USGS 7.5-minute *Mount Rose, Martis Peak*

see map on p. 322

HIGHLIGHTS The section of the Tahoe Rim Trail (TRT) between Tahoe Meadows and Brockway Summit was the last link of the 164-mile trail to be completed before the official opening in 2002. Offering some of the route's finest views, as well as the trail's high point atop Relay Peak (10,338 feet), one wonders how we got along without this part of the trail for so long. The 18-mile distance at relatively high altitude is a difficult one-day hike, but a reasonable expectation of solitude in the middle section is a fine trade-off for those who are up to the task. Backpackers will find good campsites at Gray Lake, a half mile off the TRT near the midpoint of the trip. Wildflowers are at their peak from mid-July to mid-August, but the spectacular views are always in season during the usually snow-free months of July through mid-October.

DIRECTIONS *Start:* From Reno, take I-580 to the Mt. Rose Highway (NV 431) and travel southwest to the Mt. Rose Summit (8,911 feet) and the large trailhead parking lot on the right. From Incline Village, the parking area is 8 miles east of the NV 28–NV 431 junction.

End: From CA 28 in Kings Beach or I-80 near Truckee, proceed on CA 267 to the TRT parking area, a half mile south of Brockway Summit. A steep dirt road (FS 16N56) on the west side leads quickly up to a small parking area.

FACILITIES/TRAILHEAD The large parking lot has a restroom building and interpretive signs at the southeast end. Signs clearly mark the beginning of the trail. The entrance to the Mt. Rose Campground is directly across the highway from the trailhead parking area. There are no facilities at the destination trailhead.

From the parking lot at Mt. Rose Summit, follow the trail on an ascending traverse above the Mt. Rose Highway across a sagebrush- and grass-covered hillside dotted with boulders and sprinkled with lodgepole and whitebark pines. Mule-ears and lupines add dashes of yellow and purple to the slopes in early to midsummer. As you continue the climb, the pines become even more widely scattered, which allows for fine views of the upper end of Tahoe Meadows and Lake Tahoe rimmed on the far shore by towering peaks. Eventually, the trail veers away from the highway and enters light forest on the way to a saddle between Tamarack Peak on your left and Peak 9201 on your right.

Beyond the saddle, the gently rising trail slices across the eastern flank of Tamarack Peak, where mountain hemlocks begin to intermix with the pines. Gaps in the trees permit periodic glimpses of meadow-rimmed Tamarack Lake 400 feet below, and the reddish-gray, volcanic summit of Mt. Rose looming above the treetops.

Near the 1.5-mile mark, the climbing ends and you begin a mild descent across steep slopes on the northeast side of Tamarack Peak. After the crossing of a seasonal stream, proceed across a forested bench before continuing the descent across another steep hillside. Soon the pleasant sound of running water propels you onward toward a significant waterfall. Reach the

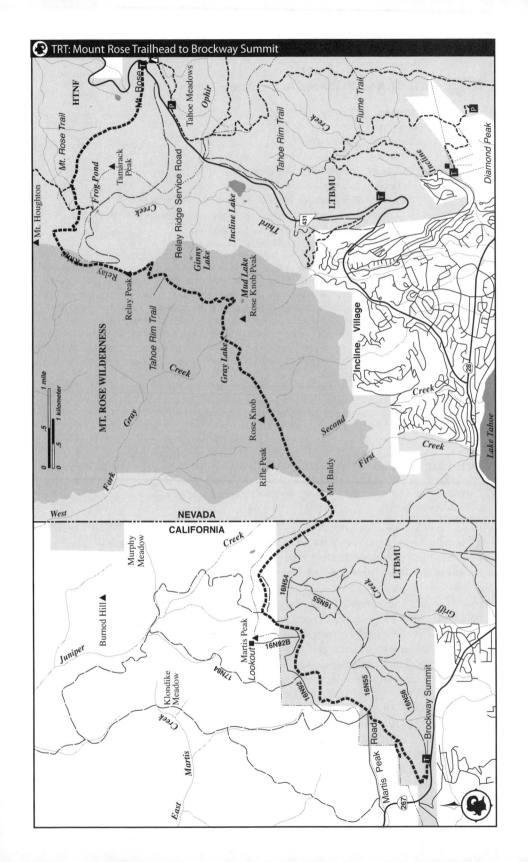

floor of Galena Creek Canyon at 2.3 miles from the trailhead and stand below this scenic gem, where multiple ribbons of water spill picturesquely down dark rock walls. Downstream, an expansive meadow provides a fine foreground view for the massive hulk of Mt. Rose. Immediately prior to the waterfall is a signed junction, where the Tahoe Rim Trail zigzags up the slope to the left of the fall.

Turn left onto the TRT and zigzag up the slope to the left of the waterfall, soon reaching the top of the fall and a fine view down the Galena Creek drainage. Continue climbing away from the waterfall through scattered forest to the crossing of an old jeep road. Before the construction of the new section of the Mt. Rose Trail in 2004, this rocky old road was part of the previous route to the summit.

Across the road, keep climbing through scattered lodgepole pines, passing below a power line and continuing up the slope. Farther above, whitebark pines replace the lodgepoles of below, heralding your entry into the upper elevations of the Mt. Rose Wilderness. Cross the wilderness boundary at the top of the ridge, where you encounter a junction with the 0.3-mile lateral to 10,490-foot Mt. Houghton to the north. Now on the west side of Relay Ridge, you follow an ascending traverse below the crest of Relay Ridge, which is littered with an array of communication towers and structures. Once past the man-made equipment, the trail returns to the crest of the ridge and reaches a junction with a very short lateral over to Relay Peak Road (your return route). From there, a moderate climb leads up the steep north ridge of Relay Peak to the 10,338-foot summit—the highest point on the Tahoe Rim Trail. The stunning vista includes a good portion of Lake Tahoe Basin, Tahoe Meadows, and a piece of Washoe Lake through the gash of Ophir Creek canyon that is backdropped by a parade of distant ranges extending east into the Great Basin. The Sierra Buttes dominate the northern skyline, but on clear days, you may be able to make out Lassen

Upper Galena Creek along the Mt. Rose Trail

Peak beyond, and on the clearest of days, Mt. Shasta. Unfortunately, the view is not all good, because immediately to the northwest you'll see the results of the extensive Martis Fire of 2001, sparked by an illegal campfire at the hands of careless campers.

Away from Relay Peak, you head down the crest of the ridge for a half mile, before a series of switchbacks leads down the southern flanks of the peak on a protracted descent toward a significant saddle, losing 800 vertical feet in the process. Along the way, you have excellent views of the Donner Summit region, the seldom-traveled terrain of the West Fork Gray Creek below, and, in the northwest, Boca, Prosser, and Stampede Reservoirs, as well as the distant, expansive plain of Sierra Valley.

More switchbacks lead to easier hiking as you approach the rocky flanks of Slab Cliffs. Nestled in the small basin below, at the head of a branch of Third Creek, is Ginny Lake, a pleasant-looking body of water only a quarter mile from the trail but virtually inaccessible without a steep, off-trail descent. Continuing, you pass through scattered conifers on a traverse across the rock outcroppings of Slab Cliffs, with more fine views as a nearly constant companion. Away from Slab Cliffs, a lone switchback drops you into the next saddle along the ridgecrest.

A series of short switchbacks leads down from the saddle to an unmarked junction with an unmaintained section of the old Western States Trail, where faint tread heads east to Incline Lake. Just downslope, a spring near a pocket of willows provides a reliable water source for much of the summer. Remaining on the TRT, you traverse the open hillside with exquisite views of Lake Tahoe and, in a quarter mile, come directly above aptly named Mud Lake. Without a natural inlet or outlet, the murky brown pond of Mud Lake stagnates in its basin, progressively shrinking over the course of the summer, disappearing altogether in drought years. Another quarter mile of gently graded trail brings you to yet another saddle along the crest, where nearby is a junction with a part of the old Western States Trail to Gray Lake, 7.5 miles from the Mt. Rose Highway.

Side Trip to Gray Lake: Unless you're in a big hurry to complete the trip, the half-mile descent to Gray Lake is a worthwhile endeavor, especially if you need a campsite. Leave the TRT and descend away from the ridge on a section of the old Western States Trail, initially through whitebark pines and mountain hemlocks. In the midst of the descent, you cross a small, flower-filled meadow and then continue to drop through a thicker forest of lodgepole pines. After hopping across the thin ribbon of a seasonal stream, you reach the floor of the small basin holding meadow-rimmed Gray Lake.

Gray Lake is a kidney-bean-shaped, shallow body of water surrounded by verdant meadows. In the natural evolution of lakes and meadows, the lake is destined to eventually become a part of Gray Meadow, as only a matter of time is necessary for silt and debris to fill the basin. On a human timetable, however, many years are left to enjoy this delightful lake. The sparkling, spring-fed water of the inlet flows down from above the lake along a rocky channel softened by rich, green moss and brilliant wildflowers. At the head of the canyon, the gray, volcanic rock of Rose Knob Peak forms a stark, contrasting background to the vibrant meadows. Over the years, numerous avalanches have swept down the side of Rose Knob Peak, delivering an ample supply of firewood to the slopes at the base of the peak.

To return to the TRT you could retrace your steps, but if Brockway Summit is your goal, you should ascend the moderately graded trail southwest from the lake to a connection with the TRT west of Rose Knob Peak, 1.2 miles from the first junction.

From the first junction to Gray Lake, the TRT skirts the east side of Rose Knob Peak, where excellent Tahoe views abound. You continue to traverse around the south side of the peak through scattered hemlocks and across talus-covered slopes before dropping to a saddle directly west of the peak, harboring a sprinkling of whitebark pines. Heading away from the saddle, traverse the ridgecrest over to the junction with the western branch of the old Western States Trail to Gray Lake, 8.9 miles from the highway.

The traverse continues across mostly open slopes, where proclaiming the excellent views starts to become redundant. Lake Tahoe glistens under the typically sunny Sierra skies, while Incline Village, the Diamond Peak Ski Area, and the Mt. Rose Highway all lie at your feet. Skirt the slopes below Rose Knob—if even grander views are desired, you can make the 300-foot climb to the top—and continue the traverse across hillsides carpeted with an extensive patch of mule-ears through midsummer. Passing below unnamed Peak 9499 and 9,271-foot Mt. Baldy, you reach the Mt. Rose Wilderness boundary amid scattered pines and then make a mild descent to an unceremonious crossing of the unsigned Nevada–California border.

A short, zigzagging descent follows the long, open traverse leading down to a rock knob, offering another grand lake view. A few switchbacks drop past some rock cliffs to a three-quarter-mile descending traverse of a northwest-trending ridge, with occasional vistas of Lake Tahoe and the mountainous terrain of the North Tahoe area. A scattered, mixed forest along the ridge begins to thicken toward the end of the traverse, where the trail leaves the ridge on a moderate descent to a saddle. From the saddle, a half mile of easy trail through open areas of rock alternating with stands of forest leads to a jeep road. The TRT follows the course of this jeep road for about 0.4 mile before singletrack trail resumes.

Side Trip to Martis Peak: For hikers interested in gaining the bird's-eye view from the lookout on Martis Peak, continue on the jeep road for 0.2 mile to a junction with the paved Martis Peak Road (FS 16N92B). (Hikers interested in shaving 4.5 miles off the total distance can arrange to be picked up here rather than at the TRT trailhead on CA 267.) Turn right and head uphill, following the paved road for 0.7 mile to the lookout, perched on a small flat, 0.1 mile northwest of the true summit. Along with the restored lookout, you'll find a picnic table and an outhouse. Thanks to the paved road, you also may find tourists as well. At one time, Martis Peak was the only staffed fire lookout in the Tahoe Basin.

Leave the jeep road and descend on the singletrack trail, quickly leaving the forest to break out into a sloping meadow carpeted with mule-ears. A short way beyond the meadow, you curve around the south ridge of Martis Peak and encounter a rocky viewpoint. Once again, the TRT hiker is blessed with a supreme vista of the Lake Tahoe Basin, including not only almost the entire lake, but the major summits surrounding the lake as well.

Tearing yourself away from the beautiful view, descend moderately back into scattered to light red fir forest, interrupted on occasion by another clearing filled with mule-ears and farther on by a patch of head-high tobacco brush. At 2.25 miles from the Brockway Summit Trailhead, you hop over a thin ribbon of water trickling down the hillside, where wildflowers, grasses, and clumps of willow add a splash of vegetation that contrasts vividly with the otherwise dry surroundings. Beyond the thin rivulet, milder trail wanders through selectively logged forest, followed by a more moderate descent that leads to the crossing of well-graded gravel FS 16N33, just 150 yards southeast of the junction with paved Martis Peak Road. After crossing the road, just over a half mile of easy hiking brings you to a junction with a spur trail to the top of Peak 7755.

Side Trip to Peak 7755: A mildly graded 0.3-mile ascent takes you through trees and shrubs, including chinquapin, tobacco brush, and huckleberry oak, up to a pile of rocks at the top of a hill. After the spectacular vistas previously encountered, this view seems fairly pedestrian. However, one last look at the lake may be warranted before you descend the last viewless mile of trail to the trailhead.

From the junction, 1.2 miles of hiking remain, as you follow the TRT on a moderate descent through a selectively logged forest of mainly white firs, mixed with a smattering of Jeffrey pines. As you near the Brockway Summit Trailhead, a trio of switchbacks leads down the hillside above CA 267, past the TRT signboard, and out FS 56 to the highway.

---

148   Incline Lake Trail to Gray Lake

see map on p. 310

Distance	8 miles (partial loop)
Hiking Time	3–4 hours
Elevation	+2,050/-2,050 feet
Difficulty	Moderate to strenuous
Trail Use	Dogs OK
Best Times	July through mid-October
Agency	Humboldt Toiyabe National Forest at 775-882-2766, www.fs.usda.gov/htnf
Recommended Maps	USGS 7.5-minute *Mount Rose*,
	HTNF *Mount Rose Wilderness* (trail not shown)

HIGHLIGHTS Formerly in the hands of private ownership, the property around what was once Incline Lake is now public land, including a section of trail climbing from the access road from the Mt. Rose Highway to a connection with the Tahoe Rim Trail (TRT). By incorporating a section of the TRT and the old Western States Trail, the route drops over the crest and heads down to a short loop around shallow but picturesque Gray Lake. Along the way are marvelous views of Lake Tahoe and the surrounding terrain. Depending on the amount of moisture that fell during the previous winter and spring, early-season hikers may have the added bonus of a fine wildflower display.

The dam responsible for the formation of Incline Lake recently failed and the Forest Service has decided not to replace the structure, allowing the area over time to return to its natural state.

DIRECTIONS Drive the Mt. Rose Highway (NV 431) to the southwest edge of Tahoe Meadows and the beginning of the Incline Lake Road, 1.5 miles from the highway summit. Park your vehicle on the shoulder as space allows—don't block the gate.

FACILITIES/TRAILHEAD There are no facilities at the trailhead. The trail begins past a locked gate on the continuation of the Incline Lake Road.

Head around the gate and follow dirt road on a descending route through a light forest of lodgepole pines. Proceed ahead at an unmarked junction with a path on the right and continue the descent, passing by small aspen groves and pockets of lush vegetation watered by some springs. Where the road makes a horseshoe bend, about 0.4 mile from the highway, an unmarked trail on the right-hand side veers away from the road to the southwest—this is your trail. You must pay close attention to this junction, as the unsigned path is easily missed. If you encounter a 15 MPH sign, you've gone too far down the road.

Descend briefly from the road to the crossing of a stream bordered by lush foliage. Just past the creek is another unmarked junction, where the trail on the left continues toward the former site of Incline Lake.

Follow the right-hand trail on a stiff climb up a hillside shaded initially by lodgepole pines but eventually by a mixed forest of western white pines, mountain hemlocks, and white firs. Mid-climb you cross over a rivulet and proceed to the signed Mt. Rose Wilderness boundary, 1.6 miles from the trailhead. Not too far from the boundary, the grade eases and the trees part along the crest of a ridge with a fine view of Lake Tahoe and some prominent Carson Range peaks, which include Slide Mountain, Mt. Rose, Mt. Houghton, Relay Peak, Slab Cliffs, and Rose Knob Peak. A brief and welcome descent leads to a junction with the Tahoe Rim Trail at 2 miles from the trailhead. Just downslope, a spring near a pocket of willows provides a reliable water source for much of the summer.

Veer to the left and climb gently along the TRT, enjoying splendid views and splashes of vibrant yellow from a preponderance of mule-ears carpeting the mostly open slopes. The trail bends into a basin holding Mud Lake below. Without a natural inlet or outlet, the murky brown pond stagnates in its own basin, progressively shrinking over the course of the summer, disappearing altogether in drought years. Near this body of water, you come to a saddle and the east junction of the Gray Lake Trail at a 4-by-4-inch post.

Leave the TRT and descend away from the ridge on a section of the old Western States Trail, initially through whitebark pines and mountain hemlocks. In the midst of the descent, you cross a small, flower-filled meadow and then continue to drop through a thicker forest of lodgepole pines. After hopping across the thin ribbon of a

Gray Lake

seasonal stream, you reach a junction with the loop trail near the floor of the small basin holding meadow-rimmed Gray Lake, 3.4 miles from the trailhead.

Gray Lake is a kidney-bean-shaped shallow body of water surrounded by verdant meadows. In the natural evolution of lakes and meadows, the lake is destined to eventually become a part of Gray Meadow, as only a matter of time is necessary for silt and debris to fill the basin. On a human timetable, however, many years are left to enjoy this delightful lake. The sparkling, spring-fed water of the inlet flows down from above the lake along a rocky channel softened by rich, green moss and brilliant wildflowers. At the head of the canyon, the gray, volcanic rock of Rose Knob Peak forms a stark, contrasting background to the vibrant meadows. Over the years, numerous avalanches have swept down the side of Rose Knob Peak, delivering an ample supply of firewood to the slopes at the base of the peak.

At the loop junction, veer right and follow the trail through lodgepole-pine forest to the far end. Near the crossing of Gray Creek are a few, seemingly little-used, campsites. Continue around the lake to the next junction, also marked by a 4-by-4-inch post, where the right-hand trail begins the climb up to the west junction of the TRT.

The moderately graded trail ascends a mostly forested slope southwest away from Gray Lake. The trail weaves through the trees on the way to another saddle on the ridge crest and the west Gray Lake junction with the TRT, 0.6 mile from the lake. Here you have more stunning views of the Lake Tahoe Basin.

Turn left and follow gently rising tread across the south slope of Rose Knob Peak, followed by an up-and-down section of trail on the way back to the east Gray Lake junction. From there, retrace your steps to the trailhead.

149 Incline Flume Trail: Mt. Rose Highway to Diamond Peak

Distance	3 miles (point-to-point)
Hiking Time	1.5 hours
Elevation	+100/-950 feet
Difficulty	Moderate
Trail Use	Dogs OK, mountain biking OK
Best Times	June through October
Agency	Humboldt Toiyabe National Forest at 775-882-2766, www.fs.usda.gov/htnf
Recommended Map	USGS 7.5-minute *Mount Rose* (trail not shown), HTNF *Mount Rose Wilderness* (trail not shown)

see map on p. 310

HIGHLIGHTS During the last half of the 19th century, the slopes of the Tahoe Basin were almost completely denuded of timber, primarily to provide lumber for the mines of the Comstock Lode and the town of Virginia City. Consequently, the trees that visitors see around the lake nowadays are almost always second-growth timber. While understanding that the forest around Lake Tahoe was the principal source of lumber for the region seems straightforward, the delivery system of that lumber to the Comstock, two mountain ranges and an intervening valley away, isn't quite as obvious.

Around 1880, an incline railroad was completed from the site of a sawmill on Mill Creek (near present-day Incline Village) to transport lumber 1,400 vertical feet up the steep mountainside to the banks of Third Creek. From there, the logs were sent several miles by flume to a tunnel beneath the crest of the Carson Range, which had been built to deliver water from Marlette Lake to Virginia City after a fire had destroyed a sizable portion of the town. A section of flume was built inside the tunnel, above the level of the water, to carry the lumber through the tunnel and into another open flume that transported it down to the community of Lakeview, at the south end of Washoe Valley. The Virginia and Truckee Railroad picked up the lumber from there, delivering the precious commodity to markets in Carson City as well as Virginia City.

For 21st-century recreationists, this shuttle trip follows a portion of the historic Incline flume trail to Incline Creek, and then down the creek to Diamond Peak Ski Area. Along the way, a short lateral provides a fine view of Lake Tahoe.

A short section of the historic Incline flume trail on the opposite side of the Mt. Rose Highway travels to the flume's origin at Third Creek, passing above the community of Incline Village. This section of the flume trail seems to be infrequently used in comparison to the described section east of the highway.

DIRECTIONS *Start:* Drive the Mt. Rose Highway (NV 431) to a wide shoulder on the west side, a half mile north of a roadside viewpoint above Incline Village.

End: Follow the Mt. Rose Highway toward Lake Tahoe and turn left (south) onto Country Club Drive (opposite the fire station). Proceed 2.1 miles, turn left at Ski Way, and drive toward Diamond Peak Ski Area. Park your vehicle in the lower parking area, outside of the area that is closed by a gate at 4 p.m.

FACILITIES/TRAILHEAD There are no facilities near the trailhead. The unmarked trail begins on a dirt road on the east side of the highway.

View from the Incline Flume Trail

Briefly follow a dirt road that quickly narrows to the width of singletrack trail and proceed on the gently graded course of the old flume through a mixed forest of Jeffrey pines and white firs. Gaps in the trees allow brief, partial views of Lake Tahoe across dry slopes covered with tobacco brush, currant, and chinquapin and sprinkled with patches of yellow mule-ears in early summer. Following the contour of the topography, swing north into the canyon of Incline Creek and reach a junction with a trail on the left that makes a serpentine climb up the hillside to a connection with the old Mt. Rose Road—a route well suited for mountain bikes. Veer right at the junction, as the trail forsakes the course of the flume and makes a brief descent to a crossing of Incline Creek on a short 2-by-6-foot bridge. Continue past the creek a very short distance to a clearing and a second junction, 1.2 miles from the highway.

Turn right (south) at the junction and head downstream a short way to cross back over the creek on another 2-by-6-foot bridge, where a fine display of lush foliage lines the sprightly stream, including grasses, willows, and corn lilies. Mildly graded trail leads away from the creek, which tumbles down a steep canyon to the east, and around lightly forested hillsides with partial views of the lake. At 1.75 miles, reach a junction with a 0.4-mile lateral to a viewpoint at the end of a ridge. Unless you're in a hurry, you should take the time to make the trip to the viewpoint and take in the fine view of Lake Tahoe. Once at the end of the ridge, you will have to drop down a bit to achieve an unobstructed vista.

From the viewpoint junction, the trail descends more steeply toward the roar of Incline Creek, coming directly above the lip of the canyon momentarily before quickly veering away. Farther on, a series of short switchbacks returns you alongside the tumbling, alder-choked creek, which is followed for the next half mile toward Incline Village. Where the rooftops of some of the homes come into view, the trail veers west and heads away from the main channel of the creek, soon crossing a 2-by-6-foot bridge over the smaller west fork. Follow this fork downstream on singletrack past the backside of several homes for a quarter mile to the end of trail at Tirol Drive.

To reach your shuttle vehicle, walk down Tirol Drive a quarter mile to the intersection of Ski Way and then follow Ski Way a short distance up to the parking area.

150 Upper Tahoe Meadows Nature Trail Loops

Distance	1.3 miles (semiloop)
Hiking Time	45 minutes
Elevation	Negligible
Difficulty	Easy
Trail Use	Good for kids, leashed dogs
Best Times	June through October
Agency	Humboldt-Toiyabe National Forest at 775-882-2766, www.fs.usda.gov/htnf
Recommended Map	USGS 7.5-minute *Mount Rose* (trail not shown), HTNF *Mount Rose Wilderness* (trail not shown)

see map on p. 310

HIGHLIGHTS The Tahoe Meadows Whole Access Trail is a wheelchair-accessible trail providing a fine opportunity to experience a part of verdant, subalpine Tahoe Meadows. Not only will the wheelchair-bound enjoy this loop, but families with small children will appreciate the wide, gently graded, 1.3-mile long path as well. The trail loops around the northeast finger of 8,700-foot Tahoe Meadows, exposing hikers to a lush meadowland environment full of plants, wildflowers, and trickling streams, bordered by a light forest of lodgepole pines. Slide Mountain and Mt. Rose provide a fine backdrop to the scenery-rich meadows.

Snow usually clears out of Tahoe Meadows by the end of June, allowing vivid wildflower displays from mid-July through August. Without the flowers, the hiking season still continues until the first significant snowfall, usually in early November.

DIRECTIONS Follow the Mt. Rose Highway (NV 431) to the Tahoe Rim Trail Trailhead parking lot on the south side of the highway, 0.7 mile west of Mt. Rose Summit (8,911 feet). From Incline Village, the parking area is about 7.3 miles east of the NV 28–NV 431 junction.

FACILITIES/TRAILHEAD The parking area has restrooms with running water. The nature trail is well signed.

From the parking lot, head east on a wide, rock-lined path for 0.1 mile to a junction. Pedestrians are encouraged to turn right at the junction, following a counterclockwise loop around the northeast finger of Tahoe Meadows. Proceed across a long wooden bridge over a marshy stretch of ground to the far edge of the meadow and then veer northeast along the fringe, passing in and out of shady stands of lodgepole pines. Around the east edge of the meadow, a series of short wooden bridges takes you across marshy areas and gurgling tributaries of Ophir Creek.

As the loop bends back around toward the trailhead, a short lateral leads onto a low hummock of granite, from where there was once a fine view of the sprawling meadow. However, since the trail was built, the surrounding forest has matured and obscured most of the view. Immediately beyond the lateral is a junction with the Tahoe Rim Trail heading northeast toward the Mt. Rose Campground access road. Turn left at the junction and follow the course of an abandoned road along the north fringe of the meadow to the junction. From there, make the easy climb back to the parking lot.

151 Lower Tahoe Meadows Nature Trail Loops

see map on p. 310

Distance	3.3 miles (loop); shorter options possible
Hiking Time	1.5–2 hours
Elevation	+300/-300 feet
Difficulty	Easy
Trail Use	Good for kids, leashed dogs
Best Time	Mid-June to mid-October
Agency	Humboldt Toiyabe National Forest at 775-882-2766, www.fs.usda.gov/htnf
Recommended Maps	USGS 7.5-minute *Mount Rose* (trail not shown), HTNF *Mount Rose Wilderness* (trail not shown)

HIGHLIGHTS Recently, the Forest Service wisely added this loop to the area's trail network, as scores of people would traipse across the fragile meadows during the summer to enjoy the colorful wildflowers, causing a significant amount of environmental damage to this sensitive meadowland. By building a lengthy stretch of boardwalk, the Forest Service ensured that visitors can still enjoy the beautiful flowers along Ophir Creek without harming the ecosystem. The first half of the 3.3-mile loop closely follows Ophir Creek through the meadows, while the second half moves into the forest and follows the Ophir Creek Trail and a short section of the Tahoe Rim Trail back to the trailhead. In addition to the trip described below, 1-mile and 2-mile loops provide options for walkers desiring shorter trips.

DIRECTIONS Drive the Mt. Rose Highway (NV 431) to the southwest end of Tahoe Meadows and park along the shoulder of the road as space allows.

FACILITIES/TRAILHEAD There are no facilities at the trailhead. The trail begins along the shoulder of the highway near a sign marked STAIRS.

Descend the stairs below the highway and follow a dirt path across the verdant vegetation of Tahoe Meadows to the start of a boardwalk near Ophir Creek that snakes across the lower end of the expansive meadows. Reach a junction and continue ahead on the boardwalk, soon passing by a park bench on a wide section of boardwalk perched above the creek. The serpentine boardwalk parallels the similarly winding stream on the way to a four-way junction at 0.2 mile with the Tahoe Rim Trail (TRT) marked by a sign and map.

Proceed ahead, remaining on the boardwalk along the course of Ophir Creek. Eventually the boardwalk bends to the right, crosses the creek, comes to an interpretive sign, and ends at the Upper Loop junction, 0.4 mile from the trailhead.

Veer left at the junction following the shared course of the Middle Loop and Lower Loop trails. Away from the boardwalk, dirt tread moves just above the meadows and wanders through scattered lodgepole-pine forest. After a short section of boardwalk over a sensitive area and the crossing of a seasonal stream, you reach the Middle Loop junction at 1 mile.

Continue straight ahead at the junction above the narrowing strip of Tahoe Meadows near the head of Ophir Creek canyon, where the rate of descent increases and the forest thickens. Where the creek plunges even more steeply down the canyon and you reach the low point of the loop, the trail bends to the south and begins the ascent back to the trailhead. Gaps in the trees allow glimpses of Slide Mountain rising above Ophir Creek canyon. Cross a tributary and proceed to a junction with the Ophir Creek Trail, 1.7 miles from the trailhead.

Turn right (west) at the junction and follow the wide track of an old road that now serves as the route of the Ophir Creek Trail through a mixed forest of Jeffrey pines, white firs, mountain hemlocks, and western white pines. Reach the Middle Loop junction at 2 miles.

Continue climbing westbound on the Ophir Creek Trail. After about 0.3 mile, the trail begins a quarter-mile descent through predominantly lodgepole-pine forest. After the grade eases, you pass the Ophir Creek Trail signboard and soon come to the Y-junction with the Tahoe Rim Trail angling back to the left.

Follow the shared route of the TRT and Ophir Creek trails ahead, breaking out of the trees and coming back alongside the fringe of Tahoe Meadows. Soon you reach the next junction at 3 miles, where the path ahead provides mountain bikers with direct access to the Mt. Rose Highway. Take the right-hand path and wind around toward the bridge over Ophir Creek and the boardwalk beyond. Just before the bridge, turn left and follow the dirt tread of single-track trail toward the highway. Just prior to reaching the road, you cross a short bridge spanning Ophir Creek and then climb the stairs up to the highway shoulder.

152 TRT: Tahoe Meadows to Twin Lakes

see map on p. 334

Distance	19 miles (out-and-back)
Hiking Time	9.5–10.5 hours
Elevation	+1,325/-2,200 feet
Difficulty	Difficult
Trail Use	Backpacking option, dogs OK, mountain biking OK (even days only)
Best Times	June through October
Agency	Humboldt-Toiyabe National Forest at 775-882-2766, www.fs.usda.gov/htnf; Lake Tahoe Basin Management Unit at 530-543-2600, www.fs.usda.gov/ltbmu
Recommended Maps	USGS 7.5-minute *Mount Rose, Marlette Lake* (trail not shown); HTNF *Mount Rose Wilderness*
Notes	Mountain bikes are allowed to use the Tahoe Rim Trail (TRT) from Tahoe Meadows to Tunnel Creek Road on even-numbered days only. Camping is limited to two designated sites inside Lake Tahoe Nevada State Park: Marlette Peak Campground, 13 miles south of the trailhead, and North Canyon Campground, 1.3 miles west of the TRT.

HIGHLIGHTS Much of this section of the TRT closely follows the crest of the Carson Range, affording travelers excellent views of the Lake Tahoe Basin to the west and the Great Basin to the east. Aside from a moderate climb from Tahoe Meadows, most of the trail follows an easy grade to Twin Lakes, a pair of shallow ponds that shrink considerably over the course of the average summer. Even considering the pleasantly graded trail, the 19-mile round-trip distance makes this a trip for hikers in good condition only. Backpackers attempting the 23-mile segment of the TRT from Tahoe Meadows to Spooner Summit should be forewarned that water is at a premium along the entire route. Lesser mortals can pick shorter turnaround points and still be more than satisfied with the superb vistas en route. Although the vast majority of trail passes across sandy soil ill suited for wildflowers, the initial segment across Tahoe Meadows is an amateur botanist's delight, with midsummer being the best time to view the blossoms.

DIRECTIONS Follow the Mt. Rose Highway (NV 431) to the Tahoe Rim Trail Trailhead parking lot on the south side of the highway, 0.7 mile west of Mt. Rose Summit (8,911 feet). From Incline Village, the parking area is about 7.3 miles east of the NV 28–NV 431 junction.

FACILITIES/TRAILHEAD The parking area has restrooms with running water. The start of the TRT is well signed at the west end of the parking lot.

Leave the TRT parking area and parallel the Mt. Rose Highway as you head southwest along the fringe of verdant Tahoe Meadows, stepping across several seeps along the way. Approaching a stand of lodgepole pines near the far end of the meadows, the trail veers south across the wildflower-carpeted meadowlands to a short wood bridge over gurgling Ophir Creek and a junction with the Lower Tahoe Meadows Nature Trail Loops. Depending on the season, you may see the blooms of buttercup, penstemon, marsh marigold, shooting star, and elephant head among the many species of wildflower that live near

the creek. Remaining on the trail to avoid damaging the sensitive flora, you continue across the meadows and into the pines, soon meeting a use trail to the Mt. Rose Highway. A short distance farther, veer right (south) at a signed Y-junction with the Ophir Creek Trail, 0.8 mile from the trailhead.

From the junction, you follow the TRT on a moderate climb of a forested hillside to a partial view of Lake Tahoe near the crest. Step across an old dirt road and begin a traverse of the sparsely forested slopes above the Incline Creek watershed, arcing southeast and then east around Peak

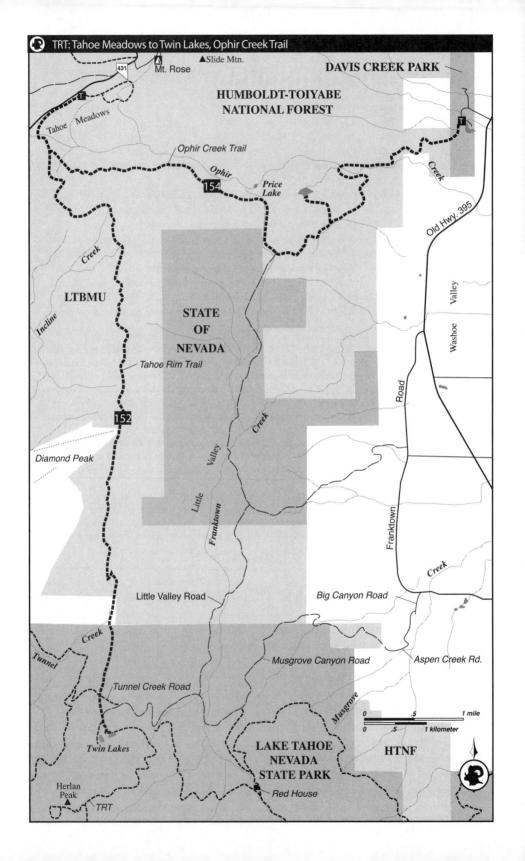

▲Slide Mtn.

Mt. Rose

DAVIS CREEK PARK

**HUMBOLDT-TOIYABE
NATIONAL FOREST**

Tahoe Meadows

Ophir Creek Trail

Ophir

154

Price
Lake

Creek

Old Hwy. 395

Creek

LTBMU

Incline

**STATE
OF
NEVADA**

Valley

Washoe

Road

Tahoe Rim Trail

152

Creek

Diamond Peak

Little

Valley

Franktown

Franktown

Creek

Little Valley Road

Big Canyon Road

Creek

Tunnel

Musgrove Canyon Road

Aspen Creek Rd.

Tunnel Creek Road

Musgrove

0   .5   1 mile

0   .5   1 kilometer

Twin Lakes

**LAKE TAHOE
NEVADA
STATE PARK**

HTNF

Herlan
Peak ▲

TRT

Red House

Sign in Tahoe Meadows

8996. Scattered western white pines allow periodic views across the lake to the peaks and ridges lining the Sierra crest and additional Tahoe landmarks around the near shore. Where the sandy trail turns south again, approximately 3 miles from the trailhead, you encounter a pair of tiny rivulets, nascent tributaries of Incline Creek. These rivulets, lined with willows, wildflowers, and young aspens, may provide the only water source along the TRT between Ophir Creek and Twin Lakes; although, late in the season of dry years, both the rivulets and the lakes could be dry.

Continue traversing along the west side of the ridge below the north-south apex of the Carson Range through sparse forest, which now includes mountain hemlocks. On a pair of switchbacks, follow descending trail to a prominent saddle north of Peak 8777. Just beyond the saddle, the trail crosses to the east side of the ridge and you have your first views of Washoe Lake, Carson Valley, and the Virginia Range.

Follow the narrow ridgecrest with alternating views to the east and west. Near the 5-mile mark, you encounter an excellent viewpoint just off the trail, where flat-topped granite boulders provide a fine perch for enjoying the Tahoe view. Away from the vista point, the trail follows the east side of the ridge into a thicker forest of western white pines and red firs. Several signs and the top of a ski lift herald your

arrival at another saddle, 5.7 miles from the trailhead, overlooking the Diamond Peak Ski Resort between Peaks 8538 and 8510.

Leaving the saddle behind, the trail follows the west side of the ridge through scattered Jeffrey pines. In between the pines, you have more excellent views of Lake Tahoe, as well as ski runs on Diamond Peak, Incline Village below, and the long ridge between Mt. Baldy and Relay Peak to the north. About 1 mile from the saddle, the trail once again crosses to the east side of the ridge and proceeds through fir forest. A little more than a mile farther, begin a moderate descent with good views to the east. Eventually, the path returns to the west side of the ridge, offering a few more lake views before entering a thick forest of red and white firs. You follow a mildly undulating trail through the trees to a well-signed junction at Tunnel Creek Road, 9.2 miles from the trailhead.

Head across the road and continue along the mildly graded TRT through a scattered forest of western white pines, red and white firs, and lodgepole pines, with an understory of pinemat manzanita. At 0.3 mile from the road, reach the eastern Twin Lake in a broad shallow bowl, rimmed by forested hills. Twin Lakes are within Lake Tahoe Nevada State Park, which allows camping only at designated campsites, the closest one being more than 4 miles away at Marlette Peak Campground.

153   Slide Mountain Summit

see map on p. 310

Distance	2.5 miles (out-and-back)
Hiking Time	1.5–2 hours
Elevation	+700 feet
Difficulty	Difficult
Trail Use	Dogs OK, mountain biking OK
Best Times	July through mid-October
Agency	Humboldt-Toiyabe National Forest at 775-882-2766, www.fs.usda.gov/htnf
Recommended Map	USGS 7.5-minute *Mount Rose* (trail not shown), HTNF *Mount Rose Wilderness* (trail not shown)

HIGHLIGHTS Ignoring the jumble of communication towers and ski-area equipment that litters the summit of Slide Mountain, hikers can have a similar view to the one from the top of nearby Mt. Rose with a fraction of the effort. From the Mt. Rose Campground, a closed service road, open to hikers, bikers, and equestrians, makes a 1.25-mile-long winding climb to the summit ridge. The 360-degree vista includes a number of significant landmarks, including the Lake Tahoe Basin, Truckee Meadows, Washoe and Eagle Valleys, and the Virginia Range. Perhaps the grandest view is that of neighboring Mt. Rose, which seemingly appears to be just a stone's throw away.

DIRECTIONS Follow the Mt. Rose Highway (NV 431) to the Mt. Rose Summit (8,911 feet) and the entrance to the Forest Service's Mt. Rose Campground on the east side of the highway (8 miles east of the NV 28–NV 431 junction in Incline Village). Follow the road past the campground to a turnaround, where a closed steel gate bars further access. Park your vehicle as space allows.

FACILITIES/TRAILHEAD The Mt. Rose Campground offers improved campsites, running water, and vault toilets. The trail follows a closed service road, signed SPECIAL SERVICE ROAD, CLOSED TO MOTORIZED USE EXCEPT BY PERMIT.

Begin climbing on the closed road through widely scattered conifers, including western white pines, mountain hemlocks, and lodgepole pines. The scattered trees allow good views of the reddish-brown volcanic rock profile of Mt. Rose to the northwest. Veer right at a Y-junction, where the left-hand road accesses equipment of the Mt. Rose Ski Area. Continue the moderate climb on a rising traverse of sandy slopes that seem unable to nourish any significant ground cover. Soon the road adopts a switchbacking course up the mountainside with improving views of the surrounding terrain.

A variety of towers, antennas, small buildings, and chairlifts greets you at the summit ridge, where views open up to the east of the Truckee Meadows and Pleasant Valley, backdropped by peaks of the Virginia Range. The road ends just below the high point, requiring a short scramble over some boulders in order to reach the actual summit of Slide Mountain. As you gain the high point, the views expand southward to Eagle Valley and to additional summits along the Carson Range, including Snow Valley Peak, South Camp Peak, Genoa Peak, and the Freel Peak group. Across Lake Tahoe, keen eyes will locate Fallen Leaf Lake and Emerald Bay, as Mt. Tallac and peaks of the Crystal Range dominate the horizon to the southwest. Closer at hand, Mt. Rose and neighboring peaks provide a dramatic scene.

154 Ophir Creek Trail

see map on p. 334

Distance	8.1 miles (point-to-point)
Hiking Time	4–5 hours
Elevation	+3,875/-350 feet
Difficulty	Difficult
Trail Use	Backpacking option, dogs OK, mountain biking OK
Best Times	July through mid-October
Agency	Humboldt-Toiyabe National Forest at 775-882-2766, www.fs.usda.gov/htnf
Recommended Map	USGS 7.5-minute *Washoe City, Mount Rose,* HTNF *Mount Rose Wilderness*

HIGHLIGHTS Although the Ophir Creek Trail does not enjoy wilderness protection from the nearby Mt. Rose Wilderness, the trail does offer many positive attributes, including two small but scenic lakes, a 2-mile-long subalpine meadow, tumbling Ophir Creek, and evidence of a major geological catastrophe.

Mark Twain, astute observer that he was, described the east flank of the Carson Range in *Roughing It*, his chronicle of life in the Far West: "The mountains are very high and steep about Carson, Eagle, and Washoe valleys—very high and very steep, and so when the snow gets to melting off fast in the spring and the warm surface earth begins to moisten and soften, the disastrous landslides commence. The reader cannot know what a landslide is unless he has lived in that country and seen the whole side of a mountain taken off some fine morning and deposited down in the valley, leaving a vast, treeless, unsightly scar upon the mountain's front to keep the circumstances fresh in his memory all the years that he may go on living within 70 miles of that place."

Twain's colorful account of history repeated itself most recently in the spring of 1983, when an entire flank of appropriately named Slide Mountain, saturated with meltwater from the thawing winter snows, broke loose and plunged into the canyon of Ophir Creek, instantly displacing the waters of Lower Price Lake. The snow-soaked debris merged with the water from the lake, forming a semi-liquid mass, which roared down the canyon with lightning quickness, consuming everything in its path and reaching the floor of Washoe Valley in a matter of seconds. One death occurred, several homes were destroyed, and acres and acres of debris were spread across the valley floor, spilling across NV 395, closing the main artery between Reno and Carson City. As a result of this enormous slide, Lower Price Lake vanished, Upper Price Lake shrank, and the canyon of Ophir Creek was visibly altered. From several spots along the Ophir Creek Trail, hikers can witness the effects of the disaster, although nature has done a lot of healing since 1983.

DIRECTIONS *Start:* From I-580, approximately 15 miles south of Reno and 10 miles north of Carson City, take Exit 50 for Bowers Mansion, NV 429, and Old US 395. Turn right onto Old US 395 (NV 439), travel 450 feet to the Davis Creek Park entrance, and turn right into the park. Follow the access road past the campground entrance to the trailhead parking area on the right.

End: Follow NV 431, also known as the Mt. Rose Highway, to the Tahoe Meadows Trailhead, 0.7 miles west of Mt. Rose Summit and 7.3 miles east of the junction with NV 28 at Incline Village. Parking is available in a lot on the south shoulder, or down a short access road.

FACILITIES/TRAILHEAD Davis Creek County Park offers improved campsites, picnic areas, and restrooms with flush toilets and running water. The Tahoe Meadows Trailhead has restrooms with running water. The trail begins near a sign at the small trailhead parking area.

From the trailhead, start up the hillside through a light forest of Jeffrey pines, soon passing by an unmarked trail coming from below. Wind over to a plank bridge across lushly lined Davis Creek and continue climbing, reaching a junction with the Discovery Trail at 0.2 mile. Proceed ahead at the junction, passing by another unmarked trail at 0.4 mile. Shortly beyond this path, the Ophir Creek Trail bends into the canyon of a tributary stream and continues the stiff ascent up this defile. The grade eases for a short time in the vicinity of a lush meadow but all too soon resumes the upward grind. After a while, another unmarked trail splits off to the left. Veer right here, where the grade eases and actually descends briefly on the way toward the lip of Ophir Creek canyon. Just before the 1-mile mark is a viewpoint, from where you can still see evidence from the 1983 slide.

Away from the viewpoint, continue the climb through a light forest of Jeffrey pines and scattered shrubs, veering slightly away from the creek for a while until reaching the edge of a rock-filled vale, where a 4-by-4-inch post offers directions for Ophir Creek ahead and Davis Creek Park behind. Nearby, a primitive campsite is just off the trail. Breaking out of the forest, angle across a boulder-strewn channel to a

ford of braided Ophir Creek, 1.6 miles from the trailhead. Usually an easy boulder hop, this ford may prove to be difficult early in the season. Up the rocky drainage, above a tangle of shrubs, is a good view of Slide Mountain, the source of all these boulders.

Away from the crossing of Ophir Creek, the trail turns downstream and descends around the nose of a forested ridge above the south side of the creek to meet the track of an old road. Climb steeply along this road up a long gully, past Point 5465, and then across a hillside above the canyon of a seasonal stream. Reach a junction with the Rock Lake lateral at 3 miles.

Side Trip to Rock Lake: Traverse north-northwest across the slope through Jeffrey pine forest for 0.2 mile before the trail makes a moderate descent down a manzanita-covered hillside to the floor of the basin holding Rock Lake, reaching the boulder-strewn shore at 0.5 mile from the Ophir Creek Trail.

Aptly named, Rock Lake reposes in a talus-filled basin, the rocky terrain interrupted only by a small grassy patch along the northwest shore, near a lone campsite. Lily pads cover the surface of the lake, while Jeffrey pines and white firs ring the shoreline. The shallow lake diminishes in size as the summer progresses, and as the park brochure warns, "don't expect the fishing to be good." Once you've thoroughly enjoyed Rock Lake, retrace your steps 0.5 mile back to the Ophir Creek Trail.

Aptly named Slide Mountain above Price Lake

A steep, winding climb leads away from the junction through moderate forest cover to the crest of a sub ridge, where scattered forest, boulders, and rock outcroppings provide some variety to the surroundings. Easy hiking on sandy tread leads across this crest and down to a signed junction with the Little Valley Road, 3.9 miles from the trailhead.

Turn right (northwest) onto the road, make an initial climb, and then traverse across the slope with good views of Rock Lake below and to the east of Washoe Lake and Valley. After a half mile, you come to another signed junction, 4.6 miles from the trailhead, where the singletrack Ophir Creek Trail bends sharply uphill. Stay on the road for a short distance, heading toward Ophir Creek. Just before the creek is a diversion ditch with a faint path alongside, which parallels the ditch to the outlet of Upper Price Lake. Either follow this path to the lakeshore, or remain on the road to a ford of the creek (may be difficult) and then head upstream to the lake. Whichever way is chosen, reach the outlet of Upper Price Lake, 4.5 miles from the trailhead.

Upper Price Lake may be just a remnant of its former self but is still with us, unlike Lower Price Lake, which was completely displaced by debris from the 1983 slide. Inexplicably, the lower lake still appears on the USGS *Washoe City* quadrangle, despite the fact that the map has a publication date of 1994, more than 10 years after the event. Judging from the picturesque beauty of Upper Price Lake, not being able to enjoy the twin as well seems a shame. Steep slopes plunge into the icy blue waters of Upper Price Lake, not nearly as large or deep after the slide. The upper canyon forms a sublime backdrop to the serene lake. Campsites are found on the north side of the creek, which means backpackers will have to carefully negotiate their way across the diversion structure as well as the creek, provided they didn't ford the creek at the road.

To continue toward Tahoe Meadows, either return to the junction of Little Valley Road and Ophir Creek Trail and climb stiffly up the trail, or follow the path on the south side of the lake on a steep ascent across the hillside through a mixed forest of Jeffrey pines, white firs, mountain hemlocks, and western white pines. After a half mile of climbing, rejoin the Ophir Creek Trail. From the junction, the path proceeds up the canyon, crossing a pair of lushly vegetated side streams along the way. The next section of trail has good views, alternating through scattered forest and pockets of verdant meadow filled with a profusion of wildflowers through midsummer.

A stiff climb leads back into moderate cover from a lodgepole-pine forest, as the course of the Ophir Creek Trail stays well into the trees, away from both the creek and Tahoe Meadows to the right. Eventually, easier hiking greets you near the upper end of the trail. Reach a junction with the Lower Tahoe Meadows Loop at 6.2 miles. Continue west at the junction and follow the wide track of an old road serving as the route of the Ophir Creek Trail through a mixed forest of Jeffrey pines, white firs, mountain hemlocks, and western white pines. Reach the Middle Loop junction at 6.5 miles.

Continue climbing westbound and, after about 0.3 mile, the trail begins a quarter-mile descent through predominantly lodgepole-pine forest. After the grade eases, you pass the Ophir Creek Trail signboard and soon come to the Y-junction with the Tahoe Rim Trail (TRT) angling back to the left.

Follow the shared route of the TRT and Ophir Creek Trails ahead, breaking out of the trees and coming alongside the fringe of Tahoe Meadows. Soon you reach the next junction, where the path ahead provides mountain bikers with direct access to the Mt. Rose Highway. Take the right-hand path and wind around toward the bridge over Ophir Creek and the loop junction at the boardwalk beyond.

From the loop junction, continue on the TRT on a mild ascent across the green, flower-dotted expanse of verdant Tahoe Meadows. Backdropped nicely by Slide Mountain, Tahoe Meadows is one of the most scenic subalpine meadows in the northern Sierra, despite the presence of a state highway near the fringe. Early-season hikers will enjoy a wide range of wildflowers, although the ground can be quite boggy then as well. Species include buttercup, shooting star, penstemon, elephant head, marsh marigold, paintbrush, and largeleaf avens. All too soon, the trail draws near to the Mt. Rose Highway and proceeds just below the busy thoroughfare for the last half mile to the end of the journey at the Tahoe Meadows Trailhead.

155 Davis Creek Park

Distance	0.6 mile (loop)
Hiking Time	30 minutes
Elevation	Negligible
Difficulty	Easy
Trail Use	Leashed dogs, good for kids
Best Times	Mid-April through October
Agency	Davis Creek Regional Park at 775-849-0684, parks.nv.gov
Recommended Map	*WCP Davis Creek Park*

HIGHLIGHTS Situated between the Sierra Nevada to the west and the Great Basin to the east, Davis Creek Park offers visitors an opportunity to explore the diverse plant and animal life found in this interesting transition zone. Armed with the *Davis Creek Naturalist Guide*, junior and amateur biologists can gather interesting tidbits of information from 10 numbered sites along the easy, 0.6-mile loop trail that circles Davis Pond. The nearby picnic grounds offer a fine opportunity for a post-hike picnic.

DIRECTIONS From I-580, approximately 15 miles south of Reno and 10 miles north of Carson City, take Exit 50 for Bowers Mansion, NV 429, and Old US 395. Turn right onto Old US 395 (NV 439), travel 450 feet to the Davis Creek Park entrance, and turn right into the park. Follow the access road past the campground entrance and past the Ophir Creek Trailhead to the parking area on the left side of the road.

FACILITIES/TRAILHEAD Davis Creek Park offers improved campsites, picnic areas, and heated restrooms with flush toilets and running water. The trail begins at the far end of the parking area near a signboard marked with a picture of a Jeffrey pinecone, the symbol of the nature trail.

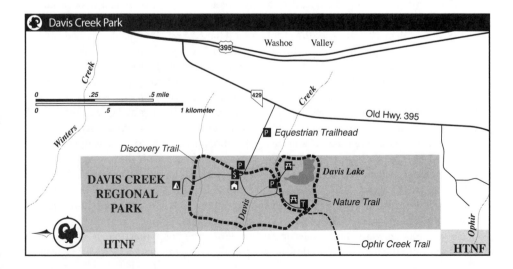

Pick up a *Davis Creek Naturalist Guide* from a box on the signboard and stroll away from the parking area through typical eastside Sierra foothill vegetation of sagebrush, bitterbrush, and widely scattered Jeffrey pines. Soon you come to post 1, corresponding to information in the naturalist's guide about the number of landslides on aptly named Slide Mountain, and a nearby trail junction.

Turn right at the junction and quickly drop down to a short wood bridge over a seasonal stream amid a tangle of alders. Head away from the stream and curve around an open hillside past posts 2 and 3, with good views of the north end of Washoe Valley and the Virginia Range beyond. Heading south, the trail leads into Jeffrey pine forest and around a picnic area to the east end of Davis Pond, with a fine view across the pond of Slide Mountain. Follow a fence line that separates the park from private homes to the east, and then veer through the trees to the south of the pond. Away from the pond, the forested trail leads across a dirt road and over a short bridge above a narrow ditch to a junction with the signed Ophir Creek Trail.

Turn right at the junction and follow the narrow ditch past post 7, soon arriving at another junction with a path between the Tent Group Camp and the restroom for the picnic area and Ophir Creek Trailhead. Here the nature trail continues ahead on a short descent past post 8 about the wild rose, and then circles behind the picnic area to a crossing of the park access road.

From the road, you follow the path to a crossing of Davis Creek, lined with willows, and continue past post 9 a short distance, to the close of the loop at the parking area.

156   Hobart Road to Hobart Reservoir

see map on p. 343

Distance	10 miles (out-and-back)
Hiking Time	5–6 hours
Elevation	+2,575/-300 feet
Difficulty	Difficult
Trail Use	Mountain biking OK, dogs OK
Best Times	June through October
Agency	Humboldt-Toiyabe National Forest at 775-882-2766, www.fs.usda.gov/htnf; Lake Tahoe Nevada State Park at 775-831-0494, parks.nv.gov
Recommended Map	USGS 7.5-minute *Carson City, LTNSP Marlette-Hobart Backcountry*

HIGHLIGHTS Definitely not for the faint of heart, the stiff, nearly 2,500-foot climb from Lakeview to Hobart Reservoir provides rugged hikers and mountain bikers with sweeping views, pleasant scenery, and a potentially refreshing dip in the relatively mild waters of the reservoir at the conclusion of the trip. Early-summer visitors will be rewarded with a fine display of seasonal wildflowers, and autumn provides a splash of golden yellow from the turning aspens along McEwen Creek. A fine network of closed roads within Lake Tahoe Nevada State Park provides a bounty of alternatives for trip extensions, especially for mountain bikers.

DIRECTIONS Drive on I-580 to the south end of Washoe Valley and take the Washoe Lake State Park–East Lake Boulevard exit. Turn west and then south onto Old 395 and proceed to Hobart Road. Proceed west on Hobart through the Lakeview Estates Subdivision for three quarters of a mile to the end of paved road and park on the shoulder as space allows.

FACILITIES/TRAILHEAD There are no facilities near the trailhead. The trail begins on the continuation of a dirt road past a closed steel gate.

Pass through the opening in a steel gate and head north on a well-traveled road, which soon bends sharply a couple of times before resuming a northward direction. Make a stiff climb through scattered Jeffrey pines, with an understory of sagebrush, bitterbrush, and manzanita. As you climb, the mostly open terrain allows improving views of Carson and Washoe Valleys and the bordering Virginia Range. Eventually, the steep ascent moderates a bit, as the road wraps around the hillside into McEwen Creek Canyon, where the din of road noise from the freeway begins to diminish. Cross willow- and cottonwood-lined McEwen Creek flowing through a pipe below the roadbed and continue upstream past luxuriant vegetation with periodic aspen stands. The road crosses over the creek a few more times on a stiff climb up the canyon before veering away across shrub-covered slopes to a vista point of Washoe Valley and the Virginia Range at a hairpin turn, 2.25 miles from the parking area.

The stiff ascent continues, soon leading past a new water tank and concrete block building with solar panels. Sweeping views of Washoe Valley and the surrounding topography, along with Slide Mountain, are plentiful along this stretch of the road. Shortly beyond the water tank, you experience a three-quarter-mile respite from the climb, as the road traverses across a hillside toward Sawmill Canyon. Early summer provides the added bonus of a variety of wildflowers in this general vicinity, including paintbrush, lupine, pennyroyal, penstemon, and mule-ears. The road comes to a closed steel gate at the boundary of Lake Tahoe Nevada State Park, comes alongside Sawmill Canyon Creek, and reaches a junction, 3.5 miles from the trailhead. Here, a less-used road branches to the right, crosses the creek, and proceeds on an arcing route toward Red House. Immediately past the junction is an interpretive sign near an old steam engine from the bygone logging days.

Veer left at the junction and enter into a light forest of Jeffrey pines, white firs, and lodgepole pines. Continue climbing up Sawmill Canyon to the crest of a minor ridge and a junction at 4.5 miles, where the left-hand road heads south for three-quarters of a mile to a signed junction with the Ash Canyon Road.

Proceed ahead from the junction and drop off the ridge on a moderate descent. Soon you can catch a glimpse of Hobart Reservoir through the trees. Reach a signboard that provides information on the fishing regulations and statistical information about the reservoir. A short distance farther, a road branches away to the lakeshore. The lakeshore is a fine place to sit and enjoy a picnic lunch, and the lake itself will tempt any swimmers in your group, especially if the steep climb happened to coincide with the area's typically hot summer temperatures.

HOBART RESERVOIR

Carson City still uses water from Hobart Reservoir as part of the municipal water supply. Anglers can test their luck on a variety of trout, including rainbow, brook, cutthroat, and hybrids. The season runs from May 1 to September 30, with a five-trout limit—only one longer than 10 inches. Anglers must use single barbless hooks only.

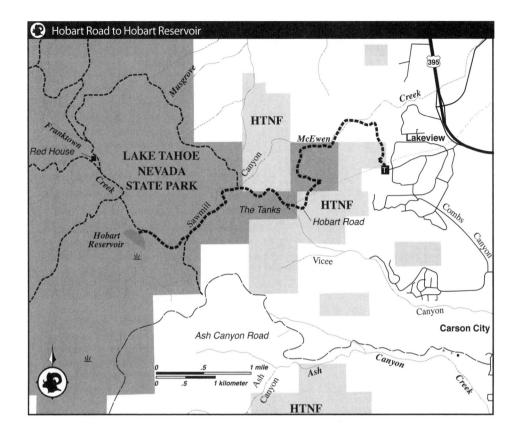

Hobart Road to Hobart Reservoir

More Hikes

Alum Creek

This route follows the Hunter Lake Road for nearly 2 miles before venturing into and up the canyon of Alum Creek to a viewpoint above Hunter Creek (9 miles).

Ash Canyon Road

The main Ash Canyon Road is open to four-wheel-drive vehicles and is steep and exposed for the first 5 miles, creating a less-than-desirable prospect for most hikers. Excellent views and more pleasant terrain in the upper elevations on the way to Snow Valley Peak might lure strong hikers who don't mind those less-desirable attributes (16 miles). A network of alternate singletrack trails has popped up in the canyon over the years, but they appeal to mountain bikers probably more so than hikers.

Kit Carson Country

Named for John C. Fremont's chief guide, the area designated as Kit Carson Country is accessed primarily from the east–west thoroughfare of NV/CA 88, which heads westbound from the Nevada towns of Minden and Gardnerville over 8,593-foot Carson Pass before reaching Jackson, California, in the foothills above the San Joaquin Valley.

The terrain varies within this area from pinyon-pine forest to alpine and just about anything in between. While most of the area appears to be volcanic in origin, in actuality, the area is largely granitic bedrock overlain by a thin veneer of volcanic rock sediment. One of the principal features, Round Top, is indeed the remnant of a volcanic cone, but the majority of the landscape is composed of granite bedrock, which explains the presence of so many lakes—volcanic rock is generally too porous to hold numerous lakes.

The easternmost trails in this chapter are lightly used paths at lower elevations that provide some early-season hiking opportunities when the higher elevations remain shrouded with winter's mantle. Autumn is an equally fine time to walk these trails,

when large stands of aspen create swaths of golden yellow. Farther west, trails in and around the 105,156-acre Mokelumne Wilderness and the proposed wilderness near Meiss Meadows offer superb hiking through montane and subalpine forests and meadows to a bounty of sparkling lakes and airy summits. Abundant wildflowers bloom in this area during midsummer, providing uplifting bursts of color that will surely satisfy even the most jaded botanist.

Backpackers planning to overnight within Mokelumne Wilderness will need a wilderness permit. Camping is limited within the Carson Pass Management Area to two-night stays at Round Top and Winnemucca lakes (three nights at Fourth of July Lake) and designated sites, available on a first-come, first-serve basis from the Carson Pass Information Station. Otherwise, permits are not required for overnighters camping outside of the wilderness or for day hikers. During the summer, a $3 day-use fee ($15 per season) is charged at the Carson Pass, Carson Pass Overflow, Woods Lake, and Meiss Trailheads. Collected fees are used to fund projects in the Mokelumne Wilderness.

Summit City Canyon from the Evergreen Trail

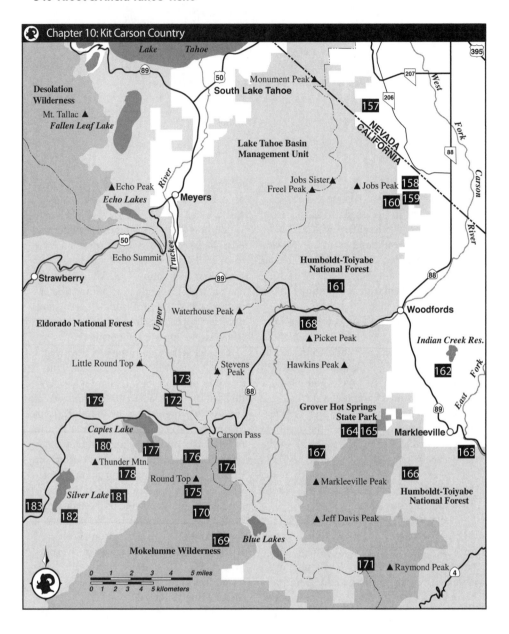

Chapter 10: Kit Carson Country

Lake Tahoe

Desolation Wilderness

Mt. Tallac ▲
Fallen Leaf Lake

South Lake Tahoe

Monument Peak ▲

157

Lake Tahoe Basin Management Unit

NEVADA
CALIFORNIA

▲Echo Peak
Echo Lakes

Meyers

Jobs Sister▲
Freel Peak ▲

▲ Jobs Peak

158
160 159

Echo Summit

Strawberry

Humboldt-Toiyabe National Forest

161

Eldorado National Forest

Woodfords

Waterhouse Peak ▲

168

▲ Picket Peak

Indian Creek Res.

Little Round Top ▲

Stevens Peak

Hawkins Peak ▲

162

173

179 172

Grover Hot Springs State Park

164 165 Markleeville

Caples Lake

Carson Pass

167

163

180 177 176

174

▲Thunder Mtn.

178

▲ Markleeville Peak

166

Round Top ▲

175

Humboldt-Toiyabe National Forest

Silver Lake 181

183 182

170

▲ Jeff Davis Peak

169 *Blue Lakes*

Mokelumne Wilderness

171 ▲Raymond Peak

0 1 2 3 4 5 miles
0 1 2 3 4 5 kilometers

157 Jobs Peak Ranch Trailhead to Fay-Luther Trailhead

see map on p. 348

Distance	3.5 miles (point-to-point)
Hiking Time	2 hours
Elevation	+500/-500 feet
Difficulty	Moderate
Trail Use	Dogs OK (leashed through easement)
Best Times	March through November
Agency	Humboldt Toiyabe National Forest at 775-882-2766, www.fs.usda.gov/htnf
Recommended Maps	USGS 7.5-minute *Minden, Woodfords* (trail not shown), CVTA Fay-Luther-Jobs Peak Ranch Trail

HIGHLIGHTS The Jobs Peak Ranch Trail represents a victory in the ongoing struggle of securing access to government land on the east front of the Carson Range in the face of the unprecedented and rapid development of western Nevada. Thanks to efforts of the Carson Valley Trails Association, a 3.5-mile hiker-only trail allows travel between Foothill Road and forest service land above, through Jobs Peak Ranch subdivision. After the subdivision is developed, the path will seem fairly civilized, with fencing delineating the boundary between the trail's easement and the private property of the upscale homes along the way. However, once recreationists reach government land, off-trail access to rugged and remote Jobs Canyon is guaranteed. Summer temperatures can be quite hot, so plan on an early-morning or early-evening hike to beat the heat.

Above the subdivision, a newer section of trail continues across forest service land to a junction with the Valley View Loop, which is a worthy 1.7-mile diversion for those with the extra time and energy. Beyond the junction, the trail continues to connections leading to the Fay-Luther Trailhead.

DIRECTIONS *Start:* From NV 395 at the north end of Minden, turn onto NV 88 and travel almost 2 miles to a right-hand turn onto Mottsville Lane (NV 207). Head west on Mottsville Lane for 3.2 miles to Foothill Road and turn left (south). Proceed on Foothill Road for 2.5 miles to the south intersection of Five Creek Road on the right. Turn onto Five Creek Road and immediately turn left into the signed trailhead parking area.

End: From the intersection of NV 88 and Fairview Lane, which is 1.4 miles north of the Nevada–California border, head west on Fairview Lane (NV 206) for 0.8 mile to where it merges with Foothill Road. Continue on Foothill another 0.9 mile to the signed trailhead parking area on the left, opposite a historical marker about Ira M. Luther.

FACILITIES/TRAILHEAD Both parking areas have equestrian loading facilities. The start of both trails is well marked.

The beginning of the trail heads south from the parking area and follows the property line behind a row of houses above Foothill Road through sagebrush, desert peach, and bitterbrush on a gently rising grade. From late spring through early summer, the area is awash in a profusion of purple lupine blossoms.

After a half mile, the trail turns sharply west and makes a moderate climb up the hillside, eventually entering a forest of Jeffrey pines. After another half mile, the route turns sharply south and makes a short drop to a year-round, unnamed creek, lined with aspens and pines.

Away from the delightful creek, follow the trail across an old road a couple of times and out onto an open slope with sweeping views of the Carson Valley below and filtered views of the Carson Range above. Back into the trees, reach a lush riparian area, where aspen, willow, wild rose, grasses and other thirsty plants flourish in the damp soils. The terrain becomes a bit steeper beyond the riparian area, as the trail soon crosses a subdivision road and continues the climb another 30 feet up the far hillside to the Nevada–California state line. Another 300 feet past the border, you stand on forest service land, where competent cross-country

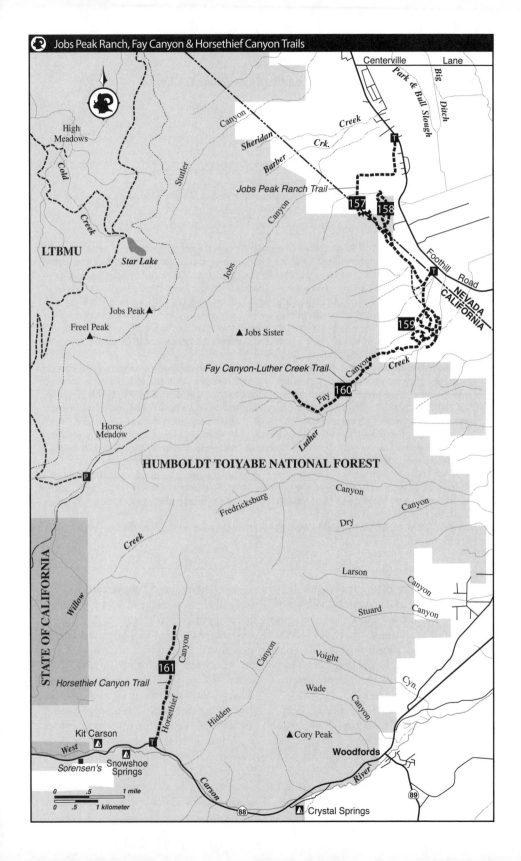

enthusiasts have legal access to the west into the wild and scenic terrain of Jobs Canyon. Unleashing dogs is now permitted.

Remaining on the Jobs Peak Ranch Trail, pass a park bench and proceed a short distance to the edge of a stream canyon, where a series of eight steep switchbacks leads down the slope. At the bottom of the switchbacks, you cross the creek via a flat-topped log in early season, or an easy hop later in the year. Away from the crossing, the winding descent continues for a brief distance before a gently descending traverse slices across the hillside through Jeffrey pine forest. After passing above a vigorous spring surrounded by lush foliage, the trail follows a rolling traverse to a junction with

the Valley View Loop on the left, 2.5 miles from the Job Peak Ranch Trailhead.

Proceed ahead from the junction, crossing an old road and entering a more open stretch of forest. At 0.4 mile from the previous junction, reach a Y-junction with the Lonesome Trail on the right.

Bear left (southwest) at the junction and make a moderate descent on sandy tread for 0.3 mile to the next junction with the Sandy Trail ahead.

Turn left (southeast) at the junction and head downhill through sagebrush scrub toward the Fay-Luther Trailhead, passing an interpretive sign about Snowshoe Thompson, crossing the state line, and strolling past an Emigrant Trail marker on the way.

158 Valley View Loop

Distance	3.7 miles (partial loop)
Hiking Time	2 hours
Elevation	+375/-375 feet
Difficulty	Easy
Trail Use	Dogs OK, mountain biking OK
Best Times	March through November
Agency	Humboldt Toiyabe National Forest at 775-882-2766, www.fs.usda.gov/htnf; BLM at 775-885-6000, blm.gov/nv/st/en/fo/carson_city_field.html
Recommended Maps	USGS 7.5-minute *Woodfords* (trail not shown), CVTA *Fay-Luther–Jobs Peak Ranch Trail*

HIGHLIGHTS A short and easy hike, particularly well suited for spring and fall, leads hikers through sagebrush scrub and Jeffrey pine forest across the eastern Sierra foothills to fine views of Carson Valley. Summer visitors will need to get an early start to beat the heat.

DIRECTIONS From the intersection of NV 88 and Fairview Lane, which is 1.4 miles north of the Nevada–California border, head west on Fairview Lane (NV 206) for 0.8 mile to where it merges with Foothill Road. Continue on Foothill another 0.9 mile to the signed trailhead parking area on the left, opposite a historical marker about Ira M. Luther.

FACILITIES/TRAILHEAD Other than an equestrian loading area, there are no facilities at the trailhead. The trail begins near a trailhead signboard.

From the parking lot, the trail follows the course of an old sandy roadbed through typical eastern Sierra foothills vegetation, primarily sagebrush. Just past the fence of the trailhead is an Emigrant Trail marker

on the left, and 200 yards farther south is a Pony Express marker. Initially, walking on the sandy tread is a bit difficult, because the frequent use this trail receives by equestrians has churned up the sandy soil quite a bit. Cross the signed border between Nevada and California and proceed past an interpretive sign about Snowshoe Thompson to a junction of the Sandy Trail on the left, a connector to the Lonesome Trail ahead, and your trail, the Fay-Luther–Jobs Peak Ranch Trail on the right, 0.3 mile from the trailhead.

Heading northeast, you make a moderate climb on sandy tread through widely scattered Jeffrey pines to a Y-junction, 0.3 mile from the previous one, with the east end of the Lonesome Trail.

Proceed ahead on a gently rolling traverse, passing across a side trail leading onto private property and continuing into slightly thicker forest. After passing above a few private homes, you reach the junction of the Valley View Loop at 1 mile from the trailhead.

Leave the Fay-Luther–Jobs Peak Ranch Trail and follow the right-hand trail away from the junction. A 0.2-mile descent leads to the crossing of an old jeep road, followed by a short climb to a usually dry gully. The sound of running water higher up the slope seems a tad unusual, but a perennial spring spills down the gully for a short distance before disappearing into the soil. A short way farther is the loop junction, 1.3 miles from the trailhead.

Follow the left-hand part of the loop on a moderate climb leading shortly to the crossing of a vigorous stream coursing down a narrow canyon lined with lush riparian foliage. Beyond the stream, you break out of the trees to grand views sweeping across the verdant plain of Carson Valley, backdropped by the Pine Nut Mountains. Near a lone Jeffrey pine, the trail loops back toward the west and begins a mild descent, still providing good views of the valley. Entering thicker forest, you cross the stream again and then make a moderate climb up to the close of the loop. From there, retrace your steps 1.3 miles to the trailhead.

159   Fay-Luther Loop Trails

HIGHLIGHTS Thanks to the efforts of the Carson Valley Trails Association, the Fay Canyon–Luther Creek area now has a fine network of trails crisscrossing the Sierra foothills through sagebrush scrub, Jeffrey pine forest, and riparian environments. Periodic views of the Carson Valley and the east side of the Carson Range provide visual treats from a variety of vantages. The three loops below are described as stand-alone trips, but they could easily be combined with one another to form one giant loop of about 5 miles, with very little backtracking necessary. The area is quite popular with the equestrian crowd, so hikers should be prepared to move off the trail as necessary. Anyone seeking a longer trip can combine any of these loops with the journey up the canyon as described in Trip 160.

DIRECTIONS From the intersection of NV 88 and Fairview Lane, which is 1.4 miles north of the Nevada–California border, head west on Fairview Lane (NV 206) for 0.8 mile to where it merges with Foothill Road. Continue on Foothill another 0.9 mile to the signed trailhead parking area on the left, opposite a historical marker about Ira M. Luther.

FACILITIES/TRAILHEAD Other than an equestrian loading area, there are no facilities at the trailhead. The trail begins near a trailhead signboard.

From the parking lot, the trail follows the course of an old sandy roadbed through typical eastern Sierra foothills vegetation, primarily sagebrush. Just past the fence of the trailhead is an Emigrant Trail marker on the left, and 200 yards farther south is a Pony Express marker.

Initially, walking on the sandy tread is a bit difficult, because the frequent use this trail receives by equestrians has churned up the sandy soil quite a bit. Cross the signed border between Nevada and California and proceed past an interpretive sign about Snowshoe Thompson to a junction with

Fay Canyon

your trail, the Sandy Trail on the left, a connector to the Lonesome Trail ahead, and the Fay-Luther–Jobs Peak Ranch Trail on the right, 0.3 mile from the trailhead.

Remaining on the Sandy Trail, turn left at the junction and continue climbing through sagebrush scrub. Farther on, beneath a Jeffrey pine, is a park bench inviting passersby to sit and enjoy the scenery. Immediately past the bench is the next junction, where the Lonesome Trail veers to the north-northeast, 0.5 mile from the trailhead.

Through scattered Jeffrey pine forest, you follow the left-hand trail away from the junction and soon come to the next junction at 0.6 mile, the point where the three loops described below begin.

Interpretive Loop

Distance	2.2 miles (partial loop)
Hiking Time	1 hour
Elevation	+350/-350 feet
Difficulty	Easy to moderate
Trail Use	Dogs OK (leashed November 15–March 30), mountain biking OK
Best Times	March through November
Agency	Humboldt Toiyabe National Forest at 775-882-2766, www.fs.usda.gov/htnf; BLM at 775-885-6000, blm.gov/nv/st/en/fo/carson_city_field.html
Recommended Maps	USGS 7.5-minute *Woodfords* (trail not shown), CVTA *Fay-Luther–Jobs Peak Ranch Trail*

see map on p. 348

The Interpretive Loop begins at the junction 0.6 mile from the trailhead. Take the left-hand path on a clockwise loop and walk a few steps to the first interpretive sign. Climb out of the forest and back into sagebrush scrub, passing the next interpretive sign and soon reaching a Y-junction with the Bitter Cherry Trail, 0.2 mile from the start of the loop.

Veer left and head toward Luther Creek on a moderate climb. Where the trail bends upstream, a short lateral provides access to the water's edge. The creek is lined with dense, thirsty vegetation, including willow, white alder, and black cottonwood. Follow the trail along the creek for a while until it bends away toward the south junction of the Bitter Cherry Trail, passing a couple more interpretive signs and use trails over to the creek on the way. Reach the Bitter Cherry junction at 1 mile from the trailhead.

Turn left and proceed south through Jeffrey pine forest for another 0.1 mile back toward the edge of Luther Creek and an unmarked, three-way junction. Here the path ahead travels along the creek for another 0.2 mile before petering out.

Turn right and double back sharply uphill on a moderate, 0.1-mile climb to the top of a minor ridge and another junction. The left-hand trail is the main route into Fay Canyon and also provides access to the Grand View Loop.

Remaining on the Interpretive Loop, you follow the crest of the ridge for a while, passing a park bench and another interpretive sign on the way. Follow descending tread across a gully and onward to the twin junctions of the Jeffrey Pine Trail, 0.2 mile from the previous one. Continuing ahead on the Interpretive Loop, you immediately encounter a junction with a short connector downslope to the Bitter Cherry Trail. A map of the Fay-Luther trail network at the junction should help to eliminate any confusion about your location.

Proceed ahead through Jeffrey pine forest with very little groundcover, soon passing an appropriately placed interpretive sign about the Jeffrey pines. Beyond, the trail follows the edge of a hillside for a while, from where there are fine views out across the valley. Pass by another sign and park bench before the path begins a more pronounced descent and passes the last interpretive sign. Follow the trail to the crossing of a couple of shallow gullies and then reach the next junction with the Jeffrey Pine Trail on the left, 0.3-mile from the previous junction.

Ahead, a short, steep descent leads to the close of the loop. From there, retrace your steps 0.7 mile to the trailhead.

Jeffrey Pine Loop

see map on p. 348

Distance	2 miles (partial loop)
Hiking Time	1 hour
Elevation	+350/-350 feet
Difficulty	Easy to moderate
Trail Use	Dogs OK (leashed November 15–March 30), mountain biking OK
Best Times	March through November
Agency	Humboldt Toiyabe National Forest at 775-882-2766, www.fs.usda.gov/htnf; BLM at 775-885-6000, blm.gov/nv/st/en/fo/carson_city_field.html
Recommended Maps	USGS 7.5-minute *Woodfords* (trail not shown), CVTA *Fay-Luther–Jobs Peak Ranch Trail*

At the start of the Interpretive Loop, take the right-hand trail steeply up the hillside for 0.1 mile to the north junction of the Jeffrey Pine Trail.

Turn right and climb moderately through a serene stretch of scattered to light Jeffrey pine forest, interspersed with some mountain mahogany and with very little groundcover. By stepping off the trail a few yards, you can obtain a good view of Fay Canyon. Eventually the trail bends away from the edge of the canyon and meanders back toward the Interpretive Trail, reaching the twin junctions after 0.3 mile. Unless you're bound for the Grand View Loop or the Fay-Luther Trail up the canyon, take the left-hand path.

Turn onto the Interpretive Loop and immediately encounter a junction with a short connector downslope to the Bitter Cherry Trail. A map of the Fay-Luther trail network at the junction should help to eliminate any confusion about your location.

Proceed ahead through Jeffrey pine forest with very little groundcover, soon passing an appropriately placed interpretive sign about the Jeffrey pines. Beyond, the trail follows the edge of a hillside for a while, from where there are fine views out across the valley. Pass by another sign and park bench before the path begins a more pronounced descent and passes the last of the interpretive signs. Follow the trail to the crossing of a couple of shallow gullies and then reach the north junction with the Jeffrey Pine Trail on the left, 0.3-mile from the previous junction. From there, retrace your steps 0.7 mile to the trailhead.

Grand View Loop

Distance	3.3 miles (partial loop)
Hiking Time	1.5 hours
Elevation	+600/-600 feet
Difficulty	Moderate
Trail Use	Dogs OK (leashed November 15–March 30), mountain biking OK
Best Times	March through November
Agency	Humboldt Toiyabe National Forest at 775-882-2766, www.fs.usda.gov /htnf; BLM at 775-885-6000, blm.gov/nv/st/en/fo/carson_city_field.html
Recommended Maps	USGS 7.5-minute *Woodfords* (trail not shown), CVTA *Fay-Luther–Jobs Peak Ranch Trail*

see map on p. 348

To reach the Grand View Loop, you must first follow a section of the Interpretive Loop from the junction 0.6 mile from the trailhead. Take the left-hand path and walk a few steps to the first interpretive sign. Climb out of the forest and back into sagebrush scrub, passing the next interpretive sign and soon reaching a Y-junction with the Bitter Cherry Trail, 0.2 mile from the start of the loop.

Veer left and head toward Luther Creek on a moderate climb. Where the trail bends upstream, a short lateral provides access to the water's edge. The creek is lined with dense, thirsty vegetation, including willow, white alder, and black cottonwood. Follow the trail along the creek for a while until it bends away toward the south junction of the Bitter Cherry Trail, passing a couple more interpretive signs and use trails over to the creek on the way. Reach the Bitter Cherry junction at 1 mile from the trailhead.

Turn left and proceed south through Jeffrey pine forest for another 0.1 mile back toward the edge of Luther Creek and an unmarked, three-way junction. Here the path ahead travels along the creek for another 0.2 mile before petering out.

Turn right and double back sharply uphill on a moderate, 0.1-mile climb to the top of a minor ridge and another junction. The right-hand trail is the continuation of the Interpretive Loop, which will ultimately be your return route.

For now, take the left-hand trail on a stiff climb for 0.1 mile to the lower junction of the Grand View Loop. Proceed ahead, climbing more steeply for another 0.2 mile to the top of a promontory and the upper junction with the main trail up Fay Canyon.

Turn right and follow the loop on a moderate descent that winds through a light forest of Jeffrey pines, mountain mahogany, and a few firs with an understory of greenleaf manzanita and sagebrush. The initial stretch of trail offers filtered views, but farther on the forest opens up to reveal a fine vista of Carson Valley and the east front of the Sierra. The grade eventually mellows out and winds back to the main trail after 0.5 mile. From there, retrace your steps 0.1 mile to the junction with the Interpretive Trail on top of the minor ridge.

160 Fay Canyon–Luther Creek

see map on p. 348

Distance	8 miles (out-and-back)
Hiking Time	4–5 hours
Elevation	+2,575 feet
Difficulty	Moderate
Trail Use	Mountain biking OK, dogs OK
Best Times	April through October
Agency	Humboldt-Toiyabe National Forest at 775-882-2766, www.fs.usda.gov/htnf; BLM at 775-885-6000, blm.gov/nv/st/en/fo/carson_city_field.html
Recommended Map	USGS 7.5-minute *Woodfords*

HIGHLIGHTS The Fay Canyon–Luther Creek Trail is one of the only routes at this end of Carson Valley where hikers, bikers, and equestrians can travel on a maintained trail from the valley floor up an eastside Sierra canyon. After a mile-long romp through sagebrush and forest, the trail generally stays a good distance away from Luther Creek on the way up Fay Canyon, so packing extra water would be a wise move. Views up the canyon toward 10,630-foot Jobs Peak are quite impressive, made even more so in autumn when the aspen-lined drainage is ablaze with color. Additional views during the ascent include the agricultural ranchlands of Carson Valley with a fine backdrop from the Pine Nut Mountains to the east.

The trail has no ultimate destination, eventually disappearing amid the steep topography near the head of the canyon, although the Carson Valley Trails Association has proposed restoring the historic connection to the Horsethief Canyon Trail (Trip 161). For more information, visit **carsonvalleytrails .org.** Strong hikers with the requisite off-trail skills can continue up the steep slopes in the upper canyon to the summit of Jobs Peak.

Mountain bikers will find the loose, decomposed granite tread in the best condition after a rain. Summers can be quite hot, so an early-morning or early-evening hike is recommended. Spring is a fine time for a trip, when snow still blankets the higher elevations; autumn is especially nice with cool temperatures and the added beauty from the fall colors.

DIRECTIONS Follow NV 88 to the intersection of Fairview Lane, which is 1.4 miles north of the Nevada–California border. Turn west onto Fairview Lane (NV 206) and proceed 0.8 mile to where it merges with Foothill Road. Continue on Foothill another 0.9 mile to the signed trailhead parking area on the left, opposite a historical marker about Ira M. Luther.

FACILITIES/TRAILHEAD The large paved parking area has equestrian loading facilities. The well-signed trail begins at the edge of the parking lot.

From the parking lot, the trail follows the course of an old sandy roadbed through typical eastern Sierra foothills vegetation, primarily sagebrush. Just past the fence of the trailhead is an Emigrant Trail marker on the left and 200 yards farther south is a Pony Express marker. Initially, walking on the sandy tread is a bit difficult, as the frequent use this trail receives by equestrians has churned up the sandy soil quite a bit. Cross the signed border between Nevada and California and proceed past an interpretive sign about Snowshoe Thompson to a junction with your trail, the Sandy Trail, on the left, a connector to the Lonesome Trail ahead, and the Fay-Luther–Jobs Peak Ranch Trail on the right, 0.3 mile from the trailhead.

Remaining on the Sandy Trail, turn left at the junction and continue climbing through sagebrush scrub. Farther on, beneath a Jeffrey pine, is a park bench inviting passersby to sit and enjoy the scenery. Immediately past the bench is the next junction, where the Lonesome Trail veers to the north-northeast, 0.5 mile from the trailhead.

Through scattered Jeffrey pine forest, you follow the left-hand trail away from the junction and soon come to the next junction at 0.6 mile, the point where the three loops described in Trip 159 begin.

Take the left-hand branch of the Interpretive Loop and very soon pass the first interpretive sign. Climb out of the forest and back into sagebrush scrub, passing the next interpretive sign and soon reaching a Y-junction with the Bitter Cherry Trail, 0.2 mile from the start of the loop.

Veer left and head toward Luther Creek on a moderate climb. Where the trail bends upstream, a short lateral provides access to the water's edge. The creek is lined with dense, thirsty vegetation, including willow, white alder, and black cottonwood. Follow the trail along the creek for a while until it bends away toward the south junction of the Bitter Cherry Trail, passing a couple more interpretive signs and use trails over to the creek on the way. Reach the Bitter Cherry junction at 1 mile from the trailhead.

Turn left and proceed south through Jeffrey pine forest for another 0.1 mile back toward the edge of Luther Creek and an unmarked, three-way junction. Here the path ahead travels along the creek for another 0.2 mile before petering out.

Turn right and double back sharply uphill on a moderate, 0.1-mile climb to the top of a minor ridge and another junction. Your route follows the left-hand trail, which is the main route into Fay Canyon.

Take the left-hand trail and make a stiff climb for 0.1 mile to the lower junction of the Grand View Loop. Proceed ahead, climbing more steeply for another 0.2 mile to the top of a promontory and the upper junction with the main trail up Fay Canyon.

Follow the roadbed on a moderate to moderately steep climb through a scattered forest of Jeffrey pines, white firs, and mountain mahogany. Farther up the canyon, shrub-covered slopes of manzanita, sagebrush, chinquapin, and tobacco brush allow good views up the canyon toward Jobs Peak and behind of Carson Valley. Near the 2.5-mile mark, the road dwindles to a footpath, briefly enters a side canyon, and makes a narrow and steep crossing of a tributary stream. After climbing out of this side canyon, continue the stiff ascent toward the head of Fay Canyon into a thicker forest of firs. After crossing a seasonal swale, the path veers northwest toward Jobs Peak, where the forest thins again and the tread becomes rocky. Headed up a gully toward a rock outcropping, the trail deteriorates and then eventually disappears. Strong cross-country enthusiasts can continue from here all the way to Jobs Peak if they so desire.

161 Horsethief Canyon

Distance	4 miles (out-and-back)
Hiking Time	2–2.5 hours
Elevation	+1,250 feet
Difficulty	Moderate
Trail Use	Mountain biking OK, dogs OK
Best Times	Mid-May through October
Agency	Humboldt-Toiyabe National Forest at 775-882-2766, www.fs.usda.gov/htnf
Recommended Map	USGS 7.5-minute *Freel Peak*

see map on p. 348

HIGHLIGHTS The Horsethief Canyon Trail provides a little-used route up a narrow canyon alongside a tributary of the West Fork Carson River. Along the way, hikers encounter lush riparian vegetation lining the creek and dry hillsides of light woodland on the slopes above. The 6,000- to 7,000-foot elevations coupled with the rain shadow effect on the east side of the Sierra make this trip a fine choice for late spring or early summer when the high country remains buried under winter's snowpack.

DIRECTIONS Follow CA 88 to a small dirt parking area signed Horsethief Canyon Trail on the north side of the highway, 3.75 miles westbound of the junction with CA 89 in the tiny community of Woodfords, and 2 miles eastbound of the CA 89 junction in Hope Valley.

FACILITIES/TRAILHEAD There are no facilities at the trailhead. The Forest Service manages the Snowshoe Springs and Kit Carson Campgrounds a short distance westbound on CA 88. The trail begins near a signboard on the downhill side of the parking area.

Head away from the trailhead on a moderately steep angling ascent across a rock- and boulder-covered hillside sprinkled with widely scattered Jeffrey pines and clumps of manzanita. A series of short switchbacks soon leads you alongside Horsethief Canyon Creek, where white firs and an occasional juniper intermix with the pines. Alder, willow, thimbleberry, and wild rose line the narrow stream banks. After the initially steep section, the canyon mellows and the grade of ascent eases to more of a moderate climb, as the trail forsakes a streamside course to climb the hillside above the creek. Volcanic rock outcrops provide some visual interest during this part of the ascent. At 1 mile from the trailhead, you pass through an open gate in a barbed wire fence and then hop over a spring-fed rivulet on its way toward the creek.

Moist soils support several stands of aspen, and lodgepole pines join the mixed forest as you proceed up the canyon. At 1.75 miles, you reach a pile of rocks supporting a wood sign that declares the end of maintained trail. Just beyond the sign, the trail intersects FS 025, an apparently well-traveled road that connects with CA 89 north of the junction with CA 88. Across the road, a jeep road continues northbound up the canyon a short distance to a clearing covered with grasses and willows, where it dies out in the boggy meadow. (The Carson Valley Trails Association has proposed to reestablish the section of trail from here to Luther Canyon.)

162 Indian Creek Recreation Area Trails

see map on p. 359

Distance	1.3 miles, loop (Curtz Lake Interpretive Trail)
	2.4 miles, point-to-point (Summit Lake Trail)
	4.8 miles, out-and-back (Carson River Trail)
Hiking Time	45 minutes (Curtz Lake Interpretive Trail)
	1.25 hours (Summit Lake Trail)
	2.5–3 hours (Carson River Trail)
Elevation	+200/-200 feet (Curtz Lake Interpretive Trail)
	+75/-650 feet (Summit Lake Trail)
	+25/-775 feet (Carson River Trail)
Difficulty	Easy to moderate
Trail Use	Good for kids, dogs OK
Best Times	Late April through October
Agency	Bureau of Land Management at 775-885-6000, blm.gov
Recommended Map	USGS 7.5-minute *Markleeville*

HIGHLIGHTS The Indian Creek Recreation Area comprises 7,000 acres of land near the eastern base of the Sierra and is managed by the Bureau of Land Management. The focal point of the area is Indian Creek Reservoir, a favorite destination for campers and anglers. At one time, the Curtz Lake Interpretive Trail must have provided a fine opportunity to learn about the natural history of the area around the lake. Unfortunately, the condition of the trail and the interpretive signs has deteriorated significantly over the years and is now in need of considerable repair. Despite this setback, the short nature trail still provides an easy stroll through varied terrain, along with a few interesting tidbits about the biology and geology of the area.

The Summit Lake Trail travels from Curtz Lake to Summit Lake on a gently graded path before descending moderately to the campground on the west shore of Indian Creek Reservoir. With shuttle arrangements, the mile-long climb from the campground back to the lake can be avoided.

The Carson River Trail is a favorite among anglers, as East Fork Carson River is a trophy stream for both rainbow and brown trout. The season runs from the last Saturday in April to November 15. Fishing is catch and release, artificial lures with barbless hooks only, and no bait allowed. Even non-anglers will find the pleasant surroundings along the river to be a fine reward for the 2.4-mile hike—just be sure to save enough energy for the return trip, which is all uphill.

DIRECTIONS From CA 89, 1.1 mile south of the junction of CA 88, turn east at Airport Road and proceed for 1 mile to Curtz Lake. The unsigned parking area for the Environmental Study Trail is on the right. The parking area for the Summit Lake and Carson River Trails is another quarter mile farther on Airport Road, where an unmarked rough road on the left soon leads to a parking area just past Curtz Lake.

FACILITIES/TRAILHEAD Within Indian Creek Recreation Lands is a developed campground on the west shore of the reservoir with running water, flush toilets, and hot showers. A day-use area offers a boat ramp and picnic areas. The reservoir is stocked with trout, making it popular with anglers.

Curtz Lake Interpretive Trail: Back when the paths of the Curtz Lake area were in good shape and well signed, hikers had the option of following three clearly marked loop trails (Curtz Lake Environmental Study Trail, Soils-Geology Trail, and Wildlife Trail) on circuits of varying lengths through the diverse topography and varied ecosystems of the area. Nowadays, with the deteriorating nature of these trails, a single loop incorporating the three trails is perhaps easier to follow than attempting to hike them separately.

The interpretive signs for the Curtz Lake Environmental Study Trail are color coded, with green signs referring to elements of plant succession, yellow signs describing the local vegetation, and red signs detailing the environmental effects of individual plants. Head southeast away from the parking area and reach the first interpretive sign about the Jeffrey pine. Continue the gentle ascent up the trail on rocky tread and an occasional wood step past more signs to a trail register. About 0.4 mile from the parking area, you reach the high point of the loop.

Follow the trail as it curves back around to the northwest and descends toward Airport Road. After a couple of switchbacks, you reach a signed junction with a trail on the right back to the parking area and the Soils-Geology Trail straight ahead. If you choose to hike only the Environmental Study Trail, turn right at the junction and walk approximately 300 yards back to the parking lot.

To continue on the full loop, angle sharply across Airport Road and find the continuation of trail on the opposite side near a sign. In similar fashion to the Environmental Study Trail, the interpretive signs for the Soils-Geology Trail are color coded, with yellow markers detailing the development of soils, red markers identifying and interpreting rock outcrops, and green markers summarizing soil development. Begin in mostly open pinyon pine forest with a sagebrush understory before entering a denser forest of primarily Jeffrey pines. Nearing the meadow that surrounds Curtz Lake, the tread of the trail disappears in the tall grasses—head toward the interpretive signs in order to stay on track.

Without fanfare, you intersect a section of the Wildlife Trail near a sign about the Pacific tree frog. Somewhere prior to this sign, the Soils-Geology Trail veered southeast back to the parking area, but this section of trail has completely disappeared. Walk past more interpretive signs before the trail curves around and then angles sharply uphill on rocky trail to reach Airport Road across from the parking area.

Summit Lake Trail: To do this trail as a point-to-point trip, you must leave a vehicle at the far trailhead by proceeding on Airport Road to a junction with the road to Indian Creek Reservoir and following signs to the campground. The trail terminates near a T-junction with a road to the tent camping area.

From the parking area near Curtz Lake, follow the continuation of the rocky road to the north of the lake, which is a meadow-rimmed, shallow body of water that tends to dry up by late season. On mildly graded trail, you head through a scattered forest of Jeffrey pine, pinyon pine, mountain mahogany, and a few firs, with an understory of sagebrush, bitterbrush, and manzanita. Pass by a trail register and continue to a Y-junction at the north end of Summit Lake, three-quarters of a mile from the trailhead.

Veer right at the junction and follow singletrack trail around the open east shore of the elliptically shaped lake toward a low gap above the far end. After a short mild climb to the forested gap, the trail follows a gentle traverse that curves east to a saddle between Peaks 6393 and 6366. Beyond the saddle, the trail continues traversing for a bit before bending north on a moderate descent. On the way, you have periodic glimpses of Indian Creek Reservoir and Stevens Lake, along with their respective dams.

Pass by another trail register and continue the descent toward the west shore of the reservoir. Following a switchback, the trail veers southeast, drops almost to the floor of the valley, and reaches the campground access road.

Carson River Trail: Walk across Airport Road from the parking area and follow a jeep road, making sure you avoid following the road that curves uphill to the right. Near a sign reading YOUTH CORPS CONSERVATION PROJECT, CARSON RIVER VALLEY TRAIL 2, singletrack trail leads past a small sign about fishing regulations on East Fork Carson River and a hiker emblem sign across grassy slopes sprinkled with white fir and Jeffrey pine. Soon the grassy slopes give way to shrubby hillsides of bitterbrush, sagebrush, and manzanita beneath a denser forest of juniper, pinyon pine, mountain mahogany, white fir, and Jeffrey pine.

Near the halfway point, the trail enters the narrow canyon of a seasonal drainage and descends toward the river. The trail eventually merges with a rocky old jeep road, as you pass a box containing angler surveys. Soon the condition of the road deteriorates so badly that most four-wheel-drive vehicles can make no further progress and a short distance farther, as the canyon narrows, the road is reduced to a singletrack path. Ultimately, the canyon widens as you approach the river. Pass a trail register and a historic sign before arriving at the north bank. The trail to the left enters a large flat holding a campsite, and faint tread continues downstream a short distance before dying out near some cliffs.

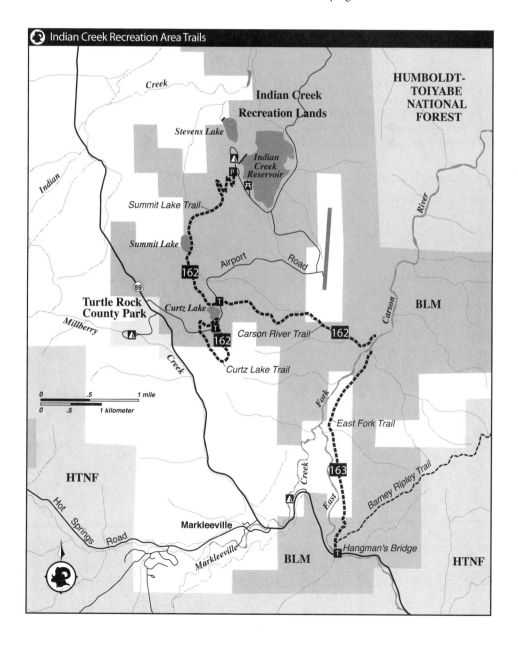

163 East Fork Carson River

see map on p. 359

Distance	5 miles (out-and-back)
Hiking Time	2.5 hours
Elevation	+75/-200 feet
Difficulty	Easy
Trail Use	Mountain biking OK, dogs OK
Best Times	Late April through October
Agency	Bureau of Land Management at 775-885-6000, blm.gov
Recommended Map	USGS 7.5-minute *Markleeville*

HIGHLIGHTS The East Fork Carson River Trail is used primarily by anglers to access some of the most extraordinary fly-fishing in the region. Even without the fishing, recreationists will find the river to be quite scenic and more than worth the effort of the straightforward 2.5-mile hike.

DIRECTIONS Follow CA 89 to Hangman's Bridge over East Fork Carson River, 1.5 miles southbound of the town of Markleeville, and turn left into the parking area just past the far side of the bridge.

FACILITIES/TRAILHEAD The parking area has vault toilets and bear-proof garbage cans. The Forest Service manages the Markleeville Campground, 0.8 mile north of Hangman's Bridge. The trail begins on a closed jeep road.

Angler plying the waters of East Fork Carson River

Hop over the gate and follow the closed road on a stiff climb up the hillside through scattered pinyon pine and Jeffrey pine with an occasional juniper. Pass a brown metal box containing angler surveys and immediately reach a Y-junction with the Barney Ripley Trail heading sharply uphill on the right. Continue straight ahead at the junction on a milder climb. Remaining a good distance away from the river, the old road passes through mostly open terrain with pastoral views to the west of the verdant meadowlands between Markleeville Creek and the East Fork.

At 1.25 miles, pass through an open gate in a barbed-wire fence and proceed through sagebrush scrub. About three-quarters of a mile farther, the road divides, with the left-hand branch heading down to a tram that crosses the river and a gauging station on the south bank. The left-hand road continues downstream, passes through another gate, and eventually narrows to the width of a trail. Shortly after, the route drops toward the river, enters a side canyon, and follows it to the end of the trail at the riverbank, where, lined with alders, willows, and an occasional cottonwood, the river glides picturesquely through the East Fork canyon.

164 Charity Valley East to Burnside Lake

see map on p. 362

Distance	5 miles (point-to-point, shuttle)
Hiking Time	2.5–3 hours
Elevation	+2,400 feet
Difficulty	Difficult
Trail Use	Dogs OK, mountain biking OK
Best Times	June through October
Agency	Grover Hot Springs State Park at 530-694-2248, parks.ca.gov; Humboldt-Toiyabe National Forest at 775-882-2766, www.fs.usda.gov/htnf
Recommended Maps	USGS 7.5-minute *Markleeville, Carson Pass*

HIGHLIGHTS This trip takes hikers on a lightly used route from the vicinity of Grover Hot Springs State Park to Burnside Lake. The trail begins just outside the park at 5,750 feet and gains only a nominal amount of elevation over the first couple of miles, providing an easy trip for families with young children, or for hikers of any age searching for an early-season alternative while waiting for the winter snowpack in the higher elevations to finish melting. Beyond the first 2 miles, the trail climbs more steeply up the canyon of Hot Springs Creek, gaining almost all of the 2,400 feet of elevation in 2 miles, before mellowing out for the last easy mile to the lake.

DIRECTIONS *Start:* From the center of Markleeville, turn west from CA 89 and follow Hot Springs Road for about 3 miles to the well-signed trailhead on the right-hand side of the road.

End: At the junction of CA 88 and CA 89 in Hope Valley, head south on Burnside Lake Road and drive 6 miles to the end of the road near the northeast shore.

FACILITIES/TRAILHEAD Grover Hot Springs State Park, three-quarters of a mile from the trailhead, has a developed campground and picnic area, as well as a natural hot springs pool. The trail begins near some trail signs.

Walk west on mildly graded trail through Jeffrey pine forest for a half mile and then skirt the north edge of Grover Hot Springs State Park's campgrounds. The trail merges with a road at the far end of the campground and continues on the roadbed near the fringe of a large grassy meadow dotted with small pockets of pines that cover the heart of the park. Reach a Y-junction with a road on the right and continue straight ahead following a sign marked simply TRAIL. Proceed past a footpath on the left and over a narrow, alder-lined seasonal stream to a well-signed junction with the Hot Springs Cutoff Trail on the left, 1.25 miles from the trailhead.

Continue straight ahead from the junction through light forest as the expansive grassy meadow is left behind. After a half mile, draw nearer to Hot Springs Creek and reach a junction with the Waterfall Trail branching to the left.

Proceed ahead from the junction, as the gentle grade is left behind on a moderate, occasionally switchbacking climb through a thick forest of white firs, incense cedars, and Jeffrey pines. Farther up the hillside, you break out of the trees onto shrub-covered slopes with fine views of the canyon. Additional switchbacks lead to a signed junction

with the Burnside Lake Trail, 3.5 miles from the trailhead.

Veer right at the junction and, leaving the pleasant grade behind, make a short switchbacking climb up a narrow and steep canyon to a crossing of Hot Springs Creek on a raised section of trail that spans a boulder-strewn channel. Beyond the crossing, make a winding climb up the canyon through a brief pocket of shady forest before emerging from the trees to continue the steep, zigzagging ascent up the south-facing canyon wall, fully exposed to the hot summer sun.

Halfway from the junction to the lake, you crest the lip of the lower canyon and follow more gently graded trail along the diminishing creek back into a thick forest of western white pines, lodgepole pines, and white firs. Soon the trail bends over to cross the main channel of Hot Springs

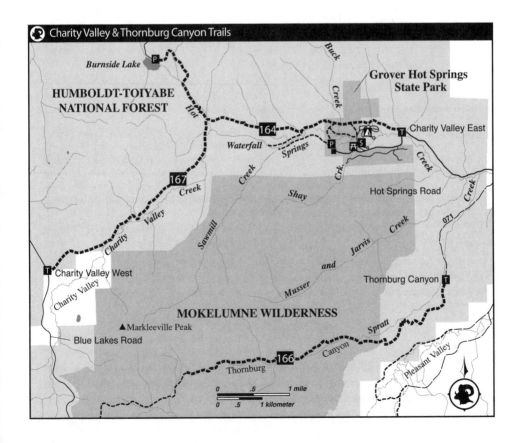

Burnside Lake

Creek and then follows the course of a tributary upstream for 0.4 mile to its crossing. Follow a mildly graded path across a verdant meadow, back into forest, and then over a low rise to the northeast shore of Burnside Lake.

165   Grover Hot Springs State Park

see map on p. 364

Distance	3 miles, out-and-back (Falls Trail)
	1.8 miles, out-and-back (Sawmill Creek Trail)
Hiking Time	1.5 hours (Falls Trail)
	1 hour (Sawmill Creek Trail)
Elevation	+200 feet (Falls Trail)
	+50 feet (Sawmill Creek Trail)
Difficulty	Easy
Trail Use	Good for kids, leashed dogs, mountain biking OK
Best Times	April through October
Agency	Grover Hot Springs State Park at 530-694-2248, parks.ca.gov
Recommended Map	USGS 7.5-minute *Markleeville*

HIGHLIGHTS Two trails emanating from Grover Hot Springs State Park provide short and easy trips for hikers of all ages. Actually, the two trails used to be a single path before a flood wiped out a bridge over Hot Springs Creek, severing the link between the two sections. Rather than rebuild the bridge and eventually risk the same fate, the north section became the Falls Trail and the south section the Sawmill Creek Trail. The Falls Trail, the more popular of the two, follows a gently graded path across the large grassy meadow in the heart of the park and then upstream to a short but picturesque fall on Hot Springs Creek. The Sawmill Creek Trail is a short, easy path that follows the fringe of the meadow into the forest and then proceeds along the tumbling creek to the site of the former bridge.

With the bonus of the nearby facilities, recreationists can enjoy a picnic lunch following their hike and then a refreshing dip in the hot-springs pool. For information on the hours of operation of the pool and fees, call 530-694-2249.

DIRECTIONS From the center of Markleeville, turn west from CA 89 and follow Hot Springs Road for about 3.75 miles to the entrance of Grover Hot Springs State Park. Veer left, following signs to the Hot Springs, drive past the hot-springs pool and park in the trailhead parking lot on the far side of the pool area.

FACILITIES/TRAILHEAD Grover Hot Springs State Park has a developed campground and picnic area, as well as a natural hot-springs pool. The trails begin at the edge of the parking area near their respective trail signs.

Falls Trail: From the parking area, follow the Hot Springs Cutoff Trail north across the meadow on sandy tread that soon leads to a stout bridge over Hot Springs Creek. Beyond the bridge, you reach a junction marked by a 4-by-4-inch post and bear left onto a fainter section of trail that immediately leads into a forest of junipers, incense cedars, and Jeffrey pines. A short way farther, you come to a three-way junction, where the more pronounced tread of the Charity Valley Trail runs east–west.

Bear left and proceed on the Charity Valley Trail up the nearly level valley for another half mile to a signed three-way junction with the Waterfall Trail. Bend left at the junction and continue through shady forest. The trail nears Hot Springs Creek and soon comes to the site of a former bridge that once spanned the creek and provided a connection between the Sawmill Canyon and Falls Trails before it was wiped out during a flood. Past the bridge site, the location of the correct trail is a bit confusing, as several use trails have developed over the years, paths that seem to randomly come and go—a good rule of thumb is to take the highest path when in doubt. Ducks and cairns may help guide you through this section, although the general route is straightforward—simply follow the creek upstream.

Climb over a rock outcropping and find more discernible tread on the far side that winds through patches of manzanita and an assortment of large boulders. Soon the roar of the fall leads you forward to a rock platform that offers a limited view of the cascading fall. To achieve a better view, you'll have to work your way a little farther up the canyon. Particularly in spring, the waterfall is quite picturesque, with ribbons of water spilling down across a cliff of dark rock.

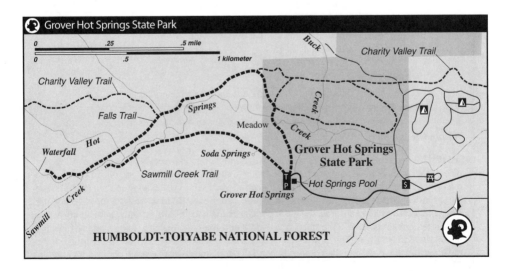

Sawmill Creek Trail: From the parking area, follow the gently graded Sawmill Creek Trail southeast around the fringe of the expansive meadow bordering Hot Springs Creek through the edge of a mixed forest of Jeffrey pines, white firs, and incense cedars. Beyond the meadow, the trail draws closer to the willow- and alder-lined creek and makes a couple of bridged crossings over a pair of thin side streams. Eventually, you reach the site of the old bridge that used to span Hot Springs Creek before being washed out several years ago in a flood. After midsummer, when the flow of the creek is low, fording Hot Springs Creek and returning to the parking area via the Falls and Hot Springs Cutoff Trails is quite possible. Although a use trail continues upstream from the old bridge site, the deteriorating path is steep, primitive, and overgrown, completely dying out a little farther upstream.

Waterfall at the end of the Falls Trail

166 Thornburg Canyon

Distance	10 miles (out-and-back)
Hiking Time	5–6 hours
Elevation	+2,375/-150 feet
Difficulty	Moderate
Trail Use	Backpacking option, dogs OK
Best Times	June through October
Agency	Humboldt-Toiyabe National Forest at 775-882-2766, www.fs.usda.gov/htnf
Recommended Maps	USGS 7.5-minute *Markleeville, Carson Pass, ENF, SNF and TNF A Guide to the Mokelumne Wilderness*

see map on p. 362

HIGHLIGHTS A seldom-trodden path leads into Mokelumne Wilderness and up Thornburg Canyon through quiet forest for quite a distance before a sweeping vista unfolds of two of the area's most prominent peaks. The trip is an excellent all-day journey for hikers in reasonable shape, and backpackers who don't mind primitive camping conditions should appreciate the abundant solitude. Peak baggers can accept the additional challenge of scaling Jeff Davis or Markleeville Peaks, but if climbing one of these peaks is the primary goal, following a route from Blue Lakes Road would be considerably shorter.

DIRECTIONS From the center of Markleeville, turn west from CA 89 and follow Hot Springs Road 1 mile to Pleasant Valley Road and turn left. Proceed a short distance to Sawmill Road and follow Sawmill an equally short way to the end of the pavement, where the dirt road becomes FS 071. Follow FS 071 across a section of private property onto forest service land and continue upstream along Spratt Creek, crossing the creek a couple of times (high-clearance vehicle recommended) before reaching a closed steel gate, 2.2 miles from Hot Springs Road. Park off the road as space allows.

FACILITIES/TRAILHEAD There are no facilities at the trailhead. The trail follows the continuation of the road beyond the gate.

Follow the old road on a mildly rising grade through a forest of mostly Jeffrey pines, with smaller amounts of juniper, white fir, and incense cedar. Initially the shady forest allows very little ground cover, but farther on, a lighter forest, which now includes aspen stands, permits enough sunlight through to nourish a sprinkling of grasses, wildflowers, willows, and wild roses in areas of sufficient moisture and a smattering of bitterbrush, sagebrush, and manzanita in drier soils. Crest a low rise and follow a moderate, winding climb

*Rock pinnacle along the
Thornburg Canyon Trail*

above the lower lip of Thornburg Canyon, with partial views below of Pleasant Valley. At 1.5 miles from the trailhead, you cross the signed Mokelumne Wilderness boundary.

From the boundary, make a brief climb and then descend toward a boulder hop of Spratt Creek, where you see evidence of a previous fire. Once across the alder- and willow-lined creek, a protracted climb up the north side of the forested canyon begins. Along the way, the trail crosses several seasonal side streams. Farther up the canyon, pockets of lighter forest allow views of some rocky cliffs rimming the canyon wall. With the increase in elevation, lodgepole pines, western white pines, and mountain hemlocks ultimately join the mixed forest.

The forest starts to thin near the head of the canyon, and soon the trail leads across open, dry slopes covered primarily with sagebrush and sprinkled with the yellow blossoms of mule-ears in midsummer. From a saddle between Thornburg Canyon and the drainage of Jeff Davis Creek, you have a remarkable view of the territory ahead, with the volcanic plug of Jeff Davis Peak to the southwest providing the focal point of the scenery, along with Mokelumne Peak to the northwest.

Unless you've arranged for pickup from Blue Lakes Road at Border Ruffian Flat, this view-packed saddle is a good turnaround point. The trail continues from the saddle on a short descent to a ford of Jeff Davis Creek, crosses a private parcel of verdant meadowlands, climbs to a saddle between ridges from Markleeville and Jeff Davis Peaks, and then descends southwest to Blue Lakes Road.

167 Charity Valley West to Burnside Lake

see map on p. 362

Distance	11 miles (out-and-back)
Hiking Time	5.5–6 hours
Elevation	+1,225/-900 feet
Difficulty	Difficult
Trail Use	Mountain biking OK, dogs OK
Best Times	June through October
Agency	Humboldt-Toiyabe National Forest at 775-882-2766, www.fs.usda.gov/htnf
Recommended Maps	USGS 7.5-minute *Carson Pass, Markleeville*

HIGHLIGHTS The gently graded Charity Valley Trail offers good views from the start of verdant Charity Valley backdropped by the rugged slopes of Markleeville Peak before following Charity Valley Creek as it glides down a forested canyon through pockets of lush vegetation and past several little ponds. The route adopts a steeper demeanor past the Burnside Lake junction but mellows again halfway to the lake. What little use this route seems to receive appears to be primarily from equestrians.

DIRECTIONS Follow CA 88 to Hope Valley and turn south onto the well-signed Blue Lakes Road. Follow paved road for 6 miles to a small parking area on the west side of the road, signed CHARITY VALLEY TRAILHEAD WEST END.

FACILITIES/TRAILHEAD There are no facilities at the trailhead. The trail begins across the road from the parking area.

Cross the road and follow the trail through a grove of lodgepole pines. Early summer provides a sprinkling of color from mule-ears and lupines in bloom. Pass through a cattle gate and continue through scattered lodgepole-pine forest with an understory of sagebrush. Start climbing across mostly open, rocky slopes dotted with an occasional juniper, crossing a number of seasonal swales along the way. The trail eventually swings around the slope below Peak 8312 and into the canyon of Charity Valley Creek, where the open topography allows fine views of the surrounding terrain, including verdant Charity Valley and towering Markleeville Peak. Follow the trail on some minor ups and downs through an increasing lodgepole-pine forest, before a steady descent leads to the floor of the grass- and flower-covered valley and along willow-lined Charity Valley Creek.

Past the edge of Charity Valley, the pleasantly graded trail follows the creek downstream through lush foliage, which now includes prominent stands of aspen, and over flower-lined side streams. The path briefly veers away from the creek into an open area of granite rock, where cairns may help guide you. A use trail leads a short distance to a fine picnic spot along the bank of the creek in full view of a stepped waterfall. The main trail drops off the area of granite and proceeds downstream through more lush foliage and around some beaver ponds.

Eventually the trail veers away from the stream into areas of drier vegetation, where Jeffrey pines join the forest and shrubs cover the slopes, including manzanita, tobacco brush, and chinquapin. Stroll along the base of some impressive cliffs below Peak 8125 and then pass by a small pond covered with lily pads. As the creek tumbles steeply down a section of the canyon, the trail moves farther north away from the creek, crossing gentler terrain on the way to a granite bench above a sharp cleft. The trail zigzags down this cleft toward the floor of the canyon to rejoin the course of the creek. Walk across the flat floor of the canyon and then make a short, mild descent to a crossing of Hot Springs Creek. Just past the stream, 3.75 miles from the trailhead, is a three-way signed junction with the Burnside Lake Trail.

Veer left (west) at the junction and make a short, switchbacking climb up a narrow and steep canyon to a crossing of Hot Springs Creek on a raised section of trail that spans a boulder-strewn channel. Beyond the crossing, make a winding climb up the canyon through a brief pocket of shady forest before emerging from the trees to continue the steep, zigzagging ascent up the south-facing canyon wall, fully exposed to the hot summer sun.

Halfway from the junction to the lake, you crest the lip of the lower canyon and follow more gently graded trail along the diminishing creek back into a thick forest of western white pines, lodgepole pines, and white firs. Soon the trail bends over to cross the main channel of Hot Springs Creek and then follows the course of a tributary upstream for 0.4 mile to its crossing. Follow the mildly graded path across a verdant meadow, back into forest, and then over a low rise to the northeast shore of Burnside Lake.

168 Hope Valley Overlook

Distance	5.8 miles (out-and-back)
Hiking Time	3–3.5 hours
Elevation	+1,200/-300 feet
Difficulty	Moderate
Trail Use	Mountain biking OK, dogs OK
Best Times	June through October
Agency	Humboldt-Toiyabe National Forest at 775-882-2766, www.fs.usda.gov/htnf
Recommended Map	USGS 7.5-minute *Freel Peak*

HIGHLIGHTS This walk up a closed fire road takes day hikers on a moderately steep climb of a forested hillside to an overlook at the edge of some vertical cliffs, which offers an expansive view of Hope Valley and the surrounding peaks and ridges. The view is grand in summer, when the tributaries of East Fork Carson River keep the verdant meadows of Hope Valley well watered. Autumn adds a brilliant touch of gold, when the numerous aspen stands are ablaze with color. Those seeking added adventures may continue along the network of back roads to Burnside Lake or Hawkins Peak or strike off cross-country toward the summit of Pickett Peak for a more expansive view.

DIRECTIONS Follow CA 88 to closed Forest Service Road 053 on the south side of the highway, 0.8 mile east of the junction with CA 89 in Hope Valley and just west of Sorensen's Resort. There is only enough space for three or four cars in front of the gate. Look for additional space in turnouts on the opposite shoulder if space is not available at the trailhead.

FACILITIES/TRAILHEAD There are no facilities at the trailhead. The trail begins along the closed road. Before or after the trip, hikers can dine on fresh dishes at Sorensen's Resort. The charming café with a quaint mountain setting is open each day from 7:30 a.m. to 9 p.m. for breakfast, lunch, and dinner. Sorensen's also offers comfortable lodging in an assortment of mountain cabins. Call 800-423-9949 or visit the website at **sorensensresort.com** for more information.

Begin a stiff, winding climb up a hillside through a mixed forest of firs, pines, aspens, and an occasional juniper. Cross a sprightly stream spilling down the hillside through a boulder-filled drainage lined with willows and aspen and then soon curve around to cross the piped stream two more times on the way up the slope. Momentarily break out of the thick forest onto a slope covered with tobacco brush and widely scattered

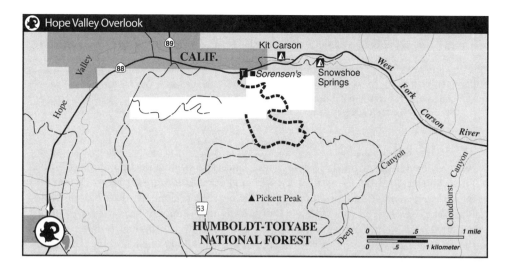

conifers, with views of peaks and ridges to the north. Near a bend in the road, you reach a promontory with a more widespread view of Hope Valley and the terrain around Luther Pass.

Head back into mixed forest, which now includes lodgepole pines and western white pines, and soon come to a Y-junction with a road coming from Deep Canyon to the east. Proceed straight ahead at the junction, as the grade eases to more of a mildly rising traverse to the west. At 2.75 miles is another

Y-junction, where the main road continues straight ahead, but you veer right (south) onto a singletrack use trail that leads a quarter mile to an overlook at the edge of some steep cliffs. Perched on this rocky aerie, you have an excellent view of the broad expanse of Hope Valley and the terrain rising up toward Luther Pass, flanked on the right by Thompson Peak and on the left by Waterhouse Peak. In autumn, the view is enhanced by extensive aspen stands that provide a sprawling burst of golden yellow.

169 Granite and Grouse Lakes

Distance	12 miles (out-and-back)
Hiking Time	6–7 hours
Elevation	+1,575/-1,125 feet
Difficulty	Moderate
Trail Use	Backpacking option, dogs OK
Best Times	July through October
Agency	Eldorado National Forest at 209-295-4251, www.fs.usda.gov/eldorado
Recommended Maps	*ENF, SNF, HTNF A Guide to the Mokelumne Wilderness*

see map on p. 370

HIGHLIGHTS Tucked well off CA 88 down the Blue Lakes Road is a series of out-of-the-way reservoirs that lures campers, boaters, and anglers. The area beyond these reservoirs presents some equally attractive backcountry that is sure to please even the most discriminating of hikers and backpackers. Day hikers searching for an easy 1-mile trip will find the walk to Granite Lake to be an excellent choice.

Nestled into a little-traveled corner of Mokelumne Wilderness, Grouse Lake sits high above Summit City Canyon. Requiring only modest effort, this longer hike offers both the spectacular scenery of sweeping vistas and the intriguing beauty of geologic diversity.

DIRECTIONS Leave CA 88 at 6.3 miles east of Carson Pass and head south on Blue Lakes Road through Hope Valley and over a divide to a junction with the Tamarack Road, 10.3 miles from CA 88. Continue straight ahead for another mile and turn right at the Mokelumne Hydro Project. Proceed past Lower Blue Lake to a small parking area on the left, just below the spillway of Upper Blue Lake, 13 miles from CA 88.

FACILITIES/TRAILHEAD Middle Creek Campground, operated by Pacific Gas & Electric, offers developed campsites just south of Upper Blue Lake, which has a boat ramp. The Grouse Lake Trail begins just south of the Middle Creek Campground, at the edge of the parking area.

Cross the seasonal channel of the spillway overflow, turn south into lodgepole-pine forest, and descend briefly to a log crossing of the perennial outflow from Upper Blue Lake. Nearly level trail leads past an unsigned lateral to the campground, before the trail swings west on a gentle ascent with tree-shrouded views of the surrounding peaks, including Round Top. The grade eases momentarily at the signed crossing of the Mokelumne Wilderness boundary. Continuing west, skirt a small pond and in about a half mile, swing next to the flower-lined, seasonal outlet from Granite Lake. Soon the lake springs into view, cradled in a small basin surrounded by weathered granite outcrops and the coarse grains of disintegrating granite rock, called grus, comes almost to the meadow-fringed shore.

Skirt the south shore of the lake past campsite laterals and veer left over a low ridge. Beyond the lake, most day hikers are left behind, as the trail winds west for most of a mile through the weathered granite landscape, passing pockets of mixed forest and a small, flower-lined creek. Farther on, a very steep climb on deteriorating tread leads to a stunning vista: clockwise from the east is the Carson Range; dark, volcanic Raymond Peak; metamorphic Highland, Stanislaus, and Leavitt Peaks; and the polished, light granite of the deep cleft of Mokelumne River Canyon.

Continue through open terrain past an old gravesite, followed by a mild descent across a verdant, flower-dotted meadow. Beyond the meadow, a lengthy ascent leads across several gullies to a sloping bench bisected by several spring-fed rills.

Descend west to a small creek, remaining on the north side, and climb through willows a short distance past the source of the creek. Continue climbing as the trail fades on an open slope. A ducked route levels off and contours northwest for a quarter mile, until multiple paths descend

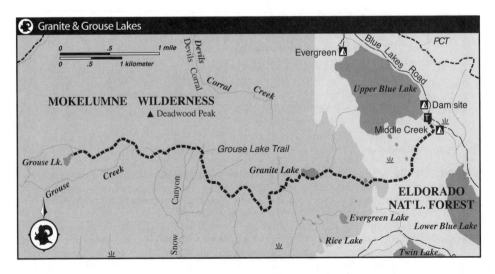

a flower-filled gully dotted with boulders, where Grouse Lake appears several hundred feet below. Eventually, the paths merge into a single trail that continues the descent into thickening forest to the shore of the secluded lake. On a hot day, Grouse Lake provides a wonderful wilderness swimming pool. Nearby viewpoints offer glimpses of Summit City Canyon below to the west, and golden eagles, which traditionally nest in the canyon, may occasionally be seen riding thermals to dizzying heights above.

Deadwood Peak towers above the Grouse Lake Trail.

170 Upper Blue Lake to Fourth of July Lake

see map on p. 372

Distance	9 miles (out-and-back)
Hiking Time	4.5–5 hours
Elevation	+1,150/-1,150 feet
Difficulty	Difficult
Trail Use	Backpacking option, dogs OK
Best Times	Mid-July through mid-October
Agency	Eldorado National Forest at 209-295-4251, www.fs.usda.gov/eldorado
Recommended Maps	*ENF, SNF, HTNF A Guide to the Mokelumne Wilderness*
Notes	Fourth of July Lake is within the Carson Pass Management Area, which requires backpackers to obtain a wilderness permit and a reservation for one of the six designated campsites, available at the Carson Pass Information Station. Fires are not allowed within the management area.

HIGHLIGHTS This route from Upper Blue Lake is definitely the back way to picturesque Fourth of July Lake, as most visitors reach the lake from the extremely popular trails emanating from Woods Lake and Carson Pass Trailheads. Potentially, your group may be the only ones on the trail all the way from the trailhead through lonely Summit City Canyon and up to the lake. Due to the area's popularity, camping at Fourth of July Lake is limited to six designated sites available only with a reservation.

DIRECTIONS Leave CA 88 at 6.3 miles east of Carson Pass and head south on Blue Lakes Road through Hope Valley and over a divide to a junction with the Tamarack Road, 10.3 miles from CA 88. Continue straight ahead for another mile and turn right at the Mokelumne Hydro Project. Proceed past Lower Blue Lake and Upper Blue Lake to the signed Evergreen Trailhead 18E21 on the right-hand side, just prior to the Upper Blue Lake Campground entrance. Limited parking is available at the trailhead.

FACILITIES/TRAILHEAD Upper Blue Lake Campground, operated by Pacific Gas & Electric, offers developed campsites and a boat ramp. The trail begins near a series of trail signs.

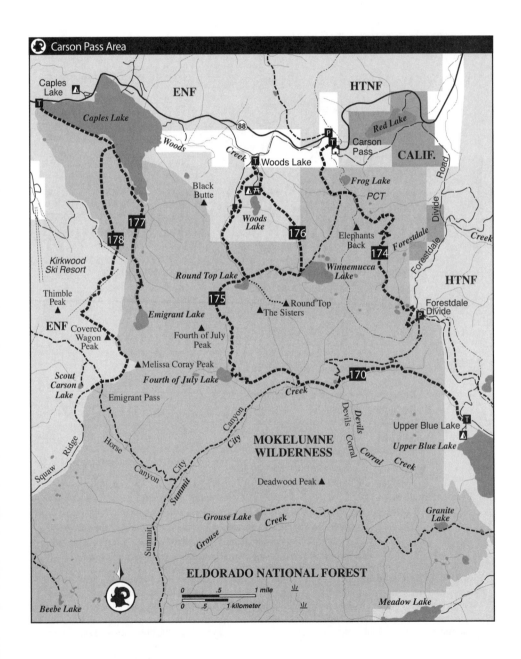

Begin hiking along an old roadbed on a moderate climb through a mixed forest of white firs, lodgepole pines, western white pines, and mountain hemlocks, alongside the thin, alder-lined inlet of Upper Blue Lake. Cross the narrow stream and continue upstream along the east bank to a small meadow filled with wildflowers in midsummer, soon returning to dense forest. Eventually, the trail moves away from the diminutive stream and crosses the signed Mokelumne Wilderness boundary. Beyond the boundary, the grade of ascent increases for a short distance to the top of a ridge, after which you start descending into Summit City Canyon.

Initially, the descent into the canyon is fairly steep, but it soon moderates on the approach to a crossing of Summit City Creek, which occurs just above the lip of a short waterfall. Just past the crossing is an obscure three-way junction with a trail that climbs up to Forestdale Divide.

Follow the creek downstream through the deep canyon. Occasional, filtered views through the trees of Deadwood Peak across the chasm of Summit City Canyon provide intriguing glimpses of some alpine-looking terrain that is deserving of a fuller view. Soon the tread becomes rocky and steep as the forest lightens a bit, allowing a ground cover of sagebrush, grasses, and drought-tolerant wildflowers to flourish, which is briefly interrupted by lush foliage where a seep trickles across the trail. Beyond the seep, the forest thickens again and the ground cover correspondingly diminishes.

Farther on, a break in the trees permits the full view of Deadwood Peak that you may have coveted before.

Continue the moderate descent on rocky trail through thick forest until the grade eases on the approach to the bottom of Summit City Canyon, where meadow-like vegetation carpets the forest floor. A gentle stroll leads past a primitive campsite to a 4-by-4-inch post marking the junction of a trail on the right to Forestdale Divide. A short distance farther, near a wide stream channel and primitive campsites, another 4-by-4-inch post denotes a junction with the trail to Fourth of July Lake, 3 miles from the trailhead.

Turn right (north) and start a moderate climb that leads out of forest cover and onto shrub-covered slopes. Soon the trail bends west and follows a rising traverse across the hillside, where the trail is nearly overgrown in places by the thick shrubs. Fine views of Summit City Canyon and Deadwood and Fourth of July Peaks abound on the ascent across this open hillside. Nearing the steep canyon holding Fourth of July Lake's outlet, the trail veers northwest and switchbacks into scattered forest and the signed Carson Pass Management Area. More short switchbacks lead to east shore of Fourth of July Lake.

Reposing in a cirque at the base of Fourth of July Peak, the lake is rimmed by steep cliffs, stands of forest, pockets of willow, and flower-filled meadows above the north shore. Camping is limited to six designated sites on the east and north sides of the lake.

171 PCT: Wet Meadows to Raymond Lake

Distance	9 miles (out-and-back)
Hiking Time	4.5–5 hours
Elevation	+1,750/-825 feet
Difficulty	Moderate
Trail Use	Dogs OK
Best Times	July through October
Agency	Humboldt-Toiyabe National Forest at 775-882-2766, www.fs.usda.gov/htnf
Recommended Map	ENF, SNF, HTNF A Guide to the Mokelumne Wilderness

HIGHLIGHTS Good views of the surrounding landscape en route and stunning scenery in the vicinity of Raymond Lake are certain to satisfy the most discriminating of travelers on this trip, which visits some of the volcanic topography for which the area is noted. Midsummer visitors will have the added bonus of a fine display of wildflowers. Despite following the famed Pacific Crest Trail (PCT) almost the entire distance, this trip utilizes a section that is not that heavily traveled.

DIRECTIONS Leave CA 88 at 6.3 miles east of Carson Pass and head south on Blue Lakes Road through Hope Valley and over a divide to a junction with the Tamarack Road, 10.3 miles from CA 88. Turn left, immediately pass a signed turnoff for the Tamarack Trailhead, and continue to a T-junction, 2.9 miles from the Blue Lakes Road. Turn right, following signed directions for Wet Meadows, and travel one-third of a mile to the next junction with a road on the right that passes through Indian Valley. Proceed straight ahead from the junction on deteriorating dirt road, which probably will require a high-clearance vehicle to negotiate some boggy sections. Continue another 1.3 miles to the small parking area for the Wet Meadows Trailhead.

FACILITIES/TRAILHEAD There are no facilities at the trailhead. The signed trail begins near a 4-by-4-inch post.

Follow a connector trail along a creek lined with willows and wildflowers for a short while, cross the creek on an easy boulder hop, and then make a brief climb up to a junction with the PCT and a signboard (backpackers can self-register for wilderness permits here). Turn right (northeast) and follow the trail upstream briefly until a moderate climb leads away from the creek and across a sagebrush-filled saddle. Away from the saddle, the trail descends through scattered forest that

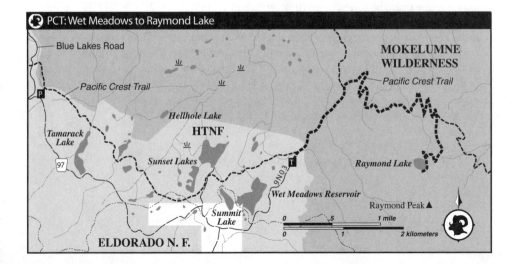

becomes thicker on the way to a log cross-ing of a tributary of Pleasant Valley Creek. Gently graded trail leads away from the creek to a Y-junction with an obscure, unmarked trail to Pleasant Valley on the left, 1 mile from the trailhead.

Remain on the well-trodden PCT as it climbs an open, shrub-covered slope and switchbacks to a rock promontory with a wide-ranging vista. Pausing travelers are treated to views of the deep cleft of Pleasant Valley beneath Thornburg Peak, the Mar-kleeville area, and the Carson Valley back-dropped by the Pine Nut Mountains. Other notable peaks in the immediate vicinity include Jeff Davis Peak and The Nipple.

Leaving the views behind, continue climbing to the crest of a minor ridge. From there, the trail follows an undulat-ing traverse of the folds and creases of the rocky topography below Raymond Peak. Along the way, the trail meets a couple of lushly lined rivulets, where seasonal wildflowers add a touch of color. Beyond the crossing of the creek from Raymond Lake, begin a moderate, switchbacking climb across predominantly open slopes on the way to a three-way junction, 3.7 miles from the trailhead.

Leave the PCT at the junction and head south on the lateral to Raymond Lake, climbing across open, sagebrush-covered slopes on the way to a forested canyon directly east of the lake. Cross a narrow and shallow seasonal stream in this can-yon and then follow an ascending traverse across the outlet and up to the lakeshore. Raymond Lake is tucked into a tight cleft below the steep north face of Raymond Peak. The clarity of the water may appear a bit murky for some tastes. Backpack-ers will find decent campsites shaded by mountain hemlocks, lodgepole pines, and whitebark pines on the east and south shores, and the sunrise is reported to be quite a treat.

Hikers take a break at vista point along the PCT.

172 Meiss Meadows Trailhead to Showers Lake

Distance	10.2 miles (out-and-back)
Hiking Time	5–5.5 hours
Elevation	+750/-675 feet
Difficulty	Moderate
Trail Use	Backpacking option, dogs OK
Best Times	July through October
Agency	Eldorado National Forest at 209-295-4251, www.fs.usda.gov/eldorado; Lake Tahoe Basin Management Unit at 530-543-2600, www.fs.usda.gov/ltbmu
Recommended Maps	USGS 7.5-minute *Carson Pass, Caples Lake*

HIGHLIGHTS Showers Lake is one of the best camping areas between CA 50 and CA 88, with numerous campsites and good angling for brook trout. En route, the trail passes through the Upper Truckee River drainage, offering panoramic views of immense volcanic formations and a fine wildflower display in season.

DIRECTIONS Follow CA 88 to the Meiss Meadows Trailhead parking area, 0.2 mile west of Carson Pass.

FACILITIES/TRAILHEAD The parking area has portable toilets. The Forest Service charges a $5-per-day fee for parking. The well-signed trail begins on the west side of the parking area.

Pass a number of signs as you leave the parking lot and follow singletrack trail on an undulating traverse across the hillside above CA 88. Continue through a light forest of western white pines, junipers, white firs, lodgepole pines, and aspens, amid scattered boulders and a sprinkling of seasonal wildflowers. Soon the trail veers north and leaves the forest on a stiff ascent incorporating a few switchbacks across an open slope carpeted with sagebrush and more wildflowers, including columbine, lupine, paintbrush, and mule-ears. Step over a couple of seasonal trickles on a climb headed toward the prominent saddle above. At the saddle, 1.25 miles from the trailhead, hikers are treated to a sweeping view to the south of such notable mountains as Elephants Back, Round Top, Sisters, Fourth of July Peak, and Thimble Peak, plus a fine view to the north of the Upper Truckee River basin.

Nearly level trail passes by a grass- and willow-lined pond before a moderate descent leads downslope through open terrain toward the headwaters of the Upper Truckee River, crossing the nascent stream a few times before reaching the floor of the canyon. Follow the course of an old jeep road on an easy stroll across flower-filled meadows to another river crossing before passing by some old cabins that were previously used by cattle ranchers. Fortunately, grazing in the Meiss Meadows area was suspended several years ago, and the surrounding meadowlands have recovered quite nicely. A short distance beyond the cabins is a well-signed junction of the Tahoe Rim and Pacific Crest Trails.

Veer left (northwest) at the junction and follow the Pacific Crest Trail (PCT) to another crossing of the Upper Truckee River, which may require an ankle-deep ford early in the season. On the near side of the crossing, a faint use trail heads northeast a half mile toward Meiss Lake. If you plan on visiting Meiss Lake, be prepared for very boggy conditions while crossing the quagmire of a meadow that exists between the trail and the lake. Not only can the meadow be a muddy mess well into summer, it also has a notorious reputation for mosquitoes early in the season. A ford of a creek on the way to the lake will likely be a wet one as well.

From the river crossing, pleasantly graded trail alternates between pockets of

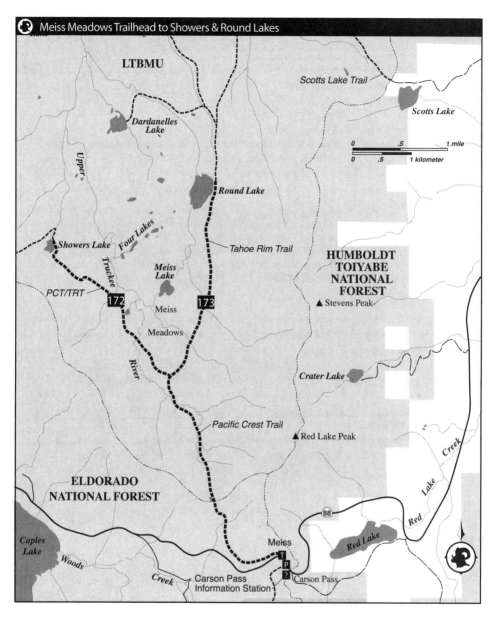

open meadow and stands of light forest. Beyond a shallow pond and the crossing of the stream draining Dixon Canyon, the trail starts an increasingly steep climb through light forest and wildflowers toward the broad crest above Showers Lake. At the top of the crest, encounter an unmarked X-junction, where abandoned trails head southwest to Schneider Cow Camp and the old alignment of the PCT travels around the south side of Showers Lake basin. Turn right at the junction and follow a realigned section of the PCT that descends to the northeast shore of granite-bound Showers Lake. Several campsites shaded by western white pines, mountain hemlocks, and lodgepole pines can be found near the outlet.

173 Meiss Meadows Trailhead to Round Lake

Distance	10.4 miles (out-and-back)
Hiking Time	5–6 hours
Elevation	+475/-950 feet
Difficulty	Moderate
Trail Use	Backpacking option, dogs OK
Best Times	July through October
Agency	Eldorado National Forest at 209-295-4251, www.fs.usda.gov/eldorado; Lake Tahoe Basin Management Unit at 530-543-2600, www.fs.usda.gov/ltbmu
Recommended Map	USGS 7.5-minute *Carson Pass, Caples Lake*

see map on p. 377

HIGHLIGHTS Round Lake is the largest of the lakes and ponds that dot the Upper Truckee River basin. In addition to the picturesque lake, this trip, utilizing segments of the Pacific Crest and Tahoe Rim Trails, leads hikers on a journey complete with grand views and wildflower-covered meadows.

DIRECTIONS Follow CA 88 to the Meiss Meadows Trailhead parking area, 0.2 mile west of Carson Pass.

FACILITIES/TRAILHEAD The parking area has portable toilets. The Forest Service charges a $5-per-day fee for parking. The well-signed trail begins on the west side of the parking area.

Pass a number of signs as you leave the parking lot and follow singletrack trail on an undulating traverse across the hillside above CA 88. Continue through a light forest of western white pines, junipers, white firs, lodgepole pines, and aspens, amid scattered boulders and a sprinkling of seasonal wildflowers. Soon the trail veers north and leaves the forest on a stiff ascent incorporating a few switchbacks across an open slope carpeted with sagebrush and more wildflowers, including columbine, lupine, paintbrush, and mule-ears. Step over a couple of seasonal trickles on a climb headed toward the prominent saddle above. At the saddle, 1.25 miles from the trailhead, hikers are treated to a sweeping view to the south of such notable mountains as Elephants Back, Round Top, Sisters, Fourth of July Peak, and Thimble Peak, plus a fine view to the north of the Upper Truckee River basin.

Historic cabins in Meiss Meadows

Nearly level trail passes by a grass- and willow-lined pond before a moderate descent leads downslope through open terrain toward the headwaters of the Upper Truckee River, crossing the nascent stream a few times before reaching the floor of the canyon. Follow the course of an old jeep road on an easy stroll across flower-filled meadows to another river crossing before passing by some old cabins that were previously used by cattle ranchers. Fortunately, grazing in the Meiss Meadows area was suspended several years ago and the surrounding meadowlands have recovered quite nicely. A short distance beyond the cabins is a well-signed junction of the Tahoe Rim and Pacific Crest Trails.

Veer right and follow a gently graded section of the Tahoe Rim Trail through scattered lodgepole pines and pockets of meadow to a seasonal stream that flows down a broad rocky swale bordered by a lush patch of grass. Head back into light forest on the way to crossings of Round Lake's inlet and a seasonal stream, and then continue the easy stroll past an aspen grove to the beginning of a moderate descent to Round Lake. Halfway down to the lake, you break out of the trees and skirt a willow-covered meadow that leads almost all the way to the shoreline.

174 Carson Pass to Forestdale Divide

see map on p. 372

Distance	10.2 miles (out-and-back)
Hiking Time	5–5.5 hours
Elevation	+1,200/-925 feet
Difficulty	Moderate
Trail Use	Dogs OK
Best Times	Late-July through mid-October
Agency	Eldorado National Forest at 209-295-4251, www.fs.usda.gov/eldorado; Lake Tahoe Basin Management Unit at 530-543-2600, www.fs.usda.gov/ltbmu
Recommended Map	ENF, SNF, HTNF A Guide to the Mokelumne Wilderness

HIGHLIGHTS Sweeping views and bountiful wildflowers will lure strong hikers who don't mind the ups and downs of this section of the Pacific Crest Trail (PCT). Forestdale Divide isn't much of a destination, but the intervening scenery and botany along the trail will satisfy photographers and amateur naturalists alike. By driving a second vehicle on the Forestdale Divide Road from Red Lake and leaving it at the informal trailhead on Forestdale Divide, you could avoid having to backtrack the 5.1 miles to Carson Pass.

DIRECTIONS Follow CA 88 to Carson Pass and park in the trailhead parking lot on the south side of the highway.

FACILITIES/TRAILHEAD The parking area has vault toilets. The Forest Service charges a $5-per-day fee for parking. The Carson Pass Information Station issues wilderness permits for Mokelumne Wilderness and camping reservations for designated sites within the Carson Pass Management Area, and also offers a limited selection of books and maps for sale. The well-signed trail begins on the west side of the Information Station.

Find this section of the PCT and Tahoe–Yosemite Trail (TRT) on the west side of the Carson Pass Information Station and head southbound on the wide, well-traveled path through a mixed forest of lodgepole pines, mountain hemlocks, and western white pines. Gently descending trail leads past a small pond surrounded by willows before a mild to moderately ascending trail crosses the wilderness boundary and switchbacks toward the Sierra crest. The forest thins on the approach to the ridge, and this allows for glimpses of such notable volcanic summits as Round Top and The Sisters. Reach an unmarked junction with a short lateral to Frog Lake, which fills a shallow depression in an open bowl dotted with widely scattered pines. Lacking a permanent inlet and outlet, Frog Lake develops a muddy bathtub ring by the end of the summer.

From the unmarked junction to Frog Lake, proceed a short way to a three-way junction, where the TYT heads south-southwest toward Winnemucca Lake. Veer left, remaining on the PCT, and make a one-third-mile winding climb to the Sierra crest, from where Forestdale Divide is now visible nearly 2 miles south-southeast.

The PCT drops steeply from the crest, arcing across east- and north-facing slopes that tend to hang onto their snowfields well into summer. Once the snow is gone, these slopes are ablaze with color from a vibrant display of a wide variety of wildflowers. After a half mile, the grade momentarily eases on top of a granite bench, but the descent soon resumes, as the trail heads south toward the floor of the basin holding the upper reaches of Forestdale Creek. Wind around some rock outcrops and drop down to the crossing of a tributary stream, where your descent comes to an end.

A steady 0.4-mile climb from the creek crossing leads to a crossing of the main channel of Forestdale Creek and onto a bench holding a handful of shallow ponds. The trail wanders through this delightful subalpine landscape before embarking on a switchbacking, mile-long ascent up to Forestdale Divide and a junction with a trail that descends into Summit City Canyon.

175 Carson Pass to Fourth of July Lake

see map on p. 372

Distance	11 miles (out-and-back)
Hiking Time	5.5–6 hours
Elevation	+1,250/-1,250 feet
Difficulty	Difficult
Trail Use	Backpacking option, dogs OK
Best Times	Mid-July through mid-October
Agency	Eldorado National Forest at 209-295-4251, www.fs.usda.gov/eldorado
Recommended Map	*ENF, SNF, HTNF A Guide to the Mokelumne Wilderness*
Notes	Fourth of July Lake is within the Carson Pass Management Area, which requires backpackers to obtain a wilderness permit and a reservation for one of the six designated campsites, available at the Carson Pass Information Station. Fires are not allowed within the management area.

HIGHLIGHTS Backpackers who don't mind regaining lost elevation will appreciate this trip through the northeast section of the Mokelumne Wilderness, experiencing several ponds and lakes, wildflower-covered slopes, sweeping vistas, and a deep canyon along the way.

DIRECTIONS Follow CA 88 to Carson Pass and park in the trailhead parking lot on the south side of the highway.

FACILITIES/TRAILHEAD The parking area has vault toilets. The Forest Service charges a $5-per-day fee for parking. The Carson Pass Information Station issues wilderness permits for Mokelumne Wilderness and camping reservations for designated sites within the Carson Pass Management Area, and also offers a limited selection of books and maps for sale. The well-signed trail begins on the west side of the Information Station.

Find this section of the Pacific Crest (PCT) and Tahoe–Yosemite (TRT) Trails on the west side of the Carson Pass Information Station, and head southbound on the wide, well-traveled path through a mixed forest of lodgepole pines, mountain hemlocks, and western white pines. Gently descending trail leads past a small pond surrounded by willows before a mild to moderately ascending trail crosses the wilderness boundary and switchbacks toward the Sierra crest. The forest thins on the approach to the ridge, allowing glimpses of the volcanic summits of Round Top and The Sisters. Reach an unmarked junction with a short lateral to Frog Lake, which fills a shallow depression in an open bowl dotted with widely scattered pines. Lacking a permanent inlet and outlet, Frog Lake develops a muddy bathtub ring by the end of the summer.

From the unmarked junction to Frog Lake, proceed a short way to a three-way junction and veer right, leaving the PCT to follow the TYT on a descent of open slopes on the west side of Elephants Back. Proceed across shrubby slopes dotted with small groves of whitebark and lodgepole pines on a mile-long descent toward Winnemucca Lake, with excellent views of hulking Round Top along the way. Reach a junction, marked by a 4-by-4-inch post, near the west shore of picturesque Winnemucca Lake, backdropped by the dark, imposing cliffs of Round Top.

Head west from the junction, cross over the lake's outlet on a flat-topped log, and begin a moderate climb up a gully covered with pockets of willow, heather, and grasses to the crossing of a stream. Continue the ascent to a saddle and then make a short descent to a three-way junction near the north shore of Round Top Lake.

Head southwest from the junction and follow an arcing, three-quarter-mile traverse around the west shoulder of The Sisters to the crest of a divide. From the crest, the trail follows a steep and rocky descent over the next 1.5 miles that loses 1,000 feet of elevation on the way to Fourth of July Lake. Colorful wildflowers should cheer midsummer hikers along this knee-wrenching descent.

Fourth of July Lake is quite scenic, cradled in a rocky amphitheater between Fourth of July Peak and Peaks 9795 and 9607. A mixture of open meadows, pockets of willow, and stands of white fir and western white pine ring the shoreline. Six designated campsites are scattered around the lake, one near the outlet, two on a forested rise above the northeast shore, and three near the edge of the meadow on the northwest side.

176   Woods, Winnemucca, and Round Top Lakes Loop

Distance	4.8 miles (loop)
Hiking Time	2.5–3 hours
Elevation	+1,200/-1200 feet
Difficulty	Moderate
Trail Use	Backpacking option
Best Times	Mid-July through mid-October
Agency	Eldorado National Forest at 209-295-4251, www.fs.usda.gov/eldorado
Recommended Map	*ENF, SNF, HTNF A Guide to the Mokelumne Wilderness*
Notes	Winnemucca and Round Top Lakes are within the Carson Pass Management Area, which requires backpackers to obtain a wilderness permit and a reservation for one of the designated campsites, available at the Carson Pass Information Station. Fires are not allowed within the management area.

see map on p. 372

HIGHLIGHTS Two picturesque, near-timberline lakes with a stunning backdrop from the craggy summits of The Sisters and Round Top are the chief attractions of this loop. The wildflower displays along the upper canyons of Woods Creek are quite colorful in season—usually from July to mid-August. Views of the Lost Cabin Mine add a touch of historical interest.

Peak baggers with basic mountaineering skills, along with some extra time and energy, may enjoy the challenge of attempting to scale 10,381-foot Round Top, the dark volcanic summit that dominates the landscape south of Carson Pass. Maintained trail will get you to the base of the peak, and from there a use trail leads on a grueling, one-hour climb almost all the way to the top. However, you will have to do a bit of scrambling, and there is some exposure involved, so this trip is not for the inexperienced, out of shape, or acrophobic. Be prepared for windy conditions at the summit, where successful mountaineers will be treated to an extraordinary view of the surrounding terrain.

DIRECTIONS Follow CA 88 to the access road for Woods Lake, 1.7 miles west of Carson Pass. Follow the paved access road for 0.8 mile to a junction and turn right, driving another 0.1 mile to the Woods Lake Trailhead parking lot.

FACILITIES/TRAILHEAD The Woods Lake Trailhead has vault toilets. The Forest Service charges a $5-per-day fee for parking. The nearby Woods Lake Campground offers developed campsites. The Round Top Lake Trail 17E47 begins a short distance down the access road from the parking area, just across a bridge.

Proceed on dirt trail through a mixed forest of white firs, mountain hemlocks, and western white pines and soon come above the access road to Woods Lake Campground. Reaching a junction, you proceed to the right following a sign for Round Top Lake. A short, moderate climb leads above the campground, where the singletrack trail merges with an old road. Follow the road on a moderate, winding climb to the Lost Cabin Mine Trailhead, a half mile from the parking lot.

Back on singletrack trail, climb amid scattered trees with a filtered view of Round Top to the southeast and Woods Lake below. After hopping across boulder- and willow-lined Woods Creek, you follow a switchbacking climb above the old structures of the Lost Cabin Mine. The mine was in operation until the early 1960s, producing copious quantities of gold, silver, copper, and lead.

Continue the ascent on a course roughly paralleling the west fork of Woods Creek. The grade eventually eases as the wilderness boundary approaches and the volcanic summits of The Sisters and Round Top spring into view. Farther upstream, the canyon widens and you pass through open, subalpine terrain carpeted with clumps of willow, patches of heather, and wildflowers in season.

Nearing Round Top Lake, a 4-by-4-inch post marks a Y-junction with a trail to Fourth of July Lake, 2 miles from the parking lot. You could follow the 2.3-mile trail on an hour-long trip to the lake easily enough (see Trip 173), but if you do, make sure you save plenty of energy for the 2,300-foot climb back to this junction. Round Top Lake is a picturesque gem lined with stands of gnarled whitebark pines, dramatically backdropped by the dark volcanic slopes of The Sisters and Round Top.

Side Trip to Round Top: From the Fourth of July junction, head away from maintained trail, on a boot-beaten path up the gully of the lake's inlet toward the saddle between east Sister and Round Top. Before reaching the saddle, the route veers into a distinct notch in a ridge and then follows the ridge toward a false summit. Many parties are content with reaching the false summit as their destination, as the true summit is not much higher and requires some exposed scrambling to reach. As expected, the view from either summit is quite extraordinary. Exercise caution and good judgment on a climb of Round Top, and be prepared for windy conditions and intense sunlight at this altitude.

From the Fourth of July junction, head east on a mildly rising climb over a granite ridge amid widely scattered, wind-battered whitebark pines and ground-hugging shrubs and grasses. From the crest of the ridge, head down a gully on a moderate descent, cross the gully's stream and continue the descent through open terrain toward Winnemucca Lake. Nearing the lake, you cross the outlet on a flat-topped log and reach a 4-by-4-inch post at a three-way junction on the west shore, 2.9 miles from the trailhead. Pockets of whitebark pine shelter designated campsites on the north shore of Winnemucca Lake, while dark cliffs rise up from the south shore beneath the towering presence of Round Top. A mile to the northeast is the rounded hump of Elephants Back.

From the junction, a 1.4-mile trail ascends the slope below Elephants Back to a connection with the Pacific Crest Trail near Frog Lake, which then heads another mile to Carson Pass. Your route veers to the north and follows the course of the east branch of Woods Creek through mostly open terrain covered with sagebrush, willows, and an assortment of seasonal wildflowers. Leave the Mokelumne Wilderness a half mile from Winnemucca Lake and continue the steady descent into a light covering of mountain hemlocks. Nearing the trailhead, you pass a lateral to Woods Lake on the left, walk across a substantial wood bridge over the creek, cross the paved access road, and then return to the parking area.

Winnemucca Lake

see map on p. 372

177 Emigrant Lake

Distance	8.2 miles (out-and-back)
Hiking Time	4–4.5 hours
Elevation	+800 feet
Difficulty	Moderate
Trail Use	Backpacking option, dogs OK
Best Times	Mid-July through mid-October
Agency	Eldorado National Forest at 209-295-4251, www.fs.usda.gov/eldorado
Recommended Map	*ENF, SNF, HTNF A Guide to the Mokelumne Wilderness*
Notes	Wilderness permits are required for overnight visits.

HIGHLIGHTS Two lakes, one large and one small, provide hikers with two distinctly different portraits of the Carson Pass environs. More than half the journey follows the shoreline of Caples Lake, a 600-acre, human-made reservoir, where scads of recreationists boat, swim, and fish. The 4-mile trail ends at Emigrant Lake, a diminutive, natural lake filling the basin of a steep cirque rimmed by 9,500-foot-plus peaks. A brilliant floral display in the cirque usually lasts from late July through August.

DIRECTIONS Follow CA 88 to the west end of Caples Lake, and park in the large parking area near the dam.

FACILITIES/TRAILHEAD The parking area has vault toilets. The trail begins near the dam.

From the parking lot, the trail makes a very brief climb to a nice view of Caples Lake and then follows the shoreline of the reservoir and the edge of the Mokelumne Wilderness on a virtually level course for the first 2.3 miles of the journey. A mixed forest of lodgepole pines, white firs, western white pines, and mountain hemlocks rims the lake, but since the trail stays so close to the lakeshore, you're guaranteed to have plenty of views across the lake of the surrounding cliffs, ridges, and peaks. Along the initial stretch of trail, you're apt to pass several anglers plying the water in search of a trophy-sized trout. Boaters on Caples Lake must observe a 5-mile-per-hour speed limit, which tends to keep engine noise to a minimum and helps to maintain a tranquil feeling around the lakeshore. Enter a more open area strewn with boulders and reach a signed junction with the Historic Emigrant Trail, 1.3 miles from the trailhead (see Trip 178).

Beyond the junction, follow the Emigrant Lake Trail back into the forest and continue the lakeshore stroll. Eventually, the path moves farther away from the shoreline. Approaching Emigrant Creek, the trail veers south and begins a moderate climb up the forested canyon. Pass through a small meadow, where senecio and corn lily brighten the surroundings. Proceed upstream along the willow- and flower-lined creek to a signed T-junction, 3 miles from the trailhead, where a newly built section of trail heads west to Kirkwood Meadows.

About 0.1 mile beyond this junction, the trail crosses Emigrant Creek and climbs more steeply upstream to a set of switchbacks. Beyond the switchbacks, the grade eases to an easy stroll through thinning forest, eventually reaching the northeast shore of Emigrant Lake.

Nestled in a deep, north-facing cirque of steep cliffs with vertical walls that hold lingering snowfields, Emigrant Lake projects a cool, alpine-like ambience that's punctuated by the chilly winds that sweep across the surface of the lake. While a few clumps of trees and pockets of willows dot the near shore, most of the shoreline is stark and exposed, which only intensifies the unprotected feeling of the surroundings. However, the austere beauty of the area is quite stunning, and you won't be disappointed with the scenery.

CAPLES LAKE

Two small lakes known as Twin Lakes occupied this area before PG&E dammed Caples Creek and created the Caples Lake reservoir. The lake and creek were named for Dr. James Caples, a physician who, in 1849, left Illinois with his family to join a wagon train bound for California. As a resident of California, Dr. Caples had stints as a miner and a merchant before managing a 4,000-acre ranch near Carson and Deer Creeks.

178 Emigrant Pass

see map on p. 372

Distance	10 miles (out-and-back)
Hiking Time	5–5.5 hours
Elevation	+1,175/-150 feet
Difficulty	Difficult
Trail Use	Dogs OK
Best Times	Mid-July through mid-October
Agency	Eldorado National Forest at 209-295-4251, www.fs.usda.gov/eldorado
Recommended Map	USGS 7.5-minute *Caples Lake*

HIGHLIGHTS In 1848, following the Mexican-American War and two years after the Donner Party tragedy, a group of Mormons discovered an alternative to the notorious Truckee River Route for their return trip to Utah (they had arrived in San Diego by a more southerly route). Their discovery would quickly become the most popular Gold Rush trail over the Sierra into California, transporting 120,000 souls between 1849 and 1852. A second flurry of travel would occur in 1859, when silver was discovered in Virginia City.

Nowadays, hikers can retrace a part of the historic Carson River Route by following this trip along the Historic Emigrant Trail from Caples Lake to Emigrant Pass. Parts of the trail are hard to follow and some of the tread is in less-than-ideal condition, but these minor inconveniences are forgotten once the wide-ranging views of the region begin to unfold on the way to Emigrant Pass.

DIRECTIONS Follow CA 88 to the west end of Caples Lake, and park in the large parking area near the dam.

FACILITIES/TRAILHEAD The parking area has vault toilets. The trail begins near the dam.

From the parking lot, the trail makes a very brief climb to a nice view of Caples Lake and then follows the shoreline of the reservoir and the edge of the Mokelumne Wilderness on a virtually level course for the first 2.3 miles of the journey. A mixed forest of lodgepole pines, white firs, western white pines, and mountain hemlocks rims the lake, but since the trail stays so close to the lakeshore, you're guaranteed to have plenty of views across the lake of the surrounding cliffs, ridges, and peaks. Boaters on Caples Lake must observe a 5-mile-per-hour speed limit, which tends to keep engine noise to a minimum and helps to maintain the tranquil feeling of the hike. Along the initial stretch of trail,

you're apt to pass several anglers plying the water in search of a trophy-sized trout. Enter a more open area strewn with boulders and reach a signed junction with the Emigrant Lake Trail, 1.3 miles from the trailhead (see Trip 177).

Veer right at the junction and follow the fainter track of the Historic Emigrant Trail on a moderate to moderately steep climb up the hillside through lodgepole pines, western white pines, and white firs. Keen eyes may spot several old California Trail historic markers periodically nailed to the trees during the ascent. About 1.5 miles from the junction, you cross into the signed Mokelumne Wilderness and soon come to the crossing of a well-graded gravel service road used to maintain the surrounding equipment for the Kirkwood Meadows ski area. Proceed past a concrete-block building and emerge onto the open slopes above verdant Emigrant Valley, with views of the surrounding peaks, including Round Top, The Sisters, Fourth of July Peak, Thimble Peak, and Covered Wagon Peak.

Across slopes carpeted with sagebrush, grasses, and wildflowers, you hop across a number of seasonal drainages, briefly enter a stand of forest, pass below a chairlift, and then angle slightly downhill to pick up the trail again on the far side of the ski run. Soon the trail becomes hard to follow—look for an Emigrant Road sign and follow the road past the Sunrise Grill and down to the bottom of the chairlift, where a trailside forest service marker indicates the resumption of singletrack trail.

Head across an open, grassy slope on faint tread to the left of the ski lift and then climb up a verdant slope covered with willows, grasses, and wildflowers, to where the trail becomes more distinct. Past a historic sign about the Carson River Route, you pass through a gate in a barbed-wire fence and continue climbing through stands of forest, which now include mountain hemlocks, alternating with open areas of verdant foliage. Farther up the slope, the conifers diminish and the views improve of the surrounding peaks and ridges, as the faint track of the trail leads across several seasonal rivulets.

Above a pair of switchbacks, the trail makes an angling ascent to the southeast across the rocky slopes below Covered Wagon Peak. Reach an unmarked junction where a sketchy use trail angles west toward the saddle between Thimble and Covered Wagon Peaks. From the saddle, either peak is a straightforward ascent. The main trail continues the climb toward the crest past a large cairn with an EMIGRANT ROAD sign attached to a steel pole. A short distance farther, you gain the crest near a broken 4-by-4-inch post and continue along a mildly rising ridge to Emigrant Pass, where a sign denotes the 9,400-foot pass as the highest point reached by emigrants during the westward migration.

179 Lake Margaret

Distance	4 miles (out-and-back)
Hiking Time	2 hours
Elevation	+225/-400 feet
Difficulty	Easy
Trail Use	Dogs OK, mountain biking OK
Best Times	Mid-July through mid-October
Agency	Eldorado National Forest at 209-295-4251, www.fs.usda.gov/eldorado
Recommended Map	USGS 7.5-minute *Caples Lake*

HIGHLIGHTS Lake Margaret is a picturesque lake tucked into the undulating terrain of the Caples Creek drainage. A short hike with minimal elevation gain leads hikers through forested terrain sprinkled with granite outcrops to the shore of the diminutive lake. Although somewhat small in stature, the lake seems to be deep enough to offer a refreshing swim and sustain a healthy population of brook trout.

DIRECTIONS Follow CA 88 to the signed trailhead on the north side of the highway, a quarter mile west of the Caples Lake Trailhead near the dam. Drive a very short distance on the access road to the small parking area.

FACILITIES/TRAILHEAD There are no facilities at the trailhead. The trail begins near some trail signs.

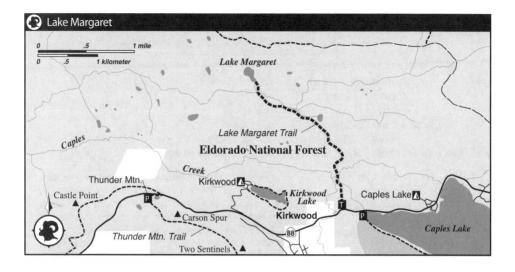

Make a winding descent from the trailhead briefly through alternating sections of open terrain and moderate forest to a pair of crossings of Caples Creek. Flooding along the creek bottom, perhaps the result of beaver activity, has inundated sections of trail in the past, so you may need to make some detours unless the problem has been resolved. After the second creek crossing, you stroll through gentle terrain and then make a short, moderate climb to a saddle between two low hills. A moderate descent leads away from the saddle and past a seasonal pond/meadow to come alongside a tributary of Caples Creek.

Gently descending trail follows the creek downstream through light forest and a grove of aspens before the trail bends and crosses the creek to the north bank. Head downstream through firs, aspens, and pines until a switchback leads up and over a series of granite slabs to the resumption of dirt trail on the far side. Soon you'll arrive at the south shore of diminutive Lake Margaret. A mixture of shrub-covered slopes, granite slabs, and scattered conifers borders the lake.

A hiker relaxes on the shore of Lake Margaret.

180 Thunder Mountain Loop

Distance	8.5 miles (out-and-back); 10.8 miles (loop)
Hiking Time	4–4.5 hours; 5–6 hours
Elevation	+1,775/-300 feet; +2,550/-2,550 feet
Difficulty	Moderate
Trail Use	Dogs OK, mountain biking OK
Best Times	Mid-July through mid-October
Agency	Eldorado National Forest at 209-295-4251, www.fs.usda.gov/eldorado
Recommended Map	*ENF, SNF, HTNF A Guide to the Mokelumne Wilderness*

HIGHLIGHTS An incredible 360-degree vista from a 9,408-foot summit should sound intriguing, especially if the trail to that summit is relatively short and not too steep. The Thunder Mountain Trail seems to fit the bill, gaining only 1,775 feet in a little over 4 miles. The view from the top lives up to its billing: a sweeping panorama that extends from the peaks of Lake Tahoe to the mountains of Yosemite. Despite these positive attributes, the trail receives less use than you would expect.

The challenging loop extension rewards hikers with sweeping vistas, picturesque canyons, and deep forests. Lying well outside of Mokelumne Wilderness, the entire route is open to mountain bikes, and a nearly 3-mile stretch of the Horse Canyon Trail is even open to motorcycles. However, the trail is lightly used by the motorized crowd, and it doesn't seem to be much used by any other groups, either, so the chance for solitude while on the trail should be fairly high. Although parts of the loop have existed for many years, the ridgeline section from Carson Spur to Thunder Mountain and down to Horse Canyon is of fairly recent origin. Not surprisingly, this newer section is in the best condition, unlike the concluding section of the loop that parallels the highway, where the actual tread is hard to locate in places.

DIRECTIONS Follow CA 88 to the roadside trailhead near Carson Spur, 1.7 miles west of the Kirkwood junction.

FACILITIES/TRAILHEAD There are no facilities at the trailhead. The trail begins near some trail signs by a wire fence.

Pass through a deteriorating cattle gate in a wire fence, and proceed through a mixed forest of red firs, lodgepole pines, and western white pines, soon encountering a T-junction with a lightly used path that heads east to cross CA 88 and then travels west to Castle Point. Continue straight ahead on a moderate climb, breaking out of the trees on a climb across a sagebrush- and wildflower-covered hillside below Carson Spur, where the rocky crags of Two Sentinels spring into view. Briefly gain the crest at a saddle before a climb across the west side of the ridge leads into thickening forest. Following a pair of switchbacks, traverse below the pinnacles of Two Sentinels to an open saddle, where the peaks of the Carson Pass area burst into view, along with Kirkwood Meadows and Caples Lake below.

Head south along the ridge toward Martin Point with additional eastward views along the way. A couple of switchbacks lead to an upward traverse around the east side of Martin Point, revealing the impressive profile of Thunder Mountain's north face, where the dark volcanic rock, punctuated with numerous clefts, gashes, pinnacles, and arêtes, creates a dramatic alpine scene. Continue the ascent along the ridgecrest toward Thunder Mountain. Approaching the northeast ridge of the peak, two more switchbacks are followed by a mild traverse around the back of the ridge to a three-way junction marked by a 6-by-6-inch post, 3.5 miles from the trailhead.

Veer to the right at the junction and follow an ascending, westward traverse through scattered lodgepole pines, western white pines, mountain hemlocks, and whitebark pines. The trees diminish near the crest as the trail angles sharply to the east to follow the ridge to the summit. The top offers an incredible view in all directions, from the mountains of northern Yosemite in the south to the peaks of Desolation Wilderness in the north. Nearby landmarks include Silver and Caples Lakes and Round Top. If the summit of Thunder

Mountain was your goal, retrace your steps to the trailhead.

To proceed on the loop trip, return to the three-way junction and head downhill across dry slopes through scattered to light timber to another three-way junction with a trail branching northeast toward Kirkwood Meadows. Continue the descent into thickening forest until breaking out of the trees

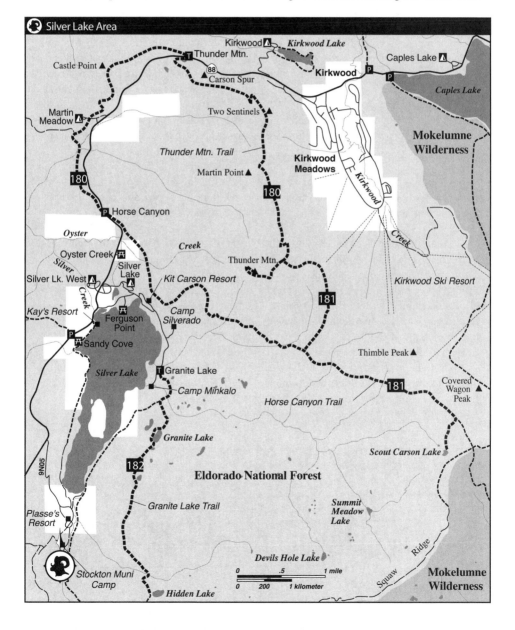

onto open, flower-filled slopes that allow excellent views of Silver Lake and Horse Canyon. Reach a junction at the bottom of the descent with the Horse Canyon Trail.

Turn right (west) at the junction and descend on a dusty trail through a light mixed forest of mountain hemlocks, white firs, and lodgepole pines. A series of switchbacks leads you into thicker forest and briefly alongside an unnamed stream bound for Silver Lake. Cross the stream and continue descending through scattered to light forest, where more open areas sport a fine display of wildflowers in season, including mule-ears, pennyroyal, cow parsnip, lupine, paintbrush, and purple thistle. Reach a Y-junction with a little-used trail on the left that provides a link to the shore of Silver Lake.

Proceed straight ahead on the main trail through predominantly fir forest with a stark absence of any ground cover, crossing a seasonal stream and passing some interesting volcanic cliffs and piles of conglomerate along the way. The descent is briefly interrupted by a short climb to the top of a low ridge, but it soon continues, as the approach to CA 88 is heralded by the sound of passing traffic. Reach a three-way junction marked by a 6-by-6-inch post, where the short path ahead leads to the Horse Canyon Trailhead along the highway.

Turn right at the junction and wind up the slope above the highway through Jeffrey pines and white firs to a disturbed area, where defined tread becomes hard to discern. Avoid the tendency to follow a dirt road and proceed straight ahead, searching for the resumption of single-track trail beyond the disturbed area. Once you're back on the trail, continue to parallel the highway for a short stretch and then descend to the highway.

Cross CA 88 on a downhill diagonal course to a road just beyond the far shoulder. Initially, you stroll on a level grade along this gravel and crumbling asphalt road, but soon you start climbing more steeply. Farther up the slope, the road passes over a pair of streams and by some primitive campsites near Martin Meadow. Walking through the camp area, keep an eye out for some 4-by-4-inch posts that mark the location of the start of a section of singletrack trail.

Follow the trail into the forest and climb up the hillside via a pair of switchbacks. You break out of the trees and continue climbing toward Castle Point and a Y-junction near the top of a ridge. To take in the view from Castle Point, follow the faint trail angling back to the left from the junction.

To return to the trailhead, continue east along the ridge with fine views to the north of the Crystal Range and to the south of nearby landmarks, such as Thunder Mountain, Carson Spur, and Martin Point. Near the end of the trail, you head back into the trees, follow the ridge to its end, cross the highway, and walk to the Thunder Mountain Trailhead.

Castle Point

181 Scout Carson Lake

see map on p. 389

Distance	13 miles (out-and-back)
Hiking Time	6.5–7 hours
Elevation	+1,775/-775 feet
Difficulty	Moderate
Trail Use	Backpacking option, dogs OK
Best Times	Mid-July through mid-October
Agency	Eldorado National Forest at 209-295-4251, www.fs.usda.gov/eldorado
Recommended Map	ENF, SNF, HTNF A Guide to the Mokelumne Wilderness

HIGHLIGHTS A lovely, small, near-timberline lake is the goal of this trip, which passes through interesting geologic scenery along the way. An optional 1-mile round-trip detour to the 9,408-foot summit of Thunder Mountain offers an expansive 360-degree vista of the Carson Pass region (see Trip 180). The route continues with fine views of the surrounding volcanic battlements on the way to Scout Carson Lake. A 1.7-mile section of the Horse Canyon Trail between the junction with the Thunder Mountain Trail and the spur to Scout Carson Lake is open to motorcycles. However, they seldom travel that far up the trail from Silver Lake.

DIRECTIONS Follow CA 88 to the roadside trailhead near Carson Spur, 1.7 miles west of the Kirkwood junction.

FACILITIES/TRAILHEAD There are no facilities at the trailhead. The trail begins near some trail signs by a wire fence.

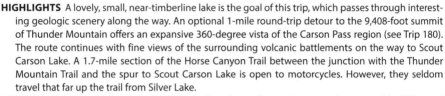

Pass through a deteriorating cattle gate in a wire fence and proceed through a mixed forest of red firs, lodgepole pines, and western white pines, soon encountering a T-junction with a lightly used path that heads east to cross CA 88 and then travels west to Castle Point. Continue straight ahead on a moderate climb, breaking out of the trees on a climb across a sagebrush- and wildflower-covered hillside below Carson Spur, where the rocky crags of Two Sentinels spring into view. Briefly gain the crest at a saddle before a climb across the west side of the ridge leads into a thick forest. Following a pair of switchbacks, traverse below the pinnacles of Two Sentinels to an open saddle, where the peaks of the Carson Pass area burst into view, along with Kirkwood Meadows and Caples Lake below.

Head south along the ridge toward Martin Point with additional eastward views along the way. A couple of switchbacks lead to an upward traverse around the east side of Martin Point, revealing the impressive profile of Thunder Mountain's north face, where the dark volcanic rock, punctuated

with numerous clefts, gashes, pinnacles, and arêtes, creates a dramatic alpine scene. Continue the ascent along the ridgecrest toward Thunder Mountain. Approaching the northeast ridge of the peak, two more switchbacks are followed by a mild traverse around the back of the ridge to a three-way junction marked by a 6-by-6-inch post, 3.5 miles from the trailhead.

From the three-way junction, head downhill across dry slopes through scattered to light timber to another three-way junction with a trail branching northeast toward Kirkwood Meadows. Continue the descent into thickening forest until breaking out of the trees onto open, flower-filled slopes that allow excellent views of Silver Lake and Horse Canyon. Reach a junction at the bottom of the descent with the Horse Canyon Trail.

Turn left at the junction and climb an open hillside, drop briefly to cross an unnamed, year-round creek, and then climb a sagebrush-dotted slope. Now at 8,800 feet, the trail follows a mile-long traverse across an open, flower-sprinkled bench on the south side of Thimble Peak. To the east of the peak are the tops of some of the ski lifts servicing Kirkwood Meadows in the next valley to the north. After passing an abandoned, overgrown path to Kirkwood Meadows, marked by an old 6-by-6-inch post with a missing sign, ascend moderately through granite boulders to a signed junction in a sandy meadow.

Turn right and stroll an easy half mile on a winding ascent through stands of mixed forest and pocket meadows to Scout Carson Lake. Perched on a small bench, ringed by meadow and surrounded by a forest of lodgepole pines, western white pines, and mountain hemlocks, diminutive Scout Carson Lake is a sweet example

of Sierra Nevada charm. Perhaps not so charming are the numerous mosquitoes buzzing through the air until late season, and less charming still is the potential for cows with their clanking bells that may be heard as they graze the nearby meadows. To an extent, one can avoid both the aural and epidermal distress by camping away from the meadow-fringed lakeshore, opting instead for drier and rockier terrain to the west. The lake supports a small but fat population of brook trout, which gratefully eat the mosquitoes. Emigrant Peak to the east is a straightforward climb offering a superb view from the summit of much of the Mokelumne Wilderness.

182 Granite and Hidden Lakes

see map on p. 389

Distance	6 miles (out-and-back)
Hiking Time	3–3.5 hours
Elevation	+475/-100 feet
Difficulty	Easy
Trail Use	Dogs OK, good for kids, mountain biking OK
Best Times	July through mid-October
Agency	Eldorado National Forest at 209-295-4251, www.fs.usda.gov/eldorado
Recommended Map	ENF, SNF, HTNF A Guide to the Mokelumne Wilderness

HIGHLIGHTS Other than the initial section of short, moderately steep trail to Granite Lake, this trip follows one of the mellowest trails in the region, making the journey well suited to families, or to hikers looking for an easy outing. Two lakes are visited, one cradled in a sea of granite and the other surrounded by cool forest. Both Granite and Hidden Lakes make fine destinations for picnickers and anglers.

DIRECTIONS Follow CA 88 to the north end of Silver Lake and turn east onto FS 10N20, signed for the Kit Carson Resort. Drive past Ferguson Point Picnic Area and proceed to the east side of Silver Lake. Find the trailhead just past a short bridge over a stream, 1.5 miles from the highway. The trailhead has only a couple of parking spaces. If those spaces are taken, continue on the road a short distance up a low hill to a wide gravel area.

FACILITIES/TRAILHEAD There are no facilities at the trailhead. The trail begins near a small sign on the east side of the road.

Head away from the trailhead on a mild to moderate climb amid patches of manzanita and a sprinkling of granite boulders and slabs beneath a scattered forest of Jeffrey pines, red firs, lodgepole pines, and aspens. Pass by a small seasonal pond/meadow on the left to a bridge spanning

Squaw Creek. Away from the bridge, you follow the trail to a three-way junction, a half mile from the trailhead.

Turn left at the junction on a stiff quarter-mile climb that briefly heads through woodland and then attacks a shrub-covered and granite-studded hillside on the way to

Granite Lake. This open area offers improving views of Silver Lake and the more distant Crystal Range to the north. Just before reaching the lake, you enter back into a light forest that now includes some western white pines and mountain hemlocks and follow alongside the lake's seasonal outlet a short distance to the north shore.

Aptly named Granite Lake is cradled in a granite depression surrounded by granite slabs, humps, and benches. Sunny slabs provide good spots for sunbathers, and a small island just off the west shore is a fine destination for swimmers. The short, easy hike ensures that the resident trout will see plenty of pressure from anglers. Although poor to fair campsites can be found scattered around the lakeshore, the easy access and resulting overuse suggests you should not camp here.

Follow the lakeshore around the west side to the far end of Granite Lake and continue past a small pond. Gently graded trail leads into a mixed forest interrupted on occasion by pocket meadows and seasonal ponds on the way to a T-junction, 1.75 miles from the trailhead, where a little-used path on the right descends toward Silver Lake.

Continuing the lightly forested route, a moderate climb away from the junction is followed by a stretch of mildly rising trail that eventually leads to a creek crossing a mile from the junction. On a winding section of trail, you climb to the crest of a rise and then follow a short, easy stroll down to Hidden Lake. Other than a small patch of willows and grasses, serene Hidden Lake is rimmed by cool forest, which shades a few decent campsites scattered around the lakeshore. Some imposing cliffs above the far end of the lake add some visual interest to the woodlands.

Beyond Hidden Lake, the trail continues through forest and flower-filled meadows to the site of Plasse's trading post on Squaw Ridge and then into the Mokelumne Wilderness.

Granite Lake

183 Shealor Lake

Distance	3.6 miles (out-and-back)
Hiking Time	2–2.5 hours
Elevation	+175/-400 feet
Difficulty	Easy
Trail Use	Dogs OK, mountain biking OK, good for kids
Best Time	July through October
Agency	Eldorado National Forest at 209-295-4251, www.fs.usda.gov/eldorado
Recommended Map	USGS 7.5-minute *Tragedy Spring*

HIGHLIGHTS A short trail leads to an attractive lake: a fine destination for a picnic lunch or a refreshing dip on a hot summer day, or a great place to skip rocks.

DIRECTIONS Follow CA 88 to the vicinity of Silver Lake and find the marked trailhead on the west side of the highway.

FACILITIES/TRAILHEAD There are no facilities at the trailhead. The trail begins near some trail signs.

From the trailhead, you climb gently through a mixed forest of lodgepole pines, white firs, and Jeffrey pines until a more moderate ascent leads into an area of granite slabs and boulders and more widely scattered conifers. A pair of short switchbacks lead over an open ridge with excellent views of Silver Lake and Thunder Mountain to the east and Shealor Lake tucked into its basin below.

Beyond the ridge, the trail angles downhill across an open granite hillside and then follows a winding descent of a shrub-covered hillside dotted with a few junipers and Jeffrey pines. Nearing the easternmost of the Shealor Lakes, you skirt a stand of lodgepole pines and white firs, on the way to a granite bench above the southeast shore.

The far shore of the largest of the four Shealor Lakes harbors an extensive area of shrubs, and a grove of trees near the south end provides a shady retreat on hot summer days. Otherwise, the shoreline is bordered by an abundance of smooth granite slabs, creating a haven for sunbathers and swimmers alike.

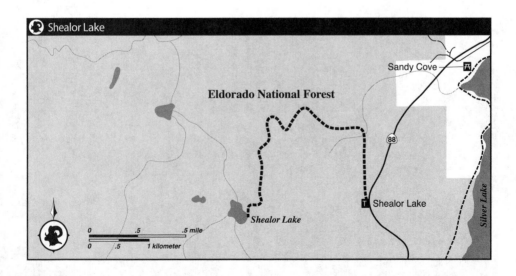

More Hikes

PCT: Tamarack Trailhead to Lost Lakes

Offers access from Blue Lakes Road to a lightly traveled section of the Pacific Crest Trail, through forest and across open slopes with fine views. The lakes area is accessible to four-wheel-drive vehicles (9.8 miles).

Castle Point

Despite some indistinct sections of tread, this trail travels from Carson Spur to a fine vista from Castle Point (2 miles).

View from the Virginia Range near Hidden Valley Park

Chapter 11

Reno–Sparks and Carson City

In recent years, the powers that be decided to showcase the greater Tahoe–Reno area as an outdoor recreation destination. This philosophical shift has resulted in action beyond just the chamber-of-commerce marketing designed to profit the casino industry. In addition to championing the area's natural treasures, several steps have already been undertaken in the pursuit of this vision. A whitewater park, developed on a stretch of the Truckee River flowing through downtown, has been so successful at attracting both events and kayakers that more whitewater parks have been proposed for the river. The 116-mile Tahoe Pyramid Bikeway project, along the length of the Truckee River, will connect existing sections (from Tahoe City to Truckee, Verdi to east Sparks, and a 15-mile section through the Pyramid Indian Reservation) into a continuous path from Tahoe City to Pyramid Lake. Recognizing the area's enthusiasm for the outdoors, Cabela's, the self-proclaimed "World's Foremost Outfitter," has opened one of its large, destination retail stores in west Reno, like its existing stores in the Midwest, which lure hordes of outdoor pilgrims.

Despite this recreational focus, perhaps no other area within the Tahoe–Reno region is in quite the state of flux as the communities of Reno–Sparks and, to a lesser extent, Carson City, in terms of rampant growth and its potentially damaging effects on open space and recreation. The wide, open spaces that once surrounded these cities is quickly vanishing, being filled with cookie-cutter homes on postage-stamp lots, and the homogenous commercial development that makes every new community look identical to every other new community in the country. While significant strides have been made in creating new trails and trailheads within suburban communities and rapidly diminishing rural areas, much more work is needed to protect the quality of life residents of the area once took for granted. See the organizations listed in Appendix 4 for ways to get involved in protecting the lands of Northern Nevada and Lake Tahoe.

Gazing out at the vast number of acres of open space surrounding these communities, one might imagine that an extensive network of trails would be available to hikers. In actuality, the number of bona fide trails in the area is quite small in comparison to the amount of open space. There are plenty of opportunities for cross-country hiking or for sharing the road with the motorized crowd, but in general, these types of routes have not been included in this guide, as the primary focus is on maintained, nonmotorized trails.

Due to the usually hot summers, most hikers will find spring and autumn to be the best times for traveling the trails in this area, although an early-morning or early-evening summertime hike can be quite enjoyable, when the daytime temperatures may not be so oppressive. The close proximity to metropolitan areas suggests that trails in the area may be filled with just as many dog walkers, joggers, strollers, and bikers as actual hikers. Trails in the area run the gamut from short, easy nature trails to all-out assaults on Peavine.

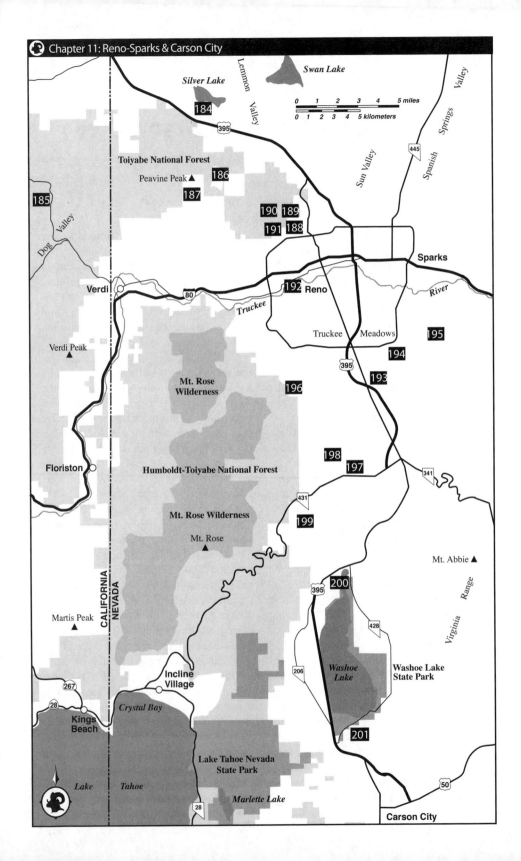

184 ## Swan Lake Nature Study Area

Distance	1.5 miles (out-and-back)
Hiking Time	45 minutes–1 hour
Elevation	+150 feet
Difficulty	Easy
Trail Use	Dogs OK, good for kids, ADA accessible
Best Times	March through November
Agency	Washoe County Regional Parks and Open Space at 775-823-6500, washoecounty.us/parks
Recommended Map	USGS 7.5-minute *Reno NW*

HIGHLIGHTS The Swan Lake Nature Study Area is the product of a joint effort between the Bureau of Land Management, Lahontan Audubon Society, Washoe County Parks and Recreation, Nevada Land Conservancy, City of Reno, Nevada Army National Guard, Nevada Department of Wildlife, and Washoe County School District. Securing reclaimed water from the nearby Reno–Stead Sewage Treatment Plant, the marshland was saved from being developed as housing, which has allowed for the continued use of this area as a layover stop on the Pacific Flyway for more than 130 different species of birds traveling between Canada and Central and South America. The preservation of this high-desert playa marsh is unique to metropolitan areas within the Great Basin.

Eventual plans for the area include an interpretive center and a loop trail around Swan Lake. Currently, a viewing boardwalk juts out above a section of the marsh, and interpretive signs offer interesting tidbits of information about the region's ecology. The Washoe County School District uses the boardwalk regularly for field trips. Nearly a mile of the loop trail has been built around the west side of the lake, offering travelers an easy stroll through alternating sections of marshlands and sagebrush scrub. Along the way are fine views across Lemmon Valley and west to Peavine Peak.

DIRECTIONS Travel on NV 395 north of Reno to the Lemmon Drive exit, head east for three-quarters of a mile on Lemmon Drive, and turn left onto Military Road. Proceed for 1.6 miles to Lear Boulevard and turn right. Reach a T-intersection after 0.4 mile at the end of paved road and turn left, following a gravel road for a quarter mile to a large parking area.

FACILITIES/TRAILHEAD The trailhead has restrooms, signage, and trash receptacles. The trail begins on the continuation of the gravel road.

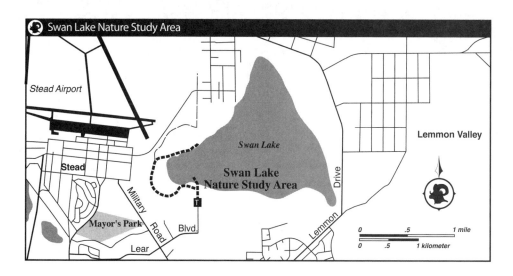

Alongside a barbed-wire fence and an irrigation ditch, you follow a closed gravel road with wide-open views across Lemmon Valley and up the slopes of Peavine Peak. Soon reach the South Side Interpretive Area, equipped with an informational kiosk, park benches, and trash receptacles. Straight ahead is a boardwalk that visitors can follow on an elevated journey out onto a marsh. The boardwalk is lined with interpretive placards with information about wetlands ecology, including some of the plants and animals endemic to the area.

After a stroll along the boardwalk, head left (west) from the South Side Interpretive Area and follow a packed gravel trail past several interpretive signs about native birds to a low rock wall, a blind where wildlife enthusiasts can be out of sight while they search for their favorite species through portals in the rock.

Continue on a westerly course away from the lush vegetation of the wetland into sagebrush scrub. Eventually, the path curves north and climbs a short way up a hillside to intersect a well-used road. Veer right at a couple of Y-junctions, as the route curves around the lake and heads east. After a while, the road deteriorates into a twin-tracked jeep road as it heads toward the wetlands again. Reach the turnaround point at a fence line, where the road turns sharply north away from the wetlands and heads toward a housing development. From there, retrace your steps back to the parking area.

On the boardwalk at Swan Lake Nature Study Area

185 Crystal Mine Trail

Distance	1.5 miles (out-and-back)
Hiking Time	45 minutes–1 hour
Elevation	+375 feet
Difficulty	Easy
Trail Use	Dogs OK, good for kids
Best Times	May through October
Agency	Humboldt-Toiyabe National Forest at 775-882-2766, www.fs.usda.gov/htnf
Recommended Map	USGS 7.5-minute Dog Valley

HIGHLIGHTS For generations, Dog Valley Road has been the back door into a serene section of Humboldt-Toiyabe National Forest for a variety of local recreationists. But with the recent explosion of growth and development in and around the Truckee Meadows, Dog Valley is no longer the quiet backwoods locale it once was. However, while the area may not offer much opportunity to get away from it all nowadays, Dog Valley may still offer the chance to get away from at least some of it. This short hike from a forest service campground to the site of an old mine atop a hill is well suited for a quick getaway, especially for families with small children. The top has an extensive pile of crystals that should provide plenty of diversion for any junior geologists in your group.

DIRECTIONS From Third Street, which is the main road through Verdi, turn onto Bridge Street and drive across a bridge over the Truckee River to the intersection with Dog Valley Road. Follow Dog Valley Road for about 8 miles to the entrance into Lookout Campground.

FACILITIES/TRAILHEAD Lookout Campground has 22 developed campsites and vault toilets. The trail begins just inside the campground entrance near some trail signs.

The short Crystal Mine Trail heads away from the shady campground in a generally northbound direction through a mixed forest. Initially, gently graded trail leads across an old road before a moderate climb heads up the hillside, aided by some switchbacks. Near the top of a hill, you reach a jeep road and then scramble to the top, where rock hounds will discover a plethora of crystals.

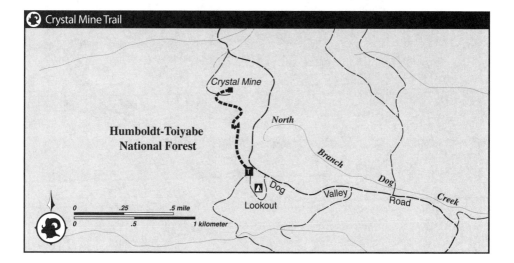

186 Poeville

Distance	6 miles (out-and-back)
Hiking Time	3–4 hours
Elevation	+500 feet
Difficulty	Moderate
Trail Use	Mountain biking OK, dogs OK
Best Times	March through June, September through December
Agency	Humboldt-Toiyabe National Forest at 775-882-2766, www.fs.usda.gov/htnf
Recommended Map	USGS 7.5-minute *Verdi*

HIGHLIGHTS After John Poe discovered a mining strike on the east slopes of Peavine Peak in the 1860s, the town of Poeville sprung up nearby. At its zenith, the town boasted 500 residents along with a post office, hotel, and stagecoach stop. Other than remnants of a few stone foundations, the most prominent reminder of the town's existence is the settling pond created by a dam in Poeville Canyon.

Modern-day visitors to Poeville will be unlikely to see five other people on their journey, let alone 500, even though the Poeville Canyon Road is open to motorized travel. Such easy access has resulted in the usual unfortunate consequences: Broken bottles and abandoned appliances are strewn about the canyon and, if brass were a high-priced metal, scavengers could get rich from collecting the copious quantities of shell casings left at the pond by indiscriminate target shooters. Despite these drawbacks, the 3-mile trip along the road to the pond and town site is a great off-season hike, when the higher terrain is blanketed with snow. Summer temperatures can be quite hot, so plan on traveling in the early-morning or early-evening hours to avoid the heat.

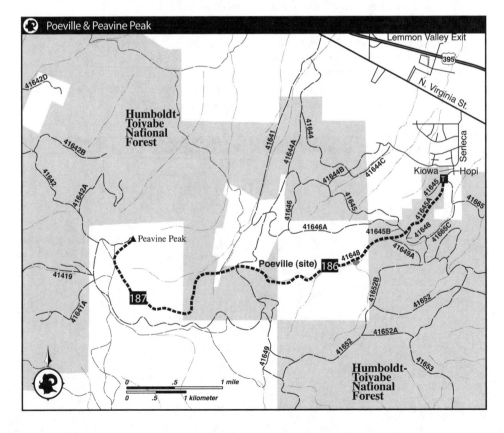

DIRECTIONS Drive on NV 395 north of Reno to the Lemmon Drive exit (exit 74). Head southwest on Lemmon Drive–Heindel Road for a half mile to North Virginia Street and turn right (northwest). Proceed a half mile to a left-hand turn onto Seneca Drive and continue for another a half mile, then turn left onto Kiowa Drive. Proceed on Kiowa a short distance to the end of the pavement and a gravel parking area.

FACILITIES/TRAILHEAD There are no facilities at the trailhead. The trip begins on the middle of the three dirt roads.

Make a moderate climb up the Poeville Canyon Road (FS 41645) through sagebrush scrub, keeping your fingers crossed that you'll encounter a minimum of motorized traffic. Pass several junctions with lesser roads on the way into the narrowing canyon, where a seasonal stream carries runoff from the eastern slopes of Peavine Peak. Patches of willow and a few cottonwoods eke out enough moisture from the damp soil in the drainage amid the otherwise drought-tolerant vegetation. Proceed ahead at a Y-junction onto FS 41645A, where FS 41645 veers to the right, about 0.5 mile from the parking area. After another 0.25 mile, continue ahead at the next junction with FS 41664, heading left across the streambed. After 1.4 miles, the steady climb arrives at the settling pond for the old mining town of Poeville.

Beyond the settling pond, the road continues the climb up the narrow canyon, past a side canyon to the left, which is about halfway between the pond and the Golden Fleece Mine site. The town site is a short distance farther. Yellowish tailing piles hint at the past mining activity, which yielded mainly copper.

187 **Peavine Peak**

see map on p. 402

Distance	10 miles (out-and-back)
Hiking Time	5–7 hours
Elevation	+2,875 feet
Difficulty	Difficult
Trail Use	Dogs OK, mountain biking OK
Best Times	June through November
Agency	Humboldt-Toiyabe National Forest at 775-882-2766, www.fs.usda.gov/htnf
Recommended Map	USGS 7.5-minute *Verdi*

HIGHLIGHTS Throngs of mountain bikers, hikers, joggers, dog walkers, equestrians, and off-roaders sprawl across the slopes of Peavine Peak, which has created a bit of a problem for a recreation area so close to a rapidly growing region. The slopes of Peavine are littered with a network of byways, ranging from a sedan-worthy summit road to faint, singletrack trail that leads nowhere—and everything in between. Virtually in Reno's backyard, an increasing number of users pursue a wide variety of activities on the slopes of the mountain, which has caused concern from recreation managers about the detrimental effects of severe overuse. Fearing that the mountain would be loved to death, the Forest Service took on the task of developing a management plan for Peavine that would identify routes for motorized and nonmotorized travel. Depending on the outcome of that process, some routes will inevitably be closed and allowed to return to a natural condition.

Any ascent of Peavine, whether by foot or bike, is a physically challenging undertaking. The 5-mile, one-way climb described here gains nearly 3,000 feet, which should properly deter the faint of heart, or at least the out of shape. Those up to the task will be rewarded with a wonderful panoramic view from the top. Beginning in typical high-desert sagebrush, the climb passes through interesting plant communities on the way to the 8,266-foot summit. Fortunate travelers may also spy some of the diverse wildlife that inhabits the area, possibly including members of a large mule deer herd.

DIRECTIONS Drive on NV 395 north of Reno to the Lemmon Drive exit (exit 74). Head southwest on Lemmon Drive–Heindel Road for a half mile to North Virginia Street and turn right (northwest). Proceed a half mile to a left turn onto Seneca Drive and continue for another a half mile, then turn left onto Kiowa Drive. Proceed on Kiowa a short distance to the end of the pavement and a gravel parking area.

FACILITIES/TRAILHEAD There are no facilities at the trailhead. The trip begins on the middle of the three dirt roads.

Make a moderate climb up the Poeville Canyon Road (FS 41645) through sagebrush scrub, keeping your fingers crossed that you'll encounter a minimum of motorized traffic. Pass several junctions with lesser roads on the way into the narrowing canyon, where a seasonal stream carries runoff from the eastern slopes of Peavine Peak. Patches of willow and a few cottonwoods eke out enough moisture from the damp soil in the drainage amid the otherwise drought-tolerant vegetation. Proceed ahead at a Y-junction onto FS 41645A, where FS 41645 veers to the right, about 0.5 mile from the parking area. After another 0.25 mile, continue ahead at the next junction with FS 41664, heading left across the streambed. After 1.4 miles, the steady climb arrives at the settling pond for the old mining town of Poeville.

Beyond the settling pond, the road continues the climb up the narrow canyon, past a side canyon to the left, which is about halfway between the pond and the Golden Fleece Mine site. The town site is a short distance farther. Yellowish tailing piles hint at the past mining activity, which yielded mainly copper. Just past the town site, the Poeville Canyon Road meets the main access road to the summit of Peavine Peak.

Mountain bikers will find that following the Peavine Road provides the most straightforward access to the summit. However, hikers who wish a more direct route that avoids any possible encounters with vehicle traffic should continue across Peavine Road and head generally west for 0.2 mile to a steep jeep road, which climbs southwest up a hillside along the course of a power line. Reach the top of a ridge after 0.4 mile, and follow sections of old road and jeep trails along the ridge as it arcs northwest toward the south summit of Peavine Peak.

Despite the plethora of communications equipment that litters the twin summits of Peavine Peak, the 360-degree view from the top is fairly remarkable.

View from Peavine Peak

188 Rancho San Rafael Park Nature Trail

Distance	0.75 mile (semiloop)
Hiking Time	30 minutes
Elevation	Negligible
Difficulty	Easy
Trail Use	Leashed dogs, good for kids
Best Times	March through November
Agency	Washoe County Regional Parks and Open Space at 775-823-6500, washoecounty.us/parks
Recommended Map	WCP&OS *Rancho San Rafael Park*

see map on p. 406

HIGHLIGHTS Rancho San Rafael Park is a beloved gem for residents of the Truckee Meadows. The large park offers a variety of resources for a wide variety of activities, including some hiking trails. The Wilbur D. May Arboretum and Botanical Garden offers a short stroll through a wide range of botanical environments that have been adapted to the Great Basin environment. The Nature Trail provides a slightly longer and more natural path through areas of common sagebrush scrub and a unique wetland. Fed by snowmelt from intermittent Evans Creek and irrigation water from the Highland Ditch, the wetland harbors a fine assortment of riparian plants and an equally diverse mixture of fauna as well—unobtrusive visitors may spy a falcon or a cottontail on their journey. Fourteen interpretive signs along the trail provide interesting tidbits about the natural and human history of the area. Hiking during the spring and fall is quite pleasant; summers tend to be quite hot, and most of the trail is shadeless—get an early start to beat the heat, or take a stroll just before the sun goes down.

DIRECTIONS Follow North Virginia Street 0.3 mile past the McCarran Boulevard intersection to the entrance into Rancho San Rafael Park Sports Complex, and proceed to the far end of the parking lot.

FACILITIES/TRAILHEAD The trailhead is located in the Rancho San Rafael Park Sports Complex. The trail begins at the northwest end of the parking lot.

Follow the marked Nature Trail on a winding course through open sagebrush past a trio of interpretive signs, and then climb up toward the National Monument to the Basque Sheepherder. Near the monument, the Nature Trail merges with a gravel-and-dirt road from the trailhead that provides the principal access to Evans Canyon (see Trip 189). Follow the dirt road around the front of the monument and down toward Evans Canyon, crossing the Highland Ditch on a short wood-plank bridge on the way to a junction on the left with the beginning of the loop section of the Nature Trail.

Proceed ahead at the junction and continue toward Evans Creek, where you enter a wetland area that is quite unique within the otherwise dry surroundings. Fed by the waters of Highland Ditch and intermittent Evans Creek, this verdant oasis harbors a wide variety of grasses, shrubs, and trees, and is a sustainable

Basque monument

environment for an equally diverse number of fauna. The trail wanders through this greenbelt for a short while to a crossing of diminutive Evans Creek near a couple of picnic tables and a park bench. Just past the stream crossing, you reach the upper junction of the Nature Trail on the left and the continuation of the Evans Creek Trail ahead.

Turn left at the junction and follow the Nature Trail as it bends to the south, roughly paralleling the course of the Highland Ditch. After a short while, the trail veers away from the ditch and swings around to the north, passing more interpretive signs along the way. Just past a picnic area, the loop is closed at the lower junction. From there, retrace your steps to the trailhead.

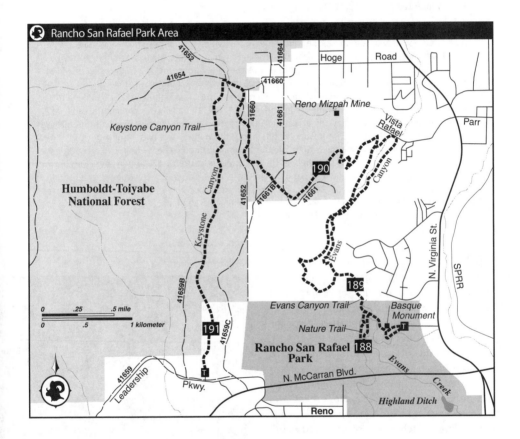

189 Evans Canyon

Distance	2.2 miles (loop); 3.4 miles (loop)
Hiking Time	1 hour; 1.5–2 hours
Elevation	+150/-150 feet; +200/-200 feet
Difficulty	Easy
Trail Use	Leashed dogs, good for kids, mountain biking OK
Best Times	March through November
Agency	Washoe County Regional Parks and Open Space at 775-823-6500, washoecounty.us/parks
Recommended Map	WCP&OS *Rancho San Rafael Park*

see map on p. 406

HIGHLIGHTS The Evans Canyon Trail is a delightful path that has become even more enjoyable with recent improvements. The riparian environment along intermittent Evans Creek, augmented by water from the Highland Ditch, is very unique amid the otherwise typically dry sagebrush zone common to the lower slopes of Peavine Peak. Beyond this lush setting, the trail snakes its way up the canyon on two loop variations of 2.2 and 3.4 miles. Thanks mainly to the efforts of volunteers coordinated by the Truckee Meadows Trail Association, the trail is in great condition, and the vegetation in the upper part of the canyon is in the process of restoration. Nearly surrounded by the signs of civilization, the Evans Canyon Trail is a magnificent getaway easily accessible to residents of the Truckee Meadows.

DIRECTIONS Follow North Virginia Street 0.3 mile past the McCarran Boulevard intersection to the entrance into Rancho San Rafael Park Sports Complex, and proceed to the far end of the parking lot.

FACILITIES/TRAILHEAD The trailhead is located in the Rancho San Rafael Park Sports Complex. The trail begins at the northwest end of the parking lot, near signs for the park's Nature Trail (see Trip 188).

Rather than follow the marked Nature Trail, veer to the right and follow either a singletrack trail or a gravel road toward the National Monument to the Basque Sheepherder, where the trail and the road will merge. Follow the dirt road around the front of the monument and down toward Evans Canyon, crossing the Highland Ditch on a short, wood-plank bridge, and passing a junction on the left with a section of the Nature Trail.

At the creek bottom, you enter a wetland area that is quite unique within the otherwise dry surroundings. Fed by the waters of Highland Ditch and intermittent Evans Creek, this verdant oasis harbors a wide variety of grasses, shrubs, and trees, and is a sustainable environment for an equally diverse number of fauna. The trail wanders through this greenbelt for a short while to a crossing of diminutive Evans Creek near a couple of picnic tables and a park bench. Just past the stream crossing, you pass by another junction with the Nature Trail on the left and pass out of the shady riparian environment into typical sagebrush scrub intermixed with nonnative grasses.

Soon a tangle of roads and paths appears to head in every compass direction imaginable—bear right at each opportunity to remain in Evans Canyon. Beyond this maze, you follow the Evans Canyon Trail through a fence and below a power line, as the wide path narrows to singletrack trail width and proceeds past a stream monitoring device. Continue up the canyon on a mild to moderate ascent to a trail junction on the left with The Snake, a challenging mountain-bike route that follows a steep, winding 0.1-mile climb up a narrow gorge to a less-difficult route along a jeep road.

A little farther up Evans Canyon, you cross the streambed on a short wood bridge and immediately reach another junction, this one with the lower end of the Miners Trail, which will be the return route for both the short and long loops. The lower part of the Miners Trail follows a side canyon up toward the white N on the hillside above. Remaining on the Evans Canyon Trail, you continue alongside the streambed another quarter mile to the upper junction with the Miners Trail, 0.9 mile from the parking lot.

Short Loop: Turn left at the junction, hop across the streambed, and immediately turn downstream on the west side of the creek to follow the Miners Trail. Climb up the slope and then follow the path as it crosses the hillside well above the floor of the canyon. Just past a low power line, the trail veers away from the main canyon into a narrow side canyon and climbs up it for a while, crosses the narrow gorge, and then proceeds from the crossing on a section of old roadbed to a T-junction. (An interesting side trip follows the right-hand road from the T-junction a short distance to a jeep trail that climbs steeply to the N.) The Miners Trail forsakes the road by angling left onto singletrack trail and descending toward the main canyon. The short descent leads to the lower junction between the Miners and Evans Canyon Trails, from where you retrace your steps back to the parking area.

Long Loop: From the junction, continue upstream on the Evans Canyon Trail, crossing the creek on the way to the upper part of the widening canyon. The course of the trail slices across the hillside above the floor of the canyon, which recently has been the focus of restoration project to rehabilitate the streambed and restore the native vegetation. Gazing up the canyon, you will see a couple of yellowish piles of mining tailings, a smattering of Jeffrey pines on the west hillside, and the fill slope below Vista Rafael Parkway. At the head of the canyon, the trail follows the base of the fill slope across the canyon and then turns downstream.

Following a path on the west side of the canyon, you soon stand atop the northernmost tailings pile, where the trail to Keystone Canyon branches to the right, away from the Evans Canyon Trail. Continue downstream below a hillside sprinkled with widely scattered Jeffrey pines with views down the canyon of a part of the Carson Range. A short climb above the streambed leads past another pile of tailings, across grassy slopes, and beneath a set of power lines spanning the canyon. A short descent veers momentarily into a side canyon and then down to the upper junction of the Miners Trail. From there, follow the Miners Trail back to the parking lot, as described in the short loop above.

190 Evans Canyon to Keystone Canyon

Distance	6.8 miles (out-and-back)
Hiking Time	2.5–3.5 hours
Elevation	+700/-700 feet
Difficulty	Moderate
Trail Use	Leashed dogs OK, mountain biking OK
Best Times	April through November
Agency	Washoe County Regional Parks and Open Space at 775-823-6500, washoecounty.us/parks; Humboldt-Toiyabe National Forest at 775-882-2766, www.fs.usda.gov/htnf
Recommended Map	Poedunks *Peavine Rides and Hikes*

see map on p. 406

HIGHLIGHTS On this loop, hikers and mountain bikers can travel the two main canyons, Evans and Keystone, in the only part of the Peavine area that is currently closed to motorized vehicles. Ongoing efforts by Washoe County, the Forest Service, and a group of dedicated volunteers have given sections of the trails a much-needed refurbishing, resulting in increased use by hikers, mountain bikers, joggers, and dog walkers. Other than some of the mountain bikers, only a small percentage of trail users seem to make the journey between the two canyons.

The route begins in Evans Canyon, where the lower part of the trail passes through a lush riparian environment along Evans Creek that is quite unique to the area. Beyond this verdant oasis, a mild to moderate ascent through typical sagebrush scrub leads up a narrow part of the canyon before widening out near the head. The trail then follows a sometimes-winding climb out of Evans Canyon through a stand of scattered Jeffrey pines and past a group of metamorphic rock outcrops. Farther up the slope, extensive views open up of the Truckee Meadows and the surrounding mountain ranges on the way toward Keystone Canyon. The route descends the narrowing canyon with views of the Carson Range and the Truckee Meadows on the way to the Keystone Canyon Trailhead.

DIRECTIONS *Start:* Follow North Virginia Street 0.3 mile past the McCarran Boulevard intersection to the entrance into Rancho San Rafael Park Sports Complex, and proceed to the far end of the parking lot.

End: From North Virginia Street, drive west on McCarran Boulevard for 1.1 miles and turn right onto Leadership Parkway. Proceed 0.3 mile to a right-hand turn into the signed Keystone Canyon parking area.

FACILITIES/TRAILHEAD The Evans Canyon Trailhead is located in the Rancho San Rafael Park Sports Complex. The trail begins at the northwest end of the parking lot, near signs for the park's Nature Trail (see Trip 188). The Keystone Canyon Trailhead has a portable toilet, park bench, and trailhead kiosk. The trail ends at the north end of the parking lot.

Rather than follow the marked Nature Trail, veer to the right and follow either a singletrack trail or a gravel road toward the *National Monument to the Basque Sheepherder*, where the trail and the road will merge. From there, follow a dirt road around the front of the monument and then down toward Evans Canyon, crossing the Highland Ditch on a short, wood-plank bridge and passing a junction on the left with a section of the Nature Trail on the way to the floor of the canyon.

At the creek bottom, you enter a wetland area that is quite unique within the otherwise dry surroundings. Fed by the waters of Highland Ditch and intermittent Evans Creek, this verdant oasis harbors a wide variety of grasses, shrubs, and trees, and is a sustainable environment for an equally diverse number of fauna. The trail wanders through this greenbelt for a short while to a crossing of diminutive, seasonal Evans Creek near a couple of picnic tables and a park bench. Just past the stream crossing, you pass by a second junction with the Nature Trail on the left and pass out of the shady riparian environment into typical sagebrush scrub intermixed with nonnative grasses.

Soon a tangle of roads and paths appears to head in every compass direction imaginable—bear right at each opportunity to remain in Evans Canyon. Beyond this confusing maze, you follow the Evans Canyon Trail through a fence and below a power line, as the wide path narrows to singletrack trail width and proceeds past a stream monitoring device. Continue up the canyon on a mild to moderate ascent to a trail junction on the left with The Snake, a challenging mountain-bike route that follows a steep, winding 0.1-mile climb up a narrow gorge to a less difficult route along a jeep road.

A little farther up Evans Canyon, you cross the streambed on a short wood bridge and immediately reach another junction, this one with the lower end of the Miners Trail. Remaining on the Evans Canyon Trail, you continue alongside the streambed another quarter mile to the upper junction with the Miners Trail, 0.9 mile from the parking lot.

Hop across Evans Creek to the trail on the far side, turn right, and make a brief climb up a gully before the trail arcs back into the main canyon and heads upstream at a gentle grade. High above the creek, the trail crosses open slopes of grasses and scattered sagebrush, as signs of civilization start to appear beyond the head of the canyon. Nearing the fill slope below Vista Rafael Parkway, you pass below a hillside sprinkled with Jeffrey pines and reach an obscure junction on top of a large pile of yellowish mining tailings, 1.5 miles from the trailhead. While your path to Keystone Canyon is clearly seen angling up the hillside, the continuation of the loop trail around Evans Canyon is somewhat hard to discern until it becomes distinct again on the far side of the tailings.

Forsaking the gentle grade of the Evans Canyon Trail, the path to Keystone Canyon attacks the west wall of the canyon, soon reaching a switchback just before running into Vista Rafael Parkway. Now heading southwest, you're treated to expanding views of Mt. Rose and the Carson Range and southwest Reno, as the trail makes an angling ascent across the hillside through grasses and widely scattered Jeffrey pines. After a while, a series of short switchbacks winds through some low rock outcroppings and leads higher up the hillside, as downtown Reno, the Virginia Range, and mountains to the north spring into view.

Near the lip of the canyon, a quarter-mile stretch of mildly descending trail provides an opportunity to recover after the moderate ascent. As you start to climb again, the trail merges briefly with a twin-tracked jeep road before singletrack veers away on the approach to a group of power poles, where power lines branch away in three different directions. Just before intersecting a road that follows one of the power lines, the trail divides, 2.5 miles from the trailhead. The right-hand path provides access to the historic site of the Mizpah Mine (an interesting side trip) and proceeds around the northeast side of some rock outcroppings and past some houses into Keystone Canyon.

Veer left at the junction and follow the path as it wraps around a power pole and angles across the power line road to the resumption of singletrack on the far side. Make a mild to moderate climb of open slopes across a couple of jeep roads toward the outcropping marked 5350 on the USGS *Reno* map, intersecting a well-traveled road just south of the outcropping that parallels a fence line and a string of power poles. Turn right and head north on this road for approximately 25 yards, and then turn right onto a stretch of singletrack that climbs up the slope and over a small pile of mining tailings to the outcrop.

Head west from the outcrop on a short descent that immediately leads across the well-traveled road and through thick sagebrush down into the upper part of Keystone Canyon. Heading in the general direction of the radio towers at the head of Keystone Canyon, you cross a well-traveled dirt road, and then wind around to intersect a less-used road for a while. Where the road curves north, you follow singletrack on an arcing route bending south to eventually merge with the old Keystone Canyon Road, 3.4 miles from the trailhead.

Similar to Evans Canyon, the upper part of Keystone Canyon starts out rather broad before narrowing considerably farther downstream. In the narrowest part of the canyon, the constricting walls force the route to veer back and forth over the streambed several times. Where the alternative presents itself, you should elect to follow the singletrack trail sections rather than the old road, as the trail generally stays out of the streambed, while the road and the streambed often share the same course.

Continue ahead at a junction with single-track trail on the right (FS 21115), 3.6 miles from the trailhead. Pass a junction on the right with FS 659C, walk below some power lines, and then come to an opening in a fence at the boundary between forest service and Washoe County lands. At 4.7 miles, you reach a junction with the Rancho Connector.

At the junction, turn left and climb steeply out of Keystone Canyon on a pair of switchbacks. Head across an old jeep road to the canyon lip and follow more gently graded tread across another old road. Pass above a water tank and travel through a gap in a fence on the way to a park bench by a rock outcrop. The bench offers an opportunity to sit and enjoy the views of the Truckee Meadows and the Virginia Range to the east. Descending tread leads away from the bench and over to a junction with the Thornton Point Loop, 5.7 miles from the trailhead.

Away from the junction, the Rancho Connector descends into a side canyon and follows the drainage east toward Evans Canyon. Veer left at a junction near Evans Creek and reach the close of the loop section. From there, retrace your steps across the creek and back down the Nature Trail to the Basque Monument and over to the parking lot.

191 Keystone Canyon

Distance	3.4 miles (out-and-back)
Hiking Time	1.5–2 hours
Elevation	+350 feet
Difficulty	Moderate
Trail Use	Leashed dogs OK, good for kids, mountain biking OK
Best Times	March through November
Agency	Washoe County Regional Parks and Open Space at 775-823-6500, washoecounty.us/parks; Humboldt-Toiyabe National Forest at 775-882-2766, www.fs.usda.gov/htnf
Recommended Map	Poedunks *Peavine Rides and Hikes*

see map on p. 406

HIGHLIGHTS As with the Evans Canyon Trail, recent improvements to the Keystone Canyon Trail have made the path a much more attractive route for a variety of trail users. A new trailhead with a portable toilet, improvements to the trail, and a vehicle closure by the Forest Service have combined to create a wonderful resource for recreationists in the Truckee Meadows. The 1.7-mile trail winds through the deep cleft of Keystone Canyon on the southwestern slopes of Peavine Peak, offering occasional views of the Truckee Meadows and surrounding mountain ranges. At the top of the canyon, the route gives way to a tangle of roads and trails frequented by mountain bikers and off-road vehicle users.

DIRECTIONS From North Virginia Street, drive west on McCarran Boulevard for 1.1 miles and turn right onto Leadership Parkway. Proceed 0.3 mile to a right-hand turn into the signed Keystone Canyon parking area.

FACILITIES/TRAILHEAD The trailhead has a portable toilet, park bench, and trailhead kiosk. The trail begins at the north end of the parking lot.

Walk a few steps to the trailhead kiosk to see an aerial photo of the Peavine area, and read about Rancho San Rafael Park and efforts to protect Keystone Canyon. From there, follow a wide, well-graded gravel path up the left side of Keystone Canyon, through open sagebrush scrub and grasses. Springtime often produces a fine sprinkling of color from a wide variety of drought-tolerant wildflowers, but the flower season in this arid environment is generally short lived. Interpretive signs along the initial stretch of trail provide information about some of flora and fauna you might encounter along the trail, the geologic formation of the canyon, and how human impact has affected the canyon environment. Continue ahead at a junction with the Halo Trail on the left. After 0.2 mile, the gravel path crosses the streambed and turns to dirt near a junction with a singletrack section of use trail that followed the right-hand side of the canyon from Leadership Parkway and the Rancho Connector heading east toward Evans Canyon.

Continue up the canyon to an opening in a wire fence at the boundary between Washoe County and forest service land. Shortly past the fence line, the trail crosses back to the left side of the drainage and passes below a set of power lines, where a road branches steeply uphill to the left. Soon the trail crosses the streambed again,

a process that will repeat itself numerous times as the canyon walls narrow farther up the gorge. Periodic rock outcroppings along the way add some visual interest to the sage-green slopes. At 0.6 mile, you reach a junction with FS 659C, veering left up the hillside.

Continue the winding ascent through the canyon. Farther upstream, the ravine starts to widen and the tops of radio towers at the head of the canyon spring into view. Along the way, some cottonwoods attempt to eke out an existence along the usually dry streambed, and a number of yellowish-orange piles of mining tailings are scattered about the canyon. Just past a jeep road on the left that climbs a steep slope out of the canyon, you reach a junction, where the road continues to the right and a section of singletrack trail veers off to the left. Veer left and follow singletrack trail up a swale towards the radio towers. After 0.3 mile, you pass by an anchor for one of the towers and intersect a service road, signaling the end of the Keystone Canyon Trail.

A maze of roads and paths litters the slopes of Peavine, offering myriad opportunities for further wanderings, particularly for mountain bikers. However, once you leave the Keystone Canyon Trail, just about every one of those routes is open to motorized vehicles.

Keystone Canyon Trailhead

192 Oxbow Nature Study Area Nature Trail

Distance	1 mile (out-and-back)
Hiking Time	30 minutes
Elevation	Negligible
Difficulty	Easy
Trail Use	Good for kids, ADA accessible
Best Times	Open all year
Agency	City of Reno Parks, Recreation & Community Services at 775-334-2262, reno.gov/government/departments/parks-recreation-community-services/parks-trails
Recommended Map	*City of Reno Oxbow Nature Study Area Guide*
Notes	The park gate closes at 8 p.m. in summer and 4 p.m. in winter.

HIGHLIGHTS Located a mere 2 miles from the downtown Reno casinos, the Oxbow Nature Study Area is an ecological oasis in the midst of urbanization, where the roar from the nearby Truckee River and a chorus of bird songs almost totally drown out the urban cacophony. A nature trail follows the course of the river upstream for a half mile along a boardwalk with interpretive signs and numbered posts corresponding to information in the park brochure, providing interesting tidbits about the ecology of the area. The trail is wheelchair accessible and flat enough to suit just about anyone, no matter their age or level of conditioning. In addition to the nature trail, observation decks, park benches, and picnic tables are scattered throughout the park, which also has a small interpretive center staffed by a knowledgeable ranger.

DIRECTIONS Exit I-80 at Keystone Avenue, head south 0.4 mile to West Second Street, and turn right. After about a half mile, Second Street becomes Dickerson Road, which you follow for 1.1 miles from the Keystone intersection to the park entrance.

FACILITIES/TRAILHEAD The park has a staffed interpretive center with attached restrooms. Picnic tables and benches are near the parking area and alongside the boardwalk. Dogs and horses are not allowed on the park grounds. The well-signed trail begins on the west edge of the parking area.

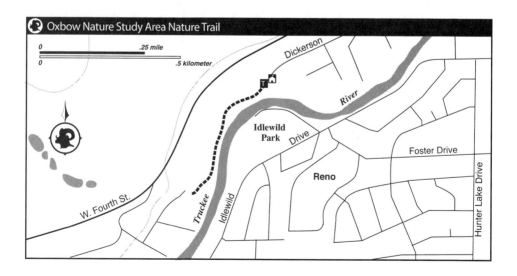

From the west edge of the parking area, follow a short path to the beginning of the boardwalk, which passes immediately below a ramp to an observation platform, from where there is a fine vantage point for viewing activity along the Truckee River. Initially, the trail passes through a mostly open area of shrubs dotted with an occasional cottonwood or Russian olive on the way past a freshwater pond to your right and the river's oxbow on the left.

The boardwalk shortly curves around to an observation deck at the river's edge, which affords more good views of the river. Beneath towering cottonwoods and through a grassy understory, the boardwalk proceeds upstream to the end at post 15 by an open, grassy meadow. A gravel path continues a short distance around the meadow to a fence at the end of the park's property. From there, retrace your steps back to the parking area.

193 Huffaker Park Lookout Trail

Distance	2 miles (loop)
Hiking Time	1 hour
Elevation	+250/-250 feet
Difficulty	Easy
Trail Use	Leashed dogs, good for kids, ADA accessible
Best Times	March through November
Agency	City of Reno Parks, Recreation & Community Services at 775-334-2262, reno.gov/government/departments/parks-recreation-community-services/parks-trails
Recommended Map	USGS 7.5-minute *Mount Rose NE* (trail not shown)
Notes	Dogs must be leashed and waste removed.

HIGHLIGHTS The Huffaker Park Lookout Trail wraps around a pair of hills that jut out of the valley high enough to provide sweeping vistas of the Truckee Meadows. Visitors have the option of hiking a three-quarter-mile or 1.6-mile loop, as well as short laterals to high points atop the north and south hills for even better views. Interpretive signs along the way provide interesting information about the ecology of the area and well-placed park benches and picnic tables offer inviting opportunities for rest stops. Nestled in the middle of suburbia, the area is a favorite not only of hikers, but of joggers and dog walkers as well.

DIRECTIONS From South Virginia Street, head northeast on Longley Lane for 0.3 mile and turn right onto Huffaker Lane. Proceed another 0.3 mile to Huffaker Park near the intersection of Offenhauser Drive. Park on Offenhauser Drive as space allows.

FACILITIES/TRAILHEAD Huffaker Park offers picnic areas, restrooms, and recreational facilities. The trail begins on the east side of the park near the tennis courts, a group picnic area, and a horseshoe pit.

Walk across a bridge over an irrigation ditch, climb sharply uphill to a switchback, and then proceed shortly to a junction with the main loop trail. Turn right at the junction and head south with improving views across sagebrush scrub of the Truckee Meadows landscape. After 0.2 mile, you reach a gazebo perched on the crest of a ridge. Just past this inviting

structure is a dirt path on the left that climbs to the top of the north hill, Peak 4705, a rocky outcrop that affords visitors a fine view from its summit of the surrounding terrain.

The trail drops gently away from the crest to a second junction near a group picnic area, where those interested in a shorter loop can turn left and wrap around Peak

4805 back to the trailhead. Those in for the long haul should proceed straight ahead toward the south hill. Near the half-mile mark is a side trail on the left that climbs 0.1 mile to the top of the south hill, where visitors can enjoy the view and a snack at a picnic table.

Continue south a short distance to a T-junction, where a lateral drops down the hillside to an access point in an apartment complex. From the lateral, the trail contours around the hillside and then heads north along the east side of the hills above recently constructed buildings of a high-tech park and newly built subdivision homes. At 1.25 miles, you reach the short loop junction and proceed on mildly rising trail around the northeast side of Peak 4805. Near the top of the climb are two viewpoints that overlook Huffaker Park and a lateral in between that provides access to a cul-de-sac in the Huffaker Hills subdivision. A short walk beyond leads to the closing of the loop trail. From there, retrace your steps to your vehicle.

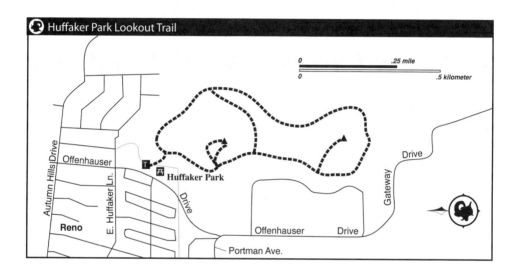

Huffaker Park Lookout Trail

194 Huffaker Hills

Distance	3.2 miles (semiloop)
Hiking Time	1–1.5 hours
Elevation	+375/-375 feet
Difficulty	Easy
Trail Use	Dogs OK, good for kids, mountain biking OK
Best Times	April through November
Agency	Washoe County Regional Parks and Open Space at 775-823-6500, washoecounty.us/parks
Recommended Maps	USGS 7.5-minute *Mount Rose NE, Steamboat*

see map on p. 416

HIGHLIGHTS The Huffaker Hills, a group of volcanic buttes sprinkled along the east side of the Truckee Meadows, provide prominent landmarks for local residents, especially the highest of the group, 6,011-foot Rattlesnake Mountain. Although beacon-topped Rattlesnake Mountain is currently privately property, the lower hills to the south are open to public use, which has become much more desirable with the recent construction of a new trailhead and accompanying trails.

Spearheaded by Washoe County Parks and the Truckee Meadows Trail Association, the paths emanating from the Huffaker Hills Trailhead offer a trio of loops well suited for short hikes during the spring and fall (hot summers necessitate early-morning or early-evening starts to beat the heat). Wet springs offer the added bonus of a fine wildflower display, which adds a burst of color amid the sagebrush scrub. Interpretive signs along the way provide interesting insights into the human and natural history of the area.

The nearly mile-long Reservoir Lookout Trail offers hikers a view of a human-made reservoir tucked between a cleft in the Huffaker Hills. The 1.2-mile-long Western Loop curves into a draw that offers a momentary escape from the presence of nearby development. The 1.5-mile Twin Peaks Loop will likely be the most popular of the trio, as the path leads to the summits of two promontories with sweeping views of the Truckee Meadows and the surrounding mountain ranges.

DIRECTIONS Head east from South Virginia Street on McCarran Boulevard, through the intersection of Longley Lane, and immediately turn south onto Alexander Lake Road. Follow the road as it winds and climbs 1 mile to a high point near a water tank; immediately turn right to the signed Huffaker Hills Trailhead.

FACILITIES/TRAILHEAD The Huffaker Hills Trailhead has a portable toilet, picnic tables, and trash receptacles.

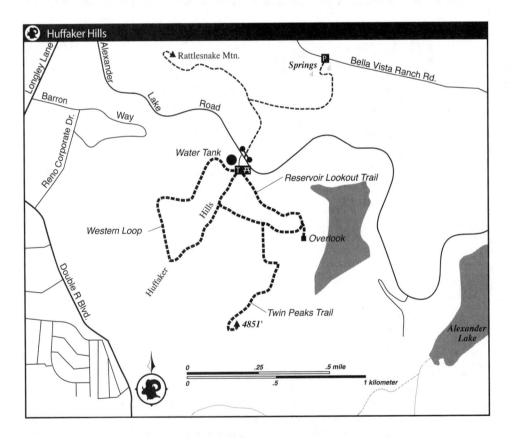

From the trailhead kiosk, follow mildly rising gravel trail through typical sagebrush scrub with a fine array of drought-tolerant wildflowers during wet springs, including daisy, balsamroot, and phlox.

At the crest of the initial climb, Mt. Rose, Slide Mountain, and the rest of the Carson Range spring into view. Gently graded trail soon leads to a Y-junction where the three trails divide.

Reservoir Lookout Trail: Head east-southeast on gravel trail, soon passing the junction with the Twin Peaks Trail. Farther on, the reservoir pops into view and a mildly descending trail wraps around the hillside to a T-junction. The right-hand path leads you on a short romp to a vista point above the reservoir, complete with park bench. Return to the T-junction and follow the course of an old roadbed before singletrack veers away from the road on a brief descent. The path bottoms out and then begins a moderate climb along a fence that leads back to the trailhead.

Western Loop: From the Y-junction, head southwest and follow a winding descent down a sage-covered hillside toward a fence that delineates the boundary between public and private property. Cross an old jeep road, turn north, and descend into a draw. While traveling down the draw, tucked between a couple of hills that block views of the city, you have a momentary sense of being away from it all. Eventually, the route forsakes the draw to make a moderate ascent of the right-hand hillside. The grade eases near a water tank, followed by a short easy walk back to the parking lot.

Twin Peaks Trail: From the Y-junction, head east-southeast on gravel trail, soon passing the west junction with the Twin Peaks Loop and proceed a short distance to the east junction. Turn south and follow the Twin Peaks Loop on a mildly rising climb through typical sagebrush scrub. The path bends sharply to the left and reaches an interpretive exhibit and an overlook of the reservoir, a piece of Alexander Lake, and the Virginia Range to the east. Soon pass another interpretive sign and proceed across a hillside above the reservoir on a moderate climb to the top of a hill. Continue climbing toward the base of the easternmost Twin Peak and follow a tight, winding climb to its summit. An expansive view from the top includes almost the entire Truckee Meadows, the Carson and Virginia Ranges, and distant hills to the north. After enjoying the view, retrace your steps back to the junction.

In the hopes that Rattlesnake Mountain will eventually become public property, a route description follows: Carefully cross the road from the Huffaker Hills Trailhead, and walk through an opening in the highway fence to access a jeep road that starts out on a mild climb of a hillside carpeted with sagebrush scrub. Soon the tread deteriorates to a twin-tracked jeep road, and the grade increases to more of a moderate ascent. Pass below a set of power lines on the way to a T-junction, where your route continues to the left on the road and a singletrack section of trail to the right heads east along the ridge and then descends steeply north to Rio Poco Road.

Follow the road on an angling ascent of the hillside below a ridge, toward the looming hulk of Rattlesnake Mountain. Pass around a steel gate near where a pair of lesser-used roads veers off the left. Take the main, higher road on a steep climb that arcs around the southwest side of the mountain, to a small flat directly northwest of the true summit. Here the road bends sharply right and proceeds a short way to the fenced airport beacon occupying the top of the peak. The high point is just past the far side of the fence. The sweeping view takes in the whole of the Truckee Meadows and the bordering mountains.

Huffaker Hills Trailhead

195 Hidden Valley Regional Park Trails

Distance	2.3 miles (loop with numerous extensions possible)
Hiking Time	1–3 hours
Elevation	+650/-650 feet
Difficulty	Moderate
Trail Use	Leashed dogs, mountain biking OK
Best Times	March through November
Agency	Washoe County Regional Parks and Open Space at 775-823-6500, washoecounty.us/parks
Recommended Map	washoecounty.us/parks/ParkTrailMaps

HIGHLIGHTS Hidden Valley Regional Park offers a lot of possibilities for people who enjoy the outdoors, including hikers. Besides the five designated trails within park boundaries, myriad unimproved use trails and old roads wind through the western front of the ochre-colored slopes of the Virginia Range. The mountains' colorful hues are the result of moisture from geothermal activity interacting with the minerals in the soil. While joggers, dog walkers, and casual hikers frequent the gently graded loop trails on the valley floor, serious hikers are drawn to the Highland Trail, a 2.3-mile loop that climbs halfway up the hillside for superb views of the Truckee Meadows and the Carson Range. Fortunate visitors also may see some of the area's wild horses.

Those who don't mind the grunt involved can select any number of routes for steep climbs up to the crest of the Virginia Range. Determining which of the many use trails to follow may be a bit challenging, as a variety of paths in various conditions crisscross the area. Only 65 of the 480 acres of parkland are developed, and most of the informal trails wander through the undeveloped portion, which creates a wilderness-like atmosphere but also forces hikers to follow a perplexing network of unmarked and unmaintained paths. Additionally, encounters with four-wheel-drive vehicles beyond the park boundaries are fairly common near the Virginia Range crest and in the neighboring canyons, especially on weekends.

DIRECTIONS From McCarran Boulevard, turn east toward Hidden Valley onto Pembroke Lane and drive 1.8 miles to a four-way stop. Turn right onto Parkway Drive and continue another 0.6 mile to the entrance of Hidden Valley Regional Park. Following a sign for equestrian parking, turn left and follow the access road around to the parking lot directly east of the arena. Park your vehicle in the dirt parking lot.

FACILITIES/TRAILHEAD Near the parking area are restrooms and picnic tables. The park has a dog park, sports field, tennis courts, horseshoe pits, and a horse arena. The trail begins across the road from the parking area.

Walk across the access road, climb up and over a berm crossing the broad track of the Perimeter Loop on the way, and then follow a path angling left toward a steel gate. Pass through the gate, making sure to close it behind you, and make a short, moderate climb to a junction with the loop portion of the Highland Trail.

Start a clockwise loop on the Highland Trail by turning right, passing above a couple of fenced water tanks and traversing south toward an unmarked Y-junction. Take the left-hand path, drop into a usually dry wash, and then follow an old road up the canyon a short distance to another unmarked junction. Leaving the road behind, head back across the wash and make a stiff climb up the hillside to the top of a rise, where you encounter a junction with a trail on the left that follows a short loop out to a viewpoint and then back to the main trail. The loop, with fine views of the Truckee Meadows and the Carson Range, is well worth the brief amount of time involved.

Continue north on the main trail, traversing across the slope and bending into and back out of a small canyon on the way to the north edge of the park. Approaching the boundary, you bend into and head up a

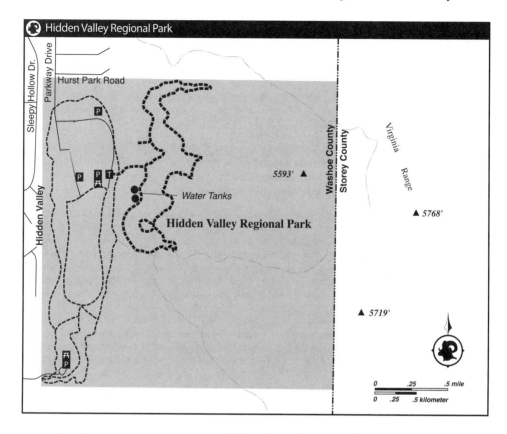

Hidden Valley Regional Park

Sleepy Hollow Dr.

Parkway Drive

Hurst Park Road

Hidden Valley

Water Tanks

Hidden Valley Regional Park

5593' ▲

Washoe County

Storey County

Virginia Range

▲ 5768'

▲ 5719'

0   .25   .5 mile

0   .25   .5 kilometer

larger canyon to a 4-by-4-inch post, where the trail, in a not particularly clear fashion, doubles back sharply in a down-canyon direction. Eventually the trail exits the canyon, bends to the south, and then comes to another junction marked by a 4-by-4-inch post. Here a short path travels west to a fine view on top of a knoll.

Proceed ahead from the junction, drop into a usually dry wash, and then return to the loop junction. From there, retrace your steps to the trailhead.

196 Ballardini Ranch Loop

Distance	2.5 miles (loop)
Hiking Time	1 hour
Elevation	+200/-200 feet
Difficulty	Easy
Trail Use	Leashed Dogs, mountain biking OK
Best Times	March through November
Agency	Washoe County Regional Parks and Open Space at 775-823-6500, washoecounty.us/parks
Recommended Map	USGS 7.5-minute *Mount Rose NE* (trail not shown); Washoe County was in the process of creating a map.

HIGHLIGHTS After years of sometimes-bitter controversy and eventual compromise, the completion of the long (2-mile) and short (0.5-mile) loops comprising the Ballardini Ranch Trail, along with corresponding trailhead improvements, was completed in 2014. The full 2.5-mile route travels across sagebrush scrub typical of the Carson Range foothills, with brief forays to riparian areas along tributaries of Dry Creek. Fine views of the surrounding countryside, including the Carson and Virginia Ranges, and a good portion of the Truckee Meadows, are available along the way. Without any shade, hikers will find the best conditions in the cooler seasons of spring and fall. Summer visitors should plan on hiking very early in the day. Proposed plans are to one day have a connection from the Ballardini Loop to the Thomas Creek Trail.

DIRECTIONS Follow South Virginia Street to the intersection of Holcomb Ranch Lane and turn west. Continue 2.2 miles on Holcomb Ranch Lane, where the road bends north and becomes Lakeside Drive. After 0.2 mile, turn left at Lone Tree Lane and continue 0.8 mile to the Ballardini Ranch Trailhead on the left.

FACILITIES/TRAILHEAD The trailhead is equipped with modern vault toilets and picnic tables. The trail begins at the west end of the parking area.

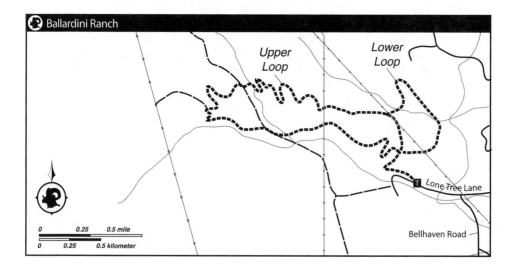

Head away from the parking area on an old road to where the road bends sharply northeast and soon comes to a junction. Turn left and follow some switchbacks up the hillside, above which the grade eases at 0.4 mile from the trailhead. After a while, you drop down and cross a tributary stream and then continue climbing up the shallow canyon through typical sagebrush scrub. Merge with an old road coming in on the left from behind and follow it for a while until you veer onto a less well-traveled road that follows the creek. Continue west-northwest across open terrain until a set of switchbacks leads up a short hill and a junction between the upper and lower loops, 1 mile from the trailhead.

Head downhill on the right-hand road, cross a well-traveled road, and then come to the crossing of a stream on a wood bridge. Winding trail away from the bridge climbs up a hill and comes to a junction with a short lateral to a viewpoint at the top of the hill, where a fine vista unfolds of the Truckee Meadows and the Carson Range. The lateral soon merges back with the main road and winds down the hillside on a half-mile moderate descent. Rising tread leads below a set of power lines and wraps around to the loop junction. Here you have the option of continuing on the lower loop, or simply backtracking to the trailhead.

To follow the lower loop, turn to the left and head northeast on a descent back toward the creek. Once at the lip of the canyon, the trail arcs around the slope above a section of the Steamboat Ditch and passes below the power lines on the way back to the east end of the parking area.

197 Lower Whites Creek Trail

see map on p. 422

Distance	3.5 miles (point-to-point)
Hiking Time	2 hours
Elevation	+925 feet
Difficulty	Moderate
Trail Use	Leashed dogs, good for kids, mountain biking OK
Best Times	March through November
Agency	Washoe County Regional Parks and Open Space at 775-823-6500, washoecounty.us/parks
Recommended Map	USGS 7.5-minute *Mt. Rose NE* (trail not shown)

HIGHLIGHTS Another successful project of the Truckee Meadows Trail Association, the Lower Whites Creek Trail offers suburbanites the opportunity to enjoy a streamside stroll during months when the nearby Sierra is cloaked with snow. (Summertime hikers should plan on either an early-morning or early-evening hike to avoid the heat of the day.) Beginning in a neighborhood park, the path follows the course of the creek, lined with aspens, alders, and willows, across sagebrush-covered slopes to the forested eastern base of the Sierra. Although the ongoing housing boom in the area will eventually see structures lining the entire length of the canyon, for now the upper half of the route is mostly devoid of homes, leaving the trail in a more natural setting. Although this description is written as a shuttle trip, hikers with only one car could easily retrace their steps 3.5 miles to the lower trailhead.

DIRECTIONS *Start:* Drive west on Mt. Rose Highway (NV 431), 0.6 mile past the intersection of Wedge Parkway, to Telluride Drive and turn right (north). After 0.2 mile, turn left onto Killington Drive, and proceed another 0.2 mile to Whites Creek Park. Continue through the park to a turnaround, and park your vehicle as space allows.

End: From the I-580 off-ramp at Mt. Rose Highway (NV 431), head westbound 2 miles on the Mt. Rose Highway to Timberline Drive and turn right. Proceed on Timberline 0.6 mile past a left-hand turn marked for Whites Creek Trail to the vicinity of a short bridge over Whites Creek. Park your vehicle on the shoulder immediately prior to the bridge as space allows.

FACILITIES/TRAILHEAD Whites Creek Park has picnic tables, a children's playground, and a playfield. The trail begins at the northeast edge of the park area, near a CLOSED TO MOTOR VEHICLES sign. The Whites Creek Trailhead has vault toilets and picnic tables.

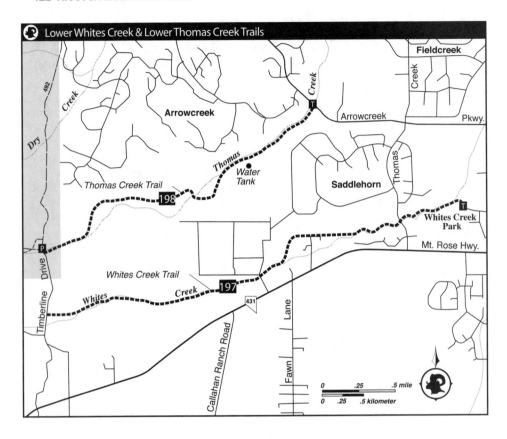

Lower Whites Creek & Lower Thomas Creek Trails

From Whites Creek Park, follow a dirt road that quickly shrinks to a single-track trail toward tumbling Whites Creek. Proceed upstream through sagebrush scrub near the edge of the riparian zone along the creek, where willows and groves of young aspens choke the streambed. The trail passes below a number of new, upscale homes on the rim of the creek's canyon. After a quarter mile, you cross the creek on a wood-plank bridge and continue up the north bank (a path continues up the south bank and could be utilized during high-water periods). Another quarter mile of hiking leads to a short climb up to a crossing of Thomas Creek Road.

Beyond the road, the trail remains on the north bank of Whites Creek and proceeds up the canyon through similar terrain. Around 1 mile from the trailhead, reach a fence that delineates a parcel of private property that includes the creek and a pair of wood bridges. The trail follows the fence line on an angling ascent out of the creek canyon and comes alongside a dirt road (Curtis Lane). Here the enjoyable creekside environment is unfortunately left behind, as the trail is forced to follow an easement through a suburban tract, and the feeling of traveling through strangers' backyards is hard to shake. Where the road soon veers away, the trail maintains a straight path headed east, along a split rail and wire fence to an unmarked T-junction with a path on the left.

Rather than continue ahead to the west, which would seem the more obvious route, turn left (south) and follow the path back into Whites Creek Canyon. Cross the creek on a short wooden bridge, and proceed upstream on the south bank to the crossing of paved Mountain Ranch Road, 1.8 miles from the trailhead, near a closed Nevada Division of Forestry building.

Walk across the well-traveled road and pick up an old jeep road that follows the south bank of the creek for a while, before narrowing to singletrack trail. Good views of Mt. Rose and Slide Mountain propel you toward the forested eastern base of the Carson Range. Just past the remnants of an old jeep road, the trail crosses the creek again, 2.8 miles from the trailhead, on a bridge made of wood planks. Proceed up the north side of the creek past a shady grove of willows and aspens, where the presence of a lone Jeffrey pine provides a hint of more conifers to come farther upstream.

Soon the trail wanders farther away from the creek, through tall mountain mahogany and ephedra shrubs that begin to intermix with the sagebrush. Reach the crossing of a well-graded road providing emergency access for one of the new subdivisions nearby. Beyond the road, the trail veers back toward the creek amid a scattered forest of Jeffrey pines, to a wooden bridge at 3.4 miles near a picturesque pool fed by the waters of a short cascade. Immediately past the bridge, the trail follows an easement across private property past a corral fence, and continues briefly upstream to Timberline Drive.

198 Lower Thomas Creek Trail

see map on p. 422

Distance	2.5 miles (point-to-point)
Hiking Time	90 minutes
Elevation	+750 feet
Difficulty	Moderate
Trail Use	Leashed dogs, good for kids, mountain biking OK
Best Times	April through October
Agency	Washoe County Regional Parks and Open Space at 775-823-6500, washoecounty.us/parks
Recommended Map	USGS 7.5-minute *Mt. Rose NE* (trail not shown)

HIGHLIGHTS The Lower Thomas Creek Trail offers hikers, mountain bikers, joggers, and dog walkers the potential for a good workout on a mildly to moderately rising path that follows the course of the namesake creek from Arrowcreek Park to Timberline Drive. The trail is especially enjoyable during the spring and fall months when the higher elevations are covered with snow. Summer users will want to do this hike either around daybreak or sunset, as shade is nonexistent, and the midafternoon temperatures usually reach into the 90s and occasionally the 100s. Although this description is written as a shuttle trip, hikers with only one car could easily retrace their steps 2.5 miles to the lower trailhead.

DIRECTIONS *Start:* From South Virginia Street, follow Arrowcreek Parkway for 3 miles to the entrance of Arrowcreek Park on the left.

End: From the I-580 off-ramp at Mt. Rose Highway (NV 431), head westbound 2 miles on the Mt. Rose Highway to Timberline Drive and turn right. Follow Timberline across a short bridge over Whites Creek, a second bridge over Thomas Creek, and past the immediate junction with the Thomas Creek Road (FS 049) on the left. Continue another 0.1 mile to the Thomas Creek Trailhead and park your vehicle in the large lot.

FACILITIES/TRAILHEAD Arrowcreek Park is equipped with a portable toilet, picnic area, children's playground, and equestrian parking. The trail begins at the northeast edge of the parking area near a kiosk and sign that reads EQUESTRIAN TRAIL, HIKERS WELCOME. The Thomas Creek Trailhead has vault toilets and equestrian facilities.

From Arrowcreek Park, follow a short lateral to the Thomas Creek Trail and turn left, heading upstream near the edge of the riparian zone, which includes willows, alders, wild rose, cottonwoods, mountain mahogany, and stands of quaking aspen. The moderate climb winds through sagebrush, rabbitbrush, desert peach, and grasses near the south bank of Thomas Creek. Approaching the Arrowcreek Golf Course, the trail veers away from the creek, crosses a gravel access road to a water tank, and continues upstream. Beyond the golf course and near a set of power lines, the trail dips down to cross Thomas Creek, 1.25 miles from the park.

The grade of ascent increases to moderate past the crossing and the trail moves farther away from the canyon of Thomas Creek. For the time being, you proceed across sagebrush-covered slopes with good views of the east front of the Carson Range, although this area seems destined to succumb to the eventual development that continues to creep up the slope toward the base of the mountains. After staying a good distance away, the trail draws near to the aspen-lined creek just before the path widens into a road and shortly meets Timberline Drive near the intersection with the Thomas Creek Road, 2.25 miles from the trailhead. Walk up Thomas Creek Road a short distance to a lateral on the right and follow it 0.1 mile north to the Thomas Creek Trailhead. To extend your journey even farther, check out Trip 131 in Chapter 9.

199 Lower Galena Creek Trail

Distance	2.6 miles (point-to-point); 5.2 miles (out-and-back)
Hiking Time	1 hour (point-to-point); 2 hours (out-and-back)
Elevation	+750 feet (point-to-point); +750/-750 (out-and-back)
Difficulty	Moderate
Trail Use	Leashed dogs, good for kids, mountain biking OK
Best Times	April through October
Agency	Washoe County Regional Parks and Open Space at 775-823-6500, washoecounty.us/parks; Humboldt Toiyabe National Forest at 775-828-6642, www.fs.usda.gov/htnf
Recommended Map	USGS 7.5-minute Washoe City (trail not shown)

HIGHLIGHTS Those who subscribe to Mark Twain's theory that golf is a good walk spoiled might enjoy this hike along Galena Creek. The trail begins in a natural setting of sagebrush scrub and Jeffrey pine forest with thick riparian foliage lining the creek, but all too soon it passes through the manicured grounds and upscale homes of the Montreux Golf and Country Club. Beyond Montreux, the surroundings return to a more natural state on the way to the Mt. Rose Highway at trail's end. The relatively low elevation makes the trip up Galena Creek a good choice for a spring or fall outing, but the mostly forested route provides enough shade that even a midsummer hike shouldn't be oppressively hot. A picnic lunch at Callahan Park may provide a fine conclusion to the adventure.

DIRECTIONS *Start:* From the Mt. Rose exit from I-580, travel approximately 3 miles westbound on NV 431 (Mt. Rose Highway) to a left turn onto Callahan Ranch Road, and proceed south-southwest for 1.5 miles to Phillip and Anne Callahan Park. Trailhead parking is available just off Callahan Ranch Road, on the north side of the park.

End: From the Mt. Rose exit from I-580, drive 6.3 miles on NV 431 (Mt. Rose Highway) to a left-hand turn onto Douglas Fir Drive. Park your vehicle in the gravel lot on the north side of the road.

FACILITIES/TRAILHEAD The park has restrooms, a picnic area, and a children's playground. The trail begins on the north edge of the park near a split rail fence.

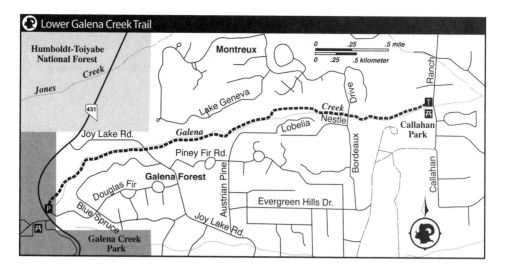

Lower Galena Creek Trail

Humboldt-Toiyabe
National Forest

Montreux

Creek

Jones

0   .25   .5 mile
0   .25   .5 kilometer

Ranch

431

Lake Geneva

Creek
Nestle

Drive

Callahan
Park

Joy Lake Rd.

Galena

Lobelia

Piney Fir Rd.

Bordeaux

Callahan

Austrian Pine

Galena Forest

Douglas Fir

Evergreen Hills Dr.

Blue Spruce

P

Joy Lake Rd.

Galena Creek
Park

Proceed on singletrack trail through a gap in a split rail fence and head upstream along Galena Creek on a winding course between the edge of the riparian area along the creek and the bordering sagebrush scrub. Jeffrey pines, cottonwoods, and pockets of aspen shade the drainage, and clumps of willow and wild rose line the creek bank. Climb along the trail at a mild to moderate grade, enjoying the woodsy ambience for the time being.

Approaching a fence corner, the mood of the surroundings changes dramatically, as the verdant, manicured grass of the Montreux golf course and the upscale homes lining the fairways spring into view. Well-maintained gravel trail leads a short distance to a crossing of Galena Creek on a stout bridge and then continues along the south bank of the creek alongside a fence meant to discourage interlopers from wandering onto the golf course. Soon the trail crosses back over the creek on a second bridge and then passes below a pair of road bridges. Continue upstream through the Montreux development, in view of the golf course and surrounding estate-like houses.

Eventually, the trail leaves the civilized surroundings behind and enters a more natural forest environment, passing through a small, grassy meadow and a head-high patch of willows and alders on the way to a crossing of Galena Creek. Beyond the crossing, you proceed upstream to the Joy Lake Road bridge. A steep path leads up to the road and down the other side to the resumption of trail. However, when the water is low, you can simply follow the streambed below the bridge and continue up the trail on the far side. Follow the trail upstream, weaving through pockets of aspens alternating with stands of Jeffrey pines and passing below some of the homes in the Galena Forest Estates subdivision. Along the way, Mt. Rose makes brief appearances through short gaps in the trees. Cross Galena Creek on a wood slat bridge at 2.3 miles. Head away from the bridge through open Jeffrey pine forest and more aspen stands, as you begin to hear traffic drifting over from the highway. Pass below and then follow a utility line for a short while, passing some dilapidated outhouses left over from an abandoned campground from a bygone era. The trail bends over to cross the creek again on a fallen log and immediately scales the steep bank up to a broad, gravel parking area on the north shoulder of Douglas Fir Drive, 2.6 miles from the trailhead and a short distance east of the intersection with the Mt. Rose Highway.

200 Little Washoe Lake

Distance	1 mile (out-and-back)
Hiking Time	30 minutes
Elevation	Negligible
Difficulty	Easy
Trail Use	Leashed dogs, good for kids
Best Times	March through November
Agency	Washoe County Regional Parks and Open Space at 775-823-6500, washoecounty.us/parks
Recommended Map	USGS 7.5-minute *Washoe City*

HIGHLIGHTS Sprawling across the broad plain of Washoe Valley, Washoe Lake and Little Washoe Lake are the centerpieces of Washoe Lake State Park, designated in 1977 in part to preserve a piece of the picturesque valley from the rapid development that has overtaken Reno to the north and Carson City to the south. Most recreationists seem to spend the majority of their time in the park around the much larger Washoe Lake boating, swimming, fishing, picnicking, or camping, leaving diminutive Little Washoe Lake to the relative few.

A 1-mile trail around the smaller lake's southeast shore provides visitors with an easy stroll to wetlands of the Scripps Wildlife Management Area at the north end of Washoe Lake. The wetlands provide forage and nesting habitat for a wide range of migratory birds and waterfowl, including pelicans, herons, and ibis (a bird checklist is available at park headquarters). While pairs of bald eagles have been known to winter in the area, red-tailed hawks are frequently seen throughout the year patrolling the skies. Along the trail, hikers will be treated to fine views across Little Washoe Lake of the Carson Range to the west.

DIRECTIONS From NV 395 at the north end of Washoe Valley, turn onto East Lake Boulevard and drive a short distance to the access road for Little Washoe Lake. Follow the road past the entrance station (fee required) to the parking lot.

FACILITIES/TRAILHEAD The trailhead has vault toilets. Nearby, Washoe Lake State Park offers a wide range of facilities, including campgrounds, restrooms with showers, picnic areas, and boat ramps. The trail begins at the south side of the parking lot near a wood post marked TRAIL.

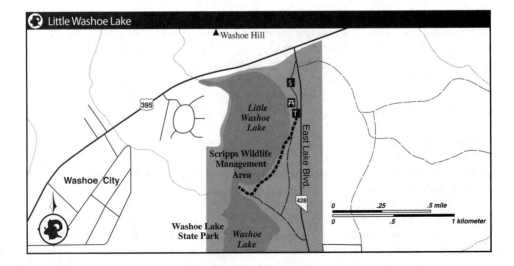

Stroll through sagebrush and other tall shrubs past picnic areas to where the trail widens to road width. Follow signs toward the lakeshore and head southwest along the shoreline, where, across Little Washoe Lake, views open up of Mt. Rose, Slide Mountain, and the rest of the Carson Range. Near the south end of the lake, the trail merges with a gravel road that leads west to a parking area (with vault toilets) near the channel between Washoe and Little Washoe Lakes. From there, retrace your steps to the trailhead. Additional roads in the area provide opportunities for extending your trip.

201 Deadman Creek Loop

Distance	2.4 miles (loop)
Hiking Time	1–1.5 hours
Elevation	+500 feet
Difficulty	Moderate
Trail Use	Dogs OK
Best Times	March through November
Agency	Washoe County Regional Parks and Open Space at 775-823-6500, washoecounty.us/parks
Recommended Map	USGS 7.5-minute *Carson City*

HIGHLIGHTS Shadeless and oppressively hot in summer, the hiker-only Deadman Creek Loop is a wonderful excursion during the milder temperatures of spring and fall. The trail begins by following a short, spring-fed stream watering a luxuriant swath of foliage that stands in stark contrast to the extensive slopes of drought-tolerant vegetation surrounding the watercourse. Beyond the stream, the trail climbs to an overlook with expansive views of Washoe Valley and the Virginia and Carson Ranges. While most hikers seem content with the overlook as their ultimate destination, the trail does continue on a circuit around Peak 5567.

DIRECTIONS From NV 395 at the south end of Washoe Valley, take the Lakeview exit and follow East Lake Boulevard northeast 3 miles to a small parking area near the start of the trail.

FACILITIES/TRAILHEAD There are no facilities immediately at the trailhead, although nearby Washoe Lake State Park offers a wide range of facilities, including campgrounds, restrooms with showers, picnic areas, and boat ramps.

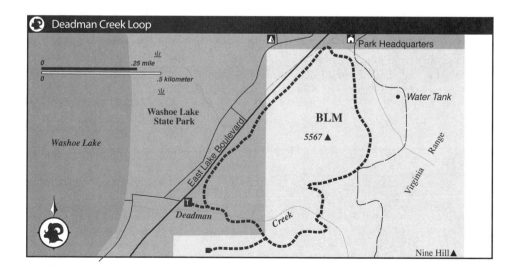

Washoe Lake as seen from Deadman Canyon Trail

Make a brief climb up the hillside to a short wood bridge across Deadman Creek and immediately reach a junction. Veer right and continue climbing up the drainage of the spring-fed creek lined with verdant riparian vegetation. Beyond the spring, the trail follows a seasonal section of the drainage on a winding ascent across drier slopes in the process of recovering from a wildfire in 1999. At the top of a 0.4-mile, 325-foot climb, a short lateral on the right leads to an overlook with a fine view of Washoe Valley and the neighboring mountains.

From the lateral junction, head roughly northeast on a winding, undulating traverse across the lower slopes of Nine Hill, following the folds and creases of the topography to a saddle. The trail briefly merges with a road in the saddle before singletrack veers away from the road at a curve.

A mildly descending traverse wraps around the hillside through sagebrush scrub until the switchbacking trail descends more steeply toward East Lake Boulevard, where you reach a junction at the bottom with a short lateral on the right that leads shortly to the park headquarters.

Turn southwest and follow the trail as it parallels the road back to the close of the loop at the junction on the north bank of Deadman Creek. From there, retrace your steps a short distance to the parking area.

More Hikes

Truckee River Bike Trail

Currently, sections of the proposed Tahoe–Pyramid Bikeway that will follow the Truckee River from Lake Tahoe to Pyramid Lake are open from Verdi to east Sparks (20 miles) and through the Pyramid Indian Reservation (15 miles). See **tpbikeway.org** for more details.

Jumbo Grade

East of Washoe Lake, a new trailhead provides access to a multiuse jeep road that heads east into the Virginia Range and travels all the way to Virginia City. Numerous side roads and trails offer plenty of options (distance varies).

McClellan Peak

At the north end of Carson City, Goni Road leads to the lookout atop the peak. This trip is a favorite of mountain bikers (10 miles).

V & T Trail

From Ash Canyon Road on the west side of Carson City, a paved and dirt path follows the course of the old Virginia and Truckee Railroad north along the base of the mountains toward NV 395 (6 miles).

C Hill

From Curry Road, a number of trails that were improved after the 2004 Waterfall Fire wander across the hill with the white *C* on it, for Carson City (distance varies).

Prison Hill and Silver Saddle Ranch

In the southeast part of Carson City, loop trails traverse the slopes of Prison Hill. Below and to the east, the Silver Saddle Ranch has easy paths that lead across the old ranchlands to the Carson River. A connector links the two areas (distance varies).

Riverview Park

At the east end of Fifth Street in Carson City, short and easy loop trips wander through wetlands directly west of the Carson River (distance varies).

Centennial Park

In the northeast part of Carson City, a number of paths lead from the park into the Virginia Range (distance varies).

Halo Trail

Perhaps the most popular mountain-bike route in the Reno–Sparks area, the Halo Trail connects the East Keystone and West Keystone Trailheads on a winding trail across the southeast slopes of Peavine Peak (8–12 miles). Although mainly used by mountain bikers, the trail is open to hikers and equestrians and closed to motor vehicles. See **poedunk.org** for more information.

Best Trips by Theme

Autumn Color

Geology

History

Peaks

Swimming

Views

Waterfalls

Wildflowers

Wildlife

Recommended Reading

History

Cline, Gloria Griffen. *Exploring the Great Basin.* Reno: University of Nevada Press, 1963.

Natural History

Charlet, David Allan. *Atlas of Nevada Conifers.* Reno: University of Nevada Press, 1996.

Clark, Jeanne L. *Nevada Wildlife Viewing Guide.* Helena, MT: Falcon Press, 1993.

Fiero, Bill. *Geology of the Great Basin.* San Francisco: Sierra Club, 1986.

Graf, Michael. *Plants of the Tahoe Basin.* Sacramento: California Native Plant Society Press, 1999.

Smith, Genny, ed. *Sierra East.* Berkeley: University of California Press, 2000.

Place Names

Carlson, Helen S. *Nevada Place Names.* Reno: University of Nevada Press, 1974.

Lekisch, Barbara. *Tahoe Place Names.* Lafayette, CA: Great West Books, 1988.

Tahoe–Reno

Castle, Ken. *Moon Handbooks: Tahoe.* 2nd Edition. Emeryville, CA: Avalon Travel Publishing, 2003.

Hauserman, Tim. *The Tahoe Rim Trail: A Complete Guide for Hikers, Mountain Bikers, and Equestrians.* 3rd ed. Birmingham, AL: Wilderness Press, 2012.

Morey, Kathy, and Mike White, with Stacy Corless and Tom Winnett. *Sierra North: Backcountry Trips in California's Sierra Nevada.* 9th ed. Berkeley: Wilderness Press, 2005.

Schaffer, Jeffrey P. *The Tahoe Sierra: A Natural History Guide to 112 Hikes in the Northern Sierra.* 4th ed. Berkeley: Wilderness Press, 1998.

Walpole, Jeanne Lauf. *Insiders' Guide to Reno and Lake Tahoe.* 4th ed. Guilford, CT: Globe Pequot, 2005.

White, Mike. *50 Classic Hikes in Nevada.* Reno: University of Nevada Press, 2006.

White, Mike. *Backpacking Nevada.* Berkeley: Wilderness Press, 2004.

White, Mike. *Snowshoe Trails Tahoe.* 2nd ed. Berkeley: Wilderness Press, 2005.

White, Mike. *Top Trails Lake Tahoe.* 3rd ed. Birmingham, AL: Wilderness Press, 2015.

Agencies and Information Sources

BUREAU OF LAND MANAGEMENT

CARSON CITY FIELD OFFICE
5665 Morgan Mill Rd.
Carson City, NV 89701-1448
blm.gov
775-885-6000

CALIFORNIA STATE PARKS

DEPT. OF PARKS AND RECREATION
1416 Ninth St.
Sacramento, CA 95814
parks.ca.gov
800-777-0369 or 916-653-6995

BURTON CREEK STATE PARK
530-525-7232

D. L. BLISS STATE PARK
530-525-7277

DONNER MEMORIAL STATE PARK
530-582-7892

ED Z'BERG-SUGAR PINE POINT STATE PARK
530-525-7982

EMERALD BAY STATE PARK
530-525-7232

GROVER HOT SPRINGS STATE PARK
530-694-2248
530-694-2249 (Pool Information)

CITY OF RENO

PARKS, RECREATION, AND COMMUNITY SERVICE
1 E. First St.
Reno, NV 89501
reno.gov/government/departments/parks-recreation-community-services
775-334-4636

U.S. FOREST SERVICE

ELDORADO NATIONAL FOREST
- *Supervisors Office*
  100 Forni Rd.
  Placerville, CA 95667
  www.fs.usda.gov/eldorado
  530-622-5061

- *Amador Ranger District*
  26820 Silver Dr.
  Pioneer, CA 95666
  209-295-4251

- *Pacific Ranger District*
  7887 Highway 50
  Pollock Pines, CA 95726-9602
  530-644-2349

- *Placerville Ranger District*
  4260 Eight Mile Rd.
  Camino, CA 95709
  530-644-2324

HUMBOLDT-TOIYABE NATIONAL FOREST

- *Supervisors Office*
  1200 Franklin Way
  Sparks, NV 89431
  www.fs.usda.gov/htnf
  775-331-6444

- *Carson Ranger District*
  1536 S. Carson St.
  Carson City, NV 89701
  775-882-2766

LAKE TAHOE BASIN MANAGEMENT UNIT

35 College Dr.
South Lake Tahoe, CA 96150-4500
www.fs.usda.gov/ltbmu
530-543-2600

TAHOE NATIONAL FOREST

- *Supervisors Office*
  631 Coyote St.
  Nevada City, CA 95959
  www.fs.usda.gov/tahoe
  530-265-4531

- *American River Ranger District*
  22830 Foresthill Rd.
  Foresthill, CA 95631
  530-367-2224

- *Sierraville Ranger District*
  317 S. Lincoln St.
  P.O. Box 95
  Sierraville, CA 96126
  530-994-3401

- *Truckee Ranger District*
  9646 Donner Pass Rd.
  Truckee, CA 96161-2949
  530-587-3558

- *Yuba River District*
  15924 Highway 49
  Camptonville, CA 95922
  530-288-3231

NEVADA DIVISION OF STATE PARKS
901 S. Stewart St.
5th Floor, Suite 5005
Carson City, NV 89701-5248
parks.nv.gov
775-684-2770

LAKE TAHOE NEVADA STATE PARK
P.O. Box 8867
Incline Village, NV 89452
775-831-0494

WASHOE LAKE STATE PARK
4855 East Lake Blvd.
Carson City, NV 89704
775-687-4319

WASHOE COUNTY REGIONAL PARKS AND OPEN SPACE
3101 Longley Ln.
Reno, NV 89502
775-328-2182
washoecounty.us/parks

BARTLEY RANCH REGIONAL PARK
6000 Bartley Ranch Rd.
Reno, NV 89509
775-828-6612

DAVIS CREEK REGIONAL PARK
25 Davis Creek Rd.
Washoe Valley, NV 89704
775-849-0684

GALENA CREEK REGIONAL PARK
18350 Mt. Rose Hwy.
Reno, NV 89511
775-849-2511

HIDDEN VALLEY REGIONAL PARK
4740 Parkway Dr.
Reno, NV 89502

RANCHO SAN RAFAEL REGIONAL PARK
1595 North Sierra St.
Reno, NV 89503
775-785-4512

Local Trails and Conservation Organizations

CALIFORNIA WILDERNESS COALITION
1212 Broadway, Suite 1700
Oakland, CA 94612
e-mail: info@calwild.org; **calwild.org**
510-451-1450

CARSON VALLEY TRAILS ASSOCIATION
P.O. Box 222
Minden, NV 89423
e-mail: info@carsonvalleytrails.org
carsonvalleytrails.org

FRIENDS OF NEVADA WILDERNESS
Northern Nevada Office
P.O. Box 9754
Reno, NV 89507
nevadawilderness.org
775-324-7667

KEEP TRUCKEE MEADOWS BEAUTIFUL
P.O. Box 7412
Reno, NV 89510
staff@ktmb.org; **ktmb.org**
775-851-5185

LAHONTAN AUDUBON SOCIETY
P.O. Box 2304
Reno, NV 89505
nevadaaudubon.org
775-562-1066

LEAGUE TO SAVE LAKE TAHOE
2608 Lake Tahoe Blvd.
South Lake Tahoe, CA 96150
e-mail: info@keeptahoeblue.org; **keeptahoeblue.org**
530-541-5388

THE NATURE CONSERVANCY
Nevada Office
1 E. First St., #1007
Reno, NV 89501

e-mail: nevada@tnc.org
nature.org/ourinitiatives/regions/northamerica /unitedstates/nevada/index.htm
775-322-4990

NEVADA LAND TRUST
P.O. Box 20288
Reno, NV 89515
e-mail: infoatnevadalandtrust.org
nevadalandtrust.org
775-851-5180

TAHOE AREA SIERRA CLUB
P.O. Box 16936
South Lake Tahoe, CA 96151
sierraclub.org/mother-lode/tahoe
530-320-1795

SIERRA CLUB TOIYABE CHAPTER
P.O. Box 8096
Reno, NV 89507
sierraclub.org/toiyabe
775-323-3162

TAHOE PYRAMID BIKEWAY
Janet Phillips
4790 Caughlin Pkwy., #138
Reno, NV 89519
email: TahoePyramidBike@aol.com
tpbikeway.org
775-825-9868

TAHOE RIM TRAIL ASSOCIATION
P.O. Box 3267
Stateline, NV 89449
email: info@tahoerimtrail.org; **tahoerimtrail.org**
775-298-4485

TRUCKEE DONNER LAND TRUST
P.O. Box 8816
Truckee, CA 96162
e-mail: info@tdlandtrust.org; **tdlandtrust.org**
530-582-4711

Index

About the Author

Mike White was raised in the southeast suburbs of Portland, Oregon, in the shadow of Mt. Hood (whenever the Pacific Northwest skies cleared enough to allow such things as shadows). As a teenager, Mike began hiking, backpacking, and climbing in the Cascades of Oregon and Washington, and he honed his outdoor skills while attending Seattle Pacific University. After acquiring a B.A. in political science, Mike and his new wife, Robin, relocated to the high desert of Reno, Nevada, from where he discovered the joys of exploring the Sierra Nevada.

After leaving his last "real" job, Mike began a full-time writing career. He is the author or coauthor of 19 outdoor guides, including award-winning books *Top Trails Lake Tahoe* and *50 Classic Hikes in Nevada*. Mike also has contributed to *Sunset* and *Backpacker* magazines and the *Reno Gazette Journal* newspaper. A former community college instructor, Mike is also a popular featured speaker for outdoor groups.